EX·LIBRIS

PALMYRA NORTH

"Princess Palmyra Geodie".
June 1. 1941.

*FM.*

## OLD FRONTIERS

The tragic story of a great people.

CHIEF JOHN ROSS AFTER THE REMOVAL
From a picture made about the time of his second marriage.

# NTIERS

*The Story of the Cherokee Indians*
*from Earliest Times to the*
*Date of Their Removal*
*to the West, 1838*

*by*

JOHN P. BROWN

1938

SOUTHERN PUBLISHERS, INC.

KINGSPORT                    TENNESSEE

MANUFACTURED IN THE UNITED STATES OF AMERICA
KINGSPORT PRESS, INC.        KINGSPORT, TENNESSEE

Without Prejudice or Sentiment,
Without Intent to Conceal His
Fault or Magnify His Virtue, This
Book is Dedicated to

THE FIRST AMERICAN

# PREFACE

Exactly one hundred years ago the Cherokee Indians were removed from their ancestral homes to what was then Arkansas. There, using the language of the United States Government, they were settled in what was to be "a permanent home that shall never in the future be embarrassed by having extended around it the lines, or placed over it the jurisdiction of any territory or state."

The Cherokees numbered, at the time of removal, not more than twenty thousand. They were surrounded by a large white population. Sequoyah had perfected his alphabet, the Scriptures had been printed in Cherokee, and the Indian nation was well advanced along the road to civilization.

Many reasons were advanced for Indian removal. The true one was that the land occupied by them and guaranteed to them by the United States, was desired by white settlers. The urgent reason at the time was that gold had been discovered on Cherokee land.

Removal was not sanctioned by the Cherokees. Calm study of the facts, after the lapse of a century, brings conviction that it was both inhumane and unnecessary. Georgia has been blamed for the injustice, perhaps with reason. The one man responsible for Cherokee removal, however, was that strong character, Andrew Jackson. Few informed people, knowing Andrew Jackson's character, will say that Georgia could have removed the Cherokees if Old Hickory had opposed the removal.

OLD FRONTIERS is not the story of the Indian removal, although that subject is treated incidentally. The book is an attempt to draw together from many sources an authentic story of the Cherokees, from earliest times. It is, mainly, the story of their struggle to hold the land of their fathers against white encroachment. If the author's sympathy has been enlisted at times for the Indian, he has tried to present the facts impartially, recognizing, as did General Henry Knox, President Washington's Secretary for War, "If the Indians are to blame, we white people have not always been without fault."

It is the hope of the author that OLD FRONTIERS may

vii

find for itself a useful place in the interest of general readers, of educational circles; and in the service of present day Cherokees, descendants of Oconostota, the Little Carpenter, Dragging Canoe, and John Watts. That these men loved the soil of America with passionate attachment cannot be denied. The title of patriot may not be denied them because it was against our own forefathers that they waged war. We may now recognize that one of the great minds of all time was possessed by the untutored Sequoyah; and surely, the pages of history reveal no finer act of patriotism than that of humble Cherokee Charlie. If the Indian scalped his enemy, or burned at the stake the man who would take his country, it was none-the-less America for which he fought, with the only means at his command. Recognizing the faults of the red man, and balancing them against his treatment at our hands, the scales tip in his favor.

The author extends grateful acknowledgment to those who have aided in preparing the manuscript, and particularly to the following: Gilbert E. Govan, Robert Sparks Walker, and Miss Zella Armstrong, for reading copy and for invaluable suggestions and encouragement; Dr. Willard Steele for assistance in visiting historical sites, and to Walter Cline for photographing them; to Rev. Sibbald Smith, Will P. Sevier, and Chief Standing Deer, for assistance in compiling an adequate Cherokee vocabulary; Hon. Sam D. McReynolds, for access to Government documents; to Judge Samuel Cole Williams, whose preliminary work has laid the foundation for thoughtful study of the early history of the Cherokee people and country; to Judge Albert V. Goodpasture, for encouragement and various items of information; to Dr. Grant Foreman, whose work has made available documentary evidence bearing on the removal of the Five Civilized Tribes, and whose books on other phases of Indian history are invaluable; to Lawson McGhee Library, at Knoxville, and to Miss Mary U. Rothrock and Miss Laura Luttrell, for use of the facilities of the library, and access to valuable historical documents and records; to Chattanooga Public Library, and to Miss Nora Crimmins and Miss Augusta Bradford, for generous cooperation.

JOHN P. BROWN

Chattanooga, Tennessee, 1938.

# CONTENTS

ix

# ILLUSTRATIONS

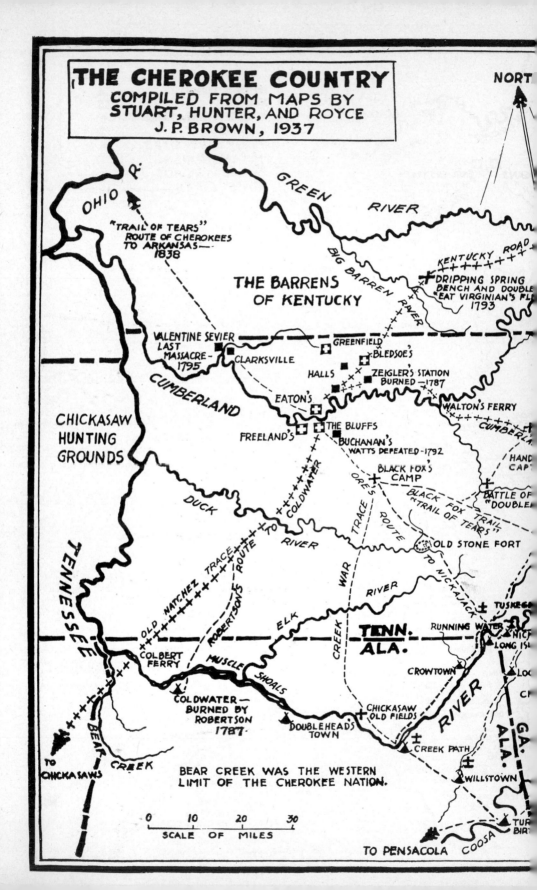

# THE CHEROKEE COUNTRY
### COMPILED FROM MAPS BY STUART, HUNTER, AND ROYCE
### J. P. BROWN, 1937

NORT[H]

OHIO R.

GREEN RIVER

"TRAIL OF TEARS" ROUTE OF CHEROKEES TO ARKANSAS — 1838

THE BARRENS OF KENTUCKY

BIG BARREN RIVER

KENTUCKY ROAD

DRIPPING SPRING BENCH AND DOUBLE [?]EAT VIRGINIAN'S FL[?] 1793

VALENTINE SEVIER LAST MASSACRE — 1795

CLARKSVILLE

GREENFIELD

BLEDSOE'S

CUMBERLAND

HALLS

ZEIGLER'S STATION BURNED — 1787

EATON'S

WALTON'S FERRY

CUMBERLA[ND]

CHICKASAW HUNTING GROUNDS

FREELAND'S

THE BLUFFS

BUCHANAN'S WATTS DEFEATED — 1792

HAND CAP[?]

DUCK

COLDWATER

BLACK FOX'S CAMP

ORE'S ROUTE

BLACK FOX TRAIL "TRAIL OF TEARS"

BATTLE OF "DOUBLE[?]

ROUTE TO COLDWATER

RIVER

OLD STONE FORT

WAR TRACE ROUTE

OLD NATCHEZ TRACE

ROBERTSON'S ROUTE

TO NICKAJACK

TENNESSEE

ELK RIVER

CREEK RIVER

TENN. ALA.

TUSKEG[?]

RUNNING WATER

NICK[?] LONG IS[?]

COLBERT FERRY

MUSCLE SHOALS

CROWTOWN

LO[?]

C[?]

COLDWATER — BURNED BY ROBERTSON 1787

DOUBLEHEAD'S TOWN

CHICKASAW OLD FIELDS

RIVER

GA. ALA.

TO CHICKASAWS

BEAR CREEK

CREEK PATH

WILLSTOWN

BEAR CREEK WAS THE WESTERN LIMIT OF THE CHEROKEE NATION.

TU[R] BIR[?]

0    10    20    30
SCALE OF MILES

TO PENSACOLA

COOSA

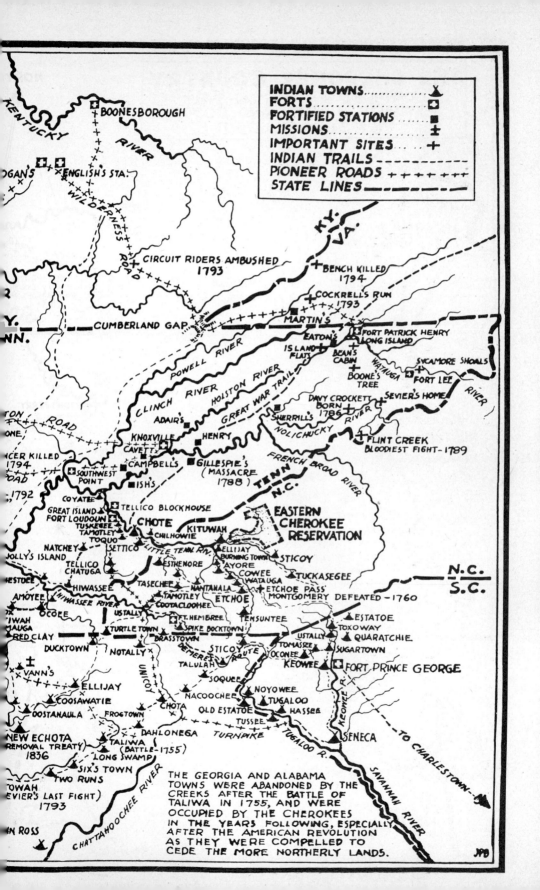

INDIAN TOWNS.............. 🛖
FORTS ...................... ⊞
FORTIFIED STATIONS ....... ■
MISSIONS ................... ‡
IMPORTANT SITES ..... +
INDIAN TRAILS ─ ─ ─ ─ ─
PIONEER ROADS + + + + + +
STATE LINES ▬ ▬ ▬ ▬ ▬

KENTUCKY

BOONESBOROUGH

RIVER

OGAN'S
ENGLISH'S STA.

WILDERNESS ROAD

KY.
VA.

CIRCUIT RIDERS AMBUSHED
1793

BENCH KILLED
1794

COCKRELL'S RUN
1793

2

Y.
NN.

CUMBERLAND GAP

MARTIN'S

EATON'S

FORT PATRICK HENRY
LONG ISLAND

ISLAND
FLATS

BEAN'S
CABIN

WATAUGA

SYCAMORE SHOALS

FORT LEE

POWELL RIVER

HOLSTON RIVER

GREAT WAR TRAIL

BOONE'S
TREE

SEVIER'S HOME

RIVER

CLINCH RIVER

DAVY CROCKETT
BORN 1786

RIVER

TON ROAD
ONE

ADAIR'S

KNOXVILLE

HENRY

SHERRILL'S

NOLICHUCKY

FLINT CREEK
BLOODIEST FIGHT - 1789

NCER KILLED
1794

OAD
,1792

CAVETT'S

CAMPBELL'S

GILLESPIE'S
(MASSACRE
1788 )

FRENCH BROAD RIVER

TENN.
N.C.

SOUTHWEST
POINT

ISH'S

EASTERN
CHEROKEE
RESERVATION

COYATEE

GREAT ISLAND
FORT LOUDOUN
TUSKEGEE
TAMOTLEY
TOQUO

TELLICO BLOCKHOUSE

CHOTE

KITUWAH

CHILHOWIE

N.C.
S.C.

NATCHEY

SETTICO

LITTLE TENN. RIV.

ELLIJAY

BURNING TOWN

STICOY

ESTHENORE

AYORE

JOLLY'S ISLAND

TELLICO
CHATUGA

HIWASSEE

TASECHEE

TAMOTLEY

NANTANALA

COWEE
WATAUGA

ETCHOE

TUCKASEGEE

ETCHOE PASS
MONTGOMERY DEFEATED - 1760

HESTOEE

AMOYEE

HIWASSEE RIVER

COOTACLOOHEE

ETCHOE

OCORE

USTALLY

FT. HEMBREE

TENSUNTEE

ESTATOE

IWAH
AUGA

RED CLAY

TURTLE TOWN

SPIKE BUCKTOWN

USTALLY

TOXOWAY

QUARATCHIE

DUCKTOWN

NOTALLY

BRASSTOWN

STICOY

DEVIER'S ROUTE

TOMASSEE

OCONEE

SUGARTOWN

VANN'S

TALULAH

SOQUEE

KEOWEE

FORT PRINCE GEORGE

ELLIJAY

COOSAWATIE

UNICOY

NACOOCHEE

NOYOWEE

KEOWEE R.

OOSTANAULA

FROGTOWN

CHOTA

OLD ESTATOE

TUGALOO

HASSEE

NEW ECHOTA
REMOVAL TREATY
1836

DAHLONEGA

TUSSEE

TURNPIKE

TUGALOO R.

SENECA

TO CHARLESTON

TALIWA
(BATTLE - 1755)
LONG SWAMP

SIX'S TOWN

TWO RUNS

OWAH
EVIER'S LAST FIGHT)
1793

CHATTAHOOCHEE RIVER

SAVANNAH RIVER

THE GEORGIA AND ALABAMA
TOWNS WERE ABANDONED BY THE
CREEKS AFTER THE BATTLE OF
TALIWA IN 1755, AND WERE
OCCUPIED BY THE CHEROKEES
IN THE YEARS FOLLOWING, ESPECIALLY
AFTER THE AMERICAN REVOLUTION
AS THEY WERE COMPELLED TO
CEDE THE MORE NORTHERLY LANDS.

IN ROSS

JPB

# BOOK ONE

## The Cherokees

# OLD FRONTIERS

## CHAPTER I

## THE SAVAGE NAPOLEON

### I

"You have bought a fair land, but you will find its settlement dark and bloody."

The speaker was *Tsu-gun-sini,* Dragging Canoe, chief of the Cherokee town of Great Island of Little Tennessee River, and the time was March, 1775. The place was beside a clear, beautiful little river in upper East Tennessee, at a point where the stream widened and bubbled and made music over numerous boulders tumbled down its current by freshets of centuries; forming a convenient crossing place, and a scene of wild beauty enhanced by sycamore trees which gave the place its name, Sycamore Shoals of Watauga, later to be historic in the old Southwest.

It was near these shoals that Daniel Boone, first and greatest of "Long Hunters," had fifteen years earlier "CillED A BAR On TREE." A few miles to the eastward, William Bean, a lusty Scotch-Irish blacksmith and gunsmith had forged the axe to build and the gun to defend a log cabin home in which the first child of English speaking parentage in all the vast region west of the Alleghenies had drawn the breath of life;[1] the full, satisfying life of frontier America, packed with danger, toil, rails split, crops made, guns forged and fired, whiskey, scalps, dogs, hate, love, happiness, and Indians.

Other men had preceded Bean into the valley of Watauga River and many were soon to follow. The first were Indian traders, Greer and Dugger. Then had come the Robertsons, Seviers, Carters, Webbs, Tiptons, Taylors, and others, seekers for liberty and opportunity, drawn by the magnet of land to be had for the taking.

Land was the occasion for the meeting at Sycamore Shoals

---

[1] Russell Bean, see note 16, Chapter VIII.

in March, 1775. Daniel Boone had explored the vast regions of "Kaintuckee," and his glowing reports had stirred the country east of the Appalachians as those of Columbus, three hundred years before, had fired the older countries of Europe.

Boone's stories sent a stream of Long Hunters over the mountains. Land hungry backwoodsmen saw visions of new homes, free from the restrictions of older settlements. Speculators, in imagination, counted fabulous profits. The westward march of America, which had halted at the mountains, again took up its way.

The man who was responsible for the beginning of the westward movement, was Richard Henderson, a young attorney of North Carolina, a man of vision. Henderson had sent Boone to explore Kaintuckee, and inspired by Boone's report, had organized the Transylvania Company to purchase title from the Indians, that the land might be peaceably settled. In the winter of 1774, Boone and Henderson visited the Cherokees, and favorably impressed them with the idea of selling the lands, to which they had, at best, but a shadowy title, for other tribes also claimed them as hunting grounds.

The great Cherokee chief, *Attakullakulla,* known to the white men as The Little Carpenter, accompanied Boone and Henderson to Watauga to see with his own eyes the goods which the Indians were to receive in payment for their title. The Little Carpenter was impressed, for Henderson's goods filled an entire house and had the substantial value of £10,000 sterling. Attakullakulla made a favorable report, and the Cherokees gathered at Sycamore Shoals to close the deal.

2

Let us picture the scene at the great council fire at Sycamore Shoals.

The Cherokee chiefs were there. Oconostota, the Great Warrior; Attakullakulla, the wise councillor; Savanukah, the Raven; Oskuah, or Abram, of Chilhowie; Kaiyah-tahee, the Old Tassel; Scolacuta, the Hanging Maw; Nooneteyah, Bloody Fellow; these were the older chiefs. Only Judd's Friend, Outacite, was absent, and he had sent word that he would abide by the decision of the others.

Of the younger chiefs, Willenawah, the Great Eagle, had achieved fame in the capture of Fort Loudoun; Tennasy Warrior, though not so famous, was well known; Tuckasee, the Terrapin, was Oconostota's son. Tsu-gun-sini, Dragging Canoe, son of Attakullakulla, was chief of Amo-yeli-egwa, Great Island, one of the smaller Cherokee towns. In addition to the chiefs, there were more than a thousand Cherokees, warriors, squaws, papooses, a colorful throng.

For the white men, Richard Henderson, known to the Indians as Carolina Dick, and his partner Nathaniel Hart, represented the Transylvania Company. Henderson's proposal to "purchase an empire" had roused violent clamor. Governors had thundered against it, and lawyers had denounced it as contrary to English law. "Has Dick Henderson lost his mind?" one of his friends inquired.

The young settlement at Watauga had its representatives, with Charles Robertson as their trustee. For a number of years, they had leased their lands from the Indians, and now they wished to buy them in fee simple. The two Robertson brothers, Charles and James, had been among the first settlers at Watauga. John Sevier, a blue eyed, handsome, vivacious young cavalier from Virginia, who was immensely popular though he had been at Watauga only a year, also attended the treaty. William Bailey Smith, Surveyor, saw much work in prospect for himself. Others from Watauga, not so renowned but all good men and true, were Jesse Benton, Tilman Dixon, William Blevins, and Thomas Price. Charles Robertson, as trustee for the Wataugans, had on hand goods to the amount of £2000 sterling with which to purchase the Indian title.

Jacob Brown, of Nolichucky, wished to buy the ground on which he lived. Parker and Carter, of Carter's Valley, whose trading store had been robbed by the Indians, were present to ask that their lands be ceded in return for the stolen merchandise. "Ugh!" said the Cherokees, "Little goods, much land." The matter was compromised by the traders throwing in a few more goods.

Captain William Twetty and seven followers attended the treaty. They were seeking adventure in the new country "Louisa," afterward called Kaintuckee. The good captain, "of great benevolence, light habited and of bodily powers unsurpassed by any man of his time," was not destined to see the new country. Adventure he did meet, but it was the Great Adventure, ushered in by a Shawnee arrow through his brain.

One of his seven followers however, Felix Walker, wrote a narrative of the captain's fate, and of the adventures met by the other members of the party.

At Richard Henderson's right hand was a man known throughout the frontier. He was of medium height, with broad shoulders and chest that proclaimed extraordinary strength. He was clothed as were the Indians, in hunting shirt, moccasins, leggins, and breech clout. His long hair was clubbed after the manner of the day. His keen eye roved the assembly, missing no detail. Daniel Boone was an Indian fighter of known repute, but never an Indian hater.[2] It was his grave and courteous diplomacy, and his reputation for fair dealing, that were responsible for Henderson's success in calling the great council at Sycamore Shoals.

Henderson, not doubting that he could purchase the land, had engaged Boone in advance, with thirty pioneers and axe-men to open a road to Kaintuckee. The men were camped at Long Island, fifteen miles on the road to the new country, awaiting the result of the treaty.

3

The first day of the treaty was occupied with the courtesies dear to the Indians. The peace pipe was smoked, and friendly talks were made. No liquor was allowed, but Henderson had provided a large number of beeves which were barbecued. Boone and Henderson circulated among their guests, kept them in good humor, and cautiously sounded them out.

On the second day, Boone explained to the Indians the boundaries desired, including all the land between Kaintuckee and Tennessee Rivers, "time out of mind the hunting ground of the Cherokees." The interpreter, Joseph Vann, explained Boone's words to the Cherokees, and Henderson, with some pride, exhibited the goods to be exchanged. A whole cabin was filled with things which were calculated to fill the savage breast with joy; guns, ammunition, clothing, blankets, beads, mirrors, bells, tomahawks, and hunting knives; such goods as the Indian most desired, to the value of £10,000.

The presents were a great temptation, but the chiefs were

---

[2] Description of Boone's personal appearance is from *Boonesborough,* by George W. Ranck, Filson Club Publications.

honest enough to warn Henderson that the Shawnees, as well as themselves, claimed the land, and that he would have trouble settling the country. "Since the battle at Point Pleasant, last year," Henderson replied, "the great Shawnee chief Cornstalk, on behalf of his people, has made peace with the white man, by which the Shawnees have given up all claims to land south of the Ohio." [3]

The Cherokees were impressed. Cornstalk was a mighty chief. He had not sought war with the white men, but when it came, he had led his followers bravely, and had fought well. All day his cry "Be strong!" had heartened his warriors and terrified the white men. Although defeated, he had drawn his forces off in good order, and the white soldiers had not dared pursue him. Stalking into the Shawnee council, he had demanded, "Now what shall we do? Will you sit here until the white man kills you, or shall we make peace?" Receiving no answer, he had struck his tomahawk into the warpole, and said contemptuously, "Since you will not make peace, I will make it myself." If so great a warrior as Cornstalk had sold his lands to the white men, who could criticize the Cherokees for doing likewise? Henderson was wise to tell them of Cornstalk. [4]

Henderson was able to convince the Indians of his own honesty and frankness, and that they were making an advantageous deal. The Little Carpenter seems always to have tried to please the white men, and his influence with the Cherokees was unbounded. Oconostota may have had doubts, but possibly he felt that the Shawnees could be depended upon to make the settlement of the land difficult. He so expressed himself to Henderson, but the cabin full of goods, and particularly the new guns for his warriors, were attractive to Oconostota, and he was willing to sign.

At the Treaty of Fort Stanwix, in 1768, the Iroquois had claimed the territory south to the Tennessee River "by right of conquest." The Little Carpenter warmly defended the Cherokee title against that claim. Felix Walker, in his Narrative, gives us a splendid word picture of the old chief.

---

[3] *Boonesborough,* Ranck.
[4] Cornstalk made the treaty as stated to the Cherokees by Henderson, but continued white encroachments sent him southward the following year, 1776, to solicit aid of the Cherokees in a proposed general Indian offensive.

"We continued at Watauga during the treaty,[5] which lasted about twenty days. Among others, there was a distinguished chief called Attakullakulla, known to the white people as 'The Little Carpenter.' As a white carpenter could bring every notch and joint to fit in wood, so this Indian could, by deep, artful, and ingenious diplomatic abilities, ably demonstrated by treaties negotiated with the white men, and his influence in their national councils, bring various minds together and fit their beliefs in the political machinery of his nation.

"He was the most celebrated and influential Indian in the tribes then known, considered as the Solon of his day. He was said to be about ninety years of age,[6] a very small man, and so light habited that I scarcely believe he would have exceeded in weight a pound for each year of his life. He was marked with two large scars on each cheek; his ears were cut and banded with silver, hanging nearly down to his shoulders, in the notion of the Indians a mode of distinction in some tribes.

"He spoke to this effect; 'He was an old man, who had presided as chief in every council, and as president of the nation for more than half a century; had formerly served as agent to the King of England on business of first importance to his nation; had crossed the big water, arrived at his destination, and was received with great distinction; had the honor of dining with His Majesty and the nobility; had the utmost respect paid him by the great men of the white people, and had accomplished his mission with success; that from long standing in the highest dignities of his nation, he claimed the confidence and good faith of all and everyone in defending and supporting

---

[5] There is some doubt as to the actual date of Boone's departure from the treaty for Kentucky. Walker, who wrote fifty years afterward, said "about March 10, 1775." Walker states, however, that his party remained at Watauga until the treaty was completed, which was March 17, 1775. A difference of a week, after lapse of half a century, would doubtless seem a small matter to an old man. Boone probably started for Kentucky after the treaty was completed, Mar. 17, 1775.

[6] Attakullakulla was certainly younger than Walker's estimate. His age is given by one authority at the time of his visit to London as 19, and by another as 30. Even the latter would make him only 75 at the time of Henderson's treaty. William Bartram visited the Cherokee country in the following year, 1776, and met Attakullakulla, who was then much too vigorous for a man of 90.

the rightful claims of his people to the Bloody Grounds, then in treaty to be sold to the white people.' " [7]

The other Cherokee chiefs readily fell in with the opinions of their principal leaders. It seemed that the plans of Henderson and Boone were assured of success, when there was an interruption among the Indians.

### 4

Dragging Canoe, chief of Amo-yeli-egwa, the Great Island, rose to his feet. Six feet tall, broad and muscular, of mature years,[8] his strong face deeply pitted with the scars of smallpox and made fiercer thereby, Dragging Canoe made an impressive appearance. This famous Indian was the son of the great chief Attakullakulla, who had been known as Ookoo-naka, the White Owl, in his youth, and whose title "The Little Carpenter" had been bestowed later by the white men.[9]

Dragging Canoe was deeply chagrined that his father, the great Attakullakulla, beloved of all the Cherokees, and Oconostota, whom he had been proud to follow upon the warpath, should consider selling, at any price, the fairest hunting grounds of his people. He rose to deliver an earnest protest.

He began by telling of the ancient flourishing state of his people; mentioned encroachments of the white men upon various nations of Indians who had left their homes and the tombs of their ancestors to satisfy the insatiable desire of the white man for more land. Whole nations had melted away like balls of snow in the sun, leaving scarcely a name except as imper-

---

[7] *Felix Walker's Narrative*, as quoted in *Boonesborough*, by George W. Ranck. *Boonesborough* contains the best description of Henderson's treaty, Deposition of Charles Robertson, and much other valuable material from original sources.

[8] Goodpasture, in his *Indian Wars and Warriors of the Old Southwest*, gives the age of Dragging Canoe at Henderson's treaty as 24. He was certainly older, as his son, Young Dragging Canoe, is mentioned by the trader Robert Dews as a grown warrior two years later, 1777. James Sevier, who saw Dragging Canoe a few years afterward, estimated him to be a man of 45.

[9] Ookoo-Naka, later known as the Little Carpenter, accompanied Sir Alexander Cuming to London in 1730, with seven other chiefs. For names and identity of the Indians who made that trip, see Drake, *Indians of North America*, 367-375; and Williams, *Early Travels in the Tennessee Country, Cuming's Journal*, 122-143.

fectly recorded by their destroyers. "Where now are our grandfathers, the Delawares?" he asked.[10]

"We had hoped that the white men would not be willing to travel beyond the mountains," he continued. "Now that hope is gone. They have passed the mountains, and have settled upon Cherokee land. They wish to have that usurpation sanctioned by treaty. When that is gained, the same encroaching spirit will lead them upon other land of the Cherokees. New cessions will be asked. Finally the whole country, which the Cherokees and their fathers have so long occupied, will be demanded, and the remnant of Ani-Yunwiya, 'The Real People,' once so great and formidable, will be compelled to seek refuge in some distant wilderness. There they will be permitted to stay only a short while, until they again behold the advancing banners of the same greedy host. Not being able to point out any further retreat for the miserable Cherokees, the extinction of the whole race will be proclaimed. Should we not therefore run all risks, and incur all consequences, rather than submit to further laceration of our country? Such treaties may be all right for men who are too old to hunt or fight. As for me, I have my young warriors about me. We will have our lands. *A-waninski,* I have spoken." [11]

The young chief drew his blanket around him and left the council circle. The Cherokees were profoundly impressed, and further proceedings were abandoned for the day. Henderson and Boone were dismayed but acted promptly. The Indians were feasted, and persuasion was brought to bear on the older chiefs.

The Cherokees, as was their custom, counseled among themselves over the events of the day. Attakullakulla advised the acceptance of Henderson's offer. Oconostota frankly admitted that he was neither orator nor diplomat, and was swayed by

---

[10] The Delawares were considered by the various eastern tribes to have been the first inhabitants of the country, hence were called "Grandfather." In 1775, the Delawares were reduced to a shadow of their former greatness, and a remnant of the tribe lived by sufferance among other nations of Indians.

[11] Roosevelt, *Winning of the West,* I, 298-303: Goodpasture, *Indian Wars and Warriors in the Old Southwest, Vol. 4, Tennessee Historical Magazine.* See also, Ramsey and Haywood. Earlier historians credited the speech to Oconostota, but Charles Robertson in his deposition, *Calendar of Virginia State Papers,* I, 283, states that it was Dragging Canoe who made it.

the opinion of his nephew Savenooka (the Raven).[12]   The
Raven was generally recognized by the Cherokees as the logical
candidate to succeed his uncle as war chief, and possibly felt
that realization of this ambition might be jeopardized by Dragging Canoe's action, for Dragging Canoe was a young chief
near his own age.   He therefore also advised acceptance, and
this was generally concurred in by the older chiefs.

It must have taken strength of character for Dragging Canoe
to deny his father and the other influential chiefs of his tribe,
and to resist the tempting display of the white man's goods.
"We will have our lands" was his stubborn reply to all appeals.
He re-entered the council, however, on the following day, and
remained bleakly silent while the negotiations moved to their
conclusion.

The treaty was read aloud and translated, sentence by sentence, by the interpreter Joseph Vann and both whites and
Indians took the precaution to have other interpreters present.[13]
Oconostota warned Henderson that he must go to Kaintuckee
at his own risk; that he could no longer hold him by the hand,
and that the Cherokees must not be held responsible for the
actions of the "Northwards," who would certainly resent the
settlement of the land by white people.   Henderson was willing
to take the risk.

As the older chiefs were on the point of affixing their sig-
natures to the document, the interpreter Vann stepped forward
and stopped Oconostota's hand.   "Take care what you are
about!" he said.   "It is what you will to sign, but clear me of
it, and do not blame me afterward." [14]   Regardless of the
protest, the treaty was signed by Attakullakulla, Oconostota,
and the Raven, in behalf of the entire Nation.

Henderson realized that the passage of settlers across Cherokee lands would cause friction.   He therefore announced to
the Indians, "I have yet more goods, arms and ammunition,
that you have not seen.   There is land between where we now
stand and Kaintuckee.   I do not like to walk over the land of

---

[12] *William Tatham, Wataugan,* Vol. 2, *Tennessee Historical Magazine.*

[13] Indian traders, Samuel Wilson, Ellis Harland, Isaac Thomas, Edward
Rogers, Richard Pearis, and Thomas Price.

[14] Deposition of James Robertson, *Calendar of Virginia State Papers,* 1,
285.   Other depositions in reference to the treaty may be found in same,
pages 277-286.   Henderson's treaty was a tremendous event, and most of the
prominent frontiersmen were present.

my brothers, and want to buy from them the road to Kaintuckee."

This was too much for Dragging Canoe.  Springing to his
feet, he stamped the ground angrily, and pointing to Kentucky,
said, "We have given you this, why do you ask more?"  Facing
Henderson, he said, "You have bought a fair land, but there
is a cloud hanging over it.  You will find its settlement dark
and bloody." [15]

He left the council, and did not return; to the day of his
death he never again entered a treaty with the Americans.  His
departure threw the council into confusion, and threatened for
a time to break off the negotiations as to the path deed.  John
Reid, one of the traders, insisted that Henderson should specify
the exact limits of the land he wanted, "for it is unfair to ask
a people to sign a deed without knowing the boundaries.  Henderson replied angrily that he hoped Reid would not be the
means of breaking the treaty, for he had been put to great
expense, and after the deed was signed he would read the
boundaries.[16]

The path deed was signed by the same chiefs who had made
the great grant.  Henderson apparently understood that he had
bought all the land lying between Holston and Kaintuckee, and
so advised the trader Richard Pearis.  Pearis asked the Indians
if they had sold the lands on Holston River.  The chiefs
thereupon informed Henderson that they had not sold him those
lands, but only a path through them to pass to Kaintuckee.
He then asked the chiefs to allow him "a small distance on each
side of the path for hunting," to which they agreed.[17]

Following the conclusion of Henderson's negotiations, the
Wataugans purchased their lands of the Cherokees; Jacob
Brown purchased a tract on Nolichucky River; and Carter and
Parker were given Carter's Valley in return for goods stolen
from them by the Indians.  The stolen goods, however, were
not considered by the Cherokees to be equal to the value of
the land.  Carter and Parker, therefore, gave additional merchandise, and burned their book of accounts against the Cher-

[15] Deposition of Samuel Wilson, *Calendar of Virginia State Papers,* I.
283.
[16] Deposition of John Reid, *Ibid.,* I, 284.
[17] *Ibid.*

okees, approximately £700, in the presence of the chiefs.[18]

Henderson's goods made an impressive appearance in bulk, but the distribution caused much dissatisfaction, for the number of Indians present at the treaty was large. One warrior who received a shirt as his portion complained, "We have sold the land, and I could have killed more deer upon it in a day than would have bought such a shirt." [19] The dissatisfaction gained followers for Dragging Canoe, the only chief who had protested the bargain. Some of the Cherokees later claimed that they had been deceived by the terms of the treaty. Dragging Canoe, though he may not have understood the treaty terms, realized that the intent of the document was to deprive the Cherokees of their hunting grounds. The Savage Napoleon had found his life work. He devoted his future to making the treaty null and void.[20]

---

[18] Deposition of James Robertson, *Ibid.*, 285. See Appendix "C."

[19] Deposition of John Reid, *Ibid.*, 284.

[20] Henderson's treaty is given in full in the appendix. It is a complicated document, and there is little likelihood that the Indians understood its exact terms, although Henderson probably made his verbal explanation plain enough. The boundaries of the vast territory ceded are vague, no southern boundary being attempted at all. James Robertson in his deposition, however, states that the Cherokees understood that Cumberland River was the southern boundary. The original deeds, of which there was a copy for each of the partners in the Transylvania Company, and also for the Cherokees, have been lost. One copy was filed for record in Rogersville, Hawkins County, Tennessee, in 1794. So far as is known, no copy of the Path Deed is in existence.

# CHAPTER II

## THE SEVEN CLANS

### I

"Time out of mind, these lands have been the hunting grounds of the Cherokees," said the Little Carpenter. He referred to Kaintuckee, sold to Richard Henderson at Sycamore Shoals.

Who were the Cherokees who had owned Kaintuckee "time out of mind?"

When the Cherokees were first found by the white man, they lived in sixty towns and villages along the streams of the Southern Appalachians. Old Kituwah, on the headwaters of Little Tennessee River, was considered the original settlement.[1] The Cherokees often used the term *Ani-Kituwah,* "Kituwah People," but their favorite name for themselves was *Ani-Yunwiya,* "The Real People." [2]

According to the myths, the tribes came from the region of the Great Lakes, and this is correct, for similarity of language has proved the Cherokees to be a branch of the Iroquoian family.

The Algonquin family of Indians once held most of the Atlantic seaboard, their strongest tribes being the Delawares and Shawnees. The Delawares were considered the original occupants of the land, and were called "Grandfather" by other Eastern tribes. They were proud of this distinction, and took delight in preserving the ancient record of their race. In 1822, Rafinesque, early student and historian of Kentucky, was fortunate enough to obtain from a remnant of the Delawares who lived in Illinois, the Walum Olum (Painted Sticks), a pictured history of the Delawares from the time of the creation to the coming of the white man.

The hieroglyphics set out in order, without dates, the names and mighty deeds of the chiefs of the Delawares. The record

---

[1] Kituwah was situated near the present Bryson City, N. C.

[2] Mooney, *Myths of the Cherokees.* Both the Iroquois and Delawares called themselves "The Real People."

14

*Picture by Walter Cline*

SYCAMORE SHOALS OF THE WATAUGA

Scene of Henderson's treaty with the Cherokees, 1775; and of the assembly of Sevier's and Shelby's forces for the march to King's Mountain. The treaty ground was situated to the right of the above view, on the South bank of the river. At the time of the treaty, it was the home of Charles Robertson, Treasurer of the Watauga Association. Sycamore Shoals was called by the Creeks, *Wetoga*, (Broken Waters.)

is divided into four songs, two of which consist of the names and deeds of the chiefs, one of the creation, and one of the deluge. At ceremonial meetings, old men delivered the songs with appropriate dances, that the younger generation might know the glories of the past. The songs were memorized by the hearers, and created intense tribal pride.[3]

The Walum-Olum tells of the warfare of the Algonquins with the Cherokees, who are called Tallegewi. The struggle lasted throughout the reign of three chiefs, after which the Tallegewi removed from their old home in Ohio, to the South. It is thought that the migration occurred during the 13th Century. Two hundred years later, in 1540, De Soto found the Cherokees in substantially the same location which they later occupied during the period of English settlement.

2

According to the Cherokee creation myth, the earth was originally flat, soft, and wet. The great buzzard, grandfather of all the later buzzards, flew over the earth while it was yet soft. When he came to the Cherokee country, he was tired, and his flapping wings touched the ground. Where the wings struck the earth, there was a valley, and where they turned up again, a mountain. Thus were formed the mountains so well loved by the Cherokees.

Fire was placed by the lightning, servant of the thunder, in a hollow sycamore stump on an island. Various animals volunteered to go to the island for the fire. The raven, *Colonah,* was the first. His feathers were scorched, and he has been black ever since.

---

[3] See Drake, *Indians of North America,* pages 720-736, for hieroglyphics, and partial translation of the Walum-Olum. A portion of Rafinesque's writings may be found in Marshall, *History of Kentucky,* 1-47. The Moravian missionary, Heckwelder, in his *Narrative,* 533, gives details of the warfare which forced the migration of the Cherokees to the South. They are called the *Tallegewi,* and are thought by some authorities to have been the builders of the Great Serpent and other effigy mounds in Ohio. Moorehead, in his *Explorations of the Etowah Site,* and after extensive excavations throughout the eastern section of the country, has reached the conclusion that these mounds are part of the culture of the Old Muscogee, an agricultural people who were forced southward by irruption of the Tallegewi. The Muscogee or Creeks originally occupied most of the valley of the Tennessee and its tributaries, as shown by Creek names of towns later inhabited by the Cherokees, such as Tuskegee, Tamotley, Tennessee, Tomassee, Chattanooga, etc.

The little Screech Owl, *Wa-hu-hu,* and the Hooting Owl, *U-gu-ku,* had their eyes burned, and could not see well thereafter.

The little blacksnake, *Uk-suhi,* crawled through a hole in the stump, was almost set on fire by the hot ashes, and after twisting and turning, found his way out the hole he went in, but without the fire. His cousin, the great blacksnake, Gulegi the climber, climbed the stump, was choked by the smoke, and fell inside. Before he could escape, he was as black as his small relative.

Fire was finally brought to the other animals by the water spider, who placed a spark in a little bowl, *Tusti,* which she still carries on her back.

### 3

The first Cherokee man was Kanati, and the first woman, Selu. Kanati became the patron of hunters, and Selu gave corn to her children. Kanati at first kept the game locked in a cave in the Great Smoky Mountains. When he needed a deer, he rolled away a stone at the mouth of the cave, let out a deer, killed it, and carried it home. Two mischievous boys followed him one day, and rolled away the stone after Kanati had left the cave. The animals escaped, and afterward had to be hunted in the woods. As punishment for the boys, Kanati overturned some covered jars, out of which swarmed insects which tortured the culprits.

Blackberries, huckleberries, and strawberries were created by the good fairies, the *Nunnehi,* in an attempt to reconcile Kanati and Selu after a quarrel.

The bears were considered one of the ancient Cherokee clans, the *Ani-Tsaguhi,* who had tired of tribal life and insisted upon living in the woods where they subsisted upon berries and roots. Their peculiar diet caused hair to grow on their bodies, and they became the *Yanu,* bears. The Cherokee hunter asked permission of the spirits of other animals before killing them, but this was not necessary with the bears, who taught the hunters two songs which indicated when food was needed in the wigwams. When these songs were heard in the woods, the bears willingly gave their bodies to their hungry brothers.

4

Jeremiah Curtin, student of the mythology of early mankind, states that there is a marked similarity in the myths of all races, because all have a common origin.

A Greek slave, Aesop, told fables to entertain the children of his master. One of the best known is that of the race between the hare and the tortoise. Probably about the same time that Aesop told this fable to Greek children, Cherokee boys and girls listened with wide-eyed interest to an almost identical myth of their favorite animal, which the story teller prefaced with the remark, *"Tsistu,* the rabbit, was the most mischievous of all the animals." The slow terrapin, as in the Greek fable, won the race from the swift rabbit, but in the Cherokee version, it was won by strategy. The course to be followed was over three hills, and the terrapin posted one of his relatives at the top of each hill to impersonate himself, for all terrapins look alike. Thus, when the fast running rabbit approached the top of a hill, he was surprised to see a slow moving terrapin going over it just ahead. The real terrapin stationed himself at the last hill, and easily won the race.

Because the rabbit lost the race, Cherokee conjurors, before a ballplay, made a soup of the hamstrings of the animal, and endeavored by stealth to pour this over the path which the opposing team would use to reach the ballground. The players might by this means, it was thought, be made tired like the rabbit, so that they would lose the game.[4]

From earliest times, the Cherokees were divided into seven clans, which were, *Ani-waya,* Wolf People; *Ani-Kawi,* Deer People; *Ani-Tsiskwa,* Bird People; *Ani-Wadi,* Paint People: *Ani-Sahini,* Blue People; *Ani-Gatu-ge-u-e,* Kituwah People;[5] and *Ani-Gilahi,* Long Hair People. Each clan was regarded as the descendants of one family, and a distinctive head-dress indicated the clan membership. Intermarriage within the clan

---

[4] The mythology of the Cherokees has been thoroughly covered by James Mooney, *19th Report, Bureau of American Ethnology.*

[5] This Clan has been rendered, by mistake, Ani-Gategewi, Blind Savannah People. The correct form is as above, Ani-Gatu-ge-u-e, which means, literally, "Beloved Town People." Kituwah was considered by the Cherokees to be the original Cherokee settlement, and as such was greatly beloved.

of the father or mother was forbidden. Each clan member owed unswerving loyalty one to another. Should a Cherokee be killed, the members of his clan were required to exact blood for blood, regardless of the circumstances of the killing.

There was no absolute authority in the Nation. The clans sent delegated chiefs to the National Council, which selected a peace and a war chief for the tribe. Each local village, however, was to a large extent a law unto itself. The daily council in which all, even the women, had a voice, was the supreme law. The Indian government was almost a pure democracy.

The Cherokees were just emerging, as were all Iroquoian people, from the matriarchal stage. "They have been a considerable while under petticoat government," Adair comments. Extraordinary respect was paid to womankind. When a Cherokee married, he took residence with the clan of his wife. His children were the property of the mother, and were classed as members of her clan. The wigwam and its contents belonged to the woman. She had a voice in the daily council, and the deciding vote for chieftanships.

The women of each clan selected a leader. These leaders constituted the Womens' Council, which did not hesitate to override the authority of the chiefs when it was thought that the welfare of the tribe demanded it. The head of the Womens' Council was the Beloved Woman of the tribe, whose voice was considered that of the Great Spirit, speaking through her.

Among some of the Iroquoian tribes, women made the marriage proposal. This was not customary among the Cherokees, though it frequently occurred. The usual custom was for the young man to kill a deer and take it to the wigwam of the chosen maiden, to indicate to her that he was a good provider. If his suit was regarded with favor, the young woman prepared for him a meal. If she chose to let the deer lie unaccepted, the lover must take it away and seek another mate.

## 5

Early writers were prone to picture the Indian women as drudges, and the men as lazy, because the women performed the tasks around the wigwam and camp. Such an arrangement, to the minds of both Indian men and women, was an honorable division of labor. The man must hunt, to supply his wigwam with meat. He must protect his family by going on the warpath for long periods of time, on scant rations, undergoing many privations. The Indian woman would have felt disgraced had her warrior husband been compelled to perform menial tasks around the dwelling.

The white pioneer mother, with her large family, was far more of a drudge than her red sister. Indian families, as a rule, were small, usually not more than two children. The Indian mother nursed her child until it was two years old. Until the white man came, with his firewater to degrade the Indian, the red man's strongest drink was the sparkling water of his mountain streams, and there were no drunken Indian fathers to abuse wives and children. There was warm affection and cooperation between the members of an Indian family. Children were taught by precept and example, and were never whipped.

Boys and girls were taught from infancy to respect age, which among all the North American tribes meant wisdom.[6]

## 6

The Cherokee dwelling was oblong in shape, and was built by setting a row of posts, filling the space between with woven wicker work, and covering the whole with a plaster of mud and grass. The roof was made of bark. The house was neatly white-washed, inside and out. The interior was furnished with couches, stools, chests of buffalo hide, and the paraphernalia of Indian house-keeping and personal possessions. Wild hemp was woven into rugs, which were painted on both sides with figures of birds and animals, "well proportioned," as Adair comments, "and with such wild variety of design that they would strike a curious eye with pleasure and admiration." [7]

A small lean-to, called the "hot house," was provided for sleeping quarters in cold weather. This was excavated to a slight depth below the surface of the earth, which afforded

---

[6] Heckewelder, in his *Indian Nations,* a delightful book that was the foundation upon which Cooper built his *Leatherstocking Tales,* specifies an instance in which a party was led into a swamp by an Indian guide who lost his way. Younger Indians realized that the leader was in error, but said nothing, for the guide was older than they. On the warpath, the oldest chief assumed command as a matter of course. In council, young men remained silent until older ones had spoken, and even in play, the oldest child controlled.

[7] Adair, 454.

protection from winds and furnished a means of defense in case of sudden attack. Port holes through which to shoot were concealed from outside view by the plaster, but could be opened quickly from within. Sleeping couches were arranged around the walls of the hot house, with skins of wild animals for bedding. A fire was kindled in the center, and as there were no windows, the hot houses proved almost unbearable to white travellers. The Indians, however, "slept soundly on their broad bed places, with their heads wrapped up." [8]

### 7

While the Indian is usually envisaged as taciturn and glum, life in the villages was far from dull. Good nature and laughter prevailed. There were times when food was scarce, but these were accepted with calm philosophy. Visits between tepees were frequent, pleasant raillery and teasing were customary, and the Indian enjoyed a joke.[9]

There was little time for idleness. Women were occupied with household tasks, preparation and serving of food, tanning, weaving of baskets, and the making of pottery. Men were engaged in the making of arrows, spears, axes, bows, tomahawks, gorgets, chungke stones, pipes, and ornaments. An incalculable number of arrowheads have been found, and other specimens are constantly unearthed by the plow. When we consider that each arrowhead was made, hafted, and feathered by hand, we are compelled to a respect for the industry of the red man.

Despite the late period of the discovery of America, the Indian was in the stone age. A few metals were used for ornament or ceremony, but the tools for utility were of stone and bone.

With limited equipment, a hammer of stone, a shaper and drill of flint, and limestone for polishing, the Cherokee workman produced pipes that required unusual skill and workmanship. He flaked flint, chert, and quartz into arrowheads and spears many of which seem impossible of accomplishment. He cut, shaped, and fitted handles to his tools, and shafts to his arrowheads, with flint knives. He shaped and polished stone axes and tomahawks, and drilled holes through stone,

[8] *Ibid.,* 452.
[9] Grinnell, Geo. Bird, *The Story of the Indian.*

using a cane for a drill.  He produced Chungke stones "with prodigious labor" that are as perfectly made as though milled by modern machinery.  With stone axes, he cleared fields that the white man uses today.

### 8

Games occupied much time with the Indians.  The ballplay was a tribal affair.  It was played on a level field, with goals two hundred yards apart.  The ball was tossed up in the center, and the object of the game was for the players to put it through the opposing goal.  "In this game," said George Catlin, "every player is dressed alike, that is, divested of all dress except the girdle and tail."

The whole population often entered into the competition of the ballplay.  "In the desperate struggles for the ball, with hundreds running together and actually leaping over each other's heads, darting between their adversaries' legs, tripping and throwing, every voice raised to the highest key in excited shrill yelps, there are rapid feats in succession that astonish and amuse one far beyond the conception of anyone who has not had the singular good luck to witness them.  The spectator loses his strength, and everything else but his senses, when the confused mass of ball sticks, shins, and bloody noses is carried off to different parts of the ground for a quarter of an hour at a time without any of the mass being able to see the ball, which they are often thus scuffling for when it has been thrown off and played over another part of the grounds.  And so on until the successful party arrives at one hundred, which is the limit of the game." [10]

### 9

A favorite game of the American Indian, played in some form by all tribes, was Chungke.  Each Cherokee village had its chungke yard, a space of an acre or more, carefully leveled and sanded.  It is said that the first activity of the Indian men when the site of a village was changed was to clear space for a chungke yard.

[10] Catlin, *Indians of North America*, 2, 126.  Catlin closes his comment on the ballplay by saying: "The winners took the stakes, and by previous agreement produced a number of jugs of whiskey, which gave them all a wholesome drink and sent them off merry and in a good humor, but not drunk."

The chungke stone, in shape similar to the Greek discus, was rolled in a wide circle, and the two or more players, after running a moment in its wake, cast "marking poles" after it; the second player attempting to strike the rolling stone, and the first to intercept his opponent's pole while in flight. Quick eyesight and skill were required. The player whose pole fell nearest to the stone where it came to rest counted two points, a hundred being the game. The poles were seven feet long, marked in spaces for measuring throws. Wagers were made on each throw, both by the players and spectators. The inventor of the game is said to have once bet his wife on the result of a throw,—and lost.[11]

## 10

A popular game around the campfire at night was "hands," which was played with stone marbles. Some of these were small, others large, and the player used one of each, the object being to guess which hand held the larger marble. Wagers were made on each play. The holder of the marbles strove to distract the attention of his opponent by singing, moving his body back and forth, and apparently changing objects from one hand to the other. The player about to choose watched closely, with right forefinger above his head. When he had decided which hand held the larger marble, he brought his finger quickly to a point, and the hand must be instantly opened for his inspection.

## 11

Buffalo, engineers of yesterday, tramped the wilderness, found the river fords, located the best routes between feeding grounds, and laid out the Indian paths for peace or war. Later, these paths became the pioneer roads, and still later, the highways of civilization. The Indian traveled afoot from lakes

---

[11] According to the Cherokee myth, the group of stars which we call the Pleiades was formed when eight boys were raised to the sky while playing Chungke. The mother of one of the boys seized him by the ankle and pulled him back to earth with such force that he disappeared beneath the ground. The mother's tears watered the spot, and an evergreen, *Natsi* the pine tree, sprouted and grew tall trying to reach his brothers in the sky.

The Cherokees were so fond of the game that Adair states that an Indian would spend the spare moments of a lifetime in the making of a Chungke stone worthy to be passed on to his son. The skill of the Cherokee workman reached its height in the making of these stones.

to gulf, and from beyond the Mississippi to the Atlantic. He did not struggle through trackless wilderness. The buffalo trails in most cases were wide, deep, and well packed. Practically every modern highway follows the route of a buffalo or Indian trail.

Along the trails by foot, and the rivers by canoe and portage, prehistoric red men carried on more commerce than we realize. Red pipe-stone, found only in Minnesota, was coveted by Indians everywhere. Pipes made of this material have been found from Maine to the Gulf, and far west of the Mississippi. Conch shells from the sea-coast were used far inland for making gorgets, beads, hair pins, and ornaments. Obsidian, the arrow-making material of the West, was exchanged for tobacco from the South. The great flint quarry in Ohio served the entire eastern section.

Commerce was thus a matter of necessity. The trader was welcomed for the wares he brought, and his person was respected though his tribe might be disdained.[12]

## 12

The introduction of new edibles to the white man's diet is the Indian's greatest contribution to mankind. The course of human life has been affected, if not entirely changed, through the addition of such products as corn, both kinds of potatoes, the tomato, pumpkin, squash, kidney bean, cocoa, and tobacco. All of these products, and many others, were introduced to the white man by the Indian. We may thank him for roast turkey, the crowning joy of Thanksgiving, for cranberry sauce, for maple sugar and syrup, and indeed for a more abundant life.[13]

## 13

Hunting, aside from war, was the principal occupation of the Indian man. Fall was the chief season for hunting, which was no haphazard affair, but a planned tribal event. The entire

---

[12] Later, the system was carried into historic times. Licensed white traders located in the Indian country, married Indian women, and wielded influence second only to that of the chiefs. Many of them among the Cherokees were Scotsmen, and we find in Cherokee history such names as Ross, McGilivray, McIntosh, Benge, Rogers, and Hicks. Sons of these men, with white fathers and Indian mothers, rose into chieftanship and power.

[13] Americana Encyclopedia, 15, 56-57.

male population, except certain elders left to protect the women and children, turned out for the pursuit.[14]

As may be said of almost every other undertaking of the Indian, hunting was preceded by ceremony and controlled by religion; fasting, prayer, going to water, and formula, always taking place beforehand.

"O great Kanati, I come where you repose. Let your bosom be covered with blood stained leaves. And you, O ancient Red, may you hover above my breast while I sleep. Let propitious dreams come. Let my hunting be good. Give me the wind, and let my trails be directed. Let the leaves be covered with blood, and may it never cease to be so." Thus sang the Cherokee hunter in the long ago as he appealed to fire and water, gods of the hunting trail.[15]

The wolf, which was considered the hunting dog of Kanati, was never killed. The meeting of a rattlesnake was considered a good omen, for his "bell," heard in the woods, meant "Look about; have a keen eye!" and of course a successful hunter must be alert.

Before killing the deer, the hunter was required to repeat a formula asking permission of the deer's spirit, assuring the animal that his wigwam was without meat, and his wife and children hungry. Should the hunter fail to observe the requirement, his house would be stricken with rheumatism, the crippler. This was because in early days, when the deer were first released from Kanati's cave, many of them were killed by men. They therefore sent word to the Indians that permission must be asked before the killing of a deer. Thereafter, when a hunter shot a deer, *Awi-Usdi,* Little Deer, king of the deer tribe, would run swiftly to the head of the animal and ask if permission had been sought. If the answer was yes, all was well; but if not, Awi-Usdi followed the trail of the hunter and

---

[14] White diplomacy on the frontier was often forced to halt and wait for the hunting season to end. Even commissioners sent by the President to negotiate treaties were occasionally compelled to return without seeing the Indians they had come to interview, because they reached the Indian country when the hunting season was on.

[15] Kanati, the great hunter who once controlled all the game, was typified by the water. Fire, typical of the sun rising in the east from whence all bravery came, was addressed as "Ancient Red." The hunter was required after each kill to offer sacrifice to these two. The blood of the game was fed to the river, dying red the leaves upon its surface; while a piece of the tongue of the slain animal was cast into the fire.

struck him with rheumatism so that he became a hopeless cripple.[16]

The deer king, being immortal, at once came to life if killed. He was easily recognized, for he was snow white, and hardly bigger than a dog. It was the ambition of every Cherokee hunter to kill him, for the possession of even the smallest portion of Awi-Usdi's antlers would make a hunter successful in his hunting for life.

## 14

Fish was an important article in the Indian's diet. The villages were located along the streams for a double reason. The sandy river and creek bottoms were easily cultivated with stone hoes, and fish and clams were at hand. The clam, or river mussel, was probably the first animal food of mankind, and the oldest Indian townsites are denoted by clam shell heaps.

Some of the Indian towns had artificial fish preserves, which are noted by De Soto's chroniclers. Usually, nothing of the sort was needed, for the streams teemed with fish for the taking. The principal fishing was done with nets made of the wild hemp, though bone fish hooks were sometimes used.[17]

Cherokee boys liked to try their prowess by spearing fish from canoes. This was practiced at night, by torchlight. The spear was a long river cane, sharpened at the end and hardened in fire. The fish, when speared, would dart away, but were impeded by the cane which soon reappeared on the surface. The boy would then plunge into the water and capture the fish. From early childhood, the Indian was almost as much at home in the water as on land.

## 15

War was the very life of the Indian, and to tread the warpath was the ambition of every brave. The Cherokees, when urged by the white people to make peace with the Tuscaroras,

---

[16] Mooney, *Myths of the Cherokees,* 250-251.

[17] A favorite form of net was one attached to two long river canes which were fastened together at the ends. Sinker stones were tied to the net to cause it to drag bottom. Two Indian youths took the flexible middle portion, and drew the open mouth through the water. When the catch was sufficient, the poles were released and sprang together by their own elasticity, imprisoning the fish. It was considered a great joke when the net was found to contain a water snake, and shouts of laughter greeted the fishermen who had such luck.

replied, "We cannot live without war. Should we make peace with the Tuscaroras, we must immediately look out for some other Nation with whom we can be engaged in our beloved occupation." Wars with the parent Iroquois, and with the Creeks whom they had displaced, became hereditary, passed down by the Cherokees from father to son as the assured means of gaining glory, and continued until white pressure forced the tribes to unite in common defense. The last fight with the Creeks was at Taliwa, Georgia, in 1755, when Oconostota, at the head of five hundred warriors, defeated his opponents and forced abandonment of Creek settlements in North Georgia. These were later occupied by the Cherokees in the years following the Revolution as they were forced to cede their more northerly lands.[18]

The Cherokee Nation, as well as each village, elected a peace and a war chief. The war chief remained in the background while peace reigned, but took command the instant war commenced. As a matter of fact, he usually began the war. When an insult was offered to his Nation, he was scorned if he failed to strike the war pole and raise the war whoop.[19]

When a leader desired to raise a party to go against the enemy, he would march three times around his house, sounding the war whoop and beating the drum. Warriors would quickly gather, to whom the chief, in rapid and commanding manner, recounted the reasons for his action. He appealed to tribal pride and reminded his hearers of the past valor of their warriors, and exhorted those who were not afraid to join him. Again sounding the war whoop, he raised his tomahawk, struck the war pole, and the dance was on.

---

[18] Ramsey, 83. Taliwa was near the present Canton, Cherokee County, Ga.

When the Cherokees and Creeks were finally overcome by the weight of the numbers of the whites, and were compelled to make a lasting peace, they were worried for fear that their young men, without opportunity to practice warfare, would grow soft. Efau Hajo, a Creek chief, speaking to Colonel Benjamin Hawkins at a treaty in 1802, stated the attitude of the four southern tribes. He said:

"Brother, if we red men fall out, dispute and quarrel, you must look upon it as two children quarreling, and you, our white friends and brothers, must remain neutral. There is among us four Nations, old customs, one of which is war. If the young men, having grown to manhood, wish to practice the ways of the old people, let them try themselves at war, and when they have tried, let the chiefs interpose and stop it. We want you to let us alone."
*American State Papers, Indian Affairs,* Vol. 1, 631.

[19] Adair, 167.

After the preliminary dance, the warriors retired to the winter house of the chief where they remained in seclusion for three days, during which time they fasted. Sentinels were stationed to see that no hungry brave endangered the undertaking by the acceptance of food. Each warrior was given doses of the sacred "Black Drink," which was believed to render him immune to the arrows of the enemy, and to increase his bravery.[20]

At the end of the fast, the warriors donned war paint, held another dance, and departed on the war trail. Shouts of defiance and threats of vengeance rang in the air while the party remained in hearing of their own village, but when the forest was entered, wild animals could not move with more caution or less noise. The men marched single file, with the chief leading. Each warrior tried to step in the footprints of the man ahead, so that if the trail were discovered, the enemy might conclude that only one warrior was in the woods.

The chief's assistant, who was called the *Ettisu,* carried the sacred war pack which was believed to bring success to the party.[21] The Ettisu had charge of rations, and issued a scant portion to each warrior daily, for it was considered that heavy eating tended to make a warrior lazy and to lessen his fighting powers.

The chief was held responsible for the loss of any of his men. "They reckon the leader's impurity to be the chief occasion for bad success. If he lose several of his warriors to the enemy, his life is in danger, or he is degraded by taking from him his drum, war whistle, and martial titles, and given again a boy's name from which he must rise by a fresh gradation."[22]

The military gradations of the Cherokees were, *Aya-tsi-gi,* a warrior; *Dayugi-da-ski,* Slave Catcher, a warrior who has made a captive; *Kolonah,* the Raven, a chief on probation; *Un-tsi-tehee,*[23] Man Killer, a warrior who has killed an enemy;

---

[20] The Black Drink, used by all southern Indians, was a distillation of the leaves of the Cussena or Yaupon tree, a species of Holly. The holly being evergreen was believed to be endowed with everlasting life, and to impart its qualities to the warriors.

[21] Adair connects the war pack of the Indians with the old Hebrew custom of carrying the Ark of the Covenant.

[22] Adair, 416.

[23] Usually rendered *Outacite.*

*Yun-ga-nu-we-u-we,* Chief; [24] *Tsi-okou-ski,* the Owl Person, a chief of first rank: [25] *Danawa-nu-gu-we-a-su,* War Chief; and *Nu-gu-we-a-su Yun-ga-nu-we-u-we,* Principal Chief.

The pinnacle of glory for the Indian warrior was to secure the scalp of his enemy, *Uska-na-gili,* "his hair." He would go a thousand miles if necessary, without regard to hardship or privation, to secure a single scalp. "They seize the head of the dead or disabled person, place one foot upon the neck, and with one hand twisted in the hair, they extend this as far as they can. With the other hand, the barbarous artists draw their sharp pointed scalping knife from a sheath at their breast, give a slash around the top of the skull, and with a few dextrous scoops, soon strip it off. As soon as time permits, they tie their trophy of blood in a small hoop with bark or deer sinews, to preserve it from putrefaction. They paint the interior part of the scalp, and the hoop all around, with red, their emblematical color of blood." [26]

## 16

Women and children were often murdered and scalped by the Cherokees in the heat of attack and massacre. When taken prisoners, however, they were usually well treated and reserved for exchange or adopted into the tribe. Male prisoners, *Da-hu-gee,* particularly those of mature years, were reserved for the torture. Those so condemned were denoted by blue stripes painted across the chest. They were stripped naked, painted black, and bearskin moccasins with the hair outward were placed upon their feet. The head was covered with clay to preserve the scalp.

---

[24] Tsi-okou-ski was usually rendered by the whites, Kitekuska or Kitegiska. The word meant "The Prince." The Cherokees explained to Sir Alexander Cuming that chiefs just below the rank of Principal Chief were designated by the word Okou, the Owl, corresponding to the word "Prince" in English. DeBrahm adds another title, *Great Warrior,* but this, it seems, was a personal appellation of Oconostota. Williams, *Memoirs of Timberlake,* 94; and Cuming's Journal, Williams, *Early Travels in the Tennessee Country,* 115-143.

[25] The word chief is probably an abbreviation of *Asgaya-Yunwi-yunwi,* "Very Great Man," the rank being emphasized by repetition. John Ross, Principal Chief, was called *Gu-wis-gu-wi.* This is the name of a large bird, possibly the egret or swan.

[26] Adair, 416.

The unfortunate victim was compelled to run the gauntlet, *"Ayetli,"* [27] between two lines of howling warriors, each of whom attempted to strike him as he fled past, being careful to hurt only, and not to kill.  He was then bound to the stake, enough slack being left to permit him to move around a few feet.  The actual punishment was left to the women, who set to with every ingenuity the savage mind could devise to break down the courage of the prisoner.  Should he show signs of fainting under tortures too horrible to describe, cold water was poured over him.  When he revived, the program was continued until death came as a welcome relief to his sufferings.

## 17

Indian diplomacy was grave, courteous, and deliberate.  The person of an ambassador was sacred.  His peace pipe, which was his passport, entitled him to full hearing and consideration.

Unless the matter was extremely urgent, it was rarely settled the first day.  The ambassador appeared before the council, gave courteous greetings from his own people, smoked the pipe, and announced that on a certain date, which might be ten days in the future, he would present a matter of importance.  He requested that the leaders should be present to hear it.

On the appointed day, the ambassador stated his case.  To show the friendly feeling of his own tribe, he presented a white wampum belt, and emphasized each point of his talk with a string of white beads.  If the matter concerned war with the white people, the Indian diplomat told of the many acts of kindness performed for that race by the red men, and how unkindly those deeds had been requited.  When he felt that his hearers were duly impressed, he brought his speech to a close by placing in the center of the assembly, a war hatchet [28] and a belt of black wampum.  He then resumed his seat.

There was a deliberate pause.  Then, if any chief considered the plea to be just, he gravely picked up the emblems of war, thus saying in effect, "I accept your talk, and will go to war with you."  If, after a suitable wait, no one in the assembly

---

[27] From the Cherokee *Ayeli,* in the middle, and *tali,* two.

[28] The War Hatchet, usually called the Ceremonial Axe, differed from the ordinary tomahawk.  It was of black material, carefully made and polished, and was for ceremonial purposes only, never for actual use as an axe.

accepted the emblems, the ambassador rose, warned his hearers that they were making a mistake, repossessed himself of his belt and hatchet, and returned to his own country.

The ceremony for peace was similar, except that a white belt was presented instead of a black one, and after long and friendly talks, the hatchet was buried. To the Indian mind, the war hatchet represented the war itself, and when it was buried, the war was at an end.

## 18

The entire life of the Cherokee was permeated and controlled by religion. "We do nothing," said the Cherokee Emperor Old Hop, "without consulting our conjurors, and always abide by what they tell us." The conjurors of whom he spoke were both physicians and priests, the *Adawehi*. The white men commonly designated them "medicine men," but the term Adawehi had a wider meaning. It indicated one skilled in the secrets of medicine and religion, a wise man and a prophet. On his chest, the Adawehi wore a gorget of conch shell, with holes which represented stars outlining a great figure in the skies. River pearls were mounted in the holes, and by the light of the camp fire, they flickered like stars. The gorget indicated that its wearer was familiar with the secrets of the stars.

Sickness and death were considered to be caused by evil spirits. The Adawehi frightened them away by uncouth songs and incantations, by rattling of gourds filled with pebbles, by dancing around his patient as he repeated sacred formulas, and by herbal remedies.

If an Indian vomited yellow bile, the Adawehi gave him an herb with yellow blossom or root. If he were forgetful, he received a concoction obtained by boiling cockle burs, for nothing will stick like a bur. The Indian remedies, used in many cases for supposed magical qualities, proved surprisingly effective. The unquestioning faith of the patient contributed to this end.[29]

There were many snakes in the Indian country, but each warrior carried in his belt pouch the "snake button root."

---

[29] Belief in "Indian herbs" is still quite prevalent throughout the country. Of twenty herbs prescribed by the Cherokee Adawehi, thirteen have been found useful in modern dispensaries, some of them, however, for very different purposes than as used by the Indian physician.

When bitten, he chewed this remedy, which caused him to vomit, and he recovered from the bite. Adair says that he never knew an Indian to die of snake bite, although he had seen them bitten by the most poisonous reptiles.

The sweat bath was a favorite remedy in all cases of sickness. A small wigwam was erected, just large enough for the patient, who seated himself with a basin of water between his feet. Stones were heated in a fire outside, but within reach, and these were transferred to the basin, causing steam to rise. The sufferer endured the heat as long as possible, then threw aside the skins of the wigwam, with a whoop to frighten away the evil spirits which had caused the illness. The treatment was completed by "going to water," a plunge in the nearest stream. The ceremony of "going to water" was practiced daily, regardless of the weather, by all Cherokees. The act, akin to the idea of baptism, was supposed to wash away evil thoughts as well as physical impurities.

Tobacco was considered a sovereign remedy for almost every disease, and its use was considered, too, an act of prayer. The smoke, floating upward, carried a petition to the Master of Life, who had given the tobacco to his beloved children, the red men.

## 19

The Indian reverenced, almost worshiped, nature. Every stone, tree, and animal was believed to have its spirit, and to have been placed in the world for a purpose, as man had been. Nature, hence, must be respected and never abused.

Ruling over all was the Master of Life,[30] *Yo-He-Wah,* who used as his messengers to mankind the four winds, east, west, north and south. Each wind was represented by a color, and each brought different fortune. From the east, red, came bravery and success. The north, blue, brought trouble and confusion to ones enemies. Death was borne on the west wind,

---

[30] Adair, in his *History of American Indians,* 102, calls attention to the similarity of the Cherokee *Yo-He-Wah* to the Jewish *Jehovah,* as proof that the Indians were of Jewish descent. A more rational explanation is that mankind, having a common origin, would retain certain names in common, particularly names of significance.

The Cherokees spoke of the Deity as *"Master of Life,"* or the *Great Man Above.* The term Great Spirit was probably of white origin. *Yo-He-Wah* may have been the Cherokee *Un,* a being, with the suffix *Egwa* added, i.e. *"Great Being."*

which was represented by black. The south, white, was the messenger of peace and happiness.[31]

<h3 style="text-align:center">20</h3>

The Green Corn Dance was the great annual religious ceremony of all southern Indians. The celebration was held in the Seventh Moon, corresponding to our September, and lasted for two weeks. All members of the tribe joined in giving thanks to the Master of Life for the gift of corn for another year's food. Enemies within the tribe, regardless of the offense, were freely forgiven. Fires were extinguished, and new fire was made by the Adawehi by means of friction. The fire on each teepee hearth was renewed from the sacred new fire, thus consecrating each Cherokee home to a new reverence for the Giver of All.

The bringing of the first fruits was an important part of the ceremony. These were deposited in the community house for the use of the poor who had no corn during the winter.[32]

<h3 style="text-align:center">21</h3>

The Cherokees believed firmly in a future life. The good were to be rewarded by being permitted to hunt and partake of enjoyments which had delighted them while on earth. The bad would be compelled to perform the most menial tasks. It was the custom to place in the grave of a deceased warrior, his cherished possessions, and food for his use on his journey to the Happy Hunting Grounds.[33]

The Cherokees, when questioned by early settlers, said that

---

[31] All American Indians believed in the Four Winds, and wore gorgets to propitiate them. The cross was sometimes used to represent the four quarters of the earth among the Cherokees. The Creeks used the "yin and yang," or whirlwind sign. The southern Shawnees used the swastika, with a picture of the ivory billed woodpecker at each of the four sides, considering that bird to be the messenger of the winds. Shawnee women wore the so called "bird stones" in the hair that they might be considered worthy of becoming mothers. Favorite shell gorgets with the Cherokees were the Rattlesnake, supposed to give its wearer the cunning of the serpent; and the Spider, intended to confuse enemies or rivals, particularly in love matters.

[32] The lives of white settlers were more than once saved by corn from the Indian community houses.

[33] Due to this habit we have been able to reconstruct many of the customs of a people who left no written record; such as ornaments, weapons, forms of pottery, etc.

they did not know who built the mounds in their country. However, they constantly used them, preserved their sacred fire in them, and their myths contain detailed description of the process of building them.[34]

22

Early settlers of America lived in a time of hard drinking, and it was perhaps natural that their first gift to the Indian was whiskey. A more unfortunate gift could not have been selected, for the white man's fire water degraded the Indian, and caused him to present his worst side to his new neighbors. It inflamed his passions, and made of him in warfare, a fiend. It contributed to the idea prevalent upon the frontier that the Indian was not human.

The frontiersman had small patience for any study of the Indian's manners, customs, or religion; and once the red man had tasted whiskey he was changed, old ideas took flight, and old customs lost their savor. Thus the opportunity for the study of the religion of the first Americans was lost. Curtin says:

"There is not a single stock of American Indians which did not possess, in beautiful form, the elements of literature, religion, and philosophy which would have thrown light on the beginnings of Aryan and Semitic thought. This knowledge is now lost to us in many cases, but we hope it may be recovered in time if civilized men, instead of slaying 'savages,' will treat them as human beings. These races possess some of the most beautiful productions of the human mind; facts not merely of great, but of unique value."[35]

---

[34] Mooney, *Myths,* 396.

[35] Curtin, Jeremiah, *32nd Report, Bureau of American Ethnology.* The Moravian missionary John Heckewelder, in his *Indian Nations,* repeatedly expresses the same thought.

# CHAPTER III

## CONQUISTADOR

### I

It was July, 1540. Sweating soldiers of Spain toiled a narrow trail, overgrown with vegetation, apparently beginning and ending nowhere, but following the course of a mighty stream called, by the natives, "The Great River." [1]  A motley crew were those Spaniards, their armor tarnished, and silken garments long since abandoned for roughly made habilaments of deerskin.

At their head, the cavalry marched two or three abreast where possible; this served to tramp down the trail and make it passable for the foot soldiers who followed. Close on the heels of the cavalry came the leader, Hernando de Soto, fanatic conquistador, joint conqueror of Peru, wealthy grandee of Spain, worn thin with unbelievable toil and disallusionment; but from whose eye flashed the determination that carried him onward in the search for the rainbow at the foot of which he might find gold and fame.

At the right of De Soto rode Luis de Moscoso, his aide; and following him, the secretary Rangel, whose priestly soul deplored De Soto's lack of effort to convert the heathen and questioned his wisdom, but who faithfully recorded the journey, nevertheless.

Juan Ortiz, a Spaniard who had been rescued from the Indians, and who knew the language of the barbarous land, rode with Rangel. His duty was to interpret the words of the chiefs into those flowing addresses which must have been pleasing to De Soto; doubtless Ortiz worded them with just that idea in view.

Behind the commander came the vanguard of the footmen. Many of them were wealthy Spaniards, who cursed the day

---

[1] The route followed by Hernando de Soto has been and may always be a disputed question. The author has chosen to follow T. H. Lewis, in *Spanish Explorations in Southern U. S.*, and J. R. Swanton, in *Early History of the Creek Indians and their Neighbors.*

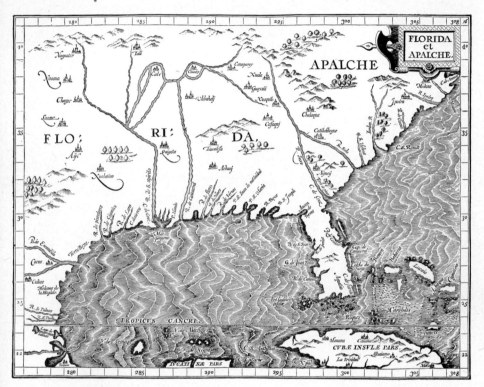

EARLIEST MAP, (1597) SHOWING LOCATION OF CHEROKEES

From Spanish Archives, *Bureau of Ethnology, 5th Report.* The map shows towns: Chalaque, or Cherokee; Xualla, the present Qualla; Guaxule or Gwa-suli, the Cherokee name for the great buzzard of the creation myth; Canasoge, the present Conasauga; and Chiaha, Otter Place, believed to be Hiwassee or Jolly's Island. The large island below Coste is either Long Island, at the present Bridgeport, Ala., or Pine Island, at Guntersville.

they had left their easy homes to embark upon this unprecedented journey. Juan Lobillo was their leader; he had served under De Soto in Peru.

The rear was covered by Juan de Anasco of Seville, mighty of girth and temper. His irascible remarks tempted more than one hot headed Spaniard to reply, as did honest Gomez Arias, "Bad luck to *you,* Juan de Anasco, and the cur that bore you!"[2] although Anasco's stout heart and active spirit commanded their respect if not their devotion. Anasco was the Contador, or Royal Accountant. One fifth of all treasure found was to be kept by him for the King of Spain. There had been little wealth for Anasco to count, but he had borne himself as became a brave man and a Spaniard, and De Soto leaned heavily upon him.

Between the rear and the van were the burden bearers, three hundred Indians furnished by the harried chiefs or "Caciques," usually as the price of the departure of De Soto and his band from their midst. "Tamenes" the bearers were called by the Spaniards, but *Tsa-gwali* by the Indians,—"He has a burden," later to become their name for horses, the strange beasts introduced to them for the first time by the haughty Spaniards.

The burden bearers, to prevent their escape, had each an iron collar. These were joined by chains, thirty Tamenes being chained together. Thus, Balthesar de Gallegos, Chief Castellan, could see that they performed their duties as slaves should for Spaniards. When they rebelled, they were put to death by burning; five were burned at one time for refusing to reveal the whereabouts of their chief.

Among the Tamenes were seven men from Coste,[3] the last town through which the Spaniards had passed. They had shown the audacity to raise their hands in violence against Christians who were despoiling their homes. De Soto had threatened them with burning, but took them along as bearers instead, a fate perhaps as bad.

---

[2] Garcillasso. Gomez Arias had been laboring several hours, most of the time in icy water, getting the horses across a swollen river. Anasco rode up and upbraided him for not making better speed. Arias replied with the above remark, and invited Anasco to take over the work himself if he chose.

[3] Coste is identified by both Lewis and Swanton as being an island in Tennessee River above the present Chattanooga. The Creek Indians were called Kusati by the Cherokees. The words Coste and Kusati are synonymous.

De Soto guarded a chest of pearls, the only spoils he had obtained thus far; but surely, Christians who had suffered so much to bring the blessed word of God into the benighted land would be more richly rewarded. Hence, De Soto's face was ever onward. The chest of pearls was later to be lost at Mauvila.

The whole party was utterly weary in July, 1540. For more than a year, the mad journey had continued; crossing rivers without bridges; through swamps and trackless forests, with here a rude trail, and there none. Tormented by insects, torn by indecision, some wished to turn back, others to turn aside, but De Soto ever to go onward. Said Rangel:

"I have often wondered at the venturesomeness, stubbornness, and persistency of firmness, to use a better word, for the way these baffled conquerors kept on from one toil to another, from one danger to many others; here losing a companion, there three, again still more; going from bad to worse without learning from experience. Wonderful God! that they should have been so blinded and dazed by a greed so uncertain, and by vain discourse which Hernando de Soto was able to utter to these deluded soldiers. He thought that his experience in the south, (Peru) was sufficient to show him what to do in the north, and he was deceived, as history will tell." [4]

The natives, scattered by horsemen, would plunge into the thickets, only to emerge and ply their bows with greater rapidity. During the time a Spaniard could fire and reload his musket, or place a bolt and send it from the cross bow, an Indian could discharge five or six arrows.

Small wonder that the Spaniards were weary as they wound over the crest of another hill on July 10, 1540. There was now no turning back. Behind them stretched twenty leagues of mountains, seemingly impassable, yet through which they had come.

Juan Terron, foot soldier, lightened his load. Of what value were six pounds of pearls in such a land? Mother of God: Whirling the sack over his head as though sowing seed, Terron scattered his pearls to the winds. It was just as well, for Juan Terron was later to lose his life in the Mississippi, with fifty arrows in his body. [5]

[4] Rangel.
[5] Garcillasso.

2

Juan de Villalobos and Francisco de Silvero, fearless scouts, had but that day, July 10, 1540, returned from the fabled country of Chisca. They reported more and more impassable mountains. The yellow metal of the caciques which they sought had proved to be but copper. They brought with them, to be sure, the hide of an ox, most curious, an inch thick, with hair as soft as the wool of a sheep; such insignificant trifles could this country produce as compared with the gold and treasure of the Incas.[6]

Disillusioned and sore of spirit, De Soto rode over the crest of the hill. Below, through the valley, stretched the river, the course of which he followed.[7] Twisting and turning, it entered a pass between two mountains from which rose the signal smoke of frightened natives. Rangel, whose duty it was to record the names of the towns visited by the conquistador, inquired of Ortiz what place they were approaching. Ortiz in turn asked of the despised Tamenes from Coste, and was told in surly syllables, "Talli-danda-ganu," (Two looking at each other.) The two mountains did indeed appear to look at each other across the great river, but despairing of the nasal, gutteral pronunciation of the natives, Rangel wrote it Talli, which means two.[8]

The Cacique of Talli, having heard of the treatment given by De Soto's men to the women of Chiaha and Coste, other towns of his people the Cherokees, strove to get his women and children away in canoes before the Spaniards could arrive. His attempt was thwarted by De Soto, whereupon the cacique stood humbly before the Spaniard and made his apology which Ortiz rendered in flowery words:

"Excellent great prince, worthy are you of being served and obeyed by all the princes of the world, for by the face one can judge the inner qualities. Who you are, and your power, I knew before you came here. I wish not to draw your attention to the lowliness in which I stand before you to make my poor services acceptable

---

[6] The hide was that of a buffalo.
[7] The Tennessee River.
[8] Talli is located by Lewis in the bend of Tennessee River below Chattanooga, now known as Moccasin Bend. The two mountains are now called Lookout Mountain and Walden's Ridge.

and agreeable; since, when the strength fails, the will instead should be praised and taken. Hence I dare to ask that you will only consider and command what you will have me do in my country." [9]

De Soto and his men spent the night of July 10th at Talli. The cacique informed the conquistador that his was the southernmost of the towns of the Cherokees; that the great captain had previously visited their towns of Xualla, Gauxale, Connesauga, Chiaha, and Coste; that on leaving Talli, he would come to the country of the Kusa people, whose first village was a few miles below Talli where there was a great cave near the river. As the Kusa, or Creek people, lived there, the Cherokees called it *Ani-Kusatiyi,* or Kusa People Place. The cacique told De Soto that the country of the Kusa people was thickly settled, with villages close together; that other towns nearby were *Amo-Yeli-Gunhita* (Long Island); *Kagunyi* (Crow Place); and *Amo-Gayunyi* (Running Water Place.) [10]

The cacique presented De Soto with thirty Tamenes and sufficient maize for his trip to Kusa, and courteously gave him directions as to his route. [11] For six days, De Soto and his men passed through towns subject to the Cacique of Kusa. On Friday, July 16, 1540, the Cacique came to meet his guests, borne in a litter on the shoulders of his followers, surrounded by attendants playing flutes and singing. He placed himself and his subjects at De Soto's service, and offered maize, beans, and such supplies as the Spaniards might need while traveling through the Kusa country.

The courtesy of the Indian chief was rewarded by the treachery all too characteristic of De Soto. The cacique was taken by stratagem, placed in chains, and held as a prisoner to insure the good conduct of his followers. Thus had De Soto treated the Inca of Peru.

That such insult could be offered to a proud Indian chief with impunity can only be explained by the fact that white

---

[9] Gentleman of Elvas.
[10] This information is based on the assumption that De Soto followed the route of the Tennessee.
[11] De Soto is believed to have left the Tennessee at Talli, and to have followed the route later known as the Willisi (Willstown) Trail; southward to the present Fort Payne, Alabama, thence eastward to the towns on Coosa River from whence a trail led to Mobile and Pensacola.

men, with their horses, armor, and haughty bearing, were utterly strange to the Indians, and were regarded as supernatural beings. As the red men became better acquainted with the Spaniards, awe gave way to resentment and hatred. A few months later, when the Father of Waters, the Mississippi, was reached, a different story was told, and the Spaniards were glad to escape the warlike Chickasaws by crossing the river. The secretary Rangel has given a vivid picture of the condition of the Spanish invaders at that time.

"I saw Don Antonio Osorio, brother to the Lord Marquis of Astorgas, wearing a short garment of the blankets of that country, torn on the sides, his flesh showing. No hat, barefooted, without hose or shoes, a buckler on his back, a sword without a shield; midst heavy frosts and cold. And the stuff of which he was made, and his illustrious lineage, made him endure his toil without lament such as many others made; for there was no one who could help him although he was the man he was, and had in Spain two thousand ducats of income from the church. And the day this gentleman saw him, he did not believe he had eaten a mouthful, and he had to dig for it with his nails to get something to eat."

So, onward to his grave in the great river which he was to discover, marched the conquistador, Hernando de Soto, until, on the banks of the Father of Waters, "finding all things against him, he sickened and died." [12]

### 3

It was the Cherokee country through which De Soto marched in July, 1540.

Talli-danda-ganu, which Rangel wrote as Talli, was the name by which the Cherokees called the two mountains near the present Chattanooga. Ani-Kusati-yi, Creek People Place, is Nickajack to this day. Amo-ga-yunyi, Running Water Place, was later the home of the greatest of Cherokees, Dragging Canoe. Amo-yeli-gunhita [13] is the present Long Island,

---

[12] The Conquest of Florida, De Soto's march, has been chronicled by four men; Rangel, Gentleman of Elvas, Biedma, and Garcillasso. The first three have been translated by E. G. Bourne, and the last by Theodore Irving. Garcillasso gives many details of personal experience, anecdote, etc., missed by the other chroniclers.

[13] The Cherokee words *Amo* (water) *yeli* (in the middle) and *gunhita* (long) form the words "Long Island."

near Bridgeport, Alabama. Kagunyi is the Cherokee word
for Crow Town. These were all old towns, probably occupied
before De Soto's time. Later, they were to be called the Five
Lower Towns of the Cherokees.[14]

---

[14] The Five Lower Towns were located:

*Nickajack,* at the present Shellmound, Tenn.

*Running Water,* on the east side of Tennessee River below the present
Hale's Bar Lock and Dam.

*Long Island,* on the island of that name at Bridgeport, Ala., and the eastern
bank.

*Crow Town,* on Crow Creek near Stevenson, Ala., one half mile from the
mouth of the creek, on the farm owned at this time, 1936, by Dr. G. L.
Austin.

*Lookout Town,* on the east side of Lookout Creek, one mile north of
Trenton, Ga.

# CHAPTER IV

## THE GREAT WHITE FATHER

### I

Following the passage of De Soto, the Cherokees held uninterrupted sway over their country for nearly two centuries. During this time, they waged vigorous warfare against surrounding tribes, Creeks, Shawnees, Catawba, and Tuscarora. They formed trading relations with the Virginians about the year 1700; and furnished one hundred warriors to aid the English against the Tuscaroras in 1712. After that war, the Tuscaroras abandoned their settlements in Carolina and joined the Iroquois League in the North.

In conjunction with the Chickasaws, the Cherokees made war on the Shawnees who possessed strong settlements on Cumberland River, forcing the withdrawal of that tribe northward to Ohio about 1715. The Cherokees thereafter claimed Middle Tennessee as their hunting grounds.

In 1721, Governor Nicholson of South Carolina, fearing that the French might gain ascendancy over the Indians, invited the Cherokees to a council at Charles Town. A treaty was concluded by which a tract of land between the Rivers Santee, Saluda, and Edisto was ceded by the Cherokees. This was their first land cession, about fifty square miles. They had no towns in the ceded territory and probably regarded it as of little importance. The chief who headed the Cherokee delegation bore the name Outacite (Man Killer), one of their war titles. By this treaty South Carolina assumed control of English trade with the Cherokees. Nine years later, through the efforts of an extraordinary character, Sir Alexander Cuming, the tribe acknowledged the complete sovereignty of King George of England.

### 2

Sir Alexander Cuming, armed with three cases of pistols, a gun, and a sword under his great coat, stood before the council house in the Cherokee town of Old Keowee, March 23, 1730.

"Your Excellency," a trader said to him, "The Indians do not come into this house with arms on their persons, and do not permit anyone else to do so."

"With a wild look, Sir Alexander replied, 'It is my intention if any of these Indians refuse the King's health to take a brand out of the fire that burns in the center of this house, and set fire to it, and guard the door myself that none escapes, but all may be consumed in ashes.' " [1]

The daring Scotsman entered the council house, overawed the three hundred Indians there assembled by his forceful eloquence, and caused them to acknowledge King George's sovereignty on bended knee. He told them that having taken the obligation in that sacred position, they would be no people should they violate it. Runners were dispatched throughout the Nation commanding the head men of the Upper, Middle, and Lower Cherokees to meet at Nequassee in fifteen days, to bow the knee to King George. The interpreter William Cooper declared:

"It is a submission they have never before made to God or man. Had I known what Sir Alexander Cuming would have ordered me to say to those Indians, I would never have ventured into that council house, nor would any of the traders have been spectators, believing that none of them could have gone out of the town house alive, considering how jealous that people has always been of their liberties. No one in South Caroline will believe this report to be true." [2]

Sir Alexander forestalled unbelief. He required each white man present to sign a declaration of what they had seen and heard, "as a testimony of His Majesty's sovereignty, regardless of what becomes of myself, for I am resolved to go on whatever shall be the consequences." [3]

Continuing the extraordinary course he had mapped out for himself, for he acted entirely without authority from any su-

---

[1] *S.C.P.R.* 27: 73-93, *Historical Relation of Facts* by Ludovic Grant.

[2] *Cuming's Journal,* Williams, *Early Travels in Tenn. Country,* 132.

[3] The witnesses were Sir Alexander Cuming, Joseph Cooper, Ludovic Grant, Joseph Barker, Gregory Haines, Daniel Jenkinson, Thomas Goodale, William Cooper, William Hatton, and John Biles. The same witnesses a few days later testified to the meeting at Nequassee, with the addition of Eleazar Wiggan, Samuel Brown, Angus McPherson, David Dowie, Francis Beaver, Lachlan McBain, and George Chicken.

perior power, Sir Alexander made a triumphant tour of the
Cherokee country. At Tellico, he met Moytoy, whom the
Cherokees had agreed to elect as their principal chief, and received from him a pledge of submission. "It was talked among
the several towns last year that they would make me chief
over all," Moytoy told him, "but now it is what you please." [4]

The amazing exploit reached its climax at Nequassee on
April 3, 1730.

"This was a day of solemnity the greatest that was ever seen in
the country. There was singing, dancing, feasting, making of
speeches, and the creation of Moytoy Emperour, with the unani-
mous consent of all the head men assembled from the different
towns of the Nation; a declaration of their resigning their crown of
Eagle Tails and scalps of their enemies, as an emblem of their owning His Majesty King George's sovereignty over them, at the desire of Sir Alexander Cuming, in whom unlimited power was
placed, without which he would not be able to answer to His
Majesty for their conduct." [5]

Cuming's achievement was so incredible that he realized that
it would not receive serious consideration at the hands of King
George and his ministers without proof. He conceived the
plan of taking the leading men of the Cherokees with him to
England to offer homage in person to the king.

The Indians hesitated at taking so unusual a journey. The
distance to be traveled over the Great Waters frightened them.
They could not be back in time for their hunting season, and
their families would be hungry. The "Emperor" Moytoy refused to go because of the illness of his wife at the time.
Finally, Oukou-naco, "The White Owl," from the town of
Tennassy, consented to go. Six others said that he should not
be compelled to go alone. Accordingly, Kitagista, Oukah-
Ulah, Tiftowe, Clogoitah, Kilonah, Onokanowin, and Oukou-
naco, agreed to accompany Sir Alexander Cuming.[6] The party
boarded His Majesty's man of war Fox at Charles Town on
May 4, 1730, landed a month later at Dover, and proceeded to
London.

---

[4] Williams, *Early Travels in the Tenn. Country,* 135.
[5] *Ibid,* 136.
[6] Eleazar Wiggan, an old trader who had been in the Cherokee country
for many years, accompanied the Indians as interpreter. Tennassy, from
which Tennessee draws its name, was a small village adjoining and later
absorbed by Echota, the Cherokee capital.

The Cherokees had the honor of dining with King George II and of kissing his hand and the hands of his sons, the Duke of York and the Prince of Wales. Sir Alexander Cuming presented to His Majesty the Indian crown, of o'possum's fur dyed red, with eagle's tails and human scalps; and gave a full explanation of what he had done.

The Indians remained in England for four months, and were entertained at the expense of the king. Articles of agreement were drawn up in flowery language. The friendship of the English was pledged to the Cherokees "as long as the mountains and rivers last, and the sun shines." [7] The phrase, used thereafter in all treaties with the Cherokees, meant in actual practice "Until the white man needs more land."

The articles of agreement were presented to the chiefs on September 9, 1730. The document recited that King George had fastened one end of a chain of friendship to his own breast, and desired the Indians to fasten the other end to the breast of Moytoy of Tellico, and to keep the chain bright and free from rust.

The Cherokees agreed to trade only with the English; to allow no other white people to settle in their country; to aid the English in war; and to permit white offenders within their nation to be punished by English law.

Okou-Ulah was chosen by the Cherokees to make their response. He wore a red jacket, but the others were naked with breech clouts only, ornamented with horse's tails behind. Each had his bow and arrows, feathers in hair, and was painted with spots of red, blue, and green.

Okou-Ulah said:

"We are come hither from a dark and mountainous country, but we are now in a place of light. The crown of our Nation is different from that which our father King George wears, but it is all one. The chain of friendship shall be carried to our people. We look upon King George as the sun, and our father, and upon ourselves as his children; for though you are white and we are red, our hands and hearts are joined together. When we have acquainted our

---

[7] The Duke of Montague desired that the Indians should have their pictures painted. The artist Hogarth accordingly made a group portrait of them. However, the Duke insisted that the savages should wear court costume for the occasion, thus depriving us of faithful representation by a great master of famous Indians in their native attire.

people with what we have seen, our children from generation to generation will remember it. In war we shall always be as one with you. The great King George's enemies shall be our enemies. His people and ours shall be always one, and we shall die together."

Laying an eagle's tail upon the table, he concluded:

"This is our way of talking, which is the same thing to us as your letters in your book are to you. We deliver these feathers in confirmation of all that we have said." [8]

The Cherokee chiefs, loaded with honors and presents, departed from London, and arrived in Charles Town on May 11, 1731, after an absence of a year. Unfortunately, Sir Alexander Cuming had become involved in financial difficulties and was not permitted to return to America with his red friends, much to their disappointment.

The treaty marked an epoch in the history of the Cherokee Indians. They had gained a Great White Father, but had lost their freedom.

England, in addition to other valuable considerations, had gained a lasting friend in the person of Oukou-naco, the youngest of the Cherokee delegation. The magnificence of what they had seen in London and the friendly reception given them by King George had deeply impressed all of the chiefs, but none of them so much as Oukou-naco. This young Indian was later to become the famous Attakullakulla, the Little Carpenter. From the date of his visit to London, he became the firm friend of the English. As he grew older his influence among his people became greater, and he was made the Peace, or Civil, Chief of his Nation. The Cherokees from time to time took up the hatchet against the English. It was always the Little Carpenter who made the overtures for peace, and he was never satisfied unless the peace was one of friendship for the English.

### 3

During the Little Carpenter's lifetime, Oconostota was War Chief of the Cherokees. Determined, brave, and haughty, he

[8] Williams, *Early Travels in the Tenn. Country,* 115-143. See also, S.C.P.R. 27; 73-93, *Relation of Historical Facts by Ludovic Grant.* Grant accompanied Sir Alexander Cuming throughout his tour of the Cherokee country.

was known as "The Great Warrior," a title well deserved and worthily borne.

The Cherokees had, in addition to the peace and war chiefs, a Principal Chief. Moytoy of Tellico occupied this position at the time of Cuming's visit, and Sir Alexander introduced the practice of calling him "Emperor."

At Moytoy's death, his son Amo-Scossite (Bad Water), claimed his father's title. The Cherokees permitted him to be called Emperor, but followed their ancient custom of choosing the head of their nation, refusing to be bound by rules of heredity. The chief selected as Moytoy's successor was Kana-gatoga of Chote, known to the white men as Old Hop because he was lame. His Cherokee name, Kana-gatoga, means "Standing Turkey."

Old Hop was an unselfish leader of his people, and was recognized by all as being the actual head of the nation. Even the Little Carpenter, whose influence was unbounded, deferred to the judgment and wishes of Old Hop.[9]

## 4

The Indian trade secured to England by Sir Alexander Cuming was immensely profitable. English traders had been among the Cherokees for many years before his visit. All early South Carolina fortunes were founded on the trade in peltries from the Indian country. In 1708, fifty thousand skins per year were exported at an estimated value of £2500 to £3000. Forty years later the annual export had grown to a million and a quarter dollars. One trader estimated that an ordinary hunting season would produce 3500 skins from his district

---

[9] Old Hop has been confused by some historians with Oconostota. His name has been variously spelled owing to the difficulty of Cherokee pronunciation, as Conacorte, Kanatuckgo, Cunnicatogue, Conogtocke, etc. The correct Cherokee form is Kana-gatoga, from *kana* (turkey) and *gatoga* (standing).

Old Hop was advanced in age when he was chosen as Moytoy's successor. There are numerous references in the correspondence of the time indicating him as an old man. Governor Lyttleton wrote him in 1756: "As I hear you are old and unable to walk to Charles Town, though I very much wish for it, I cannot expect to see you."

Old Hop had a nephew, also named Standing Turkey, an active warrior who at his uncle's death served a short time as his successor. It was the younger Standing Turkey who conducted a four day assault upon Fort Loudoun in 1760, and who signed the articles of capitulation of the stronghold.

alone. It was inevitable that such slaughter, with the ever increasing number of traders, should deplete the game and narrow the hunting grounds.[10]

Importance of the Indian trade required that it be strictly regulated. Traders were compelled to secure license and to post bond for good behavior. They agreed not to obtain furs from the Indians by threats or abuse; not to sell rum to the red men; and not to sell ammunition to enemy Indians. In 1716, the trade had grown to such proportions that it was taken over by South Carolina as a government monopoly, and a Superintendent of Indian trade was appointed.[11]

Probably the first Carolina traders among the Cherokees were the Cooper brothers, William and Joseph, who began trading in the lower towns about 1698. William, on account of his knowledge of the country, acted as guide to Sir Alexander Cuming.

Eleazar Wiggan, the "Old Rabbit," incited the Cherokees to war against the Euchees in 1711, for which action his license was temporarily suspended. It was Wiggan's friendship for the Little Carpenter that enabled Sir Alexander to persuade the chiefs to visit London.

Robert Bunning and Cornelius Doherty located among the Cherokees about the same time as did Wiggan. Haywood credits Doherty with having taught the Cherokees to "steal horses from Virginia, which were the first horses they owned."

Ludovic Grant, scion of a noble Scotch family, was as faithful an ambassador as England ever possessed. Anthony Deane of Chote was a Jesuit and "a very learned man." Samuel Benn, of Tennassy, was "a very honest trader," beloved by the Indians. James Adair was a shrewd merchant, a close observer, and an able reporter, as is proved by his remarkable book, *History of North American Indians*.

Robert Goudy of Fort Ninety Six was a hard bargainor. John Elliott of Chote was disliked by the Indians because he would not extend credit or part with goods except at a high

---

[10] Indian trade among the Cherokees has been admirably covered by Mary U. Rothrock, in *Carolina Traders among the Overhill Cherokees, East Tennessee Historical Society Publications,* 1934.

[11] Colonel George Chicken, who accompanied Sir Alexander Cuming in his tour of the Cherokee country, occupied the position of Superintendent of Indian Trade.

profit, but he performed valuable service for England and eventually lost his scalp.

All transactions in the Indian trade depended upon credit. London merchants credited dealers in Charles Town, who in turn credited the traders with their season's stock of goods. The traders advanced supplies to the Indians to be repaid in peltries from the year's hunt.

Profit tempted outsiders who dealt with the Indians without license. Adair, Grant, and other reputable traders complained bitterly that the operations of outlaw traders had ruined profits for those who obeyed the regulations. There was rivalry between the English provinces for the Indian trade. South Carolina considered the Cherokees under her jurisdiction, and intrusion of traders from Virginia or other provinces was deeply resented.[12]

While profits from the trade were large, the risks were also heavy. A bad season's hunting meant that the trader would receive little for the goods he had advanced. Adair comments on the inability of the Indians to understand the obligation arising from a debt. If they were unable to pay, that should satisfy the matter. They ridiculed the white custom of placing men in jail because of debt, thus making it impossible for them to pay.

Most of the traders, after long years of work, were poor men. Ludovic Grant wrote to Governor Glen in 1755:

"As I am to come down with the Indians (to Charles Town,) I humbly pray that I may be included in one of your Excellency's protections, without which I cannot safely appear. Altho' my creditors can recover nothing of one in my circumstances, being utterly incapable to pay the least mite, yet a prison sentence might cost me my life, tho' but a short one."[13]

---

[12] Goods handled by the traders included guns, powder, lead, flints, tomahawks, knives, hatchets, hoes, clothing, match coats (a combination blanket and overcoat), blankets, shirts, petticoats, stockings, ribbons, bracelets, anklets, beads, bells, scissors, awls, pipes, etc. Vermilion, used as war paint, was in much demand. Salt, tea kettles, and looking glasses were so highly desired by the Indians that they were placed on the "free list," the traders being allowed to get what prices they could for them. The looking glasses were for the men. No warrior's outfit was complete without a looking glass slung by a rawhide thong over his shoulder. It was used to see that his paint was properly applied to his face.

[13] S.C.I.A., 5, 53-59.

5

Ancient rivalry between France and England, dating back to Agincourt and Cressy, was brought over into the New World. The Allegheny Mountains furnished a natural barrier to the westward expansion of the English seaboard colonies. France, from her settlements in Canada and Louisiana, sought to gain control of the Mississippi Valley by a chain of forts. Fort Du Quesne was built in the north at the present site of Pittsburg; and Fort Toulouse in the south where Montgomery, Ala., is now situated.

The natural courtesy of the French people was well suited to Indian diplomacy. They were successful in gaining the friendship of powerful tribes in the south, Creeks and Choctaws; and of the Iroquois, Shawnees, and Illinois in the north. Only the small tribe of Chickasaws, friendly to the English, prevented the Mississippi from becoming a French river from source to mouth.

6

The friendship of the Cherokees was sought both by French and English. The visit of the chiefs with Sir Alexander Cuming to London had won the friendship of the Little Carpenter, but he was only the peace chief of his tribe. He was opposed by the war party, headed by the powerful Oconostota.

French emissaries asked the Cherokees, "Why do you go naked, when you might come to the French fort and be clothed as are the Creeks and Choctaws?" The Cherokees were told; "The English plan to build a fort in your country, and as soon as it is done they will kill your head men and warriors, and make slaves of your women and children." [14]

The Cherokees were warned that if they did not make friends with the French, an army would be sent to destroy their towns. The Indians were surprised to find that there were others, as well as King George, anxious to act as their Great White Father. They were invited to send their head men to the French fort to hear a good talk. "Considering it well to be friendly with all kings," a number of chiefs accepted the invitation, and among them was Oconostota. One of the traders wrote to Governor Glen:

[14] *S.C.I.A.* 5: 188-190.

"Oconostota is returned from the French fort with powder and ball, accompanied by some Frenchmen, how many I cannot say";

and again,

"Since Oconostota has returned from the French with goods and ammunition, and has had those assurances from the Creeks, he says, 'What nation or what people am I afraid of? I do not fear all the forces which the great King George can send against me in these mountains." [15]

### 7

The winning of the friendship of the Cherokees by the French would have been the end of English trade with the Indians; hence, each English trader became a missionary of hate against the French. Ludovic Grant wrote:

"As for my part, every opportunity that suitably offers, I fail not to tell and endeavor to persuade these people that the very name of a Cherokee is abominable to the French; and that they, with their Indians, want to patch up a pretended peace with the Cherokees that they may have the safer and surer opportunity to destroy them and in time cut them off from being a people." [16]

In 1736, Christian Priber, a Jesuit priest of German descent, but acting in the interest of the French, appeared among the Cherokees. He was an educated man, acquainted with seven languages. He located at Tellico, abandoned European attire for the breech clout and moccasins, and learned to speak the Cherokee tongue. In a short while, he was established in the good graces of Moytoy the Cherokee Emperor, and with his permission attempted the organization of the tribe into a form of government based on the European pattern. High sounding titles were invented for the chiefs, and bestowed on them by the Emperor at Priber's suggestion. This tickled their vanity and bound them to his aims, for nothing pleased an Indian more than to receive a name from one of his white fathers.

Priber himself took the title "His Majesty's Principal Secretary of State," and under this designation sent communications to Governor Glen of South Carolina. The surprised governor sent word to Ludovic Grant, upon whom he relied for such

[15] Thatcher, B. B., *Indian Biography*, 2, 151.
[16] *S.C.I.A.* 5: 14-20.

matters in the nation, to take the august secretary into custody and send him to Charles Town for examination.

"He, well knowing that I could not take him, laughed in my face until I could hardly bear it," Grant reported.[17]

Colonel Fox was then sent with a body of Carolina troops to arrest Priber. Unexpected opposition from the Cherokees was encountered. They took the sending of troops very much amiss, and told Fox that their country being their own, they could do as they pleased. They asked that he leave at once, and "earnestly requested that the English send no more of those bad papers to their country on any account; nor to reckon them so base as to allow honest friends to be taken out of their arms, and carried into slavery." [18]

Priber, in his capacity of "Principal Secretary of State," was obliging enough to grant Fox and his men "safe passport" from the Cherokee country to Charles Town.

Priber planned a communistic republic among the Cherokees. All were to be equal; goods were to be held in common; there was to be no marriage contract; men and women were to be equal and to enjoy the same privileges; children were to be the property of the state; each individual was to work for the common good according to his talents, and to have as his only property, books, pen, paper, and ink.

It is hardly likely that the Cherokees understood Priber's plan, but he came to possess tremendous influence with them, and would have won them to French interests had he not been captured by some English traders while on his way to Fort Toulouse, after he had been in the Cherokee country about three years. He died in captivity at Frederica, S. C.[19]

During Priber's stay among the Cherokees, the nation was visited by a scourge of smallpox, their first experience with the disease. Within two years, the population of the tribe was reduced one half. The malady was contracted from negroes imported into Charles Town as slaves, but French agents spread the report that the English had placed germs of the disease in goods intended for the Cherokees. The rumor was

[17] *S.C.P.R.* *27*: 73-93.

[18] *Ibid.* See also Williams, *Early Travels in Tenn. Country,* 149 et seq.

[19] Among Priber's effects when captured was a Cherokee dictionary compiled by him, which he had planned to have printed in Paris. This would have been a worth while achievement, for there is no dictionary of the Cherokee language in existence.

credited by some of the Indians, but the medicine men, the Adawehi, ascribed the calamity to the anger of the Great Spirit at the evil conduct of their young people. The attempted treatment was the sweat bath followed by a cold plunge, usually fatal.

## 8

Threats of the French to send an army against the Cherokees, and continued propaganda of the English traders, alarmed the Indians, and they persistently pressed Governor Glen to build a fort in their nation to protect them from their enemies. In 1754, he granted the request by going to the town of Keowee, where, for £500 in goods, he purchased the land upon which to build Fort Prince George, though the Indians offered to donate the site without cost. The governor supervised in person the building of the fort.

The Cherokees of the lower towns were much pleased with the fort. Old Hop and the Little Carpenter, however, felt that it was of no protection whatever to the Overhill towns, and asked that another fort be built in the Overhill country.

Governor Glen took the matter up with London, and also wrote to Governor Dinwiddie of Virginia. He felt that the Overhill country was closer to that state than to Carolina, with an easier line of communication, and suggested that Virginia should build the desired fort. The royal government authorized Dinwiddie to cooperate with Glen in the matter. However, the Cherokees had long been under the supervision of South Carolina, and Dinwiddie had no desire to shoulder the additional burden. Glen had estimated the cost of the fort at £7000, and Dinwiddie sent him £1000 as Virginia's portion.

The Seven Year's War was just beginning in Europe. Frederick the Great of Prussia coveted the Austrian province of Silesia. He repeatedly defeated the forces of the Austrian Empress Maria Theresa, who appealed for aid to her allies France and Russia. Those countries declared war on Prussia, and Frederick, in spite of his wonderful fighting qualities, might have been annihilated had not England come to his rescue. Thus, the English and French colonies in America were involved in the tremendous struggle in Europe. The part played by America was small, but it determined whether this continent should be French or English.

## 9

George Washington, in command of Virginia militia in 1753, realized that much of the French strength lay in their Indian allies. He urged Governor Dinwiddie to send his friend Christopher Gist to the Cherokees and Catawbas to ask their aid for the English. He wrote, "Without Indians to oppose Indians, we shall have little hope for success."

In the spring of 1754, Governor Dinwiddie wrote to Oconostota, "Emperor and King of Chote," inviting him and other prominent chiefs to visit him at Winchester, promising them presents and arms. The message was sent by Abram Smith, and failing to receive a satisfactory reply, a second request was sent by Richard Pearis. The correspondence was noted by the trader Ludovic Grant, who at once notified Governor Glen of South Carolina. He wrote:

"Old Hop said he was much obliged to the Governor of Virginia for his correspondence, but as he was promised by the first messenger, ammunition and war materials, and these not being sent according to promise, neither he nor his people could make powder and bullets, and paper alone (meaning the letters) would not defend them from their enemies." [20]

A third invitation from Governor Dinwiddie, with substantial presents of powder and ball, had the desired effect. Early in August, 1754, Oconostota and a number of chiefs visited the governor at Williamsburg. They expressed a willingness to aid the Virginians provided a fort was built in their country to protect their women and children while the men were at war. Dinwiddie promised the fort, for he was already in correspondence with Governor Glen about the matter. After much entertainment, Oconostota and his party, accompanied by Richard Pearis, returned to Chote. [21]

---

[20] S.C.I.A. 5: 14-20.

[21] An amusing controversy resulted from the visit. Governor Dinwiddie had addressed Oconostota as "Emperor and King of Chote." Old Hop, who rightfully held the title, was offended. Pearis informed the governor, who hastened to repair the damage. He wrote, "I always, until now, understood the Emperor (Oconostota) was their chief man. If Old Hop is a greater, I shall hereafter notice him as such." Thereafter, Dinwiddie's letters were punctiliously addressed to "Old Hop, King, Emperor," etc.

The ablest chief of all, and the firmest friend of the English, was the Little Carpenter. who felt that he had been slighted by Dinwiddie because

## 10

The news that Governor Dinwiddie was corresponding with the Cherokee chiefs spurred Governor Glen into action, and he arranged that a treaty should be held with the tribe at Saluda in the summer of 1755.[22]

Old Hop, Oconostota, the Little Carpenter, and the Raven were the leading chiefs who attended, with five hundred followers. The ceremonies lasted seven days, and on the sixth, as they approached conclusion, Old Hop summoned a council. As the business in hand was of great importance to the nation, he suggested that a speaker should be selected for the occasion. He himself, he said, had never been accustomed to speak to white people, besides, he was old and fatigued from his long journey, and did not feel that he could speak either to his own satisfaction or to the credit of his nation.

Attakullakulla was unanimously selected to speak for the Cherokees. His talk is a model of Indian oratory, forceful and dramatic. He first told of his trip, as a young man, to England. He said:

"I am the only living Cherokee that went to England.[23] Sir Alexander Cuming said that it would have a much better effect if some of us would go with him. But after some questions were asked about England, and how far it might be to it, not one of us would consent to go. At night, the interpreter Chestoo Kaiere, 'the Old Rabbit,'[24] came to my house and told me that the warrior Cuming had a particular favor for us; that if I would consent to

he had not been included in the list of chiefs invited to Winchester. Pearis informed the governor, and he sent a special invitation to the Little Carpenter, "the second greatest warrior," to pay him a visit. Somewhat disgusted, Dinwiddie wrote to Governor Glen, "The seldomer they come the better, for it is a great expense." *Dinwiddie Papers*, 1, 267.

[22] On Saluda River, 20 miles west of the present Columbia, S. C.

[23] Oconostota is said by some authorities to have been one of the chiefs who visited London with Cuming. This is disproved by the statement of the Little Carpenter. Oconostota was not mentioned by Cuming, and he was alive much later than 1756, when the Treaty of Saluda was held. The Carpenter was mistaken, however, in saying that he was the only living Cherokee who made the trip. Tiftowe of Hiwassee, who was one of the Cuming party, was alive in 1756, for he visited Governor Lyttleton two years later and presented to him the identical string of beads that had been given him by King George. Tiftowe was reported to have been killed at the Battle of Etchoe Pass, in 1760.

[24] The trader Eleazer Wiggan.

go, he would be indifferent whether any other went, and Mr. Wiggan pressed me very much to accept the invitation. He assured me that the distance was very much magnified and that I should be back by the end of the summer or at least some time in the fall, upon which assurance I agreed to go. Early next morning one of our people came to me and said that I should not go alone, for he would accompany me and he knew of two or three others he could persuade to go; accordingly they were spoken to and agreed, making six. We immediately got ready and started off." [25]

"What I now speak," the Little Carpenter continued, "the great King should hear. We are brothers to the people of Carolina, and one house covers us all."

Taking a boy by the hand, he presented him to the governor, saying: "We, our wives and children, are all children of the great King George. I have brought this child, that when he grows up he may remember our agreement this day and tell it to the next generation that it may be known forever." [26]

Then, opening a bag of earth, he laid it at the governor's feet. "We freely surrender part of our possessions," he said. "The French want our lands, but we will defend them while one of our nation is alive."

Holding his bow in one hand, and a sheaf of arrows in the other, he continued: "These are all the arms we have for our defense. We hope the Great King will pity his children the Cherokees, and send us guns and ammunition. We fear not the French. Give us arms, and we will go to war against the enemies of the great King."

In confirmation of his remarks, the Little Carpenter handed to Governor Glen a string of wampum. "My speech is at an end. It is the voice of the Cherokee Nation. I hope the governor will send it to the great King that it may be kept forever."

Governor Glen told the Cherokees that the best way to assure a strong fort in their country would be for them to cede all their lands to King George and declare themselves to be his subjects, as the great king would surely defend his own people. The Indians agreed to the proposal, and the treaty was concluded. Glen positively promised that a fort should be built at once in the Overhill towns.

---

[25] Drake, *Indians of North America,* 367: Williams, *Early Travels in the Tenn. Country,* 127.

[26] The child was probably his grandson, Young Dragging Canoe.

## II

In the meantime, General Edward Braddock, with two thousand British regulars, had been sent to crush French ambitions in America while France was occupied with other business on the continent. It was hoped, with the assistance of American militia, to raise fifteen thousand men, and to expel every Frenchman from America.

Washington, who was Braddock's aide de camp, realized as he had done from the first, the need for Indian help if the effort was to prove successful. Governor Dinwiddie at Washington's request sent an express to the Cherokees early in 1755, only to be informed that all the head men had gone to South Carolina for a talk with Governor Glen.

General Braddock marched against Fort Du Quesne without the hoped for Indian help. Possibly he would not have used the Indians if they had come, for he so despised the whole Indian race that Washington's friend the Half King said, "General Braddock looks upon Indians as dogs."

Braddock was defeated and lost his life with that of six hundred of his men. Dinwiddie laid the disaster at Glen's door. He wrote to authorities in England bitterly condemning the South Carolina governor.

"If that gentleman, agreeable to promise, had prevailed over a number of Cherokees and Catawbas to join our forces, we should not in all probability have been defeated, as they would have attacked the French Indians in their bush way of fighting, which the regulars are strangers to. But I notice he had a meeting with those two nations of Indians at the very time they should have joined our forces. He has all along, I think, done everything contrary to his duty and the service of the expedition." [27]

On the same day that he dispatched the above letter, Dinwiddie wrote to Glen and reproached him for Braddock's disaster. Glen replied with some heat that by the treaty just concluded, he had added forty million acres of land to His Majesty's American possessions. "Forty million acres,"

---

[27] *Dinwiddie Papers*, 2, 118.

sneered Dinwiddie, "Of what value are they to the King? Suppose the French invite these Indians farther west, and offer them double the quantity of land?" [28]

Land was cheap in 1755.

## 12

The French and northern Indians, after Braddock's defeat, harassed the Virginia border. Five thousand people fled from the frontier to the more settled portions of Virginia. At Washington's earnest request, Nathaniel Gist was sent to the Cherokees to again beg their aid in a counter-offensive against the Shawnee towns. Gist's mission was successful principally because the Shawnee war parties had penetrated the Cherokee country as well as Virginia, and the Cherokee warriors thirsted for revenge. Washington was delighted to receive the news that more than a hundred Cherokees under Judd's Friend, a brave and capable chief, were coming to his assistance. [29] He wrote to Dinwiddie:

"These Indians coming should be shown all possible respect, and the greatest care taken of them, as upon them much depends. It is a critical time, they are very humorsome, and their assistance is very necessary. One false step might lose us all that, and even turn them against us." [30]

Major Andrew Lewis, an experienced Indian fighter who was well known to the Cherokees, was placed in command of the red warriors, with Richard Pearis as interpreter. The party set off in high hopes for the Shawnee towns on Feb. 6, 1756, with this parting shot from Governor Dinwiddie:

"To Major Lewis: I am glad the Cherokees are in so high spirits. I desire you particularly to show proper regard and respect for the head warrior, (Judd's Friend) and take care that Mr. Pearis behaves well and keeps himself sober." [31]

To cement the friendship thus formed, Dinwiddie sent Colonels William Byrd and Peter Randolph to make a treaty with the Cherokees in behalf of Virginia. They arrived at Chote in March, 1756.

[28] *Ibid.*, 2, 383.
[29] Judd's Friend was otherwise known as Outacite and Ostenaco.
[30] *Dinwiddie Papers*, 2, 320.
[31] *Ibid.*, 2, 320.

The Lewis expedition was a failure. Boats containing the supplies were overturned in crossing a river filled with floating ice. The Cherokee warriors were compelled to eat their horses to avoid starvation. Dinwiddie in a letter to Old Hop mentions some disorder as the party returned to their homes.[32] It is probable that the Indians took horses and supplies from the inhabitants to replace those they had lost.

The fact that each state offered substantial rewards for Indian scalps was a constant temptation to rough characters on the border. A certain frontiersman offered food to a party of Lewis' Indians. While he thus distracted their attention, he sent a number of border ruffians to form an ambuscade for his guests. Several of the Indians were killed. A runner arrived at Chote with this information while the negotiations of Byrd and Randolph were in progress.

The Little Carpenter, realizing the danger, warned the commissioners to keep closely within their tent while he addressed the council, which had been thrown into an uproar by the news. He delegated to Saloue, a young chief of Estatoe, the duty of guarding the commissioners. A number of the warriors were determined to kill the white men forthwith, and had laid hold of Colonel Byrd with that intention when Saloue interposed. "If you kill him," he said, "you must first kill me, and my death will not go unrevenged."

The Little Carpenter begged the council not to violate the old Indian law of hospitality which guaranteed the safety of ambassadors. "Never shall the hatchet be buried until the blood of our countrymen is atoned for," he said, "but let us not violate our faith by imbrueing our hands with the blood of those who are now in our power. They came to us in the confidence of friendship, with belts of wampum to cement a perpetual alliance with us. Let us carry them back to their own settlements, then take up the hatchet and endeavor to exterminate the whole race of them." [33]

The Little Carpenter's advice was accepted, and the commissioners in the meantime had not been idle. Friends and relatives of the slain men were placated with words of sympathy and presents. When the accounts of the commissioners were

---

[32] *Ibid.*, 2, 445.
[33] Drake, *Indians of North America,* 373.

audited, it was found that they had spent the substantial sum of £1319—15s.—8d., the principal item being, "For soothing the Indians." [34]

### 13

At the conclusion of Byrd and Randolph's treaty, the Indians again brought up the matter of a fort in their country, without which they were unwilling to send more warriors to help Virginia.

When this was reported to Governor Dinwiddie, his wrath boiled over. "I sent Mr. Glen, eighteen months ago, £1000 Sterling to build that fort, and he has not begun it. Mr. Glen has always acted contrary to the King's interest, and has embarrassed our relations with the Cherokees and Catawbas." [35]

Major Andrew Lewis was ordered by the Virginia governor to assemble sixty artisans, to proceed to the Cherokee country, arrange for a suitable site, and build the fort. He was instructed to cooperate with the Carolinians if they came, but to build the fort! Dinwiddie again wrote London authorities criticizing Glen, and did not mince words in expressing his feelings to Glen himself.

The defeat of Braddock had created a sensation in London, and Dinwiddie's criticism of Glen, it was thought, deserved investigation. Glen was ordered to report to England to explain all his actions in regard to Indian matters, and William Henry Lyttleton was sent to Charles Town as his successor.

### 14

Major Lewis energetically executed the task given him by Governor Dinwiddie. He arrived at Chote in June, 1755, and was received by Judd's Friend, his old companion in arms. A site was selected on Little Tennessee River opposite Chote, and within a month Lewis wrote Dinwiddie that the fort was ready for its garrison.

The governor had supposed that the Cherokees wanted the fort as a place of refuge for their women and children while the men were away fighting. He considered it much too far

---

[34] *Calendar of Virginia State Papers,* 1, 252. This incident was the beginning of the bad feeling between the Cherokees and the English that was later to lead to the war of 1760-1761.

[35] Dinwiddie Papers, 2, 382.

from Virginia for that state to furnish a garrison, but took the matter up with the Assembly, which authorized him to send fifty men. Dinwiddie then wrote to Governor Dobbs, of North Carolina, to suggest that as the fort was within that state, Dobbs should furnish twenty-five men, and Virginia twenty-five, making a garrison of fifty. He told Governor Dobbs: "I have a letter from Major Lewis among the Cherokees. He has finished the fort I sent him to build, much to the satisfaction of the Indians, and without the least assistance from South Carolina."

The governor wrote congratulating Lewis on his work, and urged that he secure at least a hundred Cherokees for service in Virginia in return for the building of the fort. "I am sending all over the country to purchase blankets, light guns, and other necessaries. My intention is to show them all possible civility," he said.[36]

---

[36] Dinwiddie Papers, 2, 475.

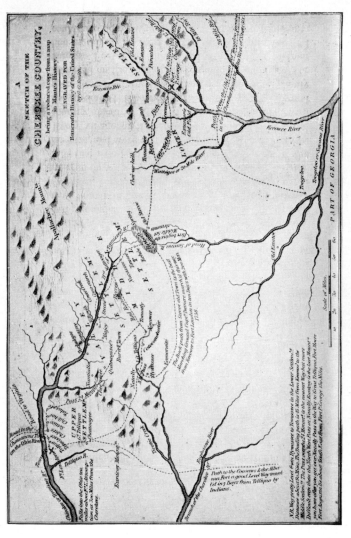

MANTE'S MAP, SHOWING DEMERE'S ROUTE TO FORT LOUDOUN. DRAWN BY MAJOR THOMAS
MANTE OF THE BRITISH ARMY FOR HIS "HISTORY OF THE LATE WAR," LONDON, 1772
From Bancroft's History of the United States, Little-Brown, Boston, 1868.

# CHAPTER V

## FORT LOUDOUN

### I

Governor William Henry Lyttleton, on his arrival at Charles Town in June, 1756, was informed that his predecessor, James Glen, was on his way to the Overhill country to build the fort that had been promised the Indians.

A council meeting was called, upon which his excellency informed the board:

"That it was incumbent upon him to put a stop to any further directions from Mr. Glen concerning the building of that fort, and therefore he proposed to send an express to Mr. Glen acquainting him therewith, and to desire him to come down to Charles Town to give information on all matters which concerned His Majesty's service; also to signify his commands to Captain Raymond Demere in command of His Majesty's Independent Company with Mr. Glen; and to write to Mr. De Brahm desiring to see him in Charles Town concerning measures which had been taken for the building of the fort, and to lay before him any plan he had prepared for the same." [1]

The council members represented to Governor Lyttleton that the Cherokees would take offense when they heard that the forces sent to build the fort had been stopped. They suggested that he should write to Old Hop that the delay was for a few days only, and that the fort would surely be built. This the governor did, and added:

"As I hear you are old and unable to walk to Charles Town, though I very much wish for it, I cannot expect to see you, but I desire that you will send some of your head men to see me and to shake hands with me and to speak with me for you, that I may be acquainted with you and your head men. Should the Little Carpenter choose to stay in the Nation to take care of the English who are to be employed in building the fort, I shall be glad to see him when he thinks it a proper time to come down." [2]

---

[1] *S. C. Council Journal, Exec. Session,* June 2, 1756.
[2] S.C.I.A., 5: 129, 130.

Lyttleton's express overtook Glen at Fort Ninety Six,[3] on his way to the Cherokee country. Glen had made all preparations for building the fort. He had sent Ensign Pearson to select a suitable site, and had with him thirty wagon loads of supplies. Two companies of Provincial troops, commanded by Captains John Postell and John Stuart, had been ordered to meet him at Fort Prince George for actual building operations.

The proposed garrison was His Majesty's Independent Company of Charles Town, two hundred men, commanded by Captain Raymond Demere.[4]

The engineer chosen for the task of locating and laying out the fort was John W. G. De Brahm, a stubborn, conceited and somewhat cowardly man, who nevertheless afterward performed good service for the American cause during the Revolution.[5]

Upon receipt of Lyttleton's instructions, Glen turned the command over to Captain Demere, and ordered several wagon loads of presents which he had intended to distribute among the Indians to be returned to Charles Town.

Captain Demere wrote Governor Lyttleton that his men being already under arms, and the fort at Ninety Six being crowded, he would march to Fort Prince George and there await further orders. He added: "I thought it necessary not to leave this place until I saw Mr. Glen into his coach for his return, for many reasons, the people here not being of the best sort."[6]

2

Captain Demere found himself in an unenviable position after Glen's departure. His health throughout his stay in the Cherokee country was unsatisfactory. The fortifications of

[3] So called because it was ninety-six miles from Keowee.

[4] Captain Raymond Demere, an officer of winning personality, had formerly commanded English forces at Frederica, Ga., and had represented His Majesty's government with distinction in negotiations with Spanish authorities at St. Augustine.

[5] For sketch of De Brahm's life, see Williams, *Early Travels in the Tennessee Country*, 187.

[6] S.C.I.A. 5: 138. James Glen was Governor of South Carolina between the years 1743 and 1756. His reputation has suffered at the hands of James Adair and the bitter criticism of Governor Dinwiddie. The criticism of Glen may be charged to personal dislike, for he was an able and energetic servant of England, with a positive genius for handling Indians and Indian affairs.

Fort Prince George were in bad condition. The Indians were expecting a French invasion, and were impatient at the delay occasioned by the change in governors. Demere's first letter to Lyttleton asked that he be relieved of his command.

"When I set out from Charles Town, I was sickly and infirm, and continue so still. My staying here long will be of great prejudice to me. Besides, your Excellency must be acquainted that I have command of the troops at Frederica where I am much wanted, and where my affairs lays in ruinous condition." [7]

He described the condition of Fort Prince George:

"This fort is in a very bad situation. For my own part, I would rather be in an open field than in it, as I should think myself more safe. The Indians may at any time pass and repass over the ditches and walls. I shall immediately begin to repair it by making the ditches wider and deeper, and repairing the breeches in the ramparts. I would have repaired it with palisadoes, but timber is at a great distance from this fort." [8]

After a week's work, he wrote: "I now assure your Excellency that this place begins to look quite another thing, and has the appearance of a fort, which before it did not." [9]

While at Fort Prince George, Demere received and forwarded to Governor Lyttleton the news that the Virginians had already built a fort among the Overhills, but that the Indians still desired the Carolina fort to be built. The Virginia fort, they stated, would intercept northern Indians who came by land, and the Carolina fort those who came by water.

On July 20, 1756, Demere had his first meeting with the Little Carpenter, whom he described to the governor as "a very sensible fellow and a well wisher of the English." His first impressions were dispelled when after a stay of ten days, the Little Carpenter became very impatient that the men were not on the march to Chote to complete the fort. He told Demere:

"I promised Old Hop to return in sixteen days, twelve of which are already gone. I will not prove worse than my word, although you need not think hard of me if I do, for Governor Glen has told me a great many lies. I now believe you, Captain Demere, to be

[7] *Ibid.*, 5: 149.
[8] *Ibid.*, 5: 150-151.
[9] *Ibid.*, 5: 153-154.

as great a liar as the governor. When you first came here, I took you for a very great warrior, but now no more than a little boy." [10]

Demere, surprised at such a talk from a chief who had professed great friendship for the English, inquired the reason for the Carpenter's sudden change of mind.

"You, Captain Demere, should ask no further questions, for you should know that Governor Glen promised me two kegs of rum which you were bringing with you."

Demere assured the angry chief that he knew nothing of the Governor's promise, but would himself give him a keg of rum to drink with Old Hop. The keg of rum was delivered with that understanding, but the temptation was too great.

"Early next morning the Little Carpenter came into the fort very drunk, supported by two young fellows from Keowee. None of his own people would come with him, for they knew him to be very troublesome when drunk. I endeavored to make myself pleasant until he made a motion to strike me in the face with a bottle he had brought with him. I desired several of the Indians from Keowee to carry him away, which they did, and I heard no more of him until next morning."

The chief appeared the following day, sober, to offer apology. He expressed himself:

"I hope you will forget the whole of it, for there was three of us together when the thing happened. Demere was the first, the Little Carpenter the second, and Rum the third. The people of Keowee have scratched me this morning, to make me remember it, and to make my blood good." [11]

Demere accepted the Carpenter's apology. "After he had expressed himself to me in that manner, I promised him I would nevermore think of it, and we became as great friends as ever." [12]

---

[10] *Ibid.,* 5: 166-168. Heckewelder, in his *Indian Nations,* comments on the invariable habit of the Indians, when setting out on a journey, to name a definite date for their return, and they were very particular to "make their word good."

[11, 12] The other Indians were concerned over the Little Carpenter's behavior. They assured Demere: "He would use his father, King George, in like manner when in drink." Demere had not been the first to experience the bad effect of liquor upon the Little Carpenter. The trader Ludovic

The Carpenter advised Demere of the trouble the Cherokees had experienced in Virginia, and of complaints received from Governor Dinwiddie of the actions of the warriors while on their way home.

"I do not know what to make of Governor Dinwiddie's letter," he said. "He has sent us a good talk and a bad one together. If he complains of the few men who were in Virginia, pray what might he expect of the great number he desires?"

The chief said that he saw no preparation for the men to go to Chote to build the fort. "I should be glad to see them getting in readiness before I leave," he said. Demere thereupon called for volunteers, a sergeant and eighteen privates, to erect buildings for those who were to come after. The Little Carpenter had the satisfaction, when he left, of taking with him Sergeant William Gibbs and eighteen privates. The men were quartered by the chief in his own house, and treated with every kindness. Sergeant Gibbs advised his commander, however, in his first letter:

"Old Hop is mighty uneasy that you do not come and build the fort according to promise. He says the Virginians have their fort done, and ours not begun yet, and he believes we shall never build one, we are so long about it." [13]

The so called Emperor, Amo-Scossite, visited Demere at Fort Prince George. He claimed title through his father, Moytoy, and having heard that a new governor had arrived in the province, was on his way to Charles Town to take him by the hand. Other chiefs assured Demere that the visit was unauthorized, and that Old Hop was the real head of the nation. [14]

---

Grant had written Governor Glen the previous year, "Your Excellency will find him impudent and unmannerly to a degree almost above what can be suffered." Grant was discouraged with Indians when he wrote, for in the same letter he said, "An Indian, I must confess, will laugh in a man's face and immediately stick a hatchet in his soul." *S.C.I.A.*, 5: 53-59.

[13] *S.C.I.A.* 5: 186-187.

[14] Amo-Scossite, on his arrival at Charles Town, proved his identity to Governor Lyttleton by producing the original treaty that had been signed by the chiefs in London at the time of Cuming's visit in 1730. He assured the governor that he had often heard the articles of the treaty interpreted to his father Moytoy, who "always said that he agreed with each of them." In the picturesque language of the Cherokees, he told the governor: "This treaty was fastened to the breast of my father by a chain of friendship, and I am now here to brighten the chain, and to remove any spots of rust that

Contact was established with the Virginia forces under Major Lewis, who wrote Demere requesting the loan of some ammunition. The object of building both the forts in the Overhill country was to secure the aid of the Cherokees in Virginia against the French, and Major Lewis assured Demere that the prospect for getting any number of Cherokees to accompany him was discouraging. "They are like the Devil's pigg, they will neither lead nor drive," he said.

### 3

The two Provincial companies enlisted for building the fort, commanded by Captains Postell and Stuart, arrived at Fort Prince George on Aug. 26th, and Demere paraded his men to receive them. They were accompanied by John Chevillette, who had been appointed commissary for the two forts; and by De Brahm the engineer. On the same day, another appeal came from Old Hop:

"All the talks from South Carolina must be lies, for when I go to bed, I expect to be alarmed by Captain Demere's guns or to see him in the morning, but I wander about the whole day, and can't see him." [15]

Captain Demere again appealed to Governor Lyttleton to be relieved of the command owing to the state of his health and the condition of his affairs at Frederica. He was promised that a successor would be sent as soon as the fort was completed, and Governor Lyttleton commended to his consideration as a possible candidate for the place, Captain John Stuart, commanding one of the provisional companies.

Demere promptly replied that Stuart would make an excellent commander. "I take him to be a very worthy gentleman, fit and capable for any sort of service. I only wish myself as capable as he is for the management of Indian negotiations." [16]

---

have gathered on it." *Ibid.* 5: 191. The name *Amo-Scossite* means bad or dreadful water. A descendant of the same name died while on the way to the west during the removal, 1838.

[15] *Ibid.*, 5: 201.

[16] Captain John Stuart, who thus appeared upon the Cherokee stage, formed a friendship with the Indians that was to endure during his lifetime. Shortly after his arrival at Fort Loudoun, he married Susannah Emory, quarter breed grand-daughter of the trader Ludovic Grant. They had one son, who inherited from his father a bushy shock of red hair, and was

4

On Sept. 21, Captain Demere marched with his little army from Fort Prince George, and arrived ten days later in the Overhill towns.

Old Hop, with two hundred warriors painted and dressed in their best, met him at a little distance from Chote. He was requested to alight from his horse, and was escorted by two warriors to Old Hop, who embraced him with every demonstration of joy and welcome.

Old Hop in his talk to Demere, gave unusual evidence of patriotism. He said:

"I am now old and lie upon a bad bearskin. My life is not more than an inch long, and I know not when a bullet may cut it short. I want my brothers Captains Demere and Stuart to remember that the Great Warrior, Oconostota, and his brother, are the only two men in the nation that ought to be thought of after my death.

"It is true that Willenawah and the Little Carpenter are my nephews, but I do not know how they would behave. If I had not remembered what I owe to a country I love, and had in mind to behave like a father, I would recommend my two sons, but I know them to be incapable, and biased by every lie that comes. I do not know how they will turn out, but I do know the others, for drunk or sober, they always admonish the Indians to love the white people." [17]

On the third day after his arrival at Chote, the chiefs informed Demere that they were ready to place him in possession of the place selected by Ensign Pearson as most suitable for the fort. The site was on the south side of Little Tennessee River, near its junction with the Tellico.

The engineer De Brahm did not approve of the place chosen, but proceeded a mile down the river to the town of Great Island, where, as he said, the river made a natural fortress. There was no place available, however, for the planting of corn and other vegetables. The Indians insisted, too, that the site was subject to enemy attacks. After some argument,

called by the Cherokees *Oo-no-dota,* Bushy-head. He was the founder of the family of that name that is still prominent among the Cherokees. His son, Rev. Jesse Bushyhead, led one of the emigrant bands to the west in 1838. See Starr, *History of the Cherokee Indians,* 577.

[17] A remarkable tribute to Oconostota, coming from his superior.

Demere mildly stated to De Brahm that there was no available
garden spot, and that the Indians were not pleased, but that he
might build the fort where he thought proper. Follows
Demere's report:

"Mr. De Brahm thereupon took one of his pistols from his
holster, and offering it to me, told me to shoot him through the
head. This he spoke with such passion and fury that the like was
never seen. I told him he might blow up his own brains if he
would.

"When Old Hop and the Little Carpenter saw this, they said
that the fort should not be built there, and after great argument he
came back to the first ground, which is a fine spot, pleasant and
agreeable, there being seven hundred acres of land, beautifully
situated, belonging to it, which I was put in possession of." [18]

Work was started on the fort the following day. The
Indians were greatly pleased, and Demere reported them
"bringing eatables by land and water, so that this place already
begins to have the appearance of a market."

De Brahm was displeased at the rejection of his ideas, and
made trouble for Demere from the start. However, Demere
wrote: "All the officers are very willing to do their utmost to
forward the work, and to put up with a little uneasiness, as well
as myself, from Mr. De Brahm." He requested that the governor send colors, and a name, for the fort. "Was this left to
me, I should be at no loss for a name," Demere wrote, meaning to flatter the governor by the intimation that he would call
the stronghold "Fort Lyttleton."

Rum was a forbidden commodity on the traders' list, but it
was the one thing most desired by the Indians. The trader John
Elliott kept a store at Chote. He was in Charles Town about the
time the expedition started for the Overhill country for building the fort, and consulted a lawyer who told him that no one
had the right to forbid the sale of rum to the Indians. Elliott
promptly loaded a hundred kegs of rum on his packhorses and

<hr>

[18] *S.C.I.A.* 5: 241-247. The site selected for the fort adjoined the Cherokee town of Tuskegee. De Brahm, in his account of the selection of the
location, gives quite another version, much to his own credit, according to
which he had the better of the argument. For his account, see Williams,
*Early Travels in the Tennessee Country*, 187-194. This also shows De
Brahm's map of the fort. This was never used, the plan being rejected
on account of the "high tower" it proposed, one of the bastions being 27
feet above the others. See *S. C. Council Journal*, July 29, 1756.

set out for the Indian country with the expectation of reaping a rich harvest of profit.

Demere seized the rum, impounded it in Fort Prince George, threatened Elliott with revocation of his trading license, and denounced him as "a crack brained fellow who does not know or care what he does."

Elliott bided his time. A little later, Demere needed supplies of corn for his workmen. Elliott agreed to furnish them, and hired Indians to bring the corn in canoes. When the task was completed, he gave the Indians orders on Demere for rum in payment for their work. He also made the principal chiefs presents of rum, and gave them orders on Demere.

Demere refused to honor the orders, and explained to the Indians that their treaty with England forbade that rum be brought into their country. Oconostota replied:

"I did not think you would refuse me so reasonable a request. The rum is justly due us. The white people expect the Indians to pay their debts, but now we will take care not to pay any of them. Goods for the fort from Charles Town must come by Tellico, and I will now go to the Tellico people and tell them to take everything that comes, and in particular, all rum. We now see that the French talk was true, and very good." [19]

To prevent an open break with the Indians, Demere gave Oconostota an order for eight kegs of rum. He wrote the governor:

"I am sure that lawyer who advised Elliott did value his fee more than the common welfare. I wish that lawyer were here among these Indians when drunk; he would soon return his fee and be gone."

Elliott, having carried his point, undertook to repeat the process a few days later. The exasperated Demere "staved his kegs," and thus brought the controversy to an abrupt close. The "crack brained" trader, however, was to perform a signal service.

Twelve cannon had been provided for defense of the fort, but had been left at Fort Prince George because of the extreme difficulty of the way. Demere wrote:

---

[19] *S.C.I.A.,* 6: 69, and same, 6: 21-25.

"I believe they will never be brought, the way being so bad; notwithstanding, Mr. Elliott has offered to bring them, for £40 a gun. He proposes to bring them in a litter between two horses. He runs the greatest hazard to lose his horses, and we, the swivels. I think it would be much better that guns should come here from Virginia, as the carriage would be easier, and they have a great many there." [20]

Elliott was given the contract. Much to Demere's surprise, he delivered the guns on November 26th, thereby raising himself in the captain's estimation in that

"He has undertook and performed what nobody else ever would have done. He has hereby served the province in a very particular manner. He knows I was not at all pleased with his former conduct, but I beg that I may have influence enough with your Excellency to hope for a forgiveness for all his past transactions, for this last important service." [21]

The trader had strapped each gun across a horse. The protruding ends often caught on rocks and trees, but the seemingly impossible feat was accomplished without the loss of a gun.

The arrival of the cannon created a sensation among the Indians, who stood in much awe of the "Great guns," and attached an exaggerated importance to their use in Indian warfare. Demere wrote:

"These guns are pretty large, some near three hundred weight. The Indians are very much pleased with them, and say the very name of our great guns will be a terror to the French and their Indians; for they never could expect that we would have brought a train of artillery from such a distance, over such prodigious mountains." [22]

## 5

The stubborn De Brahm continued to give trouble, and Demere commented in one of his letters to the governor:

"I doubt not that Mr. De Brahm has wrote a little too much, and is not able to make his assertions good; notwithstanding this gentle-

---

[20] *S.C.I.A.* 5: 291-294.

[21] Elliott, whose nature seems to have been a curious mixture of good and bad, was thereafter to cause Demere and the province much worry. He was also to perform other service of valuable and unselfish nature. Eventually, he was to give his life and scalp in the English cause.

[22] *S.C.I.A.* 5: 291-294.

man is constantly bawling out that he is acting for the King and the good of the Publick, the Publick, &ca. The men are daily threatened that he has wrote to Charles Town, and will write again if he is obliged to do it for the King and the good of the Publick, the Publick, the Publick.

"God knows what Mr. DeBrahm can write, when every gentleman does what he can for the good of the service. He has said so often that he would go away and leave us that we begin to think this is his intent. He insults and abuses people, thinking that a return of like usage would be a sufficient excuse for him to go away." [23]

A rumor that a French army was on its way to attack the fort before it could be completed caused De Brahm to remove his headquarters to Tomotley, two miles distant, to the contempt of Demere and the other officers.

"He also sent all of his things to Keowee, and it's the opinion of everyone that he intended to march off himself if anything had happened. It is said that he is visited in his room at Tomotley by Red painted faced companions, whose colour he does not dislike.
"His wife wrote him that it was reported in Charles Town that he had gone over to the French. I wish he had gone over to them, or anywhere else, before he came here." [24]

De Brahm was a pompous, strutting fellow, who felt that the project rested entirely upon his shoulders. He ignored Demere, gave out talks to the Indians that they should refuse to pay the traders for goods that the King intended them to have free; and actually promoted mutiny among the provincial troops.

The latter had been enlisted for the building of the fort only, and not in regular service. About the middle of December, De Brahm told Captains Postell and Stuart that as the fort would be completed in three days they could hold their men in readiness for discharge, after which they would receive no pay. Demere confronted the engineer and told him that it was most unusual for anyone to discharge men in the service of the province, while their commanding officer, bearing the king's commission, was on the ground. He demanded the reason for De Brahm's action. The engineer replied that he had a letter

[23] *Ibid.*, 5: 280-283.
[24] *Ibid.*

from the governor instructing him to be frugal. "I have the same instructions," said Demere, "but no man shall leave the fort until it is completed and I discharge him."

The two provincial captains were questioned by Demere. Stuart agreed to stand by Demere, but Postell told him that he would march his men to Charles Town as soon as discharged by De Brahm. He was informed that any such attempt would be followed by his confinement. One of his men, Henry Hammon, said "By God if they confine my captain there will be bloody noses!" Hammon was court martialed and given two hundred lashes. A council of officers agreed that the three companies be paraded the following morning under arms; that the articles of war be read; that Captain John Stuart, an officer of the provincials, should read his commission and instructions; that the men be warned against any attempt at insubordination; and that Captain Postell be privately admonished against the step he intended to take.

De Brahm, finding the situation beyond his control, left in the night. He sent back a runner from the nearest Indian town with "final instructions for completing the works, which should take about three days." "He means three months," a sergeant commented.

The officers, including Captain Postell, signed a message to De Brahm:

"Sir: To my great surprise I received a paper from you last night, 20th December, marked "Final directions for accomplishing the works." I lost no time in calling the officers together. All of them, as well as myself, think you might as reasonably have stayed in Charles Town and sent final directions with the people that came to build the fort, as to send them now when nothing appears but a heap of unformed dirt.

"Can you call this a fort? No guns nor platforms; no barracks; no guards; no necessary houses or drains; no requisition for the health of the garrison; no houses for the officers but miserable hovels built at their own expense, altho' denied by you a little dirt to clay the walls with; no store houses capable of holding any quantity of provisions; in short, nothing yet deserving the name fort.

"The outworks which you say are near finished are no ways defensible, the breast work being in places not three feet high. Nothing but palisadoes can hinder a man from galloping into the fort ahorseback, and after the vast labour and expense bestowed on the

place called by you Glen's Fort, it is to be abandoned and left unfinished.

"I and the rest of the officers acquaint you that the moment you
leave the fort, the work ceases until such time as the governor shall
send a proper person to inspect the present state of the works.

"We are your humble servants,

RAYMOND DEMERE,
JOHN STUART,
JOHN POSTELL,
ROBERT WALL,
JAMES ADAMSON,
RICHARD COYTMORE,
MAURICE ANDERSON.[25]

It was concluded by the officers that the safety of the entire
force required that the unfinished works should be occupied,
each company to finish fortifications to meet their own needs;
that palisadoes be cut, and the fort placed in defensible condition.

Governor Lyttleton was notified of De Brahm's action, and
was requested to send a competent person to see the condition
of the fort when abandoned by the engineer. "I send you Mr.
De Brahm's false plan of the work," Demere wrote; "your
Excellency may have a use for it." [26] "We are no engineers," he
said, "but will do our best for the fort, which scarce deserves
the name of a camp. The Indians call it the fort to keep
horses and cows in. They say Mr. De Brahm ran away to keep
from being killed." [27]

The provincials were set to work cutting palisadoes, which
were to be fifteen feet long, to project eight feet above the
breast-works, with loop holes for firing. The guns were to be
mounted on platforms so they could be fired over the top.

The fort received its name in the midst of the trouble.
Governor Lyttleton instructed that it be called Fort Loudoun
after the new English commander who had just arrived in
America.[28]

"The name of the fort," Demere wrote, "is more agreeable
to everyone than the name Mr. De Brahm had given. As soon

[25] *Ibid.*, 5: 320-321.
[26] *Ibid.*, 6: 42-45. See also Note 18 of this chapter.
[27] *Ibid.*, 5: 366-370.
[28] Another fort, in Virginia, was also called Fort Loudoun.

as the colours come and the guns are mounted, we shall celebrate the name and the day." [29]

Three months of labor were required before Demere could write to Governor Lyttleton, on March 26, 1757:

"Our palisadoes are up, and will last for six years. We are about putting up the fort gates, which are made very strong. What has been done to this fort since that De Brahm went off, and what is yet to be done, I shall refer to other people to inform your Excellency. I have spared no pains in making it as defensible as I could, with all kinds of conveniences in it." [30]

### 6

Work on the fort was spurred by constant reports of French activities, which came mostly from Tellico. The Man Killer, of that town, had visited Fort Toulouse and returned loaded with presents, and had at once hoisted the French colors on their council house. The Man Killer told Demere boldly that he had not gone to the French fort on his own initiative, but by the orders of Old Hop and the Little Carpenter. Demere confronted the Carpenter with this statement. The chief "started up, and said it was a Lye, and that he would go by the other path that he knew, and would see if his father, King George, would remember him."

"Perhaps the Mankiller will give you a French talk that will change your mind," said Demere.

"Do you look upon me as a man and a warrior," said the Carpenter; "I am not a boy, but the head man of this nation. I give talks to the Mankiller, and not him to me. My mind has always been straight. I always think one way. I now take you by the hand, and you hear what I say, and if I perform it not, make me a Lyar." [31]

While Demere was talking to the Little Carpenter, Old Hop, who had also been accused by the Mankiller, came into the fort with a letter in his hand which he wished interpreted. The Carpenter asked him, sternly: "Is that the letter you have received from the French?"

<hr>

[29] De Brahm had proposed that it be called Fort Glen.
[30] *S.C.I.A.* 5: 295-298. One of the defences of the fort was a locust hedge planted in the outer ditch, the long thorns of which were counted on to repel any attack of naked savages.
[31] *S.C.I.A.,* 5: 303-304.

Taken aback at being thus publicly accused, Old Hop replied: "No,—that we will talk of another time." "I want
nothing to do with that stolen affair," the Carpenter retorted,
"it is your affair," and he again asked: "What letter is that you
have in your hand?" "It is a letter from the place of lies!"
Old Hop replied, which displeased the other chiefs, for they
knew that he had designated Charles Town as "the place of lies"
because of the delay in building the fort.

Demere, who had been slyly enjoying the by-play between
the two chiefs, then interpreted the letter, which proved an
invitation from Governor Lyttleton for the principal men to
visit him. Good feeling was restored. Old Hop announced
that the Carpenter would set out in nine days, and Demere wrote
the governor: "The Little Carpenter is a great man in the
Nation,—he is worth gold to us."

The defection of the Tellico warriors was serious, for the
path from Charles Town ran through their town, and so long
as they were hostile, it was necessary to follow a devious path
across the mountains. Demere therefore sent Judd's Friend
to invite the Mankiller and his people to visit him at Fort
Loudoun, where he arranged a barbecue, although provisions
were scarce. In return, the Mankiller invited Demere to visit
Tellico. Friendly chiefs warned him that the trip might prove
dangerous, but the doughty captain was undaunted.

To his surprise, he was received with the eagle tail dance,
evidence of highest esteem, and the Mankiller personally danced
for him until two o'clock in the morning. Demere distributed
presents, and the chiefs told him, "We thought the English had
thrown us away, but as you have now shown us as much affection as other towns of the nation, our fears are over; we see the
error by which our path was darkened, and we cannot possibly
go it again." [32]

The rumor that Postell intended to "run away" as De Brahm
had done, spread among the Indians, and Demere wrote the
governor:

"This has confirmed them in the opinion that all the officers will
run away at the approach of the French, but they mistake in their
way of thinking. As long as I can crawl about and have a drop of

[32] *Ibid.* 5: 341-344.

blood in my veins, I shall fight, and I flatter myself that I have as much courage as any man that ever wore a head." [33]

Old Hop brought to Demere another appeal from Governor Dinwiddie for warriors to assist him against the French. The governor, however, failed to send the presents and ammunition which the Indians always expected with such requests, and Old Hop commented:

"My people's guns are old and good for nothing. I cannot send my warriors to fight the French with their fists, for the French wear shoes and will kick them, and I am sure that would not be agreeable to the governor or to me; and some of my people might leave their scalps behind instead of bringing French scalps home." [34]

Chevilette, the commissary, delivered his first lot of supplies to the fort, and promised to return with a second in two weeks. Nothing had been heard of him five weeks later, and the fort was reduced to one day's supply of corn and no meat. Demere included in the day's orders:

"As this expedition is for the good of the province and the credit of us all, our honour now lies at stake. Therefore, let there be no grumbling among you, that His Majesty's service may not suffer, and the work go on as usual. If people can't exist a few days without meat, I am ready to kill all my horses for them, and by experience I can assure you that horses are very good meat. I shall not fail to partake with you, and it will not be the first time I have eat horse's beef." [35]

Demere's letters to the governor repeatedly expressed the plea: "I am sickly and infirm; I beg your Excellency may send me a successor." It was with genuine joy that he welcomed his brother, Captain Paul Demere, who arrived at the fort on August 6, 1757, to take over the command by Governor Lyttleton's orders.

Captain Raymond Demere wrote the governor a final account of his stewardship; assured him that the Cherokees were firmly attached to the English cause, and made preparations for his departure.

---

[33] *Ibid.*
[34] *Ibid.* 5: 291-293.
[35] *Ibid.*, 5: 291-293.

"On the 14th instant, I had the garrison under arms and delivered up my command to Captain Paul Demere; and on the 19th I set out from Fort Loudoun with Captains Stuart and Postell and Ensign Loyd, accompanied by the Little Carpenter and Willenawah." [36]

Captain Raymond Demere had performed a worth while service in the building of Fort Loudoun, but his greatest achievement was in patiently building up the good will of the Cherokees at a time when they were wavering between French and English influence, and were actually inclined toward the French.

[36] *Ibid.*, 6: 78-81. The Indians, with Stuart as interpreter, were on their way to visit Governor Lyttleton.

# CHAPTER VI

## FRENCH OR ENGLISH?

### I

The long promised Cherokee fort had been built and garrisoned, and there was no longer any excuse for the Cherokees to refuse to go to Virginia. The Little Carpenter promised that they would set off immediately after the Green Corn dance in September. He requested that ammunition and war hatchets be prepared, and that a keg of rum be furnished the warriors of each town to infuse them with proper fighting spirit. Wauhatchie, chief of three of the lower towns, called upon Ensign McIntosh at Fort Prince George, stating "The Indians have dreamed that they must have a keg of rum before they go to war, or they will have no success."

"I am well acquainted with their way of dreaming," McIntosh wrote; "they have dreamed me out of a good many pounds of beef and salt since I came here. I am afraid they will dream for some of this fresh pork before they go to war," referring to a consignment of hogs he had just received. Upon McIntosh's refusal to supply the dreamed for rum, Wauhatchie informed him that he had a great mind to join the French, and spoke of King George with contempt. "He is one of the greatest villains unhung," McIntosh wrote.[1]

About the middle of September, the Cherokees began leaving in large numbers for Virginia. All were under general command of Judd's Friend, although each chief was a law unto himself. Other chiefs were: Wauhatchie, Willenawah, Round O, Scolacuta, Oskuah, Moytoy, the Raven, Saloue, Ucahala, and Tiftowe. Lieutenant Richard Pearis accompanied Judd's Friend as interpreter.

The Little Carpenter, although he was the peace or civil chief

---

[1] *S.C.I.A.* 6: 134-135. The desire of the Indians for rum was cause for constant friction, and caused Captain Demere endless trouble. Samuel Benn, a reliable trader who had been among the Cherokees for twenty years, was assaulted and robbed of his packtrain of goods because he refused to comply with a request from the warriors of Tellico for "a keg of rum." The warriors returned the goods at Demere's command and demanded the rum as a reward for so doing.

JUDD'S FRIEND, OTHERWISE KNOWN AS OUTACITE (MAN-KILLER), AND OSTENACO

A sketch made by the court artist, Sir Joshua Reynolds, while the chief was visiting London in company with Lieutenant Henry Timberlake in 1762.

of his nation, was not barred from the warpath. In company with Oconostota, he led a war party against the French fort at Toulouse. Six French scalps, and two prisoners, were taken. The Carpenter wrote Demere of his success: "I hope you will have white shirts ready for our return. Make them large. Our paint is all gone. Please send two pounds of paint by the bearer, and four bottles of rum. I think it long until I see you." [2]

Oconostota and the Carpenter added a diplomatic triumph to their victory in the field. A party of Cherokee warriors, scouting along the Ohio, had killed five Chickasaws, thinking them to be enemy Shawnees. The incident threatened inter-tribal war. The Carpenter returned with his war party by way of the Chickasaws, and appeased that tribe with his usual eloquence, aided by the gift of two of the French scalps, a string of beads, and a war hatchet. He plead in defense of the offending Cherokees that "they were young fellows, and could not come back without something to show." [3]

The Carpenter set off for Charles Town on his arrival at Fort Loudoun, to present the scalps to Governor Lyttleton. He deemed the occasion appropriate, too, for registering complaint against the trader John Elliott, who had "charged the Indians outrageous prices, particularly on womens' wearing apparel, and who threw the goods at them as if they were dogs." The Carpenter introduced a number of Cherokee women to the governor to bear witness to Elliott's conduct, with the remark:

"It is customary among the red men to admit women to our councils. As the white people, as well as the red, are born of women, is not that the custom among them, also?"

Presenting the French scalps, the Carpenter said:

"When I was last in Charles Town, your Excellency desired me to take up the hatchet against the French and their Indians and to

---

[2] *Ibid.*, 6: 115. The white shirts were desired by the Indians on their return from the warpath for the ceremony of purification. The shedding of blood rendered unclean the garments worn at the time. A fast of three days was required for cleansing, with drinking of the Black Drink, and ceremonies by the Adawehi or conjurors. The white shirts would indicate that the warriors had put away their war clothes and were at peace, white being the peace color.

[3] *Ibid.* 6: 95 and 115.

take their scalps. I always regard the orders of my brothers the
English, and did take up the hatchet and now bring to your Excellency the scalps of the French. As your Excellency is the representative of the great king over the water, I expect you to make
him acquainted therewith."

The governor replied that the king should be informed not
only of the scalps, but of the Little Carpenter's constant friendship for the English, and that the trader Elliott would receive
adequate punishment. The chief then desired that his Excellency "would be pleased to order a little red trunk for each of
the warriors, which being promised, they shook hands and
withdrew." [4]

On his return trip to Fort Loudoun, the Little Carpenter met
the trader Elliott at Keowee and told him that he had complained of him to the governor. Elliott begged for another
chance, and the Carpenter, with his usual kindness of heart,
wrote the governor:

"The Little Carpenter says that he made a complaint against
Mr. Elliott, but meeting him at Keowee, he hath agreed with Old
Hop for Elliott to have his yard longer; and all shirts to be 3
pounds weight of leather apiece; likewise he hath agreed to sell
all kinds of striped cotton at 4 pounds weight of leather and a
fathom likewise of calico; so the Carpenter and the Great Warrior
desire that you would not say anything to Mr. Elliott concerning
the complaint the Carpenter made, for they have agreed among
themselves. I desire that you send me a cloak for my wife." [5]

---

[4] S. C. Council Journal, Feb. 9, 1757; and Apr. 11, 1758.
Many writers have commented on the childlike quality of Indian reasoning and desires, of which the Carpenter's request for "a little red trunk"
for his warriors may be considered an example. Curtin, in his Seneca
Legends and Myths, has pointed out that such instances should not be considered as applicable to the Indians alone, but to the entire human race in
its earlier stages. The Indian was in the Stone Age, and reasoned as a
Stone Age man. It is permissible to assume that our own forbears, when
in the Stone Age, reasoned much the same. As Curtin remarks, the
American Indian offers an excellent opportunity for the study of the childhood of humanity.
[5] Ibid. This communication of the Little Carpenter is particularly interesting because it was written and signed for him by the interpreter John
Watts. This was the first appearance of the father of Chief John Watts,
who was later to make the name famous in Cherokee annals.

3

Following Braddock's defeat, General John Forbes had been assigned the duty of expelling the French from their frontier forts. Forbes apparently learned nothing from his predecessor's disaster as to the value of Indian help. Washington and Dinwiddie wrote him, and placed the blame for Braddock's failure upon lack of Indian allies. Forbes continued to regard Indians with supreme contempt, and his attitude was seconded by his aides, Colonels Bouquet and St. Clair. Bouquet wrote his chief:

"It is a great humiliation for us to suffer the repeated insolence of such rascals. I think it would be easier to make Indians of our white men than to coax that damned tanny race."

St. Clair likewise wrote that he "would have nothing to do with the unreasonable nation of Indians." [6]

Washington, however, had different ideas of the Indians. Writing to Dinwiddie, he said:

"They are more serviceable than twice their number of white men. Their cunning and craft cannot be equaled. Indians are the only match for Indians. If they return to their nation, no words can tell how they will be missed, for upon these people the safety of our march very much depends. However absurd it may seem, it is certain that five hundred Indians have it in their power to more annoy the inhabitants than ten times their number of white men." [7]

There was at the time quite a controversy as to the matter of scalping. Many people, while they had no objection to paying white frontiersmen for Indian scalps, scrupled at paying Indian

[6] The quotations are from Rupert Hughes' *Life of Washington.* Colonels Bouquet and St. Clair could have profited by an attempt to understand the "damned tanny race."

Bouquet later in the campaign commanded Forbes' advance guard against Fort Du Quesne. Hearing that the fort was defended by a small garrison only, he foolishly detached Major James Grant with eight hundred men to reconnoiter the position. Grant was surprised by French Indians, lost three hundred of his men, and was himself taken a captive.

General Arthur St. Clair was later to meet with disaster at the hands of the "unreasonable nation of Indians" that was comparable to that of Braddock.

[7] Dinwiddie Papers.

allies for such work.[8] Washington, knowing Indians, and valuing them on their own terms, shared no such feeling. A party of Cherokees under Ucahala lying in ambush near Fort Du Quesne, took the scalps of an Indian and a French officer, Washington forwarded the scalps to Dinwiddie for the reward, saying:

"I hope, though one is not an Indian's, they will meet with adequate reward, as the Monsieur's is of much more consequence."

Dinwiddie justified scalping by claiming that the French had introduced the practice.

"There are come to our assistance, near four hundred Indians of the Catawbas, Cherokees, and Tuscaroras. I've ordered them out in parties to discover the motions of the enemy, and to scalp those they can overcome, a barbarous method of conducting war introduced by the French, which we are obliged to follow in our own defense." [9]

Edmund Atkin, who had been appointed His Majesty's Indian Agent, brought the accusation: "The Cherokees, in particular, have got the art of making four scalps out of one man's hair." He was not so far wrong. There were rogues among the Cherokees as among all people, and the heavy reward for scalps was a temptation. The Head Warrior of Estatoe informed Governor Lyttleton in a letter that while on the way to Virginia he had met a party of Overhill Cherokees who had killed and scalped two men.

"After the Headman had killed the two men, he scalped them and made four scalps out of the two, and forced every one of his gang to make a promise not to divulge it on pain of being immediately killed; and so made the best of his way toward Winchester to there get the same reward for them as if they had taken that many French scalps." [10]

---

[8] Virginia had a standing offer of fifteen pounds for each Indian scalp, and a bonus for extra scalps in the same year. Other states, notably Pennsylvania, offered more, and were accused by the Virginians of enticing the Indian allies by greater inducement.

[9] Dinwiddie Papers.

[10] S.C.I.A. 6: 137.

4

With the feeling that existed upon the part of General Forbes and his aides; and the additional fact that Cherokee chiefs led war parties into Virginia at will and without interpreters, it was natural that trouble should arise between the Virginians and their red allies. Richard Pearis was the official interpreter. He was compelled to accompany Major Lewis, who commanded both provincials and Indians, in order that the officer might communicate his wishes.

It often happened that a war party of Cherokees, returning from a scouting trip, would find Pearis absent. They were thus unable to explain their wants. Secrecy being an essential of scouting, they were compelled to leave their horses at headquarters. The regular officers treated them with contempt, and they could not recover their horses until the return of the interpreter. One such party consisting of ten warriors was seized and held in confinement for ten days until identified by Judd's Friend.[11]

The Cherokees had come to the assistance of Virginia with the promise of receiving good treatment and substantial reward. Being insulted and even denied their horses, after the service they had rendered, stung their pride and roused them to bitter resentment.

In the month of May, 1758, Moytoy of Settico, at the head of a band of warriors who had served in Virginia, left for the Cherokee country. He was in an ugly mood. A number of his men had lost their horses or had been unable to recover them from English authorities. They took others to the number of twenty to replace their own. Affidavits of various Virginia citizens indicate that the Cherokees took the first horses available, used little ceremony in taking them, and posed as Shawnees to divert suspicion from their own nation.

Among the Virginians whose horses were taken were William Verdiman, his son William Verdiman Jr., John Hall, Richard Thompson, Robert Jones, and Henry Snow, all of

---

[11] See Calendar of Virginia State Papers, 2: 245, 252, 260, 268. The incident caused Washington much embarrassment, and he wrote to Governor Dinwiddie that but for his own efforts, it would have cost the province dearly. He suggested that no Indian war party be permitted to enter Virginia without an interpreter. Lachlan McIntosh, Commander at Fort Prince George, made the same suggestion.

Halifax County. These men gathered some reinforcements and followed the Indians, hoping to recover the animals.

The elder Verdiman, a man of advanced years, led the white men into the Cherokee camp. With hat in hand, he bowed and accosted the savages courteously. "Gentlemen," he said, "we have come to you in a brotherly manner to ask you for the horses and other goods you have taken from us."

The Indians could not understand the words, but perceived that the white men wanted the horses. Thereupon, they began painting themselves, primed and cocked their guns, struck trees with tomahawks, and attempted to encircle the white men. The Virginians took to trees, and a general firing was commenced by both sides. John Hall, a white man, was killed, and three Indians. Verdiman and his companions retreated and alarmed the country. The local militia under command of Captain Mead, to the number of forty, pursued Moytoy's party. The Indians had moved toward Staunton River, plundering the settlers' cabins as they proceeded.

Realizing that their actions might bring on a general Indian war, the Virginians made an effort to parley with the Cherokees. Two men, Hawkins and Tarbro, were sent for that purpose. They found Moytoy and his followers camped on the opposite bank of Staunton River, hallooed, and ten of the savages crossed to meet them.

Hawkins acted as spokesman. He could not make himself understood, but the Indians caught the word "brothers," whereupon they slapped themselves upon their chests and answered, "No, no, no, brothers! English damned rogues!" The two white men were seized, stripped of clothes and beaten, and signs were made to them that they must run or be killed. They ran.

Captain Mead and his men, on the advice of one Shote who acted as guide, placed themselves in ambush at a pass through which the Indians must go, and awaited the savages.

The Indians captured three white men before reaching the pass. John Wallacks, whose affidavit states that he was moved by curiosity to see the Indians, had his wish more than gratified. He was discovered as he hid near the road to watch them pass, and was stripped and beaten. The Indians then shook tomahawks over his head and ordered him to run. As he ran, pleased to escape with his life, an Indian threw a rock which cut his back severely, and well nigh killed him.

John Yates and Philip Preston, who were riding along the road, had heard nothing of the Indian outbreak. Their horses were taken, and they too were stripped, beaten, and ordered to run, which their affidavit states they "instantly obeyed."

A running fight ensued when the Indians reached the pass where Mead's men were posted. Three Indians were left dead on the field and others were carried away. Moytoy afterward stated that the Indian loss was nineteen. After much firing, "both parties fled from each other."

Moytoy hastened a runner to Chote to inform Old Hop of the trouble. Burning for revenge, he led his warriors to the Yadkin River settlements of North Carolina, where he left a trail of blood and destruction. When he returned to his town of Setticoe, he brought with him nineteen scalps of men, women, and children. The victims were poor German emigrants who had nothing whatever to do with the wrong the Cherokees had suffered in Virginia, but to Moytoy's mind, a scalp balanced a scalp.

There were many Cherokee war parties in Virginia during the summer of 1758. Without doubt, there were other cases of horse stealing, although the chiefs, in correspondence with both Lyttleton and Dinwiddie, placed entire blame upon Moytoy of Settico.[12] An ugly feeling against all Indians developed on the Virginia frontier. At least one party of Virginians, under Captain Robert Wade, followed a band of Cherokees and killed

---

[12] For affidavits of various Virginia citizens relative to trouble with Cherokee Indians passing through their country, June 1, 1758, see *S.C.I.A.* 6: 153-183.

Historians generally have followed Hewatt in reference to the matter. His version is favorable to the Cherokees and he is corroborated by Adair. The writer, however, has followed affidavits of Virginia citizens compiled by Governor Dinwiddie immediately after the trouble, and forwarded by him to Governor Lyttleton of South Carolina, *S.C.I.A.* 6: 153-183. The affidavits show plainly that the Virginians had ample provocation, and could hardly have acted other than they did. Hewatt's account is as follows:

"As the horses in those parts ran wild in the woods, it was customary both among Indians and white people on the frontiers to lay hold of them and convert them to their own purposes.

"While the savages were returning through the back parts of Virginia, many of them, having lost their horses, laid hold of such as came in their way, never imagining that they belonged to any individual in the province.

four, who were scalped. Wade's men were required by their leader to take an oath to testify that the victims were not Cherokees, but Shawnees.[13]

5

Early in 1758, Governor Dinwiddie had sent Colonel William Byrd to the Cherokees to encourage the sending of additional warriors to Virginia. Byrd had met the Little Carpenter while the chief was on his way to Charles Town to deliver the French scalps to Governor Lyttleton. The chief had promised Byrd that immediately upon his return to Fort Loudoun he would use his influence to secure warriors from the entire nation, and relying on the promise, Byrd had returned to Virginia. He left his deputy, George Turner, to accompany the Indians.

The chiefs had given Turner hearty cooperation, and announced that they would lead a large number of warriors to Virginia. The date of departure had been set, when the runner arrived from Moytoy with the news of his fight with the Virginians.

The Little Carpenter waited upon Turner at Fort Loudoun, and told him he need not prepare his baggage for departure. He was, instead, requested to attend a talk at Old Hop's on the following day. Turner, in surprise, told the Carpenter that he was ready to set out for Virginia the next day. "One day will break no squares," the chief retorted, and insisted that Turner be at Old Hop's as requested.[14]

When the warriors were assembled, the Little Carpenter told Turner that their conjuror had advised them not to go to Virginia at that time, that the way was beset by danger; that sickness and death would overtake many, and great fatigue be the portion of all, if they were to go.

Turner protested that presents and ammunition had already been distributed. "I can hardly credit," he said, "that so many

The Virginians, however, instead of asserting their rights in a legal way, resented the injury by force of arms, and killed twelve or fourteen of the unsuspicious warriors."

The evidence shows, however, that the horses taken by Moytoy were not wild, but domestic horses taken from their owners by force.

[13] *Calendar of Virginia State Papers*, 1: 254-257.

[14] An expression derived from the practice of the English soldiers of fighting in squares.

valiant warriors will be diverted from their purpose by the words of a conjuror."

The chief replied that the Indians never undertook anything of consequence without consulting their conjuror, "that they might know the will of the Great Man above; and that they never departed from the conjuror's opinion." [15]

Turner asked for an escort out of the country, and was told that he would have to wait two weeks. The Cherokees were disturbed at the killing of their people in Virginia, and wanted further details before taking action.[16]

## 6

The chiefs, after consideration, sent this letter to Governor Lyttleton, requesting him, "Brother, when you read this, send it to our brother the Governor of Virginia, that he may read it and think well."

"BROTHER: The Governor of Virginia has acquainted you with our people's behaviour, and we now hear it from you. We are ashamed and sorry to find how they have behaved, but it was not our orders. Since it has happened contrary to our desire, we beg that it may from this time be forgot, and hope that the path will still be open between us, and everything be as usual.

"What has happened seems as if it was done by people in their sleep, who dreamed a bad dream, but are now awakened out of it, and we hope that this talk, (to confirm which we send some beads) will make everything up, and let us live as before." [17]

The communication was signed by Old Hop, Standing Turkey, the Little Carpenter, and Willenawah. Governor Lyttleton in reply warned the Cherokees that the armies of the great king were strong; that the English were the only people who could supply the Cherokees; that he had been informed that war parties had set out from the Cherokee towns to take revenge, and they must be recalled, or the Cherokees would regret their action when it was too late.

---

[15] *S.C.I.A.* 6: 162-166.

[16] *Ibid.* The trader John Elliott came to Turner's assistance. He loaned the Virginia deputy horses for the trip through the Catawbas, the Virginia road being unsafe; sent Turner's baggage over the mountains on his own horses so that the Virginian might have fresh mounts, and when Turner asked the amount of his charges, replied, "Not a farthing!"

[17] *S.C.P.R.* 28: 86-87.

The difficulty happened at a critical time for Virginia, for Governor Dinwiddie felt that Indian assistance was essential to a successful campaign against the French. He therefore returned a conciliatory reply to the Indians, stating that he had given orders that Cherokee war parties must not be molested; that white people who had lost relatives in the fighting must not attempt to take revenge and that the state would make good their property loss. He informed the Cherokees that Virginia had repealed the act offering rewards for Indian scalps, lest friendly Indians might suffer.[18] He invited the Cherokees to send their head men to see him that all differences might be adjusted.

Accordingly, the Little Carpenter departed for Virginia. Tiftowe of Hiwassee, one of the chiefs who had visited England with Sir Alexander Cuming, proceeded to Charles Town to present to Governor Lyttleton as a token of the desire of the Cherokees for peace, the very string of beads which had been given him in London by King George II.[19]

## 7

By the fall of 1758, General Forbes' campaign against Fort Du Quesne was well under way. Colonel Bouquet, in command of the advance, detached Major James Grant with 800 Highlanders and 200 Virginians, and Indian scouts, to reconnoiter the fort. As they drew near unobserved, the thought occurred to Grant that he might take the fort by surprise, and thus anticipate his commander. Major Lewis, in command of the provincials, remonstrated, and was ordered to remain with his men in the rear. Grant camped near the fort during the night. The next morning he caused Donald Macdonald, commander of the Highlanders, to sound reveille and advance to the attack. This aroused hostile Indians, 1500 in number, who were lying on the opposite side of the river. Soon, the Highlanders were surrounded by overwhelming numbers of savages. The work of death went forward in a manner novel to the Scotsmen, who, in European warfare had never seen men's heads skinned.

Lewis, in the rear, advanced quickly to Grant's aid. Meeting

---

[18] According to Adair, this had actually happened in the case of the Cherokee warriors killed in Virginia. Virginia citizens turned in the scalps as those of enemy Indians, and collected the reward.
[19] *S. C. Council Journal, Exec. Sess.,* Nov. 14, 1758.

a Highlander in rapid flight, he asked how the battle went, and received the reply, "We're a' beaten, and I saw Donald Macdonald up to his hunkers in mud, wi' the skeen aff his heed!" More than a third of Grant's forces were killed, and both Grant and Lewis were taken prisoners.[20]

Two months later, in November, Forbes advanced with his entire army, and the French, outnumbered, burned and abandoned Fort Du Quesne. The English soldiers marching into the blackened ruins were saddened to note the skulls of Grant's Highlanders, mounted on poles, with kilts twisted underneath to represent skirts.

In the meantime, the Cherokees, a few of whom had remained with Forbes' army, received a final insult. The Little Carpenter, after interviewing Governor Dinwiddie at Winchester, and feeling that all differences between the Cherokees and Virginia were adjusted, had proceeded to Forbes' camp about ten days before the fort was taken.

The trouble with the Indians had confirmed Forbes' previous opinion of Indians in general. He declared the Little Carpenter "as consummate a dog as any of them, exceeding all of them in his avaricious demands." He thought it bad policy, however, "after laying out so many thousands of pounds, to lose him and all the rest for a few hundred more." He upbraided the Carpenter, however, in so ungracious a manner that the entire body of Cherokees abandoned the army a few days before Du Quesne was occupied.[21]

When word of the "villanous desertion" was brought to Forbes, he dispatched orders to all British posts that the Cherokees be apprehended, disarmed, and conducted to their own country. The Little Carpenter, however, returned by the back country of Virginia and reached the Cherokee towns without molestation.

8

The resentment of the Cherokees for their ill treatment in Virginia became intensified when, early in 1759, the Mortar, a prominent Creek chief attached to French interests, took up his

---

[20] A stirring account of Grant's disaster, and of Braddock's defeat, may be found in Henry Howe's *The Great West*, pages 58-64.

[21] Goodpasture, *Indian Wars and Warriors in Old Southwest, Tennessee Historical Magazine*, 4: 10.

residence at Chote in spite of Demere's protest.  The Mortar ridiculed the Cherokees for not taking up the hatchet against the English.  The Frenchman Lantagnac was sent to Tellico by Governor Kerleric to fan Cherokee dissatisfaction into action. He urged particularly that the Cherokees should destroy Fort Loudoun.  The weeping of the Cherokee women over their slain warriors increased the general bad feeling.

In April, 1759, Lieutenant Richard Coytmore was sent to Fort Prince George to succeed Lachlan McIntosh.  The change was unfortunate, for McIntosh had treated the Indians kindly, and had their confidence.  Coytmore and Ensign Bell intensified the dissatisfaction while on a drunken spree by forcing their way into a Cherokee house in Keowee while the men were away, and grossly mistreating the women therein.  The offense was repeated a few days later.

Lantagnac, in an impassioned talk, urged the Cherokees to war.  Seizing a tomahawk, he struck the war pole and cried: "Who is there that will take this hatchet for the King of France?  Let him come forth!"

Saloue of Estatoe answered: "I will take it!  The spirits of our dead warriors call.  He is less than an old woman who will not answer them!"

Wauhatchie, chief of three lower towns, followed Saloue and took the hatchet.  The example was followed by the warriors generally, and a war dance was soon in full swing.  The excitement swept through the lower towns.  War parties departed for the frontier to gain glory by "killing swarms of white dung-hill fowls, in the corn fields and asleep." [22]

The chiefs responsible for the outbreak are said to have instructed their followers to go to Virginia and take scalps from the people who had shown such ingratitude to the Cherokees. The impatient young warriors could not wait, and the force of the attack fell on the Carolina frontier.  Governor Lyttleton, in his report to the council on Oct. 20, 1759, summed up the loss: "twenty-two killed, two scalped but yet alive, and the entire frontier terrorized."

The outrages were committed entirely by warriors from the lower towns.  Not a warrior among the Overhills took up the hatchet.  At Fort Loudoun, Old Hop, Willenawah, and the

[22] Adair, 263.

Little Carpenter delivered to Captain Demere the scalps taken by Moytoy, and they were given burial.

Early in December, Governor Lyttleton advised the council that he was determined to lead a force to chastise the Cherokees into a lasting peace. The council authorized an army of fifteen hundred men. Colonels Beale, Pawley, Byrne, Hayward and Rivers were ordered to "fire the alarm and draft one half of their regiments."

9

In the midst of busy preparations, Oconostota, the Great Warrior, with twenty-two leading men from the nation, arrived at Charles Town. The council advised the governor that the chiefs should not be received with the usual marks of friendship, "Nevertheless, as your Excellency has in some talks lately sent to them assured them that if any of their head men should come hither to treat upon any matter, they shall come and go to their nation in safety." The council also advised the governor to tell the chiefs that as he was himself about to set out for the Cherokee country, they might return under his protection.

The Cherokees were admitted to the council chamber, and after smoking, Oconostota delivered a frank and straightforward appeal for peace. He said:

"Your Excellency is the beloved man; I am come to talk with you. I come from my governor, Old Hop, at Chote. There has been bad doings at the towns thereabouts, but I was not the beginner of them. Old Hop, my governor, has always loved the white people, and I am come hither to prove it. The path has been a little bad, but I am come to make it straight from your Excellency to my governor. There has been blood spilled, but I am come to clean it up. I am a warrior, but want no war with the English. Like a cloudy morning that clears away again, I am endeavoring to clear away all that is bad."

He laid some deerskins at the governor's feet, and continued:

"Your warriors have carried the hatchet to war against us. We have done the same against them, and both have acted like boys. I am willing to bury the hatchets of my young people, and put weights on them never to be taken off again. I have heard that the

Great King over the water talks good, and wants all matters to be straight between the white people and the Indians, and that they shall not hurt one another. I have now finished my talk, and reckon myself as one with your Excellency." [23]

Governor Lyttleton replied: "Oconostota, I have permitted you to lay down those skins, but I do not accept them in token of the peace you propose." He sternly asked Oconostota if he came in behalf of the whole Cherokee nation. The Great Warrior replied that while he spoke for the whole nation, three other chiefs desired to make talks, viz., Tiftowe of Keowee, the Head Warrior of Estatoe, and the Black Dog of Hiwassee. The Indians spoke, and Tiftowe, in particular, complained of the conduct of the officers at Fort Prince George.

The chiefs were dismissed while the council considered their talks. Governor Lyttleton advised the board that in his opinion Oconostota was not authorized to ask for peace; that the chiefs were only seeking ammunition and presents, and had come to Charles Town because they had been refused at Fort Prince George. He suggested that the expedition to the Cherokee country should be set in motion, and that a number of the chiefs then in Charles Town should be held as hostages until an equal number of Cherokees should be surrendered to be put to death for the murders committed. This was a radical idea. The persons of ambassadors were sacred by the rules of both savage and civilized warfare. The council put the governor's proposal to a vote, and were evenly divided, four to four. This left the decision to his Excellency.

On the following day, Lyttleton informed the chiefs that they were not authorized to treat for peace by the entire nation. He told them that he would immediately set out for their country, where, if he were not given the satisfaction to which he was entitled, he would take it with his army. Addressing himself to the Great Warrior, he said:

"You, Oconostota, and all with you, shall return safely to your country, and it is not my intention to harm a hair of your heads; but having put many of my warriors under arms who well know the mischief the Cherokees have done to the people of this province, there is but one way I can insure your safety. You shall go with

[23] *S. C. Council Journal,* Oct. 15, 1759.

my warriors that will accompany me to your country, and they will protect you. I have nothing further to add, and the conference is finished." [24]

Oconostota rose to reply. He was denied the right, which was a deadly insult to an Indian orator. The chiefs then withdrew.

### 10

Governor Lyttleton had spoken bravely in Charles Town, but after the fatiguing march to Fort Prince George, he began to be discouraged. Smallpox broke out among the troops. Desertion thinned the ranks, and grumbling and dissatisfaction filled the air. The rank and file of the army felt that the war was unnecessary.

The Cherokee chiefs, under heavy guard, had sullenly accompanied the army. The governor sent for the Little Carpenter, hoping to extricate himself from an embarrassing position. Peace was offered the Cherokees if they would surrender twenty-two warriors to be put to death for murders committed, and the governor proposed that the chiefs be held as hostages until the others had been brought in.

The Little Carpenter was a firm friend of the English, but the terms appalled him. He frankly told the governor that he could not fulfill them himself, but thought he might do so if some of the chiefs were released to add the weight of their authority to his own.

Accordingly, Oconostota, Judd's Friend, Tiftowe of Keowee, and Saloue of Estatoe were released. The Little Carpenter actually delivered to the governor two warriors; one of whom was the unfortunate Indian whose wife had been mistreated by Coytmore and Bell.

The other Cherokee chiefs were imprisoned in Fort Prince George, in a cabin hardly large enough for half of them. This was a direct violation of the governor's promise to Oconostota, but Lyttleton felt no regrets. He returned to Charles Town, to be received as a conqueror.

### 11

Oconostota had no thought of surrendering other friends to Governor Lyttleton. No sooner was he at liberty than he

[24] *S. C. Council Journal*, Oct. 22, 1759.

began to plan to secure the release of the captives. To his credit, he first tried to accomplish this by peaceable means.

On Feb. 14th, he appeared at Fort Prince George accompanied by the Little Carpenter and the Raven of Chote, with John Caldwell as interpreter. Smallpox was raging in the fort, and the Indians except Oconostota halted at a distance. He advanced to the parade ground and delivered several letters from Fort Loudoun, and told Coytmore that he had come for the hostages; that the Overhill towns had remained peaceful, and would so continue if the prisoners were released.

Coytmore replied that he was under the orders of the governor, and that Oconostota well knew the agreement made by the Cherokees in reference to the hostages. "I have made no agreement," said Oconostota, and he withdrew much dissatisfied. The interpreter Caldwell went into the fort and warned Coytmore that if the hostages were not released the Cherokee towns would go to war with every man that could carry a gun.[25]

A few nights later, on Feb. 15th, Oconostota placed thirty warriors in ambush in the cane near the fort. Early next morning, he sent a squaw to request a talk with Coytmore about important matters. Coytmore with two soldiers and an interpreter advanced to the river bank, on the opposite side of which Oconostota stood. The chief carried a bridle in his hand. He informed Coytmore that he was on his way to Charles Town to secure the release of the hostages, and requested that a white man should accompany him. "As the distance is great," he said, "I will try to catch a horse." He swung the bridle over his head. There was a burst of fire from the concealed warriors; Coytmore was mortally wounded, and the soldiers slightly so. All three, however, managed to regain the fort. The Indians opened fire from all sides, and the fort guns were turned in retaliation upon the nearby town of Keowee. No great damage was done on either side.

Coytmore died in the afternoon, and his place was taken by Ensign Alexander Miln. The men of the garrison swore that they would kill every Indian in the fort in revenge for their commander. Miln warned them against such action, but to pacify them, agreed that they might put the hostages in irons.

---

[25] *S.C.I.A.* 6: 219-224.

The Indians resisted, and two soldiers were mortally wounded. With that, in spite of Miln's frantic efforts to prevent it, their comrades shot down every hostage within a few minutes. They were all prominent head men of the Cherokees. The soldiers tried to excuse their action by saying that they had found a bottle of poison beneath the cabin in which the Indians were confined, with which the captives had intended to poison the water.[26]

12

The murder of the Cherokee hostages sealed the fate of Fort Loudoun, and embroiled the whole frontier in warfare. Among the first to fall was the trader John Elliott of Chote. He was scalped and his supplies, particularly ammunition, were seized for carrying on the war. Communication of Fort Loudoun with the outer world was severed, as the only practical route lay through the town of Tellico. A week after the death of the hostages, Ensign Miln wrote Lyttleton:

"I should be very desirous of forwarding your dispatches to Fort Loudoun, but it is really an impossibility. I have several traders now in the fort that I importuned to go, but not one would dare run the risque." [27]

Snipers constantly lay in the hills around Fort Prince George, and it was worth any soldier's life to show himself above the fortifications. Oconostota led his warriors to the frontier, and early in March made a determined attack upon Fort Ninety Six. The commander James Francis had been warned of the Indian advance, and Oconostota was repulsed with the loss of five warriors. The dead Indians were scalped, and Francis wrote the governor: "We have the pleasure to fatten our dogs upon their carcasses, and to display their scalps, neatly ornamented, on our bastions." [28]

In the meantime, Willenawah and Standing Turkey laid close siege to Fort Loudoun. Commencing on March 4th, a four day assault was made, which was repulsed without loss to the garrison. The Little Carpenter, despairing for the lives

---

[26] S.C.I.A. 6: 224. The Indians knew nothing of poison. The bottle probably contained whiskey.

[27] *Ibid.,* 6: 226.

[28] *Ibid.,* 227-228.

of his friends, retired to the woods with his wife and children.

Early in April, Lyttleton received notice of his appointment as Governor of Jamaica. He departed for that place, and was succeeded, temporarily, by Lieutenant Governor William Bull. About the same time the Carolinians were cheered by the arrival of Colonel Archibald Montgomery with 1500 men, with orders to chastise the warring Cherokees.

Governor Bull placed all Carolina provincial forces at Montgomery's disposal; also a force of Chickasaws and Catawbas under the trader James Adair, to act as scouts.[29]

It was known that the garrison at Fort Loudoun was in desperate straits, and by early June, Montgomery was at Fort Prince George. A forced night march surprised the towns of Keowee and Estatoe which were burned with a loss to the Cherokees of sixty killed and forty prisoners.

13

A message from Fort Loudoun dated June 6th showed that the garrison was holding out in good spirits, although rations had been reduced to a quart of corn for three men per day. The trader Doherty of Hiwassee had managed to slip through four head of cattle which greatly refreshed the men. The Little Carpenter continued faithful to his friends. He came into the fort and dined with Captain Demere on June 2nd. When asked, "What news of the towns?" he replied: "I am not the man to ask for news. The Indians hide everything from me, and say that I am the white people's friend." He informed Demere that Oconostota was planning a night attack. "I wish they would attempt it," said Demere, "we should then have the satisfaction of destroying a good number of them;" which the Carpenter said would give him much pleasure also.

On the same day, Dr. Anderson and another man had

[29] Montgomery's forces consisted mainly of Highlanders, who made a tremendous impression upon the Indian allies. Hewatt says:

"It is impossible to describe how much the savages were delighted with the dress, manners, and music of that regiment. Their sprightly manner of dancing, their dexterity in the use of arms, and natural vivacity and intrepidity the savages greatly admired, and expressed a strong inclination for attending the Scotch warriors to the field.

"Lieutenant Kennedy, to encourage them, dressed and painted himself as an Indian. They gave him a squaw, and the nation to which she belonged made him a king. No small service is expected from the alliance."

ventured outside the fort gates, and were killed and scalped within fifty yards by Indians lying in ambush. Demere wrote:

"The Indians never cease, day or night, lurking about the fort to hinder us from having any intelligence. It is impossible to get anything from the towns. The Indians that are watching us have got orders to kill any woman that comes to the fort."

Certain of the soldiers had married Indian women, who smuggled small supplies of beans and pork to their husbands and defied Willenawah when he threatened them with death. "If you kill us," they told him, "Our relatives will kill you according to our law." The amount of food thus received within the fort was too small, however, to affect the final result of the siege.

Through the Little Carpenter, the garrison received news of Montgomery's advance and of the destruction of Estatoe and Keowee. When sufficient time had elapsed, the men eagerly watched the trail and listened for the sound of guns that would herald the approach of British troops.

### 14

James Grant, Montgomery's aide, wrote to Governor Lyttleton from Fort Prince George:

"Tis next to impossible for us to think of proceeding over the mountains. The whole country is the strongest and most difficult I ever was in. A few men, properly conducted, might retard the march of an enemy army." [30]

Montgomery, however, was determined to relieve Fort Loudoun if possible. He advanced without opposition to a place called the Crow's Pass, about six miles south of the town of Etchoe.[31] The trail at that place wound between the river and an overhanging hill. The intervening space, thickly covered with cane and undergrowth, offered an ideal setting for the favorite method of Indian fighting, *U-dis-klungi*, the ambush.

On approaching the pass, Montgomery sent Captain Morrison with a body of rangers to reconnoiter. The white men

[30] *S. C. Council Journal*, June 10, 1760.
[31] Near the present Franklin, N. C.

were well within the dangerous position when the yelp of the
war whoop sounded on all sides, and Morrison and nearly
half of his men were killed.  The Highlanders closed up to
his rescue, but crowded in the narrow space they offered an
excellent target for the Indian marksmen.  As the fight raged,
a white man, with a drum strapped over his shoulder, advanced
from behind a hill ahead of Montgomery's men and played
the Grenadier's March, with a shouted invitation to come on
and be killed.  It was the renegade Hawkins, who had lived
for some time among the Indians and considered himself one
of them.

Montgomery lost a hundred men at the pass, in killed and
wounded.  The ammunition of the Indians began to run low,
and they retired slowly, but kept up a fire from the hills.
Montgomery pushed on to Etchoe, which he burned.  He remained there two days.  Encumbered as he was with wounded,
and with almost impassable mountains ahead, he decided to
retreat to Fort Prince George, sixty miles away.  Surplus
baggage was destroyed in order that the horses might be used
to transport the wounded.  The march was made difficult at
every step by the triumphant savages.

Montgomery advised Governor Bull that he felt that his
orders from General Amherst had been fulfilled.  He had
invaded the Indian country, had defeated the Cherokees in
battle, and had destroyed their lower towns.  He felt that
they would sue for peace, and as he had no orders to garrison
the frontier, he proposed to re-embark his forces for New
York.  Of the condition of his forces, he said:

"Their horses are worn out, not able to crawl, and fresh ones
must be got and the others have time to recruit, before I can leave
this place.  The list of sick has increased, the wounded are distressed with the long march, and indeed the detachment is almost
worn out with fatigue." [32]

Montgomery's decision roused consternation in South Carolina.  "Tell it not in Gath," the *South Carolina Gazette*
thundered, "nor publish it in the streets of Askalon, that the
army which came here under command of the Hon. Col.
Montgomery, and penetrated into the heart of the Cherokee

[32] S.C.P.R. 28: 372-380, Bull to Lords of Trade.

country, NEVER WERE DESIGNED to go to Fort Loudoun, but expected to effect the release of that garrison by a PEACE; the roads being horrible, etc." [33]

Governor Bull protested to Montgomery that the Cherokee war was rather inflamed than extinguished by the attack upon their towns and the retreat of the army; that the Fort Loudoun garrison must be lost to the savages who would then advance and take Fort Prince George; and that a war with the Creeks was daily expected.

Montgomery replied that his troops could be of no further use during the summer months, and that he could not remain idle because of the mere possibility of a war without severe criticism from General Amherst. He therefore marched his men to Charles Town and embarked; but as a concession to the province, left four companies of the Royal Regiment to cover the frontier.

Governor Bull wrote to Amherst and appealed for troops to complete the task that Montgomery had begun. He called attention to the need for the rescue of the Fort Loudoun garrison, and the certainty of continued bloody Indian warfare.

15

In the meantime, the men at Fort Loudoun had been reduced to last shifts. Demere sent off a courier in the night, hoping to meet Montgomery's advance. He reached Fort Prince George on July 10th, and learned of the fight at the pass and the retreat of Montgomery's force.

Indian warriors at the fort exposed themselves to shout that they had beaten Montgomery and driven him from their country; that they had taken from him two drums, a horse load of ammunition, and plenty of flour; and that they had "killed and scalped so many that their hands were sore."

Demere found opportunity to send a courier to Charles Town on July 29th. He described the garrison as miserable beyond description, feeling that it was abandoned by God and man, without hope of relief, and without even horse flesh upon which to subsist. He made ineffectual attempts to negotiate with the Indians, but Oconostota retorted: "We

[33] *Ibid.*

are sure of the fort and all within it, for they are almost starved." A few of the soldiers tried to escape in the night, in which effort they were encouraged by Demere. One of these groups, consisting of four men, reached the camp of Colonel William Byrd in Virginia after wandering a month in the wilderness.

On Aug. 6th, Demere called a council of officers. It was unanimously agreed that it was "impracticable to maintain the fort any longer, and that such terms as could be procured from the Indians, consistent with honor, should be immediately accepted and the post abandoned."

Captain John Stuart, who had won the friendship of the Indians, was selected to go to Chote and endeavor to secure terms. He set off at once, accompanied by Lieutenant Adamson.

Favorable terms were obtained. It was agreed that the men should march out with arms and drums, each soldier to have as much powder and ball as the officers should think necessary for the march, and what baggage he chose to carry. They were to be permitted to march to Virginia or to Fort Prince George, unmolested. A number of Indians should accompany them and hunt to supply them with meat. Soldiers who were sick and unable to travel were to be received into the Indian towns and treated kindly until they recovered. The Indians were to supply as many horses as they conveniently could for the march. The great guns, powder, ball and spare arms were to be delivered to the Cherokees without fraud on the day appointed for the abandonment of the fort.

The articles of capitulation were signed on Aug. 7th, by Captain Paul Demere for the garrison, and by Oconostota and Standing Turkey for the Cherokees.

16

Captain Demere sent his last dispatch to Governor William Bull on Aug. 8, 1760, acquainting him with the capitulation of the fort. He hoped, considering the great distress they were in, that the surrender would be approved. He assured the governor that they would have been compelled in any event to abandon the fort that day, come what would. "The garrison," he advised, "will set out early tomorrow for Fort Prince George, flattering ourselves that the Indians will do us no harm. We will make all the dispatch that our starved condition will permit."

By the surrender of the fort, the Cherokees came into possession of twelve cannon, a thousand pounds of powder and ball in proportion, and about eighty small arms.

On the morning of the 9th, the garrison was paraded for the last time. The English colors were hauled down from above Fort Loudoun, and the force, consisting of one hundred and eighty men, sixty women, and some children, took up the march to Fort Prince George, distant one hundred and forty miles.

The day's march was fifteen miles. Camp was made at Cane Creek where it empties into Tellico River. Oconostota and Judd's Friend had promised to accompany Demere upon his march. They failed to do so, but Judd's Friend came into camp late in the afternoon, talked with Demere, and departed toward the town of Tellico which was about two miles away.

A watch was maintained during the night. Reveille was sounded next morning, and the men prepared for another day's march. Lieutenant Adamson was receiving instructions for the day from Demere when the two officers were fired upon from ambush. Demere was wounded. Adamson returned the fire, and wounded an Indian. Instantly, the war whoop was sounded. Volleys from small arms and showers of arrows poured on the garrison. Seven hundred painted fiends surrounded the camp, firing and yelling. Demere's men were thrown into greatest confusion, and enfeebled by the long siege, could make little effective resistance. Seeing that their efforts would end in death, they called to each other not to fire, and surrendered themselves to the mercy of the savages.

Captain Demere and twenty-three of his men were killed. The Indians later claimed that they were particular as to the number, for it was the exact number of hostages who had been killed in Fort Prince George.

The fate of Demere was appalling. Wounded at the first fire, he was scalped alive and forced to dance for the amusement of his captors. His arms and legs were then cut off, and his mouth stuffed with dirt, the savages saying, "You want land, we will give it to you."

In the early part of the action, Onatoy, brother to the well known chief Round O, seized Captain John Stuart and forced him across Cane Creek, thus saving his life.   He was the only officer who escaped.

Judd's Friend saved the lives of many of the white men. As soon as Demere was dead, the chief ran to all parts of the field, and shouted, "Stop your hands; we have got the man we want!"

The Indians stripped the prisoners and carried them to the Cherokee towns; as they marched they were beaten in the faces with the scalps of their dead comrades.   On arrival at the towns, they were taken to the Chungke yards [34] where they were beaten and abused in inhuman manner.   For several nights they were compelled to "dance with rattles," this being a custom for prisoners condemned to death.

Luke Croft, a soldier of the garrison, was taken to the town of Setticoe and slowly tortured to death in most shocking manner.   His comrade Frederick Mouncy was compelled to stand and watch, and was told that the same fate awaited him as soon as Croft expired.   The Indians burned Croft's body, and set his head upon a stake in the chungke yard as a spectacle for the other prisoners.   A runner arrived from Oconostota forbidding Mouncy's execution, just in time to save his life.

The cannon, guns, and spoils from Fort Loudoun were removed to Chote.   All the prisoners were taken to that town and compelled to dance before the Mortar, the Creek chief who had aided in the reduction of the fort, to whom the Cherokees paid greatest respect.[35]

The Cherokees claimed that their reason for violating the terms of the surrender of Fort Loudoun was that Captain Demere had, contrary to his agreement, buried ten casks of powder and a large amount of ball within the fort, and that when it was discovered, the young warriors could not be controlled.   The real reason was probably the old Indian rule, a scalp for a scalp; revenge for their hostages.   It is probable, too, that they secured whiskey among the spoils from the fort. Liquor made fiends of the Indians.

After the excitement occasioned by the massacre had sub-

---

[34] The Chungke yard was a cleared and sanded space adjacent to every Indian village for playing the game of Chungke, for description of which see Chapter II.

[35] The foregoing description of the Fort Loudoun massacre is taken from S. C. Gazette, Oct. 18th and 22nd, 1760; and from Draper Mss., 2-D-1-21.

sided, the prisoners were treated well. They were told that they would not be made slaves, and would be returned to their own people at the end of the war.

### 17

The escape of Captain John Stuart is one of the most remarkable in Indian warfare, and is a tribute to Indian friendship.

On the morning after the massacre, the Little Carpenter, who was at Fort Loudoun, was agreeably surprised when Onatoy waited upon him with his prisoner. Stuart told the Carpenter how his captor had saved his life. The chief took Stuart by the hand and told him that he was exceedingly glad to see him, and would take particular care of him. He gave to Onatoy as ransom, his rifle, coat, and all that he possessed except his flap. He conducted Stuart to Demere's residence, which he had adopted as his own, and treated his prisoner in every way as a brother.[36]

Oconostota, flushed with victory, called a council at Chote to devise means for the capture of Fort Prince George. Captain Stuart was ordered to attend. He was reminded of his obligation to the Indians for sparing his life. He was told that Oconostota was determined to take the captured cannon across the mountains, and turn them upon Fort Prince George.

"You, Captain Stuart, must go with me and write such letters to the commandant as I shall dictate to you. If the officer at Fort Prince George shall refuse to surrender, I am determined to burn the prisoners, one by one, before his face, and try if he will be so obstinate as to hold out when he sees his friends expiring in the flames." [37]

Stuart preferred to die rather than fire on his comrades. He resolved to attempt an escape, and communicated his intent to the Little Carpenter. The chief took him by the hand, and told him that he need not be afraid. "I have given you one

[36] Hewatt, *Development of Carolina and Georgia*, 239-240.

It was a custom for a Cherokee to adopt a favored white man as his "eldest brother," and he was afterward regarded the same as of blood kin. There is no doubt that this relationship existed between the Little Carpenter and Captain John Stuart.

[37] *Ibid.*, 240.

proof of friendship," he told Stuart, "and I propose to give you another."

The Carpenter announced to the other Indians that he was going with his friend into the woods for a hunt, for Stuart was weak and had tasted no deer's meat during the siege; and that he would return in six days. He included in the party the surviving physician of the garrison, an elderly man; William Shorey the interpreter; a soldier, three warriors, and two squaws.

Instead of hunting in the woods, the Carpenter guided his friends through the wilderness to the Virginia settlements. Colonel William Byrd was in command of Virginia troops which had intended to invade the Cherokee country in co-operation with Montgomery. On receipt of news of the latter's "fatal retreat" Byrd had halted his men at Reedy Creek near Long Island of Holston River, and had built a stockade which he called Fort Patrick Henry.

On Sept. 3rd, Byrd rescued in the woods four members of the Fort Loudoun garrison who had left the fort in the night a few days before the surrender with the scant hope of reaching Virginia. The men, who as Byrd reported were "just starved to death," told him that other members of the garrison would attempt to reach Virginia. Major Andrew Lewis, with three hundred men, was ordered to "scout toward the fort and save as many of these unhappy wretches as possible." [38]

On the 6th, Lewis fell in with the Carpenter and Captain Stuart, who had been nine days upon their journey. They advised him of the surrender of the fort. Lewis at once fell back to Fort Patrick Henry, where, after a few days' rest, the Little Carpenter departed for his own country to continue his efforts for peace. He had given proof of friendship that has rarely been equaled.[39]

### 18

The news of the surrender of Fort Loudoun was received at Fort Prince George by a letter from Judd's Friend to Governor Bull, which was placed upon a stick by the river.

---

[38] British Colonial Papers.

[39] The survivors of the Fort Loudoun garrison were eventually delivered up, generally at heavy expense, to Virginia and the Carolinas, mainly through the efforts of Captain Stuart. Some of the men who had married Indian women chose to remain among the Cherokees. See *Draper Mss.*, 2-D-1-21.

"This is to acquaint you with the bad news. Captain Demere is killed, and twenty-three of his command. Captain Stuart and all the rest of the men are saved for to manage the Great Guns. The Man Killer (Judd's Friend) says they are determined to take Fort Prince George, since they have already taken a much more defensible fort.

"The Man Killer and Saloue say there is no peace belt in the world strong enough to hold them; that they are coming down with all the cannon from Fort Loudoun and all the white men with them, and 200 Creeks from the lower towns, and 200 from the upper, and the Mortar with them.

"The Man Killer says he does not want to hurt you, and it would be very good for you to go off in the night, and take such provisions as will serve you to the settlements, and you will not be hurt, not one of you. Don't think I am a fellow telling you lies. What one or two sees may be believed, but what all see must be truth." [40]

The letter was signed by Judd's Friend and Saloue.

Governor Bull, on receipt of the letter, hastened supplies and ammunition to Fort Prince George for the expected siege. He also wrote General Amherst and to the Lords of Trade setting forth the desperate condition of the frontier, and saying particularly that Fort Prince George would be taken unless help was sent.

"The Indians have expressed a determined resolution to oblige all those English, many of them sailors expert in the use of cannon, to transport the guns from Fort Loudoun and plant them against Fort Prince George; to which they are strongly tempted not only with the hope of getting into their possession the officers who commanded there when their hostages were put to death in February last; but also by the large quantities of presents left there by Governor Lyttleton; particularly 6000 weight of gunpowder, and a large number of arms." [41]

19

French authorities at Fort Toulouse were advised of the taking of Fort Loudoun by a runner from the Mortar, who suggested that the site be taken over by France. Lantagnac hastened to Tellico to offer the Cherokees his assistance with the guns against Fort Prince George, and in the meantime

---

[40] British Colonial Papers.

Judd's Friend was usually referred to by his Indian name, Outacite, from the Cherokee *U-tsi* (man) and *teehee* (killer).

[41] *S.C.P.R. Bull to Lords of Trade,* Sep. 9, 1760.

hurried a runner to Governor Kerleric at New Orleans with
the Mortar's suggestion. Kerleric thought well of the scheme.
A large boat with necessary supplies was dispatched from New
Orleans, and its commander was ordered to make all possible
speed to the site of Fort Loudoun, and to take it over in the
name of the French king.

The boat successfully negotiated the Mississippi, Ohio, and
the Muscle Shoals of Tennessee River, but on reaching the
Whirl and Suck at the present Chattanooga was unable to
pass.

"The waters rolled down with prodigious rapidity, dashed against
opposite rocks, and from thence rushed off in impetuous violence
on a quarter angle course. It appeared so shocking and insur-
mountable to the Monsieurs that after staying there a considerable
length of time in the vain expectation of seeing some of their
friends, necessity compelled them to return to New Orleans, to
their inconsolable disappointment." [42]

The French attempt to take over the site of Fort Loudoun
thus ended in failure, but the trading post which they established was the nucleus around which was later to rally the
branch of the Cherokees known as the Chickamaugas.

Despite French encouragement and the Man Killer's threats,
the Cherokees made no serious attempt to take Fort Prince
George.[43] Most of the chiefs felt that enough English scalps
had been taken to revenge the hostages, and the score thus
being even, peace should be made. The few months of warfare had shown the Cherokees that they were wholly dependent
upon the English for supplies.

Early in October, Samuel Terron, a soldier of the Fort
Loudoun garrison, was sent by Oconostota with a talk to
Governor Bull requesting peace. Judd's Friend asked Terron
to assure Governor Bull that if peace could be obtained, there
would be no more war with the English during his lifetime.

On Sept. 26th, a meeting was held at Nequassee which was

[42] Adair, 269-283. This was the first white settlement at the present
Chattanooga, which is shown on old maps as "French Trading Post." The
adjacent town of Tuskegee, now Williams Island, is believed to be the home
of the Mortar, who removed from the lower Creek towns to this site to be
closer to the Fort Loudoun activities.
[43] When they killed John Elliott, there was probably no other man capable
of carrying the great guns over the mountains.

attended by two thousand Cherokees. The English colors were raised, and Oconostota and Judd's Friend spoke for peace. Orders were given that any Englishman who came into the nation should be allowed to pass at will without molestation.

20

Governor Bull may have been disposed to grant peace to the Cherokees. In October, 1760, however, General Jeffrey Amherst completed the successful campaign by which the English had taken Canada from the French. Force of arms had decided that North America should be English. To that end, the fort on the Little Tennessee had contributed its part, although its garrison had suffered defeat and disaster. Had Fort Loudoun not been built, the Cherokees would have joined the French, and the result of the war might have been different.

When General Amherst received from Governor Bull the news of the surrender of Fort Loudoun, he wrote: "I must own I am ashamed, for I believe it is the first instance of His Majesty's troops having yielded to the Indians." [44] The French and Indian war being concluded, General Amherst had ample troops at his disposal. He ordered Montgomery's former aide, Colonel James Grant, to proceed to Charles Town with two thousand men, to invade the Cherokee country, and to wipe out the disgrace the Indians had inflicted upon His Majesty's arms.

[44] *British Colonial Papers.*

# CHAPTER VII

## ELDER BROTHER

### I

Lieutenant Colonel James Grant had served as Montgomery's aide in his campaign against the Cherokees. He had also led the premature attack on Fort Du Quesne in which he had been taken prisoner by the savages, and later exchanged. Experience had made Grant extremely wary in Indian warfare. With caution gained from disaster, he planned his Cherokee campaign in minute detail with General Amherst before leaving New York.

Grant arrived in South Carolina in January, 1761. His force consisted of a regiment of Highlanders and two companies of light infantry one of the latter being Major Robert Rogers' Rangers, notable Indian fighters of the day. Governor Bull placed at his disposal a provincial regiment commanded by Colonel Henry Middleton, who counted among his officers Henry Laurens, William Moultrie, and Francis Marion, names later to become famous in South Carolina.

Grant had hardly landed at Charles Town before he realized that the war was unnecessary. News of the French collapse had reached the Cherokee towns. The Indians had come to depend upon foreign sources for their supplies, and realized that these must now be secured from the English or not at all. They desired peace.

In his first letter to General Amherst, Grant stated his opinion that the war existed only in the heated imagination of provincial officers at Fort Prince George; and in the selfishness of certain people who would promote it for their own ends.

"Some think it will bring money into the province; others are anxious about their frontier plantations, and nobody thinks of the expense of government, for which reason peace is an unfashionable topick, and would be a most disagreeable event in the province."

Grant, however, had his orders, and executed them with a thoroughness that made his campaign a model for future operations against the Indians.

*Picture by Walter Cline*

SITE OF FORT LOUDOUN MASSACRE

At Mouth of Cane Creek, near Tellico Plains, Monroe County, Tenn.

The English army arrived at Fort Prince George on May 27, 1761, where Grant was met by the Little Carpenter with a plea for peace. "I am and have always been a friend to the English," he said, "although I have been called an old woman by the warriors. The conduct of my people has filled me with shame, but I would interpose in their behalf and bring about peace."

Grant refused to concede terms until the Cherokees had been punished for the Fort Loudoun affair. On June 7th, the English force marched from Fort Prince George for the Middle Towns, "without baggage except bear skins, blankets, and liquor." Forced marches brought Grant within two days to Etchoe Pass, scene of Montgomery's defeat.

Lieutenant Francis Marion with thirty Carolina rangers was sent ahead to explore the pass, closely followed by Captain Kennedy with ninety provincials and some friendly Indian scouts.

Oconostota, hoping to repeat his previous victory, had placed his warriors in ambush along the trail and on the overhanging hill. He was forced to begin the action prematurely when Grant's Indians who were acting as flankers ran into a body of his warriors. It had been his intention to wait until the English were well within the pass. Upon being discovered, the Cherokees sounded the war whoop and began a brisk fire.

Grant promptly threw a platoon of light infantry along the riverside with orders to take what cover they could and pick off the Indian sharp shooters who were firing as usual from behind trees. Major Monypenny was sent to the rear to order the Highlanders to continue their march, and "to throw a fire into the enemy when it should appear necessary, which was done in very good order." At the same time, Marion and Kennedy in the advance were ordered to secure the ford of a small river, (the Cullasaja) across which the trail passed about half a mile from the point where the attack began.

"Stopping and forming on disadvantageous ground, against an invisible enemy, could answer no good end," Grant reported: he therefore ordered the march to continue as though no attack were in progress, although his loss was severe, being eleven men killed and fifty one wounded. The firing commenced at 8:30 in the morning, and as Grant says "was pretty smart until 12 o'clock, and popping shots continued until after 2 P.M."

The Cherokees were forced to discontinue the action for lack of ammunition. While they had secured a large amount at Fort Loudoun, it had been distributed throughout the nation, and had been exhausted in the annual hunting season. Adair says, "Had the Cherokees been fully supplied with ammunition, twice the number of Grant's men could not have defeated them."

By 3 o'clock, the last of the English forces were across the river, and the Cherokees withdrew. The wounded were given attention. Those with broken bones were carried in litters by their comrades, and the slightly wounded were provided with horses. The army arrived at Etchoe at 9 o'clock and made camp. The wounded were placed in the town house, which as Grant reports "made an excellent hospital."

2

The lower Cherokee towns were destroyed by Grant with thoroughness and dispatch. He kept a daily journal of the campaign, a typical entry, that of June 12th and 13th, being given:

"We halted (at Etchoe). Corn about the town was destroyed. parties were sent out to burn the scattered houses, pull up beans, peas, and corn, and to demolish everything eatable in the country. Our Indian scouts, with one of our parties, destroyed the towns of Neowee and Kanuga. A scout of our Indians killed a Cherokee and wounded another at Ayore. A miserable old squaw from Tasso was brought in and put to death in the Indian camp by one of the Catawbas."

On June 25th, Grant placed his wounded and sick, and supplies, under a guard of 1000 men, in the old Cherokee town of Cowe. With his remaining forces, he made a night march across the mountains to the Middle Towns.

The path was so narrow and dangerous that the men were compelled to march single file, each man touching the next ahead. "Never was an army in so dangerous a position," says Grant; "this part of the country is impenetrable if defended by fifty men who know how to take advantage of the situation."

It was the first time that the Middle Towns of the Cherokees had felt the foot of the invader. In five days, not a cabin or a stalk of corn was left standing. The destruction roused the pity of Grant's men. Lieutenant Marion wrote:

"We proceeded, by Colonel Grant's orders, to burn the Indian cabins. Some of the men seemed to enjoy this cruel work, laughing heartily at the curling flames, but to me it appeared a shocking sight. Poor creatures, thought I, we surely need not grudge you such miserable habitations. But when we came, according to orders, to cut down the fields of corn, I could scarcely refrain from tears. Who, without grief, could see the stately stalks with broad green leaves and tasseled shocks, the staff of life, sink under our swords with all their precious load, to wither and rot untasted in their mourning fields.

"I saw everywhere around, the footsteps of the little Indian children, where they had lately played under the shade of their rustling corn. When we are gone, thought I, they will return, and peeping through the weeds with tearful eyes, will mark the ghastly ruin where they had so often played. 'Who did this?' they will ask their mothers, and the reply will be, 'The white people did it,—the Christians did it!'"

Marion, like Grant, realized that the war was unnecessary and prompted for selfish purposes, for he concludes his letter:

"Thus, for cursed mammon's sake, the followers of Christ have sowed the selfish tares of hate in the bosoms of even Pagan children." [1]

On July 1st, Grant's men rested, their work of destruction being complete. He reports:

"Our men were so fatigued they could hardly crawl. Even our Indians were knocked up. The list of sick increased. Numbers of our men were footsore and a great many had no shoes. Luckily, nothing was left to be done on this side. Our provisions were almost expended, and our men worn out and unable to act." [2]

Fifteen Indian towns had been destroyed, fifteen hundred acres of crops had been cut down, and 5000 Cherokees driven into the mountains to starve.

---

[1] Horry, P., *Life of Gen. Francis Marion.*
[2] The quotations, and description of Grant's campaign, are from his official report, a daily journal, in *British Colonial Papers,* Lawson McGhee Library, Knoxville.

Grant's army returned to Fort Prince George on July 9th, at which time he reported:

"Our men have suffered more fatigue than can be imagined. Near a thousand are absolutely without shoes. Without the help of our pack horses, the lame, who daily increased, could not have been taken care of."

### 3

Grant, on reaching Fort Prince George, dispatched a runner to the Cherokees requesting the head men to come in for a peace talk. In a few days, the Little Carpenter, Judd's Friend, the Raven of Chote, Old Caesar of Hiwassee, and fifteen other chiefs, appeared at the fort. Oconostota, dubious because of his previous experience with English diplomacy, did not attend.

Grant received the chiefs in a bower built for the purpose. He first asked the Little Carpenter if he had come for peace, and by the authority of the entire nation. The chief replied that he had, and the others stated that they would confirm any agreement the Carpenter might make.

Grant drew up a treaty, to which the Carpenter agreed save one clause: "Four Cherokee Indians shall be delivered to Colonel Grant to be put to death in front of his camp; or four green scalps be brought to him in the space of twelve nights." [3]

The Little Carpenter said that he had no authority to make such a concession. Grant allowed him a day to think it over. He still refused, and asked permission to go to Charles Town and lay the matter before Governor Bull.

The Cherokee ambassadors were met by the governor at Ashley's Ferry on Sept. 15, 1761. Bull realized that his predecessor's failure to recognize the sacredness of Indian diplomacy had caused the late war, and he accorded the Indians every courtesy.

Addressing the Little Carpenter, he said:

"Attakullakulla, I am glad to see you. As you have always been a good friend to the English, I take you by the hand, and not only you, but those with you, as a pledge of their security while under

---

[3] S. C. Council Journal, Sep. 15, 1761. By "green scalps" Grant intended that the Cherokees must surrender four warriors for execution, or kill them and present their scalps instead.

my protection. Colonel Grant has acquainted me that you have applied for peace. I am now met with my beloved men to hear what you have to say, and my ears are open for that purpose." [4]

The Carpenter asked for fire to light his pipe. When this was brought, he smoked and passed the pipe to the governor and to each member of the council. He then spoke:

"I am come to see you as a messenger from the whole nation. I have seen you, smoked with you, and hope we shall live as brothers together."

He delivered to the governor a string of wampum.

"You live at the water side and are in light. We are in darkness, but hope that all will yet be clear with us. I have been constantly going about doing good, and though I am tired, yet am come to see what can be done for my people, who are in great distress."

He then delivered a string of wampum from each of the Cherokee towns, signifying that each of them desired peace, and continued:

"I always speak one way, and am not double minded. As to what has happened, I believe it has been ordered by the Great Father above. We are of a different color from the white people. They are superior to us, but one God is the father of all, and we hope what is past will be forgiven. The Great Father above made all people, and there is not a day but some are coming into, and some going out of the world. I hope that the path, as the Great King told me, will never be crooked, but straight and open for all to pass."

He delivered a final string of wampum, and concluded:

"I hope, as we all live in one land, we shall all live as one people." [5]

Governor Bull took the chief by the hand, and said:

"You, Attakullakulla, have been sent to me as a messenger from the whole nation, to sue for peace. I know your heart is straight. I take you by the hand, not only because of the errand for which

[4] Ibid.
[5] Ibid.

you came, but as an old acquaintance. On the advice of my beloved men, I have decided to leave out that clause by which four Cherokees should be put to death. I therefore expect, as the Cherokees have been well dealt with upon that head, they shall be faithful and punctual in the performance of all the other articles."

"I am extremely well satisfied with everything your honor has proposed and said," the Carpenter replied.[6]

The South Carolina Gazette of Sept. 23, 1761, stated:

"On this day Attakullakulla had his last public audience, when he signed the treaty of peace and received an authenticated copy under the great seal. He earnestly requested that Captain John Stuart might be made chief white man (Indian Agent) in their nation. 'All the Indians love him,' he said, 'and there will never be any uneasiness if he is there.' His request was granted. This faithful Indian afterward dined with the governor, and tomorrow sets out for his own country."[7]

By the treaty all English prisoners held in the Cherokee towns were first to be released, after which Indian prisoners would be released, and trade resumed as formerly. As a special favor to the Carpenter, however, and to convince the entire nation that the English had granted a peace, he was permitted to choose two Cherokee prisoners to return with him to the nation.

Another requirement was that the head men of the nation, Oconostota being mentioned specifically, were to assemble at Charles Town on December 16th to ratify the treaty, and this they did. Oconostota, however, was still wary of trusting himself within the power of the English, but sent his brother Kitegista with a peace pipe to represent him. Judd's Friend and Willenawah likewise declined to attend. However, the Little Carpenter, with his usual eloquence and undoubted friendship for the English, was able to convince the council that the Cherokees sincerely desired peace. He said, in part:

"It is so long since I heard the talk of the Great King over the water that I cannot say whether any of my nation remembers it, but I have always kept that talk, and will to the last day of my life.

---

[6] *Ibid.*
[7] Drake, 375: Thatcher, 2, 155: *S. C. Council Journal,* Sep. 22, 1761.

The paper upon which it is wrote is still in our nation. There is none other in the nation alive but myself that heard the talk. A great deal of blood has been spilled in the path, but it is now wiped away."

He then produced an eagle's tail and a string of wampum which he presented to the governor, saying:

"I now leave these feathers and beads with the governor as a sure token that no other blood shall be spilled by us."

Old Hop, the Cherokee emperor, had died shortly before the conclusion of hostilities, and had been succeeded by his nephew Standing Turkey. His death was announced to the council by the Little Carpenter in these words:

"Our Headman, Old Hop, is gone to sleep, and the Standing Turkey is come in his room, but he has little to say, being just come to the government. The other chiefs present will remember how strongly Old Hop recommended to the nation to live in peace and friendship with the white people."

Speaking for himself, the Carpenter said:

"I have suffered great hardships, going about continually, often naked and starved, to convince my people of their error in falling out with the English. They are now convinced of their folly, and hope the governor and his beloved men will not remember what is past, seeing that it has been so ordered by the Great Man above."

The chief mentioned that a member of the Fort Loudoun garrison desired to remain in the nation:

"One of the King's soldiers of the independents, who was at Fort Loudoun and has afterward lived in the nation, being a carpenter, is of great service in making many things we want. He is very willing to live among us, and we are desirous that he should, and we will take it as a great favor if your Honor will permit him to settle among us. Great care shall be taken of him and his family." [8]

Thus ended the Cherokee-English war of 1760-1761. It was forced upon the Indians by the act of Governor Lyttleton in

[8] *S. C. Council Journal,* Sept. 23, 1761, and Dec. 18, 1761.

imprisoning the Cherokee chiefs to whom he had promised
safe conduct: and by Grant's campaign, which he himself
acknowledged to be unnecessary.

A fair historian feels a sense of regret that the Cherokees
failed to attempt the defense of their country following Grant's
victory at Etchoe Pass. As Grant himself remarks, fifty
determined men could have prevented the passage of the army.
The Indians were without ammunition, however. They might
have offered formidable resistance with their ancient weapon
the bow, but they had come to depend upon the white man's guns
and ammunition.[9]

## 4

The Virginia frontier had not been overlooked in the early
stages of the war. Washington, after the conclusion of the
Fort Du Quesne campaign, had resigned his commission in
the militia and retired to the life of a gentleman farmer. He
was succeeded by Colonel William Byrd III, who was ordered
to march against the Cherokees in cooperation with Montgomery's movement from Carolina. Adair remarks:

"The Virginia troops kept far off in flourishing parade without
coming to our assistance or making a diversion against those warlike towns which lie beyond the Appalachian Mountains, the chief of
which are Tennassy, Chote, Great Tellico, and Highwassey." [10]

Colonel Byrd had little heart for the Cherokee campaign.
He resigned early in 1761, and was succeeded by Colonel
Adam Stephen.

The Little Carpenter and Old Hop came to Stephen's camp
at Fort Patrick Henry in July, 1761, to ask for peace. The

---

[9] The white man's gun held a fascination for the Indian, and he desired
it greatly, although the bow was quite as effective at close range as the
firearm of the time. The writer has himself seen Indians on the Eastern
Reservation in North Carolina perform feats with the bow that would put
to shame the modern rifle.

[10] Adair, 268. His comment was justified. The Virginia militia of the
time was described by Washington as "obstinate, perverse, self willed, and
of little or no service to the people. Every mean individual has his own
crude notion of things and must undertake to direct. If his advice is neglected, he thinks himself slighted and abused, and to reduce his wrongs will
depart for home. These, sir, are matters of fact, chiefly from my own observation."
Washington to Dinwiddie, *Dinwiddie Papers*, 2, 221-226.

Cherokees had just sustained their first great defeat in their own mountains at the hands of Colonel Grant. "Oconostota and Judd's Friend," the Carpenter told Stephen, "are now sensible of their error, and are ready to bury the hatchet." [11]

Stephen advised the Little Carpenter that the Cherokees must first make peace with Grant in South Carolina. Having done so, as has been detailed, the Carpenter and Standing Turkey returned to Stephen's camp in November, 1761, and smoked the pipe of peace with Virginia.

The campaign of the Virginians thus ended, as Adair observed, "in a flourishing parade." It had, however, one happy result.

The treaty having been signed, the Little Carpenter begged Colonel Stephen to send an officer among the Cherokees to convince his people of the sincerity and good will of the English. Stephen hesitated to order an officer upon so dangerous and uncertain a mission. Lieutenant Henry Timberlake volunteered for the service, and his offer was accepted. Timberlake, taking with him Sergeant Thomas Sumter and William Shorey the interpreter, journeyed by canoe to the Cherokee towns early in 1762, where he spent several months. In his *Memoirs,* he has given an accurate map of the Overhill country, and a delightful picture of the Cherokees while they were yet in the glory of their native customs. [12]

Timberlake was kindly received in the Cherokee towns by Judd's Friend. (Oconostota was in temporary disfavor owing to his recent defeat by Colonel Grant.) The town of Settico, which had instigated the war, asked the privilege of according the English officer a special reception, of which he gives a vivid account.

Setting out in company with Judd's Friend and the interpreter, he was met at Settico by four hundred warriors headed by Cheulah (The Fox) chief of the town. [13]

Cheulah first staged for his guest the war dance, by himself

---

[11] Timberlake, *Memoirs,* 36.

[12] *Memoirs of Lieutenant Henry Timberlake,* London, 1765, reprinted in 1927 by Judge Samuel C. Williams.

[13] Moytoy, of Setticoe, had caused the war by taking the horses in Virginia and his subsequent scalping raid in the Yadkin region. He was war chief of the town. Upon conclusion of peace, the civil chief automatically took charge, and this was evidently the office filled by Cheulah. Cheulah later accompanied Timberlake to England.

and twelve warriors, naked except for flaps, painted red and black, the war colors, but evidencing their peaceful intent by eagle's tails, used by them as an emblem of welcome. Cheulah, bearing a rusty broad sword from Fort Loudoun, "cut two or three capers, . . . waved his sword over my head, and stuck it in the ground about two inches from my foot," Timberlake comments.

The chief presented his guest with a string of beads and bade him a hearty welcome, congratulating him on his safe arrival through the numerous parties of Northern warriors who were accustomed to hunt the way he came. The whole party then adjourned to the council house where he was entertained by the same warriors with the Eagle Tail Dance, evidence of highest esteem. He was then presented with the peace pipe, which he describes as "of red stone, curiously cut with a knife, the stem about three feet long, finely adorned with porcupine quills, dyed feathers, deer's hair, and such like gaudy trifles." Timberlake comments:

"After I had performed my part with this (the peace pipe), I was almost suffocated with the pipes presented to me on every hand. They might amount to about 170 or 180; which made me so sick I could not stir for several hours. This ceremony I would have waived, as smoking was always very disagreeable to me, but it was a token of their amity, and they might be offended if I did not comply: I put on it the best face I was able, though I dared not even wipe the end of the pipes that came out of their mouths, which, considering their paint and dirtiness, are not of the most ragoutant, as the French term it." [14]

## 5

Timberlake left the Cherokee country in May, 1762, and was accompanied to the Virginia capital, Williamsburg, by Judd's Friend. The chief had fought valiantly against the English, but having made peace with them, he gazed long and earnestly at a picture that was shown him of the new King of England, George III. He reflected that the Little Carpenter had once visited England, and entreated the governor that he too might have that experience, that he might see if the wonderful stories told by the Carpenter were truth or lies. Pointing to the picture of His Majesty, he said:

[14] Timberlake, *Memoirs*, 63-66.

"Long have I wished to see my father the Great King. This is his resemblance, but I am determined to see himself. I am now near the sea, and will never depart from it until I have obtained my desire." [15]

Permission was given by the Virginia governor, and Judd's Friend and two warriors whose names are not now known, journeyed to England in company with Timberlake. The interpreter William Shorey died en route, and while the Indians were granted an audience with George III, they could only converse with him by signs. The Cherokees were presented to the king by Lord Eglinton, who, as Colonel Montgomery, had conducted the unsuccessful campaign against them in 1760.

The Cherokees were visited by distinguished men, were feasted, and shown much attention. Sir Joshua Reynolds, who was at the height of his fame as an artist, made a group sketch of them, and a separate picture of Judd's Friend. The expense of entertainment was heavy, and the stay of the Cherokees grew irksome to their hosts before they re-embarked "in one of the king's canoes" on Aug. 25. They reached Charles Town on Nov. 3, 1762, where Judd's Friend delivered to Governor Bull the address he had been unable to deliver to the king owing to the death of the interpreter. He requested that the talk be sent to His Majesty.

"Some time ago, my nation was in darkness, but that darkness is now cleared up. My people were in great distress, but that is ended. There will be no more bad talks in my nation, but all will be good talks. If any Cherokee shall kill an Englishman, that Cherokee shall be put to death. Our women are bearing children to increase our nation, and I will order those who are growing up to avoid making war with the English. If any of our head men retain resentment against the English for their relations who have been killed, and if any of them speak a bad word concerning it, I shall deal with them as I see cause. No more disturbance will be heard in my nation. I speak not with two tongues, and am ashamed of those who do." [16]

The chief gave his impressions of the trip:

[15] *S. C. Council Journal*, Statement of Judd's Friend, Nov. 3, 1762. See also Timberlake, *Memoirs*, 130.

[16] *S.C.P.R.* 3: 557-563. *S. C. Council Journal*, Nov. 3, 1762.

"Although I met with a good deal of trouble going over the wide water (he was seasick), that is more than recompensed by the satisfaction of seeing the king and of the reception I met from him, being treated as one of his children, and finding the treatment of everyone there good toward me.

"The number of warriors and people all of one color which we saw in England far exceeded what we thought possibly could be. That we might see everything which was strange to us, the king gave us a gentleman to attend us all day, and at night till bed time.

"The head warrior of the canoe who brought us over the wide water used us very well. He desired us not to be afraid of the French, for he and his warriors would fight like men, and die rather than be taken." [17]

The chief concluded his remarks by saying, "I shall tell my people all that I have seen in England." He did this to good purpose, for a letter from John Stuart says: "Judd's Friend, who was in England last year, returned with such amazing accounts of His Majesty's power and grandeur as greatly effaces the impressions made by the insinuations of the French."

The Little Carpenter was jealous of the glory gained by Judd's Friend, and asked that he himself be permitted to visit England a second time. His request was refused:

"It is the King's pleasure not to comply with the request of Attakullakulla, as such visits are attended by expense and trouble, and are productive of little or no advantage." [18]

## 6

The stay of the Cherokees in England had been far from pleasant to Timberlake. As he was a stranger in London, Mr. Cacanthropus was appointed to attend the Indians. That gentleman conceived the idea of charging admission of the crowds which came out of curiosity to see the Cherokees. He also turned in padded expense accounts.

These irregularities were at first charged to Timberlake, and he had difficulty in clearing himself. Sergeant Sumter, who had accompanied him to the Cherokee country, came to blows with the servant of Cacanthropus over the matter of

[17] S. C. Council Journal, Nov. 3, 1762.
[18] British Colonial Papers.

charging admission fees to see the Indians. The crowds displeased the Cherokees, and they begged Timberlake to take them to various places that they might escape the curious sightseers. He was thus put to much expense, and by the time the visit was concluded, his finances were so reduced that he did not feel able to accompany the Cherokees to Charles Town. Sergeant Thomas Sumter agreed to go with them, and his name was later to become well known in South Carolina.[19]

Lord Egremont, in recognition of Timberlake's services, procured for him a Lieutenant's commission in the colonial forces under General Amherst. Timberlake pawned his watch to secure passage to New York. On his arrival, General Amherst, having no vacancy at the time, retired him on half pay. Timberlake proceeded to Williamsburg to attempt to secure partial reimbursement from Virginia, as Colonel Stephen of that state had sent him into the Cherokee country, and Virginia's governor had instructed him to accompany the Indians to England. His plea was denied on the flimsy pretext that he had gone to the Cherokee country "not by any order, but for his own profit and pleasure."

Timberlake soon afterward took a step that was to lead to his ruin. He arranged with Mr. Trueheart, a wealthy planter of Hanover County, Virginia, to take a shipload of tobacco to England for sale and exchange. While he was engaged in that work, he was visited by a delegation of Cherokees headed by Cheulah of Settico.[20] They had applied to the Governor of Virginia for permission to visit England to lay their troubles before King George. White men in large numbers were encroaching on their lands, they said, and they would soon have no hunting grounds left. Their petition had been denied.

Mr. Trueheart was moved by the plea of the Cherokees, and told them that they might accompany him, with Timberlake, on his tobacco ship, and they made the journey, but unfortunately Trucheart died soon after reaching London. Timberlake was left with the Cherokees on his hands. Lord Halifax, Secretary for Indian Affairs, refused to see either Timberlake

---

[19] He was afterward General Sumter of Revolutionary war fame, for whom Fort Sumter was named.

[20] Timberlake's *Memoirs,* as printed, renders the name of this chief as Chacutah. Timberlake wrote of course in long-hand, and the writer is of the opinion that Cheulah, well known chief of Settico, is meant. Timberlake would scarcely have taken an unknown chief to London.

or the Indians, "taking it ill that he should be worried with such affairs, the Indians not having come over by authority." He stated curtly that as Timberlake had brought the chiefs, he could return them.

Timberlake was soon reduced to extremity. The Indians were taken in hand by a showman who exhibited them at so much per head. Lord Hillsborough, touched by their distress, arranged for them to appear before the House of Commons on Feb. 14, 1765. Trifling presents were distributed among them, and they were sent back to Charles Town in company with two Moravian missionaries who were making the journey. Timberlake died broken hearted. His *Memoirs* were published after his death.[21]

### 7

By the Treaty of Paris, Feb. 10, 1763, all of North America east of the Mississippi came into the possession of England, and a large Indian population was acquired. Sir William Johnson was given the management of Indian affairs for the northern tribes. Captain John Stuart was appointed His Majesty's Indian Agent for the Southern District, which comprised the Cherokees, Chickasaws, Creeks, and Choctaws. He was told to make his headquarters at Mobile or Pensacola.

Stuart's first official act was to send an expression of gratitude to the Little Carpenter, to whom he owed not only the appointment, but his life.

His new appointment required that he should leave his friends the Cherokees. He therefore sent as his deputies to that nation, Alexander Cameron and John McDonald. Cameron first lived at Keowee, near Fort Prince George, but later removed to Toquo on the Little Tennessee, in the Overhill country. He married an Indian woman, and established an estate which he called Lochaber, where he lived like a Scottish

---

[21] Details of Timberlake's visits to London with the Indians are from his *Memoirs,* published originally in London in 1765, and reprinted by Judge Samuel C. Williams in 1927. Timberlake died Sept. 30, 1765. He probably wrote his *Memoirs* during the unhappy months he spent in England with the second Cherokee delegation, in the hope of improving his financial condition. His *Memoirs* closes with this paragraph:

"My circumstances are now so much on the decline that when I can satisfy my creditors, I must retire to the Cherokees or some other hospitable country, where unobserved I and my wife may breathe upon the little that yet remains."

nobleman among his clansmen. Cameron was a great favorite with the Cherokees. On all occasions, whether in friendly talk or serious treaty, they called him "Scotchie."

John McDonald located at Chickamauga. He married Anna, daughter of the interpreter William Shorey who had died while on the way to England. Their daughter, Mollie McDonald, became the mother of Chief John Ross.

On his arrival at Mobile, Stuart was welcomed by the former French agent, Chevalier de Monberaut, with whom he lived for several months. As a means of reconciling those Indians formerly friendly to France, Stuart called a great congress of all southern Indians at Mobile during March and April, 1764.[22]

Monberaut, who was a liberal entertainer, was of great help to Stuart with the Indians. During the Indian congress, he daily laid covers for thirty or more of the chiefs. His lavish service impressed the Indian diplomats, and helped to make Stuart's venture a success.[23]

Stuart was at the time in his sixty-fourth year, and spry, though troubled continuously with gout. There was no sham in his friendship with the Indians. He loved them, and they knew it, and thus he came to wield tremendous influence over them. All of the tribes called him "Father."

Due to Monberaut's assistance, most of the Indians accepted the transfer from French to English authority with calmness. The Mortar, the Creek chief who had assisted in the reduction of Fort Loudoun, was an exception.

The Mortar at the time of Stuart's Indian Congress was residing in the Cherokee country. A special embassy was sent by Stuart to invite him to attend the meeting. As a gesture of contempt for the English, the Mortar, before leaving for Mobile, burned the house of the Little Carpenter. On his way through the Creek territory, he was told by traders that Stuart

---

[22] Stuart's address to the Indians at the opening of the congress may be found in Hewatt, 2, 283-288.

[23] See *Colonial Mobile*, by P. J. Hamilton, for a lively account of Stuart by Monberaut, who states that "Stuart was more used to a wigwam than a house, for his first act was to set the house afire."

Of Stuart's personal habits, Monberaut says: "Drinking had a peculiar effect on the Superintendent. He often drank all night. Usually he could hardly walk for the gout, but when the bacchic enthusiasm prevailed, he could dance long and violently to the music of instruments, and resembled a man bitten by a tarantula."

intended to poison him, and but for the good offices of Monberaut he would not have attended the council.

Stuart's skill in handling Indians was never more clearly shown. He placed the Mortar in a chair facing himself, around which he had previously laid a number of silver gorgets bearing the insignia of King George. He told the chief that there would be no more French, Spanish, and English people in America, but all would be English. The King of England, he said, had sent a greatly beloved man to reside among the Indians to give and receive all talks, and he was that beloved man.

The king, he said, had decided to confer medals and gorgets upon the Indian chiefs, not as gifts, but as emblems of rank and distinction. Medals were to be given to chiefs of lesser rank, but only the greatest chiefs could expect a gorget, so that when a chief wore one of these, all the Indians would know that he was a very great man, and would respect him accordingly.

The Mortar said that he would like to have one of those gorgets. Monberaut was amazed. He told Stuart that the Mortar had been so jealous of his freedom that he had never accepted a French medal, "for he valued himself on being great in the eyes of his own people, and owing his power to them only."

On King George's birthday in 1764, the various chiefs formerly loyal to France, in a great ceremony at Mobile, surrendered the medals that had been given them by the French, and accepted instead the medals and gorgets of King George. Stuart wrote of the Mortar:

"He is sensible and manly. Love of his country, and jealousy for his people's lands and independence, actuated him. He adhered to the French merely from motives of necessity and interest." [24]

## 8

Following the peace of 1762, the Indian country was flooded with irresponsible traders, the offscourings of humanity. Old traders such as James Adair, Samuel Benn, and Ludovic Grant had reflected credit upon their avocation. They were

[24] *Colonial Mobile,* Hamilton.

not only traders, but diplomats, loyal Englishmen and friends to the Indians. Of the new traders, Alexander Cameron wrote:

"No nation was ever infested with such a set of villains and horse thieves. They are enough to create disturbance among the most civilized people. A trader . . . will invent and tell a thousand lies; and he is indefatigable in stirring up trouble against all other white persons that he judges his rivals in trade." [25]

Continued slaughter of game for the artificial purpose of trade was taking its toll. Deerskins and other furs could not be procured in sufficient quantities to cover the goods advanced by the traders. The Cherokees some years before the Revolution found themselves hopelessly in debt to the traders, who suggested payment in land. The Indians agreed, and actually ceded certain tracts, but the transactions were vetoed by Stuart as contrary to the policy of the crown which forbade cessions to private persons. The matter involved long correspondence with London, and was evidence of the constantly growing tendency on the frontier to settle upon Indian lands, regardless of rules or treaties.

## 9

The absence of Stuart from the Cherokee country did not lessen the affection of the Indians for their "Father." In 1767, they were delighted to learn that he contemplated a visit to them, and they wrote him:

"We have assembled in the town house of our beloved Chote to talk to our brother Scotchie about affairs that concern our nation. Our friend here told us that you promised yourself this summer a little ride to Keowee. It would give us great pleasure to see you once more in this nation, and we warriors and beloved men should all take you by the hand, and it is what you would to shake hands with our young men." The letter was signed by "Oconostota, Speaker of the Assembly." [26]

[25] *British Colonial Papers,* Stuart to Pownall, Aug. 24, 1765.

[26] *British Colonial Papers.* This is the first time the title "Speaker of the Assembly" was used among the Cherokees. The speaker announced decisions of the National Council, and spoke for the Nation in treaties. The expression used in the letter, "what you would," meant, "you would be free to do as you please."

Stuart, however, was not to enjoy the visit among his old friends. He suffered greatly from gout, induced by continual drinking. He wrote to Lord Hillsborough in April, 1767:

"The state of my health is so impaired by the repeated attacks of a general gout that I am reduced to the necessity of begging your Lordship's intercession with His Majesty for his gracious permission to have me absent from my duty for some months, that I may go to England with a view to obtaining some relief. I am at present entirely crippled and deprived of the use of my limbs. Nothing but the state I am reduced to could have induced me to give your Lordship this trouble." [27]

The permission was given, and Stuart evidently obtained relief, for he was back at his post of duty in November of the same year.

In the meantime, Sir William Johnson called a general congress of all Indians, both north and south, to meet at Fort Stanwix in New York. On Stuart's return to Charles Town, he found the Cherokee delegation awaiting him. "The persons employed for this occasion," he wrote, "are the most respectable and of greatest consequence in their nation, viz.: Oconostota, distinguished by the name of Great Warrior; Attakullakulla, commonly called the Little Carpenter; and the Raven of Nequassee." [28]

Stuart procured passage for the chiefs on one of His Majesty's ships to New York, and they arrived at Sir William Johnson's on April 28, 1768. Peace was signed between the Cherokees and Iroquois, ending a warfare which had existed so long as to be traditional. [29]

Oconostota and the Raven returned to Charles Town in an English war ship. The Little Carpenter, accompanied by an escort of his new friends, the Iroquois, set out to Fort Pitt to endeavor to secure a peace with the Shawnees, Delawares, and other tribes living on the Ohio River. The Cherokees could not understand why their country should continue to be har-

[27] *British Colonial Papers.*
[28] *Ibid.*
[29] Treaty of Fort Stanwix. Oconostota is said to have conceded at this treaty that the Iroquois owned all territory north of the Big River (Tennessee) by right of conquest. The treaty provided, however, that these lands might be used by Cherokees and Chickasaws as hunting grounds.

assed by Indians who were also under English control. The Carpenter's mission, however, was not a success. The western tribes continued to raid the Cherokee towns, and as soon as he returned to his own country, he raised a war party to retaliate. He had his brother, "Scotchie," write to Stuart:

"The Little Carpenter continues as staunch a friend as ever. Before setting out on the warpath against the western Indians, he sends you a string of beads to remember him and his two sons by, in case he does not return." [30]

## 10

The fact that England had acquired all land east of the Mississippi as the result of the French and Indian war was a tremendous stimulation to emigration. Pressure on the established Cherokee boundary became irresistible, and Stuart in his correspondence speaks of numerous parties passing down the Tennessee with intent to settle on the lower Mississippi and Florida.[31] A steady stream of settlers passed up the trail from Charles Town to the Cherokee country, with slight attention to treaty lines. Stuart found it necessary to call the Cherokees into council in October, 1768, at Hard Labour, S. C., to arrange for a revision of boundary. A tract consisting of one hundred square miles was ceded.[32]

Oconostota was principal speaker for the Indians. He said:

"My father sent word to me, and I listened with attention to his call. I arose from my white seat in Chote. I gathered together the chiefs and warriors of my nation and hastened to meet my father, that we might smoke on affairs of peace, and that the Great Being above might bear witness to our talk and see the uprightness of our intentions.

"The land is now divided for the use of the red and the white people, and I hope the white people on the frontier will pay attention to the line marked and agreed upon. I recommend to them to use kindly such of their red brothers, the Cherokees, as chance

---

[30] British Colonial Papers.

[31] One such party, which left the Cherokee towns on April 17, 1768, numbered among its members, Peter Holston, for whom Holston River was named.

[32] This was the second land cession of the Cherokees. It included all the tract between Wateree and Savannah Rivers, from near the present Columbia to within two miles of Greeneville.

to come down into the settlements. We have now given the white men enough land to live upon, and hope in return to be well used by them.

"We have not demanded any payment for the land, and shall be content with what our father chooses to give, for he knows that we are poor, and the value of the land is great."

Probably no other man than John Stuart could have procured so large a tract of Indian land without striking a bargain in advance.

Oconostota paid remarkable tribute to Stuart's deputy, Alexander Cameron.

"I am now going to talk to you concerning Mr. Cameron. He has lived among us as beloved man. He has done us justice. He has told us the truth. We all love and regard him, and hope he will not be taken from us. When a good man comes amongst us, we are sorry to part with him.

"Our beloved brother, Mr. Cameron, has got a son by a Cherokee woman. We are desirous that he may educate the boy like the white people, and cause him to be able to read and write, that he may resemble both white and red, and live among us when his father is dead. We have given him for this purpose a large piece of land, which we hope will be agreeable to our father." [33]

The gift of land to Cameron's son caused severe criticism from London authorities, and was near to losing the deputy his position, as English law did not permit cessions save to the crown. Stuart defended his deputy on the ground that it was not a cession but a gift to one of their own people, for the Indians regarded the child as a member of its mother's clan, regardless of the father's people.

II

The Treaty of Hard Labour was the signal for an inrush of settlers toward the Cherokee country, not only from South Carolina, but from Virginia and North Carolina. In March, 1769, the first glimpse is had of the Watauga settlement, when Oconostota wrote Stuart that settlers from Virginia were over the line, and wished to buy land. "If my father desires," he

---

[33] Proceedings at Treaty of Hard Labour, Oct. 14, 1768, British Colonial Papers.

said, "I will sell them the land, but a few presents are as nothing compared to good land, which will last forever." [34]

The first settler at Watauga was one Honeycut, who built a cabin in which he entertained James Robertson, then a young man dissatisfied with political conditions in North Carolina, and in search of better conditions for himself and his family.

Robertson was delighted with the beauty of the Watauga site. He planted a crop and started for the Yadkin to bring his family to the new country. He lost his direction, and wandered in the wilderness for fourteen days, being rescued at the point of starvation by some hunters.

His description of the land across the mountains fired the enthusiasm of his neighbors. Accompanied by his brother Charles, and several families from the Yadkin section, Robertson returned to Watauga and settled, early in 1769. About the same time Captain William Bean settled upon Bean's Creek, and his son, Russell Bean, was the first white child born west of the Alleghenies. John Carter settled in Carter's Valley, and Jacob Brown upon Nolichucky River. Colonel Gilbert Christian led a party from Virginia into Holston Valley on an exploratory trip. On their outward journey, they found wilderness. Returning, they found a cabin at every spring. Daniel Boone was in demand as a guide from North Carolina to the new country.

All of these settlements were on Cherokee land, and created consternation in the Cherokee towns. Oconostota wrote Stuart in July, 1769:

[34] The one man who inspired the settlement of the country west of the Alleghenies more than any other was Christopher Gist, of the Yadkin River settlement of North Carolina. Gist was a man of ability, and of more education than was customary at the time. He was employed in 1750 by the Ohio Company to explore the Ohio Valley. It was while engaged in this work that he was propounded the question by an Indian chief: "The French claim all the land north of the Ohio, and the English all to the south. Where do the Indian's lands lie?"

Gist made two trips to the Ohio, visited the principal tribes of Indians, made friends with them, and had gathered a band of a hundred pioneers to settle upon the Ohio when the French and Indian war disrupted his plans. His proposed settlers were shifted to Washington's militia, and served at Great Meadows and Fort Necessity.

On his second trip to the Ohio, Gist returned by way of the Kentucky River and brought with him a great curiosity, the tooth of a mastoden. It was his description of the Kentucky country that later sent his friend and neighbor Daniel Boone over the same path that he had explored. See affidavit of John Shaw, *S.C.I.A.* 5: 1-4.

"FATHER: The white people pay no attention to the talks we have had.  They are in bodies hunting in the middle of our hunting grounds.  Some of our people went as far as Long Island of Holston River, but were obliged to come home, for the whole nation is filling with hunters, and the guns rattling every way on the path, both up and down the river.  They have settled the land a great way this side of the line." [35]

Richard Pearis, interpreter to the Cherokees in the French and Indian war, desired to buy 200,000 acres of land direct from the Cherokees.  Oconostota wrote Stuart:

"Who is this Pearis?  He certainly must be a great man, greater than the Governor of Virginia, for when the Governor wanted land, we had to ask the King's liberty first, but Pearis wants to ask nobody.  He, being a great man, it is for him to do as he pleases." [36]

The rapid settlement of the Watauga was facilitated by trouble between the Cherokees and Chickasaws which distracted, for the time being, the attention of the Indians. Oconostota, for real or fancied insults, led his warriors against the Chickasaws, and was badly defeated at Chickasaw Old Fields.  Captain Stuart soon made peace between the two tribes.

Alexander Cameron, Stuart's resident deputy, was disturbed by the encroachment of the Watauga settlements on Cherokee land.  He ordered that the settlements be abandoned, which the Wataugans refused to consider.  They offered, however, to pay the Cherokees a fair rental for the ground.  Cameron submitted the matter to Stuart, who recommended that the offer be accepted by the Indians, for he well recognized the impossibility of removing settlers once over the Indian line. Stuart's advice being accepted, the Little Carpenter was appointed by the nation to go to Watauga and arrange details.

The Carpenter wrote his friend:

"Father, when I go to Virginia I will eat and drink with my white brothers, and will expect friendship and good usage from them.  It is but a little spot of ground that you ask, and I am willing that your people should live upon it.  I pity the white people, but

[35] Oconostota to Stuart, July 29, 1769, *British Colonial Papers.*
[36] *Ibid.,* June 27, 1769.

the white people do not pity me. Captain Guess comes into our country hunting, with fifty men. When we tell him of it, he threatens to shoot us down. The Great Being above is very good, and provides for everybody. It is He that made fire, bread, and the rivers to run. He gave us this land, but the white people seem to want to drive us from it." [37]

The Little Carpenter arrived in Watauga and successfully concluded his mission by signing a lease to the Wataugans for their lands for a period of eight years, for which the Cherokees received goods amounting to £2000.

A horse race was arranged to celebrate the conclusion of the agreement, and the Indians were invited to participate. There were rough characters on the border, who hated all Indians, and were angered at the implied equality of the contestants. Upon this pretext, one of the Indians was killed, and the Little Carpenter withdrew in great dissatisfaction and disappeared with his followers toward the Cherokee towns.[38]

The Watauga men, fearing an Indian war, sent James Robertson to Chote to make apology and restitution. Robertson's bravery and frankness won the Cherokee admiration. He distributed presents to relatives of the slain warrior, and promised that the offender would be punished when apprehended. The Indians were appeased, and Robertson from that day became a marked man, not only among the white men, but among the Cherokees as well.

Having leased the ground, the Wataugans proceeded upon the principal that they owned it. The settlement grew rapidly in numbers, and the line established by the lease was soon

[37] *British Colonial Papers.* The Captain Guess referred to by the Carpenter was Nathaniel Gist, son of Christopher Gist. Captain Gist later became well liked by the Cherokees. He was the father of Sequoyah.

[38] John Sevier was among the spectators at the horse race, it being his first trip to Watauga. He had planned to settle, but was disgusted at the action of a frontier bully named Shote, who took a horse by force from a smaller man, claiming to have won it although the owner insisted that he had made no bet. Sevier mounted his horse and started for Virginia, determined that he would not settle in so barbarous a community. He met General Evan Shelby, who was also looking over the country with a view of settling, and told of the incident. "Never mind those rascals," Shelby told him, "They'll soon take poplar and push off," (meaning that they would take canoes and leave.) The frontiersmen had their own methods of dealing with horse thieves, and Shote was soon apprehended and hung.

passed.    Cameron protested in vain.    He wrote Stuart in August, 1774:

"The inhabitants of Watauga still remain unmolested by the government of Virginia.   When the Indians found they would not remove without the shedding of blood, to which they are averse on account of the daily representations made to them on the subject, they at length agreed to take some compensation for the rent of the land, and now the settlers will not allow that the Indians have any rights to the land."

The question was soon to be settled by the greatest land purchase of all.   The Cherokees, without consulting Cameron or Stuart, were to sell all of Kentucky and Middle Tennessee to Richard Henderson for the Transylvania Company.   The Watauga people, taking advantage of the great treaty, were to buy their "little spot of ground" outright, on March 17, 1775, at the Treaty of Sycamore Shoals.[39]

## 12

Early in 1776, the naturalist William Bartram visited the Cherokee country.   As he rode over the trail from Keowee to Tellico, he observed a group of Indian horsemen, headed by a chief whom he recognized from the description that had been given him as the Little Carpenter.   He respectfully stepped aside to permit the Indians to pass, when the Carpenter dismounted to speak a courteous word to the stranger in his country.   Extending his hand, he said, "I am Attakullakulla,— did you know it?"

Bartram replied: "The Good Spirit who goes before me told me that you were Attakullakulla.   I am of the tribe of white men who live in Pennsylvania, who esteem themselves the friends and brothers of the red men, and particularly the Cherokees.   The name of the great Attakullakulla is dear to his brethren in Pennsylvania."

The chief was pleased.   "Do you come from Charles Town?" he asked, and "Is John Stuart well?"   Bartram replied that he had a letter from the Superintendent asking the friendship and protection of the Cherokees for himself while in their country.

[39] See Chapter I.  *Draper Mss.,* 22-S-140-180.

"You are welcome in my country as a friend and brother," the Carpenter said, which the members of his party confirmed by a shout. The chief shook hands heartily with Bartram, and informed him that he was on his way to see his Father, Captain Stuart, at Charles Town. He mounted his horse, and the Indian cavalcade quickly disappeared.

The Revolution, however, was at hand. The Little Carpenter was not to be permitted to visit Charles Town, and was never again to see his father Stuart. Bartram, fearing for his own safety, turned back before reaching the Overhill country. The world was the loser, for had he continued his journey we would have had a description of the Overhill towns rendered in Bartram's delightful style.[40]

----

[40] Bartram, *Travels,* 295: Thatcher, *Indian Biography,* 2, 154.

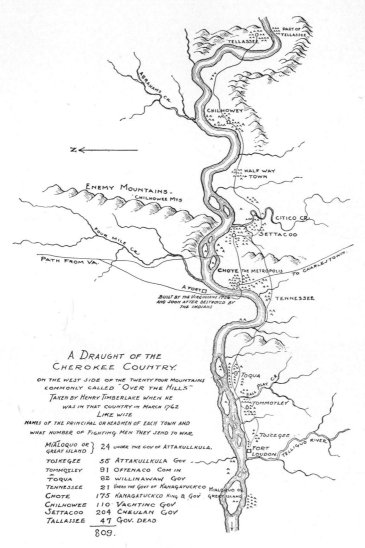

## A DRAUGHT OF THE CHEROKEE COUNTRY.

ON THE WEST SIDE OF THE TWENTY FOUR MOUNTAINS
COMMONLY CALLED "OVER THE HILLS"
TAKEN BY HENRY TIMBERLAKE WHEN HE
WAS IN THAT COUNTRY IN MARCH 1762
LIKE WISE
NAMES OF THE PRINCIPAL OR HEADMEN OF EACH TOWN AND
WHAT NUMBER OF FIGHTING MEN THEY SEND TO WAR.

| | | |
|---|---|---|
| MIALOQUO OR GREAT ISLAND | 24 | UNDER THE GOV OF ATTAKULLKULA. |
| TOSKEGEE | 55 | ATTAKULLKULA GOV |
| TOMMOTLEY | 91 | OFTENACO COM IN |
| TOQUA | 82 | WILLINAWAW GOV |
| TENNESSEE | 21 | UNDER THE GOV OF KANAGATUCKCO |
| CHOTE | 175 | KANAGATUCKCO KING & GOV |
| CHILNOWEE | 110 | VACHTINO GOV |
| SETTACOO | 204 | CHEULAN GOV |
| TALLASSEE | 47 | GOV. DEAD |
| | 809. | |

TIMBERLAKE'S MAP OF THE OVERHILL COUNTRY, LONDON, 1765

The towns shown were along the Little Tennessee River, in the present Monroe County, Tenn.  Scale, about one half inch to the mile.

# BOOK TWO
## Dragging Canoe

# CHAPTER VIII

## AN AMERICAN TAKES HIS STAND

### I

The ten years which followed Richard Henderson's treaty at Sycamore Shoals in 1775 were to witness the rise of a great war leader among the Cherokees, Dragging Canoe, worthy successor to Oconostota.

His prinicipal opponent, John Sevier, was to ride down the Great Warpath to fame.

The Wilderness Road was to see the first trickle that was to become a mightly stream of immigration flowing to new homes in Kentucky and Middle Tennessee, "a fair land," its settlement "dark and bloody."

The State of Franklin, lost star in our flag, was to rise and fall.

The American Revolution was to begin and end; to which end the frontiersmen were to contribute by winning the Battle of King's Mountain.

Organized Indian warfare, incited by British agents, was to terrorize the frontier from Canada to the Gulf; and the Cherokees were to play a willing part.

The United States, a free nation, was to conclude its first treaty with the Cherokees at Hopewell; and the treaty was to be damned by the frontiersmen.

The exit of British influence with the Indians was to bring a more ominous, intolerant Spain, bent on ownership of the Mississippi and all lands west of the great river.

These subjects will be considered in Book Two.

### 2

The Cherokees returned from Henderson's treaty to be caught in the whirlwind of passion caused by the beginning of the American Revolution. The Indians, as wards of Great Britain and dominated by English agents, were under grave suspicion. Stuart and Cameron were said to be inciting them to fall upon the frontier settlements and kill all, regardless of age and sex. These rumors were accepted at face value. Stuart's deputy among the Creeks, Thomas Brown, was tarred and feathered at Augusta.

Stuart, who was living at Charles Town, wrote General Haldimand, "Our people here are so inflamed with political enthusiasm that anywhere else in America they would be deemed proper inhabitants of Bedlam." [1]  Stuart was in his seventy-fifth year, and in bad health, but was compelled to flee for his life to an English ship lying in Charles Town harbor. He wrote to the Earl of Dartmouth from St. Augustine on July 25, 1775:

"I narrowly escaped falling into the hands of an incensed mob at a time when my state of health rendered me very incapable of bearing rough usage. My family and property are still in their power. The latter they threaten to confiscate, and I anxiously wish the former from among them, although I hope their sex and innocence will entitle them to mild treatment from a people among whom they have lived so long respectably. I beg to assure your Lordship that no consideration shall induce me to abandon the trust inposed in me." [2]

Supplies which the Cherokees had long received from South Carolina were stopped. The Indians were deeply perplexed. They could not imagine a war between brothers who spoke the same language. If such a war was to be, however, there was no question as to which side the Cherokees would take. Their chiefs had visited England, and had seen with their own eyes the might of the English king, who had been their Great White Father and had supplied their needs for a generation. His agent John Stuart was their friend, and of Stuart's deputy Cameron Oconostota had said: "He has done us justice; he has told us the truth; we all regard and love him." That the Cherokees would remain loyal to the English was a foregone conclusion.

3

From St. Augustine whence he had fled, John Stuart wrote to the Cherokees that he was sending his brother Henry Stuart to Pensacola with goods to take the place of those stopped by

[1] Hamer, P. M., *Mississippi Historical Review*, December, 1930.
[2] *North Carolina Colonial Records*, 10, 117.

South Carolina. He told them that his brother would explain to them the trouble between the king and his rebellious children the Americans.

Most of the chiefs were content to await the arrival of Henry Stuart. Dragging Canoe, however, still smarting from his experience at Henderson's treaty, gathered eighty warriors and departed to Pensacola to meet the king's agent. Henry Stuart arrived at Mobile on March 1, 1776, and found Dragging Canoe awaiting him.

The chief inquired the reason of the quarrel between the king and his subjects, and why the Indian supplies had been stopped. He complained bitterly of white encroachment:

"The white men have almost surrounded us, leaving us only a little spot of ground to stand upon, and it seems to be their intention to destroy us as a Nation." [3]

Stuart replied that he realized the inconvenience to which the Cherokees had been put by the stopping of their supplies and by the intrusion of the Virginians on their lands, but affairs were such that the Americans trampled upon the king's orders, and nothing could be done with them. He reminded Dragging Canoe that the Indians were themselves to blame for selling their lands to Henderson without knowledge of the king's agent. Dragging Canoe replied:

"I had nothing to do with making that bargain; it was made by some of the old men, who are too old to hunt or to fight. As for me, I have a great many of my young warriors around me, and they mean to have their lands."

Stuart told the chief he would proceed to the Nation and see how things were, and where a good interpreter could be had so they might understand each other better. He would leave at once with thirty horse loads of ammunition, and would go through the Chickasaw country, for the Creeks and Choctaws were at war which made the usual path unsafe. He requested Dragging Canoe to meet him at Tennessee River to escort him to the Cherokee towns.

After a tedious trip to the Tennessee, Stuart found Dragging

---

[3] Henry Stuart's Report, *N. C. Colonial Records*, 10, 763-783.

Canoe awaiting him.[4] He was also met by Captain Nathaniel Gist and a number of white men who had planned to settle upon the Mississippi.[5] Gist accompanied Henry Stuart to Chote. He had much to say of the rapid growth of the American settlement at Watauga, and Dragging Canoe announced his firm intention to drive the white men off Indian lands. The chief dispatched runners to towns which he thought were friendly to his purpose, urging preparations for immediate war.

Stuart by no means wished indiscriminate warfare against the American frontier. He recognized that American sentiment was divided, and that many loyal subjects of the King would suffer in such a war. The Revolution was just beginning, and loyal Englishmen hoped that the Colonies might be won back to the King by persuasion rather than by force. Stuart's instructions from his brother read:

"HENRY: You will understand that an indiscriminate attack on the Province is not meant, but to act in the execution of any concerted plan, and to assist His Majesty's troops and friends in distressing the Rebels and bringing them to a sense of their duty." [6]

Stuart therefore endeavored to dissuade Dragging Canoe from an immediate attack. He told the chief there were many white men on Indian land who thought the land had been honestly bought, and who would remove when they knew their mistake. He reminded the chief that the white settlements might easily have been prevented in the beginning, but their removal after seven years of occupancy would spill much blood. He promised to write the Wataugans on his arrival at Chote, requesting them to remove.

Dragging Canoe replied that he would wait until Stuart had written, and if the settlers did not then remove, he would advise

---

[4] At Muscle Shoals, where the Old Chickasaw trail crossed the Tennessee River.

[5] Gist, through his friendship for the Cherokees, sided at first with the English. Later, when sent as a messenger by the Indians to the camp of Colonel Christian of Virginia, he remained with the Americans and rendered loyal service to the American cause. At the close of the Revolution, he was in command of one of the frontier Virginia forts, and was granted land in Kentucky for his services.

[6] John Stuart to Henry Stuart, as quoted by Hamer in *Mississippi Valley Historical Review*, December, 1930.

the old chiefs of his intention to remove them by force. If the chiefs approved, all would be well, but if not, he and his young warriors would have their way.

### 4

Henry Stuart was received at Chote with the Eagle Tail Dance. He made a conciliatory talk, and secured permission from Oconostota and the Little Carpenter to write to the Watauga settlers. This gave him opportunity to warn loyal subjects of the King, that they might not be caught in the net of Indian warfare.

Isaac Thomas, a trader, was sent with a letter to the Wataugans, and one to loyal British subjects. The Cherokees also sent a talk to the Watauga settlers.

Stuart's letter to British loyalists fell into American hands. It contained the startling information that an English army was on its way from Pensacola with fifteen hundred Creeks, Choctaws, and Chickasaws, to be joined by the entire force of the Cherokee Nation; which formidable army would fall on the Watauga settlements and destroy them unless they were promptly removed.[7]

To such a communication there could be but one reply. The Cherokees were in turn threatened with a war of extermination. The older chiefs were worried, but Dragging Canoe and his followers painted themselves black and struck the war pole. War parties departed toward the white settlements, and in a few days one of these returned with four American scalps. War being apparently inevitable, Stuart dispatched William Colbert with one hundred packhorses to Pensacola to bring a full supply of ammunition.

### 5

The great Shawnee chief Cornstalk arrived at Chote at this opportune time, with a delegation of fourteen chiefs from northern tribes, the Iroquois, Mohawks, Delawares, Ottawas, Nantucas, and Shawnees, to ask the assistance of the Cherokees in united warfare against the Americans. The northern ambassadors stated that they would give their "grand talk" in ten

---

[7] Henry Stuart later claimed that the contents of the letter were altered before circulation among the Americans. He knew of course that no such force was on the way from Pensacola.

days, and requested that the head men of all the Cherokee Nation be present to hear it. They gave an account of their journey:

"We have been seventy days upon our way. When we passed through the country between Pittsburgh and our nations, lately Shawnee and Delaware hunting grounds, where we could once see nothing but deer and buffalo, we found the country thickly inhabited and the people under arms. We were compelled to make a detour of three hundred miles on the other side of the Ohio to avoid being discovered. We saw large numbers of white men in forts; and fortifications around salt springs and buffalo grounds. We noted traces of large bodies of men with horses and cattle on the road from Holston to Kaintuckee." [8]

The Mohawk deputies stated that white people had come into their towns and killed many of their people, among them the son of their English Agent Sir William Johnson, who had been put to death by immersion in hot tar.[9] They said:

"The French have given us plenty of ammunition. All of the Northern tribes have agreed to take satisfaction. The King's troops will soon fall on our enemies toward the sea, and if we, the red men, unite and fall on them on this side, we will find them as nothing."

After these talks, nothing was heard in the Overhill towns but war, and the warriors were busy repairing moccasins and making spears, clubs, and scalping knives.

The anxious Stuart sought to dissuade the Indians until cooperation could be had with English troops. The older chiefs readily agreed to what he said, but Dragging Canoe reproached him:

"It would have been better to have attacked the Wataugans at once, without writing them the letters. The letters served only to put them on guard, and caused them to prepare to come against the Cherokees. By this time, they will have all their people removed.

"You told us to assist the King. Now, when there is a white army coming against our towns, we want to keep them back. One

---

[8] *N. C. Colonial Records*, 10, 763-783.
[9] The frontier practice of "Tar and Feathers."

of the white men who lived among us, a trader, has gone away, and we are convinced it is to give information to our enemies of what has passed in the Nation. Let there be no more letters wrote, nor any more people suffered to leave the Nation."

Stuart reminded the chief that he had gone to great trouble to supply the Cherokees with ammunition. If they did not appreciate his efforts, he might as well go about his business. The older chiefs intervened, and asked Stuart to pay no attention to the talk of the young men; but agreed that no other trader should leave the towns lest he give information that the Northern Indians were among them.[10]

### 6

On the day appointed for the "grand talk" with the Northern Indians, Stuart went with the Cherokees to the council house, where he found the flag pole and posts painted black and red, the war colors.

The Mohawk deputy, who spoke also for the Six Nations, arose. He produced a belt of white and black wampum with strings of the same color attached. He said:

"I suppose there is not a man present who cannot read my talk. These white beads are my people, who were at peace. The black beads are the Long Knives, who came into our towns without provocation and killed our people, and the son of our greatly beloved man, Sir William Johnson. The strings of white and black wampum are our people who were killed.

"What is the case of my people one day may be the case with any nation another day. My people the Mohawks are fighting the Long Knives. They have sent me to secure the friendship of all Nations of Indians, for the interests of all red men are one. The red men must forget their quarrels among themselves, and turn their eyes and thoughts one way. I now offer you this belt, and if my brothers the Cherokees agree with what I have said, let them take it."[11]

The Mohawk belt was promptly accepted by Dragging Canoe.[12]

---

[10] Stuart's Report, *N. C. Colonial Records,* 10, 763-783.

[11] *Ibid.*

[12] Acceptance of the belt meant: "I agree with what you have said, and I will go to war with you."

The Ottawa deputy arose, and likewise produced a black and white belt. He expressed the desire of his people to form a true and lasting friendship with all their red brethren.

"We have been almost constantly at war, one nation with another, and the white people have taken advantage of this situation. The French in Canada have found means to supply us with ammunition, and will assist us. The Ottawas are willing to drop all former quarrels and join in a common cause, and hope that all the Nations will feel the same."

The Ottawa belt was accepted by Dragging Canoe.

The talk of the Delawares was much to the same effect, and their belt was accepted by the Raven of Chote, nephew of Oconostota.

The great chief Cornstalk, of the Shawnees, concluded the talks. He produced a magnificent purple war belt, nine feet long and six inches wide. Over this he poured vermilion to represent blood, a dramatic gesture that caused a sensation among his hearers.

Cornstalk began by enumerating the afflictions of his own and other red nations.

"In a few years, the Shawnees, from being a great Nation, have been reduced to a handful. They once possessed land almost to the seashore, but now have hardly enough ground to stand upon.

"The lands where the Shawnees have but lately hunted are covered with forts and armed men. When a fort appears, you may depend upon it there will soon be towns and settlements of white men. It is plain that the white people intend to extirpate the Indians. It is better for the red men to die like warriors than to diminish away by inches. The cause of the red men is just, and I hope that the Great Spirit who governs everything will favor us."

Cornstalk told the Indians that the French, who had long seemed dead, had supplied the Northern Nations with arms, ammunition, and provisions, and continued:

"Now is the time to begin. No time should be lost. If we fight like men, we may hope to enlarge our bounds. The Cherokees have a hatchet that was brought to you six years ago. Your brothers, the Shawnees, hope that you will take it up and use it immediately.

"If any nation shall refuse us now, we shall hereafter consider them the common enemy of all red men. When affairs with the white people are settled, we shall then fall upon such nations and destroy them." [13]

The great war belt of Cornstalk was accepted by Dragging Canoe also.

It was some minutes before any of the Cherokees rose to reply to the talks. Then, Osioota of Chilhowie, who had lived in the Mohawk Nation and whose wife had lived in Sir William Johnson's house, rose and took the great belt from Dragging Canoe in token that he, too, accepted the war talk. Drawing his tomahawk, he struck the war pole, and sang the war song.

"Wherever earth is brightened by the sun,
    Moon shines by night, grass grows or waters run,
Be it known we go like men, afar,
In hostile fields, to wage destructive war.
Like men we go to meet our country's foes,
Who, womanlike, shall fly our dreadful blows.

We'll leave our clubs, dewed with their country's showers,
And if they dare bring them back to ours,
Their painted scalps shall be our step to fame,
And grace our country's glorious name.
Or if we warriors spare the yielding foe,
Torments at home the wretch must undergo." [14]

The young men of the Cherokees and the northern chiefs joined with wild enthusiasm in the dance. With war whoops ringing around them, Oconostota and the Little Carpenter, remembering the calamities brought on the Cherokees by the last war with the white men, sat dejected and silent. [15]

The northern deputies proposed that Stuart and Cameron, the King's representatives, should accept the war belts also,

---

[13] Stuart's Report, *N. C. Colonial Records,* 10, 763-783.

Cornstalk was a great chief, respected among all the Indian nations. He had led the allied Indians in battle against the Virginians at Point Pleasant in 1774, in which his warriors acquitted themselves with bravery and distinction, the result being a drawn battle. A fort was built on the battleground. Cornstalk and his son Elinipsico were treacherously killed while under a flag of truce at the fort in 1777.

[14] *Memoirs of Timberlake,* 81.

[15] Stuart's Report.

signifying that they, too, would go to war with the Americans.
Stuart firmly but courteously declined:

"The red men do not understand the written talks of the white
men. Even so the white men do not understand the belts of the
red men. I am determined not to sanction a war that is likely to
bring destruction on the Cherokees. When the Indians were twice
as strong as they are now, and had the French to help them, they
were withstood by the Virginians, who had then but few warriors.

"You northern Indians have proper white men to direct you,
but the Cherokees have not. If they go over the border and kill
women and children, and fall on the King's friends as well as his
enemies, they will draw against themselves all the forces that were
intended to be used against the King's troops; and will rouse the
resentment of those who otherwise might have been their friends."

"Your father (Captain Stuart) is willing to support you while
you pay regard to his talks; but we do not consider it time for the
Cherokees to go out until they are certain an army is coming against
them. We therefore cannot give our consent to their going to
war." [16]

The young warriors were displeased that Stuart would not
accept the belts. He had forgotten, they said, what happened
at Cane Creek, when his brother's life was saved. It was true
that he had brought the Cherokees ammunition, but now he
wanted them to keep it until it had fallen into the hands of the
Virginians.

The Raven of Chote, speaking for Oconostota, told the
Northern Indians that the Cherokees would give them an answer to their talks on the following day, at Settico. Stuart
did not attend the meeting, for he was warned by the older
chiefs that his life, and the lives of all the white men in the
Nation, were in grave danger. The white traders, most of
whom had Indian wives, were warned also, and most of them
hid in the woods.

### 7

The next day Dragging Canoe, in war paint, called upon
Stuart. "Why have the traders left the towns?" he demanded;
"and why are you, my brother, talking of leaving, after you

---

[16] *Ibid.*

have brought trouble on the Cherokees by writing the Virginians?"

Stuart replied that the traders could not be expected to remain when their lives were in danger. "As for myself, I told the Cherokees from the first that I would return to Pensacola as soon as possible, and I expect to leave as soon as I can procure horses. You, Dragging Canoe, are the cause of the trouble that has come on the Cherokees, and it does not look well to throw the blame upon me."

Stuart suggested that a general council of the Nation be called, and all the traders be requested to attend. At the meeting, Dragging Canoe promised the traders security if they would remain in the towns, and continued:

"I hope you will not in the future pay attention to idle dreams. If any of you choose to join the war, I will be glad, but I will not insist upon any of you going. Those who do not go, however, will be expected to furnish the warriors with ammunition and supplies."

Turning to Alexander Cameron, the chief said, "I will always pay attention to what my brother says, and will hold fast to his talks."

Stuart took the opportunity to force Dragging Canoe to admit that it was he alone who was responsible for the war. The chief, apparently proud of the distinction, had no objection to making the admission, and proclaimed it publicly.

Cornstalk spoke a few words of farewell for the northern delegation before setting out for their own country. Dragging Canoe, as an assurance of his friendship and cooperation in the war against the whites, presented the Shawnee chief with the four American scalps which his followers had taken on the Kentucky road.

8

Stuart realized that hope for peace was useless. He warned the Cherokees, however, that they must not cross the white boundaries or kill women and children; and that they must not harm the King's subjects. He took his departure from Chote on July 12, 1776. In the Creek country, he was advised that Colbert had reached Chote with a plentiful supply of ammunition. He sent a runner with a final warning to Dragging Canoe that the Cherokees must abide by any advice given them by the King's Agent, Cameron. Should they fail to do, no more ammunition would reach them from the English. "I have gone to great trouble to open a path to your country from Pensacola," Stuart told the Cherokees, "and if you misbehave, a word from me will close it forever."

The older chiefs had told Stuart that the decision for war rested with Oconostota, the war chief. There was doubt among the red men as to Oconostota's attitude, for he was known to be averse to war. A date was set for his talk, but the day before the Cherokees were to meet for that purpose, word was received that the lower Cherokee towns had already commenced war against the Carolina frontier. The arrival of Colbert at Chote with 100 horseloads of ammuntion, set the Overhill towns in a frenzy. Cameron wrote to John Stuart: "All our rhetoric could no longer dissuade them from taking up the hatchet." [17]

9

The Cherokee plan of campaign contemplated a simultaneous attack on the frontiers of Virginia, the Carolinas, and Georgia. Virginia was assigned to the Overhill warriors, numbering seven hundred.

Dragging Canoe was selected to head the principal body of three hundred, which was to destroy the Holston settlements and continue on to Virginia. Abram of Chilhowie was at the same time to attack Watauga; and the Raven of Chote was to scour Carter's Valley. The campaign was planned with utmost secrecy, and had the attack fallen on the frontier without warning, the white settlements could not have survived. But there occurred an act that changed the course of destiny.

Nancy Ward was *Ghigau* (Beloved Woman) of the Cherokees.[18] Her duties were the preparation of the sacred Black

---

[17] The foregoing account, where not otherwise indicated, is taken from Henry Stuart's report to John Stuart, *N. C. Colonial Records,* 10, 763-783.

[18] Nancy Ward first came into prominence at the Battle of Taliwa in 1755, by which the Creeks were defeated by the Cherokees and driven out of North Georgia. She was at that time the wife of the warrior Kingfisher, and had accompanied him on the warpath. Her husband was killed, and Nancy Ward took up his rifle and fought as a warrior in his place during the rest of the battle. She was given the title of Beloved Woman in recognition of her bravery. She soon afterward married Brian Ward a

Drink of which the warriors partook before going on the war-path. She thus came into possession of the plans of the chiefs.

Nancy Ward had married a white trader. She felt friendly to the white people, and decided to warn them of the proposed attack. She revealed the plan of campaign to the trader Isaac Thomas and arranged for his escape from the towns in company with two other white men, William Fawling and Jarrett Williams, on the night of July 8, 1776. On the morning of the 11th, they reached Watauga and delivered the message to John Sevier.

A Cherokee war was not unexpected by the Wataugans, for the correspondence with Cameron had warned them, but the definite information given by Nancy Ward caused consternation on the frontier. There had been no Indian warfare since the settlement had begun, seven years before. There was not a complete fort or blockhouse from the Wolf's Hills[19] of Virginia westward. Sevier lost no time. Within a few minutes, messengers had mounted and were spreading the word as rapidly as horseflesh could move. Sevier's letter to the officers of Fincastle County, Virginia, is typical:

"Fort Lee, July 11, 1776.

"DEAR GENTLEMEN: Isaac Thomas, William Fawling, Jarot Williams, and one more, have this moment come in by making their escape from the Indians, and say six hundred Indians and whites were to start for this fort, and intend to drive up the country to New River before they return.

JOHN SEVIER." [20]

Feverish activity followed; couriers rushed in all directions, warning and aiding isolated settlers. Militia was called out, and blockhouses were erected hastily at strategic points. Within

---

trader who had served with English forces in the French and Indian War. Ward later left the Cherokee country and in 1791 was living upon Tugaloo River, Pendleton District, S. C., with his white family. Nancy Ward occasionally visited him there, and was received with respect by his family. William Martin, who was a son of General Joseph Martin, lived near Ward, and saw Nancy on her occasional visits. He says "She was, I think, one of the most superior women I ever saw." Nancy Ward died in 1822 in the present Polk County, Tenn., and her grave, about five miles from Benton, has been marked. See Draper Mss., 3-XX-4 for an extended statement by William Martin as to his father's relations with Nancy Ward.

[19] Wolf's Hills was later called Abingdon.
[20] Ramsay, 150.

ten days, the entire population of more than three thousand was gathered in stockade forts. There was sickness, suffering, and discouragement. Many of the settlers planned to leave the country as soon as safety would permit, but for the moment all energy was directed toward meeting the Indian invasion.

A small stockaded fort had been erected at Eaton's Station about five miles below the junction of the two forks of Holston, in advance of the settlements. It was on the Great War Trail, the natural route of the Indian army to the Holston settlements.

Five companies of militia, about one hundred and seventy men, had gathered at Eaton's, under their captains James Thompson, William Cocke, James Shelby, William Buchanan, John Campbell, and Thomas Madison. The inactivity of waiting for the foe was irksome to the turbulent frontiersmen. They feared, too, that the Indians might pass the station and destroy their homes and crops which lay beyond. It was decided to march out and meet the enemy rather than wait to be attacked. Authority was so divided among the officers that there was really no one in charge, but James Thompson was the senior captain.

On July 20, 1776, the men marched from Eaton's Station in two columns, single file, Indian fashion. The route followed was down the Great War Trail. At a place called Island Flats, about six miles below the fort, the advance guard met a party of twenty Indians coming along the trail toward them. The Indians fired and retreated.

Captain Thompson called a council of officers, and the entire force gathered around to hear the proceedings. It was late in the afternoon. Some of the officers, notably Captain William Cocke, felt that it would be prudent to retire to the fort rather than go into battle with night so near. This opinion prevailed, and the men were placed in position for retreat.

The American militiaman of the time furnished his own equipment and served at his own expense, and felt free to criticize anything that did not meet his approval. To have met the Indians only to retreat without a fight filled the members of the little army with wrath, and they expressed in no uncertain terms their opinion of the fighting qualities of any officer who would display such cowardice. Captain Cocke smarted under the censure as long as he could bear it. He then halted the men

and harangued them in defense of his reputation for bravery.[21]
Just as he had finished speaking and the lines were reforming,
the scouts ran in with the news that the main body of the Indians was coming.

Captain Thompson hastily filed his men to left and right and
formed a line of battle among the trees. The Cherokees, led
by Dragging Canoe, thought that the white men were retreating. Indian caution was dropped in the desire to secure scalps.
"Come on," the chief yelled; "The Unacas are running, come
and scalp them!" For once, the Cherokees received a dose of
their own favored method of fighting, the ambush. Dragging
Canoe fell at the first fire with a ball through both thighs. He
was borne to the rear by his followers, fiercely exhorting them
to action. A hand to hand struggle among the trees followed.

Lieutenant Moore, of Sullivan County, wounded a Cherokee
chief, his ball striking the savage in the knee. Moore sprang
forward, butcher knife in hand, to secure his scalp. The chief
threw his tomahawk and missed, and the two men grappled.
The Indian seized Moore's knife by the blade and attempted to
twist it from his hand, and persisted although his own hand
was almost severed. Moore managed to free his own tomahawk and sink it in the head of his opponent, whom he promptly
scalped.

The Cherokees retired slowly, taking their wounded with
them. Thirteen of their number were left dead on the field.
The American loss was four wounded, none killed.[22]

### 10

This serious defeat, early in his career, taught Dragging
Canoe a lesson that he never forgot. Thereafter, he did not
attempt to "fight in armies" as the white men fought, but employed the old method of Indian warfare; surprise, attack,

---

[21] William Cocke served against the Shawnees in Virginia in 1774, and
accompanied Richard Henderson on his first trip to Kentucky in 1775 at
which time he displayed signal bravery. This was later confirmed on many
fields. He was suspended by Virginia under the charge of cowardice at
the Battle of Island Flats, but was quickly acquitted. He later served as
Brigadier General of the forces of the State of Franklin. He volunteered
for the Creek war in 1813, though then 66 years of age, and was cited for
bravery in action by Andrew Jackson. He served two terms in the United
States Senate. For detailed sketch see Williams, *Lost State of Franklin,*
287-291.

[22] For official report of the battle, see Ramsey, 154.

scalp, and disappear. He put that plan into effect immediately. Small parties of Indians were dispatched to the Holston, Powell, and Clinch Valleys. Their appearance at widely separated points made pursuit impossible. Death and destruction were carried far beyond the Virginia line.

Had Dragging Canoe returned to the Cherokee towns with thirteen warriors missing, his reputation would have been in grave danger. He returned, however, despite his wound, with eighteen scalps and much loot. He had wrought victory from defeat, and was in position to defy the older chiefs.[23]

II

At daylight on the same day of the Island Flats engagement, Old Abram and his followers attacked Fort Lee at Watauga. The fort was crowded with women and children, but there were only forty men. James Robertson was in command, with Sevier as Lieutenant.

In the confusion of the first attack, the fort gates were shut before all the people had gained admittance. Catherine Sherrill, a beautiful young woman, ran for the gates and found them closed. John Sevier leaned over the palisades and shouted, "Jump for me, Kate!" His strong arms pulled her to safety. "Bonny Kate" had found her future husband.

The siege lasted for two weeks. Parched corn was the main sustenance of the inmates of the fort. A few, tempted by the irksome monotony, ventured out hoping to obtain a variety of food. James Cooper and son, and one Tucker, thus lost their

---

[23] At least one of the scalps was taken while the victim was alive, and he survived. Rev. Jonathan Mulkey, one of the first settlers in Carter's Valley, was working in the field with a companion when they were surprised by Indians. Mulkey swam Holston River and escaped. His companion was knocked down, scalped, and left for dead. Mulkey made his way to Eaton's Station, where he was amazed to learn that his friend, minus his scalp, had beaten him to the fort.

Rev. Charles Cummings, of Wolf Hills, now Abingdon, Va., was surprised while on his way to church with William Creswell. Creswell was killed, but the doughty pastor beat off his assailants and brought Creswell's body in, unscalped. Thereafter, it was Cummings' regular custom each Sabbath to put on his shot pouch, shoulder his rifle, and ride to church. He would gravely ascend the pulpit, place his rifle in handy position, lay his shot pouch on the altar, and proceed with the service. Ramsey, 160: *Notable Southern Families, Crockett,* 494, Armstrong & French.

lives.[24]   James Moore, a young man of eighteen, was taken prisoner.

Mrs. William Bean was captured as she rode on horseback toward the fort, and was taken to the Cherokee camp on Nolichucky River.   She was told that she would be killed, and a warrior advanced with cocked gun as if to shoot her.   She was then questioned by the Indians through a white man who lived among them;[25] "Where are the forts?   Have the white men any powder?   Can they be starved out?"

Mrs. Bean replied with spirit, giving her captors to understand that the white men were amply able to care for themselves.   Old Abram then told Mrs. Bean that she would not be killed, but would be expected to teach the Cherokee women to make butter and cheese.

The Cherokees found it impossible to take Fort Lee by assault or siege.   Discouraged by the news from Island Flats, Old Abram drew off his warriors and retreated on the approach of a party of a hundred Virginians marching to the relief of the fort.

The Raven of Chote, who commanded the third body of Cherokees, led his warriors to Carter's Valley, where he found the white people shut up in forts.   He burned a few cabins, picked up such loot as could be secured, and returned to the Cherokee towns when a runner notified him of the result of the Island Flats fight.

The two prisoners taken by Old Abram, James Moore and Mrs. William Bean, were taken to the towns along Little Tennessee River, and were condemned to death by fire.   Moore was taken to Tuskegee, and his sentence was executed with horrible torture.[26]

Mrs. Bean was taken to Toquo and tied to a stake at the top of a large mound which is still standing.   The fire had been lighted around her, and she had resigned herself to death, when the Beloved Woman, Nancy Ward, arrived on the scene.

The soul of Nancy Ward revolted that the Cherokees should torture a squaw.   She hastened to the top of the mound and

---

[24] Draper Mss., 32-S 140-180.

[25] Probably Captain Nathaniel Gist.

[26] The Cherokee Chief Old Tassel afterward stated that Moore was the only white man ever burned at the stake in Tennessee.   The statement is open to doubt.

scattered the burning brands. She cut the bonds which fastened the prisoner, and took Mrs. Bean to her own house, where she was treated kindly. She did instruct Nancy Ward, and through her the other Cherokee women, in the making of butter and cheese.[27]

## 12

While the Overhill warriors harassed the Virginia border, their brethren in the middle and valley towns spread desolation on the Carolina and Georgia frontiers. Cattle and horses were driven off, cabins burned, and men, women, and children were terrified or massacred.[28] Tories suffered as well as Americans. The Indians were too crazed by blood to attempt to distinguish between a tory and a rebel. A wave of resentment swept the frontier, not only against the Cherokees, but against the English who had incited the Indians to war. Indian warfare did more to unite the American colonies than did the soldiers of the King.

Swift preparations were made for reprisals. Georgia, the Carolinas, and Virginia arranged that expeditions should march simultaneously from each of the states into the Cherokee country before the British could arrive to help the Indians.

## 13

Colonel Samuel Jack, at the head of two hundred Georgians, was first in the field. He destroyed the Cherokee towns around the headwaters of Tugaloo River during the month of July.

South Carolina, to tempt volunteers for the campaign, offered the substantial rewards of £75 for each Cherokee scalp, and £100 for each prisoner taken alive.[29] On Aug. 1, 1776, eleven

---

[27] The Indians had previously regarded with disapproval "the white man's buffalo," the cow. Due to Mrs. Bean's training, Nancy Ward introduced the raising of cattle, she herself owning the first herd.

[28] A particularly terrible atrocity occurred on the Georgia frontier. Lieutenant Grant, commanding a body of Georgia militia, pursued one of the marauding bands of Indians. He was drawn into an ambush and was captured. His body was later found tied to a tree with scalp and ears cut off. A gun barrel, supposed to have been red hot, had been thrust into his body. Twelve arrows were sticking in his chest, and above them was a painted war club. A painted hatchet was laid above his head. The men who discovered the body were so affected by the scene that they fled in panic. (British Colonial Papers.)

[29] Roosevelt, *Winning of the West*, 1, 358.

hundred South Carolinians took the field under Colonel Andrew Williamson.

Williamson led his men over the trail to the site of the abandoned Fort Prince George. He made a forced march on Aug. 31st, and with three hundred and fifty men attacked the old Cherokee town of Seneca, where Alexander Cameron was encamped with a body of tories and Indians under Dragging Canoe.

The town was situated on both sides of Keowee River. It was found apparently abandoned, but as Williamson's force marched through to the river ford, they were assailed by a heavy fire from Indians who had concealed themselves in the cabins. Five men were killed, and thirteen wounded. The startled troops began a disorderly retreat, which would have developed into a rout but for the bravery of Colonel Hammond, Williamson's aide. Hammond taunted the men for their flight, and swore that he would cross the river alone and attack the Indians. He plunged his horse into the stream. Two or three volunteers followed. The whole army caught the spirit, cheered, and crowded after him. The Cherokees were put to flight, and the town, including Cameron's residence, was burned.[30]

The Indians fell back to Neowee Pass near the town of Estatoe, a narrow opening between two steep and lofty mountains, where Dragging Canoe laid a new ambush.

As Williamson's men struggled along the almost impassable path, the Indians poured into them a close and destructive fire, which killed seventeen and wounded twenty-nine men. Wild confusion resulted. Colonel Hammond again saved the army from rout. He rallied the men by voice and action, got thirty men together and sent them under Lieutenant Hampton to charge the enemy in front, while he himself led a force to clamber over the rocks and outflank the position of the Indians. Hampton's men ran forward at the shouted command, "Loaded guns advance; empty guns fall down and load!" The Indians fled before the force of the attack, and the nature of the surrounding country made pursuit impossible.

The distance from Neowee Pass to the Valley towns was only twenty miles, but it required five days of incredible toil

---

[30] *Ibid.*

for Williamson to cover the distance. At the Valley towns, he was joined by General Griffith Rutherford of North Carolina at the head of two thousand men. Rutherford had crossed the Blue Ridge at Swannanoa Gap, and had marched into the Cherokee country by the old traders' path which led to Virginia. It was later known as Rutherford's Trace.

The combined Carolina armies utterly destroyed the Middle and Valley towns. The campaign was marked by the ferocity that attended border warfare. Near the town of Tomassee, a body of Indians was surprised and cut off from retreat. Sixteen dead warriors were found in a ravine when the fighting ceased, and all were scalped. Women, as well as men, were shot down, and if wounded, were "helped to their end." A number of women and boys were captured, and the captors proposed to put them up for sale as slaves. Some of the officers objected, and the men replied: "If we cannot sell them for slaves, we will kill them and scalp them now." [31]

The Carolina armies marched for home about the middle of September. Rutherford, who had encountered but little opposition, lost only three men. Williamson's loss was ninety-four, killed and wounded. His men, however, had taken seventy-five Cherokee scalps, for which they were enriched by the reward of £75 each offered by South Carolina. [32] The bulk of the population of the Middle and Valley towns fled to the Overhills.

### 14

Virginia troops, under Colonel William Christian, gathered at Long Island of the Holston to the number of 1800, and marched for the Overhill towns on Oct. 1, 1776. Williamson and Rutherford had completed their work and returned to their homes.

The warriors from the Middle and Lower towns who had fled to the Overhills were more of a menace than an aid. Panic stricken from their experience with the Carolina troops, they counseled retreat in the face of the new invasion. The Raven of Chote, nephew and adviser of Oconostota, who had grown very old, advised an attempt to make peace with Christian, and sent the trader Ellis Harlan with a flag of truce to arrange for a talk. Dragging Canoe advocated resistance, and

[31] Mooney, *Myths of the Cherokees*, 51.
[32] Roosevelt, *Winning of the West*, 1, 354-358.

defying the older chiefs, gathered every available warrior to oppose Christian at the crossing of French Broad River.

Harlan, on reaching Christian's camp, attempted to frighten him with the information that the entire force of the Cherokees was at hand ready to attack the Virginia army; and that they had instructions from Cameron, "Never make peace: retreat and fight on."

Christian conducted Harlan through his camp and permitted him to see the strength of his force, and sent him back to the Raven with the answer:

"How can you expect peace before you have delivered up to me Alexander Cameron, that enemy of the white men and the red? How can you ask for peace when you have assembled your men to fight me should you dislike my terms?

"I shall cross the river and come to your towns. I will distinguish between those towns which have behaved well toward us, and those which have not." [33]

Christian's bold message caused violent disagreement in the Cherokee council. His demand for the surrender of Cameron filled Dragging Canoe with rage, for the chief had adopted Cameron as his "eldest brother," a relationship regarded as sacred. Christian's army was vastly superior to the Cherokees in numbers and equipment. It would have been suicidal for them to oppose him in open battle. The Canoe therefore proposed that the Little Tennessee towns be abandoned, and that the Cherokees should hold fast to Cameron's talk, "Retreat and fight on."

The older chiefs could not reconcile themselves to the loss of their beloved towns. A trader Caleb Starr harangued the Indians, and told them that the Great Spirit had destined the white men to triumph over the red, and resistance would be useless. The Raven insisted that another attempt be made to appease Christian, and sent Captain Nathaniel Gist to the camp of the Virginians for that purpose. Dragging Canoe violently opposed the action, and announced that he would have the scalp of both Gist and Harlan for their action in attempting to make peace. He demanded that the towns be abandoned and the war continued, and was backed as a whole by the warriors of

---

[33] Christian's Report, *N. C. Colonial Records,* 10, 844.

Big Island, Tellico, Settico, and Chilhowie. The Raven thereupon withdrew from the camp with his followers, and hastened to the towns to begin removal of the women and children and such supplies as could be saved quickly.[34]

Alexander Cameron, after urging the Cherokees to make no peace with the Americans, departed for Pensacola to secure additional ammunition.

Captain Gist, sent by the Cherokees to treat with Christian, had lived for many years among the Cherokees, and had married a sister of the well known chief Old Tassel by whom he had a son, later the celebrated Sequoyah. Gist had accompanied the warriors on the Watauga campaign. The horrors of Indian warfare had so roused his repugnance that he determined to have nothing further to do with such matters. He welcomed the opportunity to reach the camp of the Virginia army under a flag of truce. Christian says:

"The flag which he brought was only an excuse for him to get with me. I believe he is sorry for what he has done. I intended to have him put in irons, but the manner of his coming, I believe, will prevent me."

Feeling ran high in the American camp against anyone suspected of inciting the Indians to war. But for Christian's authority, Gist would have been scalped by the soldiers. He seems thereafter to have supported the American cause loyally.[35]

Colonel Christian advanced rapidly to the Little Tennessee

[34] Letter, Dragging Canoe to Cameron, Nov. 14, 1776, *British Colonial Papers;* see also Christian's Report, *N. C. Colonial Records,* 10, 844. One of the chiefs, Hanging Man of Chote, stated later that the Raven's talks with Christian were only a "make-haste," to enable the Cherokees to secure time to remove their women and children and save their crops.

[35] Nathaniel Gist first appeared among the Cherokees as a messenger of Governor Dinwiddie in 1755. Following the French and Indian War he formed a trading partnership with Richard Pearis and lived in the Cherokee country for several years. During that time, he took as his Indian wife, Wurteh, sister of Chief Old Tassel, and became the father of Sequoyah. Gist was informed on reaching Christian's camp in 1776 of Dragging Canoe's threats against his life. He did not therefore return to the Cherokee towns, but entered American service. He was mentioned by the Indians at the Treaty of Long Island in 1777, by which the Cherokees ceded all their land north of Nolichucky River, but reserved Long Island itself as a treaty ground, "for their use and that of Colonel Gist." Chiefs Old Tassel and the Raven requested that Colonel Gist might be permitted to "sit down" on the island whenever he pleased, and to remain as long as he desired.

River without opposition.  He crossed at Tomotley Ford, and found the towns abandoned.  Headquarters were established at Great Island from which expeditions were sent out to burn those towns known to be hostile, Tellico, Chilhowie, and Settico.  Chote, out of respect to Nancy Ward, was spared.  The work of destruction was completed and Christian sent four messengers into the Nation with the request that the Little Carpenter, Oconostota, and Dragging Canoe should come into his camp for a peace talk.

Dragging Canoe replied that he would not listen to the talks of the Virginians, for his ears were open only to talks that came from his father Stuart, and his eldest brother Cameron.[36]

The Carpenter called on Christian as requested.  Christian, disappointed that Dragging Canoe had not come also, told the Carpenter that he did not want to talk to old men, but to young warriors.  He demanded that the Cherokees surrender to him Cameron and Dragging Canoe as the price of peace.  The old chief replied that Cameron was at Pensacola, and Dragging Canoe at Chickamauga.  "Send for Cameron and bring him back, and bring us Dragging Canoe's scalp, or we will burn all your towns," Christian replied.

Oconostota appeared while the talks were in progress, and was told by Christian to "keep nothing from him."  Oconostota replied that he would not.  He was asked if he would be willing to surrender Cameron and Dragging Canoe to the Virginia army, and answered, "Yes."

"Who is this man Stuart that you call Father," Christian asked.  "What was he a few years ago, that you reckon him now so great a man?"  He ridiculed Stuart by suggesting that the issue between the Cherokees and Americans be settled by a ballplay.

"Tell Stuart from me to raise all the men he can, both white and red, and bring a great many goods with him, and we will lay

Gist commanded an American frontier fort in Virginia at the close of the Revolution, and was granted a large tract in Kentucky for his services, to which he moved from Long Island.  Sequoyah, when a young man, occasionally visited Colonel Gist in Kentucky, and was recognized by him as his son.  (See Williams, *Gist, the Father of Sequoyah, East Tennessee Historical Society Publications.*)

[36] Letter Dragging Canoe to Cameron, Nov. 14, 1776, *British Colonial Papers.*

our lands, negroes, and stock, against all he brings, and will have a great ballplay. Whoever wins, let them take all.

He further told the Cherokees:

"You are told that the Americans cannot make powder and cloth. It's all lies. This powder you see is of our own make, and we can make all goods necessary to support ourselves, as well as traders to the Indians. We can beat King George and all his people, for they do not know how to fight as we do. We can fight behind trees, and in any way whatsoever." [37]

After considerable discussion, Christian offered the Indians a substantial reward for Cameron and Dragging Canoe, dead or alive. He arranged for the chiefs to meet with him at Long Island in July of the following year to sign a treaty of peace. He told the chiefs that before leaving their country, he would burn the town of Tuskegee where James Moore had been tortured. Mrs. William Bean, the other prisoner who had been taken in the campaign, was surrendered to the Virginia forces.

One of the interpreters, McCormick, had a half breed son called the Big Bullet, who desired to hear the proceedings, but was afraid to come near the white soldiers. He climbed a tree at some distance from which he could see Christian's headquarters.

Robert Young, a Virginia soldier, observed the Indian climbing and was convinced that some act of treachery was intended. He shot and killed the Big Bullet, an act which caused great excitement and broke up negotiations for a time. The chiefs withdrew from the camp, feeling sure that they would all be killed. Christian assured them that he greatly regretted the incident, and would punish the murderer as soon as apprehended. To convince the Indians of his sincerity, he offered a reward to any soldier who would reveal the identity of the guilty person. [38] Young, however, kept his secret, and the chiefs finally agreed to meet at Long Island of Holston in July, 1777, for the signing of a treaty.

Dragging Canoe wrote Cameron:

"I am glad you are where you are, for our great man Oconostota

[37] *Ibid.*
[38] *James Sevier to L. C. Draper, Draper Mss.*, 32-S 140-180. Robert Young was a brother-in-law of Colonel Valentine Sevier, to whom he later confessed the shooting.

wanted to take your life as well as mine. While I live, you shall never be hurted, for I shall never forget your talks to us, nor our Father, who finds us everything we want. I will never consent to a peace until our Father and you agree to it, and make it for us."

"They offered at last £100 for you, and £100 for me, to have us killed. Let them bid up and offer what they will, it never disturbs me. My ears will always be open to hear your talks and our Father's. I will mind no other, let them come from where they will. My thoughts and my heart are for war as long as King George has one enemy in this country. Our hearts are straight to him and all his people, and whoever is at war with us." [39]

"I shall immediately set out for war," the chief concluded. "I will stick close to these Virginia warriors, for I do not understand their crooked talks."

Colonel Christian left the Cherokee country in December, 1776. Cameron removed to Chickamauga, where he used all of his powerful influence to induce the Cherokees to continue the war. He announced that no town which treated with the Americans should receive any English supplies or ammunition.

The older chiefs reproached Dragging Canoe with the trouble he had brought upon his people, but he still had "plenty of his young men around him, who were determined to have their lands." Finding that the head men of his Nation were determined to make peace with the Americans, and to cede part of the Cherokee hunting grounds as the price of the peace to be obtained, Dragging Canoe reached a radical decision. With his followers, he seceded from the Cherokee Nation and withdrew a hundred miles down the Tennessee River where he organized a new tribe. Those Cherokees who met in treaty with the Americans, he denounced as "rogues," or worse, as "Virginians." His own followers called themselves, proudly, *"Ani-Yunwiya,"* the Real People.

---

[39] Dragging Canoe to Cameron, Nov. 14, 1776, *British Colonial Papers.*

# CHAPTER IX

## THE WAR CHIEF

### I

Governor Patrick Henry of Virginia, possibly not understanding that Colonel Christian had set the month of July for a treaty with the Cherokees at Long Island, sent a message by Captain Gist requesting the chiefs to assemble at Fort Patrick Henry in April. A delegation of eighty-five attended, headed by The Little Carpenter, Oconostota, and the Raven. They were asked if they were willing to form an alliance with the Americans, and the Carpenter replied, "We cannot fight our Father, King George. Colonel Christian promised that if we would make peace, we might remain neutral."

It was agreed that the treaty be held as had been arranged, in July, and the chiefs promised to use their influence to induce Dragging Canoe to attend.[1]

That chief, while the talks were being held, was raiding the vicinity of Long Island as if to show his contempt for the negotiations. A letter from Isaac Bledsoe to Colonel Joseph Martin on April 8, 1777, states:

"On Wednesday night about sun sett Frederick Calvitt was skelped about one and a half miles from his own house. He is still living, and there is hopes that he will recover."[2]

The war party which scalped Calvitt was headed by Dragging Canoe. Within fifteen miles of Fort Patrick Henry where the talks were in progress, they stole ten horses from James Robertson. Robertson pursued the marauders with a

---

[1] A number of Indian women who were present, in conversation with the trader Thomas Price, said that the talks of the chiefs were a blind to give the Indians time to secure ammunition and.guns to continue the war. They told Price that should attempts to persuade Dragging Canoe to attend the treaty prove fruitless, they intended to lay the blame for his activities on the Creeks. As a matter of fact all of the prominent chiefs sympathized with Dragging Canoe's efforts, but hated to desert their Little Tennessee towns.

[2] *Draper Mss.*, 1-XX-21.

*Picture by Walter Cline*

THE OLD CHARLESTON TRAIL AT CHOTE, NEAR VONORE,
MONROE COUNTY, TENN.

party of neighbors and recovered his horses, but was compelled to retreat by a counter-attack which wounded two of his men. Dragging Canoe moved over to Carter's Valley, and murdered David Crockett and family on the site of the present Rogersville,[3] and took in all twelve scalps during the month of April.

2

Spring of 1777 in the Cherokee country was like the days of old when the Nation had broken away from their fathers the Iroquois. The towns of Settico, Great Island, Tellico, Toquo, and Chilhowie were depopulated. Afoot and mounted, by canoe, packhorse, and travois, the Cherokees with their worldly possessions poured southward to find new homes with Dragging Canoe, the chief who would fight for their lands.

The chosen site, Chickamauga Creek, was already the home of Stuart's deputy John McDonald. Dragging Canoe and his people from Great Island settled at the old town of Chickamauga,[4] two miles from the mouth of the creek. His brother Little Owl chose a site farther up the stream, near the present Graysville, Ga. The Settico people located on Tennessee River near the creek mouth, at a beautiful old townsite which they renamed Settico after the home they had abandoned on the Little Tennessee.[5] The Toquo warriors likewise gave the name of their old town, Toquo, to the new home.

Such a wholesale removal was not accomplished without turmoil and bitterness. The seceders felt that those of the Cherokees who remained on the Little Tennessee were traitors and rogues. The peace party, on the other hand, were convinced that Dragging Canoe's course would bring destruction upon the Nation.

---

[3] David Crockett was the grandfather of the noted Davy Crockett. The Indians killed Crockett, his wife, and several small children. Two sons, Joseph and James, were carried prisoners to the Chickamauga towns, and James Crockett was not released until the general peace seventeen years later, in 1794. John Crockett, the father of Davy, was serving at the time with his brother Robert in the Revolutionary militia and thus escaped the fate of his family. See Crockett's autobiography; also *Notable Southern Families, V, Crockett,* Armstrong and French.

[4] An old Creek townsite. The name was of Creek derivation, and meant, appropriately enough, "Dwelling Place of the War Chief." The Creek pronunciation was Chukko-mah-ko, from *Cukko,* dwelling place, and *Micco,* war chief.

[5] Now called Citico, within the limits of the present Chattanooga.

Judd's Friend, the old chief who had visited England, gave his support to the new movement. He was seventy-five years of age, but wielded powerful influence. Other prominent chiefs who joined Dragging Canoe were Willenawah, who had helped to starve the Fort Loudoun garrison into submission; Bloody Fellow; Scolacuta or Hanging Maw; Kitegiska, brother of Oconostota; Young Tassel, later to become famous as John Watts; Lying Fish; Tsaladihi, and the Buck. Old Tassel, who had succeeded Oconostota as speaker for the Nation, sympathized with the seceders, although he did not actively cooperate.

3

In the midst of the turmoil and confusion attendant upon the apparent ruin of his people, the Little Carpenter laid down his cares forever. His great soul took its flight so unobtrusively that his last resting place is unknown, though it is probably in the soil of his beloved Chote.[6]

That so great a Cherokee could pass to his reward without official mention in the dispatches of the time is eloquent of the disorder in his Nation which probably hastened his end. He was present at the peace talk at Fort Patrick Henry in April, 1777. Shortly thereafter, Colonel John Carter, who had been appointed to command the militia of Washington County, wrote to Governor Caswell that the Little Carpenter had stated that he had five hundred warriors ready to come to the assistance of the Americans against the British.[7]

It is not likely that the Little Carpenter made such a statement, or, if he did, it was what the Indians called a "make-haste," a subterfuge. To have furnished five hundred warriors to fight the English, the chief would have had to take up the hatchet against his friend John Stuart. This the Little Carpenter would never have done. He himself had said, "The talk of my father King George will remain with me while I live. I speak not with two tongues, and am ashamed of those who do."[8]

---

[6] The location of Chote is shown accurately upon Timberlake's map. It is in the present Monroe County, Tenn., about nine miles from Madisonville, on the Griffith Farm on Little Tennessee River.

[7] Ramsey, 177.

[8] S. C. Council Journal, Dec. 18, 1761.

4

The Cherokees gathered at Long Island of Holston, the be-loved old treaty ground, in July, 1777. The Little Carpenter was dead, and Oconostota was very old. Old Tassel and the Raven were therefore chosen to speak for the Indians. The Raven was recommended by Oconostota with the candid state-ment:

"I am no speaker and not much of a statesman, but I have high confidence in the ability of my nephew and representative, Save-nooka or the Raven, of Chote, and shall set my hand to whatever the Raven says. I reserve to myself the privilige of setting him right if he should go astray. This indeed is a liberty I would take with any man, however great or powerful." [9]

The commissioners chosen to negotiate the treaty with the Cherokees were Colonels Christian, Preston, and Evan Shelby, of Virginia; and Avery, Winton, and Lanier, for North Caro-lina.

Colonel Richard Henderson was present, in behalf of his Transylvania project. The State of Virginia had declared his purchase void, but had granted him 200,000 acres on Kentucky River in recognition of his services toward settling the west. Henderson presented a memorial to the treaty commissioners asking that his purchase be considered part of North Carolina in order that he might proceed with its settlement. His re-marks provoked reply from the aged Oconostota:

"You, Carolina Dick, have deceived your people. Why are you always telling lies? We told you that those lands were not ours; that our claim extended not beyond the Cumberland Mountains, and that all land beyond Cumberland River belongs to our brothers the Chickasaws. It is true you gave us some goods, for which we promised you our friendship in the affair. More, we never prom-ised. You have deceived your people." [10]

The commissioners reproached the Cherokees for murders recently committed, and Colonel Christian asked the where-

---

[9] Personal relation of William Tatham, who was present at the treaty and took notes of the various talks. Williams, *Tennessee Historical Maga-zine*, Vol. 2, 154-179.
[10] *Ibid.*

abouts of chiefs of the war party who were absent, Dragging Canoe, Judd's Friend, and Young Tassel. The chiefs explained that Dragging Canoe had withdrawn from the Nation and had removed to Chickamauga, where other chiefs had accompanied him. They had been unable to induce him to attend the peace talks, and disclaimed responsibility for his actions.

As punishment for beginning the war, the Cherokees were asked to cede all their land lying north of the Little Tennessee River.

The reply of Old Tassel was patriotic and eloquent, a model of Indian oratory. He said:

"It is surprising that when we enter into treaties with our fathers the white people, their whole cry is more land. Indeed it has seemed a formality with them to demand what they know we dare not refuse. But on the principles of fairness of which we have received assurance during the conduct of this treaty, I must refuse your demand.

"What did you do? You marched into our towns with a superior force. Your numbers far exceeded us, and we fled to the stronghold of our woods, there to secure our women and children. Our towns were left to your mercy. You killed a few scattered and defenceless individuals, spread fire and desolation wherever you pleased, and returned to your own habitations.

"If you term this a conquest, you have overlooked the most essential point. You should have fortified the junction of Holston and Tennessee Rivers, and thereby conquered all the waters above. It is now too late for us to suffer from your mishap of generalship. Will you claim our lands by right of conquest? No! If you do, I will tell you that WE last marched over them, even up to this very place; and some of our young warriors whom we have not had opportunity to recall are still in the woods and continue to keep your people in fear.

"Much has been said of the want of what you term 'Civilization' among the Indians. Many proposals have been made to us to adopt your laws, your religion, your manners, and your customs. We do not see the propriety of such a reformation. We should be better pleased with beholding the good effect of these doctrines in your own practices than with hearing you talk about them, or of reading your papers to us on such subjects. You say, 'Why do not the Indians till the ground and live as we do?' May we not ask with equal propriety, 'Why do not the white people hunt and live as we do?'"

Old Tassel reminded the commissioners that white hunters came into Cherokee lands continually to kill game, but said:

"We wish, however, to be at peace with you, and to do as we would be done by. We do not quarrel with you for the killing of an occasional buffalo or deer on our lands, but your people go much farther. They hunt to gain a livelihood. They kill all our game; but it is very criminal in our young men if they chance to kill a cow or a hog for their sustenance when they happen to be in your lands.

"The Great Spirit has placed us in different situations. He has given you many advantages, but he has not created us to be your slaves. We are a separate people! He has stocked your lands with cows, ours with buffalo; yours with hogs, ours with bears; yours with sheep, ours with deer. He has given you the advantage that your animals are tame, while ours are wild and demand not only a larger space for range, but art to hunt and kill them. They are, nevertheless, as much our property as other animals are yours, and ought not to be taken from us without our consent, or for something of equal value." [11]

The appeal of Old Tassel had its effect, for after considering it the commissioners revised their demands. The Cherokees ceded all land north of Nolichucky River, reserving only the Great Island of Holston. This they said they wished to keep forever as a beloved treaty ground, but they permitted its use to their friend Captain Nathaniel Gist, "desiring that he might sit down upon it whenever he wanted to, and to stay as long as he cared." [12]

5

The Cherokee war party declined to have anything to do with Christian's negotiations at Long Island. Dragging Canoe was encouraged to receive a talk from Cameron that he was on his way from Pensacola with plenty of ammunition and supplies, none of which were to be distributed among the

[11] William Tatham, who translated Old Tassel's speech, says that "it was bereaved of much of its native beauty by the defects of interpretation, for the manly and dignified expression of the Indian orator loses nearly all its energy and force in translation." He describes Old Tassel as a "stout, mild, and decided man, rather comely than otherwise, who, through a long and useful life in his own country, was never known to stoop to a falsehood."

[12] Haywood, *Civil & Political History of Tennessee,* Appendix.

"rogues" who attended the treaty. Cameron urged that the Little Tennessee towns be abandoned and the war continued.

Robert Dews, a white trader, interpreted the talk for Dragging Canoe, and thus learned its contents. He feigned agreement with the plans of the war party. The Indians, however, were suspicious of the traders, and watched Dews closely lest he escape and communicate with the Americans. He was at the house of a trader named Campbell, at Hiwassee, when the door was partially opened, and a half breed named John Arch, almost naked and his countenance expressing terror, was thrust into the room. The door slammed behind him, and the startled traders asked whence he came. He replied, "Chickamauga." "Have you seen Dragging Canoe lately?" Dews asked. Arch, looking at the trader wildly, answered "No!"

At that moment, the door was opened, and Dragging Canoe strode in. He regarded the traders sternly, said not a word, sat down, and remained in that position without speech for an hour. The Indians had been testing the pretended friendship of Dews, and took this means of informing themselves of the white men's talk. No word was spoken until the trader Campbell asked all of them to eat supper. The meal was partaken of in silence, but afterward, Dews followed Dragging Canoe out of the door, and asked Arch to interpret his words to the chief.

He told Dragging Canoe what had occurred during the stay of Christian's army at the Cherokee towns, and the talks the white commander had left for him, Dragging Canoe, and the other chiefs of the Nation. The chief answered angrily: "I suppose I am looked upon as a boy, and not a warrior." Dews assured him to the contrary, and begged him as a warrior and a chief to go to Long Island for the talks. "There is no occasion for me to go; I have already heard the talks," he retorted. Two runners arrived the next day with the news that Christian had offered a reward for Dragging Canoe's scalp, and the chief departed for Chickamauga.

Dews left Hiwassee for Toquo with the idea of escaping to Long Island to warn Christian of the attitude of the war party. He was watched closely and found escape impossible. A warrior leveled a gun at him and threatened his life. To his protest, Old Tassel replied, "Such things cannot be prevented, the

Indians regard you as a Watauga man," and Willenawah added: "The young fellows hate you because you have come in from the woods and joined the rogues."

Dews protested his friendship, and to divert suspicion, offered to write and deliver the reply of the chiefs to Cameron's letter. He was accordingly given two letters to Cameron, one from the warriors of Toquo and Tellico; and one from John Watts. He set off for Chickamauga, accompanied by Lying Fish of the war party, who showed him a black belt he was taking to Cameron from Toquo and Tellico to indicate that those towns were for war.

Fifteen miles beyond Hiwassee, two runners from Chickamauga met Dews with another talk from Cameron to be read only to Toquo and Tellico warriors. Lying Fish was from Toquo, and could not resist turning back to hear the talk. He requested Dews to await him three days at Hiwassee.

John Watts, Young Eagle, and Hanging Man arrived at Hiwassee while Dews waited. They had heard the details from Old Tassel of the peace talks at Long Island, and were on their way to Chickamauga to pass the information to Dragging Canoe. Hanging Man, in conversation, referred to the "Dreadful People" at Long Island, the Americans. The trader Campbell retorted, "You know the King of England has many more dreadful people than the rogues," at which Hanging Man laughed. "I was only joking when I spoke of 'dreadful people,' " he said; and turning to Dews, "This man is our friend, and knows our plans, but we are not telling them to any other trader lest word get to the Virginians. They might then return and destroy our towns before we can get help from the King."

A runner arrived at Hiwassee with the news that two messengers from Christian, Newell and Ewins, had arrived at Chote, and that Dews was wanted to interpret the letters they had brought. He handed the letters for Cameron to John Watts for delivery, and returned to Chote. After the letters were interpreted, the Indians requested a day to formulate an answer, and Dews took the envoys to his own house. This made the warriors very nervous. They warned him not to communicate their plans to the white men, and Dews promised, but considering the lives of Christian's envoys to be in danger, he told them all he knew.

Newell, one of the envoys, was a pig-headed, obstinate fellow. No sooner did he hear the intelligence, given him in strict confidence, than he informed the chiefs that he knew their plans. The word spread like wildfire, and the lives of all white men in the Indian towns were in danger. The next day, Dragging Canoe arrived with the demand that Dews and the trader Harlan who had carried the first friendly message to Christian, be surrendered to him to be put to death.

The trader John Benge had married a Cherokee woman, and had sons who were warriors. He was therefore not under suspicion. Dews called upon him in the hope of securing information. He told Benge that he had decided to return to Long Island with Christian's envoys. Benge pointed to an iron pot that would hold about two gallons, and replied, "I believe no one will go there in two or three days. I expect as much Christian blood will be shed as will fill that."

"You talk of Christian blood as though it were the blood of a bullock," replied Dews. "Tell me, who is it that is to be killed." "It would cost me my life if I told you," Benge replied; but after some urging, informed Dews that Dragging Canoe had been sent by Cameron to demand the scalps of all white traders, particularly those of Dews and Harlan. "In four days," he said, "an order will be issued for all Cherokees to leave the Little Tennessee towns and move to Chickamauga. You have not a friend in the Nation, and if you can possibly escape, you had better do so quickly."

Dews was thoroughly frightened. He had so conducted himself, however, as to win the friendship of Chiefs Old Tassel and Bloody Fellow, and was to learn the staunchness of Indian friendship. The Cherokee council agreed to surrender him to Dragging Canoe, and Old Tassel sent Bloody Fellow to the trader's house to help his escape. "Cover yourself with a blanket and follow me," he was told by Bloody Fellow. He was led to a thicket some distance from the town, where Bloody Fellow told him to sit down. Placing himself close to the trader, the chief said; "Dragging Canoe has demanded your scalp, and the council has agreed. Stay here. Do not move until I return. I will go and get intelligence of the Canoe's intentions. If the town is determined to throw you away, I will bring your horse and provisions, and will go with you myself to Broad River." Thus spoke Bloody Fellow, Indian friend.

In about three hours, Bloody Fellow returned to the place of concealment and conducted Dews to his own hot house where he hid him. On the second morning, he took the trader by the hand and told him that the warriors had decided to let him return to Long Island with the Raven, who was going to finish the talks with Colonel Christian. Dews arrived safely at Fort Patrick Henry, where he filed affidavit on January 22, 1777, covering his experience.[13]

## 6

During the years 1777 and 1778, Henry Hamilton, British governor of the Northwest Territory, with headquarters at Detroit, conducted an energetic Indian warfare against the American frontier. He offered substantial rewards for American scalps and was hated by the frontiersmen, who called him "The Hair Buyer."

The British general staff planned an attack on Georgia and the Carolinas in the spring of 1779. Hamilton was instructed to cooperate by promoting a general Indian offensive to distract American opposition from the movement on the seaboard. In furtherance of the plan, Hamilton called an assembly of all Indian chiefs who were friendly to the British to be held at the mouth of Tennessee River early in 1779.

Hamilton planned to use Dragging Canoe's forces as the spearhead of the proposed offensive. By the end of 1778, the Chickamauga band numbered a thousand warriors, and Dragging Canoe was the most powerful Indian leader in the South. John Stuart, southern Indian agent, was requested to assemble supplies at Chickamauga for the spring campaign. A pack train of three hundred horses wound over the trail from Pensacola with goods valued at £20,000 which were stored at the house of John McDonald, Stuart's deputy at Chickamauga.

Hamilton's plans received a rude jolt when George Rogers Clark, most daring of frontier leaders, conquered the Illinois country. Hamilton advanced against Clark in October, 1778, and retook Fort Vincennes; but Clark, in a winter campaign that makes a glorious chapter in American history, surprised Vincennes, captured the "Hair Buyer," and sent him a prisoner

---

[13] Affidavit of Robert Dews, *N. C. State Records,* 22, 995.

to Virginia. His plans for a general Indian offensive collapsed.[14]

British forces, as had been planned, captured Savannah in December, 1778, and advanced to Augusta, but they did not receive the expected Indian cooperation. Following the Treaty of Long Island, James Robertson had been sent as American Agent to the Cherokees. He was as shrewd as any man on the border, and was said to sleep with one eye open. He soon obtained details of the planned Indian offensive. These he communicated to Joseph Martin who was acting as Indian Agent for Virginia, and Martin set out hastily for that state to warn Governor Henry.

On Jan. 8, 1779, Henry wrote to Governor Caswell of North Carolina, asking cooperation in a campaign for the dstruction of the Chickamauga towns. He called attention to many indications of an early Indian offensive; to murders committed by the Chickamaugas on the citizens of both states, and to the "navigation of Tennessee River, in which your state, as well as ours, seems deeply interested, which is rendered unsafe and impracticable so long as these banditti go unpunished."

"Justice and necessity," said the Virginia governor, "demand that proper measures be taken to chastise these people, and by doing that, to anticipate the evils they meditate against us." [15]

About the same time, James Robertson wrote to Governor Caswell:

"I cannot change my sentiments with respect to a war with the Chickamoggy Indians the ensuing spring, except good methods are used to prevent it. If it should be thought requisite to permit a party of men to go against them, which I am humbly of the opinion is the only step that can be possibly taken to prevent a bloody and expensive war, I believe on leave being given a sufficient number of men will go at their own expense." [16]

7

A joint campaign by Virginia and North Carolina against the Chickamauga towns was arranged for the spring of 1779.

[14] For a detailed and stirring account of Clark's campaign, see Roosevelt, *Winning of the West*, 2, 23-149.

[15] Henry to Caswell, *N. C. State Records*, Jan. 8, 1779.

[16] Martin to Caswell, *Ibid.*, 17, 11-13. The frontiersmen fought habitually "at their own expense."

Evan Shelby, of Virginia, was given command. There was no money available, and his father, Isaac Shelby, raised the amount necessary on his personal security. Troops assembled at the mouth of Big Creek, on Clinch River, and built boats for the trip down the river. Colonel John Montgomery, who had raised 150 men to aid Clark in Illinois, permitted their use in the expedition. Shelby's army, numbering about nine hundred, left Big Creek on April 10, 1779. The current was high with spring rains, and the descent was rapid.

An Indian fisherman was captured near the mouth of Chickamauga Creek as he was setting his nets early in the morning. He was forced to guide the white men to Dragging Canoe's town. Shelby's men waded half a mile through a partially inundated canebrake and completely surprised the Indians. Approach on their settlements by water was something new to them. A short but furious resistance permitted escape of the women'and children, and the Chickamauga warriors fled to the hills. Four Indians were killed in the skirmish.[17]

Two weeks were spent by Shelby in systematic destruction of the Chickamauga towns. Eleven in all were burned. The British war supplies formed rich spoils, and McDonald's collection of furs which he had gained in trade with the Indians was captured. After completing his task, Shelby crossed the river, burned his boats, and returned to the upper East Tennessee country by land. He halted on the banks of a little creek thirty miles from the Chickamauga towns and sold the British goods to the men at public outcry.[18]

## 8

About the time that Shelby's men embarked on their invasion of the Chickamauga towns, John Stuart, the Cherokees' best friend, was lying at the point of death in Pensacola. The following letter marks the end of an honorable career of a conscientious servant of his king.

---

[17] Cameron's report, quoted by Roosevelt, 2, 292.

[18] The place has been called Sale Creek to the present time. A receipt which has been preserved shows the approximate date Shelby left the Indian country. It reads:

"Chickamauga Town, April 29, 1779. This is to certify that Colonel Evan Shelby bou't a black horse branded thus, L, about six years old, for £120. (Signed) Aaron Lewis and William Parker."

Armstrong, *History of Hamilton County, Tennessee*, 167.

"Pensacola, 26th March, 1779.

"My Lord (Germaine):

We think it our duty to acquaint your Lordship that on Sunday the 21st instant, about 3 o'clock in the afternoon, Colonel Stuart, His Majesty's sole agent for and Superintendent of Indian Affairs for the Southern District of North America, departed this life after a long and painful illness, which he bore with resignation for several months. We are with greatest respect,

Your Lordship's most humble
and most obedient Servants,
Alexander Cameron
Charles Stuart."

On receiving notice of Captain Stuart's death, Lord Germaine appointed two agents to take over his work. Alexander Cameron was assigned to the Chickasaws and Choctaws; and Thomas Brown was placed in charge of the Cherokees, Creeks, and Catawbas. The Revolution, however, was drawing to a close. The appointments had little weight, and Alexander Cameron continued to reside among the Cherokees.[19]

## 9

Dragging Canoe has been called the Savage Napoleon. After the destruction of his towns by Shelby, he justified the title. Another Indian leader, after so crushing a defeat, would have asked for peace, but it was not so with Dragging Canoe.

Shelby's campaign had been successful, but the Indian loss in manpower had been small. Crops had not been planted, and the scanty stores carried through the winter were the only food-stuffs destroyed. The British supplies had been taken, but new supplies could be brought quickly from Pensacola. Cameron himself appeared with fifty Tories, to encourage the Indians.

The most serious feature of Shelby's campaign for Dragging Canoe was that the white warriors had found their way to his towns; but for that the Great Spirit had provided a remedy. Across the course of Tennessee River at Chickamauga, towered Chatanuga Mountain.[20] The swift current,

---

[19] *British Colonial Papers.*

[20] Chatanuga Mountain, later Lookout Mountain, gave its name to the city afterward located at its base. The word is of Creek derivation, *Chado,* rock, *na,* it or that, *ugsa,* comes to an end: (Rock that comes to an end.)

dashing against the mountain, recoiled upon itself, and hemmed in between steep banks, fought its way through the great Whirl and Suck to the wilds of Cumberland Mountains. The swirling course of the river, called by the Cherokees *Untiguhi,* the Boiling Pot, could not be passed by boats except with grave danger. Chatanuga Mountain was two thousand feet high, rough and impassable. The path between mountain and river could be defended by few against a host.

The towns destroyed by Shelby were partially reoccupied, but the Savage Napoleon led the bulk of his warriors around the base of Chatanuga Mountain and located in the sites which soon came to be known as the Five Lower Towns of the Cherokees. They were, *Amo-Gayunyi* (Running Water), *Ani-Kusati-yi* (Nickajack), *Amo-yeli-gunhita* (Long Island), *Stecoyee* (Lookout Mountain Town), and *Kagunyi* (Crow Town). Another settlement was later built by the red headed half-breed Chief Will,[21] which was called *Willisi* (Willstown).

The sites of the towns were in Creek territory. This probably made little difference, for many of Dragging Canoe's followers were Creeks. However, he punctiliously observed the etiquette of Indian diplomacy by sending a delegation headed by his brother Little Owl to request permission of the great Creek Chief Alexander McGilivray. "Considering them an oppressed people," McGilivray gladly gave his consent to the settlements.[22] The Five Lower Towns were old Indian townsites, extending back to and beyond De Soto's time.

## 10

Dragging Canoe gathered around him at the town of Running Water, which he chose as his headquarters, a formidable array of chiefs, all bitter foes of the Americans. Some of them deserted him later, discouraged by defeat or tempted by the white man's presents, but Dragging Canoe, regardless of desertion or defeat, carried on. He was friendly with the British, French, and Spanish; but for the Americans who would take his hunting grounds, he had only undying hatred, tomahawk, bullet, and arrow. For fifteen years, he made good his boast to Henderson: "You have bought a fair land, but you will find its settlement dark and bloody."

---

[21] Otherwise known as Will Webber.
[22] *American State Papers, Indian Affairs,* Vol. 1, 19, 28, 30.

In July, 1779, he addressed a Shawnee delegation:

"We cannot forget the talk you brought to this Nation some years ago, which was to take up the hatchet against the Virginians. We heard and listened to your talk with attention, and before the time that was appointed to lift it, we took it up and struck the Virginians. Our Nation was alone and surrounded by them. They were numerous, and their hatchets were sharp. After we had lost some of our best warriors, we were forced to leave our towns and corn to be burned by them, and now we live in the grass as you see us. But we are not yet conquered, and to convince you that we have not thrown away your talk, here are four strings of wampum that we received from you when you came before as messengers to our Nation." [23]

Thus Dragging Canoe, in the face of defeat, kept the faith.

---

[23] *Haldeman Mss.*, quoted by Roosevelt, 2, 293.

# CHAPTER X

## THE SAGA OF THE RIVER

### I

The fall of 1779 was marked by two events that were to affect the future of the Cherokees. John Sevier was appointed Colonel of Militia of Washington County; and the Cumberland settlement was founded.

The beautiful section around the future Nashville had been visited for many years by Long Hunters. Casper Mansker had gone to the site each hunting season for ten years. Thomas Sharpe Spencer, a gigantic man, had spent three winters in a great hollow sycamore on the north bank of Cumberland River. Tracks of his moccasin clad feet had frightened a French trapper into swimming the Cumberland and leaving the country in terror, convinced that it was inhabited by a new species of giant bear.[1]

Henderson's Transylvania title had been denied by Virginia in 1776, and after a fruitless legal struggle, he had bent his energies to the establishment of a settlement within the recognized limits of North Carolina. The boundary between the two states was in doubt. It was thought that the Watauga settlements, and at least a portion of the Middle Tennessee country, lay within Virginia. Through Henderson's efforts, a boundary commission was appointed, consisting of Daniel Smith and Thomas Walker for Virginia; and Richard Henderson, John Williams, and William Bailey Smith for North Carolina. The commission began its work in 1777, and concluded the task in 1779.

Henderson was jubilant to find that the Cumberland region was within North Carolina. He wrote from Holston on Sept. 12, 1779:

"The Virginia commissioners, Dr. Walker and Major Daniel Smith, who from some inaccurate observations before we came had given out in speeches that the Long Island would be miles within

---

[1] Ramsey, 194.

Virginia, and thereby had blown up the inhabitants with hopes of great extension of territory, are brought to bed. Indeed the people here in general look as if they had lately miscarried, and hourly are making applications for land from our company. Men who two years ago were clamorous against Richard Henderson and Company, and damning their title, are now with pale faces haunting our camp and begging our friendship with regard to their land." [2]

Henderson was a man of tremendous vision, capable of inspiring others with enthusiasm akin to his own. He was, as the above letter shows, at Watauga and Holston in the fall of 1779, apparently riding the tide of success and in full control of the lands on Cumberland. As soon as the work of the boundary commission had shown that the site would fall within North Carolina, Henderson had begun preaching its advantages for a new commonwealth. His plea met with ready response, particularly with James Robertson and John Donelson, leaders at Watauga. They were poor men, ambitious to establish a future for themselves and their families. No Indians lived within a hundred miles of the Cumberland, and the Chickamaugas having been chastised earlier in the year, danger from the red men was considered negligible.

2

Robertson, accompanied by eight other pioneers, visited Cumberland early in 1779 to look over the site. They were delighted with the beauty of the country. Level land, excellent for farming, extended to the horizon, in contrast to the East Tennessee mountains and narrow valleys. Evidence of ancient occupancy was everywhere, but the country was deserted except for buffalo and other game. Robertson and his companions planted corn and fenced it in to save it from the wild animals. Three of the men volunteered to remain to look after the crop, and Robertson with the others returned to Watauga to prepare for the removal of settlers and their families.[3]

---

[2] *Richard Henderson, Author of Cumberland Compact,* by Archibald Henderson, Vol. 2, *Tennessee Historical Magazine.*

[3] The eight men who accompanied Robertson on his first trip to Cumberland were George Freeland, William Neely, Edward Swanson, James

Transportation of the women and children occasioned earnest consultation. The route to Cumberland by land was over Boone's road to Kentucky, thence by an Indian trail to the new settlement. It was a perilous road for womankind to travel, for Northern Indians were fighting to prevent white occupancy of their hunting grounds. Men on the road would find increased safety in numbers, but the greater the number of women and children, the greater the hazard. It was decided, therefore, that Robertson should go by land with the men, and Donelson would conduct the families by boat down Tennessee River to the Ohio, thence to the Cumberland, and up that stream to French Lick which was the chosen site. The arrangement permitted the women to carry household goods and valued possessions which would have been impossible had they gone by land.

The water route was not unknown. Settlers had passed through the Cherokee country as early as 1768 to settle in the newly acquired Florida. Ten years later, in 1778, the story of George Rogers Clark's conquest of Illinois had stirred the Holston settlements, and forty boats loaded with emigrants had floated down the Tennessee to locate in the conquered country. So large a party could not have failed to have friends and relatives to whom they would send news of their safe arrival, and a description of the perils of the journey.[4] Donelson was thus fore-warned of the dangers incident to navigation of the river. That pioneer women were willing to undertake such a journey speaks much for their bravery and determination.

---

Handley, Mark Robertson, Zach White, William Overall, and a negro servant.

Some years earlier, while the country had been considered part of Virginia, George Rogers Clark had entered under that state, 1000 acres of land on Cumberland River, including the site of the new settlement. Although the boundary commission had decided the country to be within North Carolina, Robertson, to prevent any dispute as to title, made the trip to Vincennes during the summer of 1779 to obtain "cabin rights" from Clark.

[4] The names of those who made this trip have not been preserved, but it is known that they reached their destination safely. A letter from Chief Colbert of the Chickasaws to John Stuart, May 25, 1779, tells of their passage through the Chickasaw country. Colbert wrote Stuart that the party were "evidently rebels." Roosevelt, *Winning of the West*, 3, 11.

## 3

James Robertson and his companions bade their families good-bye and started over the Kentucky Road for their new homes in the fall of 1779. Two of the party, Rains and Dunham, drove herds of cows. This was insisted upon by the women, for pioneer families were large and milk and butter were important articles of diet. The cattle delayed the emigrants, particularly as winter arrived early, with a severity which caused that particular season to be referred to for years as the "Cold Winter."

The animals continually strayed from the trail and had to be rounded up in rough country, and they required close watching at night. John Dunham's herd "nearly drove him mad," and finally in hopeless disgust he abandoned the cows in the wilderness.[5] John Rains, with the assistance of all the party, succeeded in reaching Cumberland with his herd of twenty-one cows; the first cattle to be brought to Nashville.[6]

Robertson's party found Cumberland River frozen over. On Christmas day, 1779, they crossed on the ice, and began to build cabins. The new settlement was called Nashborough, after Francis Nash, a brave officer from North Carolina who had lost his life at Germantown while fighting under Washington.

Robertson established the principal station at the Bluffs on the south side of Cumberland River. John Freeland established one two miles to the westward, and Amos Eaton chose a site north of the river. The three stations were within a few miles of each other, and formed a triangle with Eaton's at the apex. The old Long Hunter, Casper Mansker, built a blockhouse on the Kentucky Road ten miles from Eaton's.

The stations consisted of log cabins, connected by a high row of stakes sharpened at the top, built in a rectangular form with blockhouses at each corner. The upper story of the blockhouses extended over the lower in order to command the walls. Each settler's cabin, however, might be called a "station," for

---

[5] His brother Daniel Dunham, who had gone with Donelson by boat, was very angry at the loss, for he had paid John Dunham £100 to drive the cows to Cumberland.

[6] Roosevelt, *Winning of the West,* 3, 10.

each of them was equipped with loopholes and built to withstand attack if need be.

Robertson had fallen in with some parties of settlers bound for Kentucky. He had convinced quite a number of these that Cumberland was a "promised land," and they had decided to cast their lot with the new venture. Colonel Richard Henderson, who had promoted the settlement, sent supplies from Kentucky for the first winter. By January, 1780, Nashborough could boast of nearly two hundred population, and almost every day brought new emigrants. The rapid increase in population depleted supplies, and corn rose to one hundred and sixty-five dollars a bushel in continental money. Without the plentiful game, the pioneers could not have survived the severe winter.

### 4

"Journal of a Voyage, intended with God's permission, in the good boat Adventure, from Fort Patrick Henry on Holston River, to the French Salt Licks on Cumberland River, Kept by John Donelson." [7]

Thus begins a saga of the Tennessee River in 1779-1780, one of the most remarkable voyages ever undertaken on the American continent, and one of the most far reaching in its effects.

Boats for the trip had been in process of building throughout the summer of 1779, on Holston River. Donelson's flagship, the Adventure, was a great scow made to hold thirty men, besides women and children. Mrs. James Robertson and her five children were among the passengers; and Captain Donelson's own family, including his daughter Rachel who afterward married Andrew Jackson.

The whole flotilla, thirty boats and two hundred people, left Fort Patrick Henry on December 22, 1779. The exceeding bitterness of the "Cold Winter" delayed the start. The party went into temporary winter camp, and the journey did not really begin until February 27, 1780.

Ten days later, on March 7th, the boats approached the Chickamauga towns. A stop was made at the mouth of Chickamauga Creek,[8] where the town had been burned by Shelby the previous year. On a bleak, blustery day, with a drizzle of cold

---

[7] Donelson's Journal is quoted in full by Ramsey, page 197.
[8] Now known as South Chickamauga Creek.

rain, Mrs. Ephraim Peyton, who was in a boat with her father
Jonathan Jennings, gave birth to a son.  Her husband had
gone overland with Robertson.

The journey was resumed early next morning, and soon the
town of Settico, which had been re-occupied after its destruction by Shelby, came into view.  The Indians made signs of
friendliness, but a half-breed named Arch Coody warned the
adventurers not to land.  He accompanied the boats a short
distance down the river, described to them the "boiling pot"
which they would soon approach, told them they were out of
danger, and left.

Presently, Donelson was alarmed to see a large number of
warriors painted black and red, the war colors, put off in
canoes and follow his boats, although they stayed close to
shore.  Before long another village, near a little island, appeared on the southern bank.  The Indians tried to induce the
white people to use the channel nearest the town, indicating that
it was better.  Donelson ordered the boats to veer off toward
the opposite shore, afterward called Moccasin Bend.  Here a
number of Indians, lying in ambush among the canes, fired on
the boats, and a young man named Payne was killed.

Thomas Stuart, his family and friends, in all twenty-eight
people, occupied the rear boat.  Smallpox had broken out among
them, and Stuart agreed to stay some distance behind the
other boats to avoid spreading the disease.  The Chickamaugas
concentrated their efforts on the lone boat, and killed or captured all of the twenty-eight passengers.  Their cries could be
heard plainly by the people in the forward boats, but the swift
current prevented aid.[9]

<h2 style="text-align:center">5</h2>

Saddened by the loss of the Stuart boat, the Donelson party
continued down the river, and soon reached the great "Whirl
and Suck" which Coody had described to them as "the boiling
pot."  The river, compressed to less than half its normal width
between two spurs of Cumberland Mountains, and filled with

[9] So far as is known, only one person in the Stuart boat survived.
Thomas Stuart, Junior, six years old, son of the owner of the boat, was
ransomed by the trader William Springston and turned over two years
later to Colonel Joseph Martin at Fort Patrick Henry.  The Chickamaugas
contracted smallpox from the captives, which caused the death of several
hundred Indians.

boulders, justified the name. The spectacle was terrifying to the travelers, torn between the hard choice of the river or savages.

John Cotton attached his canoe, loaded with goods, to the larger boat of Robert Cartwright. Cotton's boat overturned. Pitying his distress at the loss of all his possessions, the party landed on the northern bank to give him what aid they could. The Indians opened fire from the bluffs above, and the adventurers hastily re-embarked.

The boat of Jonathan Jennings was caught on a large rock. His passengers were his daughter and her day old baby, his wife, two young men one of whom was his son, and a negro man-servant. The savages observed Jennings' predicament, and concentrated their fire on his boat. He was an excellent marksman and returned the fire. At the same time, he ordered the two young men and the negro to throw the goods into the river in order to lighten the boat. They tried to execute his command, but being wounded or terrified, jumped into the river and attempted to swim ashore. The negro was shot. Young Jennings and his companion were captured.[10]

The boat was finally released by the efforts of Mrs. Jennings and her daughter. Both of them, although Mrs. Peyton was but one day removed from child-birth, sprang into the water and pushed. Mrs. Jennings was nearly lost when the boat was suddenly released and jerked away by the swift current. The little baby lost its life in the confusion, probably by drowning. Three days later, Donelson and his party were overjoyed to hear behind them cries of "Help poor Jennings!" and to greet the occupants of the Jennings boat, whom they had given up for lost.[11]

Four persons were wounded in the boat of Abel Gower, who was James Robertson's brother-in-law. The crew was thrown into confusion. Nancy Gower, a young woman, seized the helm and steered the boat. Shot through the thigh, she made

---

[10] The trader John Rogers ransomed young Jennings. The other young man, whose name is not known, was burned at the stake.

[11] A sad sequel to the Jennings story is that three months later Jonathan Jennings, scarcely a month in the new land he had sacrificed so much to reach, was killed and scalped by the Indians. His body was chopped up, and pieces of it were stuck in derision on surrounding bushes. Mrs. Jennings, a devout Christian woman, said, "There is no rest save in Heaven." (Putnam, 148.)

no outcry and continued to steer. When calmer water was reached, her mother discovered the injury by the blood flowing through Nancy's clothing.[12]

## 6

Four days later, the weary travelers came within sight of Muscle Shoals. Colonel Robertson had promised to meet them at that point, but there was no sign of him, and they were sorely disappointed. Donelson's journal describes their emotion, and the perilous journey through the shoals.

"Captain James Robertson was to come across from the Big Salt Lick to the upper part of the Shoals, and there to make such signs that we might know that it was practicable for us to go across by land. But to our great mortification, we can find none, from which we conclude it would not be prudent to make the attempt, and are determined knowing ourselves to be in such imminent danger, to pursue our journey down the river.

"After trimming our boats in the best manner possible, we ran through the shoals before night. When we approached them, they had a dreadful appearance to those who had never seen them before. The water, being high, made a terrible roaring which could be heard at some distance. Among the driftwood heaped frightfully at the head of the islands, the current running in every possible direction, we knew not how soon we would be dashed to pieces and all our troubles ended at once.

"Our boats frequently dragged upon the bottom, and appeared constantly in danger of striking. They warped as much as in a rough sea. By the hand of Providence, we are now preserved from this danger also. I know not the length of this wonderful shoal; it had been represented to me to be twenty-five or thirty miles. If so we must have descended it very rapidly, as indeed we did, for we passed it in about three hours." [13]

## 7

The voyagers were fired upon by the Indians a number of times after passing the Shoals. On the night of March 14th, they made camp, lighted fires, and were preparing to retire when they were terrified by sudden barking of the dogs. They

---

[12] Nancy Gower survived, reached Nashborough, and married Anderson Lucas. Her father, Abel Gower, and her brother Abel Gower Jr., were among the first to be killed by the Indians after reaching Cumberland.

[13] Donelson's Journal, Ramsey, 197.

took it for granted that Indians were attempting to surprise them, and ran headlong for the boats. They moved down river and made camp on the opposite shore. In the morning, three men re-crossed and cautiously approached the former camp. Sleeping by one of the fires was a negro who had slept through the excitement of the preceding night. The men wakened the surprised black, recovered various utensils that had been abandoned in the flight, and returned to the boats.

The mouth of Cumberland River was reached on March 24th. The spirits of the party were lightened by the killing of a buffalo, the meat of which, "though poor, was palatable." Donelson also killed a swan, which was "very delicious," and gathered some herbs on the river bottoms which some of the company called "Shawnee Salad." [14]

On Friday, March 31st, the travelers were rejoiced to meet Colonel Richard Henderson, who was running the line between Virginia and North Carolina. He had visited the new settlement, and gave them welcome information of loved ones. He told them that he was sending corn from Kentucky to serve until a crop could be raised. Donelson and his party felt that they were nearing their destination, but it required nearly a month of further rowing until, on Monday, April 24th, they at last reached Nashborough. The closing entry in Donelson's journal is of that date.

"Monday, April 24th. This day we arrived at our journey's end, at the Big Salt Lick, where we have the pleasure of finding Captain Robertson and his company. It is a source of satisfaction to be enabled to restore to him and others, their families and friends who were entrusted to our care, and who some time since, perhaps, despaired of ever meeting again. Though our prospects at present are dreary, we have found a few log cabins which have been built upon a cedar bluff above the Lick, by Captain Robertson and his company." [15]

---

[14] The Shawnees were the last known Indian occupants of the region around Nashville. The Cumberland River was originally known as the Chauvanon, or Shawnee River. The "Shawnee Salad" was probably the well known "Poke Salad," *Phytolacca Decandra*.

[15] Donelson's Journal.

# CHAPTER XI

## NOLICHUCKY JACK RIDES

### I

In the year 1663, Charles II of England granted to eight Lords Proprietor all the lands in his North American possessions lying between the 29th and 36th degree of North Latitude, from the Atlantic to the Pacific. In honor of the king, the vast tract was called Carolina.

The lines were never run to the Pacific. A century later, in 1777, they were run west of the Alleghenies by a boundary commission appointed by Virginia and North Carolina, and the chagrined settlers on Watauga and Holston found themselves in North Carolina and not in Virginia as they had supposed.

Many of the settlers were from North Carolina, but their migration had been to escape the misrule of that state, which had brought its citizens into armed conflict with its authority. On the other hand, those of their number who were from Virginia felt an abiding loyalty to their mother state, and the news that they were citizens of a less favored commonwealth was to them gall and wormwood. For a number of years, however, the Wataugans had governed themselves through their own association, with little interference from either state.

Upon the decision of the boundary commission, the Wataugans forwarded a petition to North Carolina asking that the settlements be accepted as a portion of that state. Their plea stated frankly:

"Many of your petitioners settled on the lands of Watauga, expecting to be within the Virginia line. To their great disappointment, when the line was run, they were left without." [1]

North Carolina accepted the Watauga petition, and erected the territory west of the Alleghenies, comprising the present State of Tennessee, into the County of Washington. It was this county of which John Sevier was appointed Colonel of Militia in 1779.

---

[1] Ramsey, 135.

Sevier had come to Watauga from Virginia in 1772. He was a gentleman by birth and breeding, the son of a Huguenot who had settled in Shenandoah Valley. He possessed more education than the average border leader, and corresponded on equal terms with Madison, Franklin, and other statesmen. He was reputed the handsomest man on the frontier, tall, fair, blue eyed, with brown hair, slender of build and with erect military carriage and commanding presence. His manners were refined and easy, and he had great natural dignity. His eager, impetuous nature, his ready tact and courtesy, his generous hospitality, and his undoubted courage, gave him unbounded influence over the backwoodsmen.[2]

John Sevier was essentially a Virginian. He accepted his Colonel's commission because he was a natural leader among the frontiersmen rather than from any feeling of loyalty to North Carolina. To him and the other Wataugans, North Carolina was a step-mother, and the treatment she accorded her western subjects was that of step-children. This feeling probably accounts for the fact that Sevier, who made many Indian campaigns, made no official report of them to the state whose commission he bore. As Colonel of Militia, he was both judge and jury as to the need of an Indian campaign. When he felt that the Cherokees needed chastising, he called out his men and chastised them. He reported two campaigns only; one to Governor William Blount, representing the United States; and one to his own State of Franklin.

2

During 1779 and 1780, English forces under Lord Cornwallis overran Georgia and South Carolina, advanced against the Old North State, and threatened Virginia. Four hundred Georgia refugees under Colonel Elijah Clark, after a march of incredible hardship across the mountains in the winter of 1779, found haven at Watauga.

The "Men of the Western Waters" were intensely loyal to the American cause, but they had been engaged in the almost superhuman task of clearing the wilderness and protecting their families against a merciless foe. The Revolution had been overshadowed by the magnitude of their own difficulties. The

---

[2] Roosevelt, *Winning of the West*, 2, 356.

arrival of the refugees forcibly impressed upon the westerners the plight of their brethren on the seaboard. In June, 1780, Cornwallis sent his aides, Tarlton and Ferguson, to the base of the mountains, burning houses and impressing or hanging American sympathizers. Other refugees fled to Watauga, with a fervent appeal for aid from General McDowell, commander of the hard pressed Carolinians.

Two hundred frontiersmen, under Isaac Shelby, responded to the appeal, and in company with McDowell, carried on a guerilla warfare against the British. On Aug. 17, 1780, Cornwallis almost annihilated the southern American army under Gates at Camden. Shelby and his followers retreated to Watauga, and Colonel Patrick Ferguson was sent to stamp out every vestige of American hopes in western North Carolina.

Ferguson learned that there were settlements west of the mountains that were harboring refugees in their midst, and that some of the backwoodsmen had already borne arms against him. By a prisoner he had captured, he sent warning to the westerners that if they did not desist, he would cross the mountains, hang their leaders, put their fighting men to the sword, and burn their settlements.

The reply of the Wataugans was as dramatic as it was unexpected. When Shelby received Ferguson's insolent message, he mounted and galloped to Sevier's. He found Sevier in the midst of a barbecue and horse race. The merry-making ceased, and when Shelby had delivered his message, a hot wave of resentment filled the hearts of the mountaineers. A plan was speedily arranged to call out the militia, cross the mountains, and strike a blow for freedom.

The appointed meeting place was Sycamore Shoals, and the date was set for Sept. 25th. Campbell of Virginia brought four hundred men, Sevier and Shelby two hundred and forty each, and refugees under McDowell numbered one hundred and sixty. Each man brought his own rifle, tomahawk, and scalping knife, and wore the fringed hunting shirt of the frontier, with coonskin cap. A Presbyterian minister, Rev. Samuel Doak, admonished them to strike the British with "The Sword of God and Gideon," and on the 26th the little army began its march across the mountains. They were joined in North Carolina by three hundred militia under Colonel Benjamin Cleavland.

Ferguson was advised of the approach of the Americans by two deserters from Sevier's forces. His own men were scattered in raiding parties. He sent couriers to hasten their return, and fell back slowly toward South Carolina to permit time for gathering his strength. He sent out a proclamation calling on all British loyalists to "grasp their arms on the moment and run to his standard if they desired to live and bear the name of men, or if they chose to be degraded and spat upon by a set of mongrels, to say so at once, that their women might turn their backs upon them and look out for real men to protect them." [3]

On October 7th, Ferguson was camped on King's Mountain, near the northern boundary of South Carolina. He had about nine hundred and fifty men. His position was strong, and he felt confident that he could beat off the "whole American army."

The American forces had trotted all the morning of the 7th through a drizzling rain. The men had wrapped their blankets around their gunlocks to keep them dry. Two tories, captured near King's Mountain, told them that Ferguson was on a ridge where some deer hunters had camped the previous fall. The deer hunters were with Sevier, and stated that they knew the ground well. The forces were divided to surround Ferguson's position, and the riflemen advanced at a gallop. Cleavland led his followers to the rear of the British; Sevier led the right wing, Campbell the center, and Shelby the left.

Ferguson's aide, De Peyster, had just informed his commander that all was quiet when the Americans swarmed up the mountainside. Firing began about three o'clock in the afternoon. Ferguson sprang upon his horse, ordered the drums to beat to arms, and had his men in battle array by the time the frontiersmen commenced the actual attack. The two forces were almost evenly matched in numbers.

The mountaineers sounded the Indian war whoop and rushed forward, each man firing at will. Ferguson's troops fired heavy volleys, and advanced with the bayonet. The Americans used methods of Indian warfare which they had learned on the border. Having no bayonets, they gave way before Ferguson's charges, and each man sought the haven of a tree to reload. As fast as the Americans were driven down one side of the mountain, their comrades advanced on the other. Ferguson

---

[3] Roosevelt, 2, 326.

was thus unabled to follow any charge through to the finish, for each time he found a fresh foe in his rear. Sevier, Campbell, and Shelby quickly rallied their men after each retirement for another advance. Throughout the engagement, the piercing, unearthly war whoop disconcerted the British. One of them later told Sevier, "We could stand your rifles, but your cursed hallooing confused us. We thought you had regiments instead of companies." [4]

Ferguson, conspicuous among the British in his hunting shirt, rode hither and thither with reckless bravery, rallying his men with a silver whistle. Two horses were shot under him. At length, he led a charge against that portion of the American line that was commanded by Sevier, sword in left hand, for he was wounded in the right. "There's Ferguson!" shouted several soldiers.

Robert Young, one of Sevier's riflemen, [5] whipped his gun to his shoulder and fired. "Let's see what 'Sweet Lips' will do," he said. Several of the Americans fired, and Ferguson fell dead as his foot hung in the stirrup, pierced with half a dozen balls.

Captain Robert Sevier, Colonel Sevier's brother, was mortally wounded about the same time and was borne to the rear. De Peyster led the British for a few more charges, but the Americans having gained the summit on all sides, and being surrounded, he hoisted the white flag. Shelby and Sevier reached the top from opposite sides at the same moment. "The British have burned off part of Shelby's hair," Sevier shouted, for it was singed on one side.

As Captain Robert Sevier, desperately wounded, was carried to the rear, Colonel Sevier's son Joseph was informed that it was his father. He rushed to the front and continued firing on the English with savage fury after the surrender. Others followed his example, with the shout "Give them Buford's play!" referring to the refusal of the British to grant quarter at a previous engagement. Colonel Campbell ran among the men with his sword pointed to the ground, calling on them for God's sake to cease firing. "They have killed my father, and I will shoot the last of the damned rascals!" young Sevier re-

---

[4] Ramsey, 597.
[5] The same who had killed the Indian Big Bullet at the Treaty of Long Island in 1777.

torted with tears streaming down his cheeks. Colonel Sevier rode up in a moment, however, and the firing ceased.[6]

About three hundred of the loyalists were killed or disabled, and the remainder were taken prisoners. Many of the rough frontiersmen had little idea of mercy to a captured foe, and insisted that tories who had served under Ferguson should be hanged. Thirty were condemned to death by a rude court martial, and nine had been hanged when Sevier and Shelby, men of bold, frank nature, could no longer stand the butchery, and peremptorily ordered the executions to cease.

The frontiersmen, having accomplished their objective, returned to their homes on Watauga, Holston and Nolichucky. They had gained a notable victory which proved the turning point of the Revolution, leading directly to the retirement of Cornwallis from the Carolinas, and his surrender at Yorktown the following year. Sevier, Campbell, and Shelby were granted swords for their valiant service.[7]

### 3

The absence of a thousand white men on the King's Mountain campaign was seized upon by Alexander Cameron to revive the hopes of the Cherokees that by a quick stroke they might regain their hunting grounds. He assured the red men that the King's soldiers would make short work of the untrained mountaineers, who would all be killed. "Now is the time to wipe out the Watauga settlements, while their warriors are over the mountains," he told the Indians. He announced, too, that no supplies would be furnished to any Cherokee town that remained at peace with the Americans.[8] The Indians having no other source of supply, this was a serious threat. Under Cameron's urging, the upper Cherokee towns "took Dragging Canoe by the arm," [9] and plotted with him to destroy the white settlements while the Americans were away fighting Ferguson.

The King's Mountain campaign was soon ended, as Cameron had predicted, but with a different result. Ferguson was killed,

---

[6] Draper Mss., 30-S 351-397.

[7] The foregoing account of the King's Mountain campaign, where not otherwise indicated, is from Roosevelt, *Winning of the West*, 2, 297-354.

[8] *N. C. State Records*, 22, 995.

[9] The Cherokee said, "I take you by the arm," instead of the white salutation, "I take you by the hand."

and his army was annihilated by the long rifles of the mountaineers. John Sevier was back at home on Nolichucky before
the Indian campaign had scarcely begun. He found the traders
Isaac Thomas and Ellis Harlan waiting him, with word from
Nancy Ward of the impending Indian invasion.[10]

Sevier realized the necessity for prompt action. He dispatched a messenger to Colonel Arthur Campbell of Virginia,
asking his assistance in an offensive against the Cherokees, and
sent out a call to his own captains to assemble their men at
Swan's Pond on Lick Creek, near his home. Within three days,
he was on his way to the Cherokee towns at the head of two
hundred and fifty men. "Every man was punctual,—there was
no dodging in those days," Sevier's son afterward wrote.[11]
Sevier had participated in Christian's offensive as a Lieutenant,
and his campaign of 1780 was his first experience against the
Cherokees as commander.[12]

The little army marched rapidly down the Great War Trail,
and crossed French Broad River on the third day. On Boyd's
Creek, a southern tributary of French Broad, scouts Joseph
Dunham and Joseph Gist, who were in the advance, discovered
Indian signs. Sevier saw the men halt, and rode forward to
investigate. His keen eye located the savages ambuscaded in a
thicket. He ordered the spies to advance and draw the Indian
fire, and then to retreat to the main body and entice the Indians
on. He rode back quietly as though he had not seen the enemy,
and arranged his men for battle in three divisions. He commanded the center, Major Walton the right, and Major Tipton
the left. The right and left wings were ordered to close in as
soon as the Indians attacked, that they might be surrounded.

The Indians fell into Sevier's ruse and fired on the spies, who
returned the fire and retreated hastily. The war whoop was
sounded, and the entire body of Cherokees, about seventy in
number, pursued Gist and Dunham. Major Walton, on Sevier's
right, wheeled his men briskly as he had been ordered. Tipton

[10] One of the other commanders is said to have asked Sevier, "How soon
can you march?" "As soon as Kate can cook some dinner for my men,"
he replied.

[11] *Draper Mss.*, 32-S 140-180.

[12] Sevier's officers in the 1780 campaign were, Majors, John Tipton and
Jesse Walton: Captains, William Bean, Landon Carter, James Hubbard,
Samuel Handley, Thomas Gist, Jacob Brown, James Stinson, Benjamin
Sharp, George Doherty, James Elliott, William Russell, and James Sevier.

seems to have misunderstood his orders. He marched his men some distance to the right of the path and fell in behind Walton. Several of his men told him he was certainly wrong. Tipton, who was a violent man, replied, "Mind your own business and be damned,—I know my orders!" Had he executed the command as given, few of the Indians would have escaped.

When the Indians attacked, Tipton's men ran forward promiscuously and arranged themselves in Walton's line. The second fire, being the united one, was much stronger than the first. The Cherokees broke and fled, leaving twenty-eight dead on the field. Six others were found buried under logs on the further march to the Indian towns.

The fugitive warriors were pursued hotly by the Americans on horseback. Sevier and Joseph Dunham located a wounded Indian who had hidden in a pine tree. When he perceived that he was discovered, he raised in a threatening posture and pointed his gun first at Sevier, then at Dunham. The white men considered this a ruse, feeling sure that the gun was not loaded. They advanced with the intention of taking the Indian alive. Within a few yards of the tree, Sevier noticed the warrior draw sight on Dunham, and called, "Take care, Dunham, that fellow will shoot you." The Indian whirled his gun on Sevier and fired. Sevier's horse reared, and the bullet missed its mark, but cut off a lock of the commander's hair. Dunham mistook the hair for Sevier's brains, and raised his own gun to kill the Indian, when to his surprise the wounded savage, with great effort, drew his knife and plunged it into his own throat. He fell from the tree and expired immediately.

Tipton excused himself for not taking the position assigned to him by saying that he had acted as he understood his orders. Sevier remarked generously that this was very possibly true. The incident, however, was the beginning of Tipton's hatred for Sevier, a hatred which was in time to become almost fanatical.[13]

The Indians who participated in the Boyd's Creek fight were later identified as being from Chote. A brother of John Watts was among the killed. Sevier's only loss was one man wounded.

Just as the guns had ceased firing, two messengers rode up with a letter for Sevier from Colonel Arthur Campbell. He

---

[13] Description of the Boyd's Creek fight, which occurred on Dec. 8, 1780, is from *Draper Mss.*, 30-S 351-397; and 30-S 140-180; by Sevier's two sons, Captain James and Major George W. Sevier.

stated that he would arrive with the Virginia troops within a week, and asked that Sevier wait until the forces could be joined before advancing to the Cherokee towns.

Sevier fell back, therefore, to French Broad River, and camped on the large island since called Sevier's Island. Supplies were exhausted in a few days. Campbell had not arrived at the end of the week, and Sevier marched his men again to Boyd's Creek where he thought there would be better opportunity for hunting. William Bean, Isaac Thomas, and other good hunters ranged the woods but could find little game. The men lived on parched acorns, haws, grapes, walnuts, and hickory nuts. A cow and calf were found, lost by some pioneer or trader. This furnished variety, though so poor and tough that some of the men declined the meat. The location on Boyd's Creek was known as "Hungry Camp" for many years afterward.

Colonel Campbell arrived on Dec. 22, 1780, with four hundred men. The only supplies he had consisted of parched corn, to the disappointment of Sevier's men. The combined force marched the same day for the Little Tennessee towns, and arrived at Chote on Christmas Eve. No Indians were in sight. The half starved men found plenty of hogs and poultry, and stayed up nearly all night cooking and feasting. A strong force of sentries was kept out, and at daybreak John Bean was dispatched with five scouts to see if any trace of the Indians could be discovered. An Indian who had evidently watched the white men until weariness overcame him was found asleep behind a log. He was killed, and Bean brought his head into camp.

The army remained at Chote a week, recruiting men and horses. Strong parties were sent up river to destroy Chilhowie and Tallassee. The white forces then marched for the Hiwassee towns by way of Tellico, where the only fatality occurred. Captain James Elliott with some men was engaged in burning the Indian houses at Tellico, when four Cherokees appeared with a flag of truce. Elliott refused to recognize the flag, suspecting a trick. He ordered his men to capture the Indians if possible, and dashed forward on that mission. The Cherokees fled and escaped. One of them hid in the top of a fallen tree, and shot Elliott as he came up. He was in turn killed by the white soldiers. Elliott was buried under an Indian hut which was burned over him to prevent the savages from mutilating his body.

Nancy Ward appeared at Hiwassee and asked for peace. Sevier and Campbell insisted, however, on first destroying the Hiwassee towns. Hiwassee was found deserted. James Sevier and a party of scouts crossed the river ahead of the army and discovered an Indian boy of about twelve who escaped into the woods. Captain Landon Carter was sent with fifty men to try and capture him for the purpose of securing information, but the boy could not be located. Carter captured, however, a warrior who proved to be the dancing instructor for the town, an important position, for dancing was a significant part of all ceremonies with the Indians. The next morning the old trader Thomas, who could speak Cherokee fluently, found the Indian boy asleep by a fire in the woods. He readily surrendered, and told Thomas that a "Unaka (white man) had chased him the day before."

The towns of Hiwassee and Chestuee were destroyed, and Campbell and Sevier returned to Chote. Hanging Maw and other chiefs begged for peace which was granted. The two Cherokee prisoners were turned over to the chiefs, and the white army left the Indian towns on New Year's Day, 1781.[14]

Colonel Arthur Campbell, in his official report, belittled the part taken in the campaign by John Sevier. William Martin, son of General Joseph Martin, afterward explained Campbell's attitude:

"Colonel Sevier, of Washington County, went on in his own behalf with three or four hundred men several days before the army, met a party of Indians, had a little fight, killed a few, and retired some distance, waiting for the main army. This was complained of at the time not only as an unauthorized move, but as apprizing the Indians of our approach before the army was in position to act efficiently. It was thought that the motive of Sevier was to get glory for himself."[15]

Campbell's criticism may be charged to personal jealousy. Sevier, who first received notice of the intended Indian invasion, acted with promptness and energy. His victory at Boyd's Creek disconcerted the Cherokees at the beginning of their

[14] *Draper Mss.*, 30-S 140-180.
[15] *Ibid.*, 3-XX-4, Martin to L. C. Draper. Campbell's report may be found in *Calendar of Virginia State Papers,* 1, 434-437.

campaign. Had they have attacked the frontier, great damage would have resulted. John Sevier did not seek glory; never was a commander less boastful. The best proof of the unselfish nature of his services was the whole-hearted acceptance of "Chucky Jack" by the rough and ready frontiersmen. They were keen judges, ready to criticize anything or anybody, and hard to deceive.

### 4

Soon after returning to Nolichucky, Sevier received advice that the Middle Cherokee towns intended to go to war to revenge the defeat of the Overhills. Early in March, 1781, one hundred and thirty of his men gathered at Greasy Cove. Sevier led them to the Little Tennessee towns, and thence over the old Fort Loudoun trail to the Middle settlements, scene of Montgomery's defeat and Grant's campaign. Fifteen villages of the Cherokees were again put to the torch by the white invader.

At Cowe, Valentine Sevier, John Bond, and Nathaniel Davis swam the river on horseback to plunder some cabins, contrary to orders, for Sevier had suspected that the Indians might be lying in ambush. A band of Indians rushed between the white men and the river. Bond was killed and scalped, and Davis severely wounded. Valentine Sevier, who had remained mounted, took Davis on his horse and gained the river, which he swam with his wounded comrade. John Sevier with fifty men dashed into the river to their assistance, but by the time they had crossed the Indians had disappeared. Davis died of his wounds. The two men, Bond and Davis, were Sevier's only loss in the campaign.

As soon as the Middle towns were destroyed, Sevier led his little force back through treacherous defiles to the Little Tennessee and thence to Watauga. Twenty-nine Cherokees were killed in the campaign, and nine prisoners were taken by Sevier to his own residence. They were treated kindly and became attached to the various members of his household, and remained until peace was made during the following year.[16]

---

[16] Sevier's indomitable energy led him into a third campaign in 1781, when he and Isaac Shelby led two hundred riflemen across the mountains to the aid of Francis Marion, the "Swamp Fox," against the British. The mountaineers captured an English garrison of one hundred at Monk's Corner, and 500 fine new muskets that were especially welcome to the American forces.

## 5

"No people are entitled to more land than they can cultivate," said Judge David Campbell; "People will not sit still and starve for land when a neighboring Nation has more than it needs."

The territory south of Nolichucky River had been guaranteed to the Cherokees in solemn treaty, but settlers followed the army in its campaigns. It was taken for granted that the land having been "conquered" in war, treaties were superseded. Soon, every spring had its little cabin and cleared field, regardless of the fact that the ground on which the cabin was built was Indian property.

The line of settlement was along Dumpling Creek, a northern tributary to French Broad River, therefore, they became known as the Dumpling settlements. No part of America's broad domain has been purchased at a more costly price of blood and terror than this little bit of country called the Dumpling.

Joseph Martin, Indian Agent, at the expense of his own popularity, protested against encroachments on land that was plainly the property of the Cherokees. In September, 1782, he forwarded to Governor Martin of North Carolina a talk from Old Tassel setting out the plea of the Indians:

"Your people from Nolichucky are daily pushing us out of our lands. We have no place to hunt on. Your people have built houses one day's walk of our towns. We don't want to quarrel with our elder brother. We therefore hope our elder brother will not take our lands from us that the Great Man above gave us. He made us, and He made you. We are all His children, and we hope our elder brother will take pity upon us and not take from us the lands our Father gave us, because he is stronger than we are.

"We are the first people that ever lived in this land. It is ours. Why will our elder brother take it away from us? It is true that some time past some people from over the Great Water persuaded our young men to do some mischief to our elder brother, which our

---

An incident at the beginning of the campaign had its effect on Sevier's future. Captain James Stinson had injured his arm and was compelled to return to his home. Major John Tipton was ordered to accompany him for a few miles, over the roughest part of the trail. Tipton, instead of returning to the army, continued on to his own home, for which breach of orders Sevier revoked his Major's commission; a link in the chain of circumstances that was to make hatred of John Sevier the ruling passion of Tipton's life. *Draper Mss.*, 30-S 140-180.

principal men were sorry for, but you, our elder brother, came to our towns and took satisfaction, and then sent for us to come in and treat with you, which we did.  We have done nothing to offend our elder brother since the last treaty, and why should our elder brother quarrel with us?  We hope you will take pity on your younger brother and send Colonel Sevier, who is a good man, to have all your people moved off our land." [17]

In reply to Old Tassel's letter, Governor Martin instructed John Sevier, as Colonel of Militia, to notify all settlers on Cherokee lands to withdraw at once, and if they should refuse, to "Pull down their cabbins and remove them, paying no attention to their entreatys." [18]

Sevier had no intention of complying.  He was one of the settlers, understood their attitude, and sympathized with them.  "It is unthinkable," he wrote, "to put these people to such inconvenience on account of a few miserable savages who would not be noticed but for their cruelties practiced upon our people." [19]  Not a settler's "cabbin" did Sevier pull down; he had in mind rather the destruction of other habitations, those of the red men.  Yet Sevier had so impressed the Cherokees with his spirit of fairness that they were willing to rest their case in his hands: "Send us Colonel Sevier, who is a good man."

6

While Old Tassel was petitioning for removal of white trespassers, the Chickamaugas took more active measures and made the relief asked by the chief impossible to grant.  War parties harassed the new settlements during the spring and summer of 1782 and deliberately passed to and fro through the upper towns making it impossible to distinguish good Indians from bad.  As a matter of fact, braves from the upper towns often joined the war parties, though Old Tassel laid all "mischief" at the door of the Chickamaugas.

In June, 1782, Governor Martin wrote:

"A tribe of Cherokees called the Chicamoggies, instigated by British emissaries and tory refugees, have been very troublesome in murdering many peaceful families of this state and Virginia.  I

---

[17] N. C. State Records, 17, 175; Ramsey, 271.
[18] Ibid., 16, 692.
[19] Sevier's Journal, Tennessee Historical Magazine.

am about to form an expedition to extirpate them if possible from that country if they cannot be reclaimed; the other tribe of their nation having disclaimed their proceedings." [20]

A resolution passed by the North Carolina Assembly in July, 1782, authorized General Charles McDowell and Colonel John Sevier to raise a thousand volunteers for the destruction of the Chickamauga towns, "all the males therein to be killed, and the females captured for exchange; supplies captured to be divided among the soldiers participating." [21]

McDowell did not take part in the campaign, and Sevier commanded. Governor Caswell later wrote to the Assembly:

"The expense of this campaign, as you so justly observe, hath equal claim to Continental credit as others of a similar nature."

The governor's message thus gave official standing to this last campaign of the American Revolution.[22]

Sevier assembled his forces at Big Island of French Broad River, two hundred and fifty men in all, and marched for the Indian towns about the middle of September.

He was met at Chote by John Watts and an Indian called Noonday, but known to the white men as Butler. They offered to guide Sevier's forces. Watts was a supporter of Dragging Canoe, but spent much of his time in the upper towns where he could obtain news of the white men which he relayed to his chief at Running Water. He was a diplomatic, smooth talking Indian, and was able to fool such experts in Indian character as Sevier, and later, Governor Blount. His intention was to mislead Sevier, and he made no effort to guide the white men to the real Chickamauga towns.

Hanging Maw met the army at Tellico, and professed peace both for that town and Hiwassee, and they were not molested.

After crossing Hiwassee River, as Sevier approached Chestuee Creek, the advance guard met two Indians who turned and ran. Major Valentine Sevier led a party in pursuit. A flanking party under James Sevier had ridden to the top of a large Indian mound to reconnoitre the country. They observed

[20] N. C. State Records, 16, 692.
[21] Ibid.
[22] N. C. State Records, 16, 692.

one of the Indians running for a nearby canebrake, dashed from the mound, and cut off his retreat. The fugitive stopped, raised his hands, and uttered an imploring cry. He was taken captive.

John Sevier rode up with Watts and Butler and questioned the Indian as to where his companion had gone. He replied that the other warrior had secreted himself under the creek bank. Sevier told Watts to call for him to surrender, and he would not be harmed. Watts raised a yell, and the Indian emerged from his hiding place and surrendered.

Sevier proceeded to Chickamauga, where he destroyed the towns that had been re-occupied after Shelby's offensive in 1779. They were, Bull Town, Settico, Vann's, Chickamauga, and Tuskegee. Edmund Kirke, who states that he received his information from early settlers, says that Sevier in this campaign fought a battle on Lookout Mountain; that after he had destroyed Tuskegee Island Town, below the present Chattanooga, its chief, Bloody Fellow, yelled defiance at the white men from the opposite bluffs of the mountain. Sevier crossed the river by a ford at the head of a small island and defeated the Indians above the bluffs. The principal chief was Wyuka, probably Little Owl, brother of Dragging Canoe. The fight lasted but a short time. The ground was rough and ideal for Indian warfare, the Indian plan of battle being to fight from cover, avoid heavy losses, and retreat if outnumbered.[23]

Sevier camped several days at Bull Town at the mouth of Chickamauga Creek while the surrounding Indian towns were destroyed. Watts sent the warrior who had been taken at Chestuee as a messenger to the Indians, and he returned with Jane Iredell, a young woman who had been captured by the Indians in the present Johnson County, Tenn.

One morning the men found a message to Sevier, scratched on the ground, from the trader John Rogers, who desired to

---

[23] Kirke, Edmund, *Rear Guard of the Revolution.*

The engagement on Lookout Mountain was fought Sept. 20, 1782. Roosevelt, in his *Winning of the West,* states that Sevier's 1782 campaign rests solely upon Haywood for authority, and strongly questions the veracity of Kirke. At the time Roosevelt wrote, the North Carolina records were not available. They cover the campaign fully. See Vol. 16, pages 450, 461, 512, 692, 697, 711; also Vol. 19, pages 905, 906, 938.

Kirke, as Roosevelt states, cannot be accepted always as authority. He is said to have received his information as to the Lookout Moutain fight from John P. Long, early settler and first postmaster at Chattanooga.

join the whites but was afraid.  Sevier wrote an answer, also
on the ground, that Rogers might come in with safety.  He
appeared the next day, and brought Jack Sivil, a negro who had
been captured on Cumberland.[24]  The feeling against white
men who had lived among the Indians ran high, and some of
the soldiers wanted to kill Rogers, but Sevier protected him.
The trader was very grateful, and afterward found opportunity
to favor the Americans.

Watts had avoided leading Sevier to the newly established
Five Lower Towns.  Sevier, therefore, thinking that he had
destroyed all of the Chickamauga settlements, followed Chicka-
mauga Creek over the mountains to Coosa River.  Patrick
Clements, a tory refugee who was living with the sister of
Archie Coody, was captured.  He broke away and tried to
escape, and was shot by Isaac Thomas.  His wife, Nancy
Coody, was kept as a prisoner.

The white army approached Spring Frog Town on Coosa
River, and saw a canoe loaded with Indians making their escape.
Sevier's men gave chase, but the Cherokees with one exception
reached a canebrake and were seen no more.  The exception was
an aged squaw who hid under the river bank.  She was noticed
by Captain William Bean, who did not disturb her, as Sevier
had ordered that Indian women and children should not be
killed.  An Irishman named Ralston, however, spied the old
woman, shot her, and took her scalp.  The Beans and their
friends tormented him unmercifully.  One of them would yell
at the top of his voice, "Who killed Granny?"  Several voices
would answer from all directions, "Ralston!"  The harassed
Ralston finally took position a hundred yards from the army to
avoid his tormentors.[25]

Ustinaula, an important town on Coosa River, was next
destroyed by Sevier's men.  It had been abandoned at the approach of the white army.  Robert Bean and a scouting party
captured a squaw and several children, and an Indian warrior
of small stature who possessed a remarkably fine shotgun.
Bean took the gun from the Indian, and gave it to Sevier's

---

[24] See note 10, Chapter XII.
[25] *Draper Mss.*, 30-S 140-180, James Sevier to L. C. Draper.  James Sevier
comments that the Bean brothers, William, Robert, John, Jesse, and Edmund
were noted Indian fighters and gunsmiths, and that they were always on
hand for a campaign.

negro servant Toby, who accompanied his master on all campaigns. The Indian was filled with wrath that his gun should be given to a negro. He berated Toby on every possible occasion, in the Cherokee dialect. Toby, who understood his meaning if not his words, would reply with equally insulting remarks in English. The war of words greatly amused the soldiers, who delighted to get the two together.[26]

Sevier destroyed two other towns on Coosa River, Ellijay and Coosawatie, and then sent word to the chiefs that he would meet them at Chote for a peace talk.

He was met by Oconostota, Old Tassel, and Hanging Maw, and the peace pipe was smoked. Twenty Indian women and children who had been taken prisoners were restored to their people, and Sevier and his men returned to their homes early in November, 1782.

One of the pioneers has written of Sevier's campaigns:

"In these wars military etiquette was but little observed. The great matter was to get the men in the field. Every man considered himself a soldier. He had his horse and rifle, which he knew well how to use, and was always ready at short notice to join his fellows in any emergency. All had a common interest, and that most vital; their homes, their families, and everything dear to man. Thus there was formed among them a pride of tacit league and covenant, which all regarded as most binding.

"When fighting came on, everyone fought for himself, officers as well as men. The best officers were those who fought best; as among the Indians, the officers were leaders rather than commanders. Command was always more nominal than real. In fighting, it was always expected that the officers would lead on; any failure to do this would be marked as cowardice, and the officer cashiered, not by court martial but by acclamation.

"It would surprise men of this generation to see the power these leaders exercised over their followers. It was a power conferred by God and nature, much more effective than that on parchment. Whenever any of those great leaders thought proper to promote a campaign for the common good, he would send out his summons, and his men would come mounted and equipped at their own expense, well knowing that they would receive no pay from the government."[27]

---

[26] Details of Sevier's campaign of 1782, where not otherwise indicated, are from the narrative of his son, James Sevier, *Draper Mss.*, 30-S 140-180. James Sevier participated in most of his father's Indian campaigns.

[27] *Draper Mss.*, 3-XX-4, William Martin to L. C. Draper.

## 7

The treaty of peace at Chote in October, 1782, was the last public appearance of Oconostota. The chief was at the time very old, and almost blind. A short time afterward, Colonel Joseph Martin, because of the scarcity of food in the Nation, took Oconostota, Nancy Ward, and some other friendly Indians to his home on Long Island of Holston, where he kept them during the winter. The old chief enjoyed talking of his past experiences with Colonel Martin and the members of his family. He told Martin that he "had never run from an enemy, but he had walked fast up a branch once." William Martin, the Agent's son, gained this impression of the aged warrior:

"I am of the opinion that Oconostota was one of the noblest and best of human kind. He had a powerful frame, and in his prime must have weighed more than two hundred pounds, with a head of enormous size. He was, when I saw him, very lean, stooped, and emaciated." [28]

As spring approached, Oconostota felt that the end of his days had come, and wished to die in his beloved Chote. Colonel Martin accompanied him by canoe, and was with him when he died. Oconostota expressed his good will toward the white men, and thanked Colonel Martin for his kindness. "My brother," he said, "I want to be buried like the white people are buried, and want my body to face the Long Knife," meaning the white people. The brave old Indian clasped his friend by the hand, and his soul, which had never known fear, took its departure.

Colonel Martin respected Oconostota's wishes. A coffin was made of a canoe in which the body was placed, and it was interred with Christian rites. [29]

## 8

The Cherokees who were punished by Sevier's campaign were not the real offenders. The Chickamaugas were left with the Five Lower towns untouched, and their manpower undiminished. It is not surprising, therefore, to read a letter from Governor Martin, written in November, 1782:

[28] *Draper Mss.,* 3-XX-4.
[29] *Ibid.*

"The Chicamoggies seem not disposed for peace, as no overtures from them have been made to me or to the officers commanding the militia. Some of their towns have been destroyed, and a few Indians killed, their principal body having fled. Our militia have returned, and await further instructions. I shall delay hostilities against these Indians until we have further cause for complaint, giving them in the meanwhile an opportunity to sue for peace." [30]

This was a forlorn hope while Dragging Canoe lived.

To Old Tassel, the governor wrote, "Brother, you have not hurt us much. The Chicamoggies have done most of the mischief." [31]

## 9

The great Indian nation the Delawares, called "Grandfather" by all eastern tribes, had split upon the question of American independence. As original owners of the soil, the Delawares had entered into a treaty of peace with William Penn which was not broken during the lifetime of the great Quaker. The growth of white population, however, had forced the red men to relinquish their lands along the seacoast. At the beginning of the Revolution, the Delawares were living by permission of the Iroquois along the Muskingum River in Ohio.

The celebrated Chief White Eyes, head of the Delaware Nation, was friendly to the Americans, and succeeded in holding the majority of his tribe to a position of neutrality between Americans and British. The warlike Minsi, or Wolf Clan, sided with the British, and led by their chief Captain Pipe, joined other northern tribes in raids on the American frontier.

Early in 1782, Colonel William Crawford led a force of frontiersmen against the hostile Delawares. He was surprised and defeated on Sandusky River by Captain Pipe, and Crawford was taken prisoner. He was burned to death with horrible tortures at Pipe's town on Tymochte Creek. Squaws thrust burning brands into his flesh, burning coals were thrown on him, and he was scalped alive. He appealed to a white renegade,

[30] *N. C. State Records,* 16, 461.
[31] *Ibid.*

Simon Girty, to shoot him. Girty answered with laughter.[32]
Death of the victim ended the terrible scene.

Among the savages who danced and yelled around the stake
to which Colonel Crawford was tied was a band of Chickamauga warriors who had been sent by Dragging Canoe to
solicit aid from the northern tribes after the burning of his
towns by Shelby in 1779. They had remained as a constant
pledge of friendship of the Chickamaugas to the northern tribes,
who had dispatched a band of their own warriors to reside at
Running Water with Dragging Canoe.[33]

A vastly different scene was being enacted about the same
time at the towns of the friendly branch of the Delawares on
the Muskingum. The great chief White Eyes had died while on
a visit to Fort Pitt, and Old Tassel and the Raven at the head of
a Cherokee delegation journeyed northward to extend the con-
dolence of their nation. The Moravian missionary Heckewelder
was present on their arrival and reported the proceedings; a
vivid picture of Indian diplomacy.[34]

The Cherokee ambassadors were met by the Delawares near
the village of Goshocking. Their hosts "drew the briars and
thorns from their legs and feet,—healed the sores and bruises
of their journey, wiped the dust and sweat from their bodies,—
cleansed their eyes and ears that they might see and hear,—
and anointed their joints that they might again be supple." [35]

On the following morning, the Cherokees marched to a "long
house" erected specially for their reception. They discharged

---

[32] Simon Girty, one of the most noted characters on the border, was born
on the Susquehanna River in 1741, son of an Indian trader of the same name.
He was taken prisoner by the Indians at an early age and grew up among
the Senecas. He was exchanged after the surrender of Fort Pitt, and
served for a time as interpreter at the fort. At the beginning of the Revolution, he fled from the fort in company with two others, Matthew Elliott
and Alexander McKee. The three men became bitter and hated enemies
of the Americans. Girty and Elliott led hostile war parties against the
frontier, and were far more merciless than their savage companions. McKee
became British Agent at Detroit, and served in that capacity for nearly
twenty years.

[33] See deposition of John Slover, *Heckewelder's Narrative*, 584. The exchange of such bands of warriors was equivalent to giving hostages. The
northern warriors at Running Water were headed by Shawnee Warrior,
and gave good account of themselves in the border warfare.

[34] Heckewelder, *Narrative*, 320-323.

[35] The services were performed figuratively.

their guns in the air before entering, and left the weapons outside. Entering, visitors and hosts seated themselves on opposite sides, and remained silent with eyes cast upon the ground for half an hour.

The Raven then rose and delivered the expression of sympathy:

"One morning after I had arisen from my sleep, and according to my custom stepped out to see what weather we had, I observed a dark cloud above the trees. It neither disappeared, nor moved from the spot, as other clouds do. Seeing the cloud successively every morning, always in the same place, I began to think what might be the cause. It having struck me that the cloud was lying in the direction that my grandfather dwelt, something might be the matter with him that caused him grief. I resolved to go myself, and see if anything was wrong with him! I accordingly went, and steered a course by the direction I had observed the cloud to be! I arrived at my grandfather's, whom I found quite disconsolate, hanging his head and tears running down his cheeks. Casting my eyes around in the hope of discovering the cause of his grief, I observed a dwelling closed up, from which no smoke appeared to ascend. Looking in another direction, I observed a mound of fresh earth on which nothing was seen growing; and here I found the meaning of my grandfather's grief. No wonder he is so grieved! No wonder he is weeping with his eyes turned toward the ground! Even myself cannot help weeping with my grandfather! I cannot proceed for grief!"

The Raven seated himself as though deeply afflicted. After a space of twenty minutes of absolute silence, he again rose and took from Old Tassel a large string of wampum which he handed to the Delaware chiefs, saying:

"Grandfather! Lift up your head and hear what your grandchildren have to say to you! They have discovered the cause of your grief, and it shall be done away with! See, grandfather! I level the ground on yonder spot of earth, and put leaves and brush on it to make it invisible. I sow seeds on that spot, that trees and grass may grow thereon.

He received another belt from Old Tassel, which he presented to mark his next point:

"Grandfather! The seed which I have sown has already taken root. Nay, the grass has already covered the ground, and the trees are growing."

Presenting a third belt, he concluded:

"Now my grandfather! The cause of your grief being removed, let me dry your tears! I wipe them away from your eyes! I place your body, which by the weight of grief and a heavy heart is leaning to one side, in its proper posture. Your eyes shall henceforth be clear, and your ears open as formerly. The work is finished!" [35]

The Tassel and his followers rose, and followed the Raven as he gravely shook hands with each Delaware. When they had resumed their seats, the Delaware chief Gelelamond replied:

"Grand-children! You did not come here in vain! You have performed a good work, in which the Great Spirit has assisted you. Your grandfather makes you welcome with him!"

On the following day the Raven and Tassel entered into a covenant with the Delawares not to take part in the conflict between the Americans and the English, but to preserve strict neutrality.[36]

---

[35] The expression "grandfather" as used by the Raven had reference to the entire Delaware Nation.

[36] Heckewelder, *Narrative,* 324.

The pledge of neutrality of the Delawares and Cherokees amounted to little. Irresponsible characters on the border, both white and red, made it impossible for any Indian to remain neutral. Old Tassel himself, one of the principals in the agreement, was to die under a flag of truce.

In the fall of 1782, ninety peaceful Delawares, converts of the Moravian missionaries, were murdered by a body of Kentuckians headed by Colonel David Williamson.

None of the border Indians were more bitter against the Americans than the war party of the Delawares, headed by Captain Pipe. They were a dispossessed, homeless people, expelled from the land guaranteed to them by William Penn, living by sufferance among the Wyandots.

"What grievance have the Delawares against the Americans?" was asked of Chief Tedescund by the Governor of Pennsylvania. The chief replied, "I have not far to go!" (He stamped upon the ground.) "This ground that I stand upon is mine, and has been taken from me by fraud and forgery!" *Ibid.,* 150.

# CHAPTER XII

## WARPATH

### I

The practice of scalping among the American Indians was of old origin. De Soto mentions the taking of scalps, "which they desired more than all else." Many of the tribes shaved the head, or plucked out all the hair except the scalp lock, which was left as a defiance to their enemies.

Torture by fire was likewise a tribal custom. The mark of a great warrior was the ability to endure the torture without complaint. The Little Carpenter, mildest of Indians, presided at a council in 1763 which debated the fate of a Shawnee captive, and calmly condemned him to death by fire, "after the amputation of certain of his parts." [1]

The white men were not blameless. They adopted the practice of scalping, and royal governors offered substantial rewards for Indian scalps, thus encouraging the red men to continue their cruelty. The frontiersmen, however, could not take a philosophic view of the matter when they saw their cabins burned and their kindred scalped. "It was inevitable, indeed in many instances it was proper, that such deeds should awaken in the breasts of the whites the grimmest, wildest spirit of revenge and hatred." [2] There developed on the frontier a blind, unreasoning hatred of the red men.

"No Indian," said the pioneer Edmiston, "can be trusted. None of them can get a lick amiss." Abraham Castleman once said, "The Indians will hack you with hatchets, riddle you with bullets, and stick arrows into you until you look like a fretted porcupine. Avoid being taken alive. If you cannot escape, sell your life dearly, and make them pay in advance." [3]

---

[1] *N. C. Colonial Records*, 7: 212. It should be borne in mind that no method of execution is beautiful, whether of hangman's noose or guillotine. Our own English forbears burned Joan of Arc at the stake. Death by fire, as practiced by the Indians, was not more inhuman than crucifixion, which was inflicted upon thousands by Roman soldiers. It is only in recent years that attempt has been made to humanize legal executions.

[2] Roosevelt, *Winning of the West*, 2: 107.

[3] Putnam, 355.

GENERAL JOHN SEVIER

"Chucky Jack" to the Cherokees

Photograph from miniature in the possession of his great-grand-son
Daniel Vertner Sevier, of Jacksonville, Texas, who sent the miniature to Calvin M. McClung of Knoxville, Tennessee, who had it
photographed by Knaffl & Brakebill of Knoxville, in January, 1918.

2

The Cumberland settlers had bought the land fairly, and felt that, aside from occasional hunting parties, they had nothing to fear from the red men, so, although the stations were but partially finished, each man selected a plot that suited his taste and built a cabin in anticipation of the arrival of his family.

Throughout the cold winter of 1779-1780, the settlers were dependent upon hunting for sustenance. Game was plentiful at first, but in a month or two there began to be an unaccountable scarcity. Hunters found it necessary to travel a long way to secure meat. They attributed this scarcity to the unusual cold, but it was the work of Indians, whose first strategy was to drive off the game and force the hunters to expose themselves far from the stations. Joseph Hay, a hunter, was found one day lying on his face, stripped, scalped, and mutilated. The stations were hastily completed and strengthened; outlying cabins were abandoned, and when the women and children arrived, instead of being escorted to their homes, they were conducted by grim husbands and fathers to the three principal strongholds, Freeland's, Eaton's, and the Bluffs.

The pioneers were cheered at this time by a consignment of corn sent by Colonel Henderson from Kentucky, and also by the arrival of Henderson and his two brothers, Pleasant and Nathaniel.

Realizing now more than ever that they were far from any organized government, and dependent entirely upon themselves, the frontiersmen gathered in mass meeting on May 1, 1780, and adopted a compact for the control of their affairs. Colonel Henderson wrote the document, and it was signed by two hundred and fifty-six pioneers. The control of the settlement was placed in the hands of a committee of Judges, or Triers, of whom James Robertson was made chairman. The settlers agreed to pay Henderson ten dollars per thousand acres for the land, conditional upon his securing good title from North Carolina.[4]

---

[4] Moore, John Trotwood, *Tennessee the Volunteer State*, 171. Henderson was never able to give title, for his claim was disallowed by North Carolina in 1783, and in lieu of the Cumberland territory, he was granted 200,000 acres of land on the Holston River. The Cumberland Compact is quoted in full by Putnam, 94-102.

### 3

The Cumberland settlements were, by their location, subject to the hostility of three nations of Indians:

To hold the country he had conquered in Illinois, George Rogers Clark had built a fort in western Kentucky on the lands of the Chickasaws without asking their permission. They were disposed to take satisfaction from the nearest white men, and their English agent, Dr. Connelly, urged them to "drive those Virginians back or make wolf bait of their carcasses." [5]

They were in the pathway of communication between the Creek tribe in the South, and their northern allies, and the Creeks would not agree to the white occupation of the Cumberland without a struggle.

The Chickamaugas had been reminded by Henry Stuart that the Watauga settlements might easily have been destroyed while new, before they had gained strength to defend themselves. Dragging Canoe was determined that the same mistake should not occur with Cumberland.

### 4

When John Donelson, with his boats, had reached the mouth of Red River in March, 1780, forty of the emigrants, attracted by the beauty of the site of the future Clarksville, decided to make their homes there. It was about forty miles from Nashville, or Eaton's, and was the most isolated of the Cumberland settlements. Those who located at Clarksville, and along the Red River, were the Renfros (Moses, Isaac, and Joseph), Mr. Johns, Nathan Turpin, and others.

In June, 1780, Nathan Turpin was killed by the Indians, which so alarmed his neighbors that they decided to leave Renfro's (as the settlement was called), and seek refuge at Freeland's. When they had made camp for the night, some of the party reproached themselves for abandoning their property, and decided to return to the station and secure the things they had left. The station was reached about daylight, and after repossessing themselves of the hidden articles the men hurried back to the camp-site, where they found their families awaiting them. The others had gone on to Freeland's, which

---

[5] Putnam, 110.

they reached in safety. Those who had stayed behind made camp that night at Battle Creek, about twenty miles from Freeland's. The Indians attacked them at daybreak, and killed the entire party of eleven or twelve, with the exception of Mrs. Johns, who escaped during the excitement. She wandered several days in the woods, and finally reached Eaton's Station. A party was sent to the scene of the slaughter to bury the dead. They found the ground white with feathers from the beds, which the Indians had ripped to secure the ticking.

With the advent of good weather, the settlers were active in locating future home sites. Jacob and Frederick Stump were "prospecting" with that purpose in view on White's Creek, about three miles from Eaton's, when they were fired on by the savages. Jacob was killed, and Frederick was chased three miles, up hill and down, to Eaton's. Relating his experience later, he said, "Py sure I did run dat time." [6] The persistent Frederick later returned and established a station and grist mill on the very site he had selected before. He made whiskey, to Robertson's dissatisfaction, for Robertson, strangely, was a prohibitionist in times when drinking was well-nigh universal. He said, "I hope the time will come when good grain will not be wasted by distilling, and souls ruined by drinking liquor." [7]

Salt, of course, was a necessity on the frontier, and, as David Hood said, "It was precious, and precious scarce." It had to be procured by boiling the water from the salt licks, a process which required several hours.

William Neely, one of Robertson's companions on the first trip to Cumberland, went out with a party to make salt. His daughter accompanied the men to cook for them. The men hunted while the water boiled, and Neely brought a fat buck into camp. He lay down to rest while his daughter prepared the meal, but never rose again. When his body was found later, it was scalped, mutilated, and stuck full of arrows. His daughter was seized and her hands were bound. It was almost dark. The savages took Neely's gun and powder horn, then, taking the captive by each arm, they compelled her to run throughout

---

[6] Stump's Distillery became a favorite place with the frontiersmen. The drinking cups were buffalo horns. Cow's horns were sometimes used, but those of the buffalo were much preferred. Other distilleries were "The Red Heifer," and "Black Joe's Place." See Putnam, 155, 168, 284, 411.

[7] Putnam, 237.

the night, the Indians supporting her, not rudely, when she became exhausted. She was carried to the Creek Nation, and spent several years there, but was eventually exchanged and reared a family in Kentucky.[8]

The men tried hard to raise a crop the first year, but Indian hostilities and a freshet in mid-summer brought their efforts to little or nothing. Captain John Donelson and Abel Gower, companions on the river trip, had planted corn on the Clover Bottom. They were attempting to secure the grain when they were attacked, and Gower was killed. Donelson escaped, but his negro, Jack Sivil, was captured and taken to Nick-a-jack.[9]

James Robertson was distressed by the unexpected warfare, but was anxious to avoid open hostilities. "Kill them, yes," he told the harassed pioneers, "but spare the innocent." George Freeland answered, "Yes, if there are any innocent ones hunting around here, notify them with powder and shot that they are too far from home, so far that a good shot will give them a short cut." [10]

New stations were built at Bledsoe's, which was at a salt lick near the place which was later called Castilian Springs; at Asher's, halfway between Bledsoe's and Mansker's; and at the Clover Bottom by John Donelson. Thereafter, outlying stations were built at many locations. It was customary for two or more families to combine their numbers, and to build and occupy a station jointly for better defense.

## 5

The Indians delighted in killing the cows, to the distress of the women; they were so few and so desperately needed. "Killing a cow was next thing to killing husband or child. A mother would shed tears for either." The Indians had an

---

[8] Putnam, 118.

[9] It has been claimed that Nickajack is a corruption of Jack Sivil's name, "Nigger-Jack" (Putnam, 119). Capture of negro slaves, however, was a common matter with the Indians. They captured negroes in preference to killing them, for they were used as slaves by the Indians just as by the whites. It is unlikely that the Chickamaugas would name a principal town for a negro slave who was one of many, and occupied no position of prominence. De Soto found the Koasati Indians on the Tennessee River, who are identified by Swanton as the Kusa, or Creek, people. The Cherokee word, *Ani-Kusati-yi* (Creek People Place), is the probable derivation of Nickajack.

[10] Putnam, 112.

aversion to the "white man's buffaloes." They brought bows and arrows for this purpose, disdaining to waste shot and powder on them. They liked to leave the cows stuck full of arrows in derision. The presence of Indians in the woods was often revealed by the nervousness of the cattle. More than one attack was thus forestalled.[11]

The Indians rarely killed horses, for the capture of horses was next in glory to the securing of scalps. The fact that most of the horses had been stolen by the Indians probably saved the infant settlement from abandonment, because if they had possessed sufficient horses, the settlers would have left the country. Indeed, a majority were in favor of so doing, but Robertson said to them,

"We have no horses, and cannot get wood for boats. The Indians are on the roads to Kentucky and Holston. Providence has so ordered it that we may not get away. Everyone decide for yourselves, and do as you please. As for me, I have come to stay. Some of us would not leave if we could, but most of us could not leave if we would. We shall not find a better country. I believe we can do better here, and be safer, than we are likely to be by flight. We have to fight it out here, or fight our way out of here." [12]

John Rains, a stout pioneer and one of the original "Long Hunters," answered, "We will fight it out here!" A few, however, decided to brave the dangers of the way, and to move to Kentucky. Strange to say, John Donelson, who had brought the women and children over the long river route, was one of them. He with his family, succeeded in reaching Kentucky, where he was a short time later killed by the Indians. His widow later returned to Cumberland with a party of emigrants.[13]

All outlying cabins were deserted. The pioneers gathered in the three stations, and discouraged, but trying to look on the good side, prepared to spend the winter of 1780-1781. There being but little corn, twenty men, the best marksmen in the settlement, were sent to Caney Fork to hunt. They used

---

[11] At the attacks upon Buchanan's and Greenfield Station, the settlers were placed on guard by the nervousness of the cows.

[12] Putnam, 160.

[13] Andrew Jackson later married her daughter, Rachael.

every precaution to avoid being surprised by the Indians, and the hunt was successful; 105 bear, 75 buffalo, and 80 deer," furnished abundant meat to be jerked for winter.[14]

### 6

Robertson realized the need for organized pursuit of Indian marauders, and also for scouts to determine their presence; he, therefore, selected fifteen men to act as "militia," under command of Captain Leiper. The militia soon showed their mettle by pursuing a band of savages who had stolen horses. The trail was followed to Harpeth River; the Indians were surprised, and the horses recovered, to the delight of the settlers, for the loss of a horse was a serious matter.

Captain Leiper felt sure that he had wounded the Indian leader, and joked about it a few days later at his wedding; the first wedding to be solemnized in Nashville. "I shot the imp, and made him limp," said the intrepid captain.

The Leiper wedding was celebrated with much ceremony. The bride was Susan Drake, a great favorite. James Robertson officiated in the absence of a minister. After the ritual, James Gamble tuned up his fiddle, and a square dance was enjoyed.[15]

### 7

As 1780 drew to a close, a new menace faced the settlers. Constant warfare, and the necessity of hunting to sustain life, had depleted the stock of ammunition. Shortage of this would mean ruin. Robertson, with two companions, therefore, made a trip to Kentucky to secure a supply. In three weeks' time, on January 11, 1781, they returned to Cumberland with plenty of powder and ball.

Their arrival was at a most opportune moment; that same day, David Hood was wounded and captured by the Indians as he was going from Freeland's to the Bluffs. Pierced by three balls, and seeing no escape, he feigned death, and his assailant scalped him. The savage took hold of his hair, sawed and tugged, took a fresh hold, tugged again, and at last jerked off

[14] Putnam, 120.
[15] The young couple did not enjoy their happiness long. Capt. Leiper was killed at the Battle of the Bluffs, April 2, 1781.

the scalp. During this process, Hood, with iron nerve, "imitated a 'possum," as he afterward said. After securing the scalp, the Indian gave his victim a disdainful kick, and departed with his trophy.[16] After a while, Hood cautiously peeped from under his arm. The Indians were gone; he rose and started toward the Bluffs, but as he mounted a hill, he saw the entire band, who laughed and jeered at a man who was scalped, yet walked! Hood fled as fast as his weakened condition would permit. Having already secured his scalp, the Indians were content to send a few bullets after him, and he was wounded again. He staggered over a log, and fell into the brush. The firing attracted help from the Bluffs. Hood was thought to be dead when found and was laid in an outhouse to be buried later.[17]

Robertson had gone to Freeland's, where Mrs. Robertson had, that day, given birth to a son; Nashville's first born, who was later known as Dr. Felix Robertson. Robertson was worn out from his trip. He distributed the ammunition; related his experiences, and retired. About midnight, he heard a slight noise at the gate, and instantly gave the alarm, "Indians!"

The Indians had gained entrance to the station, but the settlers were in the cabins, prepared to give a good account of themselves. Hundreds of shots were fired, and when the sound of the swivel gun at the Bluffs announced the approach of help, the Indians retired. The only casualties were Major Lucas and his negro servant, who were sleeping in a cabin which had not been chinked. They were killed as they leaped from their beds. The attackers were later discovered to be Chickasaws.[18]

The day following the attack on Freeland's, Robertson returned to the Bluffs, and was told of the death of David Hood. He went to the outhouse, and to his surprise, found the supposedly dead man to be alive, though very weak and numb with cold. "If I had half a chance," he said to Robertson, "I believe I could get well." Robertson replied, "You shall have a whole chance." Help was summoned, and friendly hands removed the wounded man to more comfortable quarters.

---

[16] The knife of the Indian was dull, being made of flint, the savages sometimes preferring to use these instead of the white man's hunting knife.

[17] Putnam, 153.

[18] Goodpasture. The swivel gun at the Bluffs was the one brought down the Tennessee on the boat Adventure.

Special treatment was necessary for his scalp. Robertson had seen many scalped people recover in the Watauga settlements. Taking an awl, he perforated Hood's wound thickly with small holes. This painful operation permitted granulation to rise and form over the exposed surface. The same operation was later performed on many scalped persons.[19]

David Hood survived this remarkable experience, and lived to a ripe old age. He was a universal favorite, especially with the women and children, for whom he was pleased to perform small tasks. He often joked of his misfortune; "True, I lost my hood," he would say, "but then I hoodwinked the Indians, thanks to the 'possum." In the course of the frequent Indian attacks, he would cheerfully remark, "Well, they can't scalp me at any rate." He was good-natured, and a great wag, and delighted to misquote scripture. Two hunting shirts flapped around his tall and lanky form in winter. With moccasins of deerskin, leather leggins, and coonskin cap, he would say, "We are doubly skinned,—from the skin out we are clothed in skin." When making an affidavit concerning his adventure, he referred to himself as "Said Hood," and was known by that nick-name to the day of his death. His tender sympathy was shown by his kindness to little Mary Dunham, who had been scalped by Indians, and also had lived. Hood was a regular visitor to the little patient. His comical appearance and remarks not only took her thoughts off her misfortune, but caused her to laugh merrily, and the two became fast friends.[20]

## 8

Another general favorite was Thomas Sharpe Spencer, known to the settlers as "Big Foot." Spencer had spent three years in his sycamore tree at Castilian Springs before there was a white settler in Nashville. A friend, John Holiday, had remained with him two years and had then taken his departure. Spencer accompanied him to the Barrens of Kentucky, and when Holiday mentioned that he had no hunting knife, Big Foot broke his own in two and gave half to his friend. It was such traits that caused the pioneers to love him, though they

[19] When Judge Haywood wrote his history, there were more than twenty people living in Nashville who had been scalped.

[20] Putnam, 143.

would have been compelled in any event to respect him for his great size, strength, and fearlessness.[21]

Spencer had two narrow escapes in 1780. He was surprised by Indians while bringing a packtrain over the Kentucky road, and saved his life only by the speed with which he moved his mighty feet. He outdistanced the savages and reached Bledsoe's, but long mourned the loss of his packhorses. A short time later, Spencer and George Espy were fired on while hunting, and Espy was killed. Spencer again outran the Indians and reached the station in safety. One of the pioneers commented on the fact that Spencer had "made tracks" that day. "He always makes tracks," said David Hood, and commented on Spencer's nick-name "Big Foot." [22]

## 9

On April 2, 1781, the Chickamaugas carried out a carefully planned attack on the Bluffs. They were commanded on that occasion by Dragging Canoe in person.

On the night of April 1st, a large body of warriors placed themselves in ambush near the fort, on the trail which ran along Wilson's Branch. Early next morning, two Indians approached the gates and fired as if in reckless bravado, and then fled. Robertson with twenty men mounted hastily, pur-

---

[21] Spencer "greased his meals with a pint of bear's oil, and felt the better for it."

On one occasion, at a general muster, two young men engaged in a fight. Bob Shaw, who considered himself a mighty man, insisted on letting them fight it out, but Spencer differed. Pushing his way through the crowd, he took each of the combatants by the collar, shook them, and commanded them to desist. Shaw took this as a personal insult, and struck Spencer in the face. "Big Foot" caught him by the collar and waistband, and tossed him over a ten rail fence. There is a tradition that Shaw rose, dusted himself off, and said politely, "Mr. Spencer, if you will be kind enough to pitch my horse over, I will be riding." Goodpasture, *Tenn. Historical Magazine,* Vol. 4, 267.

[22] Spencer's fearlessness under fire was shown on a later occasion when he was escorting Mrs. Parker, who had been Mrs. Anthony Bledsoe before her second marriage, over the Kentucky Road, in company with David Shelby, Robert Jones, and William Penny. The Indians ambushed the party near the present Gallatin, Tenn., killed Jones, and wounded Mrs. Parker.

Spencer dismounted and passed his arm through his bridle rein. He then broke off a switch and handed it to Mrs. Parker, telling her to whip her horse until out of danger. Spencer took to a tree and halted the Indians until she was safe, and then mounted and galloped down the trail with bullets singing around him. He escaped without injury.

sued the two Indians, and ran into the ambush. Captain Lieper, Zach White, Peter Gill, Alex. Buchanan, and George Kennedy were killed, and two others were wounded.

The white men dismounted to fight, and to try to save the bodies of their companions. Their horses were stampeded by the infernal din and yells of the savages, and fled toward the fort. In the meantime, another body of warriors who had been lying concealed at the rear of the fort rushed around and placed themselves between Robertson's men and the gates. Fortunately, at that moment the stampeding horses broke through the Indian line. In their desire to capture the animals, some of the savages left a breach in the line through which Robertson and his party passed.

The dogs of the settlers, penned within the fort, were wild to get at the Indians. They had been trained to hunt the savages as they would other wild denizens of the forest.

Mrs. Robertson, seeing the danger that her husband and the other men were facing, instructed the sentry to open the gate and send the dogs to their aid. "They out-noised the Indians, ran like mad, and attacked them fiercely." The unexpected outbreak occupied the savages until Robertson and his men had regained the fort, from the cover of which they instantly opened fire on the attackers.

Edward Swanson had a narrow escape. As he ran for the fort, he was pursued by an Indian. So close was the latter that he punched his gun into Swanson's back, and pulled the trigger; but the force of his thrust knocked the powder from the pan, and the gun was useless. The Indian then clubbed Swanson down, and was about to scalp him, when John Buchanan, seeing the plight of his friend, rushed from the fort to aid him. He emptied his rifle into the chest of the Indian, who gritted his teeth in rage and pain, and took refuge behind a stump. The trace of a heavy body being dragged and a trail of blood were later found leading from the place.[23]

Finding that the white men had regained the fort, the Indians gathered up their killed and wounded, and withdrew. They captured the nineteen horses of the Robertson party.

The service rendered by the dogs at the Bluffs, was typical

___

[23] Description of the fight at the Bluffs is from Putnam, 129-134.

of pioneer times. Putnam, middle Tennessee's historian has paid tribute to "man's best friend."

"The pioneers had great packs of watchful and faithful dogs. The number of dogs exceeded the number of people. The early settlers never complained, however, of the music of the hounds. The dogs were playmates of the children, companions of the men, and guardians of all. Invaluable to the pioneers was the faithful cur and hound."

Abraham Castleman had a dog that was famous. Old "Red Gill" never failed to open on an Indian's trail if leave were given. She would indicate silently to her owner the nearness of an Indian, then, leaving the trail of bear, buffalo, deer, or elk, would pursue the red man. The savages disliked to be trailed by dogs. If they fired at the animals, their own location was betrayed; if the dogs were only wounded, they were the more fierce, and allowed no opportunity for reloading. Then was the time for the pioneer to rush into the fray. Many Indians were killed in such encounters.

The settlers often risked their lives to save those of their dogs. Rains and Castleman had an encounter with a female bear with cubs, which was treed by their dogs. The animal was getting the best of the fight, until the two men took a hand with their hunting knives. They afterward said they would rather combat half a dozen Indians.[24]

## 10

The attack on the Bluffs was the most determined attempt that was made on the settlements. The Indians remained in the vicinity, and kept the three stations in a state of siege. On the night after the attack a number of them congregated west of the station, and opened fire. The settlers loaded the swivel gun with rocks and scrap-iron, and discharged it into the midst of the savages, who abruptly ceased firing and kept quiet

---

[24] Putnam, pages 296, 340. The dogs used by the pioneers were mongrels, probably a mixture of the hound and the bull, or mastiff. They thus obtained the wonderful nose of the hound, plus the fighting qualities of the larger breed. Such mixed breed dogs are used at this time in the swampy regions of Louisiana and Florida for hunting bear.

the rest of the night. For several days, however, it was dangerous to pass from one fort to another. Men went in pairs, and stood back-to-back in order to watch in all directions. When one worked, another watched. Thus, as Putnam says, "hemmed and hindered, hunted and herded, with no safety for anyone outside the forts and little within," it was natural for the settlers to bring pressure to bear on James Robertson to abandon the settlements, and retire to Kentucky.

Robertson acknowledged the difficulties in which they found themselves, but pointed out that the land had been bought and paid for with the blood of their relatives and friends. He also reminded them that the dangers to be encountered on leaving would be greater than those on staying. Gradually, he won most of the settlers to his way of thinking.[25]

II

On November 30th, 1782, the treaty was signed at Paris, by which England acknowledged the independence of the United States. The word had to reach Philadelphia by ship; thence by "horse express" to the frontier outpost of Nashborough; a two weeks' trip. "When we heard this news," said Andrew McEwen, "Robertson and the rest of us felt a foot taller." Men shouted with joy, long rifles were fired; and the happy frontiersmen congratulated themselves that their troubles were over at last. Events, however, were to prove far different.

12

When France entered the Revolution to aid the American colonies, Spain, as the ally of France and hoping to regain Gibraltar, had also declared war on England.

The Spanish Governor of Louisiana west of the Mississippi, Senor Bernard de Galvez, was a young man of unbounded enthusiasm and energy, with an ambition worthy of a Cortez or Pizarro; and when he received word of the Spanish declaration of war, he raised a force of fourteen hundred men, and attacked the British forts at Baton Rouge and Natchez. Both places were captured. Galvez then sailed to attack Mobile, but most of his vessels were lost by shipwreck. Undaunted, he proceeded to Cuba, and, by his energy and fervor, secured

---

[25] Putnam, 160.

other vessels, and continued the war. Mobile and Pensacola were captured. When the Revolution ended, Spain was in full possession of Florida by right of conquest. The treaty of peace between England and the United States awarded Florida to Spain, but did not define the boundaries. The Americans were afterward of the opinion that the oversight was intentional, and meant to involve them in trouble with Spain.[26] Don Esteban Miro was the first Spanish Governor of Florida.

Spain, having been the ally of France, and thus in a sense, the ally of America, it was hoped that her policy would be friendly to the United States. England had supplied arms and ammunition to the Southern Indians throughout the Revolution. With this source of supply shut off, it was believed that the red men must come to terms, for they had no means of obtaining munitions except through a foreign power. Spain, however, was jealous of the navigation of the Mississippi River, and considered the Cumberland settlements a menace on that score.

Miro's first concern was to obtain the co-operation of the southern Indians. In the meantime, he wrote flattering letters to Robertson, and invited the Cumberland settlers to locate within Spanish territory, where they were offered liberal land grants and protection from the Indians.[27]

Many of the settlers were worn out by the continual Indian warfare, and were ready to abandon Cumberland. A few, allured by Miro's promises, removed from Cumberland to Natchez. They were soon dissatisfied with Spanish restrictions, but made themselves useful by keeping Robertson privately advised of Spanish intrigues.

North Carolina had shown but little interest in the protection of the far-removed Cumberland settlements, and this indifference was resented by the frontiersmen. No more loyal American than James Robertson ever lived, but he realized that Spanish friendship must be cultivated if Americans were to enjoy the vital navigation of the Mississippi.

Governor Miro issued a call for all Southern Indians to attend a conference at Pensacola in June, 1783. Chickamauga chiefs, among others, attended. Miro said to the Indians, in open treaty,

---

[26] Whitaker—*Spanish American Frontier.*
[27] Robertson Correspondence, *American Historical Magazine.*

"Do not be afraid of the Americans. You, our brothers the red men, are not without friends. The Americans have no king, and are nothing of themselves. They are like a man that is lost and wandering in the woods. If it had not been for the Spanish and French, the British would have subdued them long ago." [28]

He promised the savages a liberal supply of arms and ammunition, and particularly urged them to "give the Cumberland settlers no rest."

Thus the year 1783, which should have brought peace to the frontier, brought the same harassing conditions as before. The settlers, however, had become used to the uncertainties of frontier life, and were beginning to feel able to take care of themselves. Dr. Felix Robertson afterward said, "So used to violence had they become that the death of one man from natural causes created more comment than the massacre of a dozen by the Indians." [29]

## 13

Every war of consequence leaves a floating population of men released from military duty to whom civil life seems commonplace and dull. Soldiers released from the Revolutionary army were attracted by the excitement of frontier life, and the years beginning with 1783 saw a rush of new settlers to Cumberland. Some, of course, were undesirable, and brought no little trouble to the pioneers, themselves.

It was necessary to know what the Indians were doing. The committee agreed early in 1783 that "six spies shall be kept out to discover the motions of the enemy, so long as we shall be able to pay them, each to receive seventy-five bushels of Indian corn per month." [30] The pay was doubtless well earned, though corn was scarce at the time. The Indians had a special antipathy for spies. When they captured a man serving in that capacity, they not only scalped him, but "chopped" his body.

Robertson cautioned the pioneers not to waste ammunition, which had to be brought over the long and dangerous trail. "Take sure aim. Don't fire unless you can kill. Make sure

---

[28] American State Papers, Indian Affairs, Vol. I.
[29] Moore, Tennessee the Volunteer State, 180.
[30] Putnam, 198.

that every ball brings down an Indian or a buck."[31] His admonition was taken in all seriousness. Nicholas Trammel and Philip Mason were surprised by the Indians as they were skinning a deer they had just shot. Both were wounded, but managed to escape. The thought of the Indians profiting at their expense was too much, so they secured help, returned to the spot, and renewed the fight; both were killed.[32]

## 14

Many of the settlers became so proficient in Indian warfare that they outwitted the redskins at their own game. A favorite Indian trick was "gobbling up" the white man. By the use of a small bone "mocker" (ayeliski) they imitated the call of a turkey with uncanny accuracy. Beale Bosley, hearing a turkey call, stalked the bird; when he arrived in the neighborhood whence the call had come, he was surprised to hear a cautious "Hist!" followed by a low whistle. "No turkey ever whistled," said Bosley to himself, and he prudently took to cover. When he returned to the fort, his belt was decorated with an Indian scalp, reward for his caution.

Jacob Castleman heard the "whoo, whoo," of an owl, which roused his suspicion. He explored and found that the call apparently came from a stump, but he could see no owl. After firing at it, he found the stump to be a living Indian.

Captain Pruett, who had succeeded Leiper in command of the militia, was a new arrival in the settlements. He was a brave man, and considered it cowardly to fight from behind trees. Early in 1783, the Indians stole most of the horses from the Bluffs. Pruett, with twenty men, followed the marauders to Duck River, and recovered the animals. Instead of pushing back to the Bluffs, he camped for the night on Duck River. The savages quietly surrounded the camp, attacked it at daybreak, retook all the horses, and killed five men. This experience converted Pruett to the advantage of fighting the Indians from cover.[33]

## 15

In November, 1783, peace with the Chickasaws brought some measure of relief to the harassed settlements. Fort

---

[31] *Ibid.*, 272.
[32] *Ibid.*, 223-224.
[33] The foregoing incidents are from Putnam, 173 and 274.

Jefferson, built by George Rogers Clark on Chickasaw land, was abandoned. Their chief, Piomingo, announced his readiness for peace, and the treaty was held at Sulphur Springs, Nashville. The Chickasaws ceded a large body of land south of Cumberland River to the settlements, and never afterward disturbed the Americans.[34]

### 16

Governor Miro held another congress of Southern Indians at Pensacola in June, 1784. He told the Indians:

"The King of Spain desires the friendship of all red nations, and looks upon them as his brothers. No other nation except Spain can now supply your wants. In a short time, the Spaniards expect to be at war with the Virginians, and we look upon the Indians as our allies to aid and assist us when called upon."

The brave and outspoken Piomingo delivered a worthy reply:

"I told the governor," he said, "that he and the Americans were both white people alike, and if they had any quarrels, to fight their own battles." [35]

The Creeks, Choctaws, and Chickamaugas, however, eagerly embraced the offer of the Spanish governor. For a short time after the Revolution, the Indians had secured supplies from the British agent at Detroit. Dragging Canoe's brothers, the Little Owl, and the Badger, made several trips to Detroit for that purpose. The road to Detroit was long, inconvenient, and dangerous, whereas, Pensacola could easily be reached through the country of the Creeks. The Chickamaugas returned from the Indian congress loaded with presents, and with a message from Governor Miro: "Drive off the Cumberland settlers, or destroy them utterly." [36]

[34] Vol. 4, *Tenn. Historical Magazine.*
[35] *N. C. Colonial Records,* 17:74-87.
[36] *Ibid.*

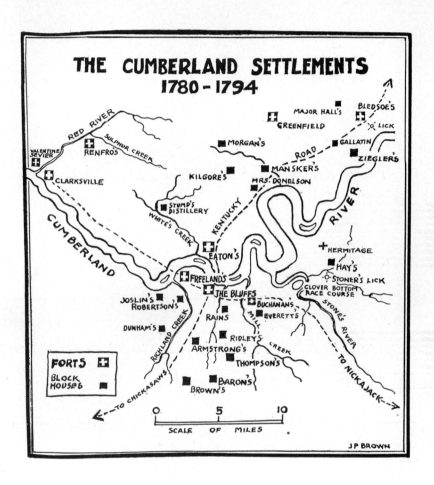

# THE CUMBERLAND SETTLEMENTS
## 1780 - 1794

RED RIVER

SULPHUR CREEK

VALENTINE SEVIER

RENFROS

CLARKSVILLE

MORGAN'S

MAJOR HALL'S

GREENFIELD

BLEDSOE'S

LICK

GALLATIN

ZIEGLERS'

ROAD

KILGORE'S

MANSKER'S

MRS. DONELSON

STUMP'S DISTILLERY

WHITE'S CREEK

KENTUCKY

RIVER

CUMBERLAND

EATON'S

HERMITAGE

HAY'S

STONER'S LICK

FREELANDS

CLOVER BOTTOM RACE COURSE

JOSLIN'S
ROBERTSON'S

THE BLUFFS

BUCHANANS

RAINS

EVERETT'S

DUNHAM'S

RICHLAND CREEK

RIDLEY'S

MILL

CREEK

STONES RIVER

ARMSTRONG'S

THOMPSON'S

TO NICKAJACK

FORTS

BLOCK HOUSES

BARON'S

BROWN'S

TO CHICKASAWS

0     5     10

SCALE   OF   MILES

J P BROWN

# CHAPTER XIII

## THE WILDERNESS ROAD

### I

The gateway to the West was Cumberland Gap, through which ran Boone's Wilderness Road, one of the most historic highways in America. The Gap and road will be forever associated with the name of Daniel Boone, but when Boone discovered this route to Kentucky, he followed a trail that had been used by the Indians for centuries. The red men had in turn followed the buffalo in their annual migration from summer to winter feeding grounds.

It was over this trail that Robertson reached Cumberland. Following him, in the years 1780-1794, more than ten thousand frontiersmen made their way over its rough and rocky course. Boone's Wilderness Road became the main artery of western travel by which the life-blood of America reached the far-flung frontier west of the mountains; and scarcely a mile of its route remained undyed with some portion of that venturesome blood. Every nook, every stream, and every spring has its tale of heroism, whether storied or unsung.[1]

### 2

Dr. Thomas Walker is believed to have been the first white man to pass through Cumberland Gap, the leader in the restless army of borderers who pushed the frontier of America from the Alleghenies to the Pacific. He did not reach the fertile portion of Kentucky discovered later by Boone. He followed the Great War Path of the Indians from Virginia to the present Kingsport, Tennessee; thence by the old Shawnee trail across Clinch River to Kane's Gap; down Powell's Valley to Cumberland Gap,[2] through which he passed into Kentucky.

---

[1] It has seemed important to the writer that the Wilderness Road, which has meant so much to America, should be resurrected in type; that we should tread its stones and ford its streams in the hunting shirt and moccasins of our ancestors. Fortunately, some few of the early travelers kept records which are available; diaries which raise the curtain of the past and enable us to glimpse the grim and picturesque frontier and the character of the men who peopled it.

[2] Walker and the various members of his party, desiring to leave some

225

Walker kept a journal of his trip,[3] which gives little description of the country or of suitable sites for settlement, but is concerned with lost awls, crippled dogs, and snake-bitten horses. Evidencing the high value set by the pioneers on their dogs, an entry reads:

"Our dogs roused a large buck elk. He killed Ambrose Powell's dog in the chase. We named the creek down which we followed him Tumbler's Creek, the dog being of that name. . . . In the evening, our dogs caught a large he-bear, which before we could come up to shoot him had wounded a dog of mine so he could not travel, and we carried him on horse-back until he recovered."

Walker's explorations were made for the Loyal Company of Virginia, of which he was a member and the moving spirit. The company had planned to begin settlement of the western country, but was discouraged by the report of the explorers, and the trip resulted in nothing of a permanent nature aside from bestowing names, which are still in use, on rivers and mountains. Cumberland River and Cumberland Mountains were named in honor of the English Duke who had just defeated Bonnie Prince Charlie at Culloden. Louisa River was named for the Duke's sister. Powell's Valley and River received its name from Ambrose Powell, a member of Walker's party.[4]

About the same time that the Loyal Company sent out Walker and his companions, the Ohio Company employed Christopher Gist, of the Yadkin settlement of North Carolina, to explore and survey the Ohio Valley. Gist made two trips, one in 1750, and another in 1751. It was Gist's description of the country that was ten years later to send Daniel Boone, the real fore-runner of western civilization, into Kentucky. Boone's first trip west of the mountains was probably made in

---

trace of their visit, carved their names on trees. The name of Ambrose Powell, on a beech tree near a river, was discovered twenty years later, and gave the river and valley his name. Walker carved his name on a tree at Cumberland Gap. He visited the gap in company with Isaac Shelby thirty years later, and proudly pointed out the evidence of his former presence.

[3] Walker's Journal may be found in Hulbert, A. B., *Boone's Wilderness Road*. His party consisted of himself, Ambrose Powell, William Tomlinson, Henry Lawless, Colby Chew, and John Hughes. The first entry in the journal is dated March 6, 1750.

[4] See Note 2.

1760. An inscription was found later carved on a beech tree near the present Jonesboro, Tennessee:

"D. Boone CillED A BAR On TrEE in THE YEAR 1760."

Colonel Richard Henderson, after his treaty with the Cherokees in 1775, sent Boone with a party of thirty woodsmen and pioneers to clear a road to Kentucky and to prepare a station for the settlers who were to follow. Henderson followed with supplies in wagons. He was accompanied by his brother Samuel Henderson, and by Thomas Hart and John Luttrell who were his partners in the venture; by William Bailey Smith, a surveyor; by Captain William Cocke; and by a party of thirty settlers.

Henderson's party left the Holston settlements on March 25, 1775, and arrived at Boonesborough on April 20th. A journal was kept of the trip, which, however, contains few details. Nothing is said of difficulties which must have been tremendous, for the wagons were taken as far as Martin's Station in Powell's Valley, and this of itself was without doubt a staggering proposition.

It is from an entry in the journal after Henderson's arrival at Boonesborough, on May 24th, that we get a glimpse of the real soul of the man. On that date, he wrote:

"No Divine Service as yet, our church not being finished."

Having penned the entry, Henderson looked up from his journal and feasted his eyes on the beautiful country to which he had led the settlers. He added:

"About fifty yards from the place where I am writing stands one of the finest Elms that perhaps Nature has ever produced in any region. The tree is placed in a beautiful plain, surrounded by a turf of fine white clover forming a green to its very stock, to which there is scarcely anything to be likened. The trunk is about four feet through to its first branches, about nine feet from the ground. From this above it extends its large branches regularly on every side at such equal distances as to form the most beautiful tree that imagination can suggest. The diameter of its branches is one hundred feet. Every fair day it describes a semi-circle on the heavenly green of upward of four hundred feet. At any time between the hours of 10 and 2 o'clock, a hundred persons may commodiously seat themselves in the shade under its branches.

"This Divine tree is to be our church, state house, council chamber, &c, but we hope by Sunday Sennight to perform Divine service for the first time in public manner, and that to a set of scoundrels who scarcely believe in God or the Devil if we are to judge by most of their looks, words, and actions."

Thus spoke the real Richard Henderson. It was civilization he sought to bring to the wilderness. It must have given him satisfaction on Sunday Sennight, two weeks later, to make the entry:

"Divine services for the first time, by the Reverend John Lyth, Minister of the Gospel, of England."

Do we find it hard to envision the difficult life of the settlers on Watauga, Holston, or Cumberland? Read in Henderson's journal:

"Wednesday, May 17th. The hunters are not returned. No meat but fat bear. Almost starved. Drank a little coffee and trust to luck for dinner. Am going to our little plant patches in hopes that the greens will bear cropping, if so, a sumptuous dinner indeed. Mr. Calloway's men got a little spoiled buffalo and elk, with which we make out pretty well, depending on an amendment tomorrow." [5]

### 3

William Calk, an illiterate member of Henderson's party, has given us a picture of pioneer travel over the Wilderness Road, set down day by day in thoroughly human fashion, with all its pleasures, perils, and hardships. Calk joined Henderson at Martin's Station in Powell's Valley, and continued on to Kentucky. His entire journal is worthy of repetition, for it portrays the experience of the men who traveled the road, whether with Boone, Henderson, or Robertson.

"WILLIAM CALK HIS JOURNAL.

"1775, Mar. 13th, Mond. I set out from Prince Wm. to travel to Caintuck. On Tuesday night our company got together at Mr. Prises on Rapadan, which was Abram Hanks,[6] philip Drake, Eanock

---

[5] Henderson's Journal is reproduced in full in *Boonesborough*, by George W. Ranck, Filson Club Publications.

[6] Abram Hanks was the grandfather of Abraham Lincoln.

Smith, Robert Whitledge & My Self.  Thear Abrams Dogs leg got broke by Drakes Dog.

"Wens. 22nd.  We start Early & git to Foart Chissel whear we git some good loaf bread & good Whiskey.

"Fryd. ye 24th.  We start Early & cross the ridge, the wind blows very hard & cold & lodge at James Loyds.

"Ye 25th.  We start Early & turn out of the Wagon Road to go across the Mountain to Danil Smiths.[7]  We lose the Drive. Come to a turabel mountain that tired us almost to death to git over it & we lodge this night on Lawrel Fork of Holston under a grait mountain & roast a fine fat Turkey for our supper & eat it without any bread.

"Ye 26th.  We start Early.  Travel over some more very bad Mountains that is called Clinche Mountain & we git this night to Danil Smiths on Clinche & thear we staid till Thursd. morning.  On Tuesday night & Wens. morning it snowed very hard & was very coald & we hunted a good deal & thear while we stayed in the rough Mountains we killed 3 Deer & 1 Turkey.  Eanock, ABram & I got lost Tuesday night & it asnowing & should have lain in the Mountains had I not had a Pocket Compas by which I got in a littel in the night & fired guns & they heard & we came in by the report.

"Thursd. 30th.  We set out again and went down to Elk Garden & thear supplid ourselves with Seed Corn & irish Tators.  Then we went on a littel way.  I turned my hors to drive befoar me & he got scard, ran away, threw down the saddel bags & broke 3 of our Powder Goards & ABrams flask.  Burst open a walet of Corn & lost a good deal & made a turabel flustration amongst the reast of the horses.  Drakes mair ran against a sapling & nockt it down.  We cacht them all agin & went on & lodged at John Dunhams.[8]

"Satrd. April 1st.  This morning there is ice at our Camp ½ inch thick.  We start Early & travel this day in a very bad hilly way. Crost one creek whear the horses almost got mired.  Some fell in & all wet their loads.  We cross Clinche River & travel until late in the night & camp on Cove Creek having with us two men that were pilates (pilots-guides).

"Sund. 2nd.  This morning a very Hard Frost.  We start Early & travel over Powells Mountain & camp at the head of Powells Valley whear thear is a very good foard.

---

[7] General Daniel Smith was later a member of the boundary commission which determined the Virginia-North Carolina line; Territorial Secretary under Governor Blount, and United States Senator from Tennessee, succeeding Andrew Jackson.

[8] John Dunham accompanied James Robertson to Cumberland with the first party of settlers, and lost his herd of cattle in the wilderness.

"Mond. 3rd. We start Early & travel down the valley. Cross Powell River & go threw some woods without any track across some bad hills. Git into Hendersons Road, camp on a creek in Powells Valley.

"Tuesd. 4th. Raining. We start about 10 o'clock & git down to Capt. Martins in the Valley where we overtake Colo. Henderson & his company bound for Caintuck & there we camp this night & they were boiling & eating beef without any bread.

"Wensd. ye 5th. Breaks away fair & we go on down the Valley & camp on indian Creek. We had this Creek to cross many times & very bad banks. ABrams saddel turned & the load all fell in. We got out this evening & killed 2 Deer.

"Thursd. 6th. This morning is Hard Frost & we wait at Camp for Colo. Henderson & Co. to come up & they come up about 12 o'clock. We join them & camp there still this night waiting for some part of the company that had lost their horses, ran away with their packs.

"Fryd. ye 7th. This morning a very Hard Snowy morning. We still continue at camp being about forty men and some negroes. This evening comes a letter from Capt. Boon at Caintuck of the indians doing some mischief & some turns back.

"Satrd. ye 8th. We all pack up & started across Cumberland Gap. About 1 o'clock this day we met a great many people turned back for fear of Indians but our company goes on still with good courage.

"Tuesd. 11th. This is a very louery morning & like for rain but we all agree to start Early. We cross Cumberland River[9] & traveled down ten miles through some turabel canebrakes. As we went down ABrams mair ran into the river with her load & swam over. He followed her & got her & made her swim back again. It is a very rainy Evening. We took our camp near Richland Creek. They kill a beef. Mr. Drake Bakes Bread without washing his hands. We keep sentry this night for fear of indians.

"Wensd. 12th. This is a very Rainy morning but we Pack up & go on. We come to Richland Creek. It is high. We toat our packs over & swim our horses & there we meet another company going back & they tell such news ABram & Drake is afraid to go any further. There we camp this night.

"Thursd. 13th. This morning the Weather seems to Brake to Be Fair. ABram & Drake turned back. We go on & git to Loral River whear we are obliged to unload & toat our packs over on a log. This day we met about 20 more turning back. We are obliged to toat our packs over Loral River & swim our horses. One horse

[9] At the present Pineville, Ky.

ran in with his pack & lost it in the river & they got in agin.

"Fryd. 14th. This is a Clear Morning & a smart Frost. We go on & have a very miry road & camp this night on a Creek of Loral River & are surprised at camp by a Wolf.

"Sund. 16th. Cloudy & warm. We start Early & go on about 2 miles down River & then turn up a creek that we crost about 50 times. Some very bad foards with a great deal of good land on it. This Evening we git over to the waters of Caintuck & go a littel down a Creek & there we keep sentry the fore-part of the night. It Rains very Hard all night.

"Tuesd. 25th. In the Evening we git us a plaise at the mouth of the Creek & begin clearing. This day we Begin to live without Bread.

"Wensd. 26th. We Begin Building us a House & Plaise of Defense to keep the indians off.

"Satrd. 29th. We git our house kivered with Bark & move our things in it & begin house-keeping, Eanock Smith, Robert Whitledge & My Self.

"Mond. May ye 1st. I go out to look for my mair & saw 4 Bufelo being the first I ever saw. I shot one of them but did not git him." [10]

The pioneer had survived the dangers of his journey, had established his home, and had shot his first buffalo, an experience for which thousands risked their lives, and many lost their all, without attaining their goal.

It is to be noted that while Calk and his companions "kept sentry," they were not molested by Indians. Not all were so fortunate. He refers to a "letter from Capt. Boon at Caintuck of the indians doing some mischief." The incident is related by Felix Walker, who accompanied Boone on the preliminary trip to clear the road and build the station. The attack occurred on March 25, 1775, within fifteen miles of Boonesborough. Captain Twetty and a negro man were killed, and Walker was desperately wounded and the party was compelled to remain in camp for twelve days before he could be moved. He pays tribute to Daniel Boone:

"He was my father, physician, and friend. He attended me as his child, cured my wounds with the medicines of the woods, nursed me with paternal affection until I recovered, and without expectation of reward."

[10] Hulbert, A. B., *Boone's Wilderness Road.*

Walker was at length carried by horse litter to the Kentucky River at the spot which Boone had chosen for the building of his fort. He describes the arrival at their destination:

"On entering the plain, a number of Buffaloes, three hundred in number, made off from the lick in every direction, some running, some walking, some loping slowly, and the young calves playing, skipping, and bounding through the plain. Such a sight some of us never saw before, and may never see again." [11]

4

Following the Revolutionary War, North Carolina paid many of her soldiers with western land grants. John Lipscomb had served as Ensign in the company of Captain Williams, Sixth North Carolina Regiment, and for his services he was granted land on Cumberland River. He left his home on April 25, 1784, in company with four other soldiers, Captain William Walton,[12] John Gatling, James Cryer, and Henry Salisbury, for the purpose of locating the lands to which they were entitled. Lipscomb kept a journal of the trip, and we thus fortunately have a record covering not only the Kentucky Road, but that part as well which was traversed by Robertson from Kentucky to Cumberland.

Lipscomb was a happy-go-lucky, waggish fellow, who managed to extract considerable fun from the journey, and like most old soldiers, maintained a lively interest in the commissary arrangements. His journal is quoted beginning with his departure from the Holston settlements in East Tennessee.[13]

"11th June. Colo. H. Murfree overtaked us.[14] We sleep in the woods constant.

"12th June. Captn. Budd bought three hens upon the north fork of holson; we got bacon at that place; came to the north fork of holson at Colo. Bledso,[15] then to Mr. Rise; staid all night.

---

[11] Walker's Narrative may be found in *Boonesborough*, by Ranck, or in *Boone's Wilderness Road*, Hulbert.

[12] Captain William Walton later secured the contract to open a short route to Nashville, known as the Walton Road.

[13] Quoted from Williams, *Early Travels in the Tennessee Country*, 272-278. The original journal is owned by the Tennessee Historical Society, Nashville.

[14] Colonel Hardy Murfree, First N. C. Regiment, for whom Murfreesboro, Tennessee, was later named. He was the ancestor of the writer, Mary N. Murfree (Charles Egbert Craddock.)

[15] Former home of Colonel Anthony Bledsoe, who had already moved to Cumberland and established a Station known as Bledsoe's.

"13th June. Left Rise's Sunday morning; came ten miles to a branch near a house; borrowed a pott & cooked the hens which had been flung away by the old Gentln., the stench being very great from the hens, but however we made our brackfast with the hens with a few slices of bacon & half a Bushel of Clabber & Buttermilk; then came to Captn. Thomas Amis 5 miles where we had an exceedingly good dinner with what grog we could hide; staid all night.[16]

"14th June. Staid at Captn. Amis. Got Oates for our horses, whiskey to drink, fared very well. In the Evening killed a Bullock & had half of him. Mr. Salisbury kild the Bullock with great dexterity. Mr. Cloud a brother traveler leaping the fence to attack the Bullock blundered & cut his hand very bad which rendered him almost an invalid, but however there is half a prospect of his recovery.[17] Staid at Captn. Amis all night.

"15th June. Rise early & cut the flesh off the bones of the beef & barbecued it to take with us on the Journey; eat the bones in a stew; got rum & whiskey. Mr. Salisbury & Roberts being the cooks & behaved exceeding well; they got plenty after the company all eating, there was some left.

"16th June. Staid at Captn. Amis fixing for the Journey. Colo. Robertson came up in order to set out for the Journey.[18] Captn. Budd got overalls & Mockersons made & that night was obliged to sleep in them both; he was afraid to pull them off for fear he could no more put them on again; nothing remarkable happened.

"17th June. Left Captn. Amis; came four miles to Mr. Wilson's; staid near three in afternoon, then came off. 8 miles over Clinch Mountain; staid all night.

"18th June. Came 15 miles over Clinch River a remarkable bad mountain & knobbs to Black Creek; halted & rested till the afternoon. No road at all & few creatures have ever been in this country from the appearances; then came over Powells Mountain, remarkable bad way through cane about 8 miles; staid all night.

"19th June. Came on the Journey. Crossed Powell River several times, very bad way. Came along the Creek some distance where the land was exceeding rich, the Buckeye 4 feet through; poplars 9 feet through; cane grew on the mountain side very thick

---

[16] See Chapter XVIII, Section 13, for comment of Bishop Asbury on Captain Thomas Amis.

[17] Lipscomb and his companions played a rude joke on the wounded man, placing his bandaged hand in a bucket of cold water while he slept. Their action "made him very angry, & he told them if they did the like again he would fling his left sledge hammer (fist) at them, which so alarmed them that they did not attempt it."

[18] Colonel James Robertson had served the Cumberland settlements as Representative to the North Carolina General Assembly, and was returning to his home.

but was much kild by the hard winter.[19]  Continued in the woods until we came to a road near Martin's Station where a few people lived.  We came on the road to a large spring; staid all night in Powells Valley; in the day about 24 miles; land very good.[20]

"20th June.  Came on the road, crossed Cumberland Mountain, 4 miles, staid all night.

"21st June.  Came to Cumberland River; crossed the river on our horses; remarkable good land; for seven miles we came through a Cain Brake; 28 miles, staid all night.

"22nd June.  Came on the Journey.  We have uncommon bad luck with our horses.  Lara tired since 19th June but kept him on; Appollo tired today but keeps on.  Salisbury kild a very fine setting turkey hen which we are to have a very good Brackfast on; she will not make very good Broath but it may be made very hott; came 28 miles, staid all night.

"23rd June.  Continued on the Journey; passed the Hazle Patch; got Brackfast; came on over Little Rock Castle eleven times; very stony & knobby for anybody on horses, but worse for mine than anybodys as they are already tired.  In the afternoon Blake Bakers Davie tired but kept him on; came 28 miles, staid all night with a party of men on there way from Kentucky to the settlements.  We have met a number of travelers on the road going to Kentucky, & others going the other way.  We met on the 22nd Inst. a man and woman traveling the road by themselves on their way from Kentucky to Hanover County, Virga; they were badly mounted, but however the road being so long before them they took second thought, & I think very wise thought, & turned back with us; the woman was a very lusty harty widow; our boys behaved very complisantly to this good woman in distress on the road; staid all night within 4 miles of Kentucky River; came 20 miles.

"24th June.  Continued on the Journey.  Came to Mr. Englishes at Kentucky, the first station in that settlement.  We got Brackfast of Bacon, Pease supe, Milk & Clabber which was fed on harty.  I never saw so much slaughter made with the Pease supe, Clabber, &c in my life, as we had short commons for several days before.  Hardy Murfree & Thos. Ward borrowed new horses.  Murfree left Lara at Mr. Englishes while he returns from Cumberland.  Walton, Murfree, Roberts & the boys went to Jno. James,

[19] A graphic description of the "forest primeval."  The section described is in the present Claiborne County, Tennessee, near Tazewell.  Lipscomb and his companions did not follow Boone's route until near Cumberland Gap.  They traveled by way of the Carter's Valley settlements through the present Rogersville.

[20] Martin's Station was a halfway settlement on the Kentucky Road established by Colonel (afterward General) Joseph Martin.

5 miles, staid all night; the rest staid at Mr. Englishes all night.[21]

"25th June. Grafton & the others came to James. We got provisions such as Corn Bacon Cheese. Murfree bought a horse of Jno. James at 25 pounds price; left Appollo at James. John Gatlin swopped horses at James with a man who lived at the station. Left James; came to an old woman's house that was built out of doors;[22] staid all night, it was only 5 miles.

"26th June. Came on the Journey. Passed several stations; the land is all exceedingly rich; came to Captn. Carpenters which is 12 miles from where we took our departure from the inhabitants of the Kentucky River settlements; came 4 miles, staid all night. We left Captn. Budd at Carpenters, his horse being tired.

"27th June. Came on the Journey; it was very rich land; came 35 miles, staid all night.

"28th June. Came on the Journey; crossed Robertson Creek & got Brackfast at a spring; the water was very good; it runs out of a stone cliff & there was a cave large enough for a family to live in; it was as cold inside as out in the month of January. Manly & Toney went ahunting to a lick near that spring where Manly made an attack on a large Buck; gave him a very heavy fire; the Buck attempted to retreat but Manly attacked him with sword in hand & put him to death tho the Buck frequently called out for quarters but all in vain. They brought that fine conquered Buck to camp. We brought him on with us till night. Crossed Green River where we fared sumptuously on the Buck. Staid all night after coming 30 miles.

"29th June. On waking in the morning one of our brother travelers Mr. Boyd had a negroe fellow named May; he frequently called May in the morning on the road; he called May as he usually did; May was very scarce; could not hear his master call; on enquiry found that May had taken his masters wallet & taken the other end of the road. Mr. Boyd with Mr. Casiter another of our brother travelers went in pursuit of May & the provision wallet; we took our departure from them wishing them well & good success in finding May & we came on the Journey to Little Barren river where there was a lick near that place.

"John Gatlin, Salisbury, & Murfree went forward & tied there horses & crept to the lick where we found that there had been a great slaughter made among the Buffelow. We had not been there long until we saw two big Buffelow Bulls coming toward us accompanyed by a wolf. We held a Council of War; it was unanimously agreed that the wolf should live longer & one of the Buffelows we

---

[21] English Station was near the present Stanford, Ky.
[22] "Out of doors"—isolated, not attached to a station.

must put to death without challenging, which was really the case, for they came along together. The wolf ran away; the Buffelow came about three yards of us; we then concluded to bring on the attack. With great spirit & activity we fired at one Buffelow; Salisbury & Murfrees guns fired, Gatlings snapped; the Buffelow much wounded stood still a small space of time while Salisbury was loading his gun & then he and Gatling was to make the second attack; the Buffelow made off.

"Salisbury & Gatling pursued him. Salisbury presently returned & said that he had lost sight of him. Gatling being active in the woods kept in sight of the Buffelow about ½ mile to a branch where the Buffelow laid down & expired. The wounds he received in the valiant attack proved fatal to him; we took parts of his Hump thigh & Tongue which we brought on to the blue spring & eat harty on it. We entered into the barrens of Little Barren River.[23]

"Came on the Journey & in the barrens there was a sink not unlike a punch bowl about 20 yards over at the top & in the bottom there was a hole made on one side, the earth being held up by the rocks; there it was away down that we got good water; suppose the water was 50 feet below the surface of the earth; came on and staid all night in the barrens; came about 34 miles.

"30th June. Proceeded on the Journey; came to the Dripping Spring; got Brackfast.[24] Colo. Robertson & Cloud two brother travelers left us & hurryed on the Journey;[25] we took it at our leisure; came on & crossed Big Barren River. Then as we came down the river Wm. Roberts & Toney went with there guns a little way off from the company where they saw 4 deer drinking in the river, the opposite side. They both prepared for the attack, but Roberts being very expirt in taking sight made the first attack on a two snagged Buck & wounded him very bad so that the Buck could not retreat. Roberts anxiety would not let him wait for

[23] The barrens of Kentucky was a favored place of the Indians for forming ambuscades. They are described by a traveler:
"North and south of Big Barren River lay the notorious Barrens of Kentucky. There were no trees here, and the trail ran through grass that grew three or four feet high. Straggling bushes showed their heads above the grass, matted over quite often with wild grape vines. In March and April there were apt to be grass fires over the Barrens, which were real dangers to travelers on the road." *The Natchez Trace*, R. S. Cottrell, *Tennessee Historical Magazine*, Vol. 2, 27.
[24] It was at the Dripping Spring, near the present Glasgow, Ky., that Captain William Overall was killed by Doublehead and Bench, who then ate his flesh that they might share his bravery. (See Chapter XXIII, Section 2.)
[25] It was typical of James Robertson that he "hurryed on" to reach his home after a long absence.

the Buck to die of the wound he had given him first, but run full drive in the river never stopping for the water & attacked the Buck with much spirit sword in hand & put him to death.

"James Cryer to get to Roberts assistance run to the bank of the river & fell in all over & got to the deer. Toney also got to the deer to assist Roberts, but Roberts put him to death, singing all the time, 'O you little deer, who made your breeches; mammy cut them out & daddy sowed the stitches, daddy sowed the stitches.'

"We fared sumptuously on the little Buck that night; staid all night near the river in the barrens; 23 miles.

"July 1st. On waking in the morning we found two of our fellow travelers Mr. Boyd & Mr. Cassiter who left us two days ago in pursuit of the negroe May encamped near us; they got the negroe; we came on the Journey; saw several deer & turkeys in the barrens.

"July 2nd. Continued on the Journey; eat Brackfast 8 miles at a small creek. Rested came on 8 miles; stayed at the rolling spring a very remarkable one; it runs out of the earth in a sunk & continues on the earth about 30 yards & then runs in a large cave; the cave was about 8 or 10 yards wide & 10 feet high all solid rock; we went in at the place where the water runs about 30 yards & then it was as big as at its mouth; some people say it is 300 or 400 yards tho it was so dark & cold in it we were afraid to go any further.

"July 3rd. Continued on the Journey; 14 miles to the north fork of Red River; continued on 8 miles to Red River Station, staid all night.

"July 4th. Continued on the Journey to Kaspers Station; 10 miles from there to the french lick or Nash Ville, where we continued in the neighborhood till the 6th of August 1784, frequently exploring the country. Out sometimes on the Harpeth where the cain was so thick a man could scarcely ride; sometimes the youngsters reconnoitering the town of Nash Ville setting up at night till 2 o'clock in the morning." [26]

5

Lipscomb's party required twenty days to complete the trip from the Holston settlements to Nashville. Their journey, fortunately, was not interrupted by Indians, although there is

[26] The trip from Holston to Nashville may be made at the present time in a few hours. Such a trip, however, cannot furnish a tenth of the relish and adventure of Lipscomb's twenty day "Journey" through the hunter's paradise that was then Kentucky. One can hardly close his journal, with its tired horses, "Brackfast," and "Buffelows" without saying, "Well done, Lipscomb."

hardly a spot described by Lipscomb that was not the scene of bloodshed at one time or another during the Indian wars.

The Kentucky Road was for several years the only route to the Cumberland settlements. In 1787, Major John Evans at the head of three hundred militia was sent by North Carolina to assist Robertson in the defense of the frontier. Evans made the trip by the Kentucky Road, but his instructions were to open a shorter route. A portion of the militia was assigned to that task, and the work was continued during the succeeding two years. The route followed in the main an old Indian trail which led from Clinch River near the present Kingston, Tenn., through Crossville, Crab Orchard, and Standing Stone (Monterey), and crossed Cumberland River near the present Carthage, thence by Bledsoe's Lick to Nashville.

In 1790, Captain William Walton, one of Lipscomb's party, was given the contract to further shorten and improve the road. He chose a more northerly route with an eastern terminus at the foot of Clinch Mountain, near Knoxville, leading through the present Wartburg, Deer Lodge, Clark Range, and joining the Evans militia road at Standing Stone. Walton himself established a ferry at Carthage. This route became known as the Walton Road, or Caney Fork Road, for the last few miles followed that river. The southern route was called the Cumberland Road. Travel over either road was very dangerous, and emigrants were accompanied usually by an escort of militia. Late in the summer of 1790, General Robertson inserted an advertisement in the State Gazette of North Carolina:

"NOTICE TO EMIGRANTS: The road is now opened from Campbell's Station to Nashville. The guard will be ready to escort parties about the first of October." [27]

Gideon Pillow, a pioneer, stated that one hundred and two people were killed by Indians on the road going to and from Nashville in the year 1792 alone.[28] As late as 1794, the rate for carrying a dispatch from Knoxville to Nashville was fifty dollars. The Kentucky Road, in spite of its additional mileage, remained the safer route for many years.

---

[27] Putnam, 310.
[28] Draper, Mss., 6-XX-15.

# CHAPTER XIV

## THE LOST STATE

### I

The expense of the Revolutionary War had been a serious drain on the original thirteen states. At the end of the long struggle, North Carolina was paying its legislators with corn instead of money.

The suggestion was made by Thomas Jefferson that states which possessed western lands might, by ceding them to the government, cancel their portion of the Revolutionary debt. On April 19th, 1784, William Blount introduced an act in the North Carolina Assembly, which was passed, whereby all the lands of that state lying west of the Alleghanies were ceded to Congress. The cession covered the counties of Washington, Sullivan, Greene, and Davidson, which had been erected from the original Washington County. The act aroused bitter opposition in North Carolina, and was repealed in October of the same year.

### 2

When the news reached Watauga that North Carolina had ceded her western lands to Congress, a convention was called which met at Jonesboro, August 23, 1784. The settlers were rather pleased than otherwise, for the majority of them cared little for North Carolina. The act of cession stated that the western lands were to be erected into states which should become members of the Federal Union. The Jonesboro convention passed resolutions petitioning Congress that the counties of Washington, Sullivan, and Greene be declared a state. It was taken for granted that Davidson County, being so far removed, would be united with Kentucky. An additional convention was called to organize the new state by adopting a constitution and electing officials. It convened on December 14th, adopted the name Franklin, and elected John Sevier as governor.[1]

---

[1] It is said that John Tipton desired the honor, and that, being denied, he opposed the new government.

*Draper Mss.*, 32-S 140-180, James Sevier to L. C. Draper.

The western settlers had no intention of antagonizing North Carolina. When they organized, they had not heard that the act of cession had been repealed. When that news reached them, they were justly indignant that they should be bandied back and forth. Popular sentiment in three counties was overwhelmingly in favor of independence. The Westerners felt that they owed North Carolina nothing. They had repeatedly assembled, at their own expense, to defend the frontier against the savages. When North Carolina was sorely oppressed by the British, they had rallied in large numbers, and had defeated Ferguson at King's Mountain.

An Indian war impended, and the Westerners knew that, as usual, they would have to take care of themselves without the help of North Carolina. So John Sevier and his associates felt impelled to carry on, regardless of the wishes of the parent state.[2]

The upper Cherokees had generally remained peaceful after Sevier's campaigns of 1782. Forty people were killed on the frontier betweeen the months of April and September, 1784, but these outrages were correctly charged to the Chickamaugas, and to Northern Indians who objected to the settlement of Kentucky.

But an incident occurred in the fall of 1784 which threatened to send the warriors of the upper towns into the hostile camp.

The corn crop in the white settlements had been scant, and a number of white men ventured into the Cherokee country to barter for an additional supply. Among them was Major James Hubbard and a companion whose name is not known.

Hubbard's parents, and all his family, had been killed in Virginia by Shawnee Indians. The experience had caused him to become an avowed enemy of the whole Indian race.

During Sevier's campaign of 1782, Hubbard had clashed with the half-breed Indian, Butler or Noonday, of Settico, who had acted, with Watts, as a guide for the white army. In the encounter, Butler had been unhorsed, and probably ridiculed as well, for he afterward nursed a bitter hatred against Hubbard.

Hubbard and his companion unfortunately met Butler as they drove their pack horses along the Indian trail near Settico. At the sight of his enemy, Butler's anger flamed. He rode up

[2] Judge S. C. Williams, *Lost State of Franklin.*

and demanded, "Why have you come into the Cherokee country?" Hubbard replied with self-control, "As the war is over, we have brought some goods we desire to barter for corn," and he opened a sack to show the truth of his remark. He drew forth a bottle of whiskey and invited the two Indians to have a drink.

In order to inspire Butler with greater confidence, Hubbard carelessly leaned his rifle against a tree; the crafty Indian promptly urged his horse between the white man and his rifle. Hubbard knew that to try to resume possession of it would be construed as an act of hostility, but he reached for the muzzle of the weapon as though he were afraid the horse might knock it down. Butler then aimed a blow at the white man which failed to land. Baffled, he cooly surveyed Hubbard, leveled his own rifle, and fired. The ball passed between Hubbard's head and ear with only slight damage, although it stunned him for a moment.

His efforts coming to nought, Butler and his friend tried to get away, but a ball from Hubbard's rifle brought him down, mortally wounded. When the white men approached, Butler said, "Let me alone, I am a dead man." Hubbard, however, raised him to a sitting posture, and placed him against a tree that he might breathe more easily. "Is your Nation for peace?" asked Hubbard. "No, they are for war, and if you go to Settico they will take your hair!" the Indian replied. "If they go to war the white people will whip them," Hubbard said, and the Indian replied, "It is a lie, it is a lie!" He added insulting remarks till Hubbard's hot temper and hatred of Indians caused him to dispatch Butler with a heavy blow of his rifle.

Hubbard's companion had been so absorbed in the quarrel between the two principals, that he permitted the other Indian to escape. Hubbard reproached him for this neglect, for he knew that the Indian would carry the news of Butler's murder to his friends and relatives, who would seek revenge.[3]

### 3

Governor Martin wrote Sevier in December, 1784, offering him the appointment of Brigadier-General of the western counties. "I am informed," he said, "that a daring murder

[3] Ramsey, *Annals of Tennessee,* 301.

has been committed without provocation on one Butler, a Cherokee Indian, by Major Hubbard of Greene County. I have directed that Hubbard be apprehended and conveyed to Burke Gaol for security until the sitting of Washington Superior Court, when he will be remanded back. I have directed Colonel Gist, of Greene County, to call on you for guards if the same be necessary." [4]

Sevier took no action, nor did he reply when Martin wrote again, urging that he accept the Brigadier's commission and asked, "Please inform me respecting the late proclamation to remove all intruders on the Indian lands, and what is done in Hubbard's case." [5]

The governor wrote to Old Tassel: "Our brothers, the white people between you and the mountains wish to have a council of beloved men and government, separate from your older brothers of North Carolina, with whom they have heretofore sat, and held their councils in common.

"Your elder brothers are not yet agreed to their separation from them, till we have held Talks together on the terms of the separation, and the Great Council at New York are agreed. Be not discouraged at this delay. Whatever disputes may be between your elder brothers, I trust it will not concern you, more than you may think the time long, we take in understanding ourselves. I, as your elder brother, request you to be peaceably disposed to all the white people who are our brothers, and not to suffer any mischief to be done to them." [6]

He informed Old Tassel that he would, by nature of the white people's government, become a private brother, but that he would pass the good talks that had been held between them to his successor, Governor Caswell.

Governor Martin's last official act was to issue a manifesto against the State of Franklin. He condemned the revolt of the western counties and the murder of Butler, and threatened the State of Franklin with force of arms should its citizens not return to the fold of North Carolina. [7]

Governor Sevier replied to the manifesto in a letter to Governor Richard Caswell, Martin's successor May 14th, 1785,

[4] *Ibid.,* 305.
[5] *Ibid.,* 306.
[6] *Ibid.,* 307.
[7] *Ibid.,* 309.

in which he defended the action of the western counties. North
Carolina, he stated, had ceded the western lands to Congress
with the express purpose that they be erected into a state. He
called attention to the services the western men had rendered
North Carolina, particularly the King's Mountain campaign.
If the Westerners had overstepped some of the rights of the
Indians, the red men, in turn, had killed forty people on the
frontier since the date of the cession of the lands to Congress.
He explained the murder of Butler:

"Alluding to Major Hubbard's killing a half-breed, we can't
pretend to know what information his Excellency had received on
the subject, or where from. This we know, that the Indian first
struck, and discharged his rifle at Hubbard. As Governor Martin
reprobates this measure in so great a degree, I can't pretend to
say what he might have done, but must believe that had any other
person met with the same insult from one of those bloody savages,
who have so frequently murdered the wives and children of the
people of this country for many years past, I say had they been
possessed of that manly and soldierly spirit that becomes an American, they must have acted as Hubbard did." [8]

### 4

The Governor of Franklin hastened to repair, so far as possible, the bad feeling caused by Hubbard's act. On May 31st,
1785, he entered into "A Treaty of Amity and Friendship begun and held with the Cherokee Indians at Dumplin Creek."
Only a certain faction of the Cherokees attended. Ancoo, of
Chote, was the speaker.

He said:

"It is agreed by us, the warriors, chiefs, and representatives of
the Cherokee Nation, that all the lands on the south side of Holston
and French Broad Rivers to the waters of Tennessee may be
peaceably inhabited and cultivated, resided on, and enjoyed by our
elder brothers, the white people, from this time forward and always. And we do agree on our part and in behalf of our Nation
that the white people shall never be molested or interrupted by
us or any of our Nation, in consequence of their settling or in-
habiting the said territory." [9]

---

[8] *Ibid.*, 315.
[9] Williams, *Lost State of Franklin*, 75-76.

The agreement, be it noted, did not actually cede the lands, but "permitted them to be settled."

Old Tassel, in a Talk to Governor Caswell, complained bitterly of the treaty:

"We are very uneasy on account of a report that is among the white people that call themselves a new state. They say they have treated with us for all the lands upon Little River. I now send this to let my elder brother know how it is. Some of them gathered on French Broad, and sent for us to come and treat with them, but as I was told there was to be a treaty held with us by orders of the great men of the thirteen states, we did not go to meet them, but some of our young men went to see what they wanted.

"They first wanted the land on Little River. Our young men told them that our head men were at home, and they had no authority to treat about lands. They then asked them liberty for those of their nation that were then living on the lands to remain there till the head men were consulted on it, which our young men agreed to. Since then, we are told they claim all the lands on the waters of Little River, and have appointed men among themselves to settle their disputes on our lands, and call it their ground. We hope you, our elder brother, will not agree to it, but will have them moved off. We also beg that you will send letters to the Great Council of America, to let them know how it is, and that if you have no power to move them off, they have, and I hope they will do it." [10]

Indian lands, once ceded, even by a small faction of the Nation, were never returned. Settlers flocked into the new territory, which was organized into the County of Blount, under the authority of the State of Franklin.

### 5

When James Robertson removed to Cumberland, Joseph Martin was appointed to succeed him as agent to the Cherokees for North Carolina. Martin was well fitted for the task. He was of a prominent Virginia family, a neighbor of Governor Patrick Henry, and had served as Virginia agent to the Cherokees while the Watauga settlements had been considered a part of that state. Martin had settled, in 1769, on the extreme western frontier, in Powell's Valley. His station was half-

[10] Ramsay, 319.

way between the Holston settlements and Kentucky. He maintained a blacksmith shop and commissary, and furnished an important service to emigrants to the new country. The station was abandoned at the beginning of the Revolutionary War, but Martin reestablished it in 1783.

Soon after he had assumed his duties as Indian Agent, Martin took an Indian wife, Betsy Ward, daughter of the Beloved Woman. The alliance was bitterly criticized by members of his family, but he defended his action as giving him great prestige among the Cherokees, and as necessary to his own safety.[11] Through his Indian wife, Martin was allied with the most influential of the Cherokee chiefs, for Nancy Ward was niece to the Little Carpenter, whose memory was revered by all Cherokees.

Joseph Martin was a man of tact, as well as of courage. He performed a real service to the American cause, often at the risk of his own reputation, by retaining the friendship of the upper Cherokees. In the controversy between Franklin and North Carolina, Martin's sympathies were with the mother state, and he did not hesitate to protest emphatically when the men of Franklin encroached upon Cherokee rights.[12]

6

Dragging Canoe and his band of Chickamaugas were gaining prestige. On January 11th, 1784, Joseph Martin wrote: "There is to be a great treaty at Chicamoggy in the spring, of all the western tribes."

At that time, there were two Shawnee chiefs at Running Water, with a great quantity of trinkets such as gorgets, arm bands, and brooches, who were supposed to be on their way to the Creeks to purchase slaves. Martin remarked: "These Shawnees have brought the war hatchet, tho' it is kept very private." [13]

[11] *Draper Mss.*, 300-XX-4, William Martin to L. C. Draper.

[12] The sincerity of Martin's friendship for the Indians won their confidence, and roused the jealousy of Alexander Cameron, who sent a warrior to assassinate the American Agent. Martin's Indian friends warned him of his danger, and when the would-be-assassin approached, Martin confronted him, fully armed, and sternly looked him in the eye for a few moments, without saying a word. The warrior's eye dropped. He returned to Cameron with this message: "If you want Martin killed, you can kill him yourself. He looks dreadful to me!"

[13] *N. C. Colonial Records*, 16: 924.

The northern Indians brought to the Cherokees the talk given them by the British at Niagara, at the end of the Revolution:

"Brothers: We are glad to see so many of our friends, the red people. We shall let you know everything that is passing amongst us. We have the war hatchet still in our hands, but are going to lay it down, and we want our brothers who fought with us in this war to lay it down with us. We do not expect that it will lie still very long, as we expect the Long Knife will be settling your country soon. If so, we advise you to strike, but not before. We will then assist you, and you shall want for nothing. In the meantime, visit all our brothers, the red men, and make everthing straight and strong." [14]

### 7

Chief Bloody Fellow, from his town of Tuskegee, defied the new State of Franklin:

"White men from Nolichucky are planting crops on lands over French Broad River. As soon as the leaves grow a little, if your government does not make them move off, I will come with a party and kill every man, woman, and child that shall be found over the river."

The chief made this statement to a party of white traders who had visited his town. He told them that he supposed they were looking for land, as most white men were, but as it was peace time, he would not concern himself with them. During the night, however, he brooded over the matter and decided that he might as well take the scalps of the white men then and there. But the men had made friends with some of the Indian women, who warned them of the imminent danger. The traders fled, leaving their guns, blankets, and ammunition. In their haste, they did not stop to saddle their horses. Disgusted at their escape, Bloody Fellow broke their guns, and burned the saddles and blankets. [15]

### 8

John McDonald and Alexander Cameron continued to reside at Running Water after the Revolution. They exercised great

---

[14] The Indians frequently referred to the Americans as "Long Knives" from their habit of wearing swords; collectively, "The Long Knife."

[15] N. C. Colonial Records, 16: 924.

influence over the Indians, and to a certain extent continued to supply them with goods which they obtained through devious channels. All the southern Indians preferred English-made merchandise. The Creek chief, McGilivray, was a member of the English trading house, Panton-Leslie & Company, and would have none of Spanish goods.

Joseph Martin wrote to Governor Martin early in 1784:

"McDonald and several others are now living at Running Water, within twenty miles of Chicamoggy. A certain Alexander Cameron is living with him, and is supplied with goods and ammunition from some merchant at Savannah or Augusta. McDonald's character is so well known that I need not say anything about it. Cameron in the course of the war has been a murderer and robber, and frequently went out with the Indians, murdering women and children. Several horse-loads of goods went to them while I was in the towns. Would it not be well for your Excellency to make known to the Governor of Georgia that no peace can be lasting while such villians among the Indians are supplied?" [16]

Martin felt, however, that if he could win the former British Agents over to the American side, peace with the Indians would be assured. He, therefore, wrote Governor Caswell:

"I have with much pains and some artifice prevailed on Mr. McDonald, the former British Agent, to correspond with me. In case of a war with any foreign power, he may be very serviceable, or very dangerous. He lives about 25 miles southwest of Chickamoggy, in what is the strongest part of the Cherokee Nation. He has great influence with the Indians, deals at Pensacola, and corresponds with Mr. Gilivray and a Mr. McClatchey at the mouth of St. Mary's, a British merchant who furnishes some part of the towns near him with goods." [17]

McDonald wrote to Martin: "Believe me, sir, I shall never turn Spaniard." However, a few years later, he accepted a commission from Governor Carondelet as "Spanish Agent to the Chickamaugas." [18]

[16] *Ibid.*, 17: 11, Cameron is referred to in some of the correspondence as Campbell.
[17] *Ibid.*, 17: 519.
[18] *Ibid.* See also Whitaker, *Spanish-American Frontier.*

9

President Washington, having gone through the grueling years of the American Revolution, was determined to have peace. He felt that a policy of fairness toward the Indians would bring this about. Benjamin Hawkins, Joseph Martin, Andrew Pickens, and Lachlan McIntosh were appointed members of a commission to take up the grievances of the southern Indians, and see if a lasting peace could not be made.

On November 18th, 1785, the commissioners met with the Cherokees at Hopewell, S. C., on Keowee River.[19] William Blount attended as commissioner for North Carolina, and John King and Thomas Glasscock as commissioner for Georgia.

Only the upper Cherokees attended the treaty. They were a brow-beaten, harassed people, and welcomed the President's wish to do them justice. Old Tassel was principal speaker for the Indians. The commissioners explained to the Cherokees that the United States had won her fight with Great Britain, and now wished to take the Indian Nations under her protection. They presented Old Tassel with a map, and asked him to mark thereon the boundary claimed by the Cherokees. They told him:

"Congress is now sovereign of all our country, which we point out for you on the map. They want none of your lands, or anything else which belongs to you. As an earnest of their regard for you, we propose to enter into a treaty perfectly equal and conformable to what we now tell you. If you have any grievances, we will hear them, and will take such measures to correct them as may be proper. We expect you to speak your minds freely, and look upon us as representatives of your father and friend, the President, who will see justice done you."

Old Tassel replied:

"The land we are now on is the land we were fighting for in the late war. The Great Man above made it for us to subsist upon. The red men are the aborigines on this country. It is but a few years since the white men found it. I am of the first stock, a native of this land. The white people are now living upon it as our friends. From the beginning of the friendship between

---

[19] A detailed Journal of the proceedings at the Treaty of Hopewell is given in *American State Papers, Indian Affairs,* Vol. 1, page 5.

white people and red, beads have been given as confirmation of friendship, as I now give you these beads." (Here he handed to the commissioners a string of white beads.)

The Tassel then explained the encroachments of white men on Indian lands in defiance of solemnly made treaties:

"The people of North Carolina have taken our lands without consideration, and are now making their fortunes out of them. I know Richard Henderson says he purchased the lands at Kentucky, and as far as Cumberland, but he is a rogue and a liar, and if he was here I would tell him so. He requested us to sell him a little land on Kentucky River for his horses and cattle to feed on, and we consented; but told him at the same time he would be much exposed to the depredations of the Northern Indians, which he appeared not to regard, provided we gave our consent. If Attakullakulla signed his deed, we were not informed of it; but we know that Oconostota did not, yet we hear his name is to it. Henderson put it there, and he is a rogue."

Taking the map which the commissioners had given him, Old Tassel marked the boundaries claimed by the Cherokees. He designated Henderson's purchase by a small circle only. The commissioners replied:

"You know, Old Tassel, that Colonel Henderson, Oconostota, and the Little Carpenter are all dead. What you say may be true, but here is one of Henderson's deeds. Your memory may fail you, but this is of record, and will remain forever. The parties being dead, and so much time having elapsed, and the country being settled upon the faith of the deed, puts it out of our power to do anything respecting it; you must, therefore, be content with it, as if you had actually sold the land, and point out your claims exclusive of this land."

The Tassel replied:

"I know they are dead, and I am sorry for it, and I suppose it is now too late to recover it. If Henderson were living, I should have the pleasure of telling him that he was a liar. We will begin at Cumberland, and say nothing more about Kentucky, although it is justly ours." He then marked the boundaries on the map with which he said the Cherokees would be satisfied.

"In the forks of French Broad and Holston," Old Tassel continued, "are three thousand white people on our lands. That is a favored spot, and we cannot give it up. It is within twenty-five miles of our towns. These people must be removed."

"They are too numerous, and cannot be removed," replied the commissioners. "They settled there when the Cherokees were under the protection of the King of England. You should have asked the King to remove them."

"Is not Congress, which conquered the King of England, strong enough to remove these people?" asked the chief.

The Tassel maintained that the Cherokees could not surrender the land in question, but agreed to leave the matter to the action of Congress. The lines finally agreed upon ran from Cumberland River forty miles above Nashville, to a point six miles south of Nolichucky, thence southward to Oconee River. Long Island of Holston was reserved by the Indians for a treaty ground.[20]

The chiefs and commissioners departed from Hopewell with thoughts of a lasting peace. The treaty, however, pleased no one.

North Carolina protested that her rights were violated, for lands had been granted to her revolutionary soldiers which were guaranteed to the Indians by the treaty. Settlers upon the Cumberland complained that lands were given back to the Cherokees which had been bought with American blood.

The treaty disregarded the boundaries of the new State of Franklin. As Old Tassel had pointed out, three thousand Americans had located in the fork of French Broad and Holston Rivers. This included the Dumplin settlements. More than five hundred families had settled south of French Broad, along the line of Boyd's Creek, and the Cherokees, by the Treaty of Dumplin, had agreed to the settlements. All of this

---

[20] Before signing the treaty, Old Tassel requested permission for the War Woman of Chote, the famous Nancy Ward, to talk to the commissioners. She said,

"I am glad there is now a peace. I take you by the hand in real friendship. I look upon you and the red people as my children. I have a pipe and a little tobacco to give to the commissioners to smoke in friendship. I have seen much trouble in the late war. I have borne and raised up warriors. I am now old, but hope yet to bear children who will grow up and people our Nation, as we are now under the protection of Congress and shall have no more disturbance. The talk that I give you is from the young warriors, as well as from myself. They rejoice that we have peace, and hope that the chain of friendship will never be broken."

territory, containing a white population of five thousand, including the town of Greeneville, which had just been selected as the Capitol of Franklin, was returned to the Cherokees by the terms of the treaty.

The document also contained a clause: "Any settler who fails to remove within six months from the lands guaranteed to the Indians shall forfeit the protection of the United States, and the Cherokees may punish him or not as they please." The commissioners must have known that it would be impossible to remove five thousand settlers from their homes. The clause was an invitation to the Cherokees to commence hostilities at their pleasure. The State of Franklin openly disregarded the treaty, and when the following spring brought Indian atrocities, the Franklinites were justified in the belief that the Cherokees were but taking advantage of the foregoing provision.[21]

### 10

John Sevier had a vision of his State of Franklin spreading over all of what is now East Tennessee. In 1785, he entered into an arrangement with the State of Georgia for the colonization of the Great Bend of Tennessee River. The Georgia assembly passed an act creating Houston County, to be located in the Bend, and Sevier was appointed one of its commissioners.

His brother, Valentine Sevier, at the head of ninety settlers, descended Tennessee River in boats, and landed late in 1785 near the present South Pittsburg where it was intended to build a blockhouse and stockade as a nucleus for the proposed settlement. Military officers and justices of the peace were elected, and land warrants were issued signed by John Donelson, Surveyor.[22]

The settlers found it impossible to accomplish anything at all, for Dragging Canoe and his warriors promptly placed them in a state of siege. After a few weeks of incessant fighting, the site was abandoned early in 1786.

### 11

Failure of the attempted settlement caused rejoicing in the

---

[21] Williams, *Lost State of Franklin*, 97.

[22] Donelson had probably noted the place as suitable for settlement on his voyage down the river in 1781. See Ramsay, 377-379, and Williams, *Lost State of Franklin*, 13-188, for attempted settlement of the Great Bend.

Five Lower Towns. Jubilant warriors followed almost at the heels of the retiring white men in a series of savage raids that were to involve the Cherokees in warfare with the State of Franklin. Colonel John Donelson, who had acted as surveyor for Houston County, was killed on the Kentucky Road. Colonel William Christian was killed a short distance north of the Ohio, and the murder was attributed to the Cherokees. An old Indian who had lost two sons in the fighting with Valentine Sevier's men hired warriors from the upper town of Coyatee to secure him two white scalps in place of those of his sons. The strange commission was executed, and the scalps were secured at the home of Ebenezer Birum in the present Greene County, Tennessee.[23] Archie Scott and four children were killed in Powell's Valley, and Mrs. Scott was taken prisoner.[24] A series of atrocities and horse stealing by warriors from Crowtown[25] near Logan's Fort sent the fiery Colonel John Logan into action. He hastily raised a force and followed the trail of the offenders across Cumberland River and down the Indian path which ran along the base of Walden's Ridge.

12

Logan was met by a party of Franklin militia who were ranging the woods under command of Lieutenant McClellan.[26] The two forces joined, and shortly afterward encountered a band of Cherokees who claimed to be from the upper towns, and friendly. They were headed, however, by a brother of Bloody Fellow, and included in their number relatives of the Fool Warrior. Both of these chiefs were known to be hostile. Logan had little doubt that he had found the warriors who had committed the murders near his fort, which may indeed have

---

[23] Ramsay, 344.

[24] The experience of Mrs. Archie Scott became a border legend. She escaped from her captors on the ninth day after she was taken, and wandered for thirty days through the wilds of Cumberland Mountains, subsisting upon roots, berries, and a fish which she caught by hand. She finally reached the Kentucky Road at Martin's Station, about forty miles from her former home. Her family having been wiped out, she soon remarried and raised another. See Collins, *Historical Sketches of Kentucky*, 550, for details of her captivity and escape.

[25] Crowtown was one of the Five Lower Towns, near the present Stevenson, Ala. It was customary after a massacre or victory for the exultant warriors to shout the name of their town, and it was by this means that Logan learned from whence the marauders came.

[26] McClellan was a son-in-law of John Sevier.

been true.  He shot the leader of the Indians, and in the ensuing
melee six of their number were killed, including a brother of
the Fool Warrior.  The survivors escaped, and Logan returned
to Kentucky.[27]

Joseph Martin, Indian Agent, on hearing of Logan's act,
sent a runner to Bloody Fellow with a request that he and the
Fool Warrior should not take revenge until they had first demanded satisfaction for the injury done.  The chief retorted:

"Demanding satisfaction from the white men has been tried,
and has produced little results; I will take my own satisfaction
for my brother."[28]

The Fool Warrior stated:

"There are white traders in the Nation.  I will kill every one
of them in revenge."[29]

The two chiefs promptly led a band of warriors toward the
Dumplin settlements.  As they neared Tellico, a friendly Indian galloped ahead and warned two white traders, Jackson
and Cade, to flee for their lives.  The war party arrived a few
minutes later.  The Fool Warrior shot the horse of the messenger, and was enraged at the escape of the white men, but
consoled himself by taking their goods.[30]

Fifteen scalps were taken by the Indians in the Dumplin
settlements.  Houses were pillaged and burned, cattle were
killed, and horses stolen.  By the body of one of the victims,
Bloody Fellow left a note addressed to John Sevier, Governor
of Franklin:

"I have now taken satisfaction for my brother and friends who
were murdered.  I did not wish for war, but if the white people
want war, that is what they will get."[31]

The challenge was promptly accepted by Governor Sevier.

---

[27] *Calendar of Virginia State Papers,* IV, 254-256.
[28] *N. C. State Records,* 18: 604.
[29] *Calendar of Virginia State Papers,* IV, 261.
[30] *Ibid.*
[31] *N. C. State Records,* Martin to Caswell, May 11, 1786.

13

Following the Treaty of Dumplin Creek, and regardless of the fact that the treaty was disapproved by the leading Cherokee chiefs, there was an inrush of white settlers south of French Broad River. Joseph Martin wrote to Governor Randolph of Virginia on Mar. 25, 1785:

"At my arrival, I found the Indians in greater confusion than I ever saw them. . . . The Franklinites have opened a land office for all the lands between French Broad and the Tennessee, which lands the legislature reserved to the Indians. It included part of their beloved town of Chote, and several of their corn fields.

"I waited on some of their leaders with a proclamation from Governor Caswell ordering them off the said lands. Their reply was that they had knowledge enough to judge for themselves, and they should not ask North Carolina or any other power how they were to be governed." [32]

The Old Tassel told Colonel Martin:

"We have held several treaties with the Americans when bounds were fixed, and fair promises made that the white people would not come over, but we always find that after a treaty they settle much faster than before. Truth is, if we had no land we should have fewer enemies." [33]

Early in August, 1786, Governor Sevier called out the Franklin militia for a campaign against the Cherokees. Sevier, being occupied with the duties of the Governorship, did not accompany the expedition, which was under the command of Brigadier General William Cocke [34] and Colonel Alexander Outlaw.

---

[32] *Calendar of Virginia State Papers,* IV, 261.

[33] *Ibid.,* 306.

[34] The organization of the Franklin militia has been one of Governor Sevier's first tasks. William Cocke was made Brigadier General. A colonel was appointed for each of the five counties composing the state. They were: Daniel Kennedy, Charles Robertson, George Maxwell, Gilbert Christian, and Alexander Outlaw. Lieutenant Colonels were: John Anderson, James Roddy, George Doherty, and Valentine Sevier. Nathaniel Evans, John McNabb, James Houston, Alexander Kelly, Landon Carter, Jacob Brown, and James Hubbard acted as Majors. It is probable that only two counties were called out in 1786, for only William Cocke and Alexander Outlaw are mentioned.

The white army, which numbered two hundred and fifty men, reached Chote on Aug. 31st. Chiefs Old Tassel and Hanging Maw protested the peaceful intentions of the upper Cherokee towns. Cocke and Outlaw readily excused them of the murders committed by Bloody Fellow's band, but charged them with the deaths of Christian and Donelson, and with the two people killed at Birum's house, located in the State of Franklin.

Old Tassel replied:

"BROTHERS: Now I am going to speak to you. We have smoked. The Great Man above sent the tobacco. It will make our hearts straight. I see you. You are my brothers. I am glad to see my brothers, and to hold them fast by the hand. The Great Man made us both, and he hears this talk.

"They are not my people that spilled the blood and spoiled the good talks. My town is not so; they will use you well whenever they see you. The men that did the murders are bad and no warriors. They live at Coyatee, at the mouth of Holston River. They have done the murders.

"My brother, Colonel Christian, was a good man and took care of everybody. He is dead and gone. It was not me or my people who killed him. They have told lies on us. I loved Colonel Christian, and he loved me. He was killed going the other way, over the river." [35]

On receipt of this information from Old Tassel, Cocke and Outlaw marched their force to Coyatee, and "luckily killed two of the very Indians that did the murder." They then returned to Chote and resumed their talks with Old Tassel and Hanging Maw.

They told the chiefs:

"The new state has bought all the Indian lands north of Little Tennessee River, and intends to settle upon it, and if any Cherokee interferes, his town will be burned."

The Tassel replied:

"I have never heard of your Great Council giving you the land you speak of. I talked last fall with your great men in Congress,

---

[35] N. C. State Records; See also Ramsey, 345. "Over the river" indicated north of the Ohio.

but they told me nothing of this. They told us nothing about the land, but now that you have spoken the truth, we hope we shall live together is friends upon it, and keep our young men at peace. I am sorry my people have done wrong to cause you to turn your backs. We will sign the terms, and agree to live together as brothers hereafter. A little talk is as good as much. Too much is not good." [36]

## 14

Such was the so-called Treaty of Coyatee. "No act of the State of Franklin is less creditable." [37] By force and without recompense, the Cherokees were obliged to surrender the rich lands between French Broad and the Little Tennessee.

A year later, with the tide of white settlement overwhelming even beloved Chote, Old Tassel was still appealing to the governors of Virginia and North Carolina for justice:

"BROTHERS: I am going to speak to you, and I hope you will hear me and take pity on me, as we were both made by the same Great Being above."

Colonel Thomas Hutchins, writing Governor Caswell early in 1787, said:

"The Franklinites have opened a land office for the sale of land south of French Broad to the banks of Little Tennessee River. The land is to be sold at 40 shillings per hundred acres; 10 shillings in hand, and two years credit on the other 30." [38]

Joseph Martin protested against the violation of Cherokee rights. His protests were met with scorn by the Franklinites, for Martin was one of the commissioners who had signed the Treaty of Hopewell, by which lands already ceded to the white people were given back to the Indians. Judge David Campbell, ardent Franklinite, wrote to Governor Caswell:

"Has not all America extended its back settlements in opposition to laws and proclamations?" [39]

---

[36] Ramsay, 345.

[37] Williams, *Lost State of Franklin*, 99. The treaty was signed on behalf of Franklin by William Cocke, Alexander Outlaw, Samuel Wear, Henry Conway, and Thomas Ingles; and for the Cherokees by Chiefs Old Tassel and Hanging Maw. (Ramsay, 346.)

[38] *N. C. State Records,* 20: 656.

[39] *N. C. State Records,* Campbell to Caswell, Nov. 30, 1786.

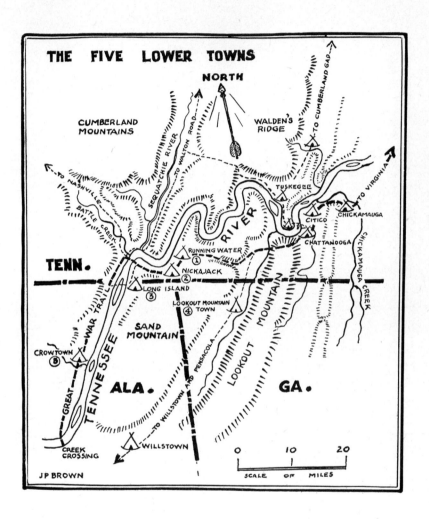

THE FIVE LOWER TOWNS

NORTH

CUMBERLAND MOUNTAINS

WALDEN'S RIDGE

TO CUMBERLAND GAP →

SEQUATCHIE RIVER

TO WALTON ROAD

TO VIRGINIA →

← TO NASHVILLE

TUSKEGEE

CHICKAMAUGA

BATTLE CREEK

CITICO

RIVER

CHATTANOOGA

RUNNING WATER
①

TENN.

NICKAJACK
②

CHICKAMAUGA CREEK

LONG ISLAND
③

WAR TRAIL

LOOKOUT MOUNTAIN TOWN
④

TENNESSEE

SAND MOUNTAIN

LOOKOUT MOUNTAIN

TO WILLSTOWN AND PENSACOLA

CROWTOWN
⑤

GREAT

ALA.

GA.

CREEK CROSSING

WILLSTOWN

0        10        20

SCALE    OF    MILES

J P BROWN

# BOOK THREE
## John Watts

# CHAPTER XV

## GROWING PAINS

### I

The close of the Revolution found the little settlement on Cumberland firmly established, but harassed by three tribes of Indians, Creeks, Chickasaws, and Cherokees.

The years immediately following were to bring war between the State of Franklin and the Cherokees; the collapse of Franklin, and the arrest of Sevier.

Old Tassel, principal chief, was to fall under a flag of truce; and the Chickamaugas were to reach high tide with the defeat of Martin's army at Lookout Mountain.

North Carolina, weary of rebellious westerners, was to drop them in the lap of Congress; and the Territory South of the River Ohio, with William Blount as Governor, was to be organized.

The coming of Governor Blount was to institute a period of diplomacy ending in more war. St. Clair's defeat was to fire hope in every wigwam of an effective Indian confederation; and the hope was to be blasted by the deaths of Dragging Canoe and McGilivray, great Indian leaders in the South.

John Watts, fighting his followers "in armies as the white men fought" was to end his spectacular career as war chief when James Robertson's hard riding followers burned Nickajack and Running Water. Spanish assistance crumbled under pressure of Revolutionary France. Mad Anthony Wayne placed a period after Indian hopes in the North; and the end of Book Three will find the fighting Chickamaugas turning to the White Path of peace.

### 2

In 1783, the General Assembly of North Carolina erected the Cumberland settlements into the County of Davidson, and changed the name Nashboro to Nashville. A log courthouse, eighteen feet square, was authorized and built. In 1786, the first merchant hung out his sign:

"LANDER CLARK, Merchant and Ordinary,
Keeper and Dealer in Dry Goods, Thimbles
and Pins for Ladies, Liquors for Men, and
Provender for Horses." [1]

Two hundred and ten militia were enlisted, each man to
furnish himself with a horse, a good rifle or smooth bore gun,
shot bag, powder horn, one pound powder, and two pounds
lead.  The annual pay was to be a good blanket, a wool or fur
hat, a pair of buckskin breeches, and a waistcoat,—plus satisfaction of serving one's country in time of desperate need.

While a member of the North Carolina Assembly in 1786,
Robertson secured the passage of an act authorizing three hundred additional militia, to be furnished by North Carolina but
to be paid out of taxes from Davidson County.  They were
ordered out in the spring 1787, under Major Thomas Evans.
He was instructed to locate and open a shorter route to Nashville; to use his militia for the purpose, making the road ten
feet wide and "fit for the passage of wagons and carts." [2]

Major Evans recruited his battalion in February, 1787, and
should have reached the Cumberland shortly thereafter, but a
series of exasperating delays ensued.  In August, Governor
Caswell was surprised to receive letters from him dated at
Richmond, which was certainly not on the route to Nashville.

The governor charged that Evans had been engaged in "making an attack on a young lady with matrimonial intent, whom
he has lately reduced into possession by making her his wife." [3]

Meanwhile, the Cumberland settlements were harassed by the
Indians, and Robertson wrote anxiously inquiring about Evans.
"I suppose he is engaged in cutting out the road that was
authorized, but we need the militia far more than the road."
Evans, however, had written Governor Caswell that he had no
funds with which to equip his men.  While the resolution in
the Assembly provided that the men were to be paid out of
taxes collected from the section they were to serve, no such
funds were available. [4]

---

[1] Putnam.
[2] Haywood, 229.
[3] *N. C. State Records*, 20: 758.
[4] Williams, *Lost State of Franklin*, 165-168. When Evans finally arrived
at Nashville on October 16th, his men were half clad and penniless.  They
performed valiant service on the border, and received in payment, the re-

3

Throughout the summer of 1786, the Cherokees continued unremitting hostilities. Robertson's militia, under Captains Rains, Castleman, and Gordon, constantly patrolled the border, but the stations were separated by forests and canebrakes, and Indian war-parties found it easy to avoid their vigilance.

John and Ephraim Peyton, with four others, were surveying a plot of ground north of Cumberland River on what was later called Defeated Creek, when Hanging Maw,[5] a supposedly friendly Cherokee chief, quietly surrounded the camp with a band of warriors. The white men noticed the excitement of the dogs, but attributed the cause to wild animals. Four were wounded at the first Indian fire. John Peyton had the wit to throw a blanket over the campfire, and they all managed to escape in the ensuing darkness; they reached Bledsoe's Station.

Peyton knew Hanging Maw. When he learned it was that chief who had attacked him, he sent word that the Indians were welcome to the plunder and horses which they had taken, but requested that his compass and chain be returned, as the red men could not use it. Hanging Maw replied, "You, John Peyton, ran like a coward and left all your property, which I took. As for your land-stealer (compass), I broke it against a tree."[6]

Rumors of an Indian confederacy, backed by Spanish money and ammunition, were constantly heard in Nashville. The Creeks were active. They wanted the Cherokees, upper and lower, to join them in a great campaign to break up the Cumberland settlements in the summer of 1787. "We want horses," they said, "and Nashville is the place to get them. Let us show the white men that we can fight in armies as well as they."[7]

ward mentioned by one of the pioneers, "A good conscience." A petition to the first legislature of the territory South of the River Ohio, in 1794, for payment of Evans' militia, was rejected on the ground that the debt was that of North Carolina and not of the new territory.

[5] Putnam. (Gov. Wm. Blount was to write a few years later, "If there is a friendly Indian in the Nation, it is Hanging Maw.") Hanging Maw's raid was in retaliation for that on his town by Cocke and Outlaw of the State of Franklin, for the inexorable Indian law required a scalp for a scalp.

[6] *Ibid.*, 245. No attempt is made in this volume to record every killing or massacre that occurred on the frontier. There were hundreds, and the circumstances of one are substantially those of all. A few which illustrate the character of Indian warfare and the spirit of the borderers are given.

[7] Putnam, 277.

4

Early in 1787, Robertson reached the decision to make a
demonstration against the Chickamaugas.  He raised a substantial body of volunteers and marched to the vicinity of the
Chickamauga towns.  But desiring not to bring on a general
Indian war, he left a message urging them to send a delegation
to Nashville for a peace talk, and retired without doing damage
to the Indian towns.[8]

The demonstration was not entirely devoid of results; Dragging Canoe sent his brother, the Little Owl, to Nashville, with
Coteatoy as interpreter, to hold a talk with Robertson.  "I
have reason to doubt their sincerity," Robertson wrote, "for
several persons were killed during their stay; one at my house,
in their sight.[9]

5

The Assembly which authorized a militia to aid the Cumberland settlers, erected the new county of Sumner from the eastern half of Davidson.  The county seat was fixed at Bledsoe's,
and Major William Hall, who lived about three miles from the
station, was made one of its first magistrates.  When the Little
Owl came to Nashville, Colonel Robertson invited Major Hall
to participate in the talks in behalf of the new county; while
Hall was smoking the peace pipe with the Chickamauga delegation, fifteen Indians formed an ambush at his home.  Ten hid
behind some logs at the roadside, and five secreted themselves
in a fallen tree at the entrance to the pasture, fifty yards beyond.

[8] Robertson's report, Ramsay, 470.  Robertson on this occasion probably
followed the Creek path to the crossing of Tennessee River near Guntersville
(present) ; a practicable route to Nickajack and Running Water was not
known until Joseph Brown discovered it in 1794.

[9] The visit of the Little Owl to Nashville was but the Indian "make-haste,"
or subterfuge.  "Dragon Canoe," wrote Joseph Martin, "is strongly attached
to Spanish interests."  The chief was earnestly seeking to establish a confederation of southern Indians.  But for the stubbornness of the Chickasaws,
who had made peace with Robertson and refused to break it, his efforts
might have succeeded.  "The Chickasaws are not now, and never will be, at
war with the Virginians," said Piomingo.  The attitude of the Chickasaws
enraged Dragging Canoe.  While his brother was in Nashville for the talk
with Robertson, two traders on their way to the Chickasaw country passed
through Running Water, and in an unguarded moment revealed their destination.  Determined that no supplies should reach the Chickasaws if he
could prevent, Dragging Canoe killed the traders, and appropriated their
goods.  N. C. State Records, 18: 604.

When the Major's two sons, William and James, went to the pasture for the horses, they had to pass the Indians hiding by the roadside. William, who was leading, turned to speak to his brother, and saw the Indians rise up behind them, with guns and tomahawks in hand. The situation looked so hopeless that William thought of surrender, but his brother also turned, and two of the savages sank their tomahawks in his head. Knowing his fate would be the same, William determined to run for his life.

He was an athletic backwoods boy of thirteen, barefooted and unencumbered. He managed to elude the Indians who had killed his brother, and ran by those concealed in the tree so close that some of them raised their tomahawks to strike as he sped past. He dashed into a canebrake, closely pursued by two warriors. A grapevine caught him under the chin and threw him flat. He was up and away in an instant. He circled, and approached the point of a ridge near his father's house, where he would have to leave the canebrake. One of the warriors attempted to head him off, but was prevented by a fallen tree. Before the savage could get around the obstruction, William was safely in the lead. The Indians chased him to within a hundred yards of the house, then withdrew.

A frontier dance had been arranged at Major Hall's that day. Half a dozen young men with their sweethearts had just arrived, and as was the custom at the time, all were armed. They brought in the body of James, then went posthaste to Bledsoe's for help. Major James Lynn with five riflemen started in pursuit of the Indians. Being familiar with the country, they were able to intercept the savages at Goose Creek, where two were wounded. The others escaped, but abandoned their equipment. James Hall's scalp was tied to one of the packs.[10]

## 6

Much of the tribulation of the Cumberland settlers in 1786 and 1787 was caused by warriors from Coldwater Town, a new settlement of the Cherokees at Muscle Shoals.

The location was convenient for the capture of boats attempting to navigate the Shoals, and from it there led an almost

[10] Narrative of William Hall, Southwestern Monthly, Vol. 1, 335.

direct trail to Nashville. The town furnished a retreat for the warriors after their raids on Cumberland. Robertson attributed the incessant Indian hostilities to war parties from Nickajack and Running Water, and did not suspect the existence of Coldwater. However, two Chickasaw warriors, while hunting on the Tennessee, came upon the new Cherokee town, and being kindly received, spent the night there. They were informed of the raids on Cumberland by their hosts.

On their return to Chickasaw Bluffs, they told Piomingo of their discovery; he sent them to Nashville with the advice to Robertson to break up Coldwater town. Robertson was in the mood for this very thing for his brother, Mark, had been killed near his home the previous day. Volunteers to the number of one hundred and thirty were called out, under Colonels Robert Hays and James Ford. Robertson, as Brigadier-General, assumed command and started for Coldwater, with the two Chickasaws for guides.

Captain David Hay was sent to the mouth of Duck River with fifty men, to intercept fugitives who might attempt to escape down the Tennessee. Hay's party went by boat, and fell into an ambush when they reached their destination. As they approached the mouth of Duck River, a hidden canoe was observed. Captain Moses Shelby, in one of the boats, attempted to secure it. A large body of Indians rose from a thicket, and let fly a volley. Eight white men were wounded, and Joseph Renfro was killed. Before the Indians could reload, the whites had put out into the Tennessee River. They returned to Nashville in order that the wounded might be treated.

Robertson's force marched rapidly to Muscle Shoals, which they reached at midday, and concealed themselves until night. Under cover of darkness they crossed the river on horseback, and were over by daylight. They found a small, deserted Indian town on the other side of the river, and stopped there for a short time to feed the horses. Then following a plain trail for eighteen miles westward, they came to Coldwater Creek. The town they were seeking was on the west side of the creek, about three hundred yards from the river. Robertson sent Rains down the east side to cut off retreat, while the main force crossed, and followed the path to the town. The Indians were completely surprised. They made a dash for canoes hidden in the river; the white force hotly pursuing. A few fled to the east side only to be met with fire from Rains' men. Twenty Indians were killed; two French traders and a French woman, who had gained the boats and refused to surrender, met the same fate. Among the killed were six Creeks, one a chief of prominence. Six French traders, an Indian woman, and one Indian child, were taken prisoner.

Robertson appropriated the supplies of the traders, consisting of sugar, coffee, clothing, blankets, beads, paints, knives, tomahawks, guns, powder and lead, and other articles. Four canoes were required to hold the spoils. The town was burned; the dead buried. Each Chickasaw guide was given a horse, a rifle and ammunition, and as many blankets and clothes from the captured spoils as they could carry. Well pleased with their treatment, they escorted the troops to a safe crossing place,[11] then departed for the Chickasaw country.

The French traders were released and given a canoe and sufficient supplies to reach the Wabash country from whence they had come. Robertson and his men returned to Nashville by way of the Chickasaw Trace, after an absence of nineteen days.

The boats with the captured goods were floated down the river. They met five French traders with laden craft on the way to Coldwater Town. These were taken also, and after reaching Nashville, the traders were given their choice of standing trial for inciting the Indians against a nation with which France was at peace, or of departing without their goods. They chose the latter course. The captured wares were sold and the proceeds divided among the soldiers.[12]

7

The killing of the Creek Indians at Coldwater caused much resentment in the Creek Nation. Although warriors from the upper towns had for years cooperated with the Chickamaugas in warfare on the Cumberland settlements, the Creeks were not officially at war with the Americans. Alexander McGilivray, with an air of injured innocence, wrote to Robertson:

---

[11] Later known as Colbert's Crossing.
[12] Ramsay, 470. Robertson wrote a report of the campaign which he forwarded to his friend, George Rogers Clark at Vincennes, from which section the traders had come.

"I will not deny that my Nation has waged war against your country for several years past, and that we had no motive in it, nor did it proceed from any sense of injuries sustained from your people. Being warmly attached to the British, and under their influence, our operations were directed by them against you in common with all other Americans.

"After the general peace had taken place, you sent us a talk of peace which I accepted, and advised my people to agree to, and which would have been finally concluded in the ensuing summer and fall.

"Judging that your people were sincere in their professions, I was much surprised to find that while this affair was pending, they attacked the French traders at Muscle Shoals and killed six of our Nation who were there trafficking for silverware. These men belonged to different towns, and had connections of first consequence in the Nation. Such an unprovoked outrage roused a most violent clamor, and gave rise to the expedition against Cumberland which soon took place." [13]

Robertson might have answered that the unprovoked outrages of the Creeks had produced a "violent clamor" in Cumberland.

## 8

In August, 1787, and during the succeeding months, small parties of Creeks overran the frontier at widely scattered places, to avenge the death of their brothers at Coldwater. Sumner County, which was more exposed than Davidson, felt the full effect of the Indian offensive.

On August 2nd, two of Robertson's spies appeared at the home of Major William Hall, and warned him that there were thirty Indians in his immediate neighborhood. He promptly prepared to remove with his family to Bledsoe's. Household goods were loaded on a large horse-drawn sled, which was the only vehicle then in use in the settlements. The sled was placed in charge of William Hall, Junior, whose fleetness had saved his life at the time his brother James was killed. William rode the horse that drew the sled; riding behind was his little brother, John. His little sister Prudence was on the sled with the goods. Mrs. Hall and an older daughter rode other horses. Richard Hall, a grown son, and a young man named Hickerson, led the

---
[13] Haywood, 245.

way on foot. Major Hall, his son-in-law, Charles Morgan, and three other men protected the rear. The little cavalcade soon came to a place where a tree had fallen in the road. Richard Hall's dog became greatly excited; and when he stepped toward the tree, a volley was fired from among its leaves. He turned, ran back a few steps, and fell dead. Hickerson, instead of taking to cover, fired from the open road. His gun missed, and he fell with six bullets in him.

William Hall jumped off the horse that pulled the sled, and led his brother and sister to a place of safety. The Indians charged, yelling like demons; the horses ridden by Mrs. Hall and daughter bolted through the Indian line in spite of efforts of the savages to stop them, and both escaped to Bledsoe's, about a mile away. Major Hall and Morgan ordered the others to scatter while they held back the Indians. Morgan was shot, but managed to escape. Hall fired his heavy rifle, turned and ran about fifty yards, then fell, pierced with thirteen balls. The Indians scalped him, took his gun and shot-pouch, and fled; well aware that the sound of firing would bring help from the near-by fort.

William had directed his brother and sister to go back to their home while he watched the outcome of the attack; knowing that the fight was lost when he heard the firing of his father's rifle, followed by the savage yells of the Indians, he started for the fort.

When the small children had reached the deserted home, the barking of the dogs so frightened them that they turned back toward the scene of the battle, but the Indians had scalped the dead and disappeared. Crying, they started down the road to the fort, and were met by a rescue party, come too late.[14]

## 9

Major John Evans arrived at Nashville soon after the Coldwater campaign with three hundred militia authorized by the North Carolina Assembly. They were divided into parties which were stationed at all exposed positions around the settle-

---

[14] Goodpasture, *Indian Wars and Warriors in the Old Southwest, Vol. 4, Tennessee Historical Magazine.* William Hall, whose experience has been related, later became Governor of Tennessee. See also *Hall's Narrative, Southwestern Monthly, Vol. 1,* 335.

ments; this left Robertson free to use his local militia as scouts and spies.

The country was covered with dense growth, and the cane along the river, while it afforded perfect cover for the Indians, also left proof of the passage of any war party. "Rains, Castleman, and other woodsmen could detect an Indian trail at a running trot. They would take the track and follow it like their own trusty hounds. Their horses, like their dogs, would "snuff" an Indian or an Indian's footprints." [15]

Notwithstanding all measures of precaution and defense, Indian war parties slipped through; scalped and burned, and all too often escaped without punishment, to return later and repeat the same offense.

Such a war party, consisting of ten warriors led by a redoubtable chief called *Ulasula-wah*, "Big Foot," was pursued by Captain Shannon. Big Foot had fought against John Sevier on Lookout Mountain in 1782. He had led his party to Cumberland in search of "hair and horses," and had secured both. Captain Shannon followed his trail to the Tennessee River, and surprised the Indians as they were eating. The scouts fired, then charged and engaged in hand-to-hand combat. Lieutenant Williams tried to club the chief with his rifle, but the powerful Indian wrested the weapon from his grasp. William Pillow, who had just reloaded, fired on Big Foot at close range, thus saving the life of Williams. The chief and five of his warriors were killed, and the other Indians, with furious yells, disappeared into the bush. [16]

10

Three days after Major Hall's death, Colonel Anthony Bledsoe, who commanded the militia of Sumner County, appealed to John Sevier for aid:

"Sumner County, Aug. 5, 1787.
"To His Excellency, John Sevier, Sir: When I last had the pleasure of seeing your Excellency, I think you were kind enough to propose that in case the perfidious Chickamaugas should infest this country, to notify your Excellency and you would send a campaign against them without delay. The period has arrived that

---

[15] Putnam, 272.
[16] *Draper Mss.*, 6-XX-15, Narrative of William Pillow.

they, as I have good reason to believe in combination with the Creeks, have done this country very great spoil by murdering numbers of our peaceful inhabitants, stealing our horses, and burning our buildings through wantonness, cutting down our corn, etc.

I am well assured that the distress of the Chickamaugas is the only way this defenceless country will have quiet. The militia being very few, and the whole country as it were a frontier, its inhabitants shut up in stations, and they in general so weakly manned that in case of an invasion one is scarcely able to help another; and the enemy daily in our country committing ravages of one kind or another, and that of the most savage kind.

"Poor Major Hall and his eldest son fell a sacrifice to their savage cruelty two days ago, near Bledsoe's Lick. They have killed about twenty-four people in this country in a few months, besides numbers of others in settlements near it. Our dependence is much that your Excellency will avenge the blood thus wantonly shed."

"ANTHONY BLEDSOE." [17]

Sevier, at the time he received Colonel Bledsoe's letter, was in the midst of his troubles with North Carolina over the State of Franklin. His beloved state was tottering, and revolt in his own ranks, led by John Tipton, prevented him from granting the assistance asked by Bledsoe.

Later, in conjunction with the State of Georgia, Sevier planned to raise a force of fifteen hundred men for a campaign against both Creeks and Cherokees. For this service, Georgia agreed to set aside the Great Bend of Tennessee River for settlement by soldiers of the State of Franklin. Major George Elmholm, a natural diplomat, was sent to Georgia to arrange for the proposed war. Elmholm conducted his mission with zeal, but Georgia hesitated, the State of Franklin soon afterward collapsed, and the campaign was never undertaken.[18]

[17] Williams, *Lost State of Franklin*, 167.
[18] *Ibid.*, 172-177.

# CHAPTER XVI

## HIGH TIDE

### I

High tide of Chickamauga power and influence was reached in the years 1788 and 1789.

As the staunch and unrelenting enemy of the Americans, Dragging Canoe's fame was spreading. He was well known to Spanish officials at Mobile, Pensacola, and New Orleans, and he maintained contact with the English at Detroit. His two brothers, Little Owl and the Badger, were his able aides. They made frequent trips representing him in the character of ambassadors, to Detroit, to the Shawnees, and to the great Creek chief, McGilivray, who was the Canoe's firm friend. John Watts, the Indian diplomat whose bluff friendliness deceived such frontiersmen as Sevier and Blount, was frequently in the American settlements. Thus, Dragging Canoe was kept advised of the progress of affairs in all directions, and with all his might he attempted to organize a confederacy of southern Indians as the only means of checking the white invasion.

### 2

Early in 1788, a party of Shawnee warriors under Cheesekau arrived at Running Water to visit Dragging Canoe. Among them was Cheesekau's younger brother, Tecumseh, who had not been, at that time, elevated to chieftanship. Cheesekau and Tecumseh were sons of the Shawnee chief Pukshinwa, who had been killed in 1774 at the Battle of Point Pleasant on the Kanawha River.[1] His widow, who was a Cherokee, had later returned to the South to live among her kinsmen. It is probable that the visit of Cheesekau and Tecumseh to Running Water was to see their mother.

The Shawnees were at the time engaged in bitter warfare

---

[1] Pukshinwa, Tecumseh's father, was born on the banks of the Sewanee River, in Florida. The river had been named for his people, "Shawanee." The Shawnees were later forced northward by hostilities of other tribes, and lived north of the Ohio River during the period of English settlement.

with the Kentuckians, and they found an ally in Dragging Canoe. Tecumseh may have derived from the Chickamauga chief the idea of an Indian confederacy that was later to become the life work of that great Shawnee.

Tecumseh and Cheesekau entered heartily into the war plans of the Chickamaugas. In February, 1788, they assisted in an attack upon an unnamed fort which it is believed was Bledsoe's. The fort was a large stockade, the entrance to which was in the runway of a double log cabin. The savages stealthily approached the cabin early in the morning. The schoolmaster, George Hamilton, was practicing the children in the songs which, among other things, he taught at station. Taking advantage of the noise, the Indians gouged the chinking from between two logs and fired at the singer, the bullet striking him in the chin. During the excitement which resulted, they chopped down one window shutter. A schoolboy, Hugh Rogan, sprang to the opening thus made and fired his rifle. Cheesekau was killed, and the savages withdrew, taking the body of their leader with them.[2]

The death of his favorite brother caused Tecumseh much grief. Cheesekau had been his companion and adviser since childhood. He had taught Tecumseh to fight bravely and to scorn all little and mean things. Tecumseh swore that he would not return to his home in Ohio until his brother had been avenged. He led a party of ten warriors to the cabin of a nearby settler, probably that of William Montgomery, on Drake's Creek. Montgomery's son and two of his brothers were killed and scalped.[3]

Tecumseh remained with the Chickamaugas nearly two years, participating in their war parties and those of the neighboring Creeks. He returned to Ohio in the spring of 1790.

### 3

In March, 1788, John Sevier's term as Governor of the State of Franklin expired. Controversy with the North Carolina party, headed by John Tipton, embittered the last few months of Sevier's administration and culminated in armed conflict at Tipton's home, February 27th. Sevier, like many strong men, had made enemies as well as friends.

---

[2] Narrative of William Hall, *Southwestern Monthly,* Vol. 1, 335.
[3] Drake, *Life of Tecumseh.*

Joseph Martin had been appointed Brigadier-General of the western counties of North Carolina by Governor Caswell. The appointment was unpopular with the westerners, who regarded John Sevier as their leader, and felt that Martin's sympathies lay with the Cherokees. Judge David Campbell, an ardent Franklinite, wrote Governor Caswell:

North Carolina has not treated us like a parent, but like a step-dame. She means to sacrifice us to the Indians. . . . She has broke our old officers, under whom we fought and bled, and has placed over us men unskilled in military adjustments, and who were none of our choice." [4]

### 4

The Cherokees were not unmindful of the differences among the Americans, and prepared to take advantage of the situation. Every trader who arrived in the settlements from the Cherokee towns brought news of an impending war in which the entire Nation would take part.

In May, 1788, the family of John Kirk was murdered at his home on Little River, twelve miles south of the present site of Knoxville, by a band of Indians headed by Chiefs Slim Tom and Red Bird, of Chilhowie.

Slim Tom was well known to the members of the Kirk family, who had befriended him on many occasions. He appeared at Kirk's home one morning, and asked for food, which was given him. He left, but had seen the defenseless condition of the cabin; for the men of the family, John Kirk and his son John Kirk, Junior, were absent. In a short time the Indian returned with Chief Red Bird and a band of warriors, and murdered the whole family, eleven in number. When Kirk and his son returned to the cabin, they found the dead and scalped bodies. [5]

### 5

The Kirk massacre roused wild excitement on the frontier, and this was intensified by the news of the capture of Colonel James Brown's boat at the Chickamauga towns, an event that

---

[4] *N. C. State Records,* 20:616. Williams, *Lost State of Franklin,* 128.

[5] *Ibid.,* 207. See letter from John Kirk, Junior, to John Watts, section 5, Chapter XVII.

had an important bearing on the future of the Chickamaugas.

Colonel Brown, of Guilford County, North Carolina, had been an officer in the Revolution, and for his military services had been given a certificate payable in the western lands of the state. He had made a preliminary trip to Nashville and selected a tract of land at the mouth of White's Creek, a few miles south of the Bluffs. Two of his sons, Daniel and William Brown, were left to clear the tract and build a cabin, while Colonel Brown returned to North Carolina to accompany other members of his family to the new country.

He built a large boat on Holston River near Long Island. Two-inch oak planks placed around the gunwales had holes for firing and it was equipped with a small swivel gun. The party consisted of the Colonel's wife, four sons, James, John, Joseph, and George; three daughters, Jane, Elizabeth, and Polly; five young men whose names are not known; and a negro woman.

They left Holston River, May 4, 1788, and five days later reached Tuskegee Island Town, opposite the present site of Chattanooga. Cotetoy, chief of Tuskegee, with two warriors, boarded the boat to look around. The Indians acted friendly, but, as soon as they could after leaving, sent messengers to Running Water and Nickajack, with instructions to attack the party.

Vann, a half-breed chief, met Colonel Brown at Nickajack. He was accompanied by forty warriors in canoes, with a flag of truce. They protested friendship and a desire to trade, but had rifles concealed under blankets. Brown permitted a few to enter his boat, with disastrous results. He, himself, his two older sons, and the five young men, were killed. Mrs. Brown, Joseph, George, Jane, Polly, and Elizabeth were taken prisoners.

Joseph was claimed by a young chief called Kiachatalee, of Nickajack. Mrs. Brown and George and Elizabeth were given to a party of Creeks, who had been of some assistance in capturing the boat. Jane and Polly were given to other warriors of Nickajack. Cotetoy, who was responsible for the massacre, claimed the negro woman as his reward.

When Joseph had been delivered to Kiachatalee's step-father, Tom Tunbridge, a white trader, and taken to his house, about a mile from Running Water Trail, a fat squaw panted up and demanded that he be killed. She maintained that he was old enough to see everything; that he would soon be grown, and might guide a white army to destroy their towns.[6] "My son will soon be here," she said, "and he will kill him."

Cotetoy arrived, and asked if there was a white man in the cabin. "No," said Tunbridge, "but there is a bit of a boy." Cotetoy replied that he knew how big the boy was, and that he must be killed. Kiachatalee's mother begged that the boy be not killed near her cabin, and to this Cotetoy agreed. "I will take him to Nickajack and have sport killing him," he said. Joseph was dragged outside and stripped. Thinking that his end had come, he fell to his knees to pray. As he prayed, Cotetoy said to his warriors: "We are doing a bad thing. I have taken a negro woman from the boat. If we kill Kiachatalee's prisoner, all of the warriors in the Nation could not keep him from killing mine, and I wish to keep the negro woman."

When Joseph opened his eyes, the faces of the Indians were wreathed in smiles. He rose rejoicing that his prayer had been answered. Cotetoy's mother, however, seized him by the hair, and hacked off a handful with a dull knife. "If I cannot have his life at least I can have some of his hair," she said. At the same time she kicked him and called him a "sorry Virginian," to the delight of the warriors.

The following day, the Breath, chief of Nickajack, arrived and was displeased with the murder of Colonel Brown. He adopted Joseph into his own family, and dressed him as an Indian boy.[7]

---

[6] This prophecy was later fulfilled to the letter.

[7] Joseph remained at Nickajack nearly a year. He was glad to go back to his people, but Polly had become attached to her Indian foster-mother, and had to be taken from her by force. His sister Jane, was at Crowtown, about thirty miles from Nickajack, and when a runner was sent for her, he returned with the information that her owner would not give her up: "Sevier is a new state man, and has not right to ask for prisoners who are North Carolina people," he had said. The old Indian runner had replied, "That is all very well, but Little John is so ugly we can do nothing with him." "Ugly" was their hardest term of abuse. Captain Bench, a formidable chief, heard the conversation; mounting his horse, he said, "I will bring the girl, or her owner's head. Early next morning, he came in with the child. Joseph and the girls were turned over to General Sevier at Coosawatie, near the present Dalton, Ga., on April 20, 1789. Mrs. Brown, Elizabeth, and George, had been taken to the Creek towns. Chief McGilivray later ransomed Mrs. Brown and Elizabeth, and restored them to their relatives in North Carolina.

In June, 1790, Chief McGilivray passed through Guilford on his way to

In April, 1789, information reached Nickajack that John Sevier had defeated the Indians on Flint Creek and had demanded an exchange of prisoners. Those taken on the Brown boat were specifically mentioned.

## 6

Following the Kirk massacre and the capture of the Brown boat, and in the face of constant rumors of a general Indian offensive, there was an insistent demand on the frontier that Joseph Martin, as Brigadier General, should lead a campaign against the Chickamaugas.

Martin held two positions: as Brigadier General of Militia, and Indian Agent to the Cherokees for North Carolina. He hesitated to conduct a campaign against the Indians without specific orders from Governor Johnston of that state.

But John Sevier had no such restraints. His term as Governor of Franklin had expired; he held no official position. Indian atrocities and the imminence of an Indian war stirred him to instant action. He called for volunteers to meet at Ish's Station, near the junction of the Holston and Tennessee Rivers; and on June 1, 1788, he marched for the Cherokee towns at the head of one hundred and fifty men. James Hubbard and Henry Conway were his majors.

General Martin was at the time living at Chote with his Indian wife, Betsy, daughter of Nancy Ward. He left Chote on May 24th, and on reaching French Broad River, learned that Sevier and his force were on their way to the towns. Martin turned back immediately to remove his negroes and horses to a place of safety. He met Sevier, and endeavored without success to dissuade him from an Indian campaign.

---

New York to make a treaty with President Washington. Mrs. Brown was living there with her brother, Colonel Gillespie. She pushed her way through the crowd that surrounded the chief, and almost overpowered him with expressions of gratitude. Her brother offered McGilivray any amount that he might think reasonable for the ransom of Elizabeth and her mother. "To accept a reward would deprive me of the pleasure and honor of having served those who were in distress," the chief said. He promised to use his influence to secure the release of her son, George, who was still a prisoner in the Creek Nation. However, he was not released till eight years later, when a general peace was made between the Americans and the Creeks, and all prisoners were surrendered.

The account of the capture of the Brown boat is from Goodpasture, *Indian Wars and Warriors in the Old Southwest, Tennessee Historical Magazine,* Vol. 4; and Joseph Brown's statement, Ramsey, 509.

Martin, thereupon, wrote Governor Johnston criticizing Sevier's action as an attempt to rally the failing fortunes of the Franklin party. "He is making a war to amuse us," said Martin.[8]

Colonel Thomas Hutchins, of Sullivan County, also wrote to the governor:

"Colonel Sevier discovers every mark of contempt for the laws of this state. Even those who are in allegiance (to North Carolina) he holds in contempt. His conduct, if not noticed, will . . . involve us in a war with the Creeks.

"He has gone out with forty men. His destination I know not, but fear the effects."[9]

## 7

On his arrival at the Little Tennessee towns, Sevier was met by Chiefs Old Tassel and Abram, who professed their peaceful intentions. "If the entire Nation takes up arms against the white men, I will remain in my house," said Abram. Sevier, therefore, marched to Hiwassee, and approached that town on June 2, 1788.

James Sevier, William Greenaway, John Cowan and Arch Lackey were sent forward as spies. They returned with the intelligence that the town was occupied and that the Indians had not discovered the approach of the white troops. Sevier arranged his force into three divisions. He commanded the left wing, Hubbard the right, and Conway the center.[10]

The town was on the north side of Hiwassee River. Sevier's left wing was the first in position to attack and, therefore, started firing. The Indians fled down the river and met with a hot fire from Hubbard's detachment, while Conway pressed the attack in the center. The Cherokees then took the only means of escape, flight across the river. Hubbard, seeing an Indian wrapped in a blanket, running for the river, fired, and was chagrined to discover that he had killed a squaw. Numbers of Indians were killed as they swam the river. The Fool Warrior, a prominent chief, reached the opposite bank

[8] Williams, *Lost State of Franklin*, 206.
[9] *N. C. State Records*, 22: 697.
[10] *Draper Mss.*, 32-S 140-180.

and was killed as he climbed to the top of the slope, and James Mawhorn crossed the river and obtained his scalp.

Major Conway captured a squaw and her small daughter, whom he placed in a cabin till the fighting was over; but when he went back to get them, they had vanished.[11]

After the town was burned, Sevier returned with his men to the Little Tennessee. Major Hubbard was sent to destroy the town of Chilhowie to punish those Indians for the Kirk massacre, Slim Tom and Red Bird being from that place. John Kirk, Junior, was in Hubbard's company.[12]

At Chote, Hubbard requested Chief Old Tassel to accompany him to Chilhowie for a talk; the unsuspecting chief readily complied. Chilhowie was situated on the north side of Little Tennessee River, and when he had arrived opposite the town, Hubbard raised a flag of truce. After they had been ferried across, they gathered at Abram's house for a "talk." As soon as all the prominent Indians present were inside, Hubbard closed the door and posted guards at the windows. Giving John Kirk, Junior, a tomahawk, he said, "Take the vengeance to which you are entitled." Kirk needed no second command.

Realizing the fate that was in store for himself and his companions, Old Tassel met it with fortitude. He bowed his head and received the death blow. The others, taking their cue from him, offered no resistance and were slaughtered, one at a time, unarmed, peaceful, and under a flag of truce. No more shameful deed is recorded in American history. The murdered Cherokees were: Old Tassel, head chief of the upper towns; Abram and his son; and the Hanging Man of Chote and his brother.[13]

Old Tassel has been described by one of the pioneers:

"He added to the reputation of a profound Indian statesman and orator, the character of being uniformly respected for his integrity and truth; in this last point it was said of him by all of his associates that through a long and useful life, he was never known to stoop to a falsehood." [14]

---

[11] *Ibid.*

[12] *N. C. State Records,* 22: 695.

[13] Haywood, 181. Ramsay, 419. *N. C. State Records,* 22: 695. See also Goodpasture and Roosevelt for account of killing of Old Tassel.

[14] Williams, *William Tatham, Wataugan; Tennessee Historical Magazine,* Vol. 2, 154-179.

John Sevier reached Hubbard's camp a short time after the Indians had been killed. He upbraided the culprits, but they defended their action. Kirk told Sevier that if he had suffered at the hands of the Indians as had the Kirk family, he would have acted the same as he, himself, had.[15]

Sevier's leniency toward the murderers of the Cherokees can be excused, for he was himself acting without official position. The campaign was entirely voluntary. His own sense of justice was recognized by both frontiersmen and Cherokees, and they realized that if he had been present the outrage would not have occurred. Old Tassel, himself, had said, "Send us Colonel Sevier, he is a good man."

When he received news of the murder of the Cherokee chiefs, Governor Johnston of North Carolina issued a warrant for Sevier's arrest, charging him with treason. "I fear that we shall have no peace in the western counties until this robber and free booter is checked," the governor said.[16]

## 8

The killing of the principal chief and others of first rank in the Nation, while they were under a flag of truce, sent every able-bodied Cherokee into Dragging Canoe's camp. John Watts abandoned diplomacy and took up the tomahawk to revenge his uncle. Bench and Tail, great nephews of the chief, and Doublehead, the chief's brother, began their retaliation. Savage warfare broke out on the frontier from Knoxville to Watauga. Settlers were compelled to desert their homes and seek refuge in the forts.

General Martin had had a fort built at Houston's Station, site of the present Maryville, and had manned its garrison under leadership of Captains Thomas Stewart and John Fain.[17] From this fort, on July 8th, Sevier and Hubbard addressed an appeal to the frontiersmen for help against the Cherokees:

To the Inhabitants in General:

"Yesterday we crossed the Tennessee (Little Tennessee) with a small party of men and destroyed a town called Toquo. On our return we discovered large trails of Indians making their way toward

---

[15] *N. C. State Records*, 22: 697.
[16] *Ibid.*
[17] *Draper Mss.*, 32-S 140-180.

this place. We are of the opinion their number could not be less than five hundred. We beg to recommend that every station be on guard; that also every good man that can be spared will voluntarily turn out and repair to this place with the utmost expedition, in order to tarry for a few days in the neighborhood and repel the enemy if possible. We intend awaiting at this place some days with the few men now with us, as we cannot reconcile it to our feelings to leave a people who appear to be in such great distress."

"JOHN SEVIER.
"JAMES HUBBARD."

"N. B. It will be necessary for those who will be so grateful as to come to the assistance of this place to furnish themselves with a few days provisions, as the inhabitants of these parts are greatly distressed by the Indians.

"J. S.
"J. H." [18]

## 9

Early in August, 1788, Captain Stewart received word that the Cherokees were planning an attack upon Houston's Station. He sent Captain Fain with thirty-one men, among them, John Kirk, Junior, to scout along the Little Tennessee River and discover if possible the movements of the Indians.

Fain crossed the river at Settico. The town had been apparently abandoned by the Cherokees, and the soldiers scattered to gather fruit in an orchard, carelessly laying aside their rifles. Indians who had been lying in ambush surrounded the orchard and also took possession of the river ford, the only possibility of retreat.

The first fire of the savages killed six men, and wounded four. The others fled in panic toward the ford, where they found the Indians in possession. They then attempted to swim the stream in deeper water. Ten were killed and several wounded in the effort. The desire of the Cherokees to secure scalps was saving grace to the others who reached the north side of the stream and fled toward Knoxville. The Indians pursued them to a point within five miles of that place.

John Kirk, Junior was one of those who escaped. He was wounded as he swam the river, but managed to reach the northern bank, where he crawled into a hollow log and was over-

---

[18] Ramsay, 419.

looked in the excitement of pursuit. Kirk waited until the Indians had departed on the trail of his comrades, then left his hiding place, and though severely wounded, reached Houston's Station.[19]

The loss of Fain's men seriously weakened the garrison at the station, and the Cherokees kept the fort in a state of siege; constantly firing upon it. The inmates, men and women, fought well. Rev. Alexander McEwen, handled a rifle with telling effect while his wife stood behind him moulding bullets. A ball passed between two logs and fell at her feet. She remelted and moulded it. Handing it to her husband, she said, "Here is a bullet that was run out of the Indian's lead; send it back to them as quickly as possible. It is their own, let them have it, and welcome." [20]

John Sevier marched to the relief of Houston's Station, defeated the Indians, and put them to flight. He then proceeded to the scene of Fain's defeat at Settico, where he was joined by Captain Nathaniel Evans who had buried the dead soldiers. The combined forces burned the town of Chilhowie and killed thirteen Indians. Sevier then returned to his home to prepare for a campaign against the Chickamauga towns, but found that General Joseph Martin already had plans under way for such a campaign.

---

[19] *Draper Mss.*, 32-S 140-180.
[20] Ramsay, 371.

# CHAPTER XVII

## SEVIER TO THE RESCUE

### I

General Joseph Martin found himself compelled, against his will, to lead a campaign against the Chickamaugas. He would have been glad to shift the responsibility to other shoulders. In June, 1788, he left the frontier for a trip to North Carolina, and wrote Colonel George Maxwell, of Sullivan County, that he was doubtful of the date of his return.

Maxwell's reply, with a naive mixture of frankness and sarcasm, expressed the sentiments of the border men:

"Sullivan County, July, 9, 1788.
GEN. JOSEPH MARTIN,
"Dear Sir:

"I received yours of the 14th of June, and am sorry to hear that you entertain the least doubt of being back in time to go on the expedition. Our country is in most distressed condition. I enclose for your satisfaction a letter from Colonel Hutchins in which is a clause relating in part to Sevier's conduct, which has so exasperated the Indians that the whole body of them is now at war with us.

"There has been a considerable number of persons killed on the frontiers since you left; at which Sevier marched against a town at Hiwassee, with 102 men; surprised the Indians, killed a number of them, which so raised him in the esteem of the people on the frontier that they began to flock to his standard.

"The next push was to Chilhowie, the relation of which you have enclosed. He then desired to go against the Chickamaugas, but when the time came he was unable, for the severity of the Indians and the disaffection of the inhabitants in consequence of such barbarity (murder of Old Tassel and other chiefs). This has reduced him to his former situation, where he remains.

"Your presence was never wanted more than on this occasion. A number of the people say you are the Indian's friend, and they warrant we will not see you until the campaign is over, while your friends assert to the contrary. Your conduct at this crisis will consummate your character in this country. I need not point out to you the bad consequences of your not being on time. I forsee a complication of evils, and I presume if you will reflect a moment you will easily determine, as necessity rules all other considerations. I am, sir, with every mark of esteem, your most obedient servant.

"GEORGE MAXWELL." [1]

Martin could not disregard hints so broad. He returned to the western country, and called a council of officers at Jonesborough on August 19th. John Sevier was not asked to participate in the campaign. To placate the Franklin party, his friend Colonel Alexander Outlaw was given the place of commissary. Colonel Robert Love commanded the soldiers from Washington County; Colonel Daniel Kenedy, those from Greene County; and Colonel George Doherty, those from French Broad section. General Martin led the men from Sullivan County, and commanded the entire expedition as Brigadier-General. Major Gilbert Christian acted as his aide. There were three companies of light horse under Major Thomas King, with Captains Miller, Richardson, and Hunter.[2]

The men assembled at White's Fort (Knoxville) to the number of approximately five hundred. A rapid march was made down the Great War Path to Hiwassee, thence to the mouth of that river, which was reached the evening of the third day. Numerous signs were found indicating that the Indians had embarked in canoes. It was thought that a night march might surprise the Chickamaugas at Lookout Mountain. Twenty miles were covered during the night, and the men proceeded at a brisk gait the next day until within two or three miles of the mountain.

Martin gave orders that the pace be increased to a gallop, hoping to be among the Indians before they could be apprised of his approach. When the town near the base of the mountain was reached, however, it was found deserted, although there was fire in several cabins. Only four of the enemy were seen. They were fired on by the troops, and one was killed. He proved to be a mulatto who had evidently been captured by the Indians, but was dressed and painted as a warrior.

The force had reached the Indian town late in the afternoon, and camp was made for the night. Captain Richardson, of the light horse brigade, proposed that as many men as cared to volunteer should cross the mountain, secure the pass, and ride to Tuskegee Town, a few miles below, where it was

[1] *N. C. State Records,* 22: 697.
[2] *Draper Mss.,* 16-DD-59: Williams, *Lost State of Franklin,* 208.

thought the Indians had conveyed their horses. The proposition did not meet with the approval of the older and more experienced Indian fighters, but Martin gave his consent and a hundred men prepared for the adventure.

The Indian trail led to the bench of the mountain, and passed between the cliffs at the mountain top, and the high bluffs along the river which flows at its base. The party of white men followed the path to the broad bench, where huge boulders seemed to have been tumbled from the cliffs above. The soldiers were strung out along the path for several hundred yards. They were greeted by a burst of fire from Indians who lay in ambush behind the boulders.

The attack was so unexpected that the white men wheeled their horses and betook themselves to rapid flight, although only one man, Major Thomas King, was wounded. He was struck in the cheek by a ball, which knocked him from his horse. His cousin, Captain John Blair, urged his own horse back up the trail and lifted the wounded man to a seat behind himself. The firing was heard plainly at Martin's camp, but George Christian, an eye witness, says, "Before we could get in readiness to succor them, those on the fleetest nags began to come in, frightened almost out of their wits."

It was dark before the confusion subsided, and nothing further was attempted that night. Guards were placed, and from dark until daylight the noise of Indian drums and the firing of guns was heard as the Chickamaugas collected their forces to repel the invaders.

Early in the morning, Captain John Beard with a company of spies was sent to reconnoiter the pass. They were fired on from the same spot where the Indians had hidden the day before. They retreated hastily. Captain Beard's horse was wounded but brought him in safely.

As soon as the firing was heard, Martin ordered the entire force to the rescue of Beard's men, thinking they were surrounded. The men galloped to the foot of the mountain, half a mile distant from their camp. There they dismounted, and leading their horses, proceeded up a trail. The way was steep and rocky, with boulders on each side which compelled the men to march single file. To avoid another ambuscade, Colonel Kenedy detached his men to the left, and marched between the trail and cliffs, but made slow progress on account of the

roughness of the ground. The men on the path had safely
passed the point where the Indians had previously been concealed, but a few moments later, they received a galling fire
from another direction. Captains Bullard, Hardin, and
Vincent were killed, and five others were wounded.

The soldiers returned the Indian fire, then retreated pre-
cipitately, carrying the wounded and dead. "It will be another
Blue Licks!" they shouted, referring to an Indian ambush in
Kentucky, where a large number of white men had lost their
lives.[3]

Most of the officers and men refused to continue the fight,
offering as their excuse that their leader (Martin), "intended
to betray them the Indians," for which statement there was of
course no foundation. Only sixty men expressed a willingness
to take further orders. There was nothing Martin could do
under the circumstances but retreat.

The three captains who had been killed were buried beneath
the council house of the Indian town at the base of the mountain to prevent the Indians from finding and mutilating the
bodies. Martin's army then retreated.

The Indian loss in the battle was two warriors, a Shawnee
and the mulatto. Chiefs who participated were Dragging
Canoe, John Watts, Bloody Fellow, Kitegisky, Glass, Little
Owl, and Richard Justice.[4]

The repulse of so formidable and well armed a body of men
was a great victory for the Chickamaugas. A reason for special rejoicing was the finding of the bodies of the three officers.
They were taken to Running Water, where a great celebration
was held. Captain Joseph Bullard strongly resembled John
Sevier, and a rumor was spread among the Indians that
"Chucky Jack" had been killed. A dance was held around
Bullard's body for a day and a night. The Indians were
chagrined when they later learned that Sevier was alive.[5]

---

[3] The Battle of Blue Licks was fought in Kentucky Aug. 19, 1782. Following a siege of Bryant's Station, the Indians retreated, leaving a plain
trail, to Licking River. They formed an ambuscade on the north bank of that
stream. A force of frontiersmen in eager pursuit crossed the river, fell into
the trap, and seventy were killed. See Roosevelt, *Winning the West*, Vol. 2:
248-259.
[4] The description is from a narrative of George Christian, a participant,
*Draper Mss.*, 16: DD-59.
[5] *Ibid.*, 30-S 351-397.

Dragging Canoe made preparations to follow up the victory immediately. Joseph Brown, who was at the time a prisoner at Nickajack, says that an Indian force of three thousand, including five hundred horsemen and a thousand Creeks, followed Martin on his retreat.[6] So large a number of Indians could not have been assembled overnight; Dragging Canoe had doubtless been informed in advance of General Martin's plans by Indian friends without the General's knowledge.

On approaching the white settlements, the Indians separated into small bands, to bring fire and terror to the entire border.

2

Unfortunate it was that General Martin had not overcome his antagonistic feeling toward John Sevier and offered him the command of the expedition. The suspicion with which the frontiersmen regarded Martin contributed toward his failure.

Sevier was at his home on Nolichucky when word was received of Martin's repulse at Lookout Mountain. He promptly rallied forty men and started for the border, knowing that the Cherokees would follow up so notable a victory.

On September 21st, as he camped with his small force on Unicoi Mountain, in the present Blount County, Tennessee, he observed a light from a burning cabin toward the region of Nolichucky, eighteen miles distant, where his father-in-law, Samuel Sherrill lived. Surmising that the Indians were there, Sevier and his men made a night march. They reached Sherrill's Station at daylight, just as the Indians were attacking it. The savages numbered not less than two hundred; but Sevier called his little force around him and announced that it was his intention to relieve the fort or die in the attempt. "Who is willing to follow me?" he asked. Every man responded, and at a given signal, charged. They had become proficient in imitating the war-whoop of the Indians, and Sevier used it in all his fights.[7]

When the determined men made their onslaught, the noise as well as their deadly fire convinced the Cherokees that a

[6] Jos. Brown's Narrative, Ramsay, 511-516.
[7] This custom is said to have originated the famous Rebel Yell, used later in the Civil War.

large number of rescuers had arrived, and they retreated. The garrison welcomed Sevier as a savior.[8]

3

It was Sevier's belief that the rich cornfields of the Valley and Middle Cherokee towns were the granary of the Nation. Destruction of crops in those sections by Montgomery, Grant, and himself had forced peace in previous times; so after the fight at Sherrill's Station, he planned an immediate expedition against the Middle Towns. Speed was necessary and he did not take time to enlist a large force, but marched with one hundred and seventy-two mounted riflemen. The officers were, Majors: Hubbard, and John McNabb; Captains: Joseph Sevier, John Sevier, 2nd, William Job, Matthew Wallace, Stephen Copeland, James Craig, John Blair, and Nathaniel Evans.

The route taken was that by which Demere had reached Fort Loudoun: by Tellico Plains, then following the trail which led up Hiwassee River and crossing the mountains to the towns of Notally, Kituwah, and Elijay. Sevier's march was observed by John Watts, who was at the head of five hundred warriors. Watts did not dare make an open attack, but sought opportunity to ambush the white men in the numerous defiles.

After marching some distance, Captain Blair protested that the path was dangerous; that the number of white men was small; the Indians knew of their coming. He informed the commander that his (Blair's) men had decided to return to their homes; that he himself was willing and even anxious to proceed, but that the men were fixed in their determination.

Sevier questioned the wisdom of one small company attempting a return: "It would be madness. You will certainly be attacked by the Indians; they are always alert to take such advantage." Blair persisted, and Sevier remarked, "It is a voluntary campaign. If the men insist upon returning, I will throw no obstacle in their way." [9] The little army had just crossed a small river and passed under a cliff. Blair and his men started off. As the first few entered the river, the Indians fired on them from the cliff tops. Had the savages delayed their fire until Blair's men were across the stream, succor would

---

[8] *Draper Mss.,* 30-S 351-397.
[9] *Draper Mss.,* 30-S 351-397.

have been cut off, and they would probably have perished. Sevier's forces, however, which were half mile away in the opposite direction, wheeled and came back to Blair's assistance. The Indians were routed and Captain Blair and his company said no more about returning to their homes.

The nature of the country made the movement of troops hazardous, and Sevier was careful to send spies in advance; he often did the scouting himself, it being his rule to ask his men to go only where he was willing to lead.

On one of these occasions, he, Enoch Carter, and two others were some distance ahead of the main body. They had just crossed a small stream by a footlog when they saw a band of warriors approaching rapidly. The white men turned to run back across the log when Sevier was seized with an attack of cramps, and reached the opposite bank with difficulty. The other men were running ahead when he called, "Boys, don't leave me, I've got cramps." Enoch Carter, a large muscular man, yelled "Get on my back, Colonel, and I'll carry you!" Sevier complied, and Carter, thus burdened, ran as rapidly as the others a distance of 150 yards, to safety.[10]

The Fort Loudoun trail after leaving Tellico passed through Unicoi Gap and thence southward to Hiwassee River at about the present Murphy, N. C., where the old town of Ustally was reached. The town seemed abandoned, but Major Hubbard with ten men were detailed to reconnoiter and found seven Indians lying in ambush in one of the cabins. Five were killed, and a boy of fifteen was captured by one of Hubbard's men, Abraham Denton. The town was burned, and the little army marched to the mouth of Valley River where a halt was made for grazing the horses. While scouting around one of the men discovered an Indian and killed him. Valentine Sevier, one of the three sons of Colonel Sevier who were with their father on this campaign, was riding a spirited horse which became excited at the firing and bolted ahead of the army. Colonel Sevier's brother Joseph, his son John, Junior, and Captain Wallace galloped after the young man to offer their assistance, and the four ran into an ambush. A hasty retreat was necessary, and Joseph Sevier was almost too late in recrossing a stream with high banks. He saved himself by

[10] *Ibid.*

dodging low on the horse's neck as it leaped across, his pursuer firing at the same moment. The army came up and gave chase to the Indians, the leader of whom was the celebrated Bench. All of them escaped, but during the excitement Thomas Christian tomahawked the boy who had been captured, with the callous remark, "Nits make lice." [11]

The Indian trail forked at Valley River. The south branch crossed Hiwassee River to the Georgia settlements. The main trail, Demere's route to Fort Loudoun, led up Valley River to its headquarters, thence through Waya Gap to the towns on Little Tennessee River, thence to Fort Prince George. On Valley River were the important towns of Coota-cloohee, Tamotley, and Tasecchee, and immediately ahead of Sevier's force were the Middle Towns, about fifteen in number, on the waters of Cheowee, Little Tennessee, and Tuckasegee Rivers.

The town of Coota-cloohee was reached late in the afternoon. The Cherokees had abandoned the place as was their custom on the approach of the white army, and Sevier's men set about destroying the corn, of which there were about one hundred acres. Twenty acres were destroyed by nightfall, and the soldiers encamped on a nearby hill. A heavy guard under John Sevier, Junior, was maintained. Rain fell during the night which extinguished campfires and made guns temporarily useless. The men were up at daybreak, dried and reloaded guns, and resumed cutting the corn. Scouts were sent out under Captain Nathaniel Evans, who returned with the alarming information that the woods were full of Indians. Five trails were found where the Indians had passed the encampment

---

[11] *Ibid.* The expression "Nits make lice," which was current on the frontier, was adopted by the Americans from a remark made by Henry Hamilton, the "Hair Buyer." In the Spring of 1782, addressing a council of Indians at Detroit, Hamilton instructed his red allies that King George expected them to take up the hatchet and "Kill all the Long Knife (Americans), and that supplies would be withheld from those who failed to heed his command." The Delaware chief Shingas, (Half King), questioned the command: "Father, only men in arms,—not women and children?" To which Hamilton replied: "All, all, kill all! Nits make lice!" Frontier warfare, brutal enough in any event, was made doubly so by Hamilton's attitude. Even the Indians revolted at such tactics. The Half King stated to another Indian: "Think not that I will do what my father commands. I will send off a party to take one prisoner, which prisoner I will deliver to my father with the charge that he be not hurt, and then I will return to him his hatchet which he has forced upon me."

Heckewelder, Narrative, 311: Indian Nations, 338.

during the night, and they were tramped down hard, indicating that the enemy were numerous.

Destruction of the corn was abandoned, and Sevier's force followed the trails which led straight to the crossing of Hiwassee River, five miles distant. Although the Indians had apparently crossed, Sevier noted that the river was choked with brush and tree tops from the recent rain, which would have rendered the passage of so large a force highly improbable. As a matter of fact Watts had placed five hundred warriors in ambush about half on each side of the ford, and planned to destroy the white army as it struggled through the swollen river.[12]

Watts' plan was betrayed by an over-eager warrior, who could not resist a shot at the white chief as he sat on his horse, a plain target, considering the possibility of an ambush. Fortunately, the guns issued to the Indians by the traders were not suitable for long range firing, and the shot missed. Sevier wheeled his horse and gave orders for instant retreat. Major James Hubbard, who had the utmost contempt for the Indians as fighters, objected strenuously, and an argument ensued. The men were highly nervous, expecting an attack any moment, and supported Sevier. During the discussion John Hicklan, one of the soldiers, noted a man whom he thought to be a spy, and galloped up to his commander in some excitement. "Colonel, there goes a man I don't know." Sevier replied irritably, "Yes, there are a thousand people in the world that you don't know." The soldier, little abashed, replied in a loud aside, "Yes, and you would like to have a thousand here, right now!" [13]

Sevier pushed his retreat throughout the day with the intention of camping at Tellico Plains, where he had fortified a position on his outward march. The soldiers were without food until about nightfall when a cow was discovered. She was slaughtered and distributed and the march resumed, the whole operation having required but fifteen minutes.

Unicoi Pass was reached about dark. One of the soldiers who had dropped his knife ran back for it. So close was the pursuit that he heard the Indians running up the opposite slope. Sevier pushed on to Tellico Plains, which was reached about

---

[12] The crossing was at the present Murphy, N. C.
[13] *Draper Mss.*, 30-S.

two o'clock in the morning, and occupied his old camp. The men built fires and commenced cooking the beef, for they had ridden sixty miles since morning, without food.

The cooking was rudely interrupted. Watts had continued to trail Sevier's forces. The Indians took position on a small ridge within shooting distance and commenced firing, aiming at the fires. Sevier hailed the enemy wrathfully and delivered this harangue:

"I have burned your towns in satisfaction for what you have done among my people. I will return home if you do not further molest my men. I am sorry to go against your towns and distress your women and children, but you provoke me to it. If you do not stop firing, I will return to your Nation and destroy every town in it."

A distant voice questioned, "Will you?" which so angered him that he replied, "Yes, I'll be damned if I don't!"[14] The Indians were impressed; the firing ceased, and Watts soon afterward withdrew, not daring to attack Sevier's position.[15]

4

John Sevier returned from his campaign against the Valley towns a discouraged man. He had many supporters, and the lower counties along the French Broad still called themselves the State of Franklin, but in the older settlements around Watauga and Nolichucky, his followers had fallen away one by one to acknowledge allegiance to North Carolina.

That state had not then accepted the Federal constitution, and the Franklinites felt that they were indeed "step children." Sevier in desperation contemplated a union of his followers with Spain, and corresponded with Spanish authorities with that in mind. In the meantime, he tried to forget his troubles in drink, the only time in his life that he drank to excess.[16]

Early in October, he visited Jonesborough. On October 9th, a council was called at that place by General Martin to consider the advisability of a second campaign against the

---

[14] *Draper Mss.,* 30-S 351-397.

[15] The incidents in Sevier's campaign of 1788 are from the narrative of his three sons, John Junior, G. W., and James Sevier,—*Draper Manuscripts,* 30-S 351-397; 30-S 140-180; and 82-S 210-233. Also, Haywood, 199-200; and Ramsay, 422-424.

[16] Statement of G. W. Sevier, *Draper Mss.,* 30-S 351-397.

Chickamaugas. Sevier was not invited to attend. He quarreled with Major David Craig, and left town in an ugly mood. Later he knocked violently at the door of David Deaderick, a merchant, and demanded liquor. He then rode to the home of the widow of one of his old captains, Jacob Brown, to spend the night.[17]

Word of Sevier's presence was carried to his enemy, John Tipton, who resolved to arrest him on the North Carolina warrant which had been outstanding for some time. Tipton collected a force of ten men and proceeded to the home of Colonel Charles Robertson, a friend of Sevier's; then to Mrs. Brown's, reaching there about daylight. On his march he was joined by Colonel Robert Love, who, although a member of the North Carolina party, desired that no harm should come to Sevier.

Mrs. Brown refused admittance of Tipton and his men. Sevier was wakened by the noise and stepped from the door. Taking Colonel Love by the hand, he said, "I surrender to you." Tipton swore that he would kill Sevier, but after some words ordered him to Jonesborough.

When they reached that place, the prisoner was handcuffed at Tipton's command. He was then sent to Morganton, N. C., the seat of government for Burke County, under guard consisting of Jacob Tipton, Tom Gorley, and George French. Colonel Love accompanied the party as far as his own home in Greasy Cove, and before he parted company, persuaded the guards to remove the irons from Sevier's wrists. He also promised to carry word to Mrs. Sevier of her husband's plight, and to ask her to send him some money and other necessaries.[18]

Tom Gorley persuaded Sevier to attempt escape on the trip across the mountains by telling him that French intended to kill him. Gorley purposely lamed the horse which Sevier was riding, so French would have better opportunity to kill him when he tried to flee. Sevier, believing that Gorley's advice was sincere, made the attempt. He might have gotten away but for a fallen tree. French fired his pistol so close to Sevier's face that it was powder burned; however, the weapon failed to discharge. Jacob Tipton, brother of John Tipton, did not share his feeling of animosity toward John Sevier. He told

[17] Williams, *Lost State of Franklin,* 226.
[18] *Ibid.,* 227; Ramsay, 426.

French and Gorley that if the prisoner had been killed, he would have blown their brains out; that Sevier had served his country well, and that his life was valuable. Jacob thereafter kept close watch on the captive and the guards.[19]

Upon arrival at Morganton, Sevier was met by old companions-in-arms, the McDowell brothers, Charles and Joseph. They accompanied him and became his sureties until Uriah Sherrill his brother-in-law was located. Sherrill made bond for his appearance at trial.

The trial was never held, however. Colonel Love had carried the message to Mrs. Sevier as he had promised, and she had immediately sent Joseph, his brother, John Sevier, Junior, Nathaniel Evans, George North, James Cozby, Jesse Green, and William Matlock to his rescue. They spent the night with Uriah Sherrill, and there learned that Sevier was staying with Major Joseph McDowell, and that he was being treated with every consideration.

The rescuers rode into Morganton next morning. Court was not in session, and the sheriff was absent. Sevier was at a tavern with Major McDowell. Joseph Sevier told his brother that they had come for him and that he must go. After tarrying an hour or so and exchanging war reminiscences with McDowell, he ordered his horse, and they started off before noon. They thought the sheriff might follow, but Morrison did not order pursuit, and made no attempt to collect the bond. The case was dropped.[20]

Sevier's return was made the occasion of a happy celebration at his Mount Pleasant home. His neighbors and friends gathered from far and near to do honor to the protector of his country. For a week a jubilee was held. Mrs. Sevier dispensed unstinted hospitality, and visiting ladies helped prepare refreshments for the large crowd. Among the visitors was an old fiddler named Black, and the Colonel and his wife led off the country dances to such tunes as the White Cockade, and the Flower of Edinburgh.[21]

---

[19] *Draper Mss.*, 82-S 210-233, Relation of John Sevier, Junior.

[20] Williams, *Lost State of Franklin*, 227: *Draper Mss.*, 82-S 210-233, Relation of John Sevier; and 30-S 351-397, Relation of G. W. Sevier. The version in Ramsay, 428, of Sevier's trial and rescue, is disproved by the statement of John Sevier, Jr., "Court was not in session, and the sheriff was absent."

[21] *Draper Mss.*, 30-S 351-397.

5

While Sevier was detained at Morganton, John Watts and a large band of warriors appeared at Gillespie's Station, which was on Holston below the mouth of Little River. He demanded the surrender of the station, which was refused. On October 17, 1788, they began a determined attack. There were only a few men in the fort; but they made desperate resistance, which was effective until their ammunition ran low. The savages then began to run over the roofs and drop inside the station. A scene of horror followed; All the white men and many of the women were killed. Two Indians seized the daughter of Colonel Gillespie simultaneously. Both claimed her as a prisoner and one, seeing that he was about to loose his prize, plunged his knife into her chest.[22] Twenty-eight women and children were captured; the fort was burned, and a defiant proclamation was left at the ruins. It was addressed: "To Mr. John Sevier and Joseph Martin, and to you, the inhabitants of the New State:

"We would wish to inform you of the accident that happened at Gillespie's Fort, concerning the women and children that were killed in the battle. The Bloody Fellow's talk is, that he is here now upon his own ground. He is not like you are, for you kill women and children, and he does not. He had orders to do it, and to order them off the land, and he came and ordered them to surrender and they should not be hurt, and they would not, and he stormed it and took it. For you beguiled the Head Man that was your friend [23] and wanted to keep the peace, but you began it, and this is what you get for it.[24] When you move off the land, then we will make peace and give up the women and children; and you must march off in thirty days. Five thousand men is our number.[25]

"BLOODY FELLOW
CATEGISKY
JOHN WATTS
GLASS"

The note being addressed to John Sevier seemed to indicate that the Cherokees held him responsible for the death of Old

[22] *Draper Mss.*, 30-S 351-397.
[23] The Old Tassel.
[24] Orders from Chief Dragging Canoe.
[25] Ramsay, 519.

Tassel. This was too much for John Kirk, Jr., who had done the actual killing; he addressed a letter to John Watts, taking the blame upon himself:

"To John Watts, now become
Chief Warrior of the Cherokee Nation:

Sir: I have heard of your letter lately sent to Chucky Jack. You are mistaken in blaming him for the death of your uncle. Listen now to my story! For days and months, the Cherokee Indians, big and little, had been fed and kindly treated by my mother. When all was at peace with the towns, Slim Tom with a party of Satigo (Settico) and other Cherokee Indians murdered my mother, brothers, and sisters in cold blood, when the children just before that were playful about them as friends. At the same instant some of them received the bloody tomahawk, they were smiling in their faces. This began the war, and since I have taken ample satisfaction, I can now make peace except as to Slim Tom.

"Our beloved men, the Congress, tells us to be at peace. I will listen to their advice if no more blood is shed by the Cherokees, and your Nation will take care to prevent such beginning of bloodshed in all times to come. But if they do not, your people may feel something more to keep up the remembrance of

JOHN KIRK, JUNIOR,
Captain of the Bloody Rangers." [26]

The capture of Gillespie's Station, following their repulse of Joseph Martin at Lookout Mountain, renewed the confidence of the Cherokees. Attacks quickly followed on Houston's and White's Stations, and while these attacks were beaten off, the Holston settlements were never in greater danger of extinction. All along, the Indians had watched with hope, the quarrel between the State of Franklin and North Carolina; if the white men fought among themselves, the Cherokees might recover their hunting grounds. Their hope was heightened by Washington's appointment of Richard Winn as Southern Indian Agent.

Winn arrived in North Carolina early in October, 1788. He wrote to the Cherokees on October 12th, deploring the violation of their treaty rights by the State of Franklin, and promising them justice from North Carolina and the United

---

[26] Williams, *Lost State of Franklin,* 208.

States; and that it was the intention of Congress to remove all settlers who were located on Cherokee lands. Even Dragging Canoe was pleased.

On November 20th, 1788, the chiefs answered Winn's letter; expressed willingness to accept peace from the United States, but used this crafty language in reference to the State of Franklin:

"We must inform you that we look upon the people who live in the new State as very deceitful. We have experienced them, and are very afraid of them. We are obliged to keep spies out on our frontiers, fearing that they will return and do us injury as they did before." [27]

The communication was signed by Dragging Canoe, for the Chickamaugas, and by the Little Turkey, who had succeeded Old Tassel, as head man of the upper Cherokees.

The intention of the Indians was evidently not so much for peace as to promote the quarrel between the white men to their own benefit.

Following up Winn's efforts, Governor Johnston of North Carolina sent Alexander Drumgoole to talk peace with the Cherokees on behalf of that state. Drumgoole denounced the oppression of the Indians by the State of Franklin, and promised them justice. In a letter to Governor Johnston, Dragging Canoe, Hanging Maw, and Little Turkey, representing all factions among the Cherokees, expressed entire willingness for peace provided their hunting grounds were restored.[28]

## 6

The General Assembly of North Carolina, at its meeting in Fayetteville in November, 1788, passed an act of oblivion and forgiveness for all Franklinites who would take the oath of allegiance to North Carolina. The act provided, however, "This shall not entitle John Sevier to the enjoyment of any office of profit, of honor, or trust in the State of North Carolina." Sevier wrote a letter to the assembly, calling attention to his record of service, and asking how long the spirit of persecution would continue to endure.[29]

---

[27] *American State Papers, Indians Affairs,* Vol. 1, 16.
[28] *N. C. State Records,* 21: 508, and various pages in same volume relating to Drumgoole's negotiations.
[29] *Ibid.,* 22: 722.

He received, about this time, cautious bids from Spanish authorities in Louisiana, looking to the union of the Westerners with Spain; and corresponded with them at some length, but the letters prove only that he sought loans for the State of Franklin, and not union with Spain. He also corresponded with the Chickasaws, and thought for a time that he might emigrate and settle among them.[30]

## 7

The inhabitants of the upper Franklin counties had generally acknowledged their allegiance to North Carolina. That state, however, had not recognized as valid the treaties made with the Cherokees by the State of Franklin. Drumgoole and Winn, in their talks with the Indians, indicated the French Broad River as the Indian boundary. This left the Dumplin settlements, the territory around Greeneville, and the settlements below French Broad, within Cherokee territory. Drumgoole and Winn assured the Indians that all this land would be restored to them; but the thousands of white settlers had entirely different ideas. They still called themselves the State of Franklin, and regarded John Sevier as their leader.

On January 12, 1789, the inhabitants of this "Lesser Franklin" met to consult on some "voluntary plan for safety and defense." They adopted articles which provided for "continuance of officers appointed under authority of Franklin." In plain language, the Westerners declared "We conceive that General Joseph Martin is a person unworthy of our confidence as an officer," and that "John Sevier shall keep the command of the inhabitants on the frontiers, . . . and shall hold all talks with the Indians."

The meeting was presided over by Alexander Outlaw, Sevier's friend and military associate. A committee was appointed to draft resolutions to Congress in the hope that the State of Franklin might still be recognized by that body. A Council of Safety was appointed, with John Sevier as president, to defend the frontier. The preamble to the proceedings makes the statement that the action taken was "a voluntary plan, not under the authority of any State, or name of any

---

[30] Williams, *Lost State of Franklin*, 229 et seq.

State, nor in opposition to the laws of any State, but purely
to defend ourselves from the savage enemy." [31]

8

The dangers from which the Council of Safety sought to
protect the State were very real. Sevier was not present at
the meeting. In January, 1789, he was at his camp on Buffalo
Creek, about ten miles from Jonesborough, recruiting his forces
for operations against the Cherokees.

Contrary to usual custom, the victorious warriors of Watts,
Bloody Fellow, and Kitegisky had not returned to their towns
at the beginning of winter. Watts was a daring and resource-
ful leader. He no doubt felt that the Indian victory was too
nearly won to be risked by the customary winter rest. He
went into winter quarters on Flint Creek, at the foot of the
Applachian Mountains about forty miles from Jonesborough.[32]
He hoped from this position to harass the settlements during
the winter months without the necessity of the long march
from the lower towns.

Sevier's spies brought the surprising information of this
encampment to him on Jan. 9, 1789, also word of a planned
attack on his forces. He went into action at once, and located
the Indian position early next morning by the smoke from their
fires. The weather was very cold, with "immense quantities
of snow." In order to surround the camp, Sevier sent General
McCarter, with the Bloody Rangers and tomahawk men, to
take position on the mountain in the only available pass by
which the Indians could retreat, while the main body of troops,
formed a line in front of the encampment.

The signal for beginning action was to be the discharge of
one of McCarter's "grasshopper" guns. Sevier had formed

---

[31] The articles of association and proceedings are given in full by Judge
Williams in his *Lost State of Franklin*, 220-223, and Appendix C. See also,
*N. C. State Records*, 22: 722.

[32] The writer bases this statement on Sevier's report, which states that
he was in camp on Buffalo Creek, which is about ten miles from Jonesboro,
and that the Indians were encamped on Flint Creek, twenty-five miles away.
He states that the Indian camp stretched along the base of the Appalachian
Mts. Flint Creek has changed its name with the passage of time, and dili-
gent inquiry has failed to discover the exact location. The writer, however,
believes that it is the creek now known as South Indian Creek, in Unicoi
County, Tennessee.

a line of "artillery" with a number of these guns at the foot of the mountain.[33]

On receipt of the signal from the pass, the engagement was opened with a broadside from the artillery. The Indians rushed from their huts and tried to save themselves by flight through the pass, where they were turned back by McCarter's force. Finding retreat cut off, they fought with desperation.

The men serving the artillery were necessarily exposed, and the Indians directed on them so hot a fire that Sevier found it advisable to "abandon that mode of attack, and trust the event to the sword and tomahawk." Colonel Loyd was ordered to mount his horsemen and charge, swords in hand. McCarter moved forward to the rear of the Indian position and the encounter became a series of hand-to-hand combats, the character of which is indicated by Sevier's report:

"Amongst the wounded is the brave General McCarter. While taking the scalp of an Indian, he was tomahawked by another, whom he afterward killed with his own hands. Death presented itself on all sides in shocking scenes."

Flint Creek was the bloodiest of all fights in the Cherokee wars. Sevier reported:

"We have buried 145 of their dead, and by the blood we have traced for miles all over the woods, it is supposed the greater part of them retreated with wounds."

Sevier's loss was five men killed, and sixteen wounded. After burying the dead, he marched his force back to Buffalo Creek, where, he says, "I must remain until I receive some supplies for my men, which I hope will be sent soon. We suffer most from want of whiskey."

Sevier's report of the action was made on January 12th, to "The Privy Council of Franklin," and was one of the only two official reports that he ever made of his twelve campaigns and thirty-five battles.[34] He credited the victory to the "arms of Franklin."

---

[33] The "Grasshopper" was a small swivel gun, carried on horseback and set up on a tripod when ready for action; the fore-runner of the present machine gun. It is believed that Sevier's fight at Flint Creek is the only instance in which artillery was used in action against the Cherokees.

[34] Williams, *Lost State of Franklin,* 218. Sevier's report in full.

A month later, on February 17, 1789, Sevier, "Governor of Franklin," with three of his loyal friends, Joseph Hardin, Henry Conway, and Hugh Weir, rode into Greeneville while the Greene County court was in session, and took the oath of allegiance to North Carolina. The State of Franklin was at an end.[35]

Among the Indians captured at Flint Creek, was Cotetoy, the chief who had been responsible for the capture of Colonel James Brown's boat; and Chief Little Turkey's daughter. Sevier took them to his home. They camped near his house, and he kept them well-supplied with corn and meat; treated them kindly, and often gave advice. The Indians came to have a feeling of affection toward the Sevier family; Cotetoy being an especial favorite of Washington Sevier, and his negro companion, Jim. He made bows and arrows for the two boys and demonstrated their use by killing small birds and animals. Cotetoy was inclined for peace, and after an elapse of two months, he was sent to Chief Little Turkey with proposals for a peace talk and an exchange of prisoners. Sevier sent word to the Indians to treat white prisoners well, and that Cotetoy would tell them how Indian prisoners had been treated.

Cotetoy went with reluctance, fearing that he would be killed while passing through the white settlements. Sevier, however, gave him a hat around which he placed a white paper, indicating a messenger of peace. Washington and Jim followed the Indian they had come to love and repeatedly called, "Farewell, Cotetoy." The chief turned and replied with regretful feeling, " 'Well! 'Well! Jim and Wash." [36] Cotetoy reached his destination in safety. The Little Turkey was overjoyed to learn that his daughter was a prisoner, and had not been killed. To secure her release, he readily agreed to a peace and an exchange of prisoners, which was effected at Coosawatie on April 20, 1789.[37]

## 9

In the fall of 1789, John Sevier was elected by Greene County to the North Carolina Senate. He appeared at Fayette-

---

[35] *Ibid.*, 225.

[36] *Draper Mss.*, 30-S 351-397.

[37] Ramsay, 515. Joseph Brown and his sisters were included in the exchange.

ville in November to take his seat, which was at first denied him because of the exception applying to him in the act of oblivion for Franklinites. The exception was withdrawn after bitter opposition on the part of Sevier's old enemy, John Tipton, who was also a member of the Senate. Sevier took his seat, and had the satisfaction of voting for a resolution restoring to him his title of Brigadier General as of date of the original commission issued to him in November, 1784.[38]

The North Carolina Assembly of 1789 passed a second act of cession to Congress of all lands of that state lying west of the Alleghenies. The cession was accepted by Congress, and the newly ceded lands were erected into the Territory South of the River Ohio. John Sevier was elected the representative of the new territory in Congress, and the years 1790 and 1791 were spent by him in Philadelphia on that service.

---

[38] The resolution ignored the fact that Sevier had declined the commission to accept the governorship of Franklin; also that Evan Shelby had been appointed Brigadier General in his stead, and had served until 1788, when Joseph Martin was appointed to succeed him. Sevier's successors had accomplished little, however, during the existence of Franklin. Shelby was inactive, and Martin's experience brought him only defeat and frustration.

## CHAPTER XVIII

## TOMAHAWK DIPLOMACY

### I

For six years following the Revolutionary War, the United States was a loose confederation of independent commonwealths, and it was not until 1789 that the Federal Constitution was adopted. Until that time, each state had dealt with its own Indian problems. In practically every case these problems sprang from encroachment of settlers on the hunting grounds of the red men. Resentment against the Americans by all Indian tribes grew daily.

Spanish governors were not slow to recognize that this was an opportune time to destroy the American settlements west of the Alleghanies. To further their purpose, three methods were used: closing the Mississippi to American commerce except at prohibitive tariffs; union of the Westerners with Spain, either by colonization or by outright annexation; and Indian warfare. By the time the United States had become a cohesive confederation, Spain had made considerable progress in this program of destruction.

The Mississippi was effectually closed, but this caused ill feeling on the part of the Westerners, who regarded its free navigation as their inalienable right.

On the question of union with Louisiana, Spain had succeeded in getting the ear of such men as John Sevier, James Robertson, and Joseph Martin. A colony of Americans had been established at Natchez, and the plan had gained even more ground in Kentucky under the auspices of General James Wilkinson, who openly favored the union. He had spent several months in Louisiana promoting this movement, also, it was generally believed on the frontier, his own interests.[1]

But Indian warfare was the most effectual of the three

---

[1] A. P. Whitaker, in his *Spanish-American Frontier* has covered Spanish attempts to separate the Western country from the United States. See also, Marshall, *History of Kentucky,* 283-313, for full discussion of Wilkinson's activities.

methods, and the savage hostilities which had terrorized the frontier from 1783 to 1789, and were to continue until the close of the century, were instigated mainly by the Spaniards, and made possible by their money and ammunition.

The United States had made one bungling attempt to promote peace with the Cherokees, by the Treaty of Hopewell, but the treaty had disregarded local conditions and had been contemptuously rejected by the frontiersmen.[2]

## 2

Thus, when North Carolina in 1789 accepted the Constitution and ceded her western lands to Congress, the stage was set for a game of diplomacy in which the stakes were nothing less than control of the great Mississippi Valley. This would mean, eventually, control of the American continent west of the Alleghanies. The protagonists in the action were varied, and their methods contradictory.

Jealous England had acknowledged American independence, but clung to Indian outposts, hoping through Indian warfare to weaken and consequently recover her lost colonies.

Catholic Spain sought to destroy Protestant America, but at the same time encouraged the settlement of Protestant Americans within Spanish borders.

The Indians, hunters for generations, cared nothing whatever for the navigation of the Mississippi as a means of trade. They saw only that their hunting grounds were diminishing daily, and turned in bewilderment from one "Elder Brother" to another, hoping in some way to regain their heritage. All too often, they sat in treaty with the white men and pretended peace, but reserved a tomahawk under the blanket; a practice which the frontiersmen aptly called "Tomahawk Diplomacy."

## 3

In 1789, the United States appointed James Seagrove as Indian Agent to the Creek Nation, most powerful of southern tribes. Alexander McGilivray, who has been described by the historian, Pickett, as the "greatest man Alabama has produced," was principal chief of that tribe. He was well educated, far more so than most Americans of his time; acquainted with

---

[2] Haywood, 226-227.

seven languages; a polished gentleman, and a member of the Masonic order. He conducted dignified correspondence, filled with lofty sentiments, with Robertson, Blount, and other Americans, while his warriors were scalping and burning on the frontier.

Seagrove found the Spaniards firmly entrenched in the favor of the Creeks, although the English firm of Panton-Leslie & Co., in which McGilivray was a partner, controlled the Indian trade for the entire South. Spain, after taking Florida from England had endeavored to wrest the trade from this firm, but after the loss of a shipload of Spanish supplies to an English war vessel, had made a virtue of necessity and had recognized Panton-Leslie & Co. McGilivray, on account of sharing the profits of the firm, would allow no Spanish goods among his people.[3]

On every section of the border, Seagrove found white settlers beyond the Indian lines. He reported to the President:

"It is to be regretted that the insatiable rage of our frontier brethren for extending their limits cannot be checked and kept within the bounds set for them by the general government. The United States, like most countries, is unfortunate in having the worst of people on her frontiers, where there is the least energy to be expected in civil government, and where, unless supported by military force, civil authority becomes a nullity."[4]

McGilivray expressed surprise that the United States had waited five years after the close of the Revolutionary War before attempting to make friends with the Indians. He wrote:

"Georgia, whose particular interest it was to have endeavored to conciliate the friendship of this Nation, I am sorry to observe, allowed violence and predjudice to take the place of good policy and reason. They attempted to avail themselves of our supposed distressed situation, being possessed with the idea that we were at their mercy. They never once reflected that the colonies of a powerful monarch nearly surrounded us, to whom we might apply for succor and protection. We deferred such proceeding, but finding no alteration in their conduct toward us, we sought the protection of Spain, and treaties of friendship and alliance were mutually entered into; they to guarantee our hunting grounds and territory.

---

[3] *American State Papers, Indian Affairs,* Vol. I, 306-308, 309.
[4] *Ibid.,* 320.

"How the boundary between the Spaniards and the United States will be determined, a little time will show. We know our own limits, and the extent of our hunting grounds; and as a free Nation, we shall pay no attention to any limits that may predjudice our claim, drawn by an American and confirmed by a British negotiator.

"We want nothing from the Americans but justice. We want our hunting grounds preserved from encroachment. They have been ours from the beginning of time, and I trust with the assistance of our friends we shall be able to maintain them against every attempt that may be made to take them from us." [5]

### 4

McGilivray refused to enter into a treaty with commissioners sent from the United States, but after much persuasion, consented to go to New York and make one with President Washington. He made the trip on horseback in 1790, accompanied by a number of chiefs, and was greeted en route by enthusiastic and curious crowds.[6]

Washington received him with the honors due a monarch. A treaty was concluded by which the Creek Nation agreed to be at peace with, and under the protection of, the United States. In return, the United States agreed to preserve the boundaries of the Creek Nation, conferred upon McGilivray the title of Brigadier-General, and granted him a salary of $1200 per year as American agent to the Creeks. A warship was provided for his return to his own country.[7]

### 5

During the absence of McGilivray in New York, there appeared in the Creek country, an adventurer, one William Augustus Bowles, who claimed to represent the King of England. In reality, he acted for an English firm headed by Lord Dunmore, last Royal governor of Virginia. Dunmore's company hoped to secure, through Bowles, the immensely profitable southern Indian trade which was controlled by Panton-Leslie & Co. An important part of Bowles' work was to discredit McGilivray, he being a partner in that firm.

George Welbanks, lieutenant of Bowles, was sent to represent

---

[5] *Ibid.*, 247.
[6] See Note 8, Chapter XVI.
[7] *Ibid.*, 308.

him among the Chickamaugas, while he himself remained among the Creeks.

Bowles discarded ordinary attire, put on the breech clout and moccasins, lived among the Indians as one of them, and learned their language. He told them that King George looked upon his red children with pity, and was determined to restore their hunting grounds.

The Indians readily accepted his talks. They had sided with England during the Revolution; she had long been their friend, and that King George would take up the hatchet in their behalf seemed to them a perfectly natural act. Bowles had brought with him, and distributed among the chiefs, posters describing himself as "Commander in Chief of the Creek and Cherokee Nations." [8]

Bowles was an ardent Englishman. His commercial rivals, Panton-Leslie & Co., being under Spanish protection, he told the Creeks that they must fight both Spaniards and Americans; that their father, King George, would aid them. His talk reached the ears of the Spanish Governor, who detailed a ship for his capture. Bowles was enticed on board by stratagem and was sent to New Orleans, thence to Havana, and eventually to Spain. His influence, however, remained a potent one for many years.[9]

## 6

When he returned from New York, McGilivray found his nation in turmoil; himself discredited; and the Spaniards jealous of his treaty with the Americans; all caused by the activities of Bowles. One of his supporters said to Seagrove: "Bowles has laid our beloved man, McGilivray, on the ground, and made him of no more consequence than a child." [10] Although Bowles himself was gone, his agent Welbank assured the Indians that his absence was temporary only, and that he would soon return more powerful than ever.[11]

---

[8] A trader noted one of these posters in the house of Richard Justice, chief of Lookout Mountain Town, in 1789. It showed Bowles with an Indian chief on either side, and bore the inscription as above. *Ibid.*, 315.

[9] *Ibid.*, 328.

[10] *Ibid.*, 296.

[11] Welbank resided at Running Water, and acted as secretary for Dragging Canoe. He attempted to carry on the activities of Bowles, and Lord Dunmore dispatched a shipload of goods to him for the Indian trade. The

Carondelet invited McGilivray to visit New Orleans, where he was feted and offered a larger salary than had been granted by the United States. A Creek chief boasted: "Carondelet has made a greater man of McGilivray than Congress did." Seagrove wrote to Secretary of War Knox:

"I have heard McGilivray say that he regretted that he had ever had any connection with the Americans, and that wherever he went in Spanish places he forbade that he should be called 'General,' the title given him by the Americans." [12]

The chief was urged by his partner, William Panton, to renounce the American treaty. Said Seagrove:

"Unfortunately, Panton hath more influence with McGilivray than any living person, and, it is said, directs all his movements. Panton, from interest as well as inclination, is an inveterate enemy of the United States." [13]

Panton hated the Americans because his estate had been confiscated by them at the beginning of the Revolution. He realized, too, that American competition would mean the end of his control of the Indian trade, and he did not fail to impress upon McGilivray that it would mean also the end of the chief's profits from the partnership. His influence, as usual, had its effect, and McGilivray, after his trip to New Orleans, expressed his sentiments. To a party of warriors who had stolen horses and committed murders on the American frontier, he said:

"You have only to say that the white people were saucy to you, and you will not be blamed. I have assurance from General Wash-

watchful Panton learned of this and arranged with Governor Carondelet to seize the goods on arrival by means of a Spanish warship.

After the Revolution, Welbank was recommended to Governor Blount as a suitable man for American Agent among the Cherokees. However, Welbank remained loyal to England, and as late as 1793 visited Governor Simcoe of Canada in behalf of "the poor Cherokees, for they are really very ill treated." Bad feeling having arisen between the Cherokees and Creeks over the hanging of a Creek warrior who had been captured by the Cherokees and turned over to the Americans, Welbank was killed while traveling through the Creek country in the fall of 1793. See *East Tenn. Historical Society Publications,* 1930; also *American State Papers, Indian Affairs,* Vol. 1, 328.

[12] *Ibid.,* 208.
[13] *Ibid.,* 296.

ington that the killing of a few people or the stealing of horses, even to the number of forty or fifty, will not cause the United States to send warriors against the Creek Nation.[14]

To Panton, McGilivray wrote:

"I have in a letter to the governor, approved his policy of settling Americans on the west side of the Mississippi. I truly wish it was in the compass of our power to drive them all from Cumberland and Ohio to seek the new asylum, out of our way."[15]

McGilivray played one nation against another, but the welfare of his own people was ever his chief concern. "If you condemn me for defending my Nation, you must also condemn your own Washington, Jefferson, and Franklin," he wrote.

### 7

In June, 1790, William Blount was appointed Governor of the Territory South of the River Ohio. Governor Blount was the friend of George Washington. He had served in the convention that framed the Constitution of the United States, and had warmly supported the cession of the western lands to Congress. His arrival ushered in an era of diplomacy with the Indians on the part of the United States; an earnest effort to substitute reason for force. Blount's position was difficult. His instructions were to make peace with the Indians, at almost any price; while the frontiersmen he was to govern were determined to have the Indian lands, a policy bound to result in warfare.

Secretary of War Knox, in a letter to President Washington, suggested the new Indian program:

"The disgraceful violation of the Treaty of Hopewell with the Cherokee Indians requires the serious consideration of Congress. If so direct and manifest a contempt for the authority of the United States be suffered with impunity, it will be vain to attempt to extend the arm of the government to the frontiers. Indian tribes can have no faith in such imbecile promises, and lawless whites will ridicule a government which shall make Indian treaties and regulate Indian boundaries, on paper only.

---

[14] *Ibid.*, 308.
[15] *Ibid.*, 308.

"How different would be the sensation to reflect that instead of exterminating a part of the human race by our modes of population, we had persevered . . . and imparted to the aborigines our knowledge. But it has been conceived to be impracticable to civilize the Indians of North America. The opinion is probably more convenient than just." [16]

Blount entered into his new duties with earnest desire and intent to carry out the wishes of President Washington, which were to bring the Indian wars to a close if humanly possible. To further this aim, the President had asked Congress for authority to negotiate a new treaty with the Cherokees, changing the boundary to include later white settlements and compensating the Indians for lands taken without authority. The Senate authorized the treaty on Aug. 11, 1790, and Blount at once opened negotiations with the Cherokees.[17]

## 8

The glory of John Sevier as an Indian fighter declined from the date of Governor Blount's arrival. He was hampered by the new policy of the Government, and his hard riding followers were succeeded by a paid militia, enlisted for a specified time. Sevier's word had hitherto been supreme. When he felt that a campaign was needed, he had called out volunteers. "Each man was personally known to the commander. They were punctual to a man, for in those days there was no dodging. They were few in number, but that few so often called together that they were like a band of brothers raised in the same family." [18] Each man "found his own horse and equipment," and fought not for pay but in defense of his home. "We traveled two hundred miles," said a pioneer in reference to one of these campaigns, "and received only a good conscience." [19]

There was little military glamor about Sevier's Indian warfare, but it saved the frontier by carrying the offensive to the Indian towns as fast as horseflesh could move. It was rare

---

[16] *American State Papers, Indian Affairs,* Vol. 1, 35 and 53. The lofty sentiments of General Knox found little favor on the frontier. Judge David Campbell expressed the sentiments of the border when he wrote: "Has not all America extended its back settlements in opposition to laws and proclamations?" Williams, *Lost State of Franklin,* 112.

[17] *Ibid.,* 35.

[18] *Draper Mss.,* James Sevier to Draper.

[19] *Ibid.,* 6-XX-46.

that actual fighting occurred, but an Indian chief, describing the effect of one of Sevier's raids, said:

"We are like wolves, ranging about in the woods to get something to eat. There is nothing to be seen in our towns but bones, weeds, and grass." [20]

## 9

Following the death of Old Tassel, those Cherokee towns which were inclined for peace had separated roughly into two groups. Hanging Maw (Scolacuta) had been selected as Principal Chief to succeed the Tassel, but the lower towns east of Lookout Mountain, Coosawatie, Elijay, Ustinali, and Etowah, recognized Little Turkey as their head man.

In June, 1791, Governor Blount sent James Robertson to the Cherokee towns to invite the Indians to a treaty to be held at White's Fort (Knoxville) early in July.

The effort of the Government to correct the wrongs the Indians had suffered at the hands of the State of Franklin was eagerly welcomed by the Cherokees. Forty chiefs and twelve hundred warriors, squaws, and children assembled at White's Fort.

The treaty was conducted with great ceremony. Governor Blount was seated in a marquee, in full dress. Trooper Armstrong acted as master of ceremonies. An interpreter introduced each chief to Armstrong, who presented him by his full Cherokee name to the governor.

Bloody Fellow and John Watts were chosen by the Indians as their speakers. Other Chickamauga chiefs present were Richard Justice of Lookout Mountain Town; Glass of Nickajack; and the famous Doublehead.

The Cherokees had looked forward to Governor Blount's treaty with great anticipation, convinced that he had been sent by Congress to right their wrongs. They were disappointed when the governor, instead of restoring their lands, suggested instead that the boundary be revised to include later white settlements. Congress was willing to pay for the lands, he told the Indians; and indicated certain presents that he had brought with him to the treaty. In addition, $1000.00 per year had been appropriated to be paid to the Cherokees for all time.

[20] *American State Papers, Indian Affairs,* Vol. 1, 13.

"Is the little handful of goods all you intend to give us for the lands?" Bloody Fellow inquired; "If so, it is nothing equal to the value of them."

"The goods are not to pay for the land, but are for presents. The $1000.00 per year is to pay for the lands," replied the governor.

"A thousand dollars will not buy a breech clout for each of my Nation," retorted the chief. Governor Blount replied that he was not authorized to offer more, but would take the matter up with Congress and see if a larger amount would be allowed.

"We Cherokees would like to send a delegation to Philadelphia to talk directly with our father, President Washington, and with Congress," was proposed by Bloody Fellow. Blount replied that such a trip would be unnecessary, for he himself was fully authorized to conclude a treaty.

Watts and Bloody Fellow repeatedly stated that they considered the annual payment of $1000.00 to be too small an amount for the lands. "It is not near so much as McGilivray obtained for the Creeks for less desirable land."

"The game on the land is all destroyed and the country settled, and the land can therefore be of no use to you," the governor said; to which Bloody Fellow replied, "It is true the land is settled, but the white people settled it without our permission."

John Watts rose and said, with earnest feeling:

"I know that the North Carolina people are headstrong. Under the sanction of a flag of truce, they laid low my Uncle, Old Tassel. It is vain for us to contend about a line. The North Carolina people will have their way, and will not observe the orders of Congress or anyone else. I wonder that you, Governor Blount, should be appointed to settle such a matter, being a North Carolinian. When you North Carolinians make a line, you tell us it is a standing one, but you are always encroaching on it and we cannot depend upon what you say. We will, notwithstanding, make you an offer of a line."

Governor Blount, somewhat nettled, replied; "The lands were taken from the Cherokees in time of war, and I do not consider the settlements to be encroachments."

The mention of the death of his Uncle, Old Tassel, so affected Watts that he wept, and could speak no more. He retired, asking Bloody Fellow to finish the talks in his behalf.

Governor Blount then repeated his observation to Bloody Fellow that the lands had been conquered. "You know, Bloody Fellow, that the Americans drove the English from this country, and the land has been purchased with American blood."

The chief replied: "It is true that the English were driven from the country, but the French assisted the Americans to do it, and the English had to come a long way to fight. There is no good purpose to be gained by bringing that up now. Such things ought to be buried."

"We remained seven days at the treaty on this business," Bloody Fellow later related, "and Governor Blount still urged us to sell our lands, the thought of which made tears come to my eyes daily."

On the seventh day, as further progress seemed impossible, Bloody Fellow again proposed that the Cherokees send a delegation to treat directly with the President. "I am fully authorized, and such a trip is unnecessary," replied the Governor. He then asked, "Have you the money for such a trip?" The question struck the chief forcibly. He reflected, he says, that the Governor had the Indians, old and young, in his power. Thinking this over, he told Governor Blount that if he would not demand too much land, and would permit the Indians to return in peace to their homes, they would sell him a little land. A treaty which the Governor had already drawn up was then signed. By its terms, the country within the forks of Holston and French Broad, the present site of Knoxville, and all land north of Little Tennessee River was ceded to the Americans. The Cherokees in beloved Chote were separated from their white neighbors only by the width of the river.[21]

---

[21] Proceedings at Treaty of Holston are from *American State Papers, Indian Affairs,* Vol. 1, 203. The Indian signers were: Scolacuta, Hanging Maw; Kunokeskie, John Watts; Nenetooyah, Bloody Fellow; Chuqualatague, Doublehead; Chuleoah, the Boots; Ocuma, the Badger; Enola, Black Fox; Nontuaka, Northward; Tekakiskee, Water Hunter; Tuckaseh, Terrapin; Kateh; Kunochatutloh, the Crane; Cauquelehanah, the Thigh; Chesqua-Telana, Yellow Bird; Chickasaw-tahee, Chickasaw Killer; Chutlow, Kingfisher; Toowa-yelloh, Bold Hunter; Tsale-oono-yeh-ka, Middlestriker; Kennesaw, the Cabin; Talli-tahee, Two Killer; Kealooske, Stopped Still; Kulsa-tahee, Creek Killer; Aquo-tague, Little Turkey's Son; Toonau-naloh; Testeekee, the Disturber; Robert McLemore; Skiuga, the Ground Squirrel; Tuckshalene; Tuskega-tahee, Tuskega Killer; Sawuteh, the Slave Catcher; Ancoowah, the Big Pigeon; Oosenaleh; Kenoteta, the Rising Fawn; Koolaqua, Big Acorn; Yona-watleh, Bear at Home; Long Will; Taloteeskee, the Upsetter; Chia-koneskie, Otter Lifter; Keshu-kaunee, She Rules.

## 10

The Cherokees were bitterly dissatisfied with the Treaty of Holston. They felt that they had been tricked, and had signed under duress. Nothing more was said to Governor Blount, but on Dec. 28, 1791, Secretary of War Knox was surprised by the arrival of a delegation of Cherokees at Philadelphia. They were, Bloody Fellow; Kingfisher; the Northward; Kitigiski the Prince; and Testeekee, the Disturber; with George Miller and James Carey as interpreters.

"After being clothed," the Cherokees were presented to President Washington, who informed them that the Secretary of War was ready to hear their grievances. The delegation gathered at the office of the Secretary on Jan. 5, 1792, and General Knox addressed them:

"Chiefs and Warriors of the Cherokee Nation: As you are now recovered from the fatigue of your journey, it is proper that I should inform you that the President gives you a warm welcome to this city. He has commanded me to assure you that your arrival makes him glad; and that he will kindly hear anything you may have to say. He hopes that you will open your hearts fully and conceal nothing from him, for it is his desire that the red and white people shall live together like brothers on the same land. Speak, therefore, like brothers, without reserve, for you speak to real friends."

Bloody Fellow said in reply: [22]

"I am come on a long journey by direction of my whole Nation and others, our neighbors, to take the President of the United States by the arm. I will explain myself fully to the satisfaction of your nation and my own, that an everlasting white cloud may be over them."

The chief then presented a string of white beads in token of his peaceful mission. So eloquently did he plead his cause that the annual allowance of the Cherokees was increased from $1000.00 to $1500.00. Bloody Fellow, in recognition of his

---

[22] Bloody Fellow, in addition to speaking for the Cherokees, delivered a talk also for the Chickasaws and Choctaws, to the effect that "North Carolina people should not be appointed to hold talks with the Indians, for they always ask for land." *Ibid.*, 303.

efforts for a lasting peace, was given by the President a new name, *Eskaqua,* meaning *Clear Sky.*[23]

"Hereafter," said Bloody Fellow, "my name shall no more be Bloody Fellow, but Clear Sky. We came to Philadelphia with our eyes full of tears, but since we have seen General Washington and have heard him speak, our tears are wiped away, and we rejoice in the prospect of our future welfare under the protection of Congress."

"The game is fast disappearing from our country," he told General Knox. "Our people must now plant corn and raise cattle. We, therefore ask the President to send us plows, hoes, cattle, and other things for farming."

Thereafter, Eskaqua or Clear Sky, was the firm friend of the Americans, although he was not entirely proof against Spanish presents. At all times there waved an American flag before his door, sometimes at the risk of his life.[24]

II

The road to Nashville ran in front of Bledsoe's Station, Sumner County, which consisted of two log houses with a runway between. On the night of July 20th, 1788, a number of Creek warriors posted themselves in ambush near the front of Bledsoe's; two warriors then galloped past, whooping and hallooing. When Colonel Anthony Bledsoe stepped into the runway to learn the cause of the commotion, he was killed. His death was a blow to Robertson, and to the entire frontier, for he was a brave and capable commander, and was one of the men who had accompanied Robertson on his first trip to Cumberland.[25]

The same party of Creeks captured George Mayfield and killed his brother; they also killed four boys at Brown's Station. Jesse Maxey was wounded and scalped near Asher's Station, and left for dead. A butcher knife was thrust into his body and

---

[23] Eskaqua is not Cherokee, but is from the Shawnee, a language with which Washington was somewhat acquainted. Galunti-yi-ga is Cherokee for Clear Sky, but the form Eskaqua, having been given, was followed thereafter.

[24] *American State Papers, Indian Affairs,* Vol. 1, 289-291.

[25] Ramsey, 479.

he was roughly treated as the scalp was jerked from his head, but he recovered.[26]

These outrages, and a series of other murders, which Robertson had reason to believe were the work of Creek warriors, caused him to write again to McGilivray and Governor Miro. He was careful to say nothing to offend, for he realized that the two men could be very dangerous to the Cumberland settlements, or very useful. He told Miro that a lot had been reserved for him in Nashville, and intimated that the Westerners might consider separation from the United States, and union with Spain.[27]

In November, 1788, growth of the population made a further division of the Cumberland necessary, and Tennessee County was erected from the western part of Davidson. The three counties, Davidson, Sumner, and Tennessee, formed a military district of which Robertson was made Brigadier-General. Realizing that navigation of the Mississippi was of vital importance, and hoping to gain it by flattery, Robertson suggested that the new district be named Mero after the Spanish Governor. His suggestion was adopted.[28]

Governor Miro replied to Robertson's letter by enclosing a list of regulations for the emigration of the Cumberland settlers to Spanish dominion. He promised each family 250 acres of land, tax free. The only requirement was that emigrants must take oath of allegiance to the King of Spain.

To McGilivray, Robertson wrote that he had just had the experience of seeing one of his own children killed and scalped. "It is a matter of no small reflection," he told McGilivray, "to a brave man to see a father, son, or brother, fall on the field of battle, but it is a serious and melancholy incident to see a helpless woman or child tomahawked in his own house." [29] He reminded the chief that if white men had encroached upon Creek

---

[26] A curious enactment was passed by the North Carolina Assembly for relief of settlers who were wounded and unable to pay for treatment. They were authorized to certify to the facts, and physicians accepted the certificates, extended treatment, then turned them in in payment of taxes.

[27] Ramsey, 480.

[28] Governor Miro spelled his name with an "i," but it was pronounced as though it were an "e." Robertson, therefore, suggested the name Mero, which followed pronunciation, rather than spelling.

[29] Ramsey, 481, Peyton Robertson was killed at his father's plantation on Richland Creek early in March, 1788.

territory, it was not men from the Cumberland; they claimed only the land bought from Henderson in 1775. It was true that he himself had led an expedition against the Indians at Muscle Shoals, but they had committed many outrages on Cumberland for which he had but "taken satisfaction."

McGilivray replied that he would have his warriors refrain from further injury to the Cumberland settlements, and would use his influence with the Cherokees to the same end. He failed to keep either promise.[30]

It seemed that Indian treaties were made only to be broken. When John Sevier made a treaty with the Little Turkey in 1789, the great Indian fighter gained temporary respite for the Holston settlements, but the Chickamaugas only transferred their attention to Cumberland. Too, many of the warriors who had been killed at Flint Creek were from the upper Creek towns, and regardless of any promise made by McGillivray, "bad young men" from those towns constantly made their way to the Cumberland to avenge their kinsmen.

The opening of a short route to Nashville by Evan's militia in 1788-1789 brought an inrush of settlers to Cumberland. Scenes of terror were enacted along the road, also scenes of bravery and cowardice. A party of twelve, seven men, a boy, and four women, whom Haywood purposely leaves unnamed, were ambushed while on their way from Southwestern Point to Nashville. At sight of the savages, the seven men set spurs to their horses and fled at top speed. The four women were too terrified to move. The Indian chief came up, shook hands with them, told them they should not be hurt, caught a horse which he tied to a tree for their use, built a fire for them, and courteously took his departure; it was probably the celebrated Bench, who spoke English well.

Four of the men continued on to Nashville. The other three turned back after a time, and escorted the women to Nashville, which they reached in safety.[31]

## 12

Religious fervor mounted in times of stress on the frontier. The first preacher who regularly served a church in the Cumber-

---

[30] Haywood, 254-255.
[31] Haywood, 270.

land settlements was Rev. Thomas Craighead,[32] who was called to the Presbyterian pastorate of Shiloh Congregation, of Sumner County, in 1787. He was an earnest man and a fervent orator, but too liberal in his views to please the strict doctrinalists of the day.

Methodist circuit riders, Rev. Benjamin Ogden, D. Combs, and B. McHenry, reached Nashville before the end of 1788. The Cumberland district was considered a part of the Kentucky Conference, of which Rev. Francis Poythress was Presiding Elder, and he, occasionally, visited Nashville.

Probably the first Baptist preachers on Cumberland were Revs. William Hickman and Lewis Craig, whose principal work was in Kentucky. Of Hickman's preaching, it was said to resemble "thunder in the distance." Craig was so determined a preacher that he had been arrested as a nuisance in Virginia before emigrating to the frontier! The prosecuting attorney had said of him, "He cannot meet a man on the road but he must ram a text of Scripture down his throat." [33]

The early preachers were circuit riders by choice. When one of them, because of ill-health, was compelled to accept "located relationship," with a single church only, it was always with keen regret. There is hardly an instance where this occurred that the preacher did not later ask to be restored to circuit work. They rode from station to station at the risk of their lives, to hold services, and gave themselves freely, not only as preachers, but as friends, confidants, and comforters. The danger to which all the frontier was constantly exposed drew the early churchmen together in undying brotherhood.

Bishop Francis Asbury, of the Methodist Episcopal Church, began his journeys west of the mountains in 1788, and in succeeding years, this frail man of strong courage crossed the Alleghanies twenty times. He journeyed to the farthest corner of his diocese, which, he wrote, was "vaster than the European continent."

---

[32] The liberal views of Rev. Thos. Craighead led to his suspension from his pastorate by the Presbyterian Synod in 1805, and it was many years before he was re-instated. The treatment of Dr. Craighead and other such men, inspired the organization of the Cumberland Presbyterian denomination a few years later.

[33] A brief account of the early church history of the Kentucky-Tennessee frontier may be found in Collins, *Historical Sketches of Kentucky,* pages 109 to 144.

He kept a journal of his travels from which we gain a vivid picture, not only of the early church, but of the frontier and the frontiersmen.[34]

Early marriages and large families was the rule on the border, and Asbury comments: "The spirit of matrimony is prevalent here." Of the preachers, he says, "I found them indifferently clad, with emaciated bodies and subject to hard fare."

The Bishop reflects often upon the "two potentates of the western country, whiskey and brandy." In his trips, he stopped frequently with Thomas Amis, who ran a tavern at the mouth of Big Creek, near the present Rogersville, Tenn. Drinking was almost universal, and Amis operated a distillery in connection with his tavern, thus collecting two profits from his guests. Asbury condemned him in plain language:

"We came to Amis', a poor sinner. He was highly offended that we prayed so loud in his house. He is a distiller of whiskey, and boasts that he gains £300 per annum by the brewing of his poison. We talked very plainly. I told him it was necessity and not choice that we were there—that I feared the face of no man. He said that he did not desire me to trouble myself about his soul."

Expressing the spirit of the circuit rider, the Bishop says:

"Live or die, I must ride. . . . Those who wish to know how rough is this way may tread in my path, over rocks, ridges, hills, stones, and streams."

One can almost hear him breathe a sigh of relief as he pens a rare entry in his journal: "I had a bed to sleep on."

Asbury found the frontiersmen "a hardened people, one degree removed from savagery, but my soul has been blessed among them, and I am exceedingly well pleased with them." Despite the roughness incident to pioneer life, there was genuine hospitality and courtesy among the settlers. The arrival of a preacher, and particularly of a bishop, was a matter of note. He was not only made to feel welcome,—he was welcome.

Of the danger of Indians, Bishop Asbury's comment is brief and to the point:

---

[34] Williams, *Early Travels in the Tennessee Country*, 289.

"I do not fear; we go armed. If God suffer Satan to drive the Indians on us, if it be His will, we will teach our hands to war, and our fingers to fight and conquer." [35]

## 13

A project was formed in 1790 for colonizing the Great Bend of Tennessee River. Georgia claimed the territory, regardless of the fact that it was guaranteed to the Cherokees by treaty. A vast tract of 300,000 acres was transferred by the Georgia Legislature to certain Tennesseeans, among whom were Thomas Gilbert, John Strother, Thomas Carr, Zachariah Cox, and James Hubbard.[36] A company was organized and called the Tennessee Company, which advertised for "Adventurers" to join an armed force which would embark from the mouth of French Broad on Jan. 10, 1791, for the purpose of settling near Muscle Shoals, under the leadership of James Hubbard. Five hundred acres were offered to each settler.[37] Governor Blount, on hearing of the project, reported it to the Secretary of War, and pointed out to him that the scheme would certainly cause trouble with the Cherokees. President Washington issued a proclamation forbidding the settlement; Blount communicated this to James Hubbard, and advised him that if the new settlement should be attempted, the Cherokees would be notified and the settlers left to their mercy. But such threats had little effect on Hubbard, who hated Indians and held them in contempt.[38]

---

[35] The work of the early preachers culminated in "The Great Revival," which swept the frontier beginning in the fall of 1800. Camp meetings were attended by thousands of people. Final services were held in Bourbon County, Kentucky, in August, 1801, daily attendance being estimated at 20,000. Collins, in his *Historical Sketches of Kentucky*, 130, gives a graphic description:
"The novelty of the manner of service, the range of tents, fires reflecting light amidst the branches of towering trees; candles and lamps illuminating the encampments; hundreds moving to and fro with lights and torches; the preaching, praying, shouting, all heard at once, rushing from different parts of the ground, was enough to swallow up all the powers of contemplation."

[36] *American State Papers, Indian Affairs*, Vol. 1, 36: Ramsay, 550.

[37] The Tennessee Company was the outgrowth of a movement first projected by John Sevier in 1787. A joint campaign by the States of Franklin and Georgia against the Cherokees and Creeks was contemplated, the Great Bend to be reserved for Franklin's soldiers. Hesitation by Georgia, and the collapse of the Franklin movement, prevented the campaign. See Section 9, Chapter XV.

[38] Ramsey 550.

On the advertised date, he, Peter Bryant, and fifteen other "adventurers" embarked at the mouth of French Broad River. Utmost precautions were used while passing through the country of the hostile Chickamaugas. They did not land for three days and nights. The Indians at one point attempted to decoy the party to land for trading; Hubbard refused, which was wise, for three hundred warriors, who had been lying in ambush, rose and poured fire into the boats. The audacious party rowed rapidly away and escaped without loss. They reached Muscle Shoals, where they erected a block-house.

As they were engaged on other defenses, they were surprised by Chief Glass, of Nickajack, at the head of sixty warriors. Hubbard was notified that he must leave Muscle Shoals immediately, or he and all his men would be killed. Taken at a disadvantage, Hubbard complied sullenly, and after they had left, the Cherokees burned the block-house.

Richard Justice, writing to Governor Blount, said,

"You may [39] think the Glass and his people are bad, but what I tell you is the truth. When it was in his power to have killed Hubbard and all his party, he, as it were, lifted them up, and told them to go in peace."

Considering Hubbard's participation in the murder of Old Tassel, this forbearance on the part of the Cherokees shows surprising patience.

### 14

Among the chiefs who had attended Governor Blount's treaty at White's Fort in 1791 were Doublehead and Bench. They took their portion of the presents that were distributed, and pledged their friendship to the Americans, but, like all the Cherokees, they were dissatisfied with the treaty. Ignoring the fact that a portion of their Nation had gone to Philadelphia to try and secure a revision of the terms, Doublehead and Bench adopted more radical measures.

To deceive Blount, Doublehead had asked and received permission to hunt on the waters of Cumberland River; he did not mention that it was scalps that he intended to hunt. After leaving the treaty, he proceeded to his town at Muscle Shoals,

---

[39] *American State Papers, Indian Affairs,* Vol. 1, 263.

then, with seven warriors, took the warpath to Cumberland.[40]

He first captured Conrad's salt boat, near the mouth of the river, and killed one man. Skulking upstream, he saw two sons of Valentine Sevier, Robert and William, and William Curtis, with two or three others, embark in a boat for Nashville. Doublehead crossed a bend of the river and concealed his warriors at a place afterward called Seven Mile Ferry. When the party came around the bend, they was showered with a volley that killed the two Seviers and Curtis. The other young men pushed the boat across the river and escaped. Doublehead scalped the men, and, the next day killed Valentine Sevier, Jr., and John Rice. He lurked near the settlement another week, and secured the scalp of a man named Boyd, who lived in Clarksville. The chief then returned to his town with seven scalps. The death of his uncle had now been more than revenged, but success only made him more avid.[41] On the very day that Doublehead killed the two Seviers, Bloody Fellow was concluding a treaty with President Washington in Philadelphia. Doublehead himself later was to go there on a similar mission.

15

When Doublehead and his nephew, Bench, parted company, following the treaty of Holston, it was with a mutual pledge to avenge the Old Tassel.[42] We have seen the revenge taken by Doublehead; that of Bench was also notable. At his town of Running Water, he struck the warpole, and beat up for volunteers. With a party of five, he departed for his favorite field of action, southwest Virginia. On Aug. 23, 1791, he surprised the house of William McDowell in Russell County, near Moccasin Gap. McDowell was absent; Mrs. McDowell was killed and scalped. Frances Pendleton, a girl of seventeen, met the same fate. Her mother, and a young brother of eight, were taken prisoners.

Three days later, Bench ambushed the house of Elisha Farris, who was mortally wounded; his wife was killed and scalped, as was their daughter, Mrs. Livingstone and her small child of three. Another daughter, Nancy Farris, was made prisoner.

[40] *Ibid.,* 274.
[41] Goodpasture.
[42] *American State Papers, Indian Affairs,* Vol. 1, 274.

Bench returned to Running Water with five scalps and three prisoners. The State of Virginia offered a reward for him, dead or alive. He became so notorious in Southwest Virginia, that mothers threatened their children: "Captain Bench will get you, if you're not good." [43]

---

[43] *Draper Mss.,* 9-DD-67.  Goodpasture, also.

# CHAPTER XIX

## ST. CLAIR

### I

William Blount's treaty with the Cherokees held at White's Fort in 1791, and called the treaty of Holston, guaranteed, among other things, the open navigation of the Tennessee River. Since the Chickamaugas did not participate in the treaty, the guaranty was of doubtful value. Blount wrote Robertson: "The Cherokees at Running Water have notified me that boats using the river must take the consequences." [1]

Dragging Canoe not only worked in close harmony with the Spaniards, but kept in touch with British authorities at Detroit through his brother, the Badger, who made frequent trips there. On April 12, 1791, he wrote to Alexander McKee, British Deputy at Detroit, requesting that he be sent one of King George's gorgets, arm bands, a war bonnet, and a French horn or fife. The letter was written by George Welbank, Bowle's able deputy at Running Water, and forwarded by the Badger.

In his letter of enclosure, Welbank said:

"You will receive a letter from the Dragging Canoe. He is one of the head warriors of this Nation, strongly attached to the English. If you answer his letter, he will be very proud, for he has a high opinion of you from what he has heard of the Indians who pass back and forward, particularly his brother, who is an exceedingly good fellow." [2]

McKee replied on July 22, 1791, addressing his answer:

"To the Dragging Canoe, Principal Chief of the Cherokee Nation:

"It gave me great pleasure to receive your letter, as I have the greatest regard for you and all your Nation, and will always

---

[1] Robertson Correspondence, *American Historical Magazine*, 2, 60.

[2] P. M. Hamer, *East Tenn. Historical Society Publications.* The Indian chiefs had adopted the custom of the white officers of using a whistle to direct their men in battle, and it was probably for that purpose that Dragging Canoe wanted the "French horn or fife."

WILLIAM BLOUNT, TERRITORIAL GOVERNOR

Photograph of original miniature from life in the possession of his great-great-grandson John C. Febles of Butte, Montana, who had a photograph made for Calvin M. McClung of Knoxville, Tennessee, for whom this two diameter enlargement was made by Knaffl & Brakebill of Knoxville, in June, 1912.

have a satisfaction when it is in my power to do them any service. Your Great Father has ordered me to assist his Indian children with clothing and provisions. He will always fulfill his engagements with his children. All the Nations here, agreeable to the advice he has constantly given them, are united in the strongest bonds of friendship and unanimity.

"Your brother who brought your letter will inform you of all that has passed at the council of the western Indians.[3] He will also deliver you a hat of feathers, two pairs of arm bands and a gorget as you desired, but I am sorry I could not send you a French horn or fife, as I have nothing of that kind here. I have sent your talk to Sir John Johnson, the Superintendent of Indian Affairs, and when any answer comes, I will take care to forward it to you. I have given clothing, provisions, kettles, ammunition, and a variety of articles to your people, and I hope they will all get safe home. I shake you by the hand, and heartily bid you farewell. A. McKEE, Deputy Agent, Indian Affairs." P.S. I have also given your brother armbands and a gorget for himself." [4]

### 2

Besides the message from McKee, the Badger brought from Detroit a talk from the Shawnees to Dragging Canoe and a similar talk and a peace pipe to be delivered to the Cherokee National Council. Their Nation, the Shawnees said, had borne the brunt of the fight to hold back the white settlement of Kentucky, which was the hunting ground of the Cherokees as well as their own. The Americans had sent General Harmar against them with a great army, and they had beaten him. They were now sending an even greater army under General Arthur St. Clair, to cut off the Shawnees as a Nation. They had lost many of their best warriors in trying to hold the common hunting ground, and they were asking the help of the Cherokees and of all red men everywhere to defeat the new army of St. Clair.[5]

Following the death of Old Tassel, the Cherokee seat of government had been removed from Chote on the Little Tennessee, to Ustanali on the Coosawatie River in Georgia, a few miles above its junction with the Conasauga. As Dragging Canoe did not attend the Cherokee Council, he instructed his

---

[3] *Ibid.* Held July 1, 1791, to devise means of resisting St. Clair's army.
[4] P. M. Hamer, *East Tenn. Historical Society Publications.*
[5] *American State Papers, Indian Affairs,* Vol. 1, 437-438.

brother to leave the Shawnee talk and peace pipe at the house of
Kitegista, the Old Prince, brother of Oconostota. When the
Badger arrived at Ustinali, he learned Kitegista was in Philadelphia with Bloody Fellow, Kingfisher, and other chiefs, ar-
ranging a treaty with the United States. He, therefore, left
the message and pipe at the house of Kingfisher, and returned
to Running Water, where he raised a party of thirty warriors
and hastened northward to aid the Shawnees against St. Clair.

When the Cherokee chiefs returned from Philadelphia, their
hearts were warm toward the United States. General Washington had "wiped away their tears." Never again, they thought,
would the Cherokees fight the Americans. Kingfisher
destroyed the pipe that had been sent by the Shawnees.[6]

### 3

The Indian tribes of the Northwest, forgetting all differences
among themselves, united to oppose St. Clair's invasion of the
Shawnee country. On July 1, 1791, the British deputy McKee
addressed a great assembly of Indians at Miami Rapids. There
were present: Shawnees, Delawares, Wyandots, Pottawato-
mies, Chippewas, Ottawas, Iroquois, Miamis, and other Nations
of the northwest. Allies, who had never seen a gun and still
fought with bows and arrows, came from beyond the Mississippi. From the south came Creeks and Chickamaugas; among
the latter was the Badger.

England was not then at war with the United States.
McKee, therefore, made the Indians a very cautious speech,
but distributed plenty of supplies and ammunition, and led the
chiefs to believe that they had a faithful friend and ally in
Great Britain.[7]

### 4

St. Clair, with fourteen hundred men, advanced against the
Indians on October 4, 1791. His troops were mostly raw
recruits. He, although a brave officer, was unfitted to command so important a movement; in addition, he was sick and
almost unable to sit upon his horse. He had been warned by
President Washington to remember the experience of Braddock,
and to beware of a surprise attack; notwithstanding this advice

---

[6] *Ibid.,* 327. See section 12, Chapter XXII.
[7] Roosevelt, *Winning of the West,* 4, 48.

he advanced in slow stages and kept out neither scouts nor outposts.

The combined Indian forces had chosen for their commander, a shrewd Miami chief, the Little Turtle. His spies watched every move St. Clair made and brought daily reports to their leader, who plotted the destruction of the white army.

With their commander sick and incapable, almost open mutiny existed among St. Clair's troops. As the army approached the Shawnee towns, a portion of the militia deserted. St. Clair sent part of the regulars to recapture them, thus weakening his force in face of a formidable enemy. The Indians observed his predicament, and attacked on the morning of November 4th as the white men were breaking camp. It was very cold and the ground was covered with snow. The troops had spent the night on Wabash River, where it was only twenty yards wide with high banks.

The militia, who were a quarter of a mile in advance of the regulars, received the first Indian attack. In spite of the bravery of their officers, they fled at the first fire and stampeded into the midst of the regulars, who were coming to their assistance. The whole army was thrown into confusion. St. Clair and his aide, Colonel Butler, displayed reckless bravery. Eight Indian bullets passed through the clothes of the commander, but he escaped without injury. When the artillery was turned on the Indians, they would quickly pick off the gunners. The commander led several charges against the savages, who would give way and fly before the charge, but were at the soldiers' heels the moment they turned. During the noise and confusion, some of the Indians advanced on the gunners and scalped them as they served the guns.

The white force was finally surrounded; and in an attempt to save at least part of his men, St. Clair ordered retreat. The roadway which the army had cut for advancing offered the only means of escape. A desperate attack in that direction caused the Indians to give back momentarily and the soldiers, militia and regulars, streamed down the passage in wild flight. Arms were thrown away, and the wounded were abandoned. The unhappy St. Clair strove in vain to stay the rout.

The Indians pursued for four miles; only their desire for spoils at the camp enabled St. Clair's men to escape. Of the fourteen hundred who had marched out with him, only five hundred returned unhurt. It was a disaster equal to Brad-dock's.

There were scenes of horror along the route of flight; many acts of bravery were performed, and some that bordered upon the ludicrous. Among the allies of the Shawnees was a young Osage, afterward the celebrated chief, Pahuska. He pursued an elderly officer who wore a white wig. The Osage seized the wig, intending to scalp his victim, when, to his amazement, the scalp came off without the use of the scalping knife! The queer scalp, then and there, became to Pahuska a thing of magic; the officer was permitted to escape while the delighted Indian showed his trophy to his admiring friends. Convinced that the scalp would serve himself as it had its former owner, the Osage thereafter fastened it to his own scalp lock while in battle and thus gained the name, Pahuska, "White Hair." [8]

The defeat of St. Clair was far-reaching in its effect. Hope again filled the Indian villages; the war-spirit flamed high; and there was rejoicing in every wigwam on the western border. The Indians had met and defeated the great American army. They were better fighters than the "Long Knives." Surely they could regain their hunting grounds. The Badger, with his thirty Chickamaugas, shared the rejoicing, and hastened home to tell the glad news. "It is nothing to meet the Americans in regimentals," he boasted. "They are such men as Montgomery brought against the Cherokees many years ago," referring to Oconostota's victory at the Pass of Etchoe. [9]

The Indians took in spoils from St. Clair's camp, horses, tents, guns, axes, powder, clothing, blankets; and, greatest of all, more than six hundred scalps.

Two months later, General Wilkinson, with 150 volunteers, visited the scene of the defeat for the purpose of burying the dead. For a distance of four miles, bodies were picked up along the frozen road. Snow was deep. Many of the victims had been partially devoured by wild animals. At the battlefield it-self, the dead were found in heaps; scalped and stripped of all clothing. The bodies, blackened by frost and exposure, were

[8] Foreman, Grant, *Pioneers and Indians,* 22.

[9] The incidents of St. Clair's campaign, except as otherwise noted, are from St. Clair's official report, *American State Papers, Indian Affairs,* Vol. 1, 137; Roosevelt, *Winning of the West,* Vol. 4, 51-72; and references in *American State Papers,* Pages 327, 329, 438.

unrecognizable. A shallow trench was dug in the frozen ground, and by the side of this common grave, Wilkinson's volunteers rendered the last obsequies to the victims of the disastrous campaign of General Arthur St. Clair.[10]

For the sake of St. Clair's courage and honorable character, he was held guiltless, by Congress and the President, for the great calamity, but Washington's anger flamed at the thought that St. Clair should have been caught by the very surprise against which he had been warned. "O God, O God!" he cried, "that he should suffer that army to be cut to pieces, hacked, butchered, and tomahawked by surprise, the very thing I warned him against!"[11]

---

[10] Among those killed at St. Clair's defeat was Colonel Jacob Tipton, who had acted as guard for Sevier when he was arrested and carried to North Carolina, a prisoner. Tipton County, Tennessee, was later named for him.

[11] Roosevelt, *Winning of the West,* 4: 72.

## CHAPTER XX

## A PATRIOT PASSES

### I

On receipt of the news of St. Clair's defeat, Dragging Canoe hastened to McGilivray, of the Creeks. "Now is the time," he told the Creek chief, "to promote a great Indian Federation, to forever banish the Americans from our hunting grounds." McGilivray was willing, and guaranteed that the Creeks and Choctaws would join such a federation. If the Chickasaws could be persuaded to abandon their friendship for the Americans, the southern Indians would, for the first time, be solidly united. He suggested that Dragging Canoe himself should go to the Chickasaws and try to persuade them to join hands with their red brethren in the attempt to expel the Americans.[1]

The Chickasaws, though few in number, were remarkable fighters. Had it not been for their brave defense of their country, France at an earlier date would have controlled the Mississippi from source to mouth.[2] The Chickasaw warrior looked with contempt on the fighting qualities of the Cherokee, Creek, and Choctaw, for he considered himself the match of four of any other tribe. The Chickasaws were firm friends of James Robertson, and had told the Spanish governor: "We are not now, and never will be, at war with the Virginians."[3]

The Dragging Canoe could not move the Chickasaws; in spite of threats and argument, they remained firm friends of the Americans. He returned to Running Water disappointed, but determined to carry on the war alone if necessary.

---

[1] *American State Papers, Indian Affairs,* Vol. 1, 264.
[2] The Chickasaws repelled three attacks by the French in the years, 1736-39.
[3] The Chickasaws alone, of all the tribes, furnished a band of warriors, under Piomingo, to assist St. Clair in his ill-starred campaign. Piomingo was dissatisfied with St. Clair's treatment and left the army the day before the defeat of the white troops. On his way to his own country, he met a northern Indian dressed in the uniform of one of St. Clair's dragoons, and killed him. *Draper Mss.,* 30-S 297-322.

2

On Feb. 17, 1792, a party of travelers, consisting of John
Collingsworth, and his family and two friends, were on the old
Chickasaw trace from Natchez to the Cumberland. A few
miles south of Nashville they walked into an ambush of
Chickamaugas, headed by the Glass of Lookout Mountain
Town. Collingsworth was wounded, but being well-mounted
managed to escape; he died later. Mrs. Collingsworth and one
child were killed; a daughter, a girl of eight, was taken prisoner.
A handsome black horse which Mrs. Collingsworth had been
riding was taken by Glass, and later afforded him much pride.[4]

About this same time, a trader named Mims who was conveying salt from Kentucky to Nashville, was waylaid near the
Dripping Spring in the Barrens of Kentucky, by Turtle at
Home, of Running Water. He was killed, and his young son
was taken prisoner.[5]

The Glass and Turtle at Home arrived among the Chickamaugas on the same day, Feb. 22, 1792. On Feb. 26th, the
scalps of Mims and the Collingsworths were taken to Lookout
Mountain Town where a great celebration and scalp dance was
held. The Glass, Turtle at Home, and Richard Justice took
the scalp of the trader, Mims, in their teeth and tore it
ferociously as they danced, representing their hatred for the
whites. The example of the chiefs was followed by the warriors generally; the scalps of the woman and child, however,
were not so treated, as the warriors did not exult in the killing
of women and children.[6]

On Feb. 28th, Dragging Canoe and other warriors from
Running Water attended the celebration, and the Mims scalp
again was exulted over with all the forms of ferocity and
hatred; in addition, the Eagle Tail dance was held in honor of
the war-chief. The dance continued throughout the night with
savage frenzy; both men and women taking part.[7]

3

On March 1, 1792, the day after the great dance at Lookout
Town, Dragging Canoe died. Whether it was the frenzy of

---

[4] *American State Papers, Indian Affairs,* Vol. 1, 330.
[5] *Ibid.*
[6] *Ibid.*
[7] *Ibid.*

the dance, or the old wound which he had received at Island Flats that caused his death, is not known. He was about sixty years of age.

The great Chickamauga chief was buried at his town of Running Water. There is no record of the rites, but being an Indian of Indians during his life-time, there is no reason to doubt that he was laid to rest according to the "beloved old custom" of his fathers. Adair has given us the burial rites used by the Cherokees at the death of a chief, prefacing his description with the remark, "When a warrior dies a natural death, which is seldom." [8]

The body was washed and dressed in finest wearing apparel. The hair was annointed with bear's oil, and the face was painted red. The dead warrior was placed in seated position on the skins of wild animals, outside his winter house, facing to the west, with his most cherished possessions around him.

A prominent old chief, preferably a relative, was selected to deliver a eulogy. The body was borne three times around the place of interment, with the Adawehi, or Medicine Man, leading, followed relatives and friends. At each complete circuit there was a pause. The Adawehi commended the body to the care of Yo-He-Wah, the master of life, and each person present repeated the sacred name in low tone, prolonged to the extent of a full breath.

The dead leader was placed in his tomb in seated position facing the east. His gun and bow, and a quiver of panther skin filled with arrows, his pipe, tobacco, and every useful article that he had possessed that might be of service to him in the next world, and food for the long journey, were placed in the grave. His wife, during the first month of mourning, was expected to sit by his warpole each day and lament with wailing notes. Thereafter, for a year, she repaired at dawn and at sunset to the place of burial, and cried in "intense, audible strains," *Yah-ah-Yo-He-ta-Wah* (Master of Life, I mourn).

4

A savage though he was, we must concede to Dragging Canoe the title of patriot. At the beginning of his public career he refused to make the hunting grounds of his people

[8] Adair, pages 19, 190 and 195.

the means of barter and sale, although his course involved the opposition of older chiefs, one of whom was his father. When his advice had been disregarded and a treaty signed, he announced his intention to make the settlement of the land that had been sold, "dark and bloody." With consistency rare in Indian annals, he followed the path he had chosen, which was the war-path to the white settlements. His hatred of white men was confined to Americans. With Spaniards and Englishmen, he was on the best of terms, and drew from them the supplies necessary for war.

There was nothing mean and small in the nature of Dragging Canoe. A warrior who had brought a woman captive, Mrs. Starke, to Running Water, addressed insulting remarks to her in the chief's presence; although by Indian law a captive was the property of the captor, to be dealt with as he saw fit, Dragging Canoe killed him. Governor Blount, when he heard of the death of the chief, commented on the incident, and said, "Dragging Canoe stood second to none in the Nation." [9]

## 5

The National Council of the Cherokees was held June 26th to 30th, 1792, at Ustanali. Chief Black Fox, *Inali,* delivered this tribute at that time:

"The Dragging Canoe has left this world. He was a man of consequence in his country. He was a friend both to his own and the white people. His brother is still in place, and I mention it now publicly that I intend presenting him with his deceased brother's medal; for he promises fair to possess sentiments similar to those of his brother, both with regard to the red and the white. It is mentioned here publicly that both red and white may know it, and pay attention to him." [10]

Dragging Canoe's brother, of whom Black Fox spoke, was Little Owl, who at the same meeting boasted of presents received from the English for himself and his brother:

"a pair of large and small armbands for each; three gorgets for his brother, and four for himself; a pair of scarlet boots and flaps, bound with ribbons, for each; four match coats, a blanket and

[9] *American State Papers, Indian Affairs,* Vol. 1, 263.
[10] *Ibid.,* 271. Black Fox was a nephew of Dragging Canoe.

two shirts, for each; and as much powder and lead as he wanted for himself and the three Cherokees who accompanied him." [11]

## 6

The death of Dragging Canoe left vacant the vital position of war-chief. A council of the Five Lower Towns was promptly held at Running Water to select his successor. There is evidence that Doublehead aspired to the honor, but the choice of the chiefs was John Watts. Doublehead was placated by election to membership in the National Council to succeed Old Tassel.[12]

Watts was a half-breed, but thoroughly Indian in his sympathies and practice. He had followed the Indian law in revenging the death of Old Tassel, his uncle. He possessed great oratorical power and considerable ability as an organizer. He talked much, but knew when to be silent.[13]

At the time of Dragging Canoe's death, Watts was at Chote, treating with Governor Blount. Two runners were sent by the council at Running Water advising him of his selection as war-chief, and requesting his presence.[14]

Before Watts left, Governor Blount invited the chiefs of the Five Lower Towns to meet him at Coyatee on May 20th, to receive their portion of the annual allowance of the government. Watts, on behalf of the chiefs, accepted the invitation, and departed from Chote with protestations of friendship for the United States, and personal attachment for Governor Blount.[15]

---

[11] *Ibid.*, 327.

[12] *Ibid.*, 271.

[13] John McKee, who was sent by Governor Blount to secure information from Watts, plied the chief with liquor until he was drunk, expecting him to talk freely while in that condition. The only information that he secured was that Watts was still his friend.

[14] *American State Papers, Indian Affairs*, Vol. 1, 263.

[15] *Ibid.*, 291.

# CHAPTER XXI

## "TO WAR WE WILL GO TOGETHER."

### I

John Watts was determined to make the meeting with Governor Blount at Coyatee one that should be memorable in the annals of Indian Diplomacy.[1] The influence of Watts over the Cherokees was never more clearly shown than at that meeting.

The date set for the gathering was May 20th, 1792. On May 19th, the chiefs of the Five Lower Towns, who were implacably hostile to the Americans during Dragging Canoe's lifetime, marched to Coyatee to participate in the treaty. They were painted black, the war color, and over the black paint they had sprinkled flour, indicating that they had been for war, but were now for peace.[2]

Governor Blount was halted half-a-mile from the treaty ground by a messenger from the chiefs, with the request that he should wait until preparations had been made to receive him. In a short time, he was asked to proceed, and found two thousand Indians forming parallel lines, at the end of which a United States flag was waving upon a high pole. As the governor rode between the Indian lines, a volley was fired in salute, followed by shouts of welcome. When he alighted at the base of the standard, he was surrounded by Indians, as he says, "with countenances demonstrative of more joy than I have heretofore been witness of."

The governor arrived at Coyatee about mid-day, and the afternoon was spent in eating, drinking, and cheerful conversation with Eskaqua, John Watts, Hanging Maw, Richard Justice, Breath, Will, and others.

On the following morning, Eskaqua waited upon Governor Blount and suggested that no public business be transacted that day. "To devote the day to happiness unalloyed with public cares will the better prepare us," he said. The day, therefore,

---

[1] Coyatee was at the mouth of the present Little Tennessee River.
[2] *American State Papers, Indian Affairs*, Vol. 1, 269.

was spent in eating, "seasonable drinking of whiskey," in holding private talks with the chiefs, and in a ballplay. The chiefs wagered heavily on the result of the game, and Eskaqua was on the losing side. "Having staked much, he bore it not quite well," the governor comments.

On the next day, Tuesday, Eskaqua again asked that Governor Blount postpone the meeting. "I have been drinking too much whiskey to be capable of public business," he said. "It is an accident that might happen to any man. I hope you will agree to the talks being postponed until another day; I will let everybody know the fault is mine and not yours."

So Tuesday was spent, as Monday had been, in eating, drinking, and another ballplay. The gambling the day before had so excited the chiefs that they staked their clothes on the second game, reserving only their flaps. Eskaqua recovered his losses. The governor comments, "His getting drunk on Monday night was supposed to be a maneuver to get some of the best players on the other side in the same situation, which he effected. He did not play himself, and none of his players drank to excess."

On Wednesday, Eskaqua, in great good humor, escorted Governor Blount to the treaty ground where the chiefs were assembled. He apologized for delaying the guest for an extra day, and asked that he be pardoned. The chiefs, he said, were ready to commence the business of the meeting.

Governor Blount thanked the Indians for their friendly reception, and read an address which he had previously prepared. He called attention to the fact that more than thirty killings had occurred on the frontiers since the Treaty of Holston, when the Cherokees had pledged their friendship to the Americans. Two hundred horses had been stolen from the Cumberland settlements alone.

"I do not say, brothers, that your people have done all of these murders, and stolen all of these horses, but, from a variety of circumstances, suspicion falls on your Lower Towns and the Creeks. My brothers, you must exert yourselves to restrain your young people from such acts. It is with difficulty that I have restrained the people whose relations have been killed from falling upon the Indians and taking satisfaction, without regard to sex or age. Your father, the President, loves you and wishes you to be happy, but he equally loves the white people and it is equally his duty to protect them. He cannot see your people kill the white people, and compel them to bear it in peace."

Hanging Maw announced that the National Council would meet in thirty nights (June 23rd) at Ustanali, and instructed all the chiefs "to attend and not be absent on any pretence whatever." He promised that reply would be made to Governor Blount at the meeting in reference to the murders he had reported, and that Eskaqua would make full report of his proceedings at Philadelphia.

The governor announced the change in Bloody Fellow's name:

"The President has been pleased to direct that Bloody Fellow shall in the future be known and designated by the more honorable title of Eskaqua, or Clear Sky."

He also announced the appointment of James Carey as official government interpreter for the Nation. The Breath, of Nickajack, rose and pointing to Eskaqua, said:

"That man induced me to come here. The people of the Lower Towns have been very deaf to your talks, but now we will take them. I have heard your charge of murders and horse stealing, and I tell you truly, I do not know who committed the whole of them, but from the Great Council at Ustanali you shall be informed of whatever has been done by our Nation."

He handed the governor a string of white beads on behalf of the Lower Towns. Richard Justice, of Lookout Mountain Town, expressed regret at the killings, and said, "I hope we shall be able to restrain our young people after the council at Ustanali."

The annual distribution of goods brought a suggestion from the Badger that as the Lower Towns had not participated in the distribution for several years, they would be entitled to the greater portion of those about to be given, to which the chiefs from the upper towns gave assent. Finding that the governor had some additional goods which were not included in the regular annual allowance, the chiefs asked that they might also be distributed "as an added inducement to their young men to preserve the peace." The governor agreed to this, "believing that the goods could never be disposed of more to the advantage of the United States."

Governor Blount concluded his report of the proceedings at Coyatee with the remark: "Eskaqua appears to have entered fully into the views of the United States; and John Watts, fully determined to second him, rejoiced much on this auspicious event. They may be said to be the champions of peace."

The governor returned to Knoxville, confident that peace had been restored to the frontier. But the chiefs of the Five Lower Towns, had perpetrated their most consummate act of tomahawk diplomacy.[3]

## 2

A few months before the death of Dragging Canoe, and before McGilivray had made his treaty with Washington at New York, the term of Don Esteban Miro as Spanish Governor at New Orleans had expired. Miro, who was well advanced in age, had asked to be allowed to return to Spain; his request was granted. He had two able deputies; Arthur O'Neal at Pensacola, and Manuel Gayoso at Natchez; either of whom, had he been promoted, would have made an excellent governor. Through family influence, however, the King of Spain was induced to appoint as Miro's successor, Hector, Baron de Carondelet, of San Salvador. His principal qualification seems to have been that his brother-in-law was Governor of Cuba.

Carondelet was a nervous, excitable person. He credited every wild rumor, and had visions of the invasion of Florida by fifteen thousand Americans. In his mind's eye, he could see the rifle of an American behind every bush between New Orleans and the Cumberland. On his arrival at New Orleans in December, 1791, Carondelet took measures to repel what he considered a menace to Spain's possessions in North America. He was determined that the American frontier must be destroyed, or come under the Spanish flag.[4]

The latter proposition was at the time not so hopeless as it would seem. The border men were bitterly dissatisfied with

---

[3] Proceedings at the Coyatee meeting are from Governor Blount's report to the Secretary of War, *American State Papers, Indian Affairs*, Vol. 1, 267-269.

[4] Whitaker, *Spanish-American Frontier*.

their treatment by the American government. The Franklinites' resentment smoldered, ready to burst into flames.
James Wilkinson of Kentucky wrote that he "would gladly
lose one arm, if he might embrace his dear friend, Gayoso,
with the other." [5] To Carondelet, Wilkinson wrote that the
time had arrived when the matter of the navigation of the
Mississippi must be settled. If not, he intimated that the
Kentuckians would invade Florida with irresistible force, but
slyly added that if the Spanish governor would advance to him
sufficient money to influence the right persons, Kentucky would
secede from the United States and become part of Spanish
America.

The simple-minded Carondelet grabbed at the opportunity to
add Kentucky to Spanish territory. He sent to Wilkinson the
substantial sum of fifteen thousand dollars, in two instalments,
to promote the separatist movement. He informed "Our Dear
Brigadier," as he called Wilkinson, that he had been placed
regularly on the Spanish payroll at $2000.00 per annum.[6]

Carondelet had no doubt that his negotiations with the
Kentuckians would be crowned with success. To insure direct
and immediate action against the American frontier, however,
he relied on Indian warfare. Northern Indians had just inflicted terrible defeat on St. Clair's army. This, to Carondelet,
indicated that the Indians were better fighters than the Americans, and he hastened to enlist the red men under Spain's
banner. Miro, for many years, had secretly incited the Indians
against the Americans; Carondelet avowed his purpose openly.

Having disposed of Bowles, who had incited the Creeks
against the Spaniards, Carondelet summoned McGilivray to
New Orleans, as has been said, and "made him a greater man
than Congress did." McGilivray drew both salaries; he did
not openly repudiate the Treaty of New York, but accepted
Carondelet's plans for destruction of the American frontier
settlements. Creek warriors were loosed on the borders of
Georgia, the Holston, and Cumberland. In his correspondence
with the Americans, McGilivray was careful to claim that
these acts were those of a "few irresponsible, bad young men."

Carondelet brought the Choctaws in line and built a fort in

---

[5] *Ibid.*
[6] *Ibid.*

their country. He sent McGilivray and Panton to confer with Dragging Canoe of the Chickamaugas at his home in Running Water. Dragging Canoe had just returned from the Chickasaw country where he had tried and failed to induce that tribe to join an Indian Confederation. Carondelet had also failed to line them up, but they eventually permitted the building of a fort at Chickasaw Bluffs. The death of Dragging Canoe occurred soon after this, and the news was carried promptly to Carondelet; also that John Watts had been elected his successor.

There were in New Orleans at the time, two American traders, Richard Finnelston and Joseph Deraque. The Spanish governor paid them $400.00 to carry a message to Watts.[7] He invited the principal Cherokee chiefs to visit Governor O'Neal at Pensacola, where they would find plenty of arms and ammunition for the taking. Fearing that the traders might not deliver the message, Carondelet sent a similar one by William Panton, head of the house of Panton-Leslie & Co.

Panton arrived in the Cherokee country while the chiefs were in conference with Governor Blount, at Coyatee.[8] He was a man of great shrewdness and long experience in dealing with the Indians. Realizing that the success of Blount's negotiations would be the death blow to his own trade with the Cherokees, he decided to forestall American influence by sending a letter to Watts before the talks were concluded.

The letter was written from the house of John McDonald, former English deputy under Stuart, who lived at Chickamauga. In it, Panton invited Watts, Doublehead, and Bloody Fellow, to visit Pensacola and to bring with them, ten packhorses. They were promised such arms and ammunition as they desired, without cost; and such other goods as they might need at a cheaper price than ever made them before.

As Watts was leaving the conference at Coyatee, he was met by a runner with Panton's letter. He went at once to McDonald's house where several days were spent. Panton convinced him that Spain was the friend to whom the Indians

[7] *American State Papers, Indian Affairs*, Vol. 1, 288.
Finnelston was a half-breed Cherokee, in the pay of Governor Blount, to whom he later gave a detailed account of his activities, and of Watts' reception of Carondelet's message.
[8] *Ibid.*, 328.

must turn if they wished to regain their hunting grounds. Together, the two visited Little Turkey, who, although he had been inclined to peace with the Americans, was not hard to convince. Bloody Fellow, who had just returned from Philadelphia with his new title Eskaqua (Clear Sky), readily fell in with the new plan. By his request, McDonald wrote for him a letter to Governor Carondelet:

"I have been to see the President where I was treated well, but am as far to seek my lands as ever. I am glad the Spaniards will supply my Nation with ammunition and assist in the recovery of our lands. I have been blind for a long time but now my eyes are open. I will let go the hand of the Americans, and will take hold of that of the Spaniards. Do not let Watts return without plenty of ammunition. I will come to see you a little later, and will bring the Little Turkey and some other chiefs." [9]

John Watts, Doublehead, and Young Dragging Canoe, son of the old chief, arranged to proceed immediately to Pensacola. McDonald wrote their credentials, highly recommending them to Governor O'Neal. Bloody Fellow accompanied them to Coosa River, spent the night with them, and regretfully turned back, as he had already agreed to meet with the Great Council on June 23rd to report on his trip to Philadelphia.[10]

The Cherokee envoys were received by Governor O'Neal with open arms. They were shown whole warehouses of supplies to be had for the asking. Their pack-horses were loaded with presents. Watts was given the title of Colonel, and was assured of Spanish support. Doublehead did not wait to get back to his own country, but applied the war paint and raised the war whoop in Pensacola.[11]

### 3

Bloody Fellow had appointed the meeting of the council at Ustanali on June 23rd, to hear his report on his Philadelphia trip, but the Spanish development arose in the meantime, and he decided not to make the report, and did not even attend the meeting. The council waited on him three days before making any transactions. Runners were sent urging him to

[9] *Ibid.*, 328.
[10] *Ibid.*, 329.
[11] *Ibid.*, 328.

come, but he replied evasively, saying that a relative was sick.[12]

The council proceeded without him. As it drew to a close, Dragging Canoe's brother, the Little Owl, appeared. He took the Little Turkey aside, and told him that Watts had returned from Pensacola, and that he would report on what he had done, at Willstown in eight nights. "The hour is come for the blow to be struck," said the Little Owl. "Watts has returned, and all things are as he wished, and he will explain fully at Willstown." He delivered a string of black war-beads from Watts to the Little Turkey.

Thus emboldened, the Little Turkey reentered the council and demanded that the old boundary between the Americans and Cherokees be restored. The Jobber's Son, sitting at a distance from the speaker, observed to those around him, "It is too late to talk on that line, for we have established a different line at the Treaty of Holston." To which a nearby warrior, Little Frog, replied: "That is nothing; we had no one to back us then. Now we have, and can get that line." [13]

4

While Watts and Doublehead were away in Pensacola, two subordinate chiefs, Bench and Shawnee Warrior, had kept the torch and scalping knife busy on the American frontier.

On April 6, 1792, Bench visited the Holston settlements and killed the wife and three children of Harper Ratliff, in Stanley Valley. He left beside the scalped bodies, a declaration of war; three war clubs; a bow; and a sheaf of arrows. The Chickamaugas used stratagen on such raids to divert the suspicion and vengeance of the whites to the upper Cherokees, and thus to force them, regardless of inclination, to take up the war-hatchet.

The Creeks helped their Chickamauga allies to harass the white settlements, particularly Cumberland.

James Thompson, his wife and two daughters, and Peter Caffrey and his wife and a son, occupied a cabin jointly, to better protect themselves from the Indians, four miles south of Nashville. Thompson was chopping wood one cold Feb-

---

[12] *Ibid.*, 328.
[13] *Ibid.*, 327.

ruary morning, when he was surprised by a party of Creeks. He managed to gain the house, but he, his wife, and Peter Caffrey were killed a few minutes later when the Indians gouged the chinking from between the logs and fired on the inmates. The savages broke in and took the other occupants captive, then headed for their town of Kialages on the Tallapoosa River. One of the Thompson girls had been wounded and could not keep the pace. She was scalped and left by the roadside, but lived long enough to tell a party of pursuing neighbors about what had happened. The older girl found it hard to keep up, being so grief-stricken, and her captor informed her that he would scratch her legs with briars, which would make her walk faster.

When the party arrived at Kialages, John O'Reilly, an Irish trader, felt so sympathetic toward the prisoners that he offered the Indians a negro each for their ransom. The Creeks retorted, "We did not bring our captives so far only to have them returned to the Virginians. We brought them to punish them by making them work to make food for ourselves. As for you, O'Reilly, we are tempted to knock you in the head for making us such a proposition. We would do so if you had not been our friend, but you must not speak so to us again." [14] The two women were put to work in the fields; Alice Thompson could not stand the hard labor, and cried. Even the savage heart was softened by the sight of the tears, and her captor put her in the house to pound corn. The generous O'Reilly, in spite of threats, persisted in his efforts to ransom the prisoners; after a time, he succeeded in securing Miss Thompson's release in exchange for eight hundred pounds of dressed deer skins, valued at $260.00; she was returned to her people.

Mrs. Caffrey was treated as a slave and kept at menial labor; she was often punished by having her limbs scratched with gar's teeth.[15] It is to the credit of the Creeks and Cherokees,

---

[14] *Ibid.*, 274.

[15] It is probable that the Indians did not regard such treatment as punishment; ballplayers were scratched in similar manner before a game to increase their strength. Mrs. Caffrey was ransomed two years later, and still bore the scars of the scratches. Her little boy was given to a Creek family and remained with them, five years. He objected to leaving his Indian playmates whom he had learned to love, when finally he was exchanged. (*Ibid.*, 274.) The gar is a species of fish.

that the white women captives, while treated as slaves, were never defiled.

## 5

Ziegler's Station was situated in Sumner County about two miles from Bledsoe's. It was occupied by the families of Jacob Ziegler, Joseph Wilson, and others. On the morning of June 26, 1792, Shawnee Warrior and Little Owl, with their followers from Running Water, and a few Creek allies, appeared at Ziegler's. Michael Shaver was killed as he worked in the fields near the station. Neighbors sallied forth to recover his body and fell into an ambush; three were wounded, but all managed to reach the fort. The Indians fired a few rounds and retired. The neighbors, except Archie Wilson, returned to their homes, thinking the fight was over.

But the Indians made a furious assault at dusk, and succeeded in setting fire to the fort. Jacob Ziegler and two negroes were killed. The flames soon became unbearable; Mrs. Joseph Wilson begged her son and husband to run for their lives, hoping that she and her daughters might be spared. The plan succeeded; Wilson and his son both were wounded, but reached the cover of the woods and escaped in the darkness. Mrs. Jacob Ziegler seized her baby, stuffed a handkerchief in its mouth to prevent it from crying, and fled into the woods; she escaped. Archie Wilson was forced into the open by the flames, and was instantly surrounded by the savages. He fought valiantly, but was killed when an Indian broke the breech of a rifle across his head.

Mrs. Wilson and her two children, Sarah and Zach; three children of Jacob Ziegler; Mollie Jones; and five negro slaves, were taken prisoners. They were divided among the Indians. Shawnee Warrior took the three Ziegler girls; Little Owl took Zach Wilson; Sarah was given to the Creeks for their assistance; and the other captives were claimed by various warriors from Running Water.

The savages crossed Cumberland River and established a base near the present Lebanon, Tenn. They carefully packed all their spoils from Ziegler's, and hung them in the branches of trees; covered with bark to protect them from the weather.

They were short of horses, therefore a small number returned to Nashville to secure them, so that they might not have to carry their booty afoot. The main body pushed ahead with the captives.

When Joseph Wilson escaped from the station he spread the alarm and a rescue party, under General Winchester, was raised. John Carr, Peter Looney, and John Hartlepool preceded the force as scouts. They located the Indian camp and the spoils, and discovered that the war-party had divided. Several men were sent back to Nashville with the spoils, and to warn the settlers to look out for their horses. Winchester, with most of the force, followed the larger trail toward Nickajack. It was easily followed as it had been raining. Seven of the prisoners were children who had been taken from their homes in the night, half-clothed. Bare-footprints were seen at every muddy place. On the second morning of the pursuit, the scouts found a dying campfire, around which were scraps of deerskin and leather thongs; the Indians had made moccasins for the children, "their feet doubtless having become sore by the hard traveling." At the next muddy spot, the white men found the print of seven pairs of small moccasins. "There was that much of kindness in them," said John Carr.

On the morning of the third day, General Winchester suggested that it would be better to permit the Indians to take their captives to the towns. "They will be killed if we attempt to take them in action," he said. The pursuit, therefore, was abandoned.

The prisoners were taken to Running Water. All of them, except the negroes, and Sarah Wilson, who had been given to the Creeks, were ransomed soon afterward through the efforts of General James White of Knoxville, Mrs. Wilson's brother.[16]

Mrs. Wilson related that when the Indians had reached Duck River, they halted to await the arrival of those who had returned to Nashville to steal horses with which to transport the stolen booty. The other Indians appeared with neither horses nor spoils, and a violent quarrel ensued. Knives were drawn, and a pitched battle was averted only by the thought that white pursuers were close on their trail.[17]

Although Robertson continued to report Indian depredations

[16] The prices paid for the release of the Wilson and Zeigler children was $58.00 each. *Narrative of John Carr, Southwestern Monthly,* Vol. 2, 74.
[17] *American State Papers, Indian Affairs,* Vol. 1, 275 and 329.

on Cumberland, Governor Blount adhered rigidly to instructions to limit Indian warfare to "defensive operations." The frontiersmen could hardly be restrained from "taking satisfaction." A volunteer company was raised in Nashville under Captain John Edmiston, with the avowed purpose of invading the Chickamauga towns. Robertson forbade the expedition, and in a few days found an anonymous letter in his mail:

"Sir: I was much surprised when I heard of your wishing to stop Captain Edmiston from going against the Indians with a volunteer company to retaliate for the damage they are daily doing to us. But hearing it generally reported in the country that it has always been your endeavor to stop all those that wish to do good to this country and damage to the Indians, I must join with the rest of my countrymen and wish Edmiston great success, and you gone from hence and a better in your place, I am, etc.,

"A Citizen of Mero District, July 10,[18] 1792.

Robertson, who had suffered as much or more than anyone on the frontier, did not deserve such a letter, and the writer was wise to sign himself anonymously.

6

After the death of Dragging Canoe, John Watts moved his residence to Willstown, which was closer to his Spanish supply, and to his Creek allies, than Running Water.[19] Warriors from all parts of the Cherokee Nation gathered at Willstown in September, 1792, to hear Watts' report of his trip to Pensacola.

Traders, Finnelston and Deraque, bearing Governor Carondelet's message to Watts, arrived at Willstown just as the Indians had gathered in the square.[20]

Watts began his report by reading a letter he had received from Governor O'Neal, reminding the Indians that the King of Spain had sent enough ammunition to Pensacola to fill four warehouses, one for each Southern tribe: "You, John Watts, have been an eye-witness to the quantity of powder, lead, and arms; if the whole of the Cherokee towns will come

---

[18] Putnam, 388.
[19] Willstown was near the present Fort Payne, Ala.
[20] *American State Papers, Indian Affairs,* Vol. 1, 289-291.

down, they shall be supplied, each town with four or five
hundred pounds of gunpowder, more if necessary, and lead
accordingly." The governor recommended to the Chickamaugas, their old friends, John McDonald and Alexander
Cameron, who had allied themselves with Spanish interests.

Watts reported his welcome by the Spanish Governor, who
had asked him:

"Did you see any Spanish settlements before you arrived at
Pensacola? Wherever the Spanish land, they sit down; even a
sandbar is sufficient for them. They never want a back-country.
They are not like the Americans, who first take your lands and
then treat with you and give you little or nothing for them."

"Now is the time for the Indians to join quickly in war with
the United States, while they are engaged in war with the northern
tribes. If you do not, as soon as the United States has conquered
the northern Indians, they will be upon the Cherokees and will
cut them off."

In reference to the visit of Bloody Fellow to Philadelphia,
the governor said:

"The talk he received was not from the heart, but from the
teeth only," and promised the Indians swords, pistols, bridles,
and saddles to support Watts' cherished plan of "fighting in
armies." He offered to build a fort in the Cherokee country,
and a magazine for ammunition at Willstown, so that the
Cherokees would always be supplied with the means of war.[21]

Having thus recapitulated the talk received from the Spanish
governor, Watts addressed his audience:

"The Cherokees have been to Hopewell, to Savannah, to Holston,
and to Philadelphia; but none of them have pleased me like what
I have seen and heard at Pensacola."

"The young fellows are always wanting war; now the time has
come when they may try themselves. There are enough of us,
and if there are not, we have friends enough back of us, Creeks
and Choctaws, and our old friends, the Spaniards. Now you
must show yourselves. All of you young men who like war, go
with me tomorrow. We have a great many more men, and will
settle matters better when we all get together."[22]

[21] *Ibid.*
[22] *Ibid.,* 328.

Eskaqua, formerly Bloody Fellow, rose to reply to Watts' talk. He strongly opposed war, not that he loved the Americans, but he did not consider the time ripe. Possibly his conscience troubled him when he remembered that Washington had "wiped his tears away."

"It is a bad step you are taking," he said, "do not go to war." He pointed to his brigadier's uniform, and to the medal given him by Washington. "Look at these thing I have fetched. When was the day you ever went to your old father, Stuart, and fetched as much as I have. You had better take my talk, and stay home and mind your children and women."

Although Eskaqua still stood to indicate that his talk was not finished, Watts' uncle, Doublehead, rose and said:

"I, too, have been to Pensacola. I have seen the governor as well as Watts. I have heard his talk and think a great deal of it, for it is good. I shall try to do as he directs me."

Doublehead resumed his seat. Bloody Fellow remained standing, but Watts advanced to the center of the stage and spoke:

"The day is come when I must bloody my hands again. Tomorrow I shall send off a runner to the Creek Nation to bring in my friends. Then I shall have enough people to go with me to Cumberland, and any place that I want to go."

At this word from their war-chief, the council dispersed, and in half an hour the warriors returned, stripped to their flaps and painted black. Bloody Fellow, in his capacity of Brigadier-General Eskaqua, had placed an American flag upon the pole in the center of the council square. Around this, throughout the night, to the beat of the tom-tom, the warriors danced the war dance.

The council reassembled the following day, and Eskaqua again stood up for peace. Taking hold of his medal, he said:

"See how my brothers have used me. This is silver, and must have cost a great deal." He called attention to his coat with silver epaulettes, and his scarlet match coat with silver lace.

"When is the day that you ever went to see your father Stuart, and brought home the like of that? I would have none of you go to war, but remain at home and lie in peace, as I mean to do. I can go over the mountains and live in peace."

When Bloody Fellow mentioned his medal, John Watts took off his own, which had been given him by the Americans, and laid it upon the ground.

Little Owl, Dragging Canoe's brother, rose and said,

"My father was a man, and I am as good a man as he was. To war I will go, and spill blood in spite of what you say. From this day I will do as I please."

Watts took Little Owl by the hand and led him forward. "You are a man and I like your talk," he said. "To war we will go together."

Eskaqua persisted:

"You had better not, for you know nothing of what you do. Look at that flag; don't you see all the stars in it? They are not towns, they are nations, and there are thirteen of them. These people are very strong, and are the same as one man. If you know when you are well, you had better stay at home and mind your women and children."

Shawnee Warrior, who had lived at Running Water with thirty Shawnee braves for several years, advanced to the center of the council, and stretched out his hands for all to see.

"With these hands, I have killed three hundred men. Now the time is come when I shall take the lives of three hundred more. Then I will be satisfied, and will sit down in peace. I will now drink my fill of blood."

"If you go to war," said Eskaqua, "I shall not." He then sat down, much dejected.

Watts advanced to the center of the council, and said:

"Tomorrow, we must go to Lookout Mountain Town, where we shall assemble together and lay off how we shall attack the frontiers of Holston."

The council dispersed, but in a short time came back with guns and tomahawks. Throughout the night the warriors danced the war-dance around the American flag. Several, in the frenzy of hatred, fired at the flag; Bloody Fellow ordered them to desist. "If you do not," he said, "I will do as I have done before," meaning that he would kill them; the firing at the flag ceased.[23]

## 7

On the third day after the council at Willstown, the Chickamaugas, to the number of six hundred, assembled at Lookout Mountain Town. It was decided, as a large number of Creek allies were expected, to attack the Holston in four divisions of two hundred each, one division to consist entirely of horsemen. The Indian army was to remain intact until the Holston had been swept as far back as Long Island; then to break up into smaller parties and destroy the settlements along the French Broad River. The warriors again went into a wardance, which lasted all night.

When Eskaqua had returned to the Cherokee Nation from Philadelphia, the President sent with him, a young man, Leonard Shaw, to instruct the Indians in agriculture and other arts, and to endeavor to train them to peace rather than to war.

Shaw had married the daughter of a chief, and had gained the confidence of the Cherokees. Through his wife, he learned of what had taken place at Willstown, and sent a runner to advise Governor Blount. The interpreter, James Carey, also sent word to the governor.

When Watts learned that Shaw and Carey had betrayed him, his plans were hastily changed. It was decided that the Cumberland, instead of Holston, should be attacked. Chief Glass, and Eskaqua, who had opposed the war, were induced to write letters to Governor Blount and counteract any information that Carey and Shaw had given him. Middlestriker, of Willstown, was assigned with sixty warriors to the Walton road, to see that no word of the intended attack should reach the Cumberland by that route. Doublehead was given the same duty on the Kentucky Road. Orders were given by Watts, that provisions be prepared and all warriors be ready to start on the second day.

About an hour after the orders had been issued, word was received that Unacatchee, the White Man Killer, was at the

---

[23] Proceeding at Willstown are from reports of Finnelston and Deraque, *American State Papers, Indian Affairs,* Vol. 1, 289-291; and report of James Carey, *Ibid.,* 328.

mouth of Lookout Creek with a quantity of whiskey. Runners were dispatched to bring the fire-water to Lookout Mountain Town. Upon its arrival, the Indians fell to drinking. On the fifth day, when the campaign was scheduled to begin, "the whole party lay generally drunk, and in the meantime, no preparations were made for the war." [24]

## 8

Finnelston and Deraque had seen enough to be convinced that the American frontier was in deadly peril. They took advantage of the drunkenness of the Indians to escape; pretending that Governor Carondelet had sent them as spies to Nashville, to report to him the number of white people who lived in the Cumberland settlements. They promised to return in ten days and give Watts full information.

The council agreed to let them go, and told them that letters would be written to Governor Blount saying that only a few drunken young fellows were for war, and that the heads of the towns, who were for peace, had stopped them. This, they said, would throw the governor off his guard, and prevent any bad consequences from the report of Carey and Shaw.

Finnelston and Deraque, thus advised of their plans, hastened toward Nashville. They traveled with such speed, fearing that the Indians might change their minds and pursue them, that Deraque killed his horse, and was compelled to continue the journey on foot.

Carey was sent a warning from Chiefs, Glass, Bloody Fellow, and the Breath, at Ustanali on Sept. 14th, that "the breath has almost gone out of your body for the report that you have given information to Governor Blount." He was notified that as he had been raised in the Nation, the chiefs would overlook his fault, but that he must "quit looking forward or giving information to the Americans"; and was informed that the chiefs had written to Governor Blount that the Lower Towns were no longer for war; "What we have written the governor is not our real intentions, but a make-haste, from the teeth outward, to deceive him until we can get ready, get our crops out of the ground, and go down to Governor O'Neal for more ammunition." Carey was invited to accompany the chiefs to

---

[24] Finnelston's report. *American State Papers, Indian Affairs.*

Pensacola, with the promise, "We will get you in a better business than you are now in." [25]

Eskaqua, who had talked so bravely at the war council, was well understood by Watts: he was not at all opposed to war with the Americans, but did not think it was an opportune time for beginning. He did not object to writing the deceptive letter to Governor Blount.

To Carey, Eskaqua wrote:

"I am going to Pensacola, and wish you would go with me and bring six or eight packhorses to assist me with the ammunition. If necessary, I shall walk back with my wife, and use our riding horses to pack more ammunition." [26]

## 9

The Little Turkey, who, following Old Tassel's death, had been chosen to head that portion of the Cherokees who lived in Georgia, was considered by Governor Blount to be a firm friend of the United States. Earlier in the year, he had written the chiefs of the Five Lower Towns, and had sent a copy of the letter to the governor:

"The Little Turkey is tired of talking to you. I have heard what you have lately done. I will no more travel the path to the Lower Towns, to hold talks. If you must go to war, go, and I will sit still and look at you, but you must stay on your own side of Chatanuga Mountain, and not mix with other parts of the Nation.[27] I will go and inform Governor Blount where you live, and that you are for war. Where will you get ammunition? Will you get it from the people you are going to kill, or will your Conjuror, Richard Justice, find it for you in the caves of the earth?" [28]

But the information that John Watts had brought back from the Spaniards had changed the attitude of Little Turkey. He, too, visited Governor O'Neal, in company with John McDonald and the Boot, to receive his share of presents and ammunition. He also traveled the path to the Lower Towns again. The Little Turkey was not different from other Indians; all of them wanted their hunting grounds restored,

---

[25] Carey's report.

[26] *American State Papers, Indian Affairs*, Vol. 1, 328.

[27] See note 19, Chapter IX.

[28] *American State Papers, Indian Affairs*, Vol. 1, 264.

and they grasped at any straw that might contribute to this result.

In a letter to the British Agent, McKee, at Detroit, written for him by Welbank, Little Turkey said:

"Father: It has been ten years now since the English have left us, and I have never heard anything since that could be depended upon. I have heard from our brothers, the Shawnees, and approve of their talks, as does all my Nation. I am in hopes of one day seeing my fathers again in this neighborhood. My Nation has been a long time in a distracted state, but I hope it will not be so any longer. I hope to receive arms and ammunition from our fathers as soon as possible, that we may prosecute the war with vigor, and sooner put an end to the dispute.

"In case any accident should happen to me, for I am old, my friend can inform you of the chief who will attend to my talks, and hold fast to the English, our fathers.

"From your friend and well-wisher, in behalf of the whole Cherokee Nation,[29]

"KANAKETAH, or The Little Turkey,
Chief of the Cherokee."

### 10

While these stirring events were happening among the Cherokees, the Spaniard, Don Pedro Oliver, was passing out ammunition to the Creeks, with the message:

"Brothers: The Spanish talk, the French talk, and the English talk are now one. When is the day they have asked you for land? But the Americans are still wanting your lands. If you need arms and ammunition to defend your hunting grounds, come to the Spaniards for them, and you shall have them."[30]

Panton, distributing guns and ammunition at Pensacola, repeatedly told the Creeks: "These guns are to kill Americans, and I would rather they would be used for that purpose than the killing of deer." He also told the Indians, with an eye to self-interest; "If any American traders come among you, rob them of their goods, for only Spanish subjects are authorized to trade with you."[31]

---

[29] *Publications of East Tenn. Historical Society,* 1930.
[30] *American State Papers, Indian Affairs,* Vol. 1, 274.
[31] *Ibid.,* 308.

Creek warriors boasted:

"It is to our interest to keep up war with the United States. When we commit ravages against them, of ever so great a nature, we can easily hold a treaty and get large presents and be at peace. We can then repeat our conduct, for the people of the United States are very good natured." [32]

When Watts' messengers reached the Creek Nation, and told that tribe what had happened at Willstown, the Creeks announced their plan: the young warriors would join Watts in the war, while the older men would go to Rock Landing and make a treaty with James Seagrove; and they did exactly that.[33]

[32] *Ibid.,* 329.
[33] *Ibid.,* 282 and 328.

# CHAPTER XXII

## FIGHTING IN ARMIES

### 1

Chief John Watts was described by Governor Blount as "unquestionably the leading man in his Nation."[1] He possessed a talent for making friends, red and white. William Martin, son of General Joseph Martin, said of him, "He was one of the finest looking men I ever saw, large of stature, bold and magnanimous, a great friend of my father's."[2] Major G. W. Sevier states: "He was a noble looking Indian, always considered a generous and honorable enemy;"[3] and other pioneers paid high tribute to his "engaging personality."[4]

Watts, a half-breed, was born at Tuskegee, on the Little Tennessee, about the year 1750. His father was a white trader, who had served Captain Demere as interpreter during the building of Fort Loudoun, and was accused at that time of stirring up trouble between the Cherokees and the English.[5] His mother was a member of a prominent Cherokee family. She was a sister of Chiefs, Old Tassel, Doublehead, and Pumpkin Boy.

### 2

John Watts had come into the War-chieftainship of the Chickamaugas, at an opportune time. Bowles had assured the Indians that King George would restore their hunting grounds. The Spanish governor had made them the same guarantee,

---

[1] *American State Papers, Indian Affairs,* Vol. 1, 443.

[2] *Draper Mss.,* 3-XX-4, William Martin to L. C. Draper.

[3] *Ibid.,* 30-S 297-332, Sevier to L. C. Draper.

[4] *Ibid.,* 6-XX-46, Joseph Brown to L. C. Draper.

[5] S.C.I.A. 5: 375-377. The Cherokees had complained to Demere of the failure of Gov. Lyttleton to send them guns and ammunition. "When the French send their Indians to war, they offer them large rewards for scalps and fit them out with everything necessary, but the English have given us only a belt of wampum, which we will return."

"I am well convinced," Demere wrote Lyttleton, "that this talk proceeded from something that was told the Indians by John Elliott and John Watts. Watts speaks their language well. Elliott and Watts are a couple of dangerous people."

and had offered unlimited amounts of arms and ammunition for that purpose. Watts' eloquence and sincerety, coupled with these promises, had roused the Cherokee and Creek towns to a frenzy of enthusiasm. He was one of the few Indian leaders who could induce the red warriors to fight together in large numbers, and their hopes flamed high under his leadership. Practically all the able-bodied Cherokees, and hundreds of Creek warriors placed themselves at his command.

The first step of Watts' campaign was the sending of deceptive letters to Governor Blount, to offset the information communicated by Carey and Shaw. The traders, Finnelston and Deraque, had reached Nashville, and Robertson had forwarded their report to Blount. The governor had also received a letter from the Little Turkey, which advised him: "Them five lower towns on the Big River have determined to go off to war.[6] It is not the consent of the whole Nation, nor any part of it only them five towns." [7]

Greatly alarmed, Governor Blount sent orders to Robertson to put his brigade in position to repel the Indian invasion, should the attack be directed at Cumberland. Captain Samuel Handley, a brave and experienced Indian fighter, was dispatched by the Walton road with forty-five men to aid in Robertson's defense.

At the height of alarm and preparation, Blount received letters from the Glass and Bloody Fellow. They were artful communications, well designed to allay his fears. The letters were dated at Lookout Mountain Town, September 10, 1792.

Chief Glass reminded Governor Blount that he had sent him a talk a few days before by Captain John Chisholm, and admonished the governor to "remember it well, as I never tell you anything but the truth"; with which auspicious beginning he proceeded with a message that was far from truthful:

"Cotetoy returned here from Nashville, and told us that Colonel Robertson said there had been a great deal of blood spilled in his settlements, and he would come and sweep it clean with our blood. This caused our young warriors to assemble together to meet him, as he told Cotetoy that the first mischief that was done, he would

---

[6] The Cherokees called the Tennessee the Hogohegee, which is a hybrid word composed of the Cherokee word, *Egwa*, Big; and the Creek word *Hatchie*, River. They invariably spoke of it as the *Big River*.

[7] *American State Papers, Indian Affairs*, Vol. 1, 277.

come. We knew it would not be long before something might happen, as there is Creeks daily going to that settlement. As our young warriors expected to suffer for the doings of others, they resolved that they would meet him, or go to the settlements and do mischief, as they were to be the sufferers, do it who would.

"With the assistance of Bloody Fellow, John Watts, and some other head-men, we have sent them to their different homes to mind their hunting, in hopes you will not suffer any more of your people to send threatening talks. We took pity on the innocent that might suffer on both sides. As I have always listened to your talks, I hope you will listen to mine, and have peace. These from your friend and brother,

THE GLASS."[8]

By the same messenger who delivered the talk of the Glass, Governor Blount received Bloody Fellow's talk:

"My brother, the Glass, has told you the reason for our young warriors being assembled together. I overtook them at this place, Lookout Mountain Town, and it was a long time before I or the other head-men could put a stop to the effusion of blood. If you was to consider well, you would see that it was more your own people's fault than mine, by daily encroaching on our lands, and sending threatening talks."

He reminded the governor that it had been but a short time since he had returned from his visit to the President:

"My tracks are scarcely yet blotted out. The President promised that the white people should not encroach upon Cherokee lands, but they are daily encroaching and building houses upon our lands, and this is not what we agreed upon. He was to let the different governors know, so they would not settle upon our lands as they had formerly done."

"I hear that you are displeased with us for holding talks with the Spaniards. Why should we not hold talks with our neighbors? We do not want to be at war with anybody if we can avoid it."

Bloody Fellow concluded his letter with this appeal:

"If there is any bad people in your land that wants to hurt us, I hope you will likewise stop them as I have done mine, that we may live in peace one with another, and hear no more of war."[9]

[8] *American State Papers, Indian Affairs,* Vol. 1, 280.
[9] *Ibid.,* 280. The letters of Glass and Bloody Fellow were probably written for them by George Welbank.

Governor Blount was delighted with the two letters. He hastened to answer both in a conciliatory manner, and closed his communications with the words:

"Now, my good friend and brother, I have answered your letter. Let me tell you that I have a great deal of love for you, and will ever be happy to see you and take you by the hand, and I shall ever be happy in seeing John Watts. I am your friend and brother,

WILLIAM BLOUNT." [10]

He canceled his order to Robertson to hold his brigade in readiness, telling him of the letters received from Bloody Fellow and the Glass. There being no further danger of an Indian offensive, he told Robertson, it was his desire that the militia should return to their homes. John Sevier remarked: "The governor is too confiding," and events proved this to be true. [11]

### 3

Bloody Fellow and the Glass were absent from home when Governor Blount's letters were delivered. Were they with John Watts? Bloody Fellow was asked afterward if he was present at the attack on Buchanan's Station. In reply, he dipped his finger in water, and, withdrawing it, asked, "You see him there?" The water leaving no trace, Bloody Fellow kept his own counsel.

The governor's letters were answered, for the absent chiefs, by the Breath and Charles. They sought still further to deceive Blount by throwing blame for all hostilities upon the Creeks; a perennial excuse of the Cherokees:

"We are sorry to inform you,—you may think it is a lie, but we assure you it is the truth;—we are sorry that four days after our people dispersed to their different homes, there was a great number of Creeks passed here for several days. It was out of our power to stop them. It is not the head men of the Creek Nation, but the young fellows instead, indeed a great number of them are boys; they said they are going to Cumberland." [12]

---

[10] *Ibid.*, 281.
[11] Putnam, 369.
[12] *American State Papers, Indian Affairs*, Vol. 1, 280.

The interpreters, almost every Indian trader, and many of the Cherokee chiefs, were in the pay of Governor Blount, and every move made by Watts was reported to the governor by one or more of his agents. On Sept. 28th, John Boggs, the messenger who had carried Blount's letters to Bloody Fellow and the Glass, returned to Knoxville. He induced Unacata, Watts' brother, to accompany him back; the governor plied them both with whiskey, hoping to secure information while they were drunk.

He learned that large numbers of Creeks had passed through Running Water for Cumberland; that they had been joined by Watts and two hundred Cherokee warriors; and that the Cherokees planned to move west of the Mississippi River, if defeated.[13]

Unacata drank freely, and "told several stories with great humor of the attentions the white people had always paid to Watts when he came among them."

Watts, he told the governor, was now for war, and had sent for him (Unacata) to join him. He said that he had replied that the white people had given to Watts a great many clothes, and he had grown saucy. All the clothes which he himself possessed had been earned and paid for. "If Watts goes to war and falls," he said, "he may lie there; I will not pick him up"; meaning that he would not avenge his brother according to the Indian law.[14]

### 4

An unaccountable delay in the appearance of the hostile Indians after they were known to have crossed Tennessee River on their way to Nashville caused Robertson to discount the information which Finnelston and Deraque had brought. Finnelston protested that: if his words were not true, Robertson might "put him in gaol and hang him."

About the middle of September, Abraham Castleman was sent out as a spy. He discovered the trail of a large party of Indians near Black Fox's Camp (Murfreesboro). He also found the camp deserted, a suspicious fact, for Black Fox had been in the habit of trading peltries in Nashville, and the hunting season was not over. He, therefore, hastened to

---

[13] This is probably the first mention by the Cherokees of removal.
[14] *American State Papers, Indian Affairs*, Vol. 1, 293.

Nashville with this information; but still the Indians did not appear.

Robertson had called out three hundred militia and stationed them at Rain's Spring, two and a half miles south of the Bluffs. The men became indignant because Castleman had "smelled a cold trail," and Robertson, concluding that this was true, marched them back to Nashville and disbanded.

Castleman, nettled, cleaned his gun, the faithful "Betsy," filled his powder horn, ran an extra number of bullets, and announced that he "was going to Buchanan's to see the enemy." [15]

Robertson, as a precaution, sent Jonathan Gee and Seward Clayton to scout the path leading to Black Fox's camp; Captains Rains and Kennedy were sent to the militia road on the same mission.

Rains and Kennedy reported "no Indians in sight." Gee and Clayton, finding fallen timber in the buffalo path they were traveling, separated, but agreed to keep within hallooing distance.

Now Watts had sent out spies, also, using John Walker and George Fields,[16] two half breeds who kept some distance ahead of the Indian army, and were dressed as white men. They heard Clayton hallooing, and Fields, who spoke English well, answered him. Clayton, thinking it was Gee, came upon their hiding place and was shot. Gee came to his aid and was quickly surrounded and scalped.[17]

Watts was thus enabled to approach within striking distance of Nashville without discovery. About dusk, Sept. 30, 1792, the Indian army approached Buchanan's Station, four miles

---

[15] Putnam, 393. Narrative of John Carr, *Southwestern Monthly*, 2, 74.

[16] *American State Papers, Indian Affairs*, Vol. 1, 293. Walker and Fields were well known to Governor Blount. Of Fields he said, "I consider him the most innocent, good natured half-breed of my acquaintance." See Note 17.

[17] Both Walker and Fields were later to become prominent in the affairs of the Nation. They served in the Creek War under Andrew Jackson. Fields was seriously wounded at Talladega, and was left behind with the expectation that he could not survive. He lived, however, through the efforts of an Indian doctor. He was to become speaker of the National Council, and emigrated to the West with his people in 1838. He related the incidents of the attack on Buchanan's Station to John Carr; see Narrative of John Carr, *Southwestern Monthly*, Vol. 1, 2-74. Chief John Walker was later active in that portion of the tribe that favored removal to the West, and was killed following a council held at Red Clay, Tenn., in 1835.

east of the Bluffs. Watts had 281 warriors. Of these, 167 were Cherokees headed by Little Owl, Kiachatalee, and other chiefs. The Creeks had sent 83 warriors under Talotiskee, of Broken Arrow Town. Thirty Shawnees who had been living at Running Water were led by their chief, Shawnee Warrior. Watts was in nominal command of the entire force. About fifty of the Cherokees were mounted, under command of John Taylor.

When the Indians had reached a place where they could hear the lowing of the cattle at Buchanan's Station, an altercation between Watts and Talotiskee arose. Watts desired to advance against Nashville, the principal fort, but Talotiskee insisted that Buchanan's should be taken first. He argued that it would be unwise to leave white warriors in their rear. "But our object, in starting, was to take Nashville," said Watts: "If we take Buchanan's first, it will put the white men at Nashville on guard. We can take the *little* fort as we come back." [18]

The fact that each group of Indians had its own head constituted their greatest weakness. Each chief was a law to himself; consequently there was no unity of thought or control between head-men and commander. Watts, about midnight, gave his consent to attack Buchanan's. "As you are determined to take the little fort, you can take it yourself, and I will stand by and see you do it," he told Talotiskee. However, not being a man who sulked in the rear when a battle was raging, he led his men to the attack. [19]

There were only fifteen white men in Buchanan's; but they were among the best marksmen in America. Having been warned by the nervousness of the cattle which had been alarmed by the Indians, they were on the alert. The warriors, however, were within thirty feet of the gate when they were discovered and fired on by the sentinel, John McRory; his first shot killed Shawnee Warrior.

Pandemonium broke loose. The firing and yelling lasted an hour. Not a man within the fort was killed. The women aided; moulding bullets, distributing ammunition, and reloading. They frequently fired the guns also. John Buchanan afterward boasted, "Mrs. Buchanan has killed buffalo and deer,

[18] and [19] Carr's Narrative; also Dr. John Shelby's Narrative, *Southwestern Monthly*, 2, 141.

and cannot now plead innocence of aim and intent to kill an Indian." [20]

The attackers were never more than fifty feet from the fort, and their fire was constant and terrific. In the ceiling above one of the loop holes, within a space that could have been covered by a hat, thirty balls were found.

John Watts was wounded, it was thought fatally, early in the engagement. He was carried to the spring house which was in the shelter of a large bake oven. George Fields, the spy, received a ball in his heel, and was the target of jest when he danced and capered about in pain. In order to bathe his wound in the spring nearby, he sought the shelter of the bake oven behind which his wounded chief lay. Watts, feeling sure that he was going to die, begged Fields to cut off his head and take it with him to the Nation, so the white men could not take his scalp.[21]

Jimmy O'Connor, a young man living in the fort, had no rifle. Buchanan, therefore, gave him a blunderbuss, or "fort gun," a weapon purposely made too heavy for hunting, so that it could be left permanently at a loop-hole for use in emergency. O'Connor loaded and snapped it several times, and, on account of the noise, failed to notice that it did not fire. On the next snap the gun fired all the charges at once. "It made a lane through the red devils, and laid Jimmy O'Connor snug under the bed on the opposite side of the room," said that Irishman.[22]

The wounding of their chief stirred the Cherokee warriors to fury. They accused the Creeks of cowardice, stating that while the Cherokees freely exposed themselves, the Creek warriors remained so far from the station that they could not fire a ball to reach it.

Kiachatalee of Nickajack taunted Talotiskee as being a "woman," vile insult to a warrior, and told him that he (Kiachatalee) would "burn the fort." [23] He dashed to the wall, climbed to the roof, torch in hand, and attempted to start a fire. He was shot, and fell to the ground. Although his thigh was broken by the fall, he kept trying, with indomitable

[20] Putnam, 396.
[21] John Carr's Narrative, *Southwestern Monthly*, Vol. 2, 74.
[22] Dr. John Shelby's Narrative, *Southwestern Monthly*, Vol. 2, 141.
[23] Narrative of Joseph Brown, *Southwestern Monthly*, Vol. 1, 10.

spirit, to start a fire; alternately calling to his warriors to continue the attack, and blowing the flames of the torch against the logs, until he died.

Stung by Kiachatalee's taunt, Talotiskee led his warriors to an assault, and was killed instantly. Little Owl, Dragging Canoe's brother, was mortally wounded, as was Unacata, the White Man Killer.[24] Four other warriors of prominence were wounded, and two of them later died at Running Water.

Toward morning, the sound of the swivel gun at Nashville warned the Indians that assistance was on the way. Bearing their wounded leader in a blanket-litter, they withdrew. John Watts' great offensive had failed miserably.

-----

The Indians removed all their dead except Kiachatalee, who had fallen so close to the wall that they were compelled to leave his body. The death of this brave young chief caused much grief among the Indians, and even among the white men. Joseph Brown,[25] who had been a prisoner at Nickajack for many months, owed his life to the fact that Kiachatalee had been his captor; he was filled with sorrow when he recognized the dead countenance of his friend and comrade, "Chatt," into whose family he had once been adopted.

Bitterness was rife on the march back to the Five Lower Towns. The Cherokees complained that the Creeks had long boasted that they were men and warriors, but had proved themselves cowards. The Creeks, though, had given Talotiskee.

### 5

On the same day that Buchanan's Station was attacked, Governor Blount received a letter from Kenoteta, or the Rising Fawn, of Hiwassee, which concerned the movements of Doublehead. Kenoteta wrote the governor:

"The mountains near you have many Indians in them for war. Take care of your people. Don't let them go out by twos or threes, even to the fields. The Lower Towns are all together, and so are the Creeks. Talotiskee [26] (Doublehead), was here a few

-----

[24] This was not Watts' brother, but another chief of the same name.

[25] Brown was a member of the Buchanan garrison, but was visiting his mother three miles away, at the time of the attack.

[26] Doublehead's name is variously spelled. The correct Cherokee form would be Tal-Tsuska, from *tali,* two, and *tsuska,* heads.

days ago, saying he was for peace. Don't you believe him, he is still for war. The Bench and another brother of his, the Tail, passed here yesterday with three other Cherokees from Willstown, declaring they were going to kill John Sevier.[27] Take care of them, they will do mischief before they return.[28]

Part of John Watts' campaign, as has been stated, was to waylay the two roads from Holston to Cumberland; Doublehead had been assigned to the Kentucky Road; and Middlestriker to the Walton Road.

Doublehead, with sixty warriors, hastened to the Kentucky Road where he met a party of six white people and took one scalp. Then, being anxious to participate in the fighting at Nashville, he took the road toward Cumberland. About the last of September, he made camp at Horseshoe Bend of Caney Fork River.

Lieutenant William Snoddy, with thirty-four militiamen from Sumner County, stumbled on Doublehead's camp while the main body of Indians were out hunting. Sixty-two warpacks were taken, each containing a blanket, lead, and a bearskin for use as a bed. A shotgun, two swords of Spanish make, and numerous bridles and halters were found. While the men were gathering up the spoils, John Peyton shouted that the Indians were surrounding the camp. The men took to trees, but it was a false alarm, and, after an hour, Snoddy decided to camp for the night. He chose a high bluff across the river for the site. The men bedded themselves in a semi-circle; the points on the edge of the bluffs, and the plunder from the Indian camp placed in the center.

The Indians had gathered on an island in the river; presently, Doublehead sounded the war-whoop, and began to harangue his warriors.

Snoddy ordered that one of their poorest horses be belled and placed outside the line. Hoping to decoy the Indians to

---

[27] *American State Papers, Indian Affairs,* Vol. 1, 293.

[28] The threat against John Sevier was not an idle one. At a later treaty, an Indian chief told Sevier that the Cherokees had at nine different times sent war parties to kill him and his family, but each time they were prevented by some unforeseen event from reaching his home. Twice they had come to his immediate neighborhood and had killed the Lewis and Headler families, but failed to locate Sevier's residence. *Draper Mss.,* 30-S, 351-397.

that point, one of the men would occasionally creep out and give the bell a ring. It failed, however.

The night was cold, with a drizzling rain; the hours of darkness seemed interminable, and none of the militia slept.

Throughout the night, they could hear the Indian commander assembling his warriors by typical signals. The howl of a wolf on one side of the camp would be answered by the scream of a panther from the other. These weird noises, coupled with the cold rain, kept the nerves of the white men taut. Just before daybreak, a horrible yell, the last signal of Doublehead to his warriors, was heard. A silence, so profound that four of the white men fled in terror, followed.

The savages had crept within forty steps of Snoddy's line, and they charged with a concerted war-whoop that could be heard for miles. The contest was close and desperate, with intrepid bravery displayed on both sides.

James Madell accounted for three Indians, one a chief, whose body the warriors tried to remove; Martin Harpool, a Dutchman, with a large English musket, poured seven charges of lead into the midst of the crowded Indians. He then jumped around in the canebrake where he was concealed, and yelled so loudly in his broken speech, that the red men were demoralized and fled; leaving the body of their chief. It was Moon, of Running Water Town.[29]

Only two of Snoddy's men were killed in the fight. The Indians blamed their defeat on Harpool, the "fool warrior of the white men."

Thirteen Indian warriors were killed; several were wounded; and all the war-packs had been lost. It was disaster indeed for Doublehead. He gathered the remnants of his force and proceeded toward Nashville. On reaching the Walton Road, he met four warriors who had been at Buchanan's, and learned from them the details of his nephew's defeat; and that Watts, supposedly with a mortal wound, was being carried back to the Indian Towns. Doublehead, scourge of the frontier, and most pitiless of Indians, wept bitter tears. Turning to his men,

---

[29] The writer has followed Goodpasture in the description of the Rock Island fight; and the address of Judge John H. Dewitt at the unveiling of a monument at the site. John Carr in his narrative, in *Southwestern Monthly,* states that the Moon was killed at another fight commanded by Gen. Winchester, but details are the same.

he said; "Divide into small parties; hunt, each man kill three or four deer; go home, get a fresh supply of provisions; and meet me at Short Mountain, equipped for war, in ten days. Vengeance I will have for Watts." [30]

### 6

Middlestriker, on the Walton Road, placed his sixty warriors in ambush in a commanding position overlooking a large spring, at which travelers were accustomed to refresh themselves. With Indian cunning, he waited in patience until rewarded.

Captain Samuel Handley, with forty-two men, who had been dispatched by Governor Blount to assist in the defense of Nashville, proceeded by the Walton Road. As they reached Spencer's Hill, they were met by a volley from Middlestriker's concealed warriors. Only three men were killed; the survivors might have made a creditable stand, but, in spite of Handley's frantic efforts, they fled in dismay.

Handley's horse was shot from under him as he attempted to rescue Lieper, one of his men. He defended himself with his sword, but was finally overcome by numbers, and surrendered to Archie Coody, a half-breed.[31] The savages were delighted to have taken so notable a prisoner. They knew him well, for he had acted as John Sevier's aide in many campaigns against them, and as a young man had fought in the battle of Point Pleasant. He was taken to Willstown, where Watts was recovering from his wound. An Indian council debated his fate for three days; then condemned him to death by fire. But, first, he was compelled to submit to the *Ayetli,* "running the gauntlet," [32] and was so seriously injured that his execution had to be postponed until he recovered. After further insults, he was tied to a stake, and the Indians gathered around for the last scene. Squaws threw sand and filth upon him, and spat in his face.

The faggots were placed, and the prisoner had abandoned hope, but kept taunting the Indians in hope that they would shoot him. Suddenly a peal of thunder was heard, followed

---

[30] *American State Papers, Indian Affairs,* Vol. 1, 329.
[31] *Ibid.*
[32] From the Cherokee, *ayeli,* in the middle, and *tali,* two.

by a downpour. The firewood was soaked; and the execution again was postponed.

In a few days the weather was propitious, and Handley was once more tied to the stake. John Watts, who was rapidly recuperating, came out to witness the burning. The captain began a conversation with him: "You are a brave chief," he said; "the white people love a brave man, and all of them love John Watts. They regret that they must fight him. I am John Sevier's aide, and he often talks of the brave John Watts. But you have a cowardly set of warriors. They are all old women; if they were not, they would shoot a warrior."

Watts' eyes filled with tears. He shouted, "Damned shame brave man die, they ought to kill cowards!" He took the prisoner by the hand and released him. The principal Indians followed Watts' example, and shook hands with Handley in the friendliest manner. He was escorted to Watts' house, fed, and treated well. Later, he was adopted into the Wolf Clan of the Cherokee.[33]

On hearing of the capture of Handley, John Sevier wrote to Watts warning him that if the prisoner were injured, the same treatment would be given to Indian captives who were in Sevier's hands.[34] Watts' was inclined for peace, however, and asked Handley to write Governor Blount to that effect. He also permitted him to write, in his own behalf, to his brother-in-law, Colonel James Scott. The letter was sent from Willstown on Dec. 10, 1792. The same runner carried Watts' message of peace to the governor. Handley was fully convinced that Watts desired peace: "If Governor Blount sends a good answer to the talk they have sent by the runner, I am confident that their talk is true and sincere. Upon the whole, we are not ripe for war with these people, for they are properly fixed for war."

Concerning his own condition, Handley wrote: "I have been much abused, and am in great distress. I beg that you and every good friend will go to the governor and try all you can to get him to send a good answer." He requested that

[33] *American State Papers, Indian Affairs,* Vol. 1, 434. See also *American Historical Magazine,* Vol. 2, —1, "Statement of Gen. Rogers, of Rock Island." The statement was evidently made by Capt. Handley, himself.

[34] Draper Mss., 30-S 351-397.

his wife be notified of his whereabouts, and that a horse be sent by the Indian runner if his release could be effected.

"If an army comes before a good answer is received," he said, "I am sure to die. Dear friends, do what you can, for I am in a distressed way,—once more I beg you to do your possibles for me, and do them as soon as you can." [35]

On receipt of Watts' message, Governor Blount returned a conciliatory reply, suggesting that Handley be exchanged for Indian prisoners who were in the hands of the white people. The chief's letter was forwarded to the Secretary of War, who wrote Blount on February 8, 1793, that the President desired that Watts and other principal chiefs of the Cherokees should visit him in Philadelphia. [36]

In the meantime, on Jan. 24, 1793, Captain Handley returned to Knoxville, accompanied by his captors, Middlestriker and Coody, and eight warriors. Governor Blount received the Indians with due ceremony, and distributed presents, consisting of a blanket, shirt, leggins, flap and match-coat, to each one. [37] During the three months that he had been a prisoner, Handley's hair had turned white. [38]

Handley advised Governor Blount that Watts desired peace except as to Cumberland settlements, which all of the Indians, Cherokees, Creeks, and Shawnees, were determined should be destroyed. The Five Lower Towns were well supplied with war materials, given them by the Spaniards together with a promise that the old boundaries should be restored.

## 7

The peace overtures of John Watts were gestures only, and were intended to lull the suspicions of Blount, thus preventing a retaliatory invasion to revenge Buchanan's Station. Immediately after his return from that disastrous campaign, Watts had sent runners posthaste to New Orleans to advise Governor Carondelet of his misfortune, and to request further supplies and ammunition. Carondelet replied with warm sympathy in November, 1792:

---

[35] Captain Handley's letter is quoted in full by Ramsey, 573.
[36] *American State Papers, Indian Affairs,* Vol. 1, 434.
[37] *Ibid.*
[38] Draper Mss., 30-S 351-397.

"The losses and misfortunes of your Nation have afflicted me. I have transmitted to the King of Spain whatever your letters to me have said. His Majesty keeps in his heart the red people. He desires their happiness, and that they shall preserve their lands."

In reference to restoring the Indians' boundaries, Carondelet wrote:

"The Great King will treat with the Americans, and obtain from them the lands necessary for your habitations. You will let me know the limits you claim, that I may immediately inform the Great King of them; and if your allies, the Nations north, will let me know theirs, I will procure that they may be comprised in the same treaty." [39]

Such positive promises, coming from high authority, were given full credence by the Indians, and encouraged them to pursue the warfare against the American frontiers.

Watts had previously sent runners to the Shawnees to inform them of his intentions for war, and early in 1793 they sent a delegation both to him and to the Creeks, to formulate plans for joint action.

The Chickamaugas prepared a new square in Running Water for the reception of the Shawnee Ambassadors. The Badger, Dragging Canoe's brother, went to Ustanali for the Shawnee pipe which he had left at the house of Kingfisher.[40] He wished to smoke the pipe with his Shawnee friends to show them that he had not thrown their talk away. But Kingfisher, believing that the Cherokees would be friendly with the Americans after his return from Philadelphia, had destroyed the pipe. He was, fortunately, away when the Badger arrived; for the Badger's wrath flamed violently. "If the Kingfisher were here," he exclaimed, "I would destroy the medal given him by the United States. His talks may henceforth be considered as those of a little boy, and not of a man and a warrior." He insisted that the chiefs at Ustanali should send immediately to a pipe-maker who lived about twenty miles distant, a description of the pipe that had been destroyed, and have him make one as nearly like it as possible. This was done and the Badger had the satisfaction of smoking it in the new square at Running Water.[41]

---

[39] Whitaker, *Spanish American Frontier.*
[40] See Section 2, Chapter XIX.
[41] *American State Papers, Indian Affairs,* Vol. 1, 430.

In memory of Talotiskee, the Creeks received the Shawnee delegation in the dead chief's town, Broken Arrow. At the same ceremony, the Creeks and Chickamaugas exchanged pledges of mutual loyalty. The Creeks sent a war club to Watts, and he accepted it, with this remark: "I will take hold of this club; will join the Creeks for war; and will take this club with me to Nashville." [42]

## 8

As soon as Blount received word from Handley that the Chickamaugas desired peace, he sent James Carey with an invitation to Watts to meet him for a peace talk.

The only man in Willstown who could read English was Leonard Shaw. Watts requested him to read the letter. Blount had begun with the phrase: "I hope you will open your ears and hear my talk for peace." When Shaw read this, Watts exclaimed,

"The white men have stopped their own ears with our lands. Let them move off our lands, and unstop their ears."

Then turning to Shaw, he asked what he thought of the governor's proposal.

Shaw replied:

"Why should you go to Governor Blount? You should go to Congress. You know I was sent here by your father, the President, to see that justice was done you, and justice you shall have, so far as is in my power. The United States has not heard how Governor Blount has wronged you out of your lands. If you treat with him, you will be as far from getting your lands as ever. I will go to Congress with you and recover your lands to the old lines, which I can easily do."

Shaw's ostentatious reply was disloyal to Governor Blount, although the governor had been very kind to him.

Watts took him by the arm:

"Are you an officer among us all this time, and never told us before that our lands were recoverable to the old lines? If you do that for us, we will take you by the hand as a brother forever." [43]

[42] *Ibid.*, 437-438.
[43] *Ibid.*, 437.

Shaw asked that the Indians be at peace for seventy-five days, so that he might have time to go to Philadelphia and return. Watts gave his word. Being in financial straits, Shaw had to knuckle under and ask the governor for funds to finance the trip. The governor knew of his duplicity, and was delighted to grant his request in order to get rid of him.[44] His mission came to naught.

## 9

Having pledged his word to Shaw that there would be no hostilities for seventy-five days, Watts had no objection to meeting the governor in treaty during his absence. He realized that no white army would invade his towns while diplomatic negotiations were in progress. Accordingly, on Feb. 4th, 1793, Blount received word that Watts was at Hanging Maw's in Coyatee, and would come to Knoxville or any other place that suited the governor, for a talk.

Governor Blount promised to be at Henry's Station on Feb. 6th.[45] Watts, accompanied by Doublehead, Hanging Maw, and many others, was there, on the day mentioned. Two days were spent at the conference; the first in "eating, drinking, and jocular conversation, of which Watts is very fond." Governor Blount, in his report, gives the expenses of the meeting as $130.00, "owing principally to the price and quantity of whiskey, of which I considered it to the interests of the United States to be liberal, as Watts and his party were thirsty." [46]

On the second day, Governor Blount asked Watts why the Creeks continued to raid the Cumberland when their nation had recently made peace with James Seagrove. Watts replied: "The Creeks have said that they will be at war with the Cumberland settlements the longest day they live, on account of their land."

But "some of the Creeks commit depredations on the frontiers of Washington district, where they have never owned any land," said the governor; and Watts replied: "It is fellows who live single, and not in towns. They are bad off for clothes, and steal horses to supply themselves."

---

[44] *Ibid.*, 440-441.

[45] Henry's Station was on the north side of French Broad River at the mouth of Dumpling Creek.

[46] *American State Papers, Indian Affairs,* Vol. I, 443.

The governor urged that Watts and a delegation of chiefs from the Lower Towns visit President Washington in Philadelphia, and offered to accompany them. Watts made no definite promise. He said: "The Nation will meet in twenty-one nights at Running Water, when the matter will be considered, and a reply given." With this evasion the governor had to be content. "Watts appeared truly friendly, and with his usual cleverness," Blount's report states. "He is unquestionably the leading character in his Nation, though he would make no promise, even to carry a representation to Philadelphia." [47]

Watts, as will be seen, was overawed by the presence of his uncle, Doublehead. That implacable chief was determined that peace should not be made with the Americans, and that negotiations with them must cease. [48]

The Creek warriors, of whom Governor Blount had inquired, spoke for themselves:

"We have done all we can to provoke the United States to war with us. We have killed and scalped men, women, and children. We have taken them prisoners and made them slaves like negroes. We have debauched their women and have taken their property, and have done it for many years, and yet we cannot make them mad. What else can we do to provoke them?" [49]

The Creeks, however, were soon to lose their great leader, Alexander McGilivray. He died February 17, 1793, while on a visit to William Panton, in Pensacola, and was buried, with Masonic honors, in Panton's garden. [50]

McGilivray was a strong man, capable, and thoroughly devoted to the welfare of the Indian tribes of the South. There was no other chief among the southern Indians who had his breadth of vision or could measure up to his ability. With him passed the hope of united action against the white people, by the four southern tribes.

The great chief, before his death, recommended that William Panton be elected as his successor. The choice, however, was

[47] Ibid., 447.
[48] Ibid., 444-445.
[49] Ibid., 378-385.
[50] Ibid., 378-385.

Charles Weatherford, McGilivray's brother-in-law. He failed to secure the united support of the Creek Nation, and while he himself was peacefully inclined the warriors of the upper Creek towns disregarded his wishes, and continued their depredations on the American frontier.

# CHAPTER XXIII

## HAIR AND HORSES

### I

*Gitlu-ale-tsagwali* "Hair and Horses" was a familiar expression on the old southwestern frontier in the stormy days when John Watts was war chief of the Chickamaugas. The two words are so often mentioned together in Governor Blount's dispatches that one wonders if they ever were used separately.

In the fall of 1792, continued Indian raids had forced Governor Blount to order out the militia under General Sevier "for a term of three weeks." Sevier made his headquarters at the mouth of Clinch River. The place was advantageous for quickly reaching any point in the territory, and for embarrassing the movements of the Indians. Sevier therefore erected a blockhouse and stockade and called it Southwest Point. Governor Blount, however, received positive orders from Secretary of War Knox to discharge the militia and to engage in no offensive operations against the Indians. He therefore instructed Sevier to march his men to Knoxville and disband, which was done on Jan. 8, 1793.[1]

That this was a short-sighted policy was quickly apparent. With no militia to oppose them, the Cherokees raided the frontier almost daily. James Carey, the interpreter in the Nation, kept Blount advised of the departure of war parties and of their return with "hair and horses." The absence of Sevier encouraged even the upper towns, and four warriors from Chilhowie gleefully exhibited to Carey a scalp they had taken on the Kentucky road. "Don't you think it is pretty hair?" one of them asked; while another proudly displayed the coat of the slain man.[2]

### 2

It was on the Cumberland that the burden of Indian warfare bore most heavily. The beautiful country around Nashville

---

[1] Haywood, 284.
[2] *American State Papers, Indian Affairs*, Vol. 1, 329.

*Picture by Walter Cline*

SPENCER'S HILL, CUMBERLAND COUNTY, TENN.

The spring, which was the scene of Spencer's death, of Handley's capture, and of McClelland's defeat, is about two hundred yards north of the highway in left foreground.

was well adapted to raising horses. Racing was a favorite sport, and the settlers took pride in improving the breed of the racers. Horses, too, were the only means of transporting goods from the older settlements to the new, and were essential in clearing and cultivating a virgin country.

The Indians were passionately fond of horses for their own use. They formed, in addition, a means of barter with Indian traders almost as staple as pounds sterling. The traders, whom Governor Blount described as "the worst of rascals," would buy all the horses the Indians brought, paying a trifling sum. The horses would then be carried out of the Nation in a different direction from whence they came, and sold at a handsome profit.[3] The only excuse for the traffic was profit, for stolen horses were easily recognized. "Persons accustomed to seeing horses raised by the white men and Indians," Governor Blount wrote, "can distinguish on seeing a drove whether their former owners have been white or red as readily as they can tell a white man from an Indian."[4]

Horse stealing has been a capital offense on all American frontiers. Cumberland settlers were filled with justifiable rage when their horses disappeared overnight and they had no redress, although Indians were known to be the offenders. The red men did not confine their thievery to workhorses and packhorses. David Gilliland, a trader, reported to Governor Blount that he had seen at Lookout Mountain Town among other horses, "Drumgold's roan race horse," a famous racer of the day. "One marauding party," he said, "returned from Cumberland mounted on sixty good horses, besides smaller ones for packhorses."[5]

James Robertson wrote:

"Horse stealing is the grand source of hostility between the white and the red people. The number of horses taken from this settlement is prodigious. I would estimate it at more than five hundred during the first ten months of 1792. It is a subject on which the whites are very sore, and with difficulty restrain themselves from taking what they call satisfaction."[6]

---

[3] Governor Blount, on asking Chief Bloody Fellow of some stolen horses, received the reply: "If the white men want to see their horses, let them go to South Carolina." *Ibid.*, 537.

[4] *Ibid.*, 265.

[5] *Ibid.*, 265.

[6] *Ibid.*, 325.

"Cumberland is the place for horses," the Indians said, and called it "The Horse Stamp." "Hair and horses" were invariably coupled, however, and besides horses, more than two hundred white scalps were taken by the red men in and around Nashville during 1792.[7]

The Cherokees were not the only offenders. James Seagrove, United States Agent to the Creeks, reported to Robertson that he had made a treaty with that nation in the fall of 1792, and that "nine tenths of the Creeks are for peace."

Robertson commented:

"That is the kind of war most to be dreaded. The other tenth, I am convinced, are daily coming to Cumberland to murder and steal. We have got common sense, and must use this against all the arts of learned diplomacy, the wiles of the Devil, and the cunning craftiness of the Indian."[8]

Sampson Williams, one of Robertson's trusted aides, remarked: "If the government will give us but half the ammunition it gives to the Indians, we will knock the hind sights off every one of the rascals."

Doublehead, uncle of John Watts, was the most cruel and blood-thirsty of the Indians who raided on Cumberland, and the most noted. As has been related, Doublehead had sworn that he would have vengeance for Watts' defeat at Buchanan Station. He recruited sixty warriors, and early in 1793, in company with his nephew Bench, a kindred spirit; and his brother, Pumpkin Boy, departed for the Kentucky Road.

On Jan. 22, Captain William Overall and a helper named Burnett were conducting nine packhorses loaded with salt, whiskey, and other goods, from Kentucky to Nashville. Overall was one of the men who had made the first trip to the site of the future Nashville with James Robertson. He had helped to plant the first crop, and was one of four men who had remained at the site while Robertson returned to Holston to bring out settlers.

Doublehead and Bench prepared an ambuscade at the Dripping Spring in the barrens of Kentucky. The barrens were described by early travelers as having few trees and little water.

---

[7] *Ibid.*, 265, 331, and *Draper Mss.*, 6-XX-15.
[8] Putnam.

The spring was just such a place as would be chosen for a cooling drink, a few moments of rest, and a chance to water stock.

Overall and Burnett walked into the Indian ambuscade and both were killed. Judging from the scene of barbarity that followed, the two white men offered desperate resistance before they were overcome. Overall had acted as one of Robertson's spies against the Indians, who cherished a particular resentment against that form of service. Spies who were killed, in addition to being scalped, were "chopped" as an insult to their nation.

After they had scalped Overall and Burnett, the Indians sampled the whiskey taken from the packhorses, which fired them to further atrocity. The flesh was stripped from the bones of the white men and cooked and eaten. This was not done to satisfy hunger, but was supposed to endow the warriors with the courage of their foes. If Burnett and Overall had shown cowardice, their flesh would not have been eaten.

Doublehead returned to Lookout Mountain Town and held a war dance over the two scalps. He had warriors, too, from Willstown, Turnip Town, and Coosawatie. The scalps were taken to each of these places, and the dance was repeated. This was Doublehead's method of stirring up the Nation for war.[9] Such scenes roused the young men to frenzied enthusiasm and sent them on the warpath to win like-glory. The upper towns were not exempt from the excitement. Hanging Maw's neighbors in his own town joined the war parties, although Governor Blount had declared, "If there is an Indian in the Cherokee Nation that is friendly to the United States, it is the Hanging Maw." [10]

During Doublehead's celebration, the runner came from Governor Blount inviting Watts and other chiefs to the conference at Henry's Station. Doublehead accompanied Watts, more to prevent peace than to secure it. Returning from the conference, he insisted that negotiations with the Americans must cease. "I want to see the face of no white man at Willstown," he told Watts, and made himself so disagreeable that Watts decided to leave the Nation. He did go some distance,

---

[9] *American State Papers, Indian Affairs,* Vol. I, 437.
[10] *Ibid.,* 430.

but Watts inspired genuine affection among his followers, and the young warriors persuaded him to return.[11]

### 3

Bench, who had participated in the Overall killing, was a typical Indian fighter. His band usually consisted of half a dozen warriors, in whom he could place implicit trust. He was a half-breed, but no Indian could have been more blood-thirsty.

After the round of dances following the affair at Dripping Spring, Bench returned with his followers to his favored field of operations, Southwest Virginia. On March 31, 1793, he met an old acquaintance, Moses Cockrell, on top of Powell's Mountain, in what is now Lee County, Virginia.

Cockrell was a border ranger famed for his size, handsome person, and activity. He had many times expressed a desire to meet the famous "Captain Bench" in personal combat, and had in no uncertain terms predicted the outcome of such an encounter. Possibly his boasts had reached the ears of Bench. At any rate, that warrior waylaid Cockrell and his companions as they were conducting a pack train across the mountain. Bench instructed his men not to shoot Cockrell as he desired to take him prisoner. The ambush was successful, and Cockrell's mates fell at the first fire.

Taken by surprise, Cockrell had no choice but flight. Two miles away, in the valley of Wallen's Creek, was the cabin of a pioneer. Cockrell was handicapped by the weight of two hundred dollars in silver which he was carrying in his belt, but he ran swift as a deer. The trail was downhill, and Bench was never more than a few steps behind; but feeling sure of capture, he made no attempt to shoot.

Cockrell reached the rail fence surrounding the settler's cabin with a few feet only to spare. The exasperated Indian threw his tomahawk just as his intended captive vaulted, but it sank in the top rail and the white man reached the cabin safely. Knowing that it would be certain death to attack him there, Bench withdrew, while Cockrell sat in the cabin and nursed his wounded pride. He had recognized his pursuer, for Bench

---

[11] *Ibid.*, 439.

was one of only two red-headed Indians in the Cherokee Nation; the other being Will, founder of Willstown.[12]

## 4

The forts of the white men were invincible strongholds against the weapons available to the Indians, but the red men skulked constantly in the hope of sniping straggling travelers.

On April 27, 1793, Greenfield's, a station two and a half miles north of Bledsoe's, was attacked.

Major William Hall, on his way to the fort, had paused for a word with John Jarvis who was guarding two negroes, Abraham and Prince, as they plowed. Hall followed Abraham as he ran a furrow, and conversed with the intelligent slave. Presently he saw the dogs of the station leap the fence and dash into a nearby canebrake. They came back with bristles erect, barking and growling. "The Indians are near!" exclaimed the major. Plowing was abandoned and the men reached the fort without mishap; but early next morning as the women were milking, a herd of frightened cattle came charging up. Jarvis was on sentinel duty. The women told him that the cattle were frightened at Indians, but he only laughed at their fears and ordered Abraham and Prince to the plowing which had been interrupted the day before.

While the negroes were hitching the horses, they saw a body of Indians rise in the canebrake. They gave the alarm and, with Jarvis, ran for the fort, the Indians in hot pursuit. Four white men ran to their assistance. A battle ensued and Jarvis and Prince were killed, but four savages paid the penalty.

The Castleman family were typical of the frontiersmen; brave, reckless, and impatient of restraint. They lived at Hay's Station, on Stone's River. As two men of the fort had been killed in February, 1793, Robertson had sent a squad to defend the fort and guard the men as they worked. On July 1st, 1793, Hans Castleman and his three sons, Jacob, William, and Joseph wanted to cut a patch of oats a short distance from the fort, and applied for a guard. This was refused as fresh Indian signs had been seen the evening before; but they disregarded the danger and went anyway. They were fired on by Indians as they gathered the oats and Jacob was killed. A

---

[12] Goodpasture, *Tennessee Historical Magazine,* Vol. 4, 259.

bullet in the breast brought Hans, the father, down, and Joseph was mortally wounded, but reached the fort. William defended his father until help came. Joseph died at sunset and the two brothers were buried outside the fort beside the graves of the two men who had been previously killed.

Abraham Castleman, a kinsman, was of the turbulent, unruly, class often found on the frontier. Robertson described him as a "disorderly person," but he was reputed to be the best shot on the border. He is the only pioneer known to have killed two Indians with one ball. One man said of him, "If I were on the other side of a hill, I would hide, for Castleman could shoot around it." [13]

Governor Blount's orders to Robertson about fighting the Indians were to limit operations to defensive measures north of Tennessee River. The war department was apprehensive that any crossing of the river would offend not only the Cherokees, but would involve the United States in war with the powerful Creek Nation.

Abraham Castleman was resolved that he would have revenge for the death of his kinsman, regardless of orders. He enlisted fourteen volunteers and after a few days' scouting reached the crossing of Tennessee River at the mouth of Battle Creek. No Indians had been found north of the river, and Castleman suggested crossing into the Indian country. Most of his companions refused. Five men, who had lost relatives by the Indians and felt as Castleman did, agreed to follow where he led. They painted and dressed themselves as Indians, and swam the river.

After traveling ten miles southward on the Willstown trail, a party of Creek warriors in war paint was discovered, seated at breakfast. Castleman and his men approached within thirty yards without creating alarm, for they were considered other Indians. Suddenly, they raised their guns and fired. Each man killed an Indian, and Castleman killed two with one shot. They fled in different directions as they had planned previously, and all reached Nashville on Aug. 21, 1793.

---

[13] Putnam. For details of Castleman's exploit, *American State Papers, Indian Affairs*, Vol. 1, 467.

The pioneer Edmiston waggishly described one of Castleman's shots: "He nicked an Indian, knocked over a catamount, brought down a flock of turkeys, laid out a buffalo, blazed a section of land, and split enough boards to cover a shanty, a mighty good shot."

Regardless of being "disorderly," Castleman was treated as a hero on his return.

### 5

In the spring and summer of 1793, Leslie, a half-breed Creek chief, son of Panton's partner, committed numerous outrages on the Holston frontier. It was his custom to return through the upper Cherokee towns after a raid and thus bring on them the revenge of the white men. This involved Cherokees who might otherwise have remained peaceful in the war with the whites.

In April, Leslie burned the house of James Gallaher near Knoxville, and retreated through Hanging Maw's town of Coyatee at the mouth of Little Tennessee. He demanded provisions but was refused. In a rage, he shot Hanging Maw's dog, and left. Soon afterward a detachment of white horsemen who had been following his trail appeared. They crossed the Little Tennessee but failed to find Leslie and returned. In re-crossing the stream one of the men, John McCullough, was drowned.

Another party of white men, also pursuing Leslie, met two friendly Cherokees and shot them down. One of them proved to be Noonday of Toquo, a close friend of John Watts and Hanging Maw. He was known to be friendly to the white people. Governor Blount apologized to the chiefs for the killing of their friend, but justified the act by saying: "He was off the path, with a gun on his shoulder, and was unfortunately mistaken for a Creek."

Watts' reply illustrated Indian reasoning, by which a scalp balanced a scalp. He said, "Noonday was a good man, and they wanted to kill him. They knew very well he was not a Creek, for they took his gun, belt, knife, and garters. As I wish for peace, let them both go together, Noonday for the man who was drowned." [14]

### 6

After his conference with Watts at Henry's Station, Governor Blount sent John McKee into the Nation to ascertain the result of the council which Watts had promised him would be

---

[14] *American State Papers, Indian Affairs,* Vol. 1, 450.

held in twenty-one days. McKee was instructed also to urge Watts and other leading chiefs to visit the President at Philadelphia. Such visits had a profound effect on the Indians, and were a potent influence for peace.

McKee was detained by rain several days at the small village of Amoyee, about ten miles south of the Hiwassee. While there, he was visited by Nontuaka, one of the delegates who had gone to Philadelphia with Bloody Fellow. Nontuaka urged the white man to go no farther into the Cherokee country, for the Indians were "very cross." "What is the reason for their crossness?" McKee asked; and Nontuaka answered, "It is their land." "Did you ever know Indians to recover land by war? Have you not observed that war is invariably followed by loss of land?" McKee inquired.

Regardless of the warning of Nontuaka, McKee continued on toward Willstown, the home of John Watts. He was met at Chatooga [15] by the trader John Benge, father of Captain Bench. "It would be certain death for you to continue," Benge told McKee. "The trader Will Webber has been at Willstown for two days trying to persuade Watts to put you to death. If you must communicate with Watts, send a trusted messenger and ask him to come for an interview."

Will Elder, a half-breed chief, agreed to carry the message to Watts. He returned two days later with the war chief.

Watts joked with McKee about his defeat at Buchanan's Station, and about his wound, from which he was almost recovered. McKee, hoping to extract information, plied the Indian with whiskey, but was compelled to report:

"With no other advantage than the conviction that neither war nor Webber's solicitations had lessened Watts' friendship for me. His professions on that head were extravagant."

Watts promised McKee that he would meet him, with Doublehead and other leading chiefs, in two days. He did not appear, and McKee, after waiting eight days, sent a messenger to inquire the reason for the delay. Watts replied with the frivolous excuse that he was detained by a ballplay. McKee then returned to Knoxville, feeling that talks with subordinate chiefs would accomplish nothing. He was met at Hiwassee

---

[15] Chatooga was located near the present LaFayette, Ga.

on his return by John Walker, who had just come from Wills-town. Walker informed him that the "ballplay" had nothing to do with the failure of the chiefs to meet him at Chatooga as had been promised. The real reason was that Doublehead was enraged at Watts' continued negotiations with the white men, and had made positive demand that they be stopped.[16]

## 7

The Chickasaws had remained friends of the Americans.[17] They had been solicited repeatedly to join the other tribes in war against the common foe, but always had firmly refused.

Early in March, 1793, James Robertson received the following letter from Piomingo, the great Chickasaw chief:

"Friend and Brother: You told me that the President well knew his friends, and would not let them suffer. On that account, I am, my brother, sending you this letter. Our talks always was to love and esteem one another. We have held you fast by the hand, and have told our young warriors they must do so, and they will as long as they are able to lift a hatchet.

"I have sent you a war club. When we both take hold, we can strike a hard blow. Although we wish to be at peace with all, the Creeks have spilled our blood, and we desire you will dispatch expresses to every head-man in America, particularly to General Washington, to let them know our agreement was to be one in regard to our friends and enemies. If one was struck, the other was to feel the blow, and be one cause.

"My brother, you must know it is on your account we have been struck, for the last talk sent to us by the Creeks, when we told them we were perfect friends with the United States and would listen to no talks against them, the Creeks said the Chickasaws were fools not to join the other Indians to cut off the Virginians, who were liars and no dependence in them. They told us the Chickasaws would soon know their mistake, for the Creeks and Shawnees would fall on them; then let their great friends, the Virginians, help them. But all their talks did not alter the minds of my people.

"I hope, my brother, when you get this we will find that what you have always told us is true. Speak strong to your young warriors; let us join, and let the Creeks know what war is. You

---

[16] *American State Papers, Indian Affairs,* Vol. 1, 445.

[17] It was due to the loyalty of this small but fighting tribe that France failed at an earlier date to secure control of the Mississippi, and the same obstinacy was later to prevent Spain from attaining that end.

make whiskey. It is good to have a little at war talks; send me some. We are now standing in the middle of a great blaze of fire. When you receive this, I hope you will be as expeditious as you can, for red people are not long preparing for war. Send us some ammunitions at once, and guns such as rifles; smooth bores will do; and flints we want; swivels and blunderbusses." [18]

The immediate cause of Chickasaw hostilities with the Creeks was that several warriors had been hunting on neutral ground, when a party of Creeks fired on them, killed one, mangled the body, and threw it in a pond. The mangling of a body was always intended by the Indians as an insult to the whole Nation of the victim, and the Chickasaws acted on this premise. On February 13, 1793, they held a council and decided for war, although they knew it meant they would have to fight the entire Creek Nation, which vastly outnumbered them.

At this council of the Chickasaws, three Cherokee chiefs, Bloody Fellow, John Taylor, and Bold Hunter, were present. Although he had talked bravely for the whites at Willstown, Bloody Fellow had not been able to resist the lure of Spanish presents. He and his fellow chiefs had visited New Orleans, and were returning through the Chickasaw country in order to try to swing the stubborn Chickasaws into line with the other Indians for war with the United States.

Bloody Fellow now stood for a cause directly opposite that for which he had plead at Willstown. With all his eloquence, he begged the Chickasaws not to declare war on the Creeks, but to join the other tribes in war on the United States, which was stealing the hunting grounds of all the red men. He threatened the Chickasaws with dire results should they not ally themselves with their red brethren.

The threat infuriated Piomingo, who interrupted the talk. "Desist!" he cried. "I am so determined for war with the Creeks that my very breath is bloody. You, Bloody Fellow, may go home, and join the Creeks if you choose. I suppose you will, for the Cherokees have long been at war with the people of the United States, though they have pretended peace and friendship." [19]

---

[18] *American State Papers, Indian Affairs,* Vol. 1, 446.
[19] *Ibid.,* 441.

8

The appeal of his friends, the Chickasaws, was embarrassing
to James Robertson. He knew that Governor Blount's instructions had been to promote peace among the different Indian
tribes and to do nothing to the contrary. He knew that the
governor would not approve of his sending them ammunition.
But he could not tolerate the idea of standing by without lending a hand. He, therefore, acted first and reported later. He
sent guns, ammunition, and even a swivel gun to their aid.

The news of this spread quickly. Governor Carondelet, at
New Orleans, protested to the Secretary of State at Washington at what he termed Robertson's violation of the friendship
between Spain and the United States. He wrote Robertson
to the same effect. Robertson replied in tactful language, assuming full responsibility for arming the Chickasaws. He
called attention to "various reports" that the Spanish government had for years supplied guns and ammunition to the Creeks
and Chickamaugas for war against Americans.[20]

Piomingo marshalled the Chickasaws for war quickly. As
a special compliment to James Robertson, he marched his warriors through Nashville on their way to fight the Creeks. It
probably was the only time that Indians ever were cheered on
the streets of Nashville or in any other frontier American
city.[21]

The doughty Chickasaws met on their way a body of Creeks
whom they defeated. Preparations were then made by the
Creek Nation to annihilate the Chickasaw tribe. Piomingo
again appealed to his white friends for aid. Washington,
though he appreciated the assistance the Chickasaws had given,
was not willing to involve the United States in war with the
Creek Nation. Robertson was compelled to advise Piomingo
that additional assistance could not be given. However he
privately raised volunteers in Nashville, and a party under
Kasper Mansker marched to the aid of the Chickasaws. The
stout-hearted Piomingo wrote Robertson:

---

[20] Putnam, 439-440.
[21] Goodpasture; *Tenn. Historical Magazine,* Vol. 4, 286.

"As what I expected of your assistance is not in your power, I hope I have made good times for you, if I have made bad for myself. If so, you shall hear that I die like a man."

Glover, another Chickasaw chief, wrote Robertson also that the Chickasaws would die bravely, for they were few in number compared with the Creeks. "Be a man ever so small, if he has a strong heart in him, it is the heart makes the man," he said.[22]

But unexpectedly Panton-Leslie & Co. came to their aid. This company controlled the trade of both tribes, and Panton was unwilling to see a customer destroyed. He would sell guns with which to kill Americans but not his own customers. Therefore, he warned the Creeks that if they persisted in fighting the Chickasaws, he would cut off their own supplies. The Creeks had already started for the Chickasaw country. On receipt of Panton's message they returned home, and the Creek-Chickasaw war came to an abrupt end.[23]

---

[22] *American State Papers, Indian Affairs,* Vol. 1, 456.

[23] *Ibid.,* 454. The valor of the Chickasaws evoked the admiration of President Washington, and he sent Piomingo, through Governor Blount, an invitation to visit Philadelphia; the chief accepted it in 1794. He met Washington and thereafter declared himself to be a citizen of the United States.

# CHAPTER XXIV

## DOUBLEHEAD AND BENCH

### I

The friendship of the Chickasaws for the Americans was not only exasperating to the Creeks and Cherokees, but was a positive menace to the success of their plans. The Chickasaws, by virtue of their location, controlled the navigation of the Mississippi and prevented free communication between southern and northern Indians.

In May, 1793, John Watts sent a delegation, headed by the redoubtable Doublehead, into the Chickasaw country for another try at convincing the Chickasaws of the error of their way. As befitted the occasion, Doublehead was in elaborate costume, and wore silver arm bands with an eagle design. He placed before the Chickasaw council, a bundle of bloody arrows, a bow, a hatchet, a scalping knife, and a treaty pipe. He asked that the Chickasaws accept these emblems of war and join the other southern tribes in a common war on the United States. He said:

"I do not doubt but that the Chickasaws and Choctaws must by this time have seen their folly, for all the other tribes have joined to cut off the Americans. If the Chickasaws and Choctaws do not now take up the hatchet, there will be nothing for them to do, for all the other tribes, during the present moon will strike the Americans.

"The northward army of the Americans, (St. Clair) is all killed. The western country is making another army, but it will be too small, and the united tribes will soon finish them. We, the Cherokees, had eaten a great quantity of the white men's flesh, but have had so much of it we are tired of it, and think it too salty."

Doublehead referred thus to the flesh of Overall and Burnett, at the Dripping Spring.

"We have plenty of guns," the Indian orator concluded, "but do not need them to kill the white men with. The bow, arrows, and scalping knife which we bring are sufficient."

Piomingo refused to attend the meeting, and the Chickasaw Council delegated Wolf's Friend to speak in his stead. When Doublehead had finished his plea, Wolf's Friend replied in emphatic manner:

"We will send your talk to the Choctaws, but think that they will take no notice of it. As for the Chickasaws, we have eaten weeds and grass, such as brutes eat, but it will be a long time before we think of eating Virginians' flesh." [1]

Finding that his war talk had not impressed the Chickasaws, Doublehead made light of their assistance. He threatened to return to a party he had left at the mouth of Bear's Creek (his own town) and waylay every crossing of the Tennessee River, so that the Chickasaws could have no communication with their beloved friends, the Americans.

After a fruitless stay of three days duration, the delegation returned to their own country, where Doublehead was to take part in a tragedy that marked the beginning of the end of the trail for the fighting Chickamaugas.

2

President Washington had requested that the leading Cherokee chiefs, and particularly those of the hostile Lower Five Towns, visit him in Philadelphia. Governor Blount had seconded the invitation, and early in June, 1793, the chiefs began to gather at the home of Hanging Maw in Coyatee to make arrangements for the trip.

Major Thomas King was in charge of the group, and Daniel Carmichael was acting for the governor.

Doublehead, a member of the National Council, was among them. Hanging Maw, Otter Lifter, Scantee, Fool Charlie, and nine other chiefs were present. Watts was daily expected.

The governor had departed before the others in order to arrange for a befitting reception of the chiefs in Philadelphia. He considered that it would be the celebration of the long-hoped-for peace with the Cherokees. But his carefully laid plans were brought to naught by an untoward event which took place at Coyatee on June 12, 1793.

---

[1] Robertson's Correspondence, American Historical Magazine; *American State Papers, Indian Affairs*, Vol. 1, 456.

### 3

On the morning of May 25th, Thomas Gillam and his son James had been killed and scalped by Indians in Raccoon Valley, eighteen miles from Knoxville. Thirty Indians were reported in the neighborhood, burning cabins and stealing horses. Two war clubs of an unusual make were left beside the mangled bodies of the Gillams, indicating that it was not the Cherokees who had committed the crime. The offenders were probably the Shawnees who lived at Running Water. Governor Blount, when he heard of the Gillam murder, ordered Captain John Beard, who had just returned from a tour of the Cumberland, to follow the trail of the war-party; but under no circumstances to cross the Little Tennessee River, the Cherokee boundary.

Governor Blount was, at the time, preparing to leave for Philadelphia, and wished nothing to interfere with his proposed peace plans. Having no idea that Beard would violate his orders, the governor departed for Philadelphia, and left his secretary, Daniel Smith, in charge.

Beard and his horsemen followed the trail of the marauders. Although the pattern of the clubs had indicated that the Cherokees had not done the damage, the trail led to the mouth of the Little Tennessee River, opposite the town of Hanging Maw, Coyatee. As a matter of fact, the war-party had passed through Coyatee, with malice aforethought, and Hanging Maw's son, over Major King's protest, had bought from them, two horses which they had stolen.[2]

Captain Beard disregarded his orders, crossed the river, and fell upon Coyatee. The attack came as a bolt out of the blue. King and Carmichael barely escaped with their lives. The friendly Hanging Maw, his wife, and a daughter of Nancy Ward, were wounded. Scantee, Fool Charlie, Betty, daughter of the old chief, Kitegista, a white man named Rosebury, and four others were killed.

Beard's act was unjustifiable. Hanging Maw had always been friendly to the United States, and even had his town been guilty, Beard had positive orders not to cross the river. The

[2] *Ibid.,* 457.

whole frontier was roused against the Cherokees, however; Beard shared the feeling and took advantage of it.[3]

Secretary Smith, governor pro tem, ordered a court-martial for Beard, and directed him to relinquish his command. Beard again disregarded an order, and continued to direct his force. The court-martial, because of the excited state of the frontier, came to nothing.[4]

Smith wrote apologetic letters to Watts, Hanging Maw, and Doublehead, assuring them that the guilty ones would be punished as soon as the matter could be presented to President Washington.

Hanging Maw replied in a letter dated at Coyatee, June 15, 1793, ridiculing the plea for delayed justice:

"Friend and Brother: It is but a few days since you were left in the place of the governor. While he was in place, nothing happened. Surely they are making fun of you. Surely you are neither headman nor warrior. I reckon you are afraid of these thieves when you talk of sending to Congress.

"If you are left in place of the governor, you ought to take satisfaction yourself. It is but a few days since I was at your house, and you told me nothing should happen to me or my people at my house. I reckon the white people are just making fun of you. Governor Blount always told me that nothing should happen to me as long as I did live, but he hardly got out of sight when I liked to have been killed. When is the day a white man was killed at my house?"[5]

He also wrote to President Washington with whom he had fought as a young man in the French and Indian War:

"I am writing the President of the United States. It is a long time since I have seen him, but I have seen him, when we were both young men and warriors."[6]

Doublehead, claiming modestly to be only a boy, although he probably had taken as many scalps as any warrior on the border, wrote:

"I am still among my people, living in gores of blood. When is the day I shall hear a full answer from you. Be strong, don't

---

[3] *Ibid.*, 459.
[4] *Ibid.*, 463, 464, 465.
[5] *Ibid.*, 459.
[6] *Ibid.*, 459-460.

be afraid, but get satisfaction for me. Why do you talk of sending to the President for advice? These people did not ask for
advice when they came and killed our people. The head man cannot give out any peace talks of going to Philadelphia until you
give us satisfaction for what is done. I am but a boy, though I
am giving out this talk. We have lost nine of our people that
we must have satisfaction for. Some of the first and principal
people of our Nation fell here. This is the third time we have
been so served when we were talking peace, and they fell on us
and killed us." [7]

Failing to get the satisfaction he desired from Smith,
Doublehead, as we shall see, took it for himself.

## 4

After Beard's massacre, John Watts found himself at the
head of a united nation. He had the active cooperation of
such chiefs as Bloody Fellow and Little Turkey, who had been
considered friendly to the Americans. The warriors of Little
Turkey's town came to his support almost to a man. His
strength was further augmented by Creek warriors from the
upper towns who flocked to his leadership.

Watts, an inspirational leader, persuaded his followers that
they should fight in large numbers as the white people fought.
The Indian was, however, by nature and training, an individual
warrior. Each chief had won his right to leadership by
personal prowess, and was concerned principally with his own
glory. Cooperation could not be expected for any length of
time.

On August 29, 1793, Watts attacked Henry's Station with
two hundred warriors. He found the station heavily defended, and did not risk another experience such as Buchanan's
Station. Lieutenant Tedford, who was outside the fort when
the firing commenced, was captured and later killed and his
body mangled. He was the only white casualty.

A month later, Watts appeared at the crossing of Tennessee
River near the present Loudon, with the amazing number of a
thousand warriors. The Indians were "fighting in armies like
the white men." Watts' force, twenty-eight files, each of

---

[7] *Ibid.* The other times referred to by Doublehead were, the massacre of
the hostages at Fort Prince George, and the killing of Old Tassel.

forty men abreast, marched all night toward Knoxville, which was the intended point of attack.

Sevier, with four hundred militia, was stationed at Ish's, within three miles of the Indian line of advance but on the opposite side of the river. Watts sent Doublehead's brother, Pumpkin Boy, and the Nettle Carrier, as spies to watch for any movement of Sevier's men. They reconnoitered the camp from the shelter of a large forked tree. An incautious movement attracted the attention of Thomas Mains who was on sentinel duty and the Pumpkin Boy was killed. The same ball apparently wounded his companion also. When the body of the dead Indian was found the next morning, his wound was stuffed with leaves as though he had attempted to stop the flow of blood. A trail of blood indicated where the wounded Nettle Carrier had retired. Pumpkin Boy was a handsome warrior, well equipped with trinkets and a pair of handsome, silver mounted pistols. These were turned over to the Sentinel Mains.[8]

Watts was accompanied on the campaign by Doublehead, his uncle, who by reason of his relationship and prowess as a warrior exercised a great influence over the younger chief.

Doublehead insisted that the Indians should burn each settler's cabin as they proceeded. Watts, realizing the importance of surprise, argued that they should push ahead with all speed to Knoxville. But for this division of opinion, so formidable a body of Indians would have caused tremendous damage.

Doublehead, fierce and sullen by nature, was angered by the death of his brother, Pumpkin Boy, and was infuriated that Watts should oppose his wishes. The quarrel between the two chiefs delayed the march. Other chiefs were drawn into it, among them Vann, who sided with Watts. Vann had a boy captive riding behind him on his horse. The ungovernable Doublehead rode up and sank his tomahawk in the boy's head. Vann taunted him with being a "baby killer," and was compelled to flee to save his own life, so great was Doublehead's rage.[9]

Daybreak of the 25th found the Indian army still eight miles

---

[8] Draper Mss., 30-S 351-397.

[9] Narrative of Rev. Stephen Foster, *Southwestern Monthly,* Vol. 2. Ramsey, 580.

from Knoxville. The opportunity for a surprise attack had been lost. Nearby, however, was a small blockhouse occupied by Alexander Cavett and his family of thirteen persons, only three being men. The Indians assaulted the place. Cavett and his companions defended it with desperate bravery. Five Indians fell before the rifles of the white men. The assault was halted, and a parley ensued.

The well known Bench, who spoke English, acted as intermediary. Watts agreed that if those within the fort would surrender, their lives would be spared and they would be exchanged for an equal number of Indian prisoners in the hands of the white people. Resistance was apparently hopeless, and the little garrison accepted the terms.

Doublehead had permitted the peace parley in sullen silence, without indicating his approval or consent. The moment the gates of the blockhouse were opened, he drew his tomahawk, sounded the war whoop, and fell on the prisoners with wild fury. Watts, startled at the sudden turn of events, seized a young white boy, Alexander Cavett, Junior, and claimed him as his own prisoner. The other captives, men, women, and children, were killed and scalped by Doublehead. Bench, who was himself a bloodthirsty warrior, begged in vain that their lives be spared, feeling that his honor was at stake. Doublehead would not be denied his vengeance, and was determined that even the boy saved by Watts should die. To save his captive, Watts spirited young Cavett away by some of his Creek allies. Three days later the boy was killed and scalped by a Creek chief.[10]

## 5

The frontier town of Knoxville had been built around the blockhouse of its founder, General James White. There were forty men in the station capable of bearing arms. They had on hand, too, three hundred muskets which had been deposited by the United States for use in emergencies.

The firing at Cavett's Station was plainly heard on the morning of the 25th, and word of the Indian invasion had already been received by General White. He hastily formed a plan of campaign. It was thought that the Indians would

[10] Ramsey, 581.

approach Knoxville by the back road over a ridge south of the town. The two oldest men, John McFarland and Robert Williams, were detailed to load the extra muskets. The remaining thirty-eight were marched to the ridge and stationed twenty feet apart. Their orders were to fire when the Indians appeared and then to scatter and make their way back to the blockhouse where the chief resistance was planned. White's men remained on the ridge throughout the 25th in hourly expectation of attack, which did not come.[11]

Sevier, at Ish's Station, had also heard the sound of the firing at Cavett's. Not knowing the number of the invaders, the extent of the mischief they had done, or the point of next attack, he sent Captain Harrison across the Holston with a company of horsemen to obtain information and if necessary to pursue the Indians.

Harrison found the smoking ruins of the station and the mangled bodies of Cavett and his family. The trail of the Indians led westward toward Clinch River. Twelve miles from Cavett's, the cabin of Luke Lea was found to have been burned. Lea and his family had sought refuge in Knoxville before the Indian advance. The forces of Watts had apparently crossed Clinch River and were retreating southward along the trail at the foot of Walden's Ridge.

General Sevier's orders from Governor Blount had been to confine operations against the Indians to defensive measures. He communicated with Secretary Smith for instructions, and in the meantime rapidly recruited his forces. Smith replied on Sept. 30th:

"In answer to yours of the 27th, I hold it would be proper to follow the trail of the large party of Indians who murdered Cavett's family on the 25th instant, and if possible inflict punishment upon them. The country is to be defended in the best manner we can, comporting with my general instructions to you of the 17th."[12]

[11] The ridge was probably the one now known as McKinney's Ridge, near New Gray Cemetery. Ramsey mentions the houses of Samuel Luttrell and Henry Lonas, which are still standing. (1935) The two houses were on the "back road" by which it was expected that the Indians would advance.

[12] Serving under Sevier on this campaign were Colonel John Blair commanding troops from Washington District; and Colonel Gilbert Christian those from Hamilton District. Major George Elmholm acted as Sevier's adjutant.

The "general instructions" were those of the Secretary of War, transmitted through Governor Blount, limiting operations to defensive measures.

John Sevier's idea of a defensive operation was a strong offensive. Within a few days, he was on his way to the Cherokee country at the head of seven hundred men.[13] The Little Tennessee was crossed at Lowery's Ferry near Chilhowie. Four wide trails leading toward the mountains were located north of the Hiwassee, indicating that the Indians had re-crossed the Tennessee at Hiwassee Island. Sevier followed the Great War Path through Hiwassee. His scouts soon located trails indicating that the Indians were concentrating at Ustanali on the Coosawatie River. That place was abandoned by the Cherokees on the approach of the white army. Large supplies of grain and meat were taken, and the town was burned. William Gaut, a sentry, was killed by the Indians during the night.

On the following night, Sevier left his campfires burning, silently withdrew his men, and marched for Etowah at the junction of Coosawatie and Coosa Rivers. He arrived at that point on the 17th, and found the Indians heavily fortified on the south bank, ready to dispute his passage.

Colonel Kelly with a part of the Knox regiment was ordered to search for a ford farther down the river. An available place was discovered within half a mile, and the men began to cross. Noting this, the Indians abandoned their breastworks and rushed to oppose Kelly's horsemen. Captain Nathaniel Evans, who was with Kelly, saw his opportunity. He turned his company and galloped back to rejoin Sevier, who immediately began crossing at the original ford. The Indians discovered their mistake too late to regain their fortifications, and hotly contested Sevier's men in the open. Only six men actually crossed at the lower ford, including George Gordon, Jesse Wallace, and Sevier's young son Richard. Firing their pistols and with swords in hand, they sounded the war whoop and galloped into the Indian rear to take part in Sevier's fight at the ford.[14]

The white army crowded the river in passing. The south bank was steep, and the path upward was so narrow that the

---

[13] *American State Papers, Indian Affairs,* Vol. 1, 622-23.
[14] Draper Mss., 30-S 351-397.

horsemen had to ascend in single file. The first man to reach
the top was Ignatius Chisholm. The firing and yelling of the
Indians frightened his horse, and probably Chisholm as well.
He found it impossible to retreat the way he had come, for
other horsemen were crowding up the trail. He therefore
jumped his horse over a twelve foot embankment into the river,
and was making his way to the rear when he met his friend
Hugh Lawson White who persuaded him to return to the
fight.[15] White urged his own horse up the ascent, and was
confronted at the top by the Cherokee Chief Kingfisher with
whom he was instantly engaged in mortal combat. Kingfisher
was killed. He was a noted chief, and his death discouraged
his followers. Following the usual Indian custom, they dispersed, carrying off their wounded with them. Several dead
warriors left on the field were scalped by the white men. In
the Indian encampment were found many guns of Spanish
make, and other spoils.

Following the battle, Sevier crossed Coosa River and
destroyed Turnip Mountain and other Cherokee villages. It
was his desire to proceed against the Five Lower Towns, but
his guides informed him that there was only one path which
would be too dangerous to follow. All surrounding towns
and crops were destroyed. The Cherokees had gone ex-
tensively into the raising of cattle, and three hundred of these
were slaughtered. Sevier marched for home about the middle
of October.

In his report of the campaign, Sevier stated:

"A number of Indian women and children were taken prisoner.
Many might have been taken, but from motives of humanity I
did not encourage it to be done, and several which were taken
were suffered to make their escape. Your excellency knows the
disposition of several that were out on this campaign, and can
readily account for this conduct." [16]

Sevier's comment was prompted by an incident which
occurred following the fight at Etowah. Wallace, one of the
men who had crossed at the lower ford, had been mortally

---

[15] *Ibid.*
[16] Sevier's Report, *American State Papers, Indian Affairs,* 1-469. This
was one of the two of Sevier's campaigns which he officially reported.

wounded, but lived until the following day. Among the Indian prisoners was a squaw with her small child. She stood under guard near where Wallace lay suffering, and looked probably in pity at the wounded man. Wallace imagined that she was smiling at his misfortune, and said, irritably, "Take her out of my sight." One of his friends, with the callous feeling toward Indians that was too frequent on the border, raised his gun and shot the Indian mother dead; and taking the child by the heels, dashed out its brains.[17]

Sevier returned with his men to Ish's Station, from which point he made official report of the campaign on Oct. 25, 1793. Pay for his troops was refused because the Secretary of War held that the moment Sevier crossed the boundary of the Indian country, his operation ceased to be defensive, and became offensive.[18]

The Etowah campaign was the last military service of John Sevier. For nearly twenty years he had been in constant service with little hope of reward except the esteem of his fellow pioneers. He was never wounded, although he fought in thirty-five engagements. He was careful of the lives of his soldiers, and thoughtful of their welfare. The rapid movement of his horsemen was a deciding factor in all his victories. He himself was an accomplished horseman, and followed the frontier tradition that commanders should be actual leaders. "Come on, boys," was his battle cry. His use of the war-whoop was so effective in demoralizing a foe, that British prisoners, after the Battle of King's Mountain, said, "We could stand your fighting, but your cursed hallooing confused us. We thought you had regiments instead of companies."

Sevier's troops were composed of his neighbors, and he was

---

[17] Draper Mss., 30-S 351-397.

[18] Three years later, after Tennessee had become a state, the matter was referred by Congress to a committee of which Andrew Jackson was chairman. The future Old Hickory called the attention of Congress to that clause in the Constitution which reads, "No state shall engage in war UNLESS actually invaded, or in such imminent danger as will not admit of delay."

He pointed out that the Indians had clearly invaded American territory; and also that the members of the militia, having been ordered out by their officers, had no choice but obedience. He moved that Sevier's men be paid for their services, and the resolution was adopted on Jan. 17, 1797.

Jackson's full report may be found in *American State Papers, Indian Affairs,* Vol. 1, 621 *et seq.*

generally accompanied on all campaigns by close relatives. The rendezvous was usually held at his house or some nearby point. His fields were pastures for his horsemen. All he had they were gladly given. In his early campaigns lead from a mine on his property was used.[19]

In his private life, Sevier was friend and father to the frontiersmen, and security notes cost him thousands of acres of his best lands. In one year, when corn was scarce, he gave a thousand bushels to the destitute. "When the wayfaring emigrant came into the country, he never passed the house of John Sevier in need of food, raiment, or information, but that he received it, and in such a way that he could never forget the kind and obliging manner in which it was dispensed."[20]

## 6

While Watts and the main body of his warriors had retreated after the capture of Cavett's Station, a body of about one hundred was left to observe the movements of the white men, and to attack the settlements when defenders were absent. One party was given the specific task of burning the house of John Sevier, and the killing or capture of his family. On Sunday, October 13th, a detachment, consisting of twenty-eight warriors, appeared in Greasy Cove, near Sevier's home, and killed Mrs. William Lewis and five of her children. One child was carried away as a prisoner.[21] Buildings and grain were destroyed. The war-party retired under the impression that they had killed Sevier's family. Another company, on the same mission, killed the family of a pioneer named Headler, who lived on Nolichucky a few miles below Sevier's residence. A party of fifty killed a woman and child in Washington County, near Dandridge. They were stuck in the throat, and the skin was entirely removed from their heads. While two neighbors, Cunningham and Jenkins, were burying the bodies, they were fired upon by Indians; Cunningham was killed. He later was buried in the same grave with the mother and child.

[19] *Draper Mss.*, 30-S 351-397.
[20] Soon after Sevier was elected governor, a pioneer passed through Knoxville with a family of thirty. Twenty of them, boys, were half-naked. Sevier's sympathy was aroused. He himself was father to eighteen children. He contributed liberally, and asked his neighbors' help; he did not cease his efforts until the unusual family was suitably clothed.
[21] *American State Papers, Indian Affairs*, Vol. 1, 469-470.

Jenkins escaped.[22] The return of Sevier and his men from the Etowah campaign, was the cue for the war-parties to disappear.

## 7

Immediately after the battle of Etowah, John Watts, the Little Turkey, Bloody Fellow, and a number of other chiefs, proceeded to Walnut Hills to tell their troubles to their friends and allies, the Spaniards. To their dismay, Governor Carondelet advised them to make peace with the Americans. Spain was having troubles of her own. Bonaparte, at the head of the Revolutionary Army of France, was conducting a campaign that caused Spain to be pressed for money to defend her frontiers. For many years, she had administered the affairs of Louisiana at a financial loss, but now she could not afford to spend money on unprofitable colonies with her own existence at stake.

During 1793, it had been difficult for Panton-Leslie & Co. to secure guns and ammunition for Spain's Indian allies. One shipload of supplies had been seized and brought into the port of Savannah by a French privateer, to the delight of the Georgians, who hated the Indians for whom the supplies were intended. To carry on the war, Watts was entirely dependent upon Spanish powder and ball. He returned to Willstown a disheartened and disillusioned man.

## 8

While Watts was away, the implacable Doublehead had not allowed the war to lag. Sevier had hardly dispersed the Indians at Etowah when Doublehead gathered a hundred warriors and left for the Kentucky road. Early in 1794, he arranged an ambush at Laurel River ford. The trail was narrow at the crossing and the Indians felled a tree across it, then concealed themselves in the bushes on each side. Thomas Ross, post rider between Holston and Cumberland, and a party of twelve travelers, among them, two Baptist preachers, Elders Haggard and Shelton, approached the crossing. They were guarded by a small militia. Ross; the two preachers; and one of the militiamen, were killed and Joseph Brown was wounded, but

---

[22] Ramsey, *Annals of Tennessee,* 500. *Draper Mss.,* 30-S, 351-397.

escaped. For years thereafter the circuit riders crossed the mountain in fear and trembling, as it was rumored that Doublehead was under oath to be avenged on the white people.[23]

During the same month, the Indian fiend killed the Wilson family, consisting of eight persons, except a boy, whom he reserved. A few days later, April, 1, 1794, Doublehead and his force were lying in wait for travelers who were passing to and from the Cumberland settlements. At the point selected, the trail wound for a mile or more between steep hills covered with undergrowth and tall trees. A large spring bubbled from the base of the northern hill; a temptation to passers-by to pause for rest and refreshment. The spot was ideal for an ambush.[24]

The noted Thomas Sharpe Spencer, with four companions, approached the ambuscade. He had been to Virginia to settle his father's estate; he had received a legacy of one thousand dollars in gold which he carried in his saddlebags. Spencer and James Walker rode in advance; as they neared the spring and were in the act of dismounting, they were fired on and Spencer was killed. His horse sprang forward as he fell, and his saddlebags dropped to the ground. These, with the scalp of so famous an opponent, furnished a rich prize for Doublehead. Spencer's companions fled, and the frequent turns of the trail enabled them to escape while the Indians scalped the mighty "Big Foot."

Doublehead was ambitious to be powerful in the councils of his Nation. He was at Hanging Maw's house preparing to leave for Philadelphia when Beard's massacre occurred, and had been wounded then. Governor Blount, on his return from Philadelphia, renewed the invitation. These visits added to the prestige of the chiefs who were priviledged to take them, and Doublehead accepted with alacrity, although his hands were scarcely dry from Spencer's blood.

Watts, at the meeting with Governor Blount at Henry's

---

[23] Goodpasture, *Indian Wars and Warriors in the Old Southwest.* Also see, Narrative of Jos. Brown, *Southwest Monthly,* Vol. 1, 10.

[24] The location, later known as Spencer's Hill, is on the present Highway 70, in Cumberland County, Tenn., between the towns of Crab Orchard and Ozone. The spring, which is yet in use, is about two hundred yards north of the main highway on the old trail.

Station in 1793, had recommended certain chiefs for the Philadelphia trip.[25]  They were, Doublehead, Glass, Little Turkey, Kitegiska, Richard Justice, Fool Charles, Breath, Water Hunter, Chuleoh, Middlestriker, and the Spider.  These were real leaders of the Nation, but some of them had been too friendly to the whites to please Doublehead.  In June, 1794, when he appeared in Philadelphia, he brought with him a number of chiefs who were not so prominent, but were all his own supporters.  His party consisted of himself; Tekakiskee, the Water Hunter; Nontuaka, the Northward; Kenesaw, the Cabin; John McLemore; Walalue, the Humming Bird; Chuleoah, the Boots; Ustanaqua, Big Head; Kulsa-tahee, Creek Killer; Kena-guna, the Lying Fawn; Chata-ka-lesa, Fowl Carrier; and Siteaha; with John Thompson and Arch Coody as interpreters.

The Cherokees were received with honor by Secretary Knox. Doublehead was the center of attention.  He proved himself to be as able a diplomat as he was a warrior.  The Cherokee annual allowance was increased from $1500.00 to $5000.00, and Double-head was permitted to take home a year's allowance in advance. Each of the chiefs was given presents.  In return for the increased allowance, the chiefs renounced in the name of the Chero-kee Nation, the lands on which the Cumberland settlements were located.

At the close of the conference, on June 14, 1794, President Washington delivered to the Indians a friendly address, beginning with the salutation "My Children."  He urged that the chiefs restrain their young men from stealing horses and murdering American citizens.  He closed his remarks:

"We mean now to bury deep and forever, the red hatchet of war.  Let us therefore forget past events.  Let us endeavor to find the means by which the path between us may be kept open and secure from all harm." [26]

9

Doublehead and his party were returned in state aboard an American warship to Savannah.  During their absence, much

[25] *American State Papers, Indian Affairs*, Vol. 1, 443.
[26] Washington's address may be found in Smith, *Story of the Cherokees*, 102.

of tremendous importance had happened to the Cherokees, Doublehead wrote to Governor Blount from Cossawatie, on October 20th, 1794:

"Friend and Brother: I send you this talk on my way home, just returned from my father the President. Now my brother, you know very well, and the rest of the white people, when I and some of my people went to Congress, we were sent by the head men of our country to go to that place. Now we have returned, and the head men and warriors, and the young men also, are satisfied with what we have done, and are determined to hold the United States fast by the hand, and keep the peace. This is the talk of all, and I am glad to inform you, my friend, it is pleasing to me that I did not send my breath for nothing. It appears now we shall have a lasting peace between us, which our old men strove a long time for. We shall live in peace now like brothers.

"My people are now wanting to go hunting, and you know it is high time to be out. You know very well where our hunting grounds are, and we hope you will keep the white people from coming to hunt the hunters.

"Now if some of our bad young men should go and steal a horse from some of your people, you must not get in a passion with us for that, but wait until the horse shall be returned to you again. That is what the great beloved man told us, to return all such horses, and not to let our young men do any bad thing to the white people. When we gave him our talk, he received it, and has taken hold of it fast. We all mean to hold the talks given us by the President and General Knox, and we hope the white people will not let our hands go, but hold us by the hand as we mean to do them. I am, your friend and brother,

DOUBLEHEAD." [27]

10

On the morning of April 6, 1794, the famous Captain Bench made his last raid on the Virginia Border.

Near the town of Mendota in Washington County, Virginia, lived Peter and Henry Livingstone and their families; the whole consisting of thirteen persons.

Mrs. Livingstone, with three of the children was in the house while the others were outside about their usual farm tasks. Suddenly the clamor of the dogs caused her to look up, and she saw seven horribly painted Indians approaching. They

---

[27] American State Papers, Indian Affairs, Vol. 1, 532.

tried to rush upon her, but she foiled them by hastily barring the door. Thereupon, they fired two balls through it, but no damage was done. Mrs. Livingstone took down her husband's gun and returned the fire. Angered at this unexpected resistance, the Indians set fire to the house. When she could stand the heat no longer, Mrs. Livingstone took her babe-in-arms and with the other children dashed outside, expecting to be tomahawked. Greatly to her surprise the Indians had rounded up all the other members of the family, including three Negro servants. Noticing her two other children, whom she had not expected to see alive, in the group, she was filled with delight. The two men, Peter and Henry, eluded the savages and managed to escape, but all the others were made prisoners.

When the Indians had retired to a secluded spot to divide spoils, Mrs. Livingstone managed the escape of her children. She had seen that the Indians were careless about the little captives, so she called softly to the eldest daughter, a girl about ten, and handing the baby to her, whispered that she must run to the house of John Russell, a neighbor. Not caring to be bothered with them on a long march, the Indians winked at their escape and allowed them to get away.

With his remaining captives, Bench headed for the wild mountainous country of Southwest Virginia. On the second day he camped at the foot of Powell's Mountain, near Big Stone Gap, far from the Livingstone home. The red-headed Indian was in great good humor, and talked freely; he boasted that he was going to capture all the negroes in Southwestern Virginia; he said, "I am coming back next summer and pay old General Shelby a visit, and take all his negroes."

Two hunters were sent ahead to get food and the march was resumed on the morning of March 9th.

In the meantime, Peter and Henry had spread the news, and Lieutenant Vincent Hobbs, one of the finest scouts on the border, started in pursuit with thirteen men. Hobbs was familiar with the whole of Southwest Virginia, and after following the trail a few miles, he realized that the Indians were headed for Big Stone Gap. Abandoning the Indian trail, they took a more direct route and reached the gap on the morning of the 9th. Fresh tracks showed that the Indians had already passed! Hobbs followed the path, and overtook the two Indians who had been sent ahead; he discovered that the main body had not gone through, so, after killing the hunters, he sped back to the gap, and placed his men in ambush. Not liking the position first chosen, but sure that it would not be long until the Indians would appear, he, and a scout named Van Bibber, advanced cautiously to select a better one. In a short while they spied the war-party approaching; Bench in the lead had charge of Mrs. Henry Livingstone. Seven warriors were conducting their prisoners in the rear of their leader; the one in charge of Mrs. Peter Livingstone being some distance behind. Hobbs and Van Bibber somewhat in advance of the other white men, each chose a man, aimed, and fired. Hobbs killed Bench, and Van Bibber the man next behind him. The other frontiersmen rushed forward, but the remaining Indians escaped into a thicket, taking with them, one of the prisoners, a negro man. The savage who had charge of Mrs. Peter Livingstone tried to kill her. He shoved her backward across a log, at the same time aiming a blow with his tomahawk; she remained unconscious for a while, but recovered. The guard escaped. While Hobbs and his men were trying to revive her, the two Livingstone men, at the head of a second rescue party, arrived; a joyful reunion followed.

The State of Virginia had offered a reward for Bench, dead or alive. Lieutenant Hobbs forwarded the red-haired scalp to his commander, Colonel Arthur Campbell, who, in turn, sent it to Governor Randolph. Colonel Campbell wrote: "I beg leave to hint that the present of a neat rifle to Mr. Hobbs would be accepted as a reward for his late services, and it will serve as a stimulus to future exertions against the enemy."

Governor Randolph adopted the hint, and at his recommendation the Virginia Legislature voted Lieutenant Hobbs a silver mounted rifle for his notable performance. The governor remarked of the scalp that there was no doubt about its being genuine, as "the hair is red." [28]

## II

During the first half of April, 1793, a series of atrocities were perpetrated by the Indians: Fifty horses were stolen

[28] Details of Bench's last exploit are from Goodpasture; *Calendar of Virginia State Papers,* 7: 111-112 and 117-118, statement of Mrs. Livingstone and Colonel Campbell's report; and Collins; *Historical Sketches of Kentucky,* 496-497.

from the various sections of the Holston settlements. Twenty-five Indians, probably a detachment of Doublehead's band, attacked the blockhouse at the mouth of Town Creek, and killed William Green. William Casteel, a Revolutionary soldier, lived south of French Broad, near the residence of Dr. James Cozby; on the morning of April 22nd, he rose early to accompany Anthony Reagan on a hunting trip; as he stepped from his door he was killed by a blow from a war club. When Reagan arrived, he found Mrs. Casteel lying on the floor dead; her scalp was torn in two places, indicating that it had taken two warriors to conquer her. An axe stained with blood was found beside her; a butcher knife had been thrust in her side; one arm was broken; and one hand almost severed. Her five children all had been scalped; Elizabeth, a ten years old daughter had received six wounds. The horrified neighbors, including Dr. Cozby and Colonel Ramsey, were making preparations to inter the family, when Elizabeth showed signs of life; Dr. Cozby without delay dressed her wounds, and she fully recovered after two years treatment.[29]

### 12

Spain had for many years offered special inducements to Americans who would settle within Spanish territory. Many on the frontier were tempted by the offers. One of these was William Scott, of Knoxville, who organized a party, in June, 1794, to settle at Natchez. A large flat-boat was built for the journey, and thirteen men and their families, with twenty negro slaves set out.

The boat was fired on at the Chickamauga Town of Running Water, but none were killed or wounded; however, Unacata, one of the chiefs who had been wounded at Buchanan's Station organized a pursuing band of three hundred. Among them was Chief Bowl. The Scott party was overtaken at Muscle Shoals, and all of the white men were killed. Now Watts was, at the time, attempting to make peace with Blount, and Bowl, who had been active in the murders and capture, felt that the action would be censured by the principal chiefs; so the slaves were distributed among the captors, and the

---

[29] Ramsey, Annals of Tennessee, 592. Elizabeth Casteel later married a settler named Dunlap, and lived for many years near the scene of the massacre.

Bowl continued down the Tennessee with the women and children. He conducted them to the St. Francis River in Arkansas, and there they settled. This was the first Cherokee Migration of importance to the country west of the Mississippi.[30]

## 13

About the middle of 1794, there occurred an incident which alienated the Cherokees from their Creek allies, and came near resulting in armed conflict between the two tribes.

On July 24th, a company of Creek warriors had killed John Ish, near his blockhouse. Major King and Lieutenant Cunningham followed the trail of the Indians, which led through Hanging Maw's town of Coyatee, and thence to Hiwassee. To show his friendliness for the Americans, Hanging Maw sent ten warriors under his son Willicoe to join in the pursuit of the offenders. At Amoyee a runner arrived from Hanging Maw with the advice that one of the Creeks had stopped at the house of a Cherokee near Hiwassee. Willicoe and his warriors had the honor of capturing him, and delivered him, bound, to the United States Agent, McKee, at Tellico Blockhouse, on July 28th. He was taken to Knoxville, and placed in jail until court should convene in August.

The Creek proved to be Obongpohego, of Oakfuskee Town. Judge Joseph Anderson presided at the trial and asked the prisoner to plead guilty or not guilty to the charge of murder. When Carey, the interpreter had explained the question, he said, "I will not plead not guilty, for the white men are determined to weigh (hang) me, anyhow." He, therefore, pleaded guilty; but the court persuaded him to withdraw the plea and make it not guilty. The jury found him guilty and when asked if there was any reason why sentence should not be passed upon him, he replied, "I have nothing to say,—I came out to take hair and horses, or to be killed. I killed John Ish, and have fallen into the hands of the whites. I would have escaped if it had not been for the Cherokees.

---

[30] Rev. Cephas Washburn, later a missionary among the western Cherokees, talked with the survivors of the Scott boat. The negroes were mentioned by Watts in his conference with Governor Blount a few months later as being "in the Nation." Mooney, Myth of the Cherokees, 100-101, Haywood, 321.

If I am now to be killed, there are enough of my Nation to avenge my death."

The Indian was taken to the outskirts of Knoxville for execution. He was mounted on a horse, placed under a tree, and a rope was looped around his neck. He being so tall, the executioner was fearful that his feet might touch the ground when the horse moved from under him, so directed the prisoner to stand up in order to shorten the rope. When the Indian complied, the horse shifted his position, and the victim's hands being pinioned at his sides, he lost balance and fell; the sheriff kept hold of the other end of the rope and the prisoner was thus executed.

The circumstances alienated the Creeks, who had stood by the Cherokees in their war against the Americans; moreover they sent warriors into the Cherokee towns to exact vengeance.[31]

---

[31] Draper Mss., 82-S 210-233, Haywood, 222-223.

# BOOK FOUR

## The White Path

# CHAPTER XXV

## MAD ANTHONY WAYNE

### I

In the last months of the Revolutionary War, General Anthony Wayne, "Mad Anthony" to his men, because he attempted feats that seemed impossible to others, had been sent by General Washington to help General Nathaniel Greene clear the British troops from the Carolinas and Georgia.

Wayne conducted himself with his usual fervor, and became so endeared to the South that the State of Georgia granted to him a rice plantation of 800 acres near Savannah.

Some time after the close of the Revolution, Wayne decided to develop the plantation, but found it hard to raise the funds with which to buy the necessary slaves. So he gave notes amounting to £4000 to Roberts Morris, the financier of the Revolution, who agreed to discount them in Holland. Wayne like most Americans, had great confidence in the financial ability of Morris. He made drafts on Holland for the anticipated credit, and proceeded with the development of his plantation.

General Wayne found the evils of peace-time more deadly than those of war: the rice crop was a failure; his estate in Waynesboro, Pennsylvania proved a liability rather than an asset; a wound he had received at Yorktown troubled him constantly; he was hounded by creditors; the drafts which he had drawn on Holland were returned protested; and he suffered with a siege of malaria.

He wrote to his wife: "God, how tired I am of being buried in a damned rice swamp!" [1]

It was about this time that Washington received news of the destruction of General Arthur St. Clair's army by the Indians.

This disaster had appalled the people of the United States, and Washington realized that only a decisive campaign could overcome the evil effects of the great Indian victory. To entrust such a campaign to St. Clair would have been unwise;

---

[1] Preston, John Hyde, *Mad Anthony Wayne*, 269.

James Wilkinson, his aide, too, suffered the odium of defeat, and was even then secretly on the payroll of the Spaniards for his efforts toward annexing the western country to Spain.

Wayne, after months of effort, had succeeded in selling his rice plantation and squaring his debts; he was penniless and in bad health. When he heard that Washington was seeking a suitable man for the western campaign, he applied for the place. Never was an application more timely. Washington not only gave him the western command, but appointed him Commander in Chief of the Army of the United States.[2]

When he reached Ohio, he found the country disorganized; Indian attacks bolder than ever; citizens discouraged; and British Agents telling the Indians to fight and they would soon have British troops to help them. With the remnants of St. Clair's troops and raw recruits sent by Congress, Wayne built up a well-trained force of three thousand men, which, after the Roman style, he called "Wayne's Legion."

The appointment of Wayne was a sore disappointment to Wilkinson, who coveted the position himself, although he did not deserve it. He was a scheming, selfish man, whose real passion was money, though he professed to want "military glory."

Wilkinson wrote letters to his influential friends criticizing his commander, and asked them to seek Wayne's removal. He instilled a mutinous spirit into the border militia, which was already resentful of Wayne's military discipline. He even plotted Wayne's death, and wrote to a friend that the finest service any man could render his country would be to hang Old Tony, as he called the commander.

Wayne ignored criticism and continued the training of his troops until ready to strike a decisive blow. Early in 1794, he advanced ninety miles beyond Cincinnati and erected a strong fort to serve as his base. In honor of his old southern commander, Nathaniel Greene, he named it Greeneville. A special force was sent to the scene of St. Clair's defeat, and there a stockade was built. As though to taunt the Indians, Wayne called it Fort Defiance. While preparations were going on, he received news that his wife had died; and it was thought he would expire when an attack of vomiting seized him. But

---

[2] *Ibid.*, 273.

news was received late in June that the Indians had attacked
Fort Defiance, and this revivified him.

On July 27th, Wayne's Legion moved toward the Miami
towns; and Indian scouts kept the British Agents informed of
his movements. He covered twice as many miles in a day as
had St. Clair, and there was no chance of surprise for he kept
scouts in advance and on all sides of his force. When General
Knox had given him instructions on that score, he had replied
laconically, "They shall not be lost." [3]

Early in August, the Legion approached the British Fort
Maumee, at Presque Isle. Near the fort, at the present site of
Toledo, the Indians had entrenched themselves behind a fortifi-
cation of fallen timbers. They were commanded by the
Shawnee chief, Blue Jacket. Wayne offered them the choice
of liberal terms of peace or battle.

Little Turtle, the crafty Miami chief who had commanded
the Indian allies in their great victory over St. Clair, was
inclined to accept Wayne's peace terms. He said:

"We have beaten the enemy twice, under separate commanders.
We cannot expect the same good luck to attend us always. The
Americans are now led by a chief who never sleeps. He is like
a blacksnake, the night and the day are alike to him. During all
the time he has been marching on our villages, notwithstanding
the watchfulness of our young men, we have never been able to
surprise him. Something whispers to me that it would be prudent
to listen to his offers of peace. Think well of it." [4]

"Has my brother turned coward?" the Shawnee chief Blue
Jacket asked scornfully. His bravery having been questioned,
the Miami chief said no more. McKee assured the Indians of
British aid, and urged them to fight, and upon this course they
decided. [5]

2

On the morning of Aug. 20th, Wayne moved his Legion
from its encampment and marched down the river to the
Maumee Rapids, in sight of the British fort. On each flank
moved the cavalry, which Mad Anthony had trained to charge

---

[3] *Ibid.*, 288.
[4] Drake, *Indians of North America*, 572.
[5] *Ibid.*

in any kind of territory. Two long lines of infantry, with guns pointing skyward and bayonets glistening in the sun, occupied the center. Each man was neatly uniformed, and Wayne had given strict orders that no man should remove his coat, regardless of the heat.[6]

Wayne's orders were: "Strike at the Indian position with the bayonet," in which he was a great believer. As soon as the trenches were taken, the troops were to fire at the backs of the Indians, and follow them so fast that they would have no opportunity to reload. The cavalry was instructed to flank the Indian line, charge with sabers, and "Put the horse's hoof over the moccasin." [7]

Wayne was a sick man on the day of the battle. He had to be lifted onto the back of his black stallion by two attendants. When the soldiers had reached the vicinity of the fallen timbers, Colonel Scott, of the Kentucky mounted-volunteers, was ordered to range to the left along the bank of the river, which was covered with breast-high prairie grass. Small reconnoitering parties were sent in all directions. The swampy ground along the river gave way after a hundred feet to higher land which was strewn with trees uprooted by a tornado. Here the Indians waited in fancied security. Warriors were ambushed also in the tall grass; they were soon located by Scott's men.

Wayne dismounted while his scouts made a preliminary survey. Suddenly there was burst of fire in front, and the Kentuckians were seen retreating, pursued by what appeared to be Indians, but on closer examination proved to be English soldiers dressed as redskins. Captain Shaumberg galloped to

---

[6] Wayne was a stickler for neat appearance of his soldiers. At Ticonderoga in 1776, after the retreat from Canada and when the spirits of the soldiers were at low ebb, he issued an order which was greeted with laughter but did much to restore morale: "A barber shall be appointed by each company for the purpose of shaving the soldiers and dressing their hair. The Colonel is determined to punish every man who comes on parade with a long beard, slovenly dressed, or dirty. He hopes the officers will think it their duty to see that their men always appear washed, shaved, their hair plaited and powdered, and their arms in good order."

He once wrote Washington: "I would rather risk my life at the head of men in elegant uniform and with soldierly appearance, merely with bayonets and a single charge of ammunition, than to take them as they appear in common, with sixty rounds of ammunition." *Mad Anthony Wayne*, 31.

[7] Roosevelt, *Winning of the West*, Vol. 4, 111.

the spot where Wayne stood. "General, we're being attacked!" he shouted. Wayne looked up. "Well? I heard it, a skirmishing party; there were six or eight guns." "Oh, sir, I heard at least a hundred and fifty guns," Shaumburg said. Wayne replied, in derision, "Great man!"

Mad Anthony mounted his horse, and a moment later the stallion carried its master headlong into battle. Wayne's hat was off; his hair stood out from all sides of his head. Saber in hand, he charged along the bank of the river behind the dragoons. "Shift to higher ground," he shouted. "Don't waste powder in tall grass, use the bayonet! the bayonet! Bear down on 'em, make 'em get up!"

The Kentucky horsemen speedily reformed, and galloped, in spite of obstructions, over the Indian breastworks. The infantry executed Wayne's orders with spirit, and used the bayonet with such vigor that the second line did not participate in the first attack.

Wilkinson irritated the commander by constantly riding back for instructions as though he questioned the wisdom of the plan of battle. "Be so very kind, sir, as to believe that I know what I am doing, and see that you do too," spoke Wayne, then spurred his horse into action. The Indian fire suddenly died down; Wilkinson, fearing that it might be a subterfuge, came to Wayne in a fever of excitement, "I think we should halt, sir," he yelled. The leader looked at him coolly, took a long breath, and pursed his lips. Then, with a shrug, he sneered, "Well, halt then! but in God's name, *General,* don't halt too long!"

At that moment, the Indians attacked in a line six deep, hoping to regain their entrenchments. They were lead by the Little Turtle; disproving the charge of cowardice. Never did redskins show greater bravery.

Mad Anthony galloped about in full view of the warriors, rallying his forces, and urging them on. "The bayonet, give them the bayonet!" he called. His cavalry rode over logs and trenches and the infantry pressed the Indians back relentlessly. Thirty Americans were killed. Still the battle raged on, and when the red men had retreated two miles, they were almost at the British fort. Whatever clothes they had had on had been torn off in the struggle. Wayne shouted, "They are fighting as naked as the day they were born!"

McKee, who had encouraged the Indians to fight, had the humiliation of seeing his savage allies stream past the British fort in full flight with the Americans at their heels.

The American chief camped within gun shot of the fort. William Campbell, commander of the garrison, dispatched a note requesting Wayne's reason for camping so near a post defended by British guns.

Wayne replied:

"I think I may without a breach of decorum, observe, sir, that, were you entitled to an answer, the most full and satisfactory one was announced to you through the muzzles of my small arms yesterday in action against the horde of savages in the vicinity of your post, which terminated gloriously to the American arms; but had the action continued until the Indians *etc.* were driven under the guns and post you mention, they would not much have impeded the progress of the victorious army under my command." [8]

By "Indians *etc.*" Wayne alluded to the disguised British soldiers. Campbell replied to Wayne's communication, saying that it was a disgusting document to receive from a gentleman," and warning him that unless the American soldiers stayed away from the fort he would fire on them. "Go ahead," Wayne wrote, "Fire! Just try it! but be advised, Major Campbell, your wisest move will be to vacate." [9] Wayne waited to see what Campbell would say. Days passed, and no reply was received. He then ordered everything destroyed to the gates of the fort, and his orders were carried out to the letter. The house of British Agent McKee went up in smoke. Indian crops and houses were destroyed. The Englishmen in the fort fumed and fretted, but dared not interfere, for they knew that that was exactly what Mad Anthony desired.

Having completed his work of destruction at the fort, Wayne marched his Legion to the heart of the Miami country. At the junction of St. Mary's and St. John's Rivers, he built Fort Wayne in order to hold the Miamis in check permanently. He then went into winter quarters at Greeneville.

As a result of the campaign, the anger of the Indians flared

---

[8] Preston, *Mad Anthony Wayne*, 320.
[9] *Ibid.*

against the English, who had promised supplies and assistance, only to fail them in time of need. Throughout the winter, parties came to Wayne asking for peace. The Shawnees were the last to come. In the spring of 1795, delegations from all northern tribes gathered at Greeneville to sign a treaty of peace dictated to them by Wayne.[10]

Blue Jacket made the assembled Indians this speech:

"Brothers: You now see me present myself as a war chief, to lay down that commission and place myself in the rear of my village chiefs, who will for the future command us. Remember, brothers, we have buried the hatchet. Your brothers, the Shawnees, now do the same good act. We must think of war no more."

General Wayne replied:

"I now take this hatchet out of your hands, and with a strong arm throw it in the center of the great ocean where no mortal can ever find it. And I now deliver to you the wide and straight path to the Fifteen Fires, the United States. This path is to be used by you and your children forever." He then handed to the Indians a wide belt of white wampum.

By the Treaty of Greeneville, the northern Indians ceded to the United States, Southern Ohio and Indiana, Eastern Michigan, the land occupied by Wayne's forts, and the Illinois country that had been taken by George Rogers Clark. In return, the United States agreed to pay annually to the Indians, ten thousand dollars.

Wayne questioned the Indians as to the true ownership of the ceded territory. A Chippewa chief rose and replied:

"Elder Brother: You ask who are the true owners of the land. If any tribe claims to own it, they lie, for our Elder Brother has conquered it!"[11]

---

[10] Proceedings at the Treaty of Greeneville are given in full in *American State Papers, Indian Affairs,* Vol. I, 579, *et. seq.*

[11] *American State Papers, Indian Affairs,* Vol. I, 579. Details of Wayne's campaign are from Preston, *Mad Anthony Wayne;* Roosevelt, *Winning of the West;* Drake, *Indians of North America;* and *American State Papers, Indian Affairs.*

3

More than a hundred Cherokees were among the warriors defeated at the Fallen Timbers by Wayne. Some of them, under their chief *Gilala* (Long Hair), had lived among the Shawnees for a number of years. The presence of such parties within an alien nation was equal to the giving of hostages; a constant pledge of mutual support. Throughout the early part of 1793, war parties constantly left the Lower Towns for the aid of their northern allies against Wayne. Watts told John McKee that fifty had departed during the month of March, and more would be leaving at once. He assured McKee that Governor Blount need not be uneasy about the Cherokees attacking the frontiers, "for most of the bad young fellows will soon be gone to the northern tribes." [12]

The Cherokees did not attend the Treaty of Greeneville. Wayne, who overlooked nothing, sent word to Gilala that unless they came in immediately to make peace, they would no longer be considered as under the protection of the United States, which would have been equivalent to their destruction.

Long Hair sent emissaries at once, with the promise that as soon as crops could be gathered, the northern band of Cherokees would return to their own people in the south. [13] In the meantime, Watts, as he returned from Pensacola with the depressing information that the Cherokees could expect no more help from the Spaniards, was met by his returning warriors with news of the disaster that had befallen his northern allies. Governor Blount, in conference with Watts a short time later, said: "I have neglected to give you details of General Wayne's victory over the Northern Indians, but if you wish to hear them, I will now give them." Watts replied: "I do not, some of my people were in the action, and they have already informed me." [14]

---

[12] *Mooney, Myths of the Cherokees,* 79; *Calendar of Virginia State Papers,* 3, 571.
[13] *American State Papers, Indian Affairs,* Vol. 1, 444.
[14] *American State Papers, Indian Affairs,* Vol. 1, 536.

*Picture by Walter Cline*

NICKAJACK CAVE

Site of the town of Nickajack (*Ani-Kusati-yi*), destroyed by Ore's expedition, Sept. 14, 1794. The town occupied an open field between the cave and Tennessee River, at the present Shellmound, Marion County, Tenn. The cave was used by the Confederacy during the War Between the States as a source of saltpetre.

## CHAPTER XXVI

## END OF THE TRAIL

### I

"When will the Lower Towns get their deserts?" James Robertson had asked General Sevier in November, 1793. He had repeatedly asked permission of Governor Blount to chastise the Chickamaugas, but this was contrary to instructions which Blount had received from the Secretary of War, so he had steadfastly refused. However, he did place the request before the President, and on July 26th, 1794, General Knox wrote to the governor:

"If the Indians have been guilty, we have not at all times been innocent. With respect to destroying the Lower Towns, however righteous such a measure might be, or whatever good consequences might result from it, I am authorized by the President specially to say that he does not conceive himself authorized to direct any such measure; nor especially as the whole matter was before Congress at its last session, and they did not think proper to authorize or direct offensive measures, notwithstanding the ideas to the contrary which prevail on your frontiers.

But the secretary added a paragraph to the foregoing, which gave Robertson some encouragement. He said:

"I would hope it were possible to strike with the highest severity any of the parties who go to Cumberland to commit depredations. It would seem that an active and intelligent partisan might find some such opportunity."[1]

General Robertson was both active and intelligent, and from the moment he read this letter, he determined to find opportunity to destroy the Chickamauga towns.

### 2

Governor Blount had, with the consent of Hanging Maw, built a blockhouse on the Little Tennessee opposite the mouth

---

[1] *American State Papers, Indian Affairs*, Vol. 1, 634.

of Tellico River. A small federal garrison under Colonel Abijah Thomas was sent to the new fort, and John McKee was stationed there as Resident Agent to the Cherokees. It proved to be an effective check to Indian raids on the Holston settlements, but caused their full activity to be turned toward Cumberland. Between the months of January and September, 1794, Haywood lists no less than forty Indian raids on the Cumberland settlements, and in practically every case, Americans were killed, houses burned, and horses stolen. The Indians made their forays in small groups, and few warriors were killed, although Robertson's militia was very active.

Occasionally retaliatory measures were successful and the record was somewhat cleansed.

A party of Creeks visited the plantation of General Robertson on February 20th, 1794, fired on his son, Jonathan and killed John Helan. Captain Thomas Murray followed their trail for one hundred and twenty miles and overtook them on the banks of Tennessee River. William Pillow, one of Murray's men wrote an interesting account of the action that ensued.

"Just after daylight we discovered the smoke from the Indian camp. We halted, and Captain Murray sent four or five men as spies, among whom were William Matlock and Robert Evans. They were to go as near as possible, and fire on the Indians. Murray would charge obliquely and strike the river below the camp, and the left would do the same, and strike above the camp. The spies fired and the charge was made as ordered. The spies killed one Indian in camp, and the others ran down the river into Captain Murray's line. Finding they were hemmed in, several of them jumped into the river and were shot there. Maclin killed one on the bank. The left wing discovered two squaws holding to the bushes in the river, and pulled them out.

"As yet I had done nothing. John Davis had lost his saddlebags which contained all our provisions, and had gone back on the trail to look for them. I heard a gunfire and hallooing, and dashed my horse up the steep bank of the river, and saw Davis running toward the camp with four Indians after him. One of them threw something at him, but when they discovered me they turned back. I put my horse at full speed and gained on them rapidly. One of them saw that I was alone and took to a tree, and raised his long axe handle in position to shoot. I saw what it was and did not stop. At that moment, two of the Indians turned to the right and ran down toward the river. I had a British musket, heavily charged with small rifle balls. I aimed nearly on the Indian and in taking my gun off my shoulder my hands very very cold, and I lost one of my bridle reins. Before I could think, my horse ran close to Indian's left side. He wheeled and struck at me with his axe, and I leaned so far over to shun the lick that I fell from my horse, I think not more than ten feet from him.

"I ran upon my hands and feet about twenty yards. I was afraid to look up, expecting to have my head split open with his axe. I think now if he had seen me upon the ground, he would have killed me. I think he struck at me with such force, and missing me, turned his face from me, and each of us were for getting away from that place as fast as possible. When I looked up I saw him running in the opposite direction, forty or fifty yards from me, which afforded me great relief. I ran after him, and being less fatigued than he, was soon within twenty yards of him. He heard me cock my gun, and jumped behind a dogwood sapling which protected his vital parts. I therefore held my gun to my face and aimed at him. He attempted to jump to a larger tree about fifteen feet from him, and as he left the sapling I fired, and he fell.

"At that moment, Captain Murray, Thomas Cox, Robert Evans, Luke Anderson and William Ewing rode up to me. I pointed in the direction one Indian had gone. They turned over the top of the ridge, and I soon heard their guns firing, but as they passed the ridge, they saw an Indian catch my horse by the bridle and jump with his breast upon the saddle. There was a blanket rolled very short which prevented him getting his leg over the horse, he however kept the horse going in a gallop until Thomas Cox put his gun almost against him and fired, shooting him through the shoulder. He held on until they were almost up with him. Luke Anderson was riding a mule, and was near him when he slipped off and it scared his mule. He ran under a bush which jerked his gun away from him. The Indian caught up the gun and snapped three or four times at them before Robert Evans shot him down.

"Just as this party left me Andrew Castleman and several more rode up, and I pointed out where I had seen the other two Indians near the river. They pursued and found them under a bluff of rocks in the river. Castleman killed one and the other dived out in the river. When he came up the men on the bank shot him. We counted eleven killed, and the squaws gave us to understand that there were only eleven men. When we had returned to the camp and eaten our breakfast, William Gresham was held by his feet and let down head foremost, to get a drink of water from the river. He saw an Indian under the bank, lying with his face out of the water. Zachariah Stull killed him, after the bank had been cleared away enough to show him. Two squaws were taken by Captain Murray to Nashville where they were kept until after peace was made." [2]

## 3

A single victory over the Indians, such as that of Captain Murray, had no effect on the Indian warfare except to intensify it. Survivors who reached the Indian towns told the story, and bands bent on vengeance left for the frontier. A sense of resentment at Blount's "defensive measures" pervaded the border, and determination to take "satisfaction" regardless of his instructions developed.

Robertson could not but share the resentment for his own family circle had suffered gravely. He resolved that the Chickamaugas should be destroyed. Secrecy was the keynote of his plans; he realized that should a word of the intended invasion reach the ears of Governor Blount, it would be prohibited. Blount's attention was, at the time, distracted by the actions of Creek war-parties resolved to revenge the hanging of the Indian who had killed John Ish. Within two days after Obongpohego was hanged, twenty-five Creeks appeared at Hiwassee River and inquired if the Cherokees who had taken part in his capture were at home.[3]

One hundred Creeks crossed the Tennessee River near the mouth of Chickamaugas Creek, and announced their intention to fall on the settlements of Knox and Hawkins counties.[4]

Hanging Maw who had been responsible for Obongpohego's undoing called out the warriors of his own town, fearing that the Creeks would destroy it. Middlestriker, of Willstown, and Willicoe, and fifty other Cherokee warriors joined in the pursuit of the Creek party. They overtook and defeated the Creeks near Craig's Station, and the Cherokees returned in triumph to Coyatee. The night was spent in dancing the scalp dance.[5]

On August 12th, twenty-five Creeks attacked Bullrun Block-

[2] Pillow's Narrative, *Draper Mss.*, 6-XX-15.
[3] Haywood, 323.
[4] *Ibid.*
[5] *Ibid.*

house, sixteen miles north of Knoxville, and kept it in a state of siege for several days. And a succession of attacks at isolated points kept the Holston frontier in an uproar throughout the month.[6]

Captain Nathaniel Evans, in charge of the local militia, detached Lieutenant John McClelland with thirty-seven men to follow an Indian trail which led toward Nashville. McClelland was camped at the foot of Spencer's Hill, and as the party which he was pursuing consisted of only a few warriors, he had no anticipation of trouble.

The men turned to the various tasks of making camp; the guns were laid aside. While they were engaged in preparing supper, a band of one hundred Creeks, who had been lying in ambush, stole into camp, and grabbed part of the guns. McClelland's men fled in confusion; and McClelland himself escaped only through the kindness of one of his men, who, seeing that his commander was exhausted, insisted that he take his horse. "Jump on, Lieutenant, I can always run," he said. Paul Cunningham, Daniel Hitchcock, William Fleniken, and Stephen Renfro were killed; and all the camp equipment, and most of the horses were taken. William Lea was captured but later escaped.[7]

### 4

Thus while Governor Blount was occupied with the Creeks, Robertson had the opportunity to complete his plans to destroy the Chickamauga Towns. He sent Sampson Williams to ask the Kentuckians for assistance; and Colonel William Whitley, whose people had suffered from the raids of Doublehead and Bench, raised 150 men and marched to Nashville. Colonel John Montgomery of Clarksville secured a large number of recruits between that town and Nashville. General Robertson

---

[6] *Ibid.*

[7] *Draper Mss.*, 30-S 351-397, Narrative of G. W. Sevier. Some years later, after peace had been declared, a party of Indians went to Knoxville to trade. "As they came opposite to Captain John Fleniken's house, one of the horses was seen to turn familiarly into the door yard, and Mrs. Fleniken recognized the animal that her son, William, had ridden away to the campaign in which he lost his life. The old lady threw her arms around the horse's neck and wept. The Indian who had the horse possessed an understanding heart for he removed his pack and left the horse there; and the beast went straight to the spot where he had been fed as a colt. He was left to roam in the pasture without working and lived for many years.

called for volunteers in his own neighborhood. Major James Ore arrived at Nashville with forty militia enlisted for protection of the Mero District, and offered his cooperation. Five hundred and fifty men assembled at the appointed rendezvous, Brown's Blockhouse, two miles east of Buchanan's Station. Robertson had engaged Joseph Brown, of the Brown's boat episode, to locate a route whereby an army could reach the Lower Towns. Brown, with a companion, traversed the proposed route, and reported to Robertson that it was practicable to use the Indian war-trail over Cumberland Mountain and down Battle Creek to the mouth of Sequatchie River. Realizing that Blount was bound to hear of so large a number of Kentuckians being in Tennessee, Robertson advised the governor that Whitley's contingent had been sent to avenge their wrongs, and that he thought it a good idea for Tennessee to cooperate in the movement.

Blount's reply was prompt and emphatic. It was marked, "PRIVATE."

Knoxville, Sept. 9, 1794.

"General James Robertson, Nashville:

"Dear Sir: You cannot conceive my surprise and mortification at being taught to believe that you would so far countenance the attempts of Colonel Whitley of Kentucky, to give sanction to muster of troops to go with him.

"You have surely paid less respect to yourself on the occasion than on any other since our acquaintance. It is not possible that the Representative in Congress from Kentucky can have had so little understanding as to have entertained the most distant hope that the perpetrators of such lawless, unauthorized acts, would expect the least pecuniary reward for their troubles, for services I cannot call them. I know not the price I would take to report such an order to the Secretary of War.

"Your letter of the 30th will be destroyed, that it may never rise in judgment. Don't suppose this too severe. It proceeds from my personal esteem and the high value at which I hold your public character. No good consequences can arise from such unauthorized expeditions. If such must be, let them be made by states who have senators and representatives in the public councils.

"You cannot conceive the pain I feel upon this occasion, not that the Indians will be injured, for God knows that is a score that, so far as affects the hostile part, I am quite easy on; but for the reputation of the people I have the honor to be appointed to govern. I am, etc., WILLIAM BLOUNT." [8]

Blount had spoken too late. The expedition had left Nashville on Sept. 7th.

Major James Ore had official standing; he was therefore given command of the troops. Robertson hoped thus to obtain public approval of the expedition. His instructions to Ore read:

"The object of your command is to defend Mero District against a large body of Creeks and Cherokees of the Lower towns, which I have information is about to invade it; also to punish in an exemplary manner such Indians as have recently committed depredations in this district."

The adroitly worded order complied with Blount's "defensive measures" and also with the letter of Secretary of War Knox as to "exemplary punishment" of marauding Indians. The next clause of the order, however, could Governor Blount have read it beforehand, would have caused him consternation. It read:

"You are to proceed along Taylor's Trace toward the Chickamauga Towns, on which you are momently to expect a large party of Creeks and Cherokees advancing to invade this district. If you do not meet this party before you reach the Tennessee, you will cross it and destroy the Lower Towns, which must serve as a check to the expected invaders."

This clause was in direct opposition to the orders of the Secretary of War, although Robertson chose to call the campaign a defensive one. Ore was instructed to spare women and children and to treat prisoners with humanity. If he should discover trails of Indian parties returning from depredations on the frontier, "which can be distinguished by the horses being shod," he was to pursue such parties "even to the towns from whence they come."

## 5

Ore's army followed the Indian war-trail by the present town of Murfreesboro, past the Old Stone Fort near Manchester, and over Cumberland Mountain, where the town of

[8] Robertson Correspondence, *American Historical Magazine*.

Monteagle is now located. The night of September 11, 1794, was spent at a large spring, now known as Martin's Spring, at the foot of Cumberland Mountain. On the 12th, about dark, the Tennessee River was reached, three miles below the mouth of Sequatchie River, near the present town of South Pittsburg.[9]

The night was unusually dark, and the river was high from recent rains. "It certainly appeared a desperate adventure to swim a river half-a-mile wide in the night to fight a horde of savages who had never been chastised," said one of the pioneers.[10]

Ore had brought along two oxhide boats, clumsy, square, affairs, stiff and unwieldy, for the purpose of transporting arms and ammunition across the river in dry condition. Richard Finnelston, one of the guides, offered to swim the river and light a fire to guide the troops. Not having much confidence in him, he being a half-breed, three of the white men, Joseph Brown, Daniel Brown, and William Topp swam the stream with him. They reached the south bank of the river and lighted a fire.[11]

The men began crossing immediately. The oxhide boats proved to be too small to carry all the arms and were kept busy moving back and forth all night. Seven men in William Pillow's squad, including his brother, Gideon, and William Montgomery, made a raft, "which carried our guns, shot bags, and clothes as snugly as a canoe would have done." William and Gideon were excellent swimmers. William attached a rope to the front of the raft, which he took in his teeth and swam ahead, while Gideon swam behind and pushed. Montgomery, who could not swim, caught hold of the raft and was thus pulled across.[12] Major Joseph B. Porter "could not swim one rod, so he got together a bunch of cane, and holding onto it kicked himself across."[13]

By daylight 268 men had crossed, and it was thought best for them to push ahead at once, for Nickajack was five miles away, and the element of surprise would probably win or lose

---

[9] Royce's Map shows the crossing at the mouth of Battle Creek.

[10] Narrative of Joseph Brown, *Southwestern Monthly,* Vol. 1, 76.

[11] At the time Brown was suffering from the wound he had received at Laurel River when the post-rider Ross was killed. He swam with one hand only.

[12] William Pillow's Narrative, Draper Mss., 6-XX-15.

[13] Joseph Brown's Narrative, *Southwestern Monthly,* Vol. 1, 76.

the day. Consequently, nearly half of the men did not participate in the battle. Colonel Gasper Mansker, however, led a
portion of those who did not cross up the north bank of the
river opposite Nickajack to prevent escape of the Indians in
that direction.

Those who had crossed pushed forward toward Nickajack,
and as they neared the town proceeded along the mountain to
the southward in order to surprise the savages.

They had been disorganized when crossing the river, and
there was but little order among them.[14] Colonel Whitley commanded the right; Colonel Montgomery the left; and Major
Ore the center. Second in command were Captains Edmiston,
Rains, Gordon, Pillow, and Johnson.[15]

Joseph Brown, with twenty men, was sent to the mouth of
Nickajack Creek in case the Indians should attempt escape at
that point. It was arranged that Colonel Montgomery, on the
right, should push ahead at a fast pace until he had passed the
town, then turn and join the other wings for the purpose of
surrounding the Indians.

The town was composed of log cabins, substantially built,
two of them about a third of a mile west of the others. A
squad was left to guard these two cabins lest the red men in
them should discover the presence of the army and raise an
alarm. Montgomery, with the remainder marched ahead with
all possible speed. The morning was foggy, and the corn grew
close around the houses, which enabled the soldiers to take position without being seen.

The group which had been left to guard the outlying cabins
started the battle. As they watched, a young woman had come
out of one of the cabins and started pounding corn. She was
joined shortly by her husband, a stalwart brave, who placed
his arm around her waist, swung her around, and assisted with
the pestle. An over-eager soldier fired, and the warrior dropped
dead at his wife's feet. She quickly opened the door and attempted to drag the body within, but by this time the whites
were upon her and she was taken captive.

The surprised savages made little resistance. Many of them
fled to the river hoping to escape by canoe, but were shot down

---

[14] Pillow's Narrative.
[15] Brown's Narrative.

as they huddled on the river bank. The three contingents closed and the battle turned into a massacre. About seventy Indians were killed, among them Chief Breath, of Nickajack. He had befriended Joseph Brown and had more than once aided the Americans, although he had written one of the deceptive letters to Blount.

A few escaped in canoes. Several frontiersmen tried their markmanship on one who was endeavoring to get away by lying low and propelling the canoe with one hand. It looked as though he would escape when Colonel Whitley said, "Let me try." At the discharge of his rifle, blood spurted from the arm of the warrior, but he continued to row. With tomahawk in his belt, Joseph Brown swam out to the canoe. The wounded Indian begged for life, saying, "I am a Cherokee," meaning that he was not one of the hostile Chickamaugas. "What are you doing at Nickajack?" asked Brown. "To visit some friends," he replied. Brown tomahawked him.

About twenty women and children were taken captive; this was customary, the prisoners being used for exchange. Not all of them were taken without difficulty. Among Whitley's men was "Big Joe Logston" whom Collins, Kentuckian historian, describes as a "rare chap." Joe was famous for his size and strength. He had boasted, "I can out-run, out-hop, out-jump, throw down, drag out, and whip any man in the country." He had the distinction of having killed an Indian warrior with his fists.[16] Logston was the butt of hilarity when he attempted to capture a large and powerful squaw who had taken refuge in a thicket. She fought, bit, scratched, and kicked. Disdaining to use his fists on a woman, he was almost as disheveled as his prisoner when finally he subdued her.

The women were temporarily confined in one of the cabins. Joseph Brown, upon going to the door was recognized. The horror stricken captives remembered that they had killed his people, five years before. At length, an old squaw ventured to remind him that his own life had been spared, and asked him to appeal for theirs. "These are white people," Brown replied. "They do not kill women and children." "Oh, that is good news for the wretched!" exclaimed the woman. When another asked if the white men came from the clouds, he said, "We

---

[16] Historical Sketches of Kentucky, Collins, 329.

have not come from the clouds, but we can go anywhere we please. We did not wish to kill the Indians. You have forced that upon us."

The prisoners were sent in a boat to the downstream crossing place. As it passed the two isolated cabins where the first brave had been killed, the young widow sprang into the water. She was rapidly getting away when a soldier raised his gun to shoot. An officer struck up the gun and made the remark, "She is too brave to be killed"; they permitted her to escape.

After completing the destruction of Nickajack, Major Ore immediately set out for Running Water, which was three miles up the river. The warriors of that town had heard the firing at Nickajack and were coming to the assistance of their friends when they met the white army at the Narrows, where the mountain juts out over the river. They made desperate resistance, but of short duration, probably to allow for the escape of the women and children. Joshua Thomas was mortally wounded in the fray, being the only white man lost on the expedition. The Indians took to the hills, and the army kept on toward Running Water. This town was found to be deserted. The dogs had been imprisoned in the cabins to prevent their giving away the secret of the retreat. When the houses were set on fire, howls filled the air.

On the same day, Ore and his men recrossed to the north side of the river and joined their comrades, then set out for Nashville. On their homeward march, they met a band of Chickasaws who told them the news of Wayne's victory over the Northern Indians. After an absence of ten days, they reached Nashville on September 17th.[17]

## 6

Among the spoils secured at Nickajack were two fresh scalps but recently taken on the Cumberland, and a large number of old ones that were found displayed before the cabins. A letter from Baron de Carondelet was found on the Breath. It proved to be a missive with passport attached. The letter had informed the Cherokees that Carondelet, with troubles of

---

[17] Details of the Nickajack campaign are from William Pillow's Narrative, *Draper Mss.*, 6-XX-15: Joseph Brown's Narrative, *Southwest Monthly*, Vol. 1, 76 *et seq.*: Account of James Collier, as quoted by Henry Howe in *The Great West*, 176; also Ramsey and Haywood.

his own, desired them to be at peace with the Americans, as he was no longer in position to furnish war material.

The full letter follows:

"New Orleans, July 14, 1794.
"To the Breath and Glass, Chiefs of the Cherokees:
"Friends and Brothers:

"The Governor of Pensacola has sent me your talk, which I have received with all the consideration and satisfaction it deserves. Be assured it is engraved on my heart. I love all the red people, and only wish for their preservation and happiness. The Great King, my master, who protects all those who implore his assistance, is desirous that the Cherokee Nation shall live in peace and multiply in the land of its ancestors, like the stars in the firmament. Open your ears and be attentive to what he has ordered me to say to the Cherokees.

"The war against the United States is of long standing, and consequently it is difficult to know whether the Cherokees are in fault or not. Since the Cherokee Nation, entering into a treaty of alliance and friendship with the Great King, desires that he shall act as mediator between the Cherokees and the United States, the Great King now requests the Cherokee and Creek Nations to suspend all hostilities, and remain on their own lands, content with defending themselves in the event of being attacked there.

"The Great King desires that the Nation shall be at peace with the United States. The powder, ball, guns, vermillion, bracelets, etc., that he gives to his Nation are only the voluntary effect of his goodness, that the Cherokee Nation may not be jealous of others. The arms are for hunting, and the clothes to protect them from the cold. He makes an annual present to the Indians who are friendly to him, as a mark of his remembrance, but not to put them in a situation of maintaining themselves without hunting or labor.

"Should an attempt be made to deprive his friends of their lands, or drive them from their villages, the Great King will give them arms and ammunition in abundance to defend themselves and make war. He will make it with them, to force their enemies to restore what they usurped.

"I wish you a good journey and a good hunt, and the observance of the treaty I have asked for you from Congress; since the first of April and until the Great King arranges all the differences in the Nation, which will be in a very short time. I cordially shake hands with you, and bear in my heart the remembrance of you and yours.

HECTOR, Baron de Carondelet." [18]

---

[18] American State Papers, Indian Affairs, Vol. 1, 540-541.

This announcement from the Spaniards that the Cherokees must cease warring with the Americans was quite as severe a blow to the hopes of John Watts as was the destruction of his towns. Wayne's defeat of the Northern Indians had destroyed the chance for an Indian federation; and without Spanish guns and ammunition, the Chickamaugas could not fight.[19]

### 7

Governor Blount received the news of the Nickajack expedition with mixed emotions of embarrassment, mortification, and pleasure. He learned from some of the prisoners that Watts, Bloody Fellow, and others had attended a scalp dance in Nickajack only two days before the town was destroyed, and had by that narrow margin missed the fate of the other Indians there.

His mind was filled with apprehension as to the attitude President Washington would take, but he himself could not help but be gratified at the punishment meted out to the Chickamaugas.

As has been recorded, the governor had written to James Robertson, "I know not the price for which I would report such an order to the Secretary of War." Under the circumstances the only thing he could do was to place the blame squarely on shoulders of Robertson. "If General Robertson had given an order for the destruction of these towns, he was not warranted in doing so by any order from me," [20] he reported. As a precaution, Blount asked for the resignation of Robertson as Brigadier-General, to be used if necessary. He did not mince words in condemning the action.

Robertson earnestly defended what he had done.

Nashville, Oct. 1, 1794.

"To Governor William Blount:

"Sir: I have to acknowledge receipt of your Excellency's letter. Enclosed you have a copy of my order to Major Ore of the 6th of

---

[19] The King of Spain had already opened the Mississippi to American trade by proclamation in July, 1794. A few years later, forced by Napoleon, Spain was to cede Louisiana to France; and France in turn, ten years after the Nickajack campaign, was to cede the territory to the United States. When this was done the United States was mistress in her own house. Indian uprisings might occur, but the hope for a federation of Southern tribes was gone forever.

[20] *American State Papers, Indian Affairs,* Vol. 1.

September. My reasons for giving it were that I had received two expresses from the Chickasaws; one from Thomas Brown, a man of as much veracity as any in the Nation, and the other by a common runner; both giving information that a large body of Creeks and Cherokees from the Lower Towns were embodying with a determination to invade the District of Mero.

"Not doubting my information, I conceived that if Major Ore did not meet this body of Creeks and Cherokees as I expected, it could not be considered otherwise than defensive to strike the first blow on the Lower Towns, and thereby check them in their advance. Nor could I suppose that the pursuit of parties who had recently committed murders and thefts in our towns, as an offensive measure, unauthorized by the usages of Nations in such cases. It cannot be necessary to add as justification, the long repeated and I might almost say daily sufferings of the people of the District of Mero at the hands of the Creeks and Cherokees of the Lower Towns.

"The destruction of the Lower Towns by Major Ore was on September 13th. On the 12th, in Tennessee County, Miss Roberts was killed on Red River forty miles above Nashville. On the 14th, Thomas Reasons and wife were killed and their house plundered near the same place. On the 16th, in Davidson County, twelve miles above Nashville, another party killed Mr. Chambers and wounded John Bosley and Joseph Davis. They burned John Donaldson's Station, and carried off several horses.

"This proves that three separate and distinct parties of Indians were out for war against the District of Mero before Major Ore's men left Nashville. Enclosed is a copy of a letter from Dr. R. I. Waters, a citizen of the United States residing at New Madrid, strongly supporting the information of the intended invasion.

"If I have erred, I shall ever regret it. To be a good citizen, obedient to the law, is my greatest pride; and to execute the duties of the commission with which the President has been pleased to honor me, in such a manner as to win his approbation, and that of my superiors in rank, has ever been my most fervent wish.

"I have engaged to pay Mr. Shute fifty dollars for going to to you express. I have the honor to be, with the greatest esteem, your Excellency's most obedient servant,

JAMES ROBERTSON, B. G."[21]

Although Governor Blount was determined that peace with the Indians should prevail, the frontier was so dangerous that

[21] *Ibid.*, Vol. 1, 633.

the rate for sending a letter from Nashville to Knoxville was still fifty dollars; regardless of the fact that the population of the Cumberland settlements had increased to ten thousand people.

In a letter written a few days later, Governor Blount refers to "the usual rate, fifty dollars." In one of his letters he says:

"Your letter sent express by James Russell was handed to me much stained with his blood, by Mr. Shannon who accompanied him. Russell was wounded by a party of Indians who ambushed him about eighteen miles from Southwest Point, which place he reached with difficulty, and was obliged to continue there several days before he could be removed. He is now under the hands of a skilled surgeon and it is hoped that he will recover. *His fifty dollars has been dearly earned,* but instead of complaining he may rejoice that he has often escaped." [22]

## 8

The letter which Russell carried was a copy of one sent on September 20th, 1794, by James Robertson to John Watts:

"Old Friend: I am glad to hear you talk as you did in the old times, that 'peace if good.' This I hear from your own people (prisoners). They say that Nickajack and Running Water were just listening to good talks. This we did not know, for our people were killed every day. The trails came and went toward them towns. One thing we do know, we found there property that was taken from our people when they were killed on the road to Kentucky, so them towns cannot plead innocence, and we have long known them to be our enemies. But if they were about to be good, we are sorry that we did not know it in time.

What is past cannot be recalled, so if friendship is to be between us, we must take care on both sides for the future. We will not listen to half-way measures. That, we are tired of. Our ears are shut to such talks; but our eyes are open, and if we see no white people killed, we shall not kill or distress the Cherokees.

"Our people are strong enough to have gone to Lookout Mountain, or Willstown; but they heard that Dick Justice was head of Lookout Mountain, and he is known to be a good man; and that the Middlestriker did live at Willstown, and you were now giving good talks; so they returned to see if enemies should come again from that way. If they do, our people will soon return the visit.

---

[22] Robertson Correspondence, *American Historical Magazine.*

This I do not tell you as a threat, but you may depend upon it, so let your people not blame us in the future if the innocent should suffer for the guilty; for when our people go to your towns they cannot distinguish the innocent from the guilty. So it will lay on your head men to send a flag, which can at all times come safe, and let us know who are enemies, that the innocent may be spared.

"Your Nation sent men to make a treaty with the President, and in the meantime, while they were talking, you killed his people. These are the talks we are done listening to. I have not heard that one of you has talked of punishing those that murdered the people in the boats taken this summer,[23] neither have I heard of you sending in the negroes taken, but it is well to say no more. We want peace and love it. If you feel as we do, take steps to bring it about. Do not let the Creeks pass through your country to make war against us. There is a new town settling below. Let them be peaceable, or it will be spoiled.

"We have got seventeen of your people prisoners, who will be well-treated until we hear from you. Our people will not go to your towns any more if you will come in and make peace. We shall wait long enough for you to come in with a flag, but if you do not come, our people will be sure to come again to war, and we have men enough to come and destroy you all, and to burn your towns.

"Four of the prisoners are taken to Kentucky by some of their men who went to war with us. They will keep them until you send in four negroes taken from General Logan, who lives in that country. He will come after his negroes if peace is not made soon. The prisoners we have will be returned if you will come in with a flag and good assurance of a peace, and you will bring in with you a girl you took prisoner (Miss Titsworth), and murdered her father and mother on their way to the Chickasaws Nation.

"I am your old friend, JAMES ROBERTSON."[24]

On October 23rd, Robertson forwarded the requested resignation as Brigadier-General to Governor Blount: "not through disgust with the public service or officers of the Government, but from matters of a domestic concern, and a conviction that a successor will be appointed whose ability and experience in tactics may better qualify him to execute its duties.[25]

Governor Blount had written that "No good can come out

---

[23] The Scott boat. See Section 12, Chapter XXIV.
[24] American State Papers, Indian Affairs, Vol. 1, 531.
[25] Robertson's Correspondence, *American Historical Magazine,* Vol. 3, 363.

of unauthorized expeditions"; and the Secretary of War had said, "The destruction of the Lower Towns stands upon its own footing. That it was unauthorized is certain. The Secretary hence rules that the soldiers participating in the Nickajack campaign should receive no pay." [26] The results of the campaign, however, were to prove so propitious that Robertson's resignation was not accepted, and he continued to discharge his duties as Brigadier-General.[27]

### 9

John Watts' cup of bitterness was full. His principal towns had been burned; his Spanish friends could furnish no more ammunition; and his northern allies had been defeated by Wayne. There was nothing left for Watts to do but to acknowledge defeat and follow the white man's path of peace. He sent word to Governor Blount that he feared to go to Knoxville because of the excited state of public feeling, and begged a meeting with the governor at Tellicoe Block House.

On October 11, 1794, Governor Blount met the chiefs at the appointed place. There were present for the Cherokees, Glass, Watts, Bloody Fellow, Hanging Maw, Richard Justice, Little Turkey, Otter Lifter, and others.[28] The chiefs expressed an earnest desire for peace, and a meeting to conclude a treaty was arranged to be held on November 7th.

Governor Blount was to discover that to have a good effect all expeditions do not have to be authorized. Frontier rifles had succeeded where his diplomacy had failed. His correspondence with the Secretary of War thereafter took on a brighter tone, almost of jubilation. "Permit me to congratulate you, sir, on these pleasing prospects." [29]

### 10

A colorful throng gathered at Tellico Block House on Nov. 7th, 1794. The Chickamaugas were represented by John

---

[26] *American State Papers, Indian Affairs,* Vol. 1, 631.

[27] Robertson received the appointment in 1795 of Agent to the Chickasaw and Choctaw Indians, but continued to reside at Nashville and served as Brigadier-General until Tennessee became a state in 1796. General James Winchester was then appointed as his successor. He died while serving as Agent to the Chickasaw Nation where he had removed, in 1814.

[28] Robertson Correspondence, American Historical Magazine, Vol. 3, 363.

[29] *American State Papers, Indian Affairs,* Vol. 1, 535.

Watts, Bloody Fellow, Middlestriker, Richard Justice, Glass, Tatlanta, and the Crier. From the Cherokee towns east of Lookout Mountain came The Little Turkey, Long Warrior, of Turnip Mountain, Standing Turkey of Ustanali, Dreadful Water of Elijay, Pathkiller of Cotokoy, Stallion of Chenee, Bold Hunter, of Connasauga, and Tuckasee of Etowah (son of the old chief Oconostota). The upper Cherokees were represented by Hanging Maw of Coyatee, Oconostota of Hiwassee, Will Elder of Toquo, and others. Four hundred warriors also attended the ceremony which was to mark the end of the long and bitter Cherokee wars. James Carey and Charles Hicks acted as interpreters.[30]

The white delegation was headed by Governor Blount and Silas Dinsmoor, who had received appointment as United States Agent to the Cherokees; John McKee, Deputy Agent resident at Tellicoe Block House; Colonel S. R. Davidson, commanding the garrison; John Sevier, and many other frontier citizens.

"This meeting," said John Watts with hopeless finality, "seems to have been ordered by the Great Spirit." He handed to Governor Blount a string of white beads. Then pointing to Hanging Maw he continued:

"There is Scolacuta. He is old enough to be my father. From my infancy he was a great man, and he is now the Great Chief of the Nation. In the spring of this year, he sent a talk to the Lower Towns, telling them that he and his upper towns had taken the United States by the hand, and inviting the Lower Towns to do the same.

"Just before Running Water and Nickajack were destroyed, I went to those towns, as well as to Lookout Mountain Town, and exerted myself for the restoration of peace. I verily believe that those towns had heard my talk and were determined for peace. I do not say those towns did not deserve the chastisement they received, nevertheless it so exasperated those who escaped from the ruins that for a time I was compelled to be silent myself. But the Running Water people told the Glass that notwithstanding the injury they had received, they remembered my good talks and held them fast, and desired me to take measures for the recovery of their prisoners. I deliver to you this string of beads as a true and public talk from the Lower Towns. Scolacuta, the head of the

---

[30] *American Historical Magazine*, Vol. 3, 367.

Nation, is sitting beside me. The Lower Towns instructed me to request him not to throw them away, but to come with me and present this talk to you." [31]

Hanging Maw then spoke:

"I too have had a talk with the Lower Towns. They were once my people, but not now, yet I cannot but think much of the talk I have now received from Watts. Before anything happened to Nickajack and Running Water, I sent those towns many peace talks which they would not hear. Now, since their destruction by Major Ore, they send me to make peace for them, together with Watts. I am the head man of my Nation, and Governor Blount is the head man of the white people. It is not the fault of either that those towns were destroyed, but their own bad conduct brought destruction upon them.

"All last winter, I was compelled to live in the woods by the bad conduct of my people drawing war upon us. In the spring, you invited me to meet your deputy, John McKee. He assured me of the disposition of the United States for peace, and told me and my party to return to our houses and fields. I could hear threats against my life for several parts of the Nation. I then asked that this fort should be built, to protect me and my party as well as the frontier inhabitants. I still heard murmurings from several parts of the Nation that they would be have nothing to do with this fort; but I see standing around me many of those very people, who are now glad to come to it." [32]

Governor Blount warned the chiefs that the Cherokees could have no lasting peace so long as they permitted the Creeks to pass through their towns to war on the American frontier. "It will be a duty you owe to yourselves as well as to the United States not to permit them to pass through your country, and if they do slip through, to seize them and bring them to this place as the upper towns did last summer."

Watts replied that it was quite true that the upper towns had captured a Creek warrior whom they had delivered to Governor Blount, and had killed two others, "but the upper Cherokees live far from the Creek towns, and have the white people to support them. The Lower Towns are but few in numbers, and live near the Creeks, too distant from the whites to be

[31] American State Papers, Indian Affairs, Vol. 1, 536.
[32] *Ibid.*

supported by them. The Creeks are a great and powerful Nation, and the Cherokees are but few. We cannot prevent them from passing through our towns to war when they please. On their passage, they kill our hogs and cattle and steal our horses, which we dare not resent."

Hanging Maw, however, declared, "I ordered the Creek seized, and ordered the two Creeks killed. I will kill my own people if they kill the white people." [33]

December 28, 1794, was the date set for the exchange of prisoners, and at that time Governor Blount and the chiefs again met. An unusually large crowd of Indians was present to receive their people. It was raining, and as all the Indians wished to hear the proceedings, they asked for a postponement till the next day. The following day Bloody Fellow said, "Yesterday was a bad day. Today is no better. All the people white and red, want to hear what is done between us, and the house is too small for the whole of them. We will be ready the first fair day." The rain continued for four days without prospect of letting up, and the chiefs reluctantly agreed to negotiate within doors.

In his opening remarks Governor Blount again warned the Cherokees that they must not permit the Creeks to pass through their towns for war against the Americans.

"Too many of your young men have joined them. To speak plainly, I advise that your Nation settle on the waters of the Tennessee at Chatanuga Mountain.[34] By this plan, should any of your Nation remain below the mountain, and join the Creeks, the innocent can be spared, and the guilty punished."

The Governor asked if the Indians were ready for the exchange of prisoners, and Bloody Fellow made reply:

"It is improper to speak before one thinks. Tomorrow I will answer your talk. I will hide nothing. I will bring forward my young warriors, and we will throw away all bad thoughts."

The parties to the treaty reassembled the following day,

---

[33] *Ibid.*, 536.

[34] Chatanuga Mountain gave its name to the city now located at its base. The mountain now is known as Lookout Mountain. See note 3, Chapter XXIII.

Dec. 31st, and as it was raining still, the exchange of prisoners had to be made indoors.

Bloody Fellow spoke on behalf of the Cherokees:

"I want peace, that we may travel our paths, sleep in our houses, and rise in peace on both sides. I now deliver to you this firm peace talk, that our people will mind their hunting, and that both parties may rise in peace each day. My talk shall be made known throughout the Nation." Here a long string of white beads was handed to the governor.

Blount delivered thirteen Cherokee prisoners, who were received and counted by Watts. The Indians presented in return only two prisoners; a little girl named Collins, and a negro girl.

"You have more than thirty of our people in captivity," said Governor Blount, "and have delivered only two." He read the names of the captives who had not been brought in.

Miss Thornton, taken by the Otter Lifter,
Five negroes, taken from Gen. Logan, of Kentucky,
Negro girl, taken from Ziegler's Station by Shawnee Warrior,
Negro, belonging to Robertson,
Negro man, in possession of John Rogers, white trader,
Twenty-two negroes, taken from Scott's boat.

Watts reminded the governor that there were Indian prisoners who had not been delivered also; and in reference to the captured negroes, he said:

"They are scattered in the Nation. Some of them have changed hands many times and will have to be bought from their present owners. We are a poor people and have no goods with which to purchase the negroes from the persons who have the possession of them. If we attempt to take them by force, they might perhaps be put to death or injured. The most proper time, I think, will be when we receive our annual allowance from the government. We can, with those goods, pay the possessors, and deliver the negroes to you. The other prisoners will be delivered as soon as possible. As to the negro in the possession of John Rogers, he is a white man, and I have nothing to do with him."

The only negro delivered, a girl, had been captured by the Crier of Nickajack and he had brought her in exchange for his own daughter who had been taken at Nickajack.

Bloody Fellow seconded Watts' remarks:

"All that can be said on the subject of exchange, has been said. If I should rush down and take the negroes by force from the persons who possess them, it might endanger their lives.

"It is well. It is best to take time and do the business effectually," said Governor Blount.

It was, therefore, agreed that prisoners on both sides would be delivered at the earliest date possible.

The subject of stolen horses was then brought up:

"We have said nothing of stolen horses," said the governor, "and I see many frontier people standing around who have come to look for their horses. I know many of these horses have been carried to the frontier stations of North and South Carolina and Georgia, but some of them must yet be in your Nation, and such as are I expect to be delivered up to the people from whom they were stolen."

Bloody Fellow replied: "Has there not been a distemper in this country? In our country many horses have died. Some have been stolen by the Creeks, and a great many have been sold at Seneca. If the white people want to see their horses, let them go to South Carolina."

John Watts spoke again: "I do not want war for my people but to live in the house of peace. When people are young, they are full of war, and do not care what becomes of themselves. I am becoming an old man. I wish to live at peace with all people."

"As my mate, John Watts, has said," spoke Bloody Fellow, "we want peace with all people. Let us bury the blood deep, that it may be see no more, and walk together in the paths of peace." [35]

## II

Doublehead did not attend the Tellico Block House Treaty. He had just returned from Philadelphia with the annual allowance of $5000.00 worth of goods which the President had

---

[35] *American State Papers, Indian Affairs,* Vol. 1, 537: Robertson Correspondence, *American Historical Magazine,* Vol. 4, 82-94.

permitted him to draw in advance. On his arrival in the Cherokee country late in October, 1794, he held a meeting at Oconee
Mountain. He distributed the goods; taking the lions share
for himself and his followers. Few of the Upper Town chiefs
were present. When he heard of the event, Hanging Maw
inquired of Deputy Agent McKee:

"Are those goods to be delivered to Doublehead and his band of
murderers, or to that part of the Nation that has given proof of
friendship to the United States by taking one Creek and killing
two others? If they are, the friendly part of the Nation will know
how to insure the reward of the United States for their services." [36]

Doublehead wrote to Governor Blount on Oct. 30th that he
was "ready to go hunting," and that he hoped the governor
would keep the white people from coming to "hunt the hunters." [37] He appeared in Nashville early in November, and
smoked the peace pipe with James Robertson while talking
over his trip to Philadelphia; and upon leaving for his town
in a canoe, they stopped over to visit with Colonel Valentine
Sevier at the mouth of Red River. [38] Sevier's son-in-law,
Charles Snyder, repaired the guns of several warriors, and
they left apparently grateful.

But a few miles from Colonel Sevier's Station they met a
band of Creeks who had committed murders in the vicinity;
and the thought occurred to Doublehead that here was an opportunity to retaliate for the many fights Chucky Jack had
waged on his people. He, therefore, proposed to join forces
with the Creeks, return to the station, and kill Colonel Sevier;
he being Chucky Jack's brother. [39]

His warriors attempted to dissuade him; reminding him
that he had smoked the pipe with Robertson in Nashville, and
that Snyder had repaired their guns without pay. Doublehead
was inflexible, and as usual when opposed, his savage temper
flared; his followers could do nothing but yield, and on Nov.

[36] *American State Papers, Indian Affairs,* Vol. 1, 535.
[37] A. S. P., I. F., Vol. 1, 535.
[38] Draper Mss., 30-S 297-332.
[39] *American State Papers, Indian Affairs,* Vol. 1, 542. Colonel Sevier
had already lost three sons at the hands of the Indians. The attack on Nov.
11th, brought the total loss in his immediate family to four grown sons,
two daughters, two sons-in-law, and several grandchildren. See Armstrong,
*Notable Southern Families,* Sevier, 41.

11, 1794, Sevier's Station was attacked. All of the men, except Sevier and Snyder, were away. Colonel Sevier and his wife successfully defended their own house, but all the others in the little enclosure were killed. Snyder and his wife, Betsy, their son, and Joseph Sevier, were killed in Snyder's house. Rebecca, one of the Colonel's daughters, was visiting in one of the cabins when the alarm was sounded; she attempted to gain her father's house, but was overtaken and scalped. She was left for dead, but eventually recovered.

An eye witness, who came to the rescue while the attack was in progress, wrote:

"Yesterday, I was spectator to the most tragical scene that I ever saw in my life. The Indians made an attack on Colonel Sevier's Station. On hearing the guns, four or five of us ran over (from Clarksville). We found the poor old Colonel bravely defending his own house with his wife. It is impossible to describe the scene. The crying women and children, the bustle and consternation of the people, being all women and children but the few that went out to Sevier's, was a scene that cannot be described. There were twelve or fifteen Indians. The Colonel prevented the savage band from entering his house, but they cruelly slaughtered all around him. Three of his own children fell dead. Charles Snyder and two children also fell. It was a horrid sight, some scalped and cut to pieces, some tomahawked very inhumanly, and the poor helpless infants committed to the torturing flames." [40]

The Creek warriors who were associated with Doublehead in the massacre were from Tuskega (the old French Fort [41] Toulouse). Doublehead, afterward, threw entire blame on the Creeks, but Joseph Sevier, son of Governor John Sevier, who was a trader in the Nation, found out the truth. However, peace had already been made, and Governor Blount had issued stern warning:

"Peace with the Indians exists now not only in name, or upon paper in form of treaty, but in fact, and he who shall violate it shall deserve the severest punishment of the laws, and execrations of his fellow citizens. Such of my fellow citizens as are sore under their former sufferings, I beg of them to recollect if they

[40] *American State Papers, Indian Affairs,* Vol. 1, 542.
[41] *American Historical Magazine,* Vol. 3, 364.

should meet the particular Indians at whose hands their friends
have fallen, that the death of such Indians will not restore their
friends to life, and that the death of even one such Indian will
bring on another war in which thousands of innocent people will
be the victims.  He who shall break peace by killing an Indian,
however improper his past conduct may have been, may be truly
said to have killed a number of innocent women and children." [42]

12

These bloody scenes were rapidly drawing to a close.
Throughout 1795, marauding bands of Creeks committed
murders on the Cumberland frontier.  On June 14th, 1796,
however, Benjamin Hawkins, George Clymer, and Andrew
Pickens, Commissioners for the United States, met in treaty
with the Creek Nation at the frontier military post of Colerain,
on St. Mary's River.  As befitted the close of an era with the
Indians, the occasion was celebrated with the old ceremonies.

"The kings, head men, and warriors, to the number of four
hundred, marched under the flag of the United States to the spot
where the commissioners, attended by the officers of the garrison,
were seated.  As they marched, they danced the Eagle Tail dance,
and the four dancers at the head of the chiefs waved the Eagle
Tail six times over the heads of the commissioners.
"Six of the principal chiefs came up and took the commissioners
by the hand.  Then they handed them their pipes and held out fire
which they had brought from their camp.  The commissioners lit
the pipes and smoked.  There was a short pause between each
dance, and the waving of an Eagle Tail, and the same interval in
the shaking of hands, and lighting the pipes." [43]

With the smoking of those pipes, the Creek Nation ended
its warfare with the Americans, and agreed, with the Cherokees, to travel the white path of peace.  The Indian wars which
had desolated the frontier for twenty years, were ended, and
the warriors had reached *Ulawistu-Nunnehi,* "The End of the
Trail."

---

[42] *American Historical Magazine,* Vol. 3, 364.
[43] *American State Papers, Indian Affairs,* Vol. 1, 551.

# CHAPTER XXVII

# THE HOUSE OF PEACE

## I

General Henry Knox, Secretary of War, in a letter to President Washington dated June 15, 1789, stated the policy of the United States toward the various tribes, which has been consistently followed to the present time.

"As the settlements of the whites shall approach near to the Indian boundaries established by the treaties, the game will be diminished, and the lands being valuable to the Indians only as hunting grounds, they will be willing to sell further tracts for small consideration." [1]

The smallness of the consideration was revealed in a letter from General Knox to James Robertson:

"The average price paid for Indian lands in various parts of the United States within the last four years does not amount to one cent per acre." [2]

The signing of a treaty by the Indians was but the beginning of further trouble for them instead of the peace they desired.

The white men in all their treaties stressed the idea advanced by General Knox that the land being devoid of game was of little value to the Indians. But a Creek chief, speaking to Benjamin Hawkins at the Treaty of Colerain, shrewdly made reply that although the land might be worth but little to the Indian, he had observed that it was worth a great deal to the white man.

"Upon this land, there is a great deal of timber, pine and oak, which are of much use to the white people. They send it to foreign countries, and it brings them a great deal of money. On this land there is much grass for cattle and horses, and much good food for hogs. On this land there is a great deal of tobacco raised, which likewise brings much money. Even the streams are found

---

[1] American State Papers, Indian Affairs, Vol. 1, 13.
[2] *Ibid.*

valuable to the white men, to grind the wheat and corn that grow on these lands. The pine trees, when they are dead, are valuable for tar.

"All these are lasting profits; but if the Indians have a little goods for their lands, in one or two seasons they are rotten and gone for nothing. We are told that our lands are of no service to us, but still, if we hold our lands, there will always be a turkey or a deer, or a fish in the streams, for the younger generation that will come after us. We are afraid that if we part with any more of our lands, the white people will not suffer us to keep as much as will be sufficient to bury our dead." [3]

2

The Cherokees, having promised to follow the white man's path of peace, were to experience an exemplification of the Indian policy of the United States as stated by General Knox. At the same time, they were to demonstrate the ability of the American Indian to adapt himself to civilization, and were to show progress unequaled in Indian history.

At the close of the Indian wars, the Cherokees owned a substantial territory in the states of Tennessee, North Carolina, and Georgia, guaranteed to them forever, by solemn treaty. The treaty, however, constructed no high fence around the territory.

A standing army would have been needed to prevent land-hungry frontiersmen from settling beyond the imaginary lines fixed by treaty. The greed of the white settlers for Indian land still was unsated.

The Government occasionally removed a few squatters; but this invariably caused controversy with the state of which they were citizens and the easier plan of making treaties with the Indians in which they ceded the additional land was usually followed.

3

Peace with the Cherokees had scarcely been signed when the State of North Carolina began to settle the claims of its Revolution soldiers by grants of land in its western territory. It

---

[3] *Ibid.*, 604. The words of the chief are literally true. The mounds, "sufficient ground to bury the dead," are cultivated, plowed down, and obliterated, that more wheat and corn may be raised by the white man on the lands that were "of little value to the Indians without game."

made no difference to the beneficiaries that this was at the expense of the Indians and they declared themselves ready to settle on such lands regardless of treaties.

Governor Blount, recognizing that such a course would lead to endless trouble, asked President Washington to take steps to protect the rights of the Cherokees to lands which had been guaranteed to them in treaty by the United States. The President presented the matter to Congress in vigorous terms on Feb. 2, 1796. He concluded his message with these words:

"The injustice of such intrusions, and the mischievous consequences which must result therefrom, demand that effectual provision be made to prevent them." [4]

But regardless of congress, the white frontier advanced steadily into the Cherokee hunting grounds.

4

The friendly old chief, Hanging Maw, died a few months after the conclusion of the peace treaty of 1794.[5] He was succeeded as Principal Chief of the Cherokees by Little Turkey.[6] Doublehead was made speaker of the National Council; and his aggressive personality overshadowed the mild and inoffensive Little Turkey. He assumed more and more authority, and was soon the controlling influence in the dealings of his people with the white men.

5

In 1797, Louis Philippe, Duke of Orleans, who afterward became King of the French, made an American tour, and expressed a desire to visit an Indian tribe in its native surround-

---

[4] *American State Papers, Indians Affairs,* Vol. 1, 584. Had a similar sense of justice animated President Jackson, forty years later, the removal of the Cherokees would not have occurred.

[5] *Ibid.,* 621. On Jan. 17, 1797, Hanging Maw's widow petitioned Congress that reparation be made for the damage she had suffered in Beard's raid, in which she was wounded, her house burned, and her property carried away. Her claim was favorably reported by the Congressional Committee. She was found two years later by Moravian missionaries, living on Hiwassee River, respected by her neighbors, and known as the Widow Maw.

[6] The Little Turkey began writing as Principal Chief in April, 1795. Doublehead was principal speaker at a treaty held at Tellico Blockhouse in 1801, and spoke for his people in all negotiations until his death in 1807.

ings.  As the Cherokees had made peace, he was conducted to Tellico Blockhouse where he was to be the guest of Little Turkey and John Watts.  He visited Chote, the old Cherokee capital and beloved town, and was entertained with a ballplay in which six hundred Cherokees participated.  The Duke entered into the spirit of the occasion by staking six gallons of brandy on the outcome.

During the excitement of the game he fell off his horse; and the usual treatment of bleeding himself was followed.  The operation proved so successful that he was asked to perform a similar one on an old chief who was ill.  It may have been imagination, but the chief instantly felt better.  As evidence of his gratitude, he accorded the Duke the privilege of sleeping between his grandmother and his great aunt, two of the most venerable of the squaws.  This was considered a distinction, for the old people of the tribe, especially the old women, were regarded with profound respect.[7]

The royal guest "smoked a diversity of pipes, ate a great many (to him) queer dishes, and enjoyed his experience among the Cherokees better than any other part of his tour of America, placing Niagara Falls second." [8]

6

The years that followed the peace treaty of 1794, were years of development for the Cherokees.  "We have long wished to live so that we might have gray hairs on our heads," said Little Turkey.[9]  The wish was gratified, for the taking of scalps was practiced no more; and the pursuit of agriculture and commerce engaged their attention.  Orchards were planted, bees were domesticated, and a thriving trade in honey and beeswax was promoted; also the raising of cattle and horses was generally followed.  While the hunting grounds were restricted, fur trading was still important and the old occupation of hunting required much time.

Slavery had become common in the Nation during the years

---

[7] The experience impressed Louis Philippe, for years later when Edward Livingstone was sent to France by President Jackson to obtain settlement of "Spoliations Claims," he was asked by the King if it still was the custom in Tennessee for worthy guests to be permitted to sleep between the hosts' grandmother and great aunt.

[8] See Williams, *Early Travels in Tennessee Country,* 433-441.

[9] *American Historical Magazine,* 4, 191.

of warfare. Several of the leading chiefs were slave holders, and the capture of negroes by warriors had been a frequent occurrence. If the captor did not wish to keep the slave for his own use, he was sold; thus the slave sometimes passed through several hands, and efforts of former owners to recover them at the end of war usually resulted in disappointment. "It is useless to expect the return of slaves captured by the Indians during the wars, as they have changed hands so many times in the Nation," wrote agent Dinsmoor. The Indian who had come into possession by purchase refused, regardless of treaties, to surrender his slaves.

Among the captives which Colonel Whitley had carried back to Kentucky to insure the return of negroes who had been taken from him in raids by the Cherokees, were relatives of the chief Otter Lifter. Peace having been declared, Otter Lifter made overtures to Colonel Whitley for an exchange. Whitley took his prisoners to Willstown for that purpose.

The Colonel's slaves were in possession of John Taylor, a half-breed who had commanded the Indian cavalry in the attack on Buchanan's Station; he objected strenuously to giving them up. "You cannot have them!" he exclaimed, and accented the statement by beating a drum and voicing the war-whoop. Warriors gathered and assumed a threatening mien. "I thought times were squally," Whitley afterward related, "but I looked at the Otter Lifter, and his face was unchanged. He told me that I should not be killed." When Taylor demanded that he "prove his property," Whitley retorted, "If I have to do that, I will go back to Kentucky and bring a thousand witnesses, each with a rifle to speak for him." The influence of the Little Turkey was required before they were surrendered. The fact that the captives of Colonel Whitley were blood-kin to a prominent chief rendered him more fortunate than most slave owners in such circumstances.[10]

7

Tennessee became a state in 1796. John Sevier was elected Governor; William Blount was sent to the United States Senate; and Andrew Jackson went to Congress.

Blount had hardly taken his seat when he was expelled. His

[10] Collins, *Historical Sketches of Kentucky,* 552.

expulsion followed the discovery of a letter he had written to James Carey at Tellico Blockhouse, asking his assistance with the Cherokees in a scheme which involved the transfer of Florida from Spain to England; and removal of the Creeks and Cherokees to the West, the United States to take over their lands. Blount had expected to go to England in further-ance of the plan, which, however, never materialized.[11]

In 1797, the State of Tennessee addressed a memorial to Congress asking that Indian titles in the state be extinguished at the earliest possible moment; that the Indians at best were but tenants at will, and that treaties guaranteeing them their lands were contrary to the rights of Tennessee.[12]

President Adams obtained authority from Congress to make a new treaty with the Cherokees, which was held at Southwest Point on June 25, 1798. Certain parcels of land on which the white men had settled were ceded. Tennessee continued to press Congress, and a meeting for another treaty was arranged, Sept. 4, 1801. Governor John Sevier attended in person, with the object of obtaining extinguishment of Indian titles North of Tennessee River. The Government also requested permis-sion to build roads from Nashville to Natchez, and from Tellico Blockhouse to Carolina.

Doublehead spoke plainly for the Cherokees:

"In behalf of my Nation I am authorized to speak to you. There are land speculators among you who say that we want to sell our land when we do not. We hope you will not listen to these speculations. They will give you fine talks which are intended to deceive, for they are for their own interest. We remember the former talks by the United States, but we suppose the head men of the United States have been forgotten by the State of Tennessee.

"There is a road that we have consented to be made, from Clinch to Cumberland, and also the Kentucky Trace. When you first made these settlements, there were paths that answered for roads. These roads which you propose, we do not want made through our country. A great many people of all description will pass over them, and you would labor under the same difficulty that you do now. We hope you will not make the roads through our country, but will use those you have made in your own limits. We hope you

[11] Blount's letter to Carey, and proceedings in the Senate at the time in reference to the so-called "Spanish Conspiracy," may be found in Heiskell, *Andrew Jackson and Early Tennessee History*, 82-103.
[12] Royce, *Cherokee Nation of Indians*, 175: *American State Papers, Indian Affairs*, Vol. 1, 625.

will say no more on this subject. I expect that you will think that we have a right to say yes, or no. I hope you will say no more about the roads, or about the lands. I am now done speaking for the day."[13]

On behalf of the United States, the Treaty Commissioners replied to Doublehead's remarks:

"Brothers, you have been alarmed by the songs of lying birds, and the talks of forked tongues. You have heard that your father would press you for further cession of lands, some have said, even as far as the Big River (the Tennessee).

"You will know how to listen to such thieves, liars, and mischief-makers, and will treat them as they deserve. Brothers, listen to us, and hear the truth. Your white brethren want land, and are willing to pay for it. If you have any to sell, they will buy it from you, but if you are not disposed to sell any more lands, not one more word will be said on the subject."[14]

## 8

In 1802, the State of Georgia ceded to the Government, her western lands, comprising the territory later erected into the states of Alabama and Mississippi. The section was then occupied by the Creeks, Choctaws, Cherokees, and Chickasaw Indians. A seemingly inoffensive clause in the act of cession was later to prove the ruin of the Cherokee Nation, and to cause the removal of the Cherokees from the land of their fathers. In consideration of the cession of the lands, the United States agreed to pay to the State of Georgia, $1,250,-

---

[13] *American State Papers, Indian Affairs,* Vol. 1, 604. The shrewd old chief was close to the truth when he spoke of "the head men of the frontier" being interested in speculation in Indian lands. Land speculation was the accepted means of acquiring wealth on the border. The "Spanish Conspiracy" was a scheme to take over the Indian lands, and William Blount lost no popularity thereby with the frontiersmen, although he was expelled from the Senate. John Sevier is said to have entered 165 tracts of land of 640 acres each. He was accused by Andrew Jackson of having stolen the books of the Entry Taker and to have entered many tracts without payment of the proper fee. The accusation led to controversy between the two men, and a challenge to a duel. Jackson's statement, and Sevier's reply, may be found in *American Historical Magazine,* Vol. 4, 373-375.

[14] *American State Papers, Indian Affairs,* Vol. 1, 657. While the treaty talks were in progress, the Cherokee chief, Glass, was in Philadelphia, trying to secure the removal of Colonel James Wofford, who had settled with a number of followers on Cherokee land.

000.00 and *"To extinguish the Indian title whenever the same can be done on peaceable terms."* [15] Georgia did not forget that clause. From the day the agreement was signed, with ever increasing pressure, fulfillment was demanded of the Government.

### 9

In 1803, the United States sent commissioners to the Cherokees to ask permission to buy the Wafford tract, and to build a road through the Cherokee country from Tellico Blockhouse to Athens, Ga. The Indians refused both demands. Then began the shameful method of bribery so often practiced thereafter. Private inducements were offered to various chiefs for their influence. Joseph Vann, near whose home the proposed road would run, was given $300.00. Other chiefs were similarly bribed, probably including Doublehead, for he later did accept special inducements at the expense of his Nation.

The Wafford tract, consisting of one hundred square miles, near Chattahoochee River in Northeast Georgia, was ceded, and the building of the road authorized. The government having no funds available for the project at the time, it was left to the States of Tennessee and Georgia for completion, and they took no action. [16]

### 10

Since before the beginning of the century, the Government had distributed among the Cherokees as a part of their annual allowance, plows, looms, spinning wheels, and agricultural tools. Their use spread rapidly, particularly among the Lower Towns, which possessed rich river bottoms to cultivate. The upper, mountaineer element clung tenaciously to their old cus-

---

[15] Theodore Roosevelt, in *Winning of the West,* has pointed out that Georgia did not actually cede the western lands, but only a disputed title to them. The lands were still under the dominion of the King of Spain by right of conquest from England during the Revolutionary War. Although "ceded" by Georgia in 1802, they did not actually become the property of the United States until purchase from Spain after the Creek war of 1814.

[16] Royce. The treaty was unaccountably lost, and was not submitted to Congress for ratification until 1825, and then only when the Cherokee chiefs produced their copy. It was the first treaty to be negotiated with the Cherokees by Return J. Meigs, who thereafter acted as United States Agent to them for many years, and became their firm and trusted friend.

toms. Upon their complaint that they had not received a just share of the tools, Watts and Doublehead replied that "the goods were there, and if the upper towns did not choose to come for them, the lower Cherokees could not be blamed for taking and using them." Watts suggested that the Lower Towns might secede, as they had done once before, and leave the Upper Cherokees to shift for themselves.[17] He continued to reside at Willstown, and was a respected leader of his people. In the journal of two Moravian missionaries, who visited the Cherokee country in 1799 in the hope of establishing a mission, he was mentioned:

"John Watts did not attend the last distribution of presents, for he is prosperous and has no need of the goods." [18]

---

[17] Mooney, *Myths of the Cherokees,* 83.

[18] Williams, Early Travels in the Tennessee Country, 448-455. Watts died at Willstown, and was buried in the cemetery later used by the Christian Mission. A marker has been placed at the cemetery which is about two miles north of the present site of Fort Payne, Alabama.

# CHAPTER XXVIII

## DOUBLEHEAD'S LAST FIGHT

### I

In October, 1805, agent Meigs, James Robertson, and Daniel Smith, acting as commissioners for the United States, negotiated two treaties with the Cherokees by which a vast territory north of Tennessee River, running from Hiwassee River to Muscle Shoals, was ceded. Southwest Point[1] and Long Island of Holston, the "Beloved Old Treaty Ground," were included in the cession. The consideration to the Cherokees was $17,000.00 cash, and $3,000.00 annually forever.

*By secret agreement,* two tracts of square mile each were reserved at the mouths of Clinch and Hiwassee Rivers *for the use of Doublehead,* who negotiated the treaties for his people. A similar tract was reserved at the mouth of Duck River for Doublehead's kinsman, Tahlonteeskee.

The secret agreement soon became known among the Cherokees, and created bitter resentment. The whole treaty was considered a betrayal of Cherokee interests, for Doublehead's action had not been sanctioned by the National Council.

### 2

The ill feeling came to a head in the summer of 1807, when the Cherokees gathered at Hiwassee Garrison for the distribution of the Government annuity. The Indians, as was their usual custom on such occasions, held a ballplay. Agent Meigs, officers from Hiwassee Fort, and numerous traders, were present. Among the latter was General Sam Dale, of Mississippi.

Doublehead had paid little attention to the criticism of his treaty with the Americans; he was present to receive his share of the annuity. Meeting General Dale, with whom he was well acquainted, he greeted him: "Sam, you are a great liar. You have never kept your promise to come to see me." With a smile illuminating his grim features, (he is said never to have

---

[1] Southwest Point is now Kingston, Tenn.

smiled during the Indian Wars) he extended a bottle of whiskey and invited Dale to drink with him.  The bottle was emptied and when Dale offered to replenish it Doublehead replied:
"When in white man's country, drink white man's whiskey,
but here, you must drink with Doublehead." [2]

After the ballplay was over, a chief named Bone Polisher
approached Doublehead.  "You have betrayed our people," he
said, "you have sold our hunting grounds."

Doublehead replied quietly: "Bone Polisher, you have said
enough.  Go away, or I shall kill you."  Bone Polisher raised
his tomahawk in a menacing manner, and Doublehead shot him
through the heart.

Shortly after dark of the same day, Doublehead entered
McIntosh's Tavern and encountered a chief named Ridge, afterward known as Major Ridge.  Ridge was accompanied by a
half-breed, Alex Saunders, and John Rogers, an old white
trader among the Cherokees.  Rogers, too, reviled the old
chief, who answered proudly: "You live among us by our permission.  I have never seen you in council or on the war path.
Be silent, and interfere with me no more."  But the trader
persisted, and Doublehead attempted to kill him.  His gun
missed fire; the lights were suddenly extinguished, and a shot
rang out.  When the light was restored, Doublehead lay on
the floor with his lower jaw shattered.  Ridge, Saunders, and
Rogers had disappeared.[3]

The chief's friends set out with him for Hiwassee Garrison,
but fearing they might be followed, concealed him in the loft
of a school maintained at the garrison by Rev. Gideon Blackburn.

Ridge and Saunders, with two members of Bone Polisher's
clan, determined to take vengeance under the clan law.  They
tracked Doublehead by his bloody trail, and found him lying
on the floor of the school loft.  Leveling their pistols at him,

---

[2] General Dale wrote an account of the proceedings.  This was Doublehead's last appearance on the stage of human activity.  Hiwassee Garrison
was on the west side of Tennessee River at Jolly's Island, now known as
Hiwassee Island.

[3] The trader John Rogers was among the Cherokees before the Revolution, and had an honorable record.  He saved the son of Jonathan Jennings
from torture, and is mentioned in Sevier's campaign of 1782.  Two of his
sons signed the removal treaty in 1836.  Will Rogers, the humorist, was a
descendant.

they missed fire, and the chief sprang upon Ridge and would have overcome him had not Saunders reprimed his pistol and shot him in the hip. Saunders raised his tomahawk to complete his destruction, but Doublehead wrested the weapon from him and again leaped upon Ridge with demoniacal rage. Just in time, Saunders sank another tomahawk in his brain and thereby saved the life of Ridge. Doublehead had fought his last fight.[4]

## 3

Following Doublehead's death, agent Meigs anticipated trouble in carrying out the treaty which the chief had signed. To prevent this, he made another secret agreement with the then principal chief, Black Fox, a nephew of Dragging Canoe.[5] Black Fox was given $1,000.00, a rifle, and an annual allowance of $100.00. Bribes were also paid to other leading chiefs to secure their acquiescence. On Sept. 7, 1807, Meigs and James Robertson met with the chiefs at Chickasaw Old Fields, near Muscle Shoals, and agreed upon the boundary for the ceded territory.

Meigs wrote:

"With respect to the chiefs who transacted this business with us, they will have their hands full to satisfy the ignorant, the obstinate, and the cunning of their own people, for which they well deserve this silent consideration. It is a handsome country, and is now settled cheap enough in all conscience."[6]

## 4

The killing of Doublehead was evidence of a growing sense of unity on the part of the Cherokees. Hemmed in as they were by the white settlements, with hunting grounds diminishing daily, they were coming to the realization that no longer could each chief be a law unto himself if they were to survive as a Nation. A still further step toward national unity was the abolishment, on April 18, 1810, of the old law of Clan

---

[4] Goodpasture, quoting Dale's Narrative. Doublehead's kinsman, Tahlonteeskee, who had participated in the treaty with him, removed to the west to avoid a like fate, and later was elected principal chief of the western band of Cherokees.

[5] American State Papers, Indian Affairs, Vol. 1, 273.

[6] *Ibid.*, 754: Royce, *Cherokee Nation of Indians*, 197.

Revenge. The law, which tallied so closely with the Mosaic requirement of "an eye for an eye and a tooth for a tooth" that James Adair accepted it as proof that the Indians were the Ten Lost Tribes of Israel, was:

"Murder, under any circumstances must be punished by the nearest relative with death. The clan may forgive, but no individual, and the privilege of forgiveness is sought only under very peculiar circumstances and very seldom. If the murderer can bring in an enemy scalp before he is taken, it will be received in full atonement; or in time of war he may give a prisoner of his own capture to be adopted in lieu of the slain." [7]

The National Council relegated the old custom to oblivion, with the sole reservation that if brother killed brother, he should be deemed guilty of murder and punished accordingly. The act provided, also; "If a man have a horse stolen and overtake the thief, and his anger shall be so great as to cause him to shed blood, let it remain on his own conscience, but no satisfaction shall be required for his life from his relatives or clan." [8]

---

[7] *John Howard Payne Mss.*
[8] *Ibid.*

# CHAPTER XXIX

## TECUMSEH AND THE PROPHET

### I

Tecumseh, one of the greatest of American Indians, had won the northwestern tribes to his plan for an Indian confederacy which would halt the white tide rolling over the red men from Canada to the Gulf. He was assisted by his brother, Tenskatawa, "The Prophet," who claimed to have been permitted in a dream to visit the Happy Hunting Grounds from whence he had brought a message that the Indians were to throw away the white man's customs and return to the old Indian habits. In a short time, he claimed, the Great Spirit would send a storm, with hailstones as large as corn mortars, which would kill all the white people, and the red men would reclaim their country as of old.

Tecumseh went from tribe to tribe, firing the Indians with his eloquence, for this untaught savage was a natural orator of great power. The two brothers established at the junction of the Tippecanoe and Wabash Rivers, a village known as "The Prophet's Town," which was to be the headquarters for the Indian federation.

In 1809, General William Henry Harrison, Governor of Indiana Territory, negotiated the Treaty of Fort Wayne, by which certain Miami chiefs ceded to the United States three million acres of land on the Wabash River, at a price which amounted to less than a third of a cent an acre.

The treaty enraged Tecumseh. In 1811, he set out on a long journey to enlist the aid of the Southern tribes for his confederation. On his way south, he talked to General Harrison at Fort Vincennes. He told Harrison that the white people need not be alarmed at the Indian confederacy, for the red men were but following the example of the thirteen American colonies, uniting for the common good. He said:

"A few chiefs have no right to barter away hunting grounds that belong to all the Indians, for a few paltry presents or a keg or two of whiskey. We do not want war with the United States, but there can be no peace until the land is returned. I would not come to General Harrison and ask him to tear up the treaty, but I would say to him, 'Sir, you have liberty to return to your country.' The late sale is bad. It was made by a part only. All red men have equal rights to unoccupied land. It requires all to make a bargain for all. Until lately, there were no white men on this continent. Then, it all belonged to the red men. Once a happy race, they have been made miserable by the white men, who are never contented, but always encroaching. They have driven us from the Sea-coast, and will shortly push us into the lakes. We are determined to make a stand where we are." [1]

General Harrison defended the treaty. He ridiculed Tecumseh's claim that the land was owned in common by the Indians. "If the Miamis wish to sell part of their lands and receive an annuity from the Seventeen Fires, the Shawnees have no right to control them in selling their own property," he said.

"It is all false!" said Tecumseh. He spoke rapidly to his warriors in Shawnee, and they sullenly withdrew from Harrison's presence.

The governor did not wish to break off the negotiations. He visited Tecumseh the following day, and was courteously received, although he found the chief quite inflexible. He told Harrison:

"I am anxious to be the friend of the United States. If you, General Harrison, will prevail upon the President to give up the lands lately purchased, and will agree never to make another treaty without the consent of all the tribes, I will be the faithful ally of the Americans, and will aid them in their wars with the English. I would much rather join the Seventeen Fires, but if they will not give up the lands, I will join the English."

Governor Harrison told Tecumseh that his talk would be faithfully reported to the President, but that he knew the President would never agree to give up lands that had been bought by the Americans in treaty.

To which the chief replied:

"As the President is to determine the matter, I hope the Great Spirit will put enough sense into his head to direct you to give up

---

[1] Drake, *Indians of North America*, 617.

the lands. It is true he is so far off he will not be injured by the war. He may sit still in his town and drink his wine, but you and I will have to fight it out."

"Is it your determination to make war unless your terms are complied with?" asked Harrison. Tecumseh replied grimly:

"It is my determination; nor will I give rest to my feet until I have united all the red men in the like resolution." [2]

Colonel Benjamin Hawkins, United States Agent to the Creeks, was present in the square at Tukabatchie, the principal Creek town, when Tecumseh arrived to make his plea for the Indian confederation. All southern tribes had been asked to send representatives to hear the talk.

Tecumseh presented to the Creeks a bundle of red sticks, typifying the united Indian tribes; a war hatchet; and a belt of wampum. He explained that he wished the red men to form a confederation, as the whites had done, in order that they might hold their hunting grounds. He said:

"The white people have no right to take the land from the Indians, for it is ours. The Great Spirit gave it to us. Let all the redmen unite in claiming a common and equal right in the land, as it was at first, and should yet be, for it never was divided, but belongs to all, for the use of each of us.[3]

"I do not want war with the Americans, but to be in peace and friendship with them. Do not do any injury to them. Do not steal even a bell from any one, of any color. Let the white people of this continent manage their affairs in their own way. Let the red men, too, manage their affairs in their own way."

He explained the vision which had been seen by his brother, the Prophet, and said:

"Kill your cattle, hogs, and fowls. Destroy the wheels and looms. Throw away the plows, and everything used by the Americans. Sing the song of the Indians of the Northern Lakes, and dance their dance. Shake your war clubs, shake yourselves, and you will frighten the Americans. The arms will drop from their hands. The ground will become as a bog and mire them, and you may knock them on the head with your war clubs. I will be with you, with my Shawnees, as soon as our friends the British are

---

[2] Drake, *Indians of North America,* 620-621, Thatcher, B. B., *Indian Biography,* Vol. I, 234.

[3] Drake, *Indians of North America,* 617.

ready for us. Lift up your war club with your right hand, be strong, and I will come and show you how to use it." [4]

Tecumseh was a man of great force of personality. He was tremendously in earnest; his dramatic appeal created a sensation in the Creek Nation, but failed to convince Big Warrior, of Tukabatchie, who presided at the council. He had accepted the emblems which Tecumseh had brought, but being a shrewd judge of character, Tecumseh looked him straight in the eye, and said:

"Your blood is white! You have taken my talk, and the sticks, and the wampum and hatchet, *but you do not mean to fight!* I know the reason; you do believe the Great Spirit has sent me. I will leave Tukabatchie immediately, and will go to Detroit. When I arrive there, I will stamp on the ground, and will shake down every house in Tukabatchie!"

He thereupon strode from the council, and left the Creek Nation. The warriors were in a furor, and counted the days which they calculated he would require to reach Detroit. On the day they had estimated that he would reach his destination, a rumbling sound was heard. It was the great earthquake of New Madrid, which formed Reelfoot Lake and created such devastation in the then thinly settled Mississippi Valley. But to the warriors of Tukabatchie, there was but one explanation. Their houses, as Tecumseh had predicted, were shaken down. "Tecumseh has reached Detroit!" said the awe-stricken Creeks.[5] Religious fervor swept the Nation, carrying on its tide all but the older chiefs.

2

The hope for a Messiah who will right all wrongs is almost universal with mankind. The Creeks, in common with all American Indians, had suffered great wrongs. They were persuaded that the Prophet was their Messiah, and that Tecumseh was the leader who was to bring them back the old

---

[4] *American State Papers, Indian Affairs,* Vol. 1, 845.

[5] Mooney, *Ghost Dance Religion, 14th Report, Bureau of American Ethnology.* There is no reason to doubt that Tecumseh himself thought that the Great Spirit had sent the earthquake to convince the Creeks of the justice of his plea.

life. Even among the lower Creek towns, which were neutral, there were hundreds of young warriors who hastened to put on the war paint, while the upper towns espoused Tecumseh's cause with passionate enthusiasm:

"We will throw away our rifles, and will take American forts with the old weapons of our fathers; the bow, arrow, and toma- hawk. We are determined to put to death every Indian who will not join us. Our prophet knows the secrets of the Americans. The Master of Breath has permitted a conquering spirit like a storm to arise among us, and like a storm it will ravage." [6]

At the height of excitement in the Creek towns, war between England and the United States was declared on June 28, 1812. While many of the Creeks believed that America might be overcome with bows and arrows, with the help of the Prophet, others felt that a plentiful supply of guns and ammunition would be required. Spain still owned Florida. A delegation of Creeks visited Don Matteo Manique, Spanish governor at Pensacola; his sympathies were strong for England, and he had little doubt that in a short time the United States would no longer exist. "I will furnish you arms and ammunition, and will assist you," he told the Indians. "If the Americans prove too much for both of us, I have sufficient boats to take us all off together." [7]

Tecumseh had judged Big Warrior rightly. He refused to go to war and was besieged in his own town. Autosse- Emautla, an old chief, declared himself to be a representative of the Prophet, and was joined by a number of warriors who began killing members of the peace contingent. He was over- powered and killed, "but we could not take him alive," Big Warrior wrote Hawkins. "His party all fought until they were killed. This is the case with all of them,—they fight until they drop." The death of the Prophet's deputy only caused the war- riors to burn with more ardor for the fight. "Prophets" ap- peared in every town; they burned the houses of peaceful Indians and killed hogs, cattle, and horses. "All who are friends to the United States are doomed to destruction," a chief wrote. Leaving the towns, the war party moved into the

---

[6] *Ibid.*

[7] *American State Papers, Indian Affairs,* Vol. 1, 854.

woods and danced the dance of the "Indians of the Lakes."
They refused to accept messages from Agent Hawkins. "I
will receive no talk from Colonel Hawkins or the white people.
I am done with him and his talks," a chief declared.

The excitement came rapidly to a climax. On Aug. 30, 1813,
a thousand Creek warriors surprised Fort Mims, on Tensas
River, near Mobile.[8] The white commander, regardless of
warnings, had carelessly left the gates of the fort open. A
horrible massacre followed. Four hundred Americans were
killed.

### 3

So much excitement on their southern border could not pass
unnoticed by the Cherokees. "Prophets," who preached a return to the old ways as the only hope for the survival of Indian
life, appeared in their towns.

A great council was called at Ustanali, where a medicine
dance was held; the new doctrine was explained by a Cherokee prophet from Coosawatie. He began by saying that the
mountain towns had abused him, and had refused to receive
his message, but that he must continue to bear testimony, regardless of what might happen. He spoke:

"We have taken the white man's clothes and trinkets. We have
beds, tables, and mills. Some even have books and cats. All this
is bad, and because of it the Great Spirit is angry, and the game is
leaving the country. If the Cherokees would live and be happy
as before, they must put off the white man's dress, throw away
the mills and looms, kill the cats, put on paint and buckskins, and
be Indians again. Otherwise, swift destruction will overtake
them."

This talk appealed to the Cherokees; they cried out that it
was good. But for the courage of Major Ridge, he who had
killed Doublehead, it would have been accepted. "Such talk,"
he told the warriors, "will lead to war with the United States,
and mean ruin for the Cherokees." His statement was so resented that he would have been killed had not his friends
spirited him away.

---

[8] They were led by Wm. Weatherford, "Red Eagle," nephew of Alexander
McGilivray.

A day of reckoning was appointed for all who failed to accept the new doctrine. "On that day," said the prophet, "the Great Spirit will send a hailstorm and destroy all but the faithful, who must assemble on the highest peak of the Smoky Mountains."

Hundreds abandoned their homes and waited in the mountains for the promised hailstorm, which never materialized.[9]

While the Cherokees were in a state of uncertainty, the issue was decided when a party of "Red Stick" Creeks killed a Cherokee woman near Etowah, in Georgia. The friendly lower Creek towns invited the Cherokees to join them and the Americans in putting down the Red Sticks. "If the prophets are allowed to have their way," said Major Ridge, "all the advancement made by the Cherokees will be lost." He called for volunteers, and soon there were four hundred in the field, commanded by Colonels Gideon Morgan and John Lowery, both half-breeds.

4

Andrew Jackson with the American army approached the Creek country from the North. Pathkiller, a Cherokee chief, at his village of Turkeytown,[10] was in danger of being cut off by the Creeks; he sent runners to Jackson for aid, and received the reply:

"The hostile Creeks will not attack you until they have had a brush with me, and that I think will put them out of the notion of fighting for some time." [11]

However, he ordered a detachment under command of General James White to join the Cherokees and relieve Pathkiller.

Another detachment of Cherokees, under Captain Richard Brown, accompanied General Coffee to attack the Creek town of Tallushatchie, which was situated on Coosa River a few miles below Turkeytown. After valiant resistance the town was taken. Coffee's report says:

"The Creeks fought as long as one existed, with savage fury, and met death without shrinking or complaining. Not one asked to be spared, but fought as long as they could stand or sit." [12]

---

[9] Mooney, *Myths of the Cherokees*, 88.
[10] On Coosa River, opposite the present Center, Ala., in Cherokee County.
[11] Drake, *Indians of North America*, 395.
[12] Mooney, *Myths of the Cherokees*, 90.

Two hundred Creeks lost their lives.

The Cherokees also assisted in the destruction of Talladega a few days later. Again the Creeks fought with reckless bravery, and three hundred were killed. It was unusual for Indians to stand and fight against odds, but the Red Sticks were so fired with religious fanaticism that they willingly risked all, convinced beyond doubt that the Great Spirit would give them the victory.

Hillabee town sued for peace, which Jackson granted. At that time, however, the Cherokees under General White were ranging the country, and, not knowing that the Hillabees had been granted peace, surrounded the town and destroyed it on Nov. 18, 1813. Sixty Creeks were killed and two hundred and fifty taken prisoners. General White's report highly praised the courage of the Cherokees under Morgan and Lowery.

The destruction of the Hillabee town proved to be the death warrant for the Creek Nation. The Creeks were not aware that the attack had been made without General Jackson's knowledge and concluded that peace overtures were hopeless.

Thereafter they fought with the desperateness of despair, neither giving nor asking quarter. At one time they inflicted defeat on the white army. At the battle of Emuckfau, Jackson was compelled to retreat; the Creek hopes rose high. But Jackson returned with stronger forces and ended the war with one final crushing blow.

At Tohopeka, or Horseshoe Bend,[13] the Tallapoosa River makes a curve, enclosing a hundred acres,—almost an island, with a narrow neck at the upper end. At this neck the Creeks erected a strong breastwork of logs across the neck, behind which a thousand warriors and three hundred women and children prepared to do or die for their country. They had no fear for the outcome; their prophets had assured them that the Great Spirit would give them the victory.

Jackson, with two thousand men, including five hundred Cherokees, approached the Bend from the north. He sent General Coffee with his cavalry and the Cherokees to surround the lower side of the bend to prevent the escape of the Creeks.

---

[13] Near the present Dadeville, Cherokee County, Alabama.

By ten o'clock in the morning, March 28th, 1814, they had them hemmed in.

As a preliminary to storming the fortifications, Jackson cannonaded the breastworks for two hours, without results. He then ordered the 39th Regulars, under Colonel John Williams, to take it by storm.[14]

The first man over was Ensign Sam Houston. He received an arrow in the thigh, but tugged it from the wound and continued fighting. While the prophets urged them on by exhortations, "Fight on! The Great Spirit will give us the victory. Fight On!" the Red Sticks fought fanatically.

A number of canoes had been placed at the lower end of the bend for use in retreat, if necessary. After swimming the river and taking away the boats, the Cherokees began a furious attack in the rear. This divided the attention of the Creeks and enabled Jackson's force to take the breastwork. Entirely surrounded now, the Creeks continued to fight. In mid-afternoon, Jackson ordered the firing to cease, and offered life to all who would surrender. During the lull a small cloud appeared in sky. The prophets had told their followers that this would be the sign of victory. The offer was refused; and fighting was resumed. By sun-down, all the Creeks had been killed except a few who had sought refuge in a ravine; these scorned suggestions of surrender. Whereupon the ravine was fired and the defenders of Horseshoe Bend died to the last man.

Five hundred and fifty-seven dead warriors were found on the field of battle, and probably two hundred more were drowned in the river.

Jackson's loss was twenty-six, killed, and one hundred and seven, wounded, of the whites; and eighteen, killed, and thirty-five, wounded, of the Cherokees.[15]

5

Jackson had intended to use the Cherokees only to prevent

---

[14] Before the attack began however, Jackson issued an order that was typical of the man. He notified the Creeks that the breastwork was about to be stormed, but that time would be allowed for the women and children to be removed to a place of safety.

[15] Mooney, *Myths of the Cherokees,* 96: Drake, *Indians of North America,* 394-401. Reports of Jackson, Morgan, and Coffee are given in full in Heiskell, *Andrew Jackson, and Early Tennessee History.*

the escape of the Creeks; not content with this passive role, they had crossed the river and attacked the Red Sticks in the rear. Morgan's report says: "As soon as we crossed the river, we were warmly assailed in every quarter except our rear, and we kept this open only by dint of hard fighting. About an hour after my arrival, I received a wound on the right side of my head which had like to have terminated my existence. I soon recovered, however, and received the heavenly news that the 39th had charged, and were in possession of the breast-works." [16]  The official reports of the battle give high praise to the Cherokees.

## 6

Tecumseh in the north, had fared no better than his Creek allies. During a visit to the Southern tribes, General Harrison had defeated the Prophet in the bloody battle of Tippecanoe. On October 5, 1813, Tecumseh and his British allies were also defeated by Harrison in a battle on the River Thames. Tecumseh might easily have escaped, but he had sworn to take the scalp of his greatest enemy, General Harrison. A hand-some officer, who wore a cocked hat and a wide wampum belt across his shoulder, to which his shot bag and powder horn were attached, had been active in the battle, galloping his horse from point to point. It was Colonel William Whitley, of Kentucky. From his activity, Tecumseh took him to be Harrison, and advanced with the intention of securing his scalp.

---

[16] Heiskell, S. G., *Andrew Jackson*, 369. Marquis James, *Andrew Jackson, Border Captain,* 59. Only a few of the names of the Cherokees who took part in the Battle of Horseshoe Bend, have been preserved. It is interesting to find among them, Young Dragging Canoe, son of the greatest foe of the Americans on the border. Others mentioned are: Colonel John Lowery, of Chickamauga; Captain Richard Taylor, who once commanded the Indian Cavalry under John Watts; Major Ridge, who had helped to slay Double-head; Adjutant John Ross, afterward Principal Chief; Major John Walker who, as a spy, had preceded Watts' army on its march to Buchanan's Station; John McLemore, of McLemore's Cove; Whitepath, of Elijay, to whom Jackson gave a medal for bravery in the battle; Pathkiller, who had been rescued at his village of Turkeytown at the beginning of the war; and others whose names would doubtlessly be recognized as once familiar on the war trails of Cumberland and Holston. Drake, 401: Mooney, and various other sources. Prominent among the Eastern Cherokees in North Carolina, was Chief Junaluska (Tsuna-Lahunski), who fought bravely at Tohopeka, and afterward remarked, "If I had known Jackson would have driven us from our homes, I would have killed him that day at the Horse-shoe Bend."

He was followed by several warriors, who spread in the shape of a triangle, with Tecumseh at the apex.

Colonel Whitley had observed the approach of the warriors, and rode to meet the attack. The two leaders raised their guns at the same instant, but the chief was quicker on the trigger, and Whitley received a mortal wound. Tecumseh sprang forward to scalp him; a volley from the Kentuckians brought him down, with a number of his warriors. Though desperately wounded, Tecumseh still endeavored to scalp Whitley, when a young man named King, who had discharged his musket, drew a pistol from his belt and shot the great chief.[17]

## 7

Soon after the Creek war, the Cherokees ceded the last of their land in South Carolina, including the sites of the old towns of Seneca, Keowee, and Sugartown. As an immediate result of the war, they granted permission to the United States to build military roads through their country, and were allowed $25,000.00 for damages caused by the American soldiers during the war.

A road was built from Old Echota, on Little Tennessee River, through the Smoky Mountains, to the headwaters of Tugaloo River. Another was built from Tellico Blockhouse to Spring Place, thence southward to Jasper and Athens, Ga. From Ross's Landing, the present Chattanooga, a road was built west of Lookout Mountain to Willstown, thence eastwardly to the present Cedartown and Marietta, Ga. Ross's Landing was also connected by road with Spring Place.

The Cherokees had proved their loyalty by service under the Stars and Stripes, which should have merited gratitude and fair treatment. Their reward was far different. Soldiers who had passed through the Cherokee country spread stories of the beauty and fertility of the land. Strong pressure by the government brought the cession in 1815 of three thousand, five hundred acres in Alabama. A commission, of which John Sevier was a member, was appointed to run the new line, and Sevier died while on this mission at Decatur, Alabama, September 24, 1815.

---

[17] Brunson, *Western Pioneer*, 1, 141. Marshall, *History of Kentucky*, 2: 494.

## CHAPTER XXX

## THE MISSIONARIES

### I

The first attempt to introduce the Christian religion among the Cherokees was made in 1784 by the Moravians of North Carolina, who sent Brother Martin Schneider to the Cherokee towns along the Little Tennessee to ask permission for the establishment of a mission within the nation.

Schneider was met on his journey by the Indian hater, James Hubbard, who viewed with suspicion any man or mission that was friendly to the Indians. He cursed Schneider and ordered him to leave the country. The missionary, however, was not easily frightened, and continued on to Chote where he was the guest of the Indian Agent, Joseph Martin. The frontier was still in the grip of Indian warfare, and nothing definite came of the attempt to establish a mission at that time.[1]

### 2

The second Moravian attempt to found a mission was made in 1799, when Abraham Steiner and Christian Schweinetz visited the Cherokees. They were unable to make final arrangements, having arrived during the hunting season when the

---

[1] Schneider's Journal, Williams, *Early Travels in the Tennessee Country,* 250-264.

Schneider's Journal gives an intimate picture of the Cherokee towns along the Little Tennessee. Speaking of the frontiersmen, he says, "They scarcely regard the Indians as human beings."

The missionary returned to North Carolina in the winter of 1784, and narrowly escaped death by drowning at the crossing of French Broad River. The following is an extract from his journal:

"Jan. 13, 1784. I breakfasted before the break of day, and put on as few clothes as possible. With our Saviour I had quite a peculiar conversation, viz., that I had deserved his displeasure in many ways, but I begged it as a favor to help me through this water.

"Three-quarters of the way it went very well, but two large flakes of ice between which I must pass got hold of my horse, and with a violent current carried him downstream to a hole twelve or fifteen feet deep, in which but lately a man had drowned.

"My horse could hardly keep up on account of the pointed rocks. I was several times in the water to my arms. There was no place for landing,

466

leading Indians were away. Little Turkey was Principal Chief at that time, and John Watts, War Chief. The missionaries mention that Watts did not attend the previous annual distribution of presents by the Government, because he was wealthy and had no need of them. His son, John Watts, Jr., acted as their guide. They visited "Grandmother Maw, widow of Scolacuta, and talked of her future welfare, but doubt if she understood." [2]

Not being able to do anything definite, they left, but returned in 1800 with better results. A Moravian school was then established. Chiefs present on the occasion were, Doublehead, Little Turkey, Glass, Bloody Fellow, and the Boot. Strangely, Doublehead favored the school, and it was through his influence that permission was granted to build it. When the negotiations were completed, he approached the missionaries and suggested that they present him with a bottle of whiskey for his aid in putting through their project! [3]

The site chosen was at the home of Joseph Vann, a progressive half-breed chief, who lived at Spring Place, Georgia.[4] Rev. John Gambold and his wife, Anna Rosel Gambold, were sent to take charge of the work in 1805, and the mission exercised great influence throughout the nation.

### 3

Many of the settlers on America's western frontier had considered that the Indians were not human. John Heckewelder, one of the Moravian missionaries, was astounded by their attitude. He was told:

"An Indian has no more soul than a buffalo; to kill either is the same thing, and when you have killed an Indian, you have done a good act, and have killed a wild beast." [5]

---

nothing but rocks straight up as a wall, some of them hollowed out twenty feet by the violent current. At last I saw a little opening in the rocks, where to my good fortune was also enough ground that my horse could stand in the water above his belly. I jumped in the water and took my things off and tied my horse to a piece of wood fastened in the ice, and climbed up through the narrow pass, but which was too straight for my horse. I must, therefore, let him stand below in the water.

"Now I had to run through the snow three miles over the hills, without road or path, in wet cloathes, to obtain help and return for my horse, but my heart was so full of joy and thankfulness to our Saviour for his wonderful help that I forgot all difficulties."

[2] *Ibid.*, 448-525.

[3] Walker, *Torchlights to the Cherokees,* 27.

[4] *Ibid.*

[5] Heckewelder, *Narrative,* 106.

With the coming of peace, the various Christian denominations reproached themselves for having failed to attempt to Christianize the red men. The conviction took root that perhaps the Indian was human after all, and had a soul to save. Much of the praise for the progress of the Cherokees from 1800 to the date of the removal may be given to the unselfish Christian men and women who toiled not only to convert, but to educate and to better in every way the Indians.

In 1803, the Presbyterian Church appointed Rev. Gideon Blackburn as missionary to the Cherokees. He was so impressed with their needs that he made a tour of the northern churches to collect offerings for the cause. Through his eloquence and zeal, he raised $5,250.00. The Presbyterian General Assembly voted additional funds to make the amount $10,000. Blackburn established two schools, one at Hiwassee Garrison, and the other at Sale Creek. He instructed the boys and men in agriculture and carpentry, and the girls and women in domestic arts. He encouraged in particular, weaving and spinning. He was compelled to abandon the work in 1810 because of ill health, but did not lose interest in the Cherokees.[6]

4

Blackburn was a member of the American Board of Commissioners for Foreign Missions, an interdenominational body. Through his influence, and with the approval and assistance of the United States Government, the board, in 1816, sent Rev. Cyrus Kingsbury to continue the work Blackburn had begun.

Kingsbury attended a council which had been called at Turkey Town by General Andrew Jackson, for settling the Creek-Cherokee boundary. He was introduced to the chiefs by General Jackson. When his plan was explained, it met with approval, and Chief Glass was appointed to assist him in the selection of a site.

The old town of Chickamauga, near the present Chattanooga was selected. The government paid John McDonald $500.00 for 160 acres on the south side of Chickamauga Creek. Return J. Meigs, Indian Agent, was instructed to build the necessary houses and to aid in the effort to gain the attendance of the Indian youths. Farming equipment and household goods were

---

[6] Armstrong, *History of Hamilton County, Tennessee,* 65.

furnished by the United States. The project was called Brainerd Mission,[7] in honor of the Rev. David Brainerd, a well-known missionary to the Northern Indians. It was a success from the start. The school consisted of approximately a hundred Indian boys and girls. A large farm was maintained.

Two years after its foundation, the Mission was honored by a visit from President James Monroe, who was so impressed by the work being done that he authorized the building of a girls' dormitory at the expense of the government.

After two years work at Brainerd, Rev. Kingsbury was transferred and Rev. S. A. Worcester was sent to take his place. Rev. Samuel Worcester, Secretary of the Board, and uncle of the resident missionary, visited the Mission in 1821, and died while there. He was buried in the Mission cemetery.[8]

With Brainerd as the Parent-Mission, branches were set up at Willstown, Oothlacoga, Guntersville, Etowah, and other places.[9] The Missions were the greatest influence for good, aside from Sequoyah's invention of the alphabet, in the progress of the Cherokees, whose advancement was not surpassed by any other tribe of North American Indians.

5

Little Turkey, Principal Chief of the Cherokees, died soon after the Brainerd Mission was instituted. He was succeeded by the aged Pathkiller, who visited the mission in 1819. When the old chief saw the bright-eyed Indian boys and girls at their tasks, and particularly when he heard them sing, tears rolled down his war-worn face, though he endeavored to restrain himself, evidently being ashamed of weeping.[10]

---

[7] *Ibid.*, 66: and Walker, Torchlights to the Cherokees, 15-24.

[8] His remains were later, in 1844, removed to his home in Massachusetts.

[9] Among the missionaries names are S. A. Worcester, Ard Hoyt, Elizur Butler, D. S. Buttrick, Cephas Washburn, A. E. Blunt, John Vail, John Thompson, and others.

[10] Rev. Elias Cornelius, agent for the Board of Foreign Missions, visited Brainerd in September, 1817. He was cordially welcomed by Charles R. Hicks, the assistant Chief, who assured him that the mission would have the co-operation of the Cherokees. While there he was introduced to the Great Council of the Nation, and his report shows the meeting was conducted with decorum, without disorder or drinking. Major Ridge, as speaker of the council, in an animated speech urged the people to give the mission their hearty support, and to send their children to be taught.

He spoke to the children in their own language, with eloquent gestures, urging them to take advantage of their opportunity, so that they might later disperse and carry the lessons which they had learned into every Indian home in the Nation. After the conclusion of his talk, he asked each boy and girl to shake his hand. "The Nation should think much of you," he told the missionaries; "I will tell the people everywhere that it is good to send their children here." [11]

---

[11] The various missions to the Cherokees are fully covered by Robert Sparks Walker, in *Torchlights to the Cherokees*.

CHIEF JOHN JOLLY, (OOLOO-TEE-SKEE)
After a sketch made by George Catlin about 1835.

# CHAPTER XXXI

## WEST OF THE MISSISSIPPI

### I

For a number of years, the government had been trying to induce the Cherokees to move west of the Mississippi.

The migration of Chief Bowl in 1794, following the capture of Scott's boat, has been mentioned.[1] Bowl settled with his followers on St. Francis River in the present Arkansas. He was joined by the influential chief Tat-si, known to the white men as Dutch, and a few years later removed to Red River in Texas, forming the nucleus of the Texas band of Cherokees.[2]

In 1809 Tahlonteeskee removed to Arkansas because of dissatisfaction caused by the treaty of 1807, for which Double-head had been killed. He was accompanied by John D. Chisholm, a white member of the tribe, and by the old and well known chief Takatoka. These men were recognized leaders among the eastern Cherokees, and their emigration was a great stimulus to the western movement. To encourage others, agent Meigs sent a delegation at government expense to inspect the western lands, and they returned with a favorable report, particularly of plentiful game. Prospect of a return to the old hunting life without white neighbors sent hundreds of Cherokees westward. William Lovely, Meigs' assistant, was sent as Government Agent to the Arkansas band. A regular tribal organization was effected, with Tahlonteeskee as Principal Chief, and Takatoka as War Chief. Within a few years, nearly six thousand Cherokees were living in the west.

Although they had left their old homes to escape the white man's influence, the Indians soon found their lands overrun by white hunters. Tahlonteeskee and Chisholm led a delegation in

---

[1] Section 12, Chapter XXIV.

[2] The Texas Cherokees increased in numbers until in 1839 they numbered probably 8000. They were industrious and peaceful, and friends of Sam Houston. Houston's second term expired in 1839, and by secret agreement contrary to his wishes, a military force was dispatched by Governor M. B. Lamar which expelled the Cherokees from Texas after a bloody battle on June 15, 1839. Bowl was killed.

1815 which protested to Governor William Clark of Missouri that that state had "swallowed the Cherokee country."

Said Tahlonteeskee:

"Under the faith of the President of the United States, we have been industrious. We have cleared nine miles on each side of Arkansas River. We wish our boundaries run according to agreement. We wish to be friendly with our brethren the whites, but at the same time we wish them to know that we walk on our own ground.

"When our father sent us here, he told us there was plenty of game. To our sorrow, the French and others destroy five thousand buffaloes every summer for no other profit than the tallow. A thousand weight of meat is thrown away for perhaps 20 pounds of tallow. This is a thing that will render the game shortly scarce, and we must then see our children suffer." [3]

2

In 1817, a treaty was concluded at Calhoun, Tennessee, by Andrew Jackson, David Meriwether, and Governor Joseph McMinn, whereby two considerable tracts were ceded by the Cherokees, they to receive in return territory of equal extent in Arkansas.

The treaty roused bitter resentment throughout the Cherokee Nation. Before it was consummated, a memorial was presented to the commissioners signed by seven prominent chiefs, one of whom was John Ross, a young man of 27 who had just been elected to membership in the National Council. The preparation of the memorial was his first service in that capacity.[4]

The memorial set forth the progress the Cherokees were making toward civilization, and their disinclination to return to savagery. "Let us, therefore, remain where we are, in the land of our fathers, without further cession of territory." [5]

[3] Foreman, *Indians and Pioneers,* 44. Governor William Clark, of Missouri, was a brother of George Rogers Clark. He had been one of the leaders of the Lewis & Clark expedition to the Pacific in 1807.

[4] Mooney, *Myths of the Cherokees,* 221.

[5] Two years later, John Ross was elected President of the National Committee, the second highest honor in the gift of the Nation. This great chief, whose story is inseparable from that of the Cherokees, was born Oct. 3, 1790. The place of his birth is in doubt, but the weight of evidence seems to indicate *Kana-gatugi* (Turkey Town) on Coosa River opposite the present Center, Ala.

The treaty was completed regardless of the protest, and within a month Agent Meigs reported that seven hundred Cherokees had enrolled for the western trip.

The most prominent of these was Oolooteeskee, known to the white men as John Jolly. Jolly was Tahlonteeskee's brother. Accompanied by his brother-in-law, the old trader John Rogers, he emigrated from his home on Hiwassee Island, where he had been a prudent, substantial farmer, respected by the white people, and called "Beloved Father" by the Cherokees. Sam Houston, when a young man, had spent three years as the guest of Jolly, who had given him the Indian name *Colonah* (The Raven).[6]

John Jolly's band of emigrants numbered 331 persons, of whom 108 were warriors. Each man was furnished by the government, a new rifle and provisions for seventy days' travel.

Upon Jolly's departure for the west, he sent the following address to the Secretary of War, John C. Calhoun, through agent Meigs:

"Father, you must not think that by removing we shall return to the savage life. You have taught us to be herdsmen and cultivators, and to spin and weave. Our women will raise the cotton and indigo, and spin and weave cloth to clothe our children. By

---

His father, Daniel Ross, had emigrated from Scotland before the Revolution, located among the Cherokees as a trader, and married the quarter blood daughter of John McDonald, deputy British Agent under John Stuart.

As a boy, John Ross was known among the Cherokees as *Tsan-Usdi* (Little John) but after attaining manhood was called *Gu-wis-gu-wi*, after a large migratory bird which was occasionally seen in the Cherokee country, possibly the egret or swan. The name is an onomatope, a repetition of the call of the bird.

John Ross received his education at Southwest Point, later Kingston, Tennessee; and under John Barbour Davis, a private tutor employed by Daniel Ross for the instruction of his children. Ross's official career began at the age of nineteen, when he was sent by Agent Meigs on an important mission to the western Cherokees. He served as Adjutant in the Cherokee regiment of Colonel Gideon Morgan in the Creek war of 1813-1814. From that time to the day of his death, he was in the constant service of his people. He filled the position of Principal Chief from 1828 to 1866. See Mooney, *Myths of the Cherokees*, 223; Foreman, *Indian Removal*, 265; Armstrong, *History of Hamilton County and Chattanooga, Tenn.*, 59.

[6] Houston, while living with Oolooteeskee, became enamored with Tiana Rogers, daughter of John Rogers and niece of his host. Later, when Houston resigned the governorship of Tennessee because he discovered that his newly wed wife loved another man, he sought the wigwam of his friend Oolooteeskee in Arkansas, and the arms of his former Indian wife, Tiana Rogers, for consolation.

means of schools here, numbers of our young people can read and write. They can read what we call 'The Preacher's Book' sent by the Great Spirit to all people. We shall live in peace and friendship with the Indian tribes west of the Mississippi if within our power. It is our wish that the differences between our people and the Osage Nation may be amicably settled." [7]

## 3

Chief John Jolly had said, "It is our desire that the differences between our people and the Osage Nation may be amicably settled."

From the first emigration of the Cherokees, they had trouble with the Osages, a fierce, uncivilized tribe. The Osages had been willing to cede a portion of their lands to the government for white settlement, believing that the white people would trade with them and teach them the arts of civilization. It was another matter when the lands, instead of being thrown open to white settlers, were given to the Cherokees.

The Osage chief, Claremore,[8] complained to the Government of the injustice of permitting one tribe of red men to settle upon lands which another tribe had ceded. He failed to obtain a satisfactory answer, and the Osages began harassing the Cherokee settlements. The Cherokees retaliated. This condition existed for a number of years, when the Cherokee emigrants, having gained in numbers, decided to end the matter by making open war upon the Osage Nation. Tahlonteeskee and Takatoka sent runners to Governor Clark of Missouri, advising him of their intention. They detailed the grievances inflicted upon the Cherokees by the Osages, "who have stolen so many of our horses that we are compelled to work the soil with our hands, and have recently killed two young Cherokee warriors, for whom we will take revenge." [9]

Governor Clark reported the Cherokee threat to the war department, and instructions were sent to General Jackson advising him to send troops to preserve order. Majors Stephen

---

[7] Foreman, *Indians and Pioneers,* 74. Jolly was visited a few years later by George Catlin, who painted his picture, and reported him an aged, dignified, and beloved leader of his people. He had then succeeded his brother Tahlonteeskee as Principal Chief.

[8] Grah-mo, "arrow going home."

[9] Foreman, *Indian and Pioneers,* 74.

Long and William Bradford were dispatched to Arkansas on that mission. They arrived in 1818, and built Fort Smith, but the Indian war had already begun.

Throughout the first half of 1817, the Cherokees were preparing for the Osage war. Runners were sent to the Eastern Cherokees to ask their aid. The call of blood was strong, and the war-whoop resounded again throughout the Cherokee villages. John McLemore led ten boats loaded with warriors down the Tennessee, headed for the Osage country. So great was their ardor that all the young braves in the Nation would have gone had not the movement been peremptorily put to an end by Government agents.[10]

The neighboring tribes of Delawares, Koasati, and Comanches, all of whom had suffered at the hands of the Osages, were asked by the Cherokees for aid; and in the fall of 1817 nearly six hundred warriors responded and advanced against Claremore's town. The Cherokee leaders were, Tahlonteeskee, Takatoka, McLemore, Black Fox, and Bowl; they were accompanied by a number of white men, among whom was John D. Chisholm.

Many of the Osage warriors were away on the annual fall hunt; their town was overwhelmed in the absence of its defenders. Fourteen warriors, and sixty-nine women and children, were killed and scalped. One hundred and four prisoners were taken; most of them being women and children. Claremore's town was burned; the Cherokees returned in triumph to their own settlements. McLemore's warriors were given all the scalps which they had taken; a portion of the spoils; and three prisoners,—a woman, and two children.

Runners were sent to the Eastern Cherokees notifying them of the victorious return of the war party. Dances and other joyous ceremonies were held. Chief Pathkiller, however, sternly forbade traffic in the prisoners. The two Osage children were placed in school at Brainerd, Pathkiller himself paying a ransom to their captors. The woman later married a Cherokee.

[10] McLemore lived in North Georgia, a few miles south of the present Chattanooga, Tenn., where a large section is still known as McLemore's Cove. McLemore fought as a captain in the Creek war. His father had fought under Watts, and his grandfather had served as messenger for Captain Demere when he was beleaguered in Fort Loudoun. See *American State Papers, Indian Affairs*, Vol. 1, 455.

Four years later, the Government succeeded in making peace between the Osages and Cherokees, whereby it was provided that all prisoners should be returned. The Osage children were saddened at having to leave Brainerd, and wept; the woman loved her Cherokee husband and begged to be allowed to stay with him. "Your father and mother wish to see you. If the Cherokee loves you, he will not fail to come after you," asserted Claremore.

The Osage war had a unifying effect on the Eastern and Western Cherokees, and caused them to feel that regardless of separation, they still were one people.

4

In November, 1818, Governor Joseph McMinn of Tennessee called a council of Cherokee chiefs. He told them it was no longer possible to protect the Cherokees from encroachments of surrounding white people, and urged them to prepare for removal to the West. "If you remain in your present location, the Government may wish to help you, but your lands will be taken, your women corrupted, and your men made drunkards." [11]

Governor McMinn praised the western paradise, and offered the Cherokees $100,000 if they would remove at once. The proposition was contemptuously rejected. He then offered double the amount; but failed and resorted to other means.

A delegation of Western Cherokees, headed by Tahlonteeskee and accompanied by Sam Houston, passed through Tennessee on the way to Washington to ask for an outlet through the Osage country to the West. [12]

McMinn seized the opportunity. He explained his intentions to Houston, who was immensely popular and influential with the Indians. Chiefs Glass and Utsala were persuaded to accompany the western delegation to Washington to represent the Eastern Cherokees. After long negotiations, the President agreed to grant the Cherokees an outlet strip through the Osage lands to the Rocky Mountains, in view of the fact that the Osages had been defeated in the war. Through the influence of Houston's glowing description of the Osage lands gained by the Cherokees,

[11] Royce, *Cherokee Nation of Indians,* 224.
[12] *Ibid.,* 77. Takatoka, the old war chief, expressed it: "We want a clear opening to the setting of the sun, with no white people in front of us."

and by direct bribery, Glass and Utsala were induced to sign a treaty for the Eastern Cherokees, by which they ceded all land north of Tennessee River, and east of a line two and a half miles above Hiwassee Old Town.

On his return to Tennessee, Houston brought a letter from the Secretary of War to McMinn, advising him of the successful conclusion of the negotiations, and of the bribery of the chiefs. McMinn replied:

"I am truly pleased to learn that the usual plans have been taken with the chiefs in purchasing their friendship, for such has been the course pursued with the natives from time immemorial, and corrupt as it may seem, we are compelled to resort to such measures." [13]

The tract ceded by the Cherokees was about six thousand square miles, more than a fourth of the land held by the Nation. The whole transaction represented a distinct loss to the Eastern Cherokees, as they received nothing for the vast territory. They were told that it was "compensation to the government for lands already ceded to those Cherokees who have removed to the West." In addition to losing a fourth of their lands, it was agreed that one-third of the annual allotment should be paid to the western band.

The preamble to the agreement naively stated: "As the commencement of those measures necessary to the civilization and preservation of the Cherokee Nation." [14]

For signing the treaty, Tahlonteeskee received one thousand dollars, and each of the other chiefs, five hundred dollars. John D. Chisholm had already been paid a thousand dollars, as Andrew Jackson wrote, "to stop his mouth." [15]

After his return from Washington, Chief Glass led a party of one hundred and sixty-seven emigrants to the west. There was much sickness on the journey. The chief lost his wife and son on the way, and did not live long himself after reaching the western country, in the fall of 1819. [16]

The outlet to the west continued to be a bone of contention with the Osages, and the two Nations engaged in intermittent warfare over a period of ten years.

---

[13] *Ibid.*, 78. See also Royce, 229.
[14] Royece, *Cherokee Nation of Indians*, 229.
[15] Foreman, *Indians and Pioneers*, 49.
[16] *Ibid.*, 73.

# CHAPTER XXXII

## TALKING STONES

### I

At the treaty of Long Island in July 1777, Chief Old Tassel had objected to giving up the beloved Cherokee treaty ground, Long Island of Holston River, "to any person or Nation whatever, except Colonel Nathaniel Gist, for whom and themselves it was reserved." Tassel's remarks were seconded by the Raven, of Chote, who desired that Colonel Gist "might sit down on Great Island when he pleased, as it belonged to him and them to hold good talks upon." [1]

Gist was the father of Sequoyah, inventor of the Cherokee alphabet.[2] The invention of an alphabet for a people who had no system of writing would in any case be a major event in their history. Sequoyah's invention enabled an Indian, after a few hours of study, whether educated or not, to read. The characters were fashioned from an English speller, though Sequoyah had no idea of the meaning of the words and never learned to speak English!

Wurteh, Sequoyah's mother, was well connected in the Nation. She was a sister to Chiefs Old Tassel and Doublehead, and was related to John Watts, Major Ridge, George Lowery, and other prominent Cherokees.[3]

Sequoyah was born about 1760, and as a boy lived at Tuskegee, adjacent to the ruins of Fort Loudoun. He was present at the treaty in 1770 which terminated the wars between the Cherokees and the Iroquois.[4]

---

[1] Haywood Appendix, 501-503.

[2] *Payne Mss.,* Newberry Library, Chicago. John Howard Payne, author of *Home Sweet Home,* spent some time among the Cherokees while gathering material for a history of the tribe. His manuscript was never published, and is now in the Newberry Library, Chicago. Much of his work consists of notes only, but the chapter on Sequoyah seems to be complete. Chapter XXXII of this book is taken mainly from an excerpt of Payne's manuscript furnished through the courtesy of Prof. Wm. R. Webb, who has a *Life of Sequoyah* in formation.

[3] Two of Wurteh's kinsmen are mentioned by Payne as being uncles of John Watts. They were: Kaiyah-Tahee, who was killed under a flag of truce and may be recognized as Old Tassel; and Tal-tsuska, the famous Doublehead.

[4] Mooney, *Myths of the Cherokees,* 109.

SEQUOYA (SIKWÂYĬ)

From McKenney and Hall's copy of the original painting of 1828

An entry in the journal of Abraham Steiner, the Moravian missionary, under date of Nov. 18th, 1799, probably has reference to Sequoyah:

"A young Indian was here today who had cleverly inlaid his tomahawk with silver, having graved a small flower design with the initial letters of his name. According to his statement, he wished to go to Philadelphia for a year to learn something in this line." [5]

2

The following story of Sequoyah's invention of his alphabet was told by his brother-in-law, George Lowery, to John Howard Payne. [6]

"Sequoyah was called George Gist by the white people. [7] It was the fashion among the Cherokees to decorate themselves with ornaments of silver, such as ear rings, armlets, bracelets, gorgets, and fine chains. George Gist decided that he would like to make these things beautiful in design. One day he requested Chief Charles R. Hicks to write "Gist," on paper in English, so that he might copy it upon silver ornaments, especially on arm bands and gorgets, to let people know that it was his work. He became so proficient in this occupation that he was well known throughout the nation."

Payne's manuscript continues:

"He now turned his attention to sketching upon paper. He could draw horses, persons, and in short, whatever happened to strike his fancy. His friend, the Bark used to be much in his company when doing this. George Gist showed Bark how to do sketching, even men. Often, when employed at their work, they would discuss the white people. The Bark thought that the most wonderful thing they did was writing down what was passing in their minds so that it would keep.

"George would remark that he saw nothing wonderful or difficult in this; he had heard that in former times, a man named Moses, who was the first man to write, would make marks upon stone, thus: upon which he would draw lines on a scrap of paper to show Bark how it was done."

[5] Williams, *Early Travels in Tennessee Country*, 488.
[6] *John Howard Payne Mss.*, Newberry Library, Chicago.
[7] Sequoyah later signed treaties as George Guess.

About 1818, after the land upon the Little Tennessee had been sold to the white men, Gist removed to Willstown. He had become, by this time, very popular in his tribe. When his friends came to call, the conversation again turned to discussion of the white man's ingenuity in writing on paper.

Gist said:

"I can see no impossibility in it. The white man is no magician. It is said that in ancient times a man named Moses made marks upon stone. I can agree with you by what name to call those marks, and that will be writing, and can be understood!"

Whereupon he took a small whetstone from his pocket, scratched marks upon it, and said, "Thus can I make characters like Moses did, which every one of you will understand."

"His friends burst into laughter. They bantered him upon his scheme to make stones talk; telling him that he would find those stones very unentertaining company, and advising him to get his reason back and settle down to a regular and rational occupation. Sitting in perfect silence, Gist repeated to himself: 'I know I can make characters which may be understood.'"

He immediately began to contrive characters; each stood for a word. He soon discovered that the number of signs required for a complete set of words would be so great that no one could memorize them. But by making the characters represent sounds, he saw that they would combine so as to form words.

About this time he acquired an English speller. The letters had no meaning whatever to him; he was never able to speak anything but Cherokee, and never attended school a day in his life. From the speller, however, he fashioned his characters. The letter "J" was used in several ways, upside down, reversed, etc.

After prodigious labor and study, Sequoyah completed eighty-six characters, and with them he began to frame sentences.

But his Indian friends were worried because of the whim that had taken possession of his mind. Turtle Fields spoke to him:

"My friend, there are a great many remarks upon this employment you have taken up. Our people are most concerned about you. They think you are wasting your life. They think,

### Sounds represented by Vowels.

*a* as *a* in *father*, or short as *a* in *rival*
*e* as *a* in *hate*, or short as *e* in *met*
*i* as *i* in *pique*, or short as *i* in *pit*
*o*, as *aw* in *law*, or short as *o* in *not*
*u*, as *oo* in *fool*, or short as *u* in *pull*
*v*, as *u* in *but*, nasalized

### Consonant Sounds

*g* nearly as in English, but approaching to *k*. *d* nearly as in English but approaching to *t*. *h, k, l, m, n, q, s, t, w, y*. as in English. Syllables beginning with *g* except *S* have sometimes the power of *k*. *A S O* are sometimes sounded to, tu, tv. and Syllables written with *tl* except *L* sometimes vary to *dl*.

THE CHEROKEE ALPHABET
Sequoyah's Talking Stones

my friend, that you are making a fool of yourself, and will no longer be respected."

Sequoyah replied:

"If our people think I am making a fool of myself, you may tell our people that what I am doing will not make fools of them. They did not cause me to begin, and they shall not cause me to stop. If I am no longer respected, what I am doing will not make our people less respected, either by themselves or others; so I shall go on, and you may tell our people." Turtle Fields said no more, and left.

Sequoyah's wife was not in sympathy with his ambition. He built a cabin apart from his family one, and there would study and contrive. He confined himself for a year; the whole charge of his farm and family devolving upon his wife. When the remonstrances of his friends availed nothing, she went in and capped the climax by flinging his whole apparatus of books and papers into the fire; and thus was lost his first labors. Undismayed, he only said: "Come, it must be done over," and after two more years of toil, completed his work.

### 3

Sequoyah first taught his alphabet to his little daughter, Eye-o-kah, who was only six years of age. He then demonstrated it to George Lowery, who had accused him of only recalling from memory the words he had written. Sequoyah called in his little child, and said: "Eye-o-kah, say over my alphabet, as I hold up the characters." She proudly repeated the sounds as rapidly as they could be shown. "Yoh!" ejaculated George Lowery, in astonishment.

The news that Sequoyah had succeeded in writing Cherokee words that could be read by another person, even at a distance, quickly spread. The scorn with which the inventor's efforts had been regarded, was instantly forgotten. Cherokees, old and young began to learn the new writing; soon messages were passing to and from the western band. Within a few months, the Cherokees became a reading Nation!

### 4

Dr. S. A. Worcester, at Brainerd Mission, wrote the American Board for Foreign Missions suggesting that the Bible be printed in Sequoyah's Cherokee alphabet. The Board approved and manufacture of the type was begun.

In the fall of 1826, the Cherokee Nation adopted a constitution with the same basic principles as that of the United States. Charles Hicks was elected Principal Chief, and John Ross, assistant chief. The Nation was divided into eight districts, with the functions of a regularly organized government.[8]

It was decided to begin the publication of a national paper, printed in Sequoyah's alphabet. On Feb. 21, 1828, the first issue of the *Cherokee Phoenix, (Tsalagi-Tsi-le-hi-sani-hi)* was printed in the capital, New Echota. Elias Boudinot, a quarterbreed Cherokee, who had been educated at an Indian school maintained by the Board of Commissioners for Foreign Missions, at Cornwall, Conn., was the editor. The printer was John F. Wheeler, who left a letter telling of his experience in setting up type in a language of which he understood not a word.

Wheeler and another printer, Isaac N. Harris, arrived at New Echota on Dec. 23, 1827. The editor, Boudinot, was on hand, but the type had not arrived. Dr. Worcester furnished the printers with a copy of the alphabet for study. Wheeler wrote:

"We had nothing to do for three or four weeks but learn the alphabet. It was more and more incomprehensible to us than Greek. For myself, I could not distinguish a single word in the talk of the Indians with each other. It seemed a continuance of sounds.

"While we were waiting for the type and press it was ascertained that no printing paper had been ordered. A two horse wagon was secured, and Harris started for Knoxville where there was a paper mill. The type did not arrive until the latter part of January, 1828. The house built for the printing office was of hewn logs, thirty feet long, twenty feet wide.

"Stands had to be made, a bank, and a case for the Cherokee type. The latter was something new, as no case to accommodate an alphabet containing 86 characters could be found. The press, a small royal size, was like none I ever saw before or since. It was cast iron, with spiral springs to hold up the plates, at that time a

---

[8] The adoption of a constitution modeled upon that of the white people was highly objectionable to many of the older Cherokees. The noted chief, Whitepath, who had fought under Jackson at Horseshoe Bend, rebelled and demanded a return to the old customs. IIis rebellion was suppressed with little difficulty, however, the majority of the Nation being progressive.

new invention. We had to use balls of deerskin stuffed with wool for inking, as it was before the invention of the composition rollers.

"The first number of the *Cherokee Phoenix* was issued about the middle of February, 1828. Harris had abandoned the effort to learn the Cherokee alphabet, and the setting up of the type fell to my lot. We had no impression stone, and had to make up each page of the paper on a sled galley, put it in the press, take proofs on slips of paper, then correct it in the press, a very fatiguing way of correcting foul proof, which was the case with my first attempt to set Cherokee type. I did not know or understand a word of the language.

"Translation of English into Cherokee was a slow business, therefore we seldom made up more than three columns each week in Cherokee. John Candy, a native half-breed, who came to us as an apprentice, could speak the Cherokee language, and was of great help to me in giving me the words where they were not plainly written. Elias Boudinot, known among the Indians as Kala-Kina, (The Buck), an Indian whose father and mother could not speak English, was the editor of the paper." [9]

## 5

Sequoyah had in the meantime removed to Arkansas to instruct the western Cherokees in the use of his alphabet. He visited Washington in 1828, and his picture was painted at that time. He was granted $500.00 by the Government in recognition of his great service to his people.[10] The Cherokee Nation, through Chief Ross, presented him a medal, with the following tribute:

"The old and the young find no difficulty in learning to read and write in their native language. Types have been made and a printing press established in the Nation. The Scriptures have been translated and printed in Cherokee. While posterity continues to be benefitted by the discovery, your name will be held in grateful remembrance. The great good designed by the author of human existence in directing your genius to this happy discovery cannot be fully estimated—it is incalculable. Wishing you health and happiness, I am, your friend,

JOHN ROSS." [11]

[9] Pilling, C. C., *Bibliography of Iroquoian Languages,* 1880, bulletin of Bureau of American Ethnology.

[10] By the same agreement the United States appropriated $1000.00 for the purchase of a printing press for the diffusion of Sequoyah's invention among the Cherokees. See Starr, 67-71 for complete treaty.

[11] *Payne Mss.*: Mooney, *Myths of the Cherokees,* 110-112.

Sequoyah was visited in his western home by John Howard Payne in 1840. He was then an old man. Many had offered to pay him for his alphabet, but he had given it freely and without cost to his people. He maintained that some could not afford to pay, and he would make no charge to anyone; he made copies for all who desired them.

Payne's description of Sequoyah is worthy of repetition:

"Guess had a turban girding his grey hairs; a dark blue robe and a checked calico tunic under it, confined by a beaded belt which sustained a wooden handled knife, and its collar apart, with a handkerchief flung around his neck and gathered within the bosom of his tunic.

"He wore plain buckskin leggings. One leg is lame and shrunken. He had a long Indian pipe, and smoked incessantly. His air was altogether what we picture to ourselves of an old Greek philosopher. He talked and gesticulated very gracefully, his voice alternately swelling and then sinking to a whisper; eye firing up, and then subsiding into a gentle and benignant smile."

Payne had hoped to secure a written statement from Sequoyah, but found the Indian orator in the midst of a discourse to an audience that was so enthralled that the talk was never translated. "I seemed entirely forgotten by the rest of the audience," says Payne. "A listener would occasionally say, 'Oh, it is beautiful,' or 'Oh, how interesting,' but no attempt was made to translate."

The Indians told Payne later that they had not interrupted Sequoyah for fear of breaking the thread of his recollection, for it seems that he was telling the story of the peace that was made between the Cherokees and Iroquois, and of the peace belts that were sent by the northern tribes. As a boy, he had witnessed the treaty.[12]

## 6

There was a tradition among the Cherokees that at a very early date a number of their people had emigrated to the Rocky Mountains. They were known as the Lost Band.

---

[12] Foreman, Grant, *Advancing the Frontier*, 322-323. The story told by Sequoyah was a well known tradition among the Cherokees, and may be found in Mooney, *Myths of the Cherokees*, 486-488. Such stories, passed down by the old men were the only historical record of the tribe. Great care was used to repeat them in the exact words of the original teller.

Picture by Walter Cline

THE PRINTING SHOP AT NEW ECHOTA

The building has been demolished since picture was made.

Sequoyah desired that every Cherokee should have the opportunity to learn his alphabet. It would be wonderful, he thought, if the lost Cherokees could be found and enabled to communicate with their kinsmen. With this idea in mind, he set out to try to locate the early emigrants; he was a very old man even then. He died in August, 1843, at the village of San Fernando, Mexico.

As a memorial, the giant redwood trees upon our western coast, probably the oldest of living things, were, in 1849, given the name of Sequoia, to honor that unselfish servant of his people.

# CHAPTER XXXIII

## A NATION WITHIN A STATE

### I

The State of Georgia had persistently pressed the Government to extinguish not only the Cherokee titles, but also those of the Creeks. William McIntosh, son of a Scottish father and an Indian mother, was chief of the Lower Creek towns. He was a cousin of Governor G. M. Troupe, of Georgia.[1] He had remained loyal to American interests during the Creek war of 1813-1814, and had led a band of followers who fought under Jackson at Horseshoe Bend.

Governor Troupe, because of his relationship with McIntosh, was able to persuade him that it would be advantageous to the Creek Nation to sell its lands east of the Mississippi, and receive in exchange, other lands in the West. The Creek National Council recognized the danger of the situation, and passed a law similar to that which had been adopted by the Cherokees, condemning to death any chief who sold tribal lands without the approval of the Nation in full council. The matter, however, was pressed by Georgia, and commissioners from that State met the Creek chiefs at Indian Spring, on January 8, 1821. McIntosh and his followers, who represented but a small part of the Nation, were inclined to make the cession. The chief of Tubabatchie rose and said:

"McIntosh knows that we are bound by our laws, and that what is not done in the public square in general council, is not binding on our people." Then turning to the Commissioners, he said, "That is the only talk I have for you, and I shall return home." He thereupon withdrew from the treaty, and was followed by thirty-five other chiefs. The Commissioners advised McIntosh, however, that Georgia would consider his signature and that of his followers binding upon the Nation. McIntosh, with thirteen other chiefs, signed a treaty ceding a large body of land in the lower Creek country.[2]

---

[1] Foreman, *Indian Removal*, 20.
[2] Drake, *Indians of North America*, 392.

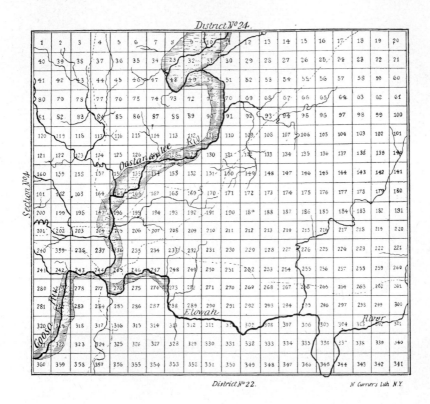

A MAP of the *23d DISTRICT 3d SECTION*
of originally Cherokee, now

A Typical Section of Georgia's Cherokee Land Lottery, Show-
ing Site of the Present City of Rome. Lot Number 237, the
Home of Chief John Ross, Was Drawn by Hugh Brown, of
Habersham County

From *Cherokee Land Lottery,* by James F. Smith, Published by Harper
& Brothers, 1838.

McIntosh forthwith lost favor with his people. It was generally thought that he had accepted a bribe, and the belief was substantiated by his further conduct. Governor Troupe seized upon the chief's loss of popularity to urge early removal to the West. He also urged McIntosh to use his influence and friendship with the Cherokees to secure the removal of that tribe, and the chief visited the Cherokee National Council in the fall of 1823, on that mission.

Pathkiller was Principal Chief of the Cherokees; John Ross was President of the National Committee; and Major Ridge was speaker. McIntosh had served with all three under Jackson. On Oct. 21, 1823, he made a proposition in writing to John Ross, looking to a joint cession of all eastern lands of both Creeks and Cherokees, to the enrichment of himself and Ross, personally:

"My Friend: I am going to inform you a few lines, as a friend. I want you to give your opinion about the treaty, whether the chiefs will be willing or not. If the chiefs feel disposed to let the United States have the land, part of it, I want you to let me know. I will make the United States Commissioners give you two thousand dollars; A. McCoy the same; and Charles Hicks, three thousand dollars, for present, and nobody shall know it. If you think the land shouldn't be sold, I will be satisfied. If the land should be sold, I will get you the money before the treaty is signed; and if you have any friend you want to receive,—they shall receive. The whole amount is $12,000.00, and you can divide among your friends, exclusive, $7000.00. I remain your affectionate friend, WM. MCINTOSH. To JOHN ROSS, (an answer return.)" [3]

The letter was handed to John Ross as he presided over the council. He consulted with the other chiefs, and it was decided that it should be read in McIntosh's presence. He was therefore called in and Ross addressed the council:

"My friends, five years have elapsed since I have been called to preside over the National Committee. Your approbation of my conduct is manifested by the successive appointments you have conferred upon me. Your trust has been sacredly maintained, and shall ever be preserved. A traitor in all nations is looked upon

[3] *Ibid.*, 393.

as more despicable than the meanest reptile that crawls the earth. An honorable character is more valuable than all the money in all the world. I would rather live as poor as the worm that inhabits the earth than to gain all the world's wealth, and have my reputation tarnished by the acceptance of a bribe.

"It has become my painful duty to inform you that a gross contempt is offered to my character, as well as to the members of the general council. The letter I hold in my hand will speak for itself, but fortunately, the author of it has mistaken our character and sense of honor."

Major Ridge, as chief speaker of the Nation, was instructed to condemn the traitor, publicly, and did not mince words, although McIntosh had been his old comrade in arms. He stated:

"McIntosh has borne a character of high moral rectitude among his people, the Creeks, but how stands his character now? I cast him behind my back! He is to be bought with money! We will not exult over fallen greatness. McIntosh may go to his own Nation, and in the bosom of his family, mourn a good name." [4]

Notwithstanding the rebuke at the hands of the Cherokees, and the dissatisfaction of his own people, McIntosh signed a treaty on February 12, 1825, ceding all the Creek lands east of the Mississippi to the United States. He realized that his life was forfeit by the law of his people, and asked protection of Governor Troupe. The governor promised protection, but evidently did not take the request seriously, as he failed to keep his promise.

On the morning of May 1, 1825, a party of a hundred warriors appeared at McIntosh's house and requested that women and children, and any white people present, should withdraw; when they had obeyed, the house was fired. McIntosh, and a faithful friend who had remained with him, ran from the burning building, and were shot down. On the same day,

---

[4] *Ibid.*, 448. William McIntosh was the son of Laclan McIntosh, commander of Fort Prince George from its erection until 1760; he was later re-appointed by Lieut.-Col. James Grant to the same post. Grant wrote: "I am sending Ensign McIntosh to the command of Fort Prince George. He is much esteemed by the Indians, had the fort before, and I shall recommend him for a lieutenant's commission." *British Colonial Records*, Lawson McGhee Library, Knoxville, Tenn.

WILLIAM McINTOSH, CREEK CHIEF

Executed May 1, 1825, by his own people, for selling Tribal Lands
without authority. From McKenney & Hall's *History of North
American Indians*.

his son-in-law, Sam Hawkins, was publicly hanged in one of the Creek towns.[5]

The killing of McIntosh enraged Governor Troupe. He pressed the Government with increasing insistence for removal of both Creeks and Cherokees. The adoption of a constitution by the Cherokees in 1826 was seized upon as a pretext that the United States had violated the Federal Constitution by permitting a Nation to be erected within the limits of a State. Governor Troupe demanded that the agreement to extinguish Indian title be fulfilled, despite the provision "when it can be done peaceably and on reasonable terms."

The Government had made every effort to comply with the agreement. In the quarter-of-a-century following the cession of the western lands by Georgia, 25,000 square miles of land had been bought from the Indians, for the sum of seven million dollars.[6]

2

In November, 1828, Andrew Jackson was elected to succeed John Quincy Adams as President of the United States. Jackson was a frontiersman. He had experienced the horrors of Indian warfare, and was firmly convinced that it was impossible for Indians and white men to live as neighbors.

Before election, Jackson had assured Georgia's representatives that if he were chosen they might count on his cooperation.[7]

Among his first acts following the inauguration, President Jackson requested that Congress pass an Indian Removal bill, which placed the matter in his own hands with power to act. The Georgia Legislature, encouraged by the President's attitude, passed an act annexing all Cherokee lands within the State.

Cherokee laws were declared null and void. Persons of Indian blood were forbidden to testify in court against a white

---

[5] A small number of Creeks, consisting mainly of McIntosh's followers, emigrated to Arkansas immediately after his death. The majority were removed forcibly in 1836. The Creek removal, a tale of horror, has been covered fully by Grant Foreman in his *Indian Removal*, University of Oklahoma Press, 1932, pages 107-190.

[6] Report of Secretary of War Calhoun, Mooney, *Myths of the Cherokees*, 115.

[7] Mooney, 117-119: Royce, 297.

man.  Georgia laws were extended over the Cherokee country. The drastic act was to take effect on June 1, 1830.  Two days thereafter, Governor Gilmer issued a proclamation declaring the provisions of the law to be in effect, and warning the Cherokees that it would be enforced.

Gold had just been discovered on Ward's Creek, near Dahlonega, on Cherokee land.  Governor Gilmer's proclamation gave notice that all the Cherokee lands, including the gold mines, were the property of Georgia.  Cherokees were forbidden to dig gold on their own lands, although white men might enter and dig at will.  Cherokees were also forbidden to hold meetings or councils.  White men residing in Cherokee territory were required to take an oath of allegiance to Georgia, agreeing to accept the enactments of the legislature.  This act was designed to drive out the missionaries.  Cherokee land was mapped into lots of 160 acres each, and "gold lots" of forty acres.  These were distributed by lottery to Georgia citizens.  Contracts between  white men and Indians were declared unenforceable without two white witnesses, which virtually canceled debts due Indians from white men.

The Cherokees appealed to President Jackson and were told that nothing could be done for them unless they were willing to remove to the West.  Government annuity payments to the tribe were stopped.  Bands of armed men from Georgia invaded the Cherokee country, taking horses, cattle, and houses from which they forcibly ejected the occupants.  Acts of injustice and oppression followed in rapid order.

In September, 1830, another attempt was made to secure removal.  The overtures were rejected by the National Council, although matters appeared more and more hopeless.  The Nation brought suit in the Supreme Court of the United States, through John Ross, asking injunction against the fulfillment of the Georgia law.  The court dismissed the paper on the ground that the Cherokees were not a foreign nation.[8]

### 3

To deter any who might be tempted to give up the fight, the National Council, on Oct. 31, 1829, adopted the resolution:

---

[8] Mooney, *Myths of the Cherokees,* 119.

"If any citizen of this Nation shall bind themselves by enrollment or otherwise as emigrants to Arkansas, he, she, or they shall forfeit all rights and privileges they have enjoyed as citizens of this Nation.

"If any citizen of this Nation shall sell or dispose of their improvements to any person so enrolled, he, she, or they shall be viewed as having disposed of said improvements to a citizen of the United States: shall be ineligible to hold any office of honor, profit, or trust in this Nation, and upon conviction shall be fined not less than one thousand dollars, and be punished with one hundred lashes." [9]

Stringent provision was made against any dealing whatsoever with persons who had enrolled for removal. Such persons were required to leave the Nation within fifteen days after enrollment, or be treated as intruders, arrested, and delivered to the United States authorities as such.

## 4

The presence of the Missionaries and their schools was offensive to the Georgians. It was felt that their influence was used to stiffen the resistance of the Indians.

Dr. S. A. Worcester, Dr. Elizur Butler, Missionaries Thompson and Proctor, and the printer, Wheeler, refused to compromise themselves by taking the oath of allegiance to Georgia, taking the position that they were agents of the Government for educating and Christianizing the Indians.

On March 12, 1831, the missionaries were arrested by the Georgia Guard, but were released upon the above plea. Governor Gilmer then asked the Secretary of War whether the Government claimed immunity for missionaries. Secretary Eaton replied that only Moravian and Baptist missionaries could claim to be agents of the Government, for it was through them that Government funds for civilization of the Indians had been expended.[10] On receipt of Eaton's reply, Governor Gilmer

---

[9] Starr, *History of the Cherokee Indians*, 64.

[10] Secretary Eaton was in error in assuming that Brainerd Mission, which was inter-denominational, had not received Government funds. The land was purchased by the Government for mission use, buildings had been erected under supervision of the Government Indian Agent, and President Monroe had authorized the building of the girls' dormitory at Government expense.

informed the missionaries that they could leave Georgia within ten days, or face arrest.

They made no move whatever and on July 7, 1831, a body of the Georgia Guard under Colonel C. H. Nelson appeared at New Echota and arrested Dr. Worcester. About the same time, other detachments arrested John Proctor, Rev. Trott, and Dr. Butler. All were treated with utmost brutality, chained together, tied to the back of a wagon, and forced to walk twenty-two miles. Two Methodist preachers, McLeod and Wells, witnessing the brutal treatment of prisoners who were making no attempt to escape, protested, and McLeod thereupon was chained to the other prisoners. Wells was struck on the head and warned by Colonel Nelson that he would receive like-treatment unless he made himself scarce. The guards heaped curses upon the prisoners, and taunted them with such phrases as "Fear not, little flock, it is the Father's pleasure to give you the Kingdom." After two days hard marching, the missionaries were placed in jail at Lawrenceville, Georgia, with a parting remark from the guards, "That is where all the enemies of Georgia land; there or in Hell!"

On the first Sabbath of their imprisonment, a note was addressed to Colonel Nelson, requesting permission to hold Divine services. It was returned with the notation:

"We view the within request as an impertinent one. If your conduct be evidence of your character and the doctrines you wish to promulgate, we are sufficiently enlightened as to both. Our object is to restrain, not to facilitate, their promulgation. If your object is true piety, you can enjoy it where you are. Were we hearers, we would not be benefitted, devoid as we are of confidence in your honesty. C. H. NELSON." [11]

The trial of the missionaries was held at Lawrenceville on September 18, 1831. They were sentenced to four years hard labor in the Georgia penitentiary at Milledgeville, but were offered pardon if they would take the oath of allegiance to the state. Thompson, Proctor, Wheeler and Trott consented, and were released. Worcester and Butler refused, and were taken to Milledgeville for confinement.

[11] Letter of Dr. Worcester to Board of Commissioners for Foreign Missions, quoted by Walker, *Torchlights to Cherokees,* 269.

By this time public sympathy in favor of the missionaries, was running high; Governor Gilmer therefore wrote to the prison authorities requesting them to "converse with each convict alone, and ascertain from them whether they are disposed to promise not again to offend the laws, if they should be pardoned." [12] Worcester and Butler, "having, as they averred, committed no crime, would accept no pardon," and were committed to the penitentiary; dressed in convict garb; and put to hard labor. The authorities soon relented however, and treated the prisoners with consideration. Permission was given them to hold religious services in the penitentiary; a visit from their wives was also permitted.

The case of Worcester and Butler was submitted to the Supreme Court of the United States on Feb. 23, 1832. Chief Justice Marshall announced the court's decision as a reversal of the Georgia judgment.

The case had been watched with intense interest by the Cherokees, and the Supreme Court's decision was celebrated with great rejoicing. "It was trumpeted forth that the decision had forever settled the controversy about their lands; that their laws and country would be restored, . . . and the Georgians expelled. Councils were held in all the towns of the Nation; rejoicing, night dances, were had in all parts, and whooping and yelling was heard in every direction." [13]

President Jackson dismissed the opinion of the Supreme Court with the remark, "John Marshall has made his decision; now let him enforce it."

Governor Gilmer had been succeeded by William Lumpkin; the new governor had no desire to go to war with the United States. When the decision of the Supreme Court was announced, he sent word to Worcester and Butler that if they would drop the case without further action, he would order their release. The missionaries agreed, after securing advice from the Board of Foreign Missions. They wrote to Governor Lumpkin that their action was not dictated by any change of views or doubt of their legal rights, but for the avoidance of troubles to their country which the continuance of the case might involve. The governor considered this disrespectful, and in a second letter the missionaries disclaimed any intention to

---

[12] Drake, *Indians of North America,* 456.
[13] Foreman, *Indian Removal,* 244.

offend. Governor Lumpkin then issued a statement that the prisoners had appealed to his executive clemency; had been pardoned; and were being released.[14]

## 5

Early in 1834, the Cherokees submitted a memorial to President Jackson, offering to cede a part of their lands to Georgia. They would remain in their country, which, the memorial stated, they would never voluntarily abandon, and within a time to be specified by the Government, would become citizens of the United States. Jackson replied: "The only relief from the Cherokees is by removal to the West." [15]

Before the Cherokee delegation had left Washington, Chief Ross was humiliated by an action of his brother, Andrew Ross; who privately suggested to Secretary of War Eaton that if he were authorized, he would bring a few chiefs or respectable individuals of the Nation to Washington, with whom a treaty could be concluded for the sale of all Cherokee lands.

His plan was approved, and he later returned to Washington with eight Cherokees, headed by William Hicks and John McIntosh. Secretary of War Eaton invited John Ross to cooperate in the making of the treaty. Ross replied:

"In the face of Heaven and earth; before God and man, I most solemnly protest against any treaty whatever being entered into with those men affecting the rights and interests of the Cherokee Nation." [16]

Realizing that no relief could be expected from President Jackson, John Ross memorialized Congress on May 17, 1834, in a document "evidencing the devoted and pathetic attachment with which the Cherokees cling to the land of their fathers, and refuse to believe that justice, prosperity and happiness

---

[14] Details of the arrest and imprisonment of the missionaries, where not otherwise specified, are from Robert Spark Walker's *Torchlights to the Cherokees,* Macmillan Company, 1931.

[15] Royce, *Cherokee Nation of Indians,* 274. The boon of citizenship, thus denied to the Cherokees, original owners of the country, advanced in civilization and the arts of peace, was in less than thirty years to be granted by the same Government to four millions of people who owned no land, could not read or write, and had no training for citizenship, The American Negro!

[16] *Ibid.,* 274.

await them beyond the Mississippi, remembering the humiliations and wrongs of the past." [17]

When the Scriptures had been translated into Cherokee, a copy was brought to the old chief, *Yonagunski* (Drowning Bear), and after hearing some of the passages read, he said, "It seems a good book; it is strange that the white man, who has had it so long, is no better than he is."

William Wirt, Attorney General of the United States, who presented the case of the Cherokees to the Supreme Court, used this language:

"We may gather laurels on the field of battle, and trophies upon the ocean, but they will never hide this fould blot upon our escutcheon. 'Remember the Cherokee Nation' will be answer enough to the proudest boasts that we can ever make." [18]

---

[17] *Ibid.*, 276.
[18] Drake, *Indians of North America,* 439.

# CHAPTER XXXIV

## BENEVOLENT INTENTIONS

### I

As the controversy lengthened into years, there grew up among the Cherokees a faction which contended that if they did not sell their lands, Georgia would take them for nothing; as a matter of fact had already taken them. They felt that the Nation should secure the best terms possible from the United States, while they could be obtained.

The life of Andrew Ross was threatened because of his efforts to execute a treaty ceding all Cherokee lands. He was spared because of the respect and affection for John Ross, which the Cherokees all had. Nevertheless, his idea took root and found converts. In February, 1835, two rival delegations appeared in Washington. One, headed by John Ross, was prepared to fight to the bitter end for their homes. The other, led by Major Ridge, announced readiness to discuss terms with the Government.

President Jackson seized the opportunity offered by Ridge and his followers. Rev. J. F. Schermerhorn was appointed to deal with the Ridge faction; John Ross's delegation was ignored.

A treaty was arranged with Ridge by which the Cherokees agreed to cede their lands for $3,250,000. John Ross discovered that the negotiations were under way, and demanded $20,000,000. The controversy was thus turned to discussion of how much, not cession, and John Ross was trapped. He finally consented to let the United States Senate fix the amount. The Senate declared $20,000,000 to be excessive, but raised the Schermerhorn consideration to $4,500,000.[1] The treaty was concluded and signed on March 14, 1835, but with the provision that it must be approved by the Cherokee Nation, in full council to make it binding.

In October, 1835, the Cherokee National Council unani-

---

[1] Royce, Cherokee Nation of Indians, 274.

mously rejected the treaty. Even Major Ridge, to Schermerhorn's surprise, voted against it. Schermerhorn, who was present, reported the outcome of the meeting to the President, adding, "The Lord is able to overrule all things for good." He notified the council that the Government would hold another meeting in December at New Echota to negotiate a further treaty.

Notices of the December meeting were printed in Cherokee, and distributed throughout the Nation, with a warning that all who did not attend would, by their absence, assent to any treaty that might be made.[2]

The commodious home of Chief Ross on Coosa River, at the present Rome, Ga., had been drawn in the Georgia lottery while the chief was in Washington in 1835. On his return, he had found his wife, who was in feeble health, restricted to one room, and Georgians in possession of the house. He retired to Red Clay, just across the Tennessee line, and built a cabin there. He was visited in the summer of that same year, by John Howard Payne, who wrote *Home Sweet Home*. Payne was profoundly impressed by the character of Ross, and the sufferings of the Cherokees. He suggested to the chief that he would be glad to put before the American people the true facts of the controversy. Ross assented and placed at Payne's disposal the records of the Nation and all his own papers.[3]

The council which had rejected Schermerhorn's treaty had authorized Chief Ross to negotiate one which would be more in accord with justice for the Nation. To prevent his departure on this mission, the Georgia guard under Colonel W. N. Bishop crossed the Tennessee line on Nov. 7, 1835, and arrested Ross and Payne.[4] The two were taken to Spring

---

[2] The council of October, 1835, was held at Red Clay, Tennessee. Schermerhorn called his later meeting in December at New Echota. Following enactment of Georgia legislation in 1830 forbidding them to meet within the state, the Cherokee capital had been moved to Red Clay in Tennessee, the temporary residence site of John Ross.

[3] Payne's statement, covering his visit to Ross and subsequent arrest, may be found in *History of Rome and Floyd County, Ga.,* by Geo. M. Battey, Jr. The arrest was supposed to have been inspired by Benjamin F. Curry, who had been sent into Cherokee country by the Government as Superintendent of Removal. Curry was engaged in taking a census of the Cherokees, and the chief was accused of interfering with the work.

[4] Mooney, 124.

Place, Ga., and confined in an outhouse at the former home of Chief Joseph Vann.

Payne, on asking the reason for his arrest, was told that statements "derogatory to Georgia" had been found among his papers, in which he had said that the Georgia guard looked more like banditti than soldiers." "A glance at them," said Payne, "made me feel that I ought to ask of any banditti a most respectful pardon."

Payne and Ross were released after two weeks' imprisonment, but Ross' arrest and detention had deprived the Cherokees of the advice and counsel of their leader at a critical moment.

Less than four hundred Cherokees attended the called meeting at New Echota in December, 1835. There was liberal use of whiskey and other inducements. As a result, the jubilant Schermerhorn departed for Washington on Dec. 29, 1835, with a treaty signed by the following Cherokees: Major Ridge, John Ridge, James Foster, Tah-ye-ske, Long Shell Turtle, John Fields, George Welch, Andrew Ross, William Rogers, John Gunter, John A. Bell, Joseph Foreman, Roberts Sanders, Elias Boudinot, Johnson Rogers, James Rogers, Stand Watie, and John Smith.[5]

None of the signers was a chief of the first rank. The most prominent were Major Ridge and Elias Boudinot. They later claimed that they were willing to sign because of a clause whereby Cherokees who so desired might remain as citizens of the United States, each of whom would received 160 acres of land. The clause was struck from the treaty by President Jackson, who remarked that it was his desire that all the Cherokees should emigrate together to the West.[6]

By the terms of Schermerhorn's treaty, for it was not that of the Cherokee Nation, all Cherokee lands east of the Mississippi were ceded to the United States for $5,000,000. In return, the Government ceded to the Cherokees, approximately seven million acres of land in the West. The Western land had already been ceded in 1828; the following is the language used in the cession:

"The United States, desiring to secure to the Cherokees

[5] Starr, 98.
[6] Mooney, 123: Drake, 460.

both east and west of the Mississippi a permanent home, *that shall never in all future times be embarrassed by having extended around it the lines, or placed over it the jurisdiction of any territory or state, nor be pressed upon in any way by any of the limits of any existing territory or state,* agrees to possess to the Cherokees, seven million acres," etc.[7]

Ross and his followers had taken no cognizance of the called meeting appointed by Schermerhorn, because, they said, the right to call a National Council was vested in the Principal Chief, and they were not aware that he had delegated his authority to anyone.[8]

Upon learning that a treaty with the Ridge faction had actually been concluded, Ross circulated a petition among the Cherokees to be signed by them, protesting that the agreement did not represent the will of the people; that the chiefs who had signed were unauthorized; and that the Cherokees were not willing to part with their lands at any price. Of a total estimated population of seventeen thousand, Ross's protest was signed by 15,964 Indians.[9]

Chief Ross presented the petitions in Washington early in the spring of 1836, and was informed that President Jackson had ceased to recognize any existing government among the eastern Cherokees. The Schermerhorn treaty was approved in the United States Senate by a majority of *one vote,* and was officially proclaimed by President Jackson on May 23, 1836. By its terms, the Cherokees were allowed two years in which to remove to the West.

2

John Ross, having returned home, entered upon a vigorous campaign of opposition to the execution of the treaty. Councils were held and resolutions adopted denouncing the actions of Schermerhorn, and declaring the treaty in all its provisions, null and void. He incited animosity against Ridge and his faction.

It was anticipated that disorders in the Cherokee country would follow ratification of the treaty; General John E. Wool, of the United States Army, was ordered to concentrate certain

[7] Royce, Cherokee Nation of Indians, 229. (The italics are the author's).
[8] *Ibid.,* 281.
[9] *Ibid.,* 283.

troops to "look down opposition." At the same time, Brigadier-General R. G. Dunlap, commanding a regiment of East Tennessee Volunteers, was ordered upon similar duty.

Gen. Dunlap disbanded his regiment in September, 1836, with the following statement:

"I gave the Cherokees all the protection in my power (the whites needed none). My course has excited the hatred of a few of the lawless rabble in Georgia who have long played the part of unfeeling petty tyrants, to the disgrace of the proud character of gallant soldiers and good citizens.

"I had determined that I would never dishonor the Tennessee arms in a servile service by aiding to carry into execution at the point of the bayonet a treaty made by a lean minority against the will and authority of the Cherokee people. I soon discovered that the Cherokees had not the most distant thought of war with the United States, notwithstanding the common rights of humanity and justice had been denied them." [10]

Major Ridge had undoubtedly been conscientious in signing the removal treaty; he was soon to repent in sack cloth and ashes. Aside from the contempt of his fellow countrymen, he was compelled to witness daily, the oppression of the Cherokees; and on June 30, 1836, he appealed to his former commander, General Jackson:

"Even the Georgia laws, which deny us our oaths, are thrown aside. Notwithstanding the cries of our people, and protestations of our peace and innocence, the lowest classes of the whites are flogging the Cherokees with cowhides, hickories, and clubs. We are not safe in our homes. Our people are assailed day and night by the rabble. Even justices of the peace and constables are concerned in this business. This barbarous treatment is not confined to the men, but the women are stripped also, and whipped without law or mercy.

"Send regular troops to protect us from these lawless assaults, and to protect our people as they depart for the West. If it is not done, we shall carry off nothing but the scars of the lash on our backs, and our oppressors will get all our money, and we shall be compelled to leave our country as beggars and in want. We speak

[10] *Ibid.*, 286.

plainly, as chiefs having property and life in danger, and we appeal to you for protection." [11]

General Wool arrived in the Nation with United States troops early in 1837, and in February of that year reported to the Secretary of War that the Cherokees to a man were opposed to the treaty, and that thousands of them would die rather than submit to it. His report stated:

"So determined is their opposition that they will receive neither rations nor clothing, however poor or destitute, lest they might compromise themselves in regard to the treaty. During the summer just past, thousands of them preferred living upon roots and the sap of trees rather than receive provisions from the United States; and, as I have been informed, had no other food for weeks.

"The whole scene since I have been in this country has been nothing but a heart-rending one, such as I would be glad to be rid of as soon as circumstances will permit. If I could,—and I could not do them a greater kindness,—I would remove every Indian tomorrow beyond the reach of the white men, who, like vultures, are watching, ready to pounce upon their prey and strip them of everything they have or expect to have from the Government of the United States. Nineteen-twentieths, if not ninety-nine out of every hundred, will go penniless to the West." [12]

Vann's fine brick residence at Spring Place, which had cost him ten thousand dollars, was claimed, under the lottery, by two Georgians. They appeared, heavily armed, at the same time. Spencer Riley took charge of the upper floor, and Colonel W. N. Bishop, of the Georgia guard, the lower. A set battle between the two followed. Vann and his family cowered in one room, where they had fled for safety. They later were driven out, and made their way through the snow to a log cabin with dirt floor, across the Tennessee line. [13]

---

[11] Mooney, *Myths of the Cherokees*, 127. The attitude of Georgia was rendered more inflexible by the removal of the Creeks which was then in progress.

[12] Royce, *Cherokee Nation of Indians*, 286.

[13] Riley's Statement, Battey, *History of Rome and Floyd County, Ga.*, 85-87. See also, Foreman, Grant, *Indian Removal*, 251. The gun battle was won by Bishop.

3

The matter of the Cherokee removal excited wide interest in the country, and bitter discussion in Congress. The Democrats upheld the course of President Jackson. The Whigs assailed it, not only for reasons of humanity, but because, as Henry Clay said, "The injustice of it has inflicted a deep wound on the American Republic." [14]

The courageous Davy Crockett of Tennessee denounced the treatment to which the Cherokees had been subjected, as "unjust, dishonest, cruel, and short sighted in the extreme." He said:

"I have been threatened that if I do not support the policy of removal, my public career will be summarily cut off, but while I am perhaps as desirous of pleasing my constituents and of coinciding with my colleagues as any man in Congress, I cannot permit myself to do so at the expense of my honor and my conscience in the support of such a measure." [15]

Congressman Henry A. Wise, of Virginia, stated that the Cherokees were probably more advanced in civilization than the surrounding people of Georgia, "and in saying that, I do not disparage the people of Georgia, far from it." He invited comparison between John Ross and Mr. Halsey, Georgia's representative in Congress. "And the gentleman from Georgia will not gain greatly by the comparison, either in civilization or morals," he said.[16]

Edward Everett of Massachusetts, repeatedly assailed the treaty as contrary to humanity, morals, and national honor.

4

In May, 1837, General Wool, commanding United States troops in the Cherokee country, was relieved at his own request, and Colonel William Lindsay was sent as his successor. Colonel Lindsay was instructed, in case John Ross further

[14] Royce, *Cherokee Nation of Indians,* 287.
[15] Crockett's public career was indeed "Summarily cut off" through influence of Old Hickory. Texas gained a recruit in her struggle for independence, and the Alamo, a hero.
[16] Royce, *Cherokee Nation of Indians,* 290.

VANN HOUSE, SPRING PLACE, GA.

Erected by Chief Joseph Vann about the year 1827. It was in an outbuilding on this place that John Howard Payne was confined after his arrest with Chief John Ross by the Georgia Guard in 1835. The builder of the house was Robert Howell, a contractor who erected also the house of David McNair in the present Polk County, Tenn. They were the first brick houses erected in what was then the Cherokee Nation.

incited a spirit of hostility to removal, to place him under arrest and turn him over to civil authorities for trial.

But Ross was not intimidated. In the spring of 1838, he placed before Congress a memorial for his people. It was laid upon the table in the Senate by a vote of 36 to 10.[17]

In March, 1838, Andrew Jackson was succeeded as President by Martin Van Buren. Public feeling on the subject of Cherokee removal had reached a high peak, and President Van Buren in May, 1838, submitted a compromise, permitting the Indians two years more for removal, subject to the approval of Congress and the governors of the States involved. Governor Gilmer of Georgia responded:

"I can give it no sanction whatever. The proposal could not be carried into effect but in violation of the rights of the state. It is necessary that I should know whether the President intends that the Indians shall be maintained in their occupancy by armed force in opposition to the right of *the owners of the soil*. If such be the intentions, a direct collision between the authorities of the state and the general Government must ensue. My duty will require that I shall prevent any interference whatever by the troops with the rights of the state and its citizens. I shall not fail to perform it." [18]

## 5

It was but natural that the Cherokees who were determined to hold their country should cherish bitter sentiments against the small minority which they felt were responsible for bringing misery upon the tribe. Major Ridge, leader of the treaty-party, felt obligated to see that the terms were observed, and was anxious to avoid open hostilities. Hence, the first party to assemble for removal included Ridge, Stand Watie, and others favorable to the cession, to the number of 466. The Indians began their journey at Ross' Landing in a fleet of eleven flat-boats, on March, 1838; and were transferred at Decatur, Ala., by railroad train, which took them around Muscle Shoals, to a waiting steamboat. The railroad had but recently been completed, and was a curiosity to the emigrants.

Dr. John S. Young, representative of the Government, was in charge of the party, and Dr. C. Lillybridge was the physi-

---

[17] *Ibid.*, 289.
[18] *Ibid.*, 290. (Italics are the writer's.)

cian. The latter left a journal of the trip, which is concerned, however, with the ailments of the Indians and the remedies used:

"Henry Clay better last night. Got him a comfortable situation near the chimney of the steamboat and breakfast of coffee and sea-bread, which appeared to afford him much satisfaction considering his case, which is consumption.

"Daughter of Young Squirrel sick with headache and fever. Gave cathartic. Arthur, son of Archila Smith, sick with influenza, gave Px. Vin. Antim. Applied a blister to chest of Henry Clay.

"Stand (Watie) has been in feeble health, cough very troublesome. James Williams taken very suddenly with inflammation of spleen; bled him and applied blister, etc." [19]

They arrived at their destination, Fort Smith, Arkansas, on March 27th, 1838, and settled on Honey Creek, in the northeast corner of the Western Cherokee Reservation, near the Missouri line.[20]

Another band, under B. B. Cannon, with Dr. G. S. Townsend as physician, went overland. It included James Starr, Charles Timberlake, James Taylor, Charles Ross, and others. Following is an excerpt from Dr. Townsend's journal:

"James Starr's wife had a child last night. Wagoners having horses shod until late at night, encamped and issued fodder and beef. Passed through Springfield, Missouri, on the 16th. Buried Elige's wife and Charles Timberlake's son, Smoker. Snowing, much colder, and sickness increasing. Buried Dreadful Waters this evening. Remained in camp at Dye's several days to attend the ill and wait for medicines to be brought from Springfield. Reached Lock's on Flat Creek, 21st. On 23rd, buried Rain Frog's daughter (Lucy Redstick's child), and halted at Reddix. Three days later camped at James Coulter's on Cane Hill, Arkansas, and next day buried Elsey Timberlake, daughter of Chas. Timberlake. Marched at 8 oc. A.M., halted at Bean's in Cherokee Nation, West. Buried another child of Timberlake's." [21]

Between 1836 and 1838, through the efforts of Benjamin F. Curry, emigrants, possibly to the number of two thousand

[19] Foreman, *Indian Removal*, 273-278.
[20] *Ibid.*
[21] Foreman, *Indian Removal*, 280-283.

in all, removed to the West, but the majority stood solidly behind Ross. They refused to believe that so infamous a treaty would be enforced, and made no preparations whatever for removal. In May, 1838, Chief Ross submitted to the President a new proposal by which the Cherokees would agree to remove upon receipt of a larger compensation for their lands, and certain minor advantages. In reply, he was assured that, while the United States was willing to extend liberality in construction of terms of the Schermerhorn treaty, the idea of a new treaty could not be considered. President Van Buren forwarded a copy of his reply to Congress, in the words:

"The accompanying copy of a communication addressed by the Secretary of War to the Cherokee delegation is submitted to Congress in order that such measures may be adopted as are required to carry into effect the *benevolent intentions* of the Government toward the Cherokee Nation, which it is hoped will induce them to remove peaceably and contentedly to their new homes in the West." [22]

General Winfield Scott, with 7000 troops, was ordered to the Cherokee country to carry into effect the benevolent intentions of the Government.

---

[22] Richardson, *Messages and Papers of the Presidents,* 3, 497.

# CHAPTER XXXV

## THE TRAIL OF TEARS

### I

General Scott arrived in the Cherokee country in May, 1838. On May 17th, he issued a proclamation from New Echota, which was made known by hand-bills scattered throughout the Nation. The Cherokees were informed that he had come with a large army by order of the President, to cause them to "join that part of your people who are already established in prosperity on the other side of the Mississippi.[1] They were reproached for permitting two years to elapse without attempting to fulfill the provisions of the removal treaty. General Scott advised:

"I have no power, by granting further delay, to correct the error you have committed. The full moon of May is already on the wane, and before another shall have passed away, every Cherokee man, woman, and child must be in motion to join their brethren in the far west.

"Will you, by resistance, compel us to resort to arms? God forbid! . . . I am an old warrior, and have been present at many a scene of slaughter, but spare me, I beseech you, the horror of witnessing the destruction of the Cherokees." [2]

The Indians were urged to make instant preparations, and to hasten to New Echota, to Gunter's Landing, or to Ross's

---

[1] Mansfield, R. E., *Life of Gen. Winfield Scott*.

The General's proclamation told the Cherokees that their brethren were living *in prosperity* west of the Mississippi, which was not the case. George Vashon, Government Agent in Arkansas, wrote in 1830:

"The five hundred Cherokees who reached here this year have been under the necessity for want of supplies of selling their claims on the government, to anyone who would furnish something to relieve their sufferings. It is to be regretted that the long delay in payment has placed these unfortunate people so much in the pitiless power of speculators."

A year later, he wrote:

"They complain most feelingly of the loss sustained when compelled by necessity to trade off their claims, continuing to inquire of me incessantly how much longer they will have to wait for their money." Foreman, *Indian Removal*, 231.

[2] Scott's Proclamation, Mansfield, *Life of Gen. Winfield Scott*.

MAJOR RIDGE

LEADER OF THE TREATY FACTION OF THE CHEROKEES. HE
WAS KILLED IN 1839, IN THE PRESENT OKLAHOMA, FOR SIGN-
ING THE REMOVAL TREATY.

From McKenney & Hall's *History of North American
Indians.*

Landing, where they would find food, clothing, and provisions, "and thence at your ease, in comfort, be transported to your new homes according to the terms of the treaty." [3]

On the same day that the proclamation to the Indians was issued, General Scott gave orders to his soldiers:

"Every possible kindness, compatible with the necessity of re-moval, must be shown by the troops. If in the ranks a despicable individual should be found capable of inflicting a wanton injury or insult on any Cherokee man, woman, or child, it is hereby made the duty of the nearest officer or good man to interpose and con-sign the guilty wretch to the severest penalty of the laws."

Soldiers were also instructed to pursue the Indians in case of flight, but not to fire except in case of resistance. "If we get possession of the women and children first, or first capture the men, the other members of the same family will readily come in on assurance of . . . kind treatment." He told them that in case of sickness, "one or more members of the family or friends of the sick person will be left in attendance with ample subsistence and remedies, and the remainder of the family removed by the troops." [4]

General Scott's orders, as may be seen, were humane enough. They were given, however, when the concentration first began and did not take into account that the Cherokees as a whole had never consented to the treaty, and regarded it as an outright fraud. Much of the rounding up of the Indians, too, was being done by militia under lesser ranking officers. This was particularly true in Georgia, from which state came most of the complaints of mistreatment.

2

While concentrating the Cherokees, General Scott made his headquarters at Amoyee Camp, on Hiwassee River near Calhoun, Tenn. Other camps were established at Ross's Landing, Gunter's Landing, and at Candy Creek. It was the intention that the Indians should be taken to the west by the water route.

Nine-tenths of the Cherokees made no movement toward the

---

[3] General Scott's proclamation.
[4] Mansfield, R. E., *Life of Gen. Winfield Scott.*

camps, still hoping that the unsanctioned treaty might not be carried into effect. General Scott proceeded, therefore, without further ceremony, to gather them up regardless. "Squads of soldiers were sent to search out with rifle and bayonet, every small cabin hidden away in the coves on the sides of mountain streams, to seize and bring in as prisoners all of the occupants, however or wherever they might be found." [5]

Families at dinner were startled by the sudden gleam of bayonets in the doorway. They were driven with blows and oaths along the weary miles of trail that led to the stockades. Men were seized in their fields or while traveling along the road. Women were taken unceremoniously from their spinning wheels, and children from their play. In many cases, on turning for a last look, the Indians saw their homes being swallowed up by flames which had been set by the rabble that followed at the heels of the soldiers to loot and pillage. So close on the scent were the outlaws that in some instances they were driving off the cattle and stock before the soldiers could start the owners in the opposite direction. Systematic hunts for Indian graves were made, to rob them of valuables deposited with the dead. A Georgia volunteer, afterward a Colonel in the Confederate Army, said, "I fought through the Civil-War, and have seen men shot to pieces and slaughtered by thousands, but the Cherokee removal was the cruelest work I ever knew." [6]

The soldiers were ordered to approach and surround each house, in order to come upon the occupants without warning, and thereby prevent escape. One old patriarch, when thus surprised, called his children and grandchildren around him, and kneeling down, bade them pray with him in their own language, while the astonished soldiers looked on in silence. Then, rising, the old man led the way into exile. [7]

"The property of many was taken and sold before their eyes, almost for nothing, the sellers and buyers having combined in many cases to cheat the Indians. These things are done at the instant of arrest and consternation; the soldiers standing by with arms in hand, impatient to go on with their work, could give

[5] Mooney, *Myths of the Cherokees,* 130.
[6] *Ibid.*
[7] *Ibid.*

little time to transact business. The captive, in a distressing state of agitation, his weeping wife frantic with terror, surrounded by crying, terrified children, without a friend to speak a consoling word, is in poor condition to make a good disposition of his property, and in most cases is stripped of the whole at one blow." [8]

The only refuge of the Indians lay in the religion taught by the missionaries. A letter from a camp at Hiwassee says: "These savages, prisoners of Christians, are now all hands busy, some cutting and carrying posts, and some preparing seats, for a temporary place of preaching tomorrow." [9]

Among the prisoners noted at the Candy Creek camp were Revs. Jesse Bushyhead and Stephen Foreman, native missionaries of the American Board of Foreign Missions. The preachers did not relax in their labors, but preached constantly. "On one Sabbath, by permission of officers in command, they went down to the river and baptized five males and five females. They were guarded to the river and back. Some whites present affirm it to have the most solemn and impressive religious ceremony they ever witnessed." [10]

The civilized white man was shamed before reputed savages, —victims of a tragedy that for terribleness has not been exceeded in American history.

General Scott wrote that he regretted the loss of property by the Cherokee consequent upon the hurry of capture and removal, "but the loss was the fault of the Cherokees, for having faith in the ability of John Ross to save them." [11]

### 3

By early June, "before another moon had passed," as General Scott had decreed in his proclamation, seventeen thousand Cherokees were assembled in the stockades, and the actual work of removal had begun.

The first detachment,[12] consisting of twenty-eight hundred,

---

[8] Foreman, *Indian Removal*, 288-289.
[9] *Ibid.*
[10] *Ibid.*
[11] Scott to Nat Smith, *Ibid.*, footnote.
[12] Hundreds of Indians died in the stockades. Uncertainty, unhappiness, imprisonment, and the enforced change of diet, were disastrous. The rations issued included flour and other staples of which many of the captives had little knowledge, and often no means of preparing.

was sent from Ross' Landing during the month of June. Sickness and discontent were rife. Government agents were unable to list the emigrants, for they stubbornly refused to give their names. They were forcibly placed on boats by a guard in command of Lieutenant Edward Deas. Lieutenant J. W. Harris was assigned the duty of conducting them to the West. The flotilla consisted of one steamboat of 100 tons, and six flatboats, one of which was constructed with a double deck cabin. One of the flatboats was smashed at the Whirl and Suck, but fortunately none of the emigrants was injured.

The Indians were transferred, as had been the Ridge party, around Muscle Shoals on the new Tuscumbia Railroad. Despite their curiosity concerning the train, more than a hundred took advantage of the transfer to escape to their native mountains. Others escaped at every landing.

The weather became extremely hot, and when the party left the boats near Little Rock, Ark., to complete the journey by ox-team, three, four, and five deaths occurred daily. The party halted on August 1, "more than half being sick." Lieutenant Harris wrote, "My blood chills as I write at the remembrance of the scenes I have gone through today." [13]

### 4

So great was the mortality among the Indians being sent to the West during the summer of 1838 that the Cherokee Council authorized Chief Ross to propose to General Scott that, as the Cherokees must be removed, they should be allowed to remove themselves in the fall, after the hot season was over. The resolution as presented to General Scott was signed by John Ross, Elijah Hicks, Edward Gunter, Samuel Gunter, Situaka, White Path, and Richard Taylor. It read:

"The present condition of the Cherokee people is such that all dispute as to the time of emigration is set at rest. Being already severed from their homes and property, their persons under the absolute control of the commanding general, and being altogether dependent upon the benevolence and humanity of that high officer, all inducements to prolong their stay in this country are taken away. However strong their attachment to the homes of their

[13] *Ibid.*, 295-297.

fathers may be, their interests and wishes are now to depart as early as possible.

"Therefore, resolved by the Nation in General Council that the whole business of the emigration of our people be undertaken by the Nation, and the delegation are hereby advised to negotiate the necessary arrangements with the commanding general for that purpose." [14]

General Scott agreed to the proposition, with the provision that every Cherokee except the sick and aged must be on their way by October 20th. A party of 1070 emigrants had left Ross' Landing three days before the agreement was made, traveling by wagons to Tuscumbia, Ala., where they expected to take boats for the remainder of the trip. Runners were dispatched to advise them that the emigration had been postponed until Autumn. General Smith refused to permit the Indians to return, and insisted that the trip should be continued. "Shortly after which about three hundred of them threw part of their baggage out of the wagons, took it, and broke for the woods." One of the Indians remarked to Smith, "All white men are liars and bad men. We will go home and shoot for John Ross." [15]

### 5

General Scott's decision to postpone the Cherokee emigration until autumn, dictated by humanity, roused a storm of protest, particularly from contractors who had procured the privilege of supplying the Indians en route, and who saw their fat profits endangered.

From the Hermitage, where Andrew Jackson had retired after serving as President, came a protest that fairly blistered. It was addressed to Felix Grundy, Attorney General of the United States.

"Hermitage, August 23, 1838.

"My Dear Sir: (Private)

"Colonel Walker has just shown me several communications from General Smith, removing agent for the Cherokees.

---

[14] Mansfield, *Life Gen. Winfield Scott*. Mansfield, in admiration of his hero, Gen. Scott, conveys the idea that the removal was almost a summer picnic.

[15] Gen. Nat Smith, of Athens, Tenn., who had been appointed to succeed Benj. F. Curry as Removal Agent. Curry died Dec. 13, 1836.

"The contract with Ross must be arrested, or you may rely upon it, the expense and other evils will shake the popularity of the administration to its center. What madness and folly to have anything to do with Ross, when the agent was proceeding well with the removal, on principles of economy that would have saved at least 100 per cent from what the contract with Ross will cost. Whilst the present appropriation for this object would have exceeded the expense, the contract with Ross will far exceed it, and compell a resort to Congress for further appropiation. What a fine excuse for Bell, Wise, and Adams.

"I have only time to add as the mail waits that the contract with Ross *must be* arrested, and Gen'l Smith left to superintend the removal.

"The time and circumstances under which Gen'l Scott made this contract shows that he is no economist, or is, sub rosa, in league with Clay & Co. to bring disgrace on the administration. The evil is done. It behooves Mr. Van Buren to act with energy to throw it off his shoulders. I enclose a letter to you under cover, unsealed, which you may read, seal, and deliver to him, that you may aid him with your views in getting out of this real difficulty.

"Your friend in haste,
ANDREW JACKSON."

"P. S. I am so feeble I can scarcely wield my pen, but friendship dictates it & the subject excites me. Why is it that the scamp Ross is not banished from the notice of the administration?" [16]

Curiosity is aroused as to the character of protest Old Hickory might have written could he have "wielded his pen" with his customary vigor.

6

Despite protests, General Scott's arrangement with Ross was allowed to stand, for disturbances on the Canadian border brought threat of war with England, and it was necessary that the Cherokee matter be disposed of quickly.

Emigration under Ross's leadership began in October, 1838. The sad procession, numbering thirteen thousand Cherokees, was divided into contingents of one thousand each, and two capable leaders were placed in charge of each detachment.[17]

---

[16] American Historical Magazine, Vol. 5, 139-140.

[17] Among the leaders chosen were John Benge, Elijah Hicks, Hair Conrad, Captain Old Field, Situaka, Rev. Evan Jones, Rev. Stephen Foreman, Rev. Jesse Bushyhead, James D. Wafford, George Hicks, Mose Daniels, Chowalooka, James Brown, John Drew, Richard Taylor, and Peter Hildebrand.

John Ross remained until the last to see that all were safely
started.  Before the first company took up its march, the
Cherokee chiefs met in solemn council for the last time in
their old homeland, and adopted a resolution which stated:

"The title of the Cherokee people to their lands is the most
ancient, pure, and absolute known to man; its date is beyond the
reach of human record; its validity confirmed by possession and
enjoyment antecedent to all pretense of claim by any portion of the
human race.

"The free consent of the Cherokee people is indispensable to a
valid transfer of the Cherokee title.  The Cherokee people have
neither by themselves nor their representatives given such consent.
It follows that the original title and ownership of said lands still
rests in the Cherokee Nation, unimpaired and absolute.  The
Cherokee people have existed as a distinct national community for
a period extending into antiquity beyond the dates and records and
memory of man.  These attributes have never been relinquished by
the Cherokee people, and cannot be dissolved by the expulsion of
the Nation from its own territory by the power of the United
States Government."

The resolution was signed by Richard Taylor, President of
the National Committee, and Going Snake, Speaker of the
Council; and by a committee in behalf of the whole people.[18]

The emigrants assembled at Rattlesnake Spring, near the
present Charleston, Tenn., and crossed Hiwassee River at
Gunstocker Creek.  They proceeded down the river to the
north end of Hiwassee Island, where the Tennessee was
crossed.  The route followed the old Black Fox Trail, south
of Pikeville, through McMinnville, and across the Cumberland
at Nashville.

The first party of 1103 Cherokees was in charge of John
Benge, son of the famous Bench who had led many war parties
against the whites.  It started Oct. 1, 1838.  William Shorey
Coody, who was present, describes the impressive scene:

"At length the word was given to move on.  I glanced along
the line, and the form of Going Snake, an aged and respected
chief whose head eighty summers had whitened, mounted his
favorite pony and passed before me and led the way in silence.

---

[18] Starr, 104: Foreman, *Indian Removal,* 302-312; Mooney, 131.

At this very moment a low sound of distant thunder fell upon my ears. The sun was unclouded, and no rain fell. I almost thought it a voice of Divine indignation for the wrongs done my poor and unhappy countrymen, driven by brutal power from all they loved and cherished in the land of their fathers, to gratify the cravings of avarice." [19]

Nine contingents of Cherokees left during October, 1838, and four during the next month. The last, conducted by George Hicks, left on Nov. 4th. On that day, Hicks reported to Chief Ross:

"We are now about to take our final leave and farewell of our native land, the country that the Great Spirit gave our fathers. It is with sorrow that we are forced by the authority of the white man to quit the scenes of our childhood. We bid a final farewell to the country which gave us birth, and to all that we hold dear.

"From the little trial we have made in a start to move, we know that it is a laborious undertaking, but with firm resolution we think we will be able to accomplish it if the white citizens will permit us. But since we have been on our march many of us have been stopped and our horses taken from our teams for the payment of unjust and past demands. The Government says we must go, and its citizens say 'you must pay me,' and if the debtor has not the means, the property of his next friend is levied upon.

"Our property has been stolen and robbed from us by white men, and no means given us to pay our debts. Our property is robbed of us in open daylight and in view of hundreds, and why are they so bold?—they know that we are in a defenseless situation." [20]

Grant Foreman has used this language:

"The Indians, more than the white people, cherished a passionate attachment for the earth that held the bones of their ancestors and relatives. The trees that shaded their homes, the cooling spring, the friendly water courses, the familiar trails, busk grounds, chungke yards, and council houses; . . . these simple possessions filled their lives; their loss was cataclysmic.

"It is doubtful if white people, with their readier adaptability, can understand the sense of grief and desolation that overwhelmed the Indians when they were compelled to leave all these behind forever; and begin the long journey toward the setting sun which they called the Trail of Tears." [21]

---

[19] Foreman, *Indian Removal*, 290.
[20] *Ibid.*, 305.
[21] Foreman, *Indian Removal*, Preface.

On December 3, 1838, President Van Buren sent his second annual message to Congress, in which he said:

"It affords me sincere pleasure to apprise the Congress of the entire removal of the Cherokee Nation of Indians to their new homes west of the Mississippi. The measures authorized by Congress at its last session have had the happiest effects. By an agreement concluded with them by the commanding general in that country, their removal has been principally under the conduct of their own chiefs, *and they have emigrated without any apparent reluctance.*" [22]

## 7

An eye witness who met and spent three days with the party of emigrants in charge of Rev. Jesse Bushyhead while passing through Kentucky, later commented on President Van Buren's message, and gave his impressions of the actual condition of the Cherokees.

"When I read the President's message that he was happy to inform the Senate that the Cherokees were peaceably and without reluctance removed, I wished that the President could have been there in Kentucky with me that very day, and have seen the comfort and willingness with which the Cherokees were making the journey." [23]

It was in mid-winter. Some of the emigrants were on horseback, and the sick and feeble were carried in wagons. By far the greater number were on foot.

"Even aged females, apparently nearly ready to drop into the grave, were traveling with heavy burdens attached to the back, sometimes on the frozen ground and sometimes on muddy streets, with no covering for the feet except what nature had given them.[24]

The party made an average of ten miles per day. Twelve to fifteen dead were buried at each stopping place. The observer was impressed by the fact that the Indians did not travel on

[22] Richardson, *Messages and Papers of the Presidents,* 3, 497. (The italics are the author's.)
[23] *A Native of Maine Traveling in the Western Country,* in *New York Observer,* Jan. 26, 1839, quoted by Grant Foreman in *Indian Removal,* 305-311.
[24] *Ibid.*

the Sabbath, which, he says, should be a lesson to the American nation.

"When the Sabbath comes, they stop, and not merely stop, they must worship the Great Spirit, too, for they had Divine service on the Sabbath, a camp meeting in truth."

Commenting on the appearance of the emigrants, the observer says:

"Some carry a downcast look bordering on despair; others a wild frantic appearance as if about to burst the chains of nature and pounce . . . upon their enemies. Most of them seemed intelligent and refined. Mr. Bushyhead . . . is a very intelligent and interesting Baptist clergyman. Several missionaries accompany the party."

Many of the Indians, through industry and thrift, had acquired means and property before the removal. The traveler comments upon such a case:

"One lady passed us in her hack in company with her husband, apparently with as much refinement as any of the mothers of New England; and she was a mother, too, and her youngest child, about three years old, was sick in her arms, and all she could do was to make it as comfortable as circumstances would permit. She could only carry her dying child in her arms a few miles farther, and then she must stop in a strange land and consign her much loved babe to the cold ground, without pomp or ceremony, and pass on with the multitude." [25]

"When I passed the last detachment of these suffering exiles," the traveler comments: "and thought that my countrymen had expelled them from their native soil and their loved homes, . . . I turned from the sight with feelings which language cannot express, and wept like childhood. I felt that I would not encounter the secret prayers of one of those sufferers, if there be a God who avenges the wrongs of the injured, for all the lands in Georgia." [26]

[25] *Ibid.*
[26] *Ibid.*

8

Henry Parker accompanied the detachment of Rev. Stephen Foreman. He wrote from Fredonia, Kentucky, on Nov. 27, 1838, to his friend Rev. John D. Wilson, at Maryville, Tennessee.[27]

"Our company consists of Dr. Hodsden, myself, Mr. Blunt,[28] Mr. Hunter, Clerk of the detachment, and our wagoner. Each individual draws daily one pound of beef or pork, or three-fourths pound of bacon; one pound of flour, or three half-pints of meal. There are issued to each hundred rations, four pounds of coffee, eight pounds of sugar, three pounds of soap, and four of salt.

"We have 950 persons, 353 horses and steers, and 50 wagons. When we encamp for the night, we extend half a mile. We have had eight or ten births on the road, but it has not hindered us any from traveling.

"The sickness in the detachment is considerably subsided. Most of the deaths of late have been relapses, or from over-eating and imprudence. The detachments which have gone before have suffered much more sickness than we have. I saw Susan Bushyhead yesterday. She said her brother Jesse lost two or three by death every night. Her brother Isaac, Dr. Powell, the physician of their detachment, and their commissary, were lying at the house where he saw her, very dangerously sick of a fever. She also showed me a letter from Dr. Butler,[29] of the second detachment, stating that he had three hundred cases of sickness in that detachment.

"Our detachment seems to be very well united. Several strangers have remarked that they did not believe that as many white people could be collected and taken through the country with as little trouble as our Indians are."[30]

The greater portion of the journey was made among people who had not supported the Cherokee removal, and many of whom had opposed it actively. The unhappy emigrants attracted, therefore, sympathy and even friends as they proceeded. Parker comments:

[27] Original owned by Mrs. R. N. Ragain, grand-daughter of Rev. John D. Wilson. Quoted by courtesy of Lawson McGhee Library, Knoxville.

[28] Rev. Ainsworth E. Blunt, missionary at Brainerd. His daughter, Mrs. T. H. Kirby, of Dalton, Ga., survives (1936).

[29] Dr. Elizur Butler, who was imprisoned with Worcester.

[30] Letter of Henry Parker, see Note 27.

"Last Sabbath and today Mr. Foreman preached to large congregations of white people who came in for that purpose. This evening he rode back five miles to preach in a village where he and his family, Mr. Blunt, and myself, dined yesterday with a stranger, though a warm friend to the missionaries and Indians.

"We have found several friends since we started. Mr. Foreman has preached several times in villages through which we passed. Four miles the other side of Nashville, he preached, and at the close of his sermon when he came to speak of the cruelties and wrongs the Indians had suffered, I think every individual was in tears, and many sobbed aloud. He was invited the next day to preach in Nashville, where he received thirty or forty dollars in money for the benefit of his detachment. The next day, Mr. Dunn, who married Eliza Boyd, invited him and his family, Dr. Blunt, and myself, to dine with him, which we did, and they appear to be a very pleasant couple." [31]

"For two weeks, we have had very cold and freezing weather, which has made it very uncomfortable for traveling, especially for the women and children. We expect much suffering before we get through, which will not be until the last of February." [32]

### 9

Among those who fell by the wayside on the frozen roads of Kentucky was the old Chief Whitepath, *Nunne-unaga,* who had once rebelled at the adoption of the white man's customs by his people. He was buried by the roadside, and a peeled pole with a white flag was erected to notify those who followed, that they might pay homage to a brave man and a chief.

The Mississippi was reached opposite Cape Girardeau in Illinois, in midwinter. Crossing was delayed by ice in the river. James Mooney, who talked to survivors fifty years later, found that half a century had not erased the memory of "the halt by the frozen Mississippi, with hundreds of sick and dying penned in wagons or stretched upon the ground with only a blanket to temper the January wind." [33]

The crossing was at last completed, and two months later, in March, 1839, the long journey was finished. Four thousand Cherokees, men, women, and children, had been left in un-

---

[31] William Dunn was originally of Sevier County, Tenn., and removed to Blount County where he married Eliza Boyd. He was later editor of a paper at Huntsville, Ala., where he died.

[32] Letter of Henry Parker.

[33] Mooney, *Myths of the Cherokees,* 133.

marked graves along the saddest trail in American history.[34] Among them was the wife of John Ross, adding the pain of bereavement to his heart-break at the ruin of his people.

Every scalp, every burning, every massacre, had been expiated. The Cherokees had given their country. They had borne their cross.

Three months after the arrival in the new home, Major Ridge, his son John Ridge, and Elias Boudinot, who had been the leaders in signing the treaty which caused the removal, were executed under the Indian law; selling tribal lands without authority. John Ross was recognized as the chief of a reunited nation which began its existence in new surroundings. It was a bitter existence for many years, finally faced again with the old question of the white man's greed for the Indian's land.

---

[34] The Cherokees called it *Nunna-da-ul-tsun-yi*, "Trail where they cried."

# CHAPTER XXXVI

## TSALI

### I

Quite a number of Cherokees had eluded General Scott's soldiers, or escaped from emigrating parties, and fled to the wilds of the Great Smoky Mountains. There were probably fifteen hundred in all. The refugees placed themselves under the leadership of a chief called *Utsala* (Lichen), and took refuge in the rough and inaccessible region around the headwaters of the Ocona-Luftee and Tuckasegee Rivers.

There is one whose story should be told, for it illustrates the undying love of the Cherokees for their mountain homes, and had an important bearing on the future of those who had escaped from the soldiers.

*Tsali* (Charley) was a middle-aged Cherokee who lived on the border-line between North Carolina and Tennessee. One morning soldiers appeared at the door of his little cabin. Tsali, his wife, brother, and two sons were started toward the stockade at Calhoun, Tenn., for removal to the West.

Tsali's wife did not walk fast enough to suit her guard; he prodded her with his bayonet, admonishing her to move faster. This treatment of his wife was beyond the endurance of Tsali. He sprang upon the soldier, wrested away his gun, and killed him with the bayonet. His brother likewise grappled a soldier and killed him. Before the others had recovered from the surprise and chagrin caused by the unexpectedness of the attack, Tsali and his family had fled. They escaped and joined the refugees under Utsala.

Immediately upon the conclusion of his agreement with Ross whereby the Cherokees were to remove themselves, General Scott had relieved three regiments from their Cherokee-removal duties. Two were sent to the Canadian border, where trouble with England threatened; the other was sent to Florida where the Seminoles were at war with the United States. Two regiments were left to complete the removal work. Scott's presence was needed elsewhere and he realized that the

JOHN ROSS (GU′WIS-GUWI′) IN 1835

From McKenney & Hall's copy of the original painting, made while Chief Ross was in Washington to protest the removal of the Cherokees.

running down of every Cherokee who was a fugitive in the mountains would require months. The Tsali incident offered opportunity for a compromise.

William H. Thomas, a lifelong friend of the Cherokees, adopted son of *Yona-Gunski* (Drowning Bear), a prominent chief, was engaged to carry a message to Utsala, proposing that Tsali, his brother, and his two sons be surrendered to him to be put to death for the killing of the soldiers. He would then permit the remainder of Utsala's followers to stay in their mountain fastness until their case could be taken up with Congress in an effort to obtain permission for them to remain permanently.

Thomas made his way over mountain paths to Utsala's hiding place and presented the proposition to the chief. The heart of Utsala was bitter; his wife and child had died of starvation on the mountainside. He considered the thousands of his countrymen in exile who had sworn never to leave the land of their fathers. Better a few should die than all; but Tsali must be convinced.

Therefore Thomas journeyed without escort to the cave where Tsali had taken refuge, and delivered Scott's ultimatum. His brother and sons agreed that if Tsali went, they would go with him. Accordingly they came in and surrendered to General Scott. History records no finer act of patriotism.

Several members of Utsala's band had accompanied Tsali to show Scott that the chief had accepted the terms of the offer. All of the Indians, in charge of a squad of soldiers, were sent to the spot on Tuckasegee River where the murders had been committed. Tsali, his brother, and eldest son, were shot. To impress the Cherokees with their helplessness, Utsala's warriors were required to act as the firing squad. The victims were buried in unmarked graves.

Tsali's younger son, a mere lad, was allowed to return to the hiding place of his people to tell the story.

Due to the sacrifice of Tsali and his kin, the refugees were allowed to remain in the remote region of western North Carolina. Later through the efforts of Major Thomas, they were allowed to buy their land in fee simple, on which approximately 2500 Cherokees live at the present time. The son who had returned, took the name of Washington, *Wasituni* in Cherokee, and his family is still prominent on the reservation.[1]

2

On June 18, 1838, General Charles Floyd, in command of Georgia militia, wrote to Governor Gilmer:

"I am fully convinced that there is not an Indian within the limits of my command. Georgia is ultimately in possession of her rights in the Cherokee country." [2]

The Cherokee titles having been extinguished in their own country, it would seem but fair that the Indians should enjoy complete security in title to the Western lands which had cost them so dearly. As early as 1824, however, when the new State of Arkansas had been organized, a section of its constitution provided the western boundaries of the State should be as originally fixed by Congress "when the Indian titles had been extinguished." [3] That ever recurring clause had pursued the Cherokees since the first agreement between the United States and Georgia, in 1802. John Ross, in conversation with President Jackson in 1833, had asked: "If you cannot protect the Cherokees against infringement on their rights in Georgia, how can you protect them against similar evils in the West?" [4]

A Creek chief, Speckled Snake, speaking at the Creek National Council in 1836, presented the plea of all the Southern Indians in words that cannot be surpassed: [5]

"Brothers: *We have heard the talk of our Great Father; it is very kind. He says he loves his red children.*

"Brothers, *when the white man first came to these shores,*

---

[1] The Tsali episode is from Mooney, *Myths of the Cherokees,* 131, and is authenticated by General Scott's official reports. Twenty-five years later, Major W. H. Thomas prepared for the use of the Confederate Government, an enrollment of the Cherokees, which contains this entry:

"Paint and Wolf Towns, Upper Qualla, Haywood County.

"#54, Charley, shot by the Cherokees in the presence of the troops on Tennessee River in 1838, for the murder of two United States soldiers. Aged 50 years."

Similar entries were made for the brother and son. Tsali's wife and younger son, Washington, were residing on the reservation at the time the enrollment was made in 1863. Washington was interviewed when an old man, by James Mooney.

[2] Foreman, *Indian Removal,* 271.
[3] *Ibid.,* 247.
[4] *Ibid.*
[5] Drake, *Indians of North America,* 450.

*the Indians gave him land, and kindled fire to make him comfortable. When the Pale Faces of the south* (Spaniards) *would have taken his scalp, our young men drew the tomahawk and protected him.*

*"But when the white man had warmed himself at the Indian's fire, and had filled himself with the Indian's hominy, he became very large. He stopped not at the mountain tops, and his foot covered the plains and valleys. His hands grasped the eastern and western seas. Then he became our Great Father. He loved his red children, but said, 'you must move a little farther, lest by accident I tread upon you.'*

*"With one foot he pushed the red men across the Oconee, and with the other he trampled down the graves of our fathers. But our Great Father still loved his red children, and soon made them another talk. He said much, but it all meant, 'Move a little farther; you are too near me.'*

*"Brothers: I have heard many talks from our Great Father, and they all began and ended the same. When he made us a talk on a former occasion, he said, 'Get a little farther; go beyond the Oconee and the Ocmulgee,—there is a pleasant country.' He also said, 'It shall be yours forever.'*

*"Now he says, 'The land you live upon is not yours. Go beyond the Mississippi; there is game; there you may remain while the grass grows and the rivers run.'*

*"Brothers: Will not our Great Father come there also? He loves his red children, and his tongue is not forked."*

THE END

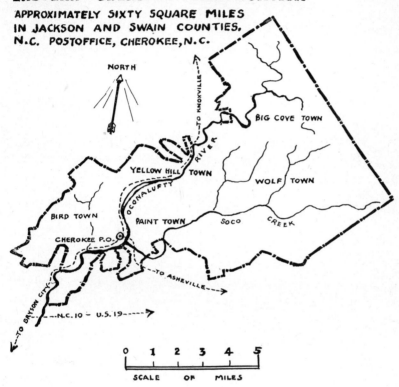

### EASTERN CHEROKEE RESERVATION
APPROXIMATELY SIXTY SQUARE MILES
IN JACKSON AND SWAIN COUNTIES,
N.C. POSTOFFICE, CHEROKEE, N.C.

NORTH

TO KNOXVILLE

BIG COVE TOWN

RIVER

YELLOW HILL TOWN

OCONALUFTY

WOLF TOWN

BIRD TOWN

PAINT TOWN

SOCO    CREEK

CHEROKEE P.O.

TO ASHEVILLE

TO BRYSON CITY

N.C. 10 — U.S. 19

0  1  2  3  4  5
SCALE    OF    MILES

THE EASTERN RESERVATION

Sole remnant of the once mighty Cherokee Hunting Grounds.

# APPENDIX A

## CHEROKEE VOCABULARY

The following Cherokee vocabulary has been compiled with the assistance of *Awi Gatoga* (Standing Deer) of Cherokee, N. C.; Rev. Sibbald Smith, Patrick, N. C.; Will P. Sevier, Hulbert, Okla.; and from Mooney and Adair.

The vowel sounds were: A, as in father; E, as in pet; I as in pique, or short as in pin; O as in note, but approaching aw as in law; U as oo in moon, or short as in pull; and nasalized as in bunt.

Consonant sounds: G, always hard, almost K; the soft G, and Ch, are represented by tsa, tse, or tsi.

Few labials were used. Isaac N. Harris, a printer who helped to set type for the first copy of the Cherokee Phoenix, stated that the Indians could talk all day without closing their lips.

Originally, there were three dialects, distinguished by a slight difference in the use of L, R, and N. The Upper Cherokee said *Ottare,* and the Lower *Atali,* both words meaning *mountain.* L was usually substituted for N, and sometimes for R; as *Tallassee* for Tennessee; and *Tsalagi* for Cherokee.

In nearly every case, the accent is on the last syllable.

Above, the sky, Galun-lati′
acorn, gu-le′; ear, the same.
across, un-tli′
adze, dega′nuda-sti′; the suffix sti indicated sharp.
aged, aga-yunli′; ancient, ka-i-ere′
afraid, daska-sti′
alligator, tsula-ski′
alighted, tsul-kila-nunyi′; he alighted there
also, nu
air, uno-lay′
ambassador, messenger, ganu-seda′
ambush, undi-skalun-gi′, hiding out place; or ahalu′na, to take unawares.
Amoyee, water place, a town on Ocoee River near its junction with Hiwassee, in the present Polk County, Tenn.
and, ale′
ant, tso-sudali′, he has six legs
antler, tsulu-nuhi′; or uskwal-gu′

apple, suguta'; crab apple, suguta-sune'

all, o-wa-sa'

arm, kano-gani'

arrow, da-cleda-ti or da-cleda-taw: the form given by Mooney, gu-ni', is apparently identical with gu-na', bullet.

arrow maker, skina-tlun-ska' da-cleda-ti', he makes arrows.

arrow shaft, ganu-sta' da-cleda-ti'

Arch, John, *Atsi,* an early Cherokee convert who helped to translate the Bible into Sequoyah's characters. His descendants are prominent in the Eastern band.

Apportioner, Ule-lalun-hi'; the sun was so called in the sacred formulas because it divides the day into morning, afternoon.

ashes, gasdu'; Gasdu-yi, ashes place, present location of Asheville.

Attakulla-kulla, Ata-gul-galu, Leaning Wood. Peace Chief of the Cherokees during period of English settlement. Known to whites as The Little Carpenter.

aunt, alu-tsi'

awl, or punch, detala-sti'

axe, man's tomahawk, galu-ya-sti' usdi', little axe.

axe, ceremonial or war hatchet, danawa' ahi' galuya-sti'

axe, woman's domestic, galuya-sti' agi'ya

Ayun-ini', Swimmer. An Eastern Cherokee priest and leader who assisted James Mooney in compiling his myths and formulas. He was very literal. "How would a Cherokee doctor treat a tooth ache?" Mooney asked him, at the same time feigning great pain. Swimmer seized a bottle of ink, sucked it into his mouth, and blew it all over Mooney's face, explaining that it was the only liquid handy, and Mooney seemed to be suffering.

baby, usdi', little; awa-ni' ta, baby deer, was often used.

bad, u-ya-i'; abbreviation of usga-astu', not good, see dreadful.

bad young man, tsun-di' usga'seti

badger, uku'na

bald, uda-wagun'ta, having reference to bald mountain top.

ball, lead bullet, gu-na'

ball, for playing, anet'sa; ball play, same.

ball player, anetsa-unski'; ball ground, anetsa-gada'

ball stick, anetsa taga-lo-de'

bank of stream, amo-ya stu-ni'

basket, talu-tsa'

bark, of tree, tsu-walu'ka; A chief of this name, Chu-wa-looka, led one of the emigrant bands to the West in 1838. He was a great friend to Sequoyah.

bat, tla-meha'

bane berry or cohosh, uda'i

bead, ade'la; beads, di-ade'la; money, same.

beans, tu-ya'

bear, ya-nu (Yonah); bear's grease, yanu-ka'i; bear's meat, yanu-hawe'ya; bear skin, yanu-gana'ki; bear grass, sa-i-qua-yi; ya-nu was pronounced yaw-nuh

beaver, da'yi; beaver dam, dayi-hun'ski, beaver made it.

beard, ahanu-lahu', face hair.

bed, atsi-sta', place to sleep

bee, gasgo-ya'; beeswax, wadule-si galu', honey container.

beloved, agi'ga-u-e', meaning literally, beloved woman. See Nancy Ward.

below, or lower, ela'di; lower dialect, era'ti

bell, ahalu'nee

beetle, large snapping, tsul-sku-wa', snaps with head.

big, or great, egwa'; the suffix ya meant principal, or great.

Big Dipper, constellation, Yan-egwa', Big Bear.

Bighead or Bullhead, Uskwale'na, a chief about 1738.

birch tree, dalaw'nega adah, yellow wood.

blow gun, tu-gwe'sti; blow gun arrow, gee'tsi

bird, tsis-kwa', pronounced chees-qua

bite, ada-skalu'tsi

bitter, tsuna-tsa-yasti', sharp tasting.

black, gune'ga

blackberry, ganu-gala'

black drink, gunega ada-ta-sti'

Black Eyed Susan, *Rudbeckia,* awi-akta, deer's eye.

Black Fox, Inali, Dragging Canoe's nephew; Principal Chief about 1819.

blackbird, gunega-tsiskwa'

blacksnake, small, uk-su'hi; large, gule'ga, the climber

blanket, unagu-hu'

blind, di-ge-wi'

blood, gi-ga'; bloody, giga-ha-i'

Bloody Ground, Kentucky, Gan-da giga-ha-i'

blood brother, dani-taga'; "standing so close together as to form one"

Bloody Fellow, Eskaqua; Yunwi-giga', Bloody Person, usually written Noone-teya. A prominent chief from about 1756 until after the Revolution. He visited Washington at Philadelphia, and the President conferred on the name Eskaqua, Algonkin for Clear Sky. In Cherokee the name would be Galunti-yiga'

blue, saha'ni; abbreviation of sa-ka-na-ga'

bone, kalu'

bouncing, as a ball, ka-sti'

bow, galo-tsa-di; usually abbreviated ga-tso'-di

bow and arrows, gatso'-di ale da-cle-datah'

bow string, gatso'di dadi'

bowl, small, tu-sti'; large, diwa'li

boy, uwagi-atsu-tsa'

brass, untsa-yi'; usually abbreviated tsu-yi'

branch, small stream, ste-wa'yi

brave, bravery, ule'tsu-ya-sti'

bread, gatu'; corn bread, tsalu' gatu'

Breath, Unli'ta, Chief of Nickajack, killed in 1794. The name indicated long winded, i.e. a good runner.

breech clout, or stroud, gato'la yatu-sulo', something to cover privates.

briar, kanu-tsu'

bright, utsi'stalu-giski'

brother, ditlu-nu-tsi', same mother. Brothers, eda-ditlu-nutsi, "we, sons of the same mother." The form ungi-nay'li or di-ginay'li, friends, was used interchangeably by the Cherokee orator for Brothers.

brown, wadi-ğa-i'

buck, male deer, gala-gi'na

bug, diga'nawa'li

bull, tsu-kana-sta'ti

Bulltown, probably same as Citico, which see. Stecoyee; a town at the mouth of Chickamauga Creek.

bullfrog, kunu'na

bullet, gu-na'

burden or pack, asgwa'lihu'; see horse

burn, atsi'la; the cedar was so called because cedar bark was used for kindling fires.

butterfly, kama'ma

buzzard, su'li; or di-la'


cairn, rock burial, dagal-gun'yi; they are piled up there

caller or mocker, to imitate bird or animal, a-yeli'ski

cane, reed used for fishing, e-ya'

cane, staff, uda-la-nu'sti

canoe, tsi-yu'

cannibals, yunwi-g̈iski', man eaters

camp, su-sti-yi'; campfire, atsila susti-yi'

carrier, diye'tsi; abbreviation of dane'tsi-ski'

cat, we-sa, Indian attempt to pronounce "pussy."

captive, ahu'tsi; the term was synonymous with slave. One of the war titles was dahu-digi'ski, slave catcher.

catch-fly, rattle-snake's master, gani-dawa'ski

catfish, tsul-stanu'yi, he has a beard.

cat tail, marsh plant, atsilu'ski, fire maker.

Catawba, Ani-tsagwa, a Carolina Indian tribe.

Catoosa, Gatu'si, a mountain. See mountain.

cave, usta-gala-yi

chair, gaski'la

charcoal, gina'ski

cedar, atsi'la

Chattanooga, from the Creek, Chado-na-ugsa, "Rock that comes to an end." The name was originally applied to Lookout Mountain.

Chatooga, probably from Tsa-tu-gi-yi, "I have crossed there," to indicate a river crossing. The name may have been simply gatu'gi, a town. The name of a settlement near the present La Fayette, Ga.; and another at Tellico Plains.

Cherokee, Tsa-lagi' or Tsal-ragi'. The name is probably derived from Atsila-gi-ga-i', Red Fire Men. Red was the emblem of bravery with the Cherokees; and bravery was derived from the East, or sunrise. The name would therefore indicate that the Cherokees were children of the sun, brave men.

chestnut, ut-ti'; western version di-le'; chestnut bread, diskwa'ni

Chestuee, Tsistu-yi, rabbit place; a town on Hiwassee River at the mouth of Chestuee Creek, Polk County, Tenn.

chickadee, tsi-ki-li-li, its cry.

chicken, tsu-ta-gu', the ruffed grouse

Chief, Un-ga-nu-we-u-we; probably abbreviation of asga-ya yunwi-yunwi, very great man; the rank is emphasized by repetition.

Chief, war, danawa'ga-we-u-we'

Chief, peace, du-we-u-we wanida'tsi

Chickasaws, Ani-tsiksa

child, ayu'le; children, dini ayu'le

Chimney Tops, Duni-skwal-guni, forked antlers, twin peaks in the Great Smoky Mountains.

chipmunk, ground squirrel, ki-u'ga

Chickamauga, Creek, Cukko-micco, pronounced Chukko-micco, dwelling place of the war chief. At the present Chattanooga, on the creek which gave its name to the seceding branch of the Cherokees in 1777.

Chote, Etsa'ti-yi, council place. The name means literally "They met there." The principal town or capital of the Cherokee Nation on Little Tennessee River near the present Von Ore, Monroe County, Tenn.; also a town on Unicoi Turnpike in Habersham County, Ga. New Echota, later the capital, was near the present Calhoun, Ga.

chosen, su-ye-ta'; he is chosen; asuyeta'; I choose, ga-su-ye-u'

chunky, the discoidal game, tsun-ge'; from tsun-gayun'yi, they are running. Chunky-yard, tsun-ge-yi'. The game was often called gata-ya-sti', sharp or hard running.

Citico, Utsu-ti-gwa-yi, fishing place, literally, big fish there. An important town on the Little Tennessee at the mouth of Citico Creek, Monroe County, Tenn.; and another at the present Chattanooga. Sometimes spelled Settico.

Clans, the seven of the Cherokees:

Ani-gatu-ge-wi', Ani Kituwah, Kituwah People.

Ani-gila'hi, Long Hair People.

Ani-kawi', Deer People

Ani-sahani, Blue People, literally Blue Paint People.

Ani-Tsiskwa', Bird People

Ani-wadi', Paint People, literally Red Paint People.

Ani-waya', Wolf People.

According to the myths, an eighth Clan, Ani-tsa-gu'hi, People-who-disappeared, became the bears.

clay, gada-gwa'la, hence Qualla, the Eastern Reservation originally.

clear, yi-ga'; also noonday, 12 M.

climb, lu-hi'; climber, gule-ga'; I am climbing, tsi-lihu'

Clingman's Dome, peak in Smokies, Kuwa'yi, huckleberry place.

clothing, agwa-nu'

clouds, or cloudy, uni-tsi-la'

closed, gewi', also blind. Constipation, tsun-de-gewi', they have them closed. They have their ears closed, tsun-gulis-gewi'

cold, u-yun'-tsa

Conahaney, kanahe'ni, sour corn mush.

Conasauga, Guna-soquo, one bullet or one arrow; probably so called from an unusual feat of marksmanship. A town reached by De Soto in the present Polk County, Tenn.

cook, ada-sta-yu-hu'ski; cooked, uwanu-suhi'; cooking, gu-ne-sti'

conceived, ne-han-du'

conjuror, ada-wehi', also dadu-ne-ski'

compass, ala-ni agada'di, land stealer.

corn, tsa-lu'; corn meal, tsalu-esi'; parched corn, tsalu-guwe-sa'; corn meal pudding, u-gana-sta'; corn tassel, utsi-tsa-ta'

Coosawatie, Kusa-watie-yi, Old Creek Place; an important town on Coosawatie River, Gordon County, Ga.

Coota-cloo-hi'; Gada-kalu'yi, bones on the ground there, a town on Valley River near the present Murphy, N. C.

council, ana-ska'; council house, ana-ska-yi'. The council house was often called gatu'yi, town house.

cow, wa-ka', from the Spanish va-ca. Cow-itch, flower, ga-ne-da'

coward, cowardice, uski-anu'

country, this land, Ani-tsalagi-ga-tohi', "Given to the Cherokees."

Cowe', Ani-kawi', Deer Place. An important town on Little Tennessee near Franklin, N. C., probably the original site of the Deer Clan.

Coyatee, Kai-eti-yi, Sacred Old Place, a town at the mouth of Little Tennessee River, Loudon County, Tenn.

cracked, unest-la'

crane, ganu-tsi-tali'

crawfish, tsistu-na, little rabbit; or tsi-ska gili', thunder's dog.

crazy, insane, una-sti-ski; or ugala-yunwi', foolish person

creation, dine'tlana'

creek, small river, amo-awa'ya

Creek, people, Ani-Kusa. Lower Creeks, Ani-Kawita

Creek Path, Kusa-nunnehi', a town at the present Guntersville, Ala.

cricket, tala-tu'; often called detala-yeski', the barber, because it gnaws hair from furs.

cross, ugly or mean, a-sga'si-ti

crossing place, ford, asa-tun'yi; I have crossed, gatu'gi

crow, ka-gu'

Crowtown, Kagun'yi, one of the Five Lower Towns, near the present Stevenson, Ala.

Currahee, gurahi'yi, water cress place, hence Currahee Mountain.

Dahlonega, Dalaw'nega, yellow; gold, atila-dalaw'nega, yellow money.

daisy, uwadu-gada'

dance, tsal-tsi-ski'; or uls-ğis-ku'

| | |
|---|---|
| Green corn dance, | tsalu'uls-ğisku' |
| Eagle tail dance, | awa'li uls-ğisku' |
| Scalp dance, | utsi-naga'uls-ğisku' |
| Victory dance, | dale-na-heda' uls-ğisku' |
| War dance, | danawa uls-ğisku' |
| They are dancing, | ana-uls-ğisku' |
| Townhouse dance, | uni-kawi uls-ğisku' |

dance ground, detsa-nun'li

dark, ule-se-ki'

daughter, a-gwe'tsi; his daughter, u-wetsi

day, e-ga'; daylight, ega-guti'

deaf, tsune-la'

dead, duha-sata'

death, of human, o-yohu'sa; of animal, u-ewa'tsu

death by fire, o-yohu'sa atsi'la

deadwood, for lighting fires, eta-wa'; hence Etowah.

debt, tsun-dan-li'ta

deer, awi'

deer caller or mocker, awi'a-yeli'ski

deer skin, awi'gana'ki

desire, a-kwi-du-lihu', I desire it very much

dew, amo-ga-i', grass water

dewberries, ha-senu-da'

die, o-yohu'si; he will die, tutsi-hu'si; she will die, tuya-hu'si

distance, the prefix w, added to a word, indicates distance.

dog, gili'; puppy, gili-usdi' or gili-ni'ta

dogwood tree, gana-si'ta

domesticated, tame; as an animal, ulu-ni'ta; as a plant, gunu-tlu'ni

doll, ana-lo'di; playing dolls, danay'loha-ski'

doodle bug, yahu'li

door, entrance, stu-ti'; abbreviation of galu-hi-sti'

Doublehead, Tal-tsu'ska, two heads. Often written Talotiskee. A noted chief, brother of Old Tassel and uncle to Watts. Active from about 1788 until his death in 1807.

Dragging Canoe, Tsi-yu'gunsi'ni, from tsi-yu, canoe, and gunsi'ni, he is dragging it. Leader of the war faction of the Cherokees and war chief of the Chickamaugas until his death in 1792. His father, Atta-kulla-kulla, was in early life called Tsi-yu'gunun'ta, "Canoe, he picks it up."

dipper, di-ta-ti'

dirt, gada'; dirty, gada-na-i'

dress, woman's, asa'ni

drill, to bore into, to make hollow, ata-lay'sti

drill, instrument for boring, de-ta-lay'sti

drink, ada-ta'sti

drown, guni'ska

Drowning Bear, Yona-gun'ski, a prominent chief of the Eastern Cherokees during and after the removal. He died in April, 1839.

drum, ahu'li

duck, kawa'na

dwell, e-hu'; dwelling, ehu'yi


eagle, awa'hi-li

ear, gu-le'

ear ornament, ring or bob, da-gule-adu'

earth, e-la'

East, nunda-yi, Sun place in sacred formulas. The ordinary form is di-galun-gun'yi, it comes up there.

eat, tsi'ski; I am eating, tsi-ski-u'; they are eating, uni-tsi-ski

eating bowl, utali'da-de'

eddy, as in water, tsuda-tsa-sun'yi

edge, as of stream, sia-stun'yi

egret, or great white heron, tsis-qua'yi

eggs, tsu-way'tsi

Elder Brother: U-dani du-tlu-nu'tsi; the form u-ginay'li, my friend; or tsun-ginay'li, my friends, was interchangeable.

elk, awi-egwa', great deer.

Ellijay, Ela-tsay'yi, earth green there, an important town on Coosawatie River, Gilmer County, Ga.

elm, dawagu'la

emphasis, to add, the suffix tsi-ki' is sometimes added; as au-stu', good, and austu-tsi-ki', best of all. The suffix -i was sometimes used, as u-ginay-li-i', very much friend, or strong friend.

enemy, danada'ska-gi'; enemy's country, u-ga-do-hi'

Estatoe, Esta-ta-wi', expelled, or put out. A town on upper Keowee River, Pickens County, S. C.

Etchoe, Itsa-hi-yi', new green place. A pass at the present Cullasaja, N. C., about two miles east of Franklin, where Montgomery and Grant were ambushed by Cherokees, 1760-1761.

Etowah, Ita-wa', deadwood place; an important town near the present Rome, Floyd County, Ga.


fairy, yine'hi; fairies, nunne-hi; water spirits, ama-yine'hi; the little people, yunwi-tsun-di'

Fall, season, Ula-ga-ha'sti

fall, to fall down, nu-gi'; I fall down, tsi-nugi'; he fell, ganu-gi'; falling
    continually, as water, gu-gala'ski
falling off, as leaves, ada-teli'
family, tsi-dana-lu'
far, the prefix w- indicates distance.
fast, to refrain from eating, ina-hi-yu'
fast, speed, ga-tsa-nu'li; he is a fast runner, yalu-anu'li
fastened, tied, tsu-ga-nun'yi
fat, ka-le-tsa'hi-di'
father, do-da'; my father, ga-doda'; your father, e-doda'
fault finder, grumbler, yan-da-ska-gi'; one of the myths contained the refrain,
    "Yandaska-gi hunya-hu'ska," The fault-finder will die.
fear, a-ska-i'
feather, u-lunu-hi'; plural tsu-lunu-hi'
feather headdress, gedala'stu-la'
feathers, eagle tail or wing, tsu-gi' duli'; abbr. of tsu-gi dawa'li
female, agi'si, see woman.
fern, yan-utse'stu, bear's bed.
field, lage'si; old field, ka-lage'si; edge of field, tla-ge'si; cultivated field,
    ga-ge'si
fight, atsi-lahu', I am fighting
Fighting Town, Walas-unul-sti-yi', a settlement on Fighting Town Creek,
    near Morgantown, Fannin County, Ga.
finished, udu-la'; unfinished, u-tulu-la'
fire, atsi'la; old fire, aya-ta-ski'; new fire, ga-taw'
fire, blaze of, adawa-la-ği-ski, it eats the deadwood.
fire, coals of, u-ge-sti-li'
fire, hunting by torch at night, atsun-sta-ti'
fire maker, atsil-sunti'
fire, sacred, atsila- galun-kwe-ti-yu'
fire place, gado-di-yi'; or atsila-yi'
fire water, amo-atsila
fish, u-tsu'ti; fishing, asu-hu-ska'; fisherman, asu-hi-ski'
fish net, de-sa-di'; fish trap, uga-yun-tu-ni'
fish, special, dak-wa', great mythical fish
            tuga-lu'na, long nose fish
            ugun-sti-li', horny nose fish
flat, aya-teni'; flats, diya-teni'
flax or hemp, u-tale'ta
flea, tsu-ga', or kase-he-la'
flea-bane, atsil-sunti', something to make fire
flint, tawi'ska-lun'ti, smooth
Flint, supernatural being, Tawiska'la
floor, aya-ditla-hu'
flower, a-tsi-law'ski; usually abbreviated tsi-law'; the flowers were called
    collectively, ani-tsila'ski, flower people.
fly, insect, ani-ska'
flyers, all insects, ani-nahili-dahi', winged people.
food, aği-ski'; foods, uni-ğis-ki'; see eat.
foot, tsu-na'; foot-prints, utsu'ni; footprints in trail, utsula-sinun'yi
foot log, asun'tli; abbreviation of asun-tlun'yi
ford, crossing place, asa-tsun'yi
forest, tsalu'yi; also swampy place.
fort, ani-ya-ska' nuna-yu-di'

forked, digu'ni; forked tongue, digun-tsu'gi

forget, tsu-ga'wa; forgotten, tsa-wo-ne-su'ga

fox, tsu'la

friend, ginay'li; plural, di-ginay'li; my friend, a-ginay'li; my very good friend, or strong friend, a-ginay'li-i'

frog, gwal-gu'; toad, wala-si'; spring frog, dut-stu'; bull frog, kunu'nuh; tree frog, da-li'

Frogtown, Wala-si-yi, a settlement on Frogtown Creek, Lumpkin County, Ga.

gall, ata-tsu'

game, wild animals, ena-ga-ya'hi

game, to play, ala'ska-le-ha'

garden, adu'ski

garter, ana-tla-sti'; plural, dina-tla-sti'

get, he-tsi'; get out, ta-yi'

girl, agi-usdi', little woman

glass, ada-ke-ti'

Glass, Tagwa-dihi'; a well known chief from about 1790 until the agitation for removal. He was one of an emigrating party in 1828, and died shortly after reaching the West.

ghost, asgi'na

go, parting salutation, hwi-la-hi'. The person departing said, "Na-hwun-yu-ga-i', *Now I am going";* and the host replied, "Hwi-la-hi'," *Go, then.*

go to sleep, hi-lu-nu'; you go to sleep, ega-si-nu'

gnat, ana-to-ga'

Going Snake, Ina-du-na-i'; an old chief at the time of removal, 1838. One of the western Districts was given his name. See Notally.

ginseng, yunwi-usdi', little person.

gobbler, kana'tsi

goat, awi-ahalu'na, bearded deer.

goiter, dule'tsi, kernels; or gata'sti

gold, dalaw'nega, yellow; hence Dahlonega.

good, as-tu'; very good, astu-tsi-ki'

goose, wild, tuga-lu'; tame, sa-sa'

gorget, breast ornament, a-hee'

grand-child, uni-si'; my son's child, so-gini-si'
                      my daughter's child, ungi-li-si'

To indicate sex, the word asga-ya'; male; or agi-ya, female.

grand-father, paternal, asga-da-du'; maternal, agi-da-du'.

grand-mother, ali-si' or ani-si'

grapes, wild, una-su-ga'; summer, talun-lati', "they hang high."

grass, guna-ski'; hay, dried grass, guna-sku'

grass hopper, tso-le-tsu-ke'

gray, unaga e-u-sti'

grease or oil, ka-i'

great, big, eg-wa'

Great Island, Amo-yeli-egwa; a town of the Overhill Cherokees on Little Tennessee one mile west of Fort Loudoun. Shown on Timberlake's map as Mialaquo.

Great Spirit, old form after Adair, Yo-he-wah'; modern form Galun-kwa-di etsi-da-du, "Beloved Old Father;" The Great Spirit was often referred to as Asgaya-Galun-lati', "The Man Above."

green, itse'hi
green snake, sa-kwa-yi
grinning, utset'sti; see o'possum and Sequatchie.
ground, ga-da'
ground hog, a'gana'
ground hog sausage, agana-sta'ta; see Oconostota.
grove, lun-yi'; forest, salun'yi
grow, ta-sun'; grown, utanu'; I am growing up, ga-ta-sun'i
gun, galo'gwa; rifle, principal gun, galo'gwa-ya; musket, unuda'na
gun sheath, a-yun-dula'di

Ha! hear, now; introductory exclamation
hack berry, ganu-sta-gwa'la
hair, gitlu'
hair and horses, gitlu ale tsa-gwa'li
hair pins, gi-lu'sti
hammer, gane-kwa-la'sti
hand, u-wa-yi'; plural, diwa'yi; hand breadth, uwa-hilu'
handle, guwa-da'di
hanging, guta'
happy, ale-hale-sti'
hard, a-sti-yihu'
Hard Mush, Gatun-wali, a chief about the time of removal; son of John
    Watts.
hat, uskwa-tewa'
hatchet, galu-ya-sti'; war hatchet, danawa' galu-ya-sti'
have, a-gwa-li-i', I have it.
hawk, tawa'di; sparrow hawk, tawadi usdi'; great mythical hawk, tlanu'wa
he, nahi'
he will die, hun'ya hu-ska'; sentence of death for prisoner.
head, uskă'la
head man, u-ga-we-u-e'
heart, una-wi'
heavy, ga-gay-de-u'
hello, greeting, a-si-yu'; usually abbreviated si-yu'
hemp, wild, gatun-lati'; flax, uta-le-ta'
here, this place, ha-ya-ni'
heron, great white, tsa-wa'yi
hickory, wa-ni'; some varieties, yahu'la
hickory nut, tsa-hi'
hide and seek, game, dana-di-ska-na-lay'
high, galun-la-ti'
hill, gatu'si; see mountain.
Hiwassee, A-hwa'si, a savannah or meadow; an important town at the
    crossing of Hiwassee River of the Great War Trail, in the present Polk
    County, Tenn.
hoe, galaga'di
hold, ti-di-neya'; hold fast, sti-yi-neya'
home, gala-tsa'di; dwelling, e-hu'
hominy, amu-tsi, hence Armuchee; with nuts, ka-nŭ'tsi
honey, wadule'si; or kulse'tsi, sugar
honest, tona-te-u'
honored, sacred, galun-kwi-ta-ga'
horn of animal, tsulu-nuhi'; see antlers.

hornet, se-wha'tu

horse, tsa-gwa'li, he has a burden.

hot, ude-le-ga'

hot house, sleeping quarters, a-si'; from atsi'la, fire.

house, ge-tsa'di

how many? or how much? hila-gu?

huckleberry, guwa-yay'

hungry, gaya-siha'; I am hungry, a-gaya-siha'

hunter, kana'ti

hunting grounds, kana-ti-yi

hunting shirt, kana-gasu-lanu'

husband, u-ya'hi

ice, una-sta-lu'

I, myself, a-ya'

I accept your talk, hiwani'sku da-go-ga'da-ne-luga'si

I am picking it up, (as a war belt) tsi-ni-u'

I am speaking, a-wani-hu'

I have spoken, a-wani-ski'

I have it, a-gwi-li-u'

I am good, (response to salutation), ga-si-u'; see hello.

I speak the truth, tsi-wani-hu' to-e-u'

I speak not with two tongues, tali tsudu-lana-yi dega-wanihu' luwu-di'

I am a friend, a-ginay'li

incomplete, not finished, a-dulu'la; complete, u-dulu'la

I am going to do something, a-yun-dega' da-neli'

Indian, Yun-wi'ya; plural, Ani-yunwi-ya; principal people.

insects, ani-ska'yi

Iroquois, Ani-nunda-wegi'; so called because the Onandagas were keepers of the sacred fire of the Iroquois.

island, amo-yeli, water, in the middle.

I take you by the hand, tsi-aya-uwa'yi

It is true, ha-yu', emphatic affirmative

It is not true, tla-u to-e-u-ha'; lie, atsi-ska-lay'; liar, gaya-ska-ğee'

It is not yet time, u-ta-lu-li'

It is what you will, hale' sku-wa te-ca-le-i'

It is what we will, di-ha-le skuwa-te-cale-i'

Jay bird, tsay-ku, its cry

Jehovah, or Great Spirit, Yo-he-wah'

John Jolly, Ahu-lu-di'ski, Oolutiskee, "He throws away the drum." A prominent chief, owner of Hiwassee Island or Jolly's Island at the mouth of Hiwassee River. He removed West in 1819, and became Principal Chief of the Western band. He was the friend of Sam Houston.

Junebug, ta-gu'; also called tuya'diski-law'stiki, "He keeps the fire under the beans." His coming was supposed to mark the ripening of the beans.

Junaluska, Tsunu-la-hun'ski, "I tried but I failed." A chief of the Eastern Cherokees who fought at Horseshoe Bend.

Kana'sta, abbr. Kana-sta-yun'yi, Running Turkey; Former old Cherokee town near the present Brevard, N. C.

Kallamuchee, a name applied at an early date to Tennessee River; probably from the Creek Tekalla-na Uchee, Uchee Crossing.

katy-did, tsi-ki-ki', its cry. The cry of the katy-did was supposed to indicate that the corn was ripe enough to eat.

keen sighted, ak-ti'na; Uk-tena, great mythical serpent.

keep, or hold to, hi-ne-yu'

key, stu-gi'

kernels, of nuts, dulu'sti; hence Dulu-stini', September, Nut Month.

Kentucky, Gan-da Giga-i', Bloody Ground. Kentucky was invariably so designated by the Cherokees.

Keowee, Kuwa-hi-yi, Huckleberry Place. An important town on Keowee River opposite Fort Prince George, Pickens County, S. C.

Kiachatalee, Tsi-aga-tali', he shot, or killed, two. A young chief of Nicka-jack, killed at Buchanan's Station in 1792.

killer, di-hi'

kill, atsi-dihi'; killed, atsi-sti';

kingfisher, tsu-la', a favorite male name. Tsula-wa-yi, Chilhowie, "Big Kingfisher Place."

knife, haya-la-sti'; The Long Knife, i.e. white people, Gunhi-yalasti'

kneeling, detsi-na-gwa'na

Knoxville, Kuwan'da-ta-lun-yi', Mulberry Grove Place

Kituwah, Gatu-gi-wa'; Principal Town; an old town, the reputed original Cherokee settlement; on Tuckasegee River below the junction with Ocona Lufty, near Bryson City, N. C. Site of the Clan Ani-Gatugi-wa, usually written Ani-Gatege-wi, rendered by mistake, Blind Savannah People. The correct form is Ani-Kituwah, the name by which the Cherokees often designated themselves.

kiss, sqa-nu'tsa


lake, uday'li

land, gada-wahi'; usually abbreviated gada'

laugh, utset'sti; I laugh, aya-utset'sti; they laugh, uni-utset'sti

lead, for ammunition, gu-na', same as bullet.

leader, ula-gu'

leaf, ugalo'tsa; leaves, utalo'tsa

lean, not fat, ula-tsa-di-u'

leaning, galu'; hence Atta-gul-galu', Tall Leaning Wood.

leather, ano-tlu'ski; hide, or skin, kanǎ-ga'

leech, tlanu'si

leggings, dela-sula'

lend, atǎl'sta; I am lending, aya-tal'sta; borrowed, aga-tal'sta

Let me carry you on my back, ka-ma'ma, (the butterfly)

Lichen, Utsay'la; chief of the refugee band during removal.

lie, to recline, u-tsi-stu'

lie, untruth, atsi-ska-lay'; the old form, go-he-ga' was much used in oratory. The person questioning asks, O-E-A? "Is it the truth?" The answer would be, Tsi-a-gohega', "I do not lie," a favorite expression of the Cherokee orator.

life, gano-du'

light, ega'hi, see day.

lightning, asgaya' gi-ga-ge-i', the red man.

like, resemblance, i-yǔ'sti

liquid, tsi-negi' yagu'li, "It is in the water, or other liquid"

listen, ha! abbreviation of ha-duda'sta

little, usdi'; the abbreviation nita, young, was often used.

Little Deer, Awi-usdi', mythical head of the deer clan.

Little Owl, Ookoo-usdi', brother of Dragging Canoe, killed at Buchanan Station, 1792.

Little Turkey, Kana-gi′ta, Principal Chief following the death of Old Tassel in 1788.

liver, uwe′la

lizard, diga-hali′; scorpion, giga-dane′ski, bloody mouth.

locust, insect, uh-lay′, its cry. The Cherokees said, "Uh-lay has brought the beans," its cry denoting the ripening of the crop.

locust, tree, kulse′tsi, also sugar. Hence Cullasaja River, N. C.

log, asi′ta; hickory log, wana-a′ta

Lone Peak, Tsuda-yi-lun′yi, a mountain near the head of Keowee River.

lonesome, na-tsi-ya′, living alone (lonely—in formulas—u-hi-sa′ti).

long, gunhi′ta

Long Island, Amo-yeli-gunhita, one of the Five Lower Towns, on the island still so called, at Bridgeport, Ala.

long eared, the mule, digu′lanahi′ta

long ago, hila′hi-yu′, the suffix u makes it emphatic.

look, dak-ta′; looking, daka-na′; I am looking, detsi-kana′

Long Winded, Unli′ta, the Breath, chief of Nickajack; killed during Ore's raid, 1794.

lose, tsagu′hi; lost, agi-ya′tsu-a-li′

love, ada-ga-u-e′; loves, uga-u-hi-u′; lover, asi-ule′ehu′

low, ala-de-u′, opposite of high, galun-la-de-u, or galun-lati

Long Hair, Gilu-gunhi′ta, a Cherokee chief who participated in the fighting against Wayne in 1794.

Lookout Mountain, Tali-danda-ganu′, "Two looking at each other," the name given by the Cherokees to the two mountains facing each other at Chattanooga, Tenn. The Creeks called the mountain Chado-na-ugsa, "Rock coming to an end," hence Chattanooga.

Lookout Mountain Town, Stecoyee, probably same as Citico, Utsuti-gwa′yi "Big Fish there." On Lookout Creek, one mile above the present Trenton, Dade County, Ga. One of the Five Lower Towns.

Lowery, George, Agi′na-gi′la, Rising Fawn, cousin of Sequoyah. Participated as Major in Creek War, 1814. Assistant Principal Chief (West) about 1840.

Lying Fish, Utsu′ti-ganago′hi, usually abbreviated Utsuta-gana; one of the seceding chiefs, 1777.


magician, priest, medicine man, ada′wehi′

make, gatlun′ska, I make it.

male, gala-gi′na, buck.

man, asga-ya′; plural, uni-asga-ya′; woman, agi′ya

Mankiller, see Outacite.

many, utsu′ti, same as fish.

marry, tsa-ya′; he will marry you, tu-tsa′ ye-si′

married, u-da-la′; the mistletoe was so called because of its attachment to the tree upon which it grew.

maple, kulse′tsi, sugar, see locust.

martin, bird, tlu-tlu′, its cry

Master of Life, Gano-du′gwaludu′ski, Life Master, a name often applied to the Great Spirit.

material, out of which to make something, ga-tsun′ti

Mayapple, unis-kwetu′ski, he has a hat.

May-pop, passion flower, Uwa-ga′-yi, hence Ocoee.

meadow lark, na-kwi′si, star.

medal, or gorget, a-hee'

Memphis, Tsundi-tali-sun'yi, where the banks are falling.

middle, ayet'li; usually abbreviated aye'li

milk, u-nun'ti

Milky Way, Gili-dine-hun'yi, where the dog ran. According to the myth, the dog stole some meal, and when pursued fled across the sky, strewing the meal behind him.

mill, for pounding corn, u-skwal-ti-ga'

mink, sun-gi'; mink family, gaw-sun-gi; see onion.

mirror, dase'ti

mischief, gu-he-yu'; you are mischievous, tsune-guhe-yu'; he is mischievous, une-gu-tsa-tu'; I am mischievous, a-gine-gu-tsa-tu'

mistletoe, uda-la', married.

mixed, u-su-ye'

moccasin, shoe, ulasu'la; boots, tsu-la-wa', big shoes.

moccasin, snake, kane-gwa'ti

mocker, for imitating call of animal, a-yeli'ski; whistle, same.

mocking bird, ska-da-gi'ski, he imitates.

money, adi'la; gold, adi'la dalaw-nega, yellow money.

Months, the twelve; The Cherokee year began with August, month of the Green Corn Dance.

   1. August, Galo'nee, End of Fruit Month.

   2. September, Dulu-stinee', Nut Month.

   3. October, Duna'na-dee', Harvest Month.

   4. November, Nuda'na'egwa', Big Trading Month.

   5. December, U-ski'ya, Snow Month.

   6. January, Unu-la-ta-nee', Cold Month.

   7. February, Gaga-lu'nee, Bony, or Hungry Month.

   8. March, Unu'lahee', Windy Month.

   9. April, Tsi-law'nee, Flower Month.

   10. May, Ana-sku'tee, Planting Month.

   11. June, Da-tsalu'nee, Green Corn Month.

   12. July, Tsa-lu-wa'nee, Corn in Tassel or Great Corn Month.

morning, suna-lee

mortar, u-skwal-tiga; often ganaw'na

mosquito, tso-si'

moss, alu'

mother, et'si; my mother, agi'tsi; his mother, u-tsi; her mother, unet-si; she is a mother, alu-et-si.

mound, ga-u-wa-tlun'yi; earth heaped up there.

moth, tun-ta-wu', "too close to the fire."

mountain or hill, gatu'si, hence Catoosa. In sacred form, ata'la, hence Attalla; or ata-lun-yi, "high there."

mouse, tsis-tĕ'tsi

mouth, aha'li; hence the colloquialism "holler", meaning to yell.

Moytoy, Amo-ada'wehi, Water Conjuror or Rainmaker; chief of Tellico made "Emperor" by Cuming in 1730. He died about 1755.

mud hen or didaper, di-gawa'ni, "they are lame," because they hop along.

mulberry, gu-wa'

mullein, tsalu-yu-sti', tobacco like.

muscadine, talun-la'di, they hang high.

mush, corn meal gruel, kana-hay'na; hence Conahaney.

mush in balls, un-wa'li

mushroom, u-wa'se

mussel, fresh water clam, da-gu'na

Mussel Shoals, Dagu'na-yi, mussel place, now Muscle Shoals.

mud, ga-da-nay'; muddy water, gada-na-amo'

Muscogee, Creeks, Mexco-ulgee, Mexican People. The X has the sound of sh. The Creeks, of Mexican origin, are believed to have landed at the mouth of the Mississippi about the beginning of the 12th Century. The Old Muscogee culture reached as far north as Ohio, and once occupied all of the Tennessee Valley section.

Nacoochee, Creek Na-ku-ce, rich; a settlement in White County, Ga., at the head of Chattahoochie River.

naked, uya-tiga'; they are naked, tsun-ya-tiga'

Nancy Ward, A-gi-ga-u-e, usually written Ghigau. The name means literally, "Greatly Beloved Woman." Nancy Ward occupied the position of Beloved Woman during the period of English settlement. She died in the present Polk County, Tenn., about 1827. Her grave has been marked.

Natchey Town, Natsi-yi, Natchez Place. A settlement on Natchey Creek, Monroe County, Tenn., occupied by Natchez refugees about 1740, when the Natchez towns were destroyed by the French. It was the birthplace of Dragging Canoe, and in later years the home of Attakullakulla.

near, nula-ti or nul'ti

needle, utsu-gwa' gatu-na-u-hi', "for making clothes." Usually abbreviated utsu-gwa'

nest, as of bird, una-sta'la

nephew, ungi-ni'si

Nequassee, Ni-kwa'si, star. An important town at the present Franklin, N. C., where Sir Alexander Cuming held council with the Cherokees in 1730. A large mound marks the townsite.

net for fishing, dasu-du-di'

Nettle Carrier, Tala-dane-giski', brother of Doublehead, killed at Ish's Station, 1793.

Nickajack, Ani-kusati-yi, Old Creek Place, one of the Five Lower Towns, at the present Shellmound, Marion County, Tenn. The cave at Nickajack was called by the Creeks Tecallassee, which means Old Crossing Place.

night, suna'yi

noon, e-ga'

no, negative, klu-nun; or ha-le-nu.

Nolachucky, Nula-tsu'gu-yi, Spruce tree place.

North, aya-stalu'yi, ice there, or ice place

nose, kaya-sa'

not, negative, same as no.

Notally, Ina'dula-i', Going Snake Place. A settlement on Notally River near the Georgia line, Cherokee County, N. C.

now, ka

nut, tsa-hee'

nuthatch, bird, tsule'na

numerals: 1, so-qua'; 2, ta-li'; 3, tsa'i; 4, nun'ki; 5, hi'ski; 6, su-tali; 7, gul-kwa'gi; 8, su'nali; 9, so'nali; 10, skä'hi;

The teens were indicated by adding the suffix *DU*, as 11, so-adu'; 12, tali-du'; 13, tsa-du', etc.

Numbers above 20 were indicated as "two tens," "three tens," as 20, tali-ska'hi; 30, tsa-ska'hi.

100 was ska-egwa, "great ten."

oak, ata-ya', principal wood.

oar, gaga-wa-sti'

Ocoee, Uwaga-hi-yi, Maypop Place. A town on Ocoee River near its junction with Hiwassee, Polk County, Tenn.

Oconee, egwa'ni, river. Sometimes written Acquone.

Ocona-lufty, Egwani-nulti, beside the river. A settlement near the present Bird Town on the Eastern Reservation.

old, aga-un'li or e'ti

Old Hop, Kana-gatoga', Standing Turkey. Chief who succeeded Moytoy as Emperor about 1755. He died in 1760.

Old Tassel, Kai-ya-tahee', Principal Chief, succeeding Attakullakulla in 1777. He was killed under a flag of truce in 1788.

old time, kai-ere'

old town, kai-gatu'gi, or e'ti-gatu'gi

old woman, aga-we'la

one who goes about, personal name, eda'hi

Ooltewah, Un-tewah', resting place. A town in the present Hamilton County, Tenn.

onion, sun'gi

Oostanaula, Usta-na'li, an important town near the junction of Coosawatie and Conasauga Rivers, Gordon County, Ga. It was the Cherokee capital about 1790; this was later moved to New Echota. The name signifies a shoals, or rock barrier, in a river, same as the Creek Watauga.

o'possum, si-kwa', or utset'sti, he grins; hence the modern Sequatchie.

Osage, Sa-see'

otter, tsi-ya'

Otter Lifter, Tsiya'hane'ski, a chief of the Chickamaugas who lived at Running Water.

Otter Place, Tsiya'hi; a town at which De Soto stopped in 1540, believed to be Jolly's Island, later Hiwassee Island. De Soto's route has not been definitely proven.

Outacite, Utsi-dihi', Man Killer. A chief who visited England with Timberlake in 1762, and was prominent until after the Revolution. Otherwise called Oostanaca and Judd's Friend.

Over the Hills, Gatoosi-deli'; The Overhill Cherokees who occupied towns along Little Tennessee River, Monroe County, Tenn.


paint, wa-di', especially red paint.

paint mortar or mixing bowl, wadi'galo-da'di

panther, tlun-tu'ski

parched, as corn, guwe-su-he'

pass, mountain, ela-di-u' gala-du-i', low ground place.

partridge moccasin, lady slipper, gugwe'ulasu'la

past tense, indicated by suffix ge-se-i'

path, nun-ne-hi'

Pathkiller, Nunnehi-dihi'; Principal Chief succeeding Black Fox about 1819. He died in 1836, and is buried at New Echota.

peace, tla-le-gwa', hence Tellico, Talequah, Peace Towns.

peas, tu-yun'sti

people, a-ni'

perch, fish, atsu'la

pheasant, tlan-ta-tsi'

persimmon, tsa-la-lu-i', pucker mouth.

person, human being, yun-wi'

personal pronouns, I, a-ya'; you, hi'; he or it, ski-na'
picture, ditli'la-sta-nuhee'; it looks like you.
pigeon, wa-yi'; abbreviation of an-ku-wa'-yi
Pine Log, Natsi-asun-tlun'yi, abbreviated Na-sun'tli; a town on Pinelog
    Creek, Bartow County, Ga.
Pay—of doctor or medicine man—u-gis-ta'-ti. "I take it."
pine tree, na'tsi
pipe, ku-nu-nuwah'; peace pipe, dayo-hee' kununawah'
planting, awe-sku-e'; to plant, awe-sku'; May, Awe-sku'hee, planting month.
please, ule-ha'lesti'
pleased, uleha-lestu-gi'; much pleased, add yu!
pleasant, yeli-u-sta'
plugged or stopped up, u-kwu-nun'ti
Pleiades, Ani-tsu-tsa', the boys.
plum, gwa-nun'sti
plural, indicated by prefix di, sometimes tsi.
poison ivy, ulun'ta, it has climbed.
poor, not rich, ule-sa-da'i
poplar, dalaw'nega utsi-lahun', yellow leaves
porcupine, tsu-tsa-ya'sti une-gwa-gu-le'; he has sharp quills.
possessive, indicated by suffix ni; as uwayi-ni, his hand.
pot, unti'ya, hence Unti-gu-yi, Pot in Water there, the Suck of the Tennessee,
    below Chattanooga.
pot, small cooking, tsu-la'ski
pot, large cooking, utanu-tsu-la'ski; jug, gada-ga-gun'
pottery, anything made of earth was called di-wa'li
pot maker, unti'ya diglu'ski
potsherds, dula-stu'ni
pot scrapings, utsale-ta, from utsala, lichen.
potato, u-li'; lower dialect nu'na; potato like, nuna-yu'sti
pouch, daga'tli
pounding mill, as for corn, u-skwal'tiga'
pounding, act of, tes-ta'ski
pounding rock, or pestle, tes-taski nun-yu'
powder, dawela'giski'
powder horn, dawela giski u-ya-na'
pretty, uwa-du-hee'
Pretty Woman, see Nancy Ward
principal or real, denoted by suffix ya
prisoner, captive, ahu'tsi
pumpkin, i'yah
punch, detala'sti
punk, tawa'li, material for fire starting

quartermaster, chief's assistant on warpath, e-ti-su'
quail, or partridge, gu-gway', its call.
queen bee, leader, u-la-gu'
quiet, daga-sa-sti'; or u-sawa-hi' atsa-wali-hu', everything is quiet.
quiver, decla-da' sto-di', arrow holder.
quiver of arrows, decla-da' tsa-yu-hi'

rabbit, tsis-tu'
race, taki-yati'; race course, un-taki ya-sti-yu', where they race.
raccoon, ku-li'

rafters, das-kwi-tu-ni'

rain, aga-skwa'; it is raining, aga-ska'; it has begun to rain, aga-na'; they make it rain, ani-ganti-ski'; the latter had reference to small lizards supposed to cause rain.

rat, tsis-ta'tsi

rattle, ganse'ti

rattle snake, utsa-na'ti

rattle snake master, campion, gani-da-wa-ski', it disjoints itself

Rattlesnake Springs, Amo-gada' Utsana'ti; a spring two miles south of Charleston, Tenn.; assembly place for removal to West.

raven, kalo'nah

raw, uncooked, ago'sti

Red Bud, Judas tree, ga-ga'ki

Red Bird, Tsisqua-ya, a chief who participated in the murder of the Kirk family, 1788.

Red Clay, Ela-wadi-yi, red earth place. Council ground of the Cherokees after being forced out of Georgia about 1830. The location was at a large spring about half a mile north of the Tennessee State line, at the present Red Clay, Ga. John Ross lived about two miles northward on the present Cleveland-Dalton pike.

The present council ground of the Eastern Cherokees at Cherokee, N. C., is also called Red Clay.

red man, asgaya' giga-ga-i', the lightning; Indian, Yunwi-ya'.

Resurrected One, Christ; Tsulehi-sanun'hi; "I was down and have risen." The name given to the Cherokee National paper at the suggestion of Rev. S. A. Worcester.

revenge, tsu-tsa'si; vengeance, same.

rest, ayi'a-wa'

rich, uwe-nahi'

Richard Justice, Uwenahi' Tsus-ti', "He has wealth, or riches." The word Uwenahi', meaning rich, was used as an abbreviation for the name Richard; "Justice" being a corruption of the Cherokee Tsus'ti, "He possesses." Chief of Lookout Mountain Town 1777, 1794.

Ridge, Major, Ganun-da-le-gi', "He follows the ridge," leader of the "Treaty Party" which advocated removal to the West.

ridge, tsa-le-gi'

ring, une-sta-gu'

Rising Fawn, Agili-gi'na, a chief of the Lower Cherokees about 1790

river, e-gwa'ni; big river, egwa'ni-ma'ya. The Cherokees so called the Tennessee River.

roast, gunta-sku'

roasting ear, tsalu'yi

robbing, sahun'sku

robin, ga-skwa'gu

rock, nun-yu'

run, at-sun'sti; running, ga-yun'yi

runner or messenger, da-tsi-da-hi'

rose, the wild or Cherokee, Tsistu'na-ğis'ka, rabbit's food.

Running Water, Amo-ga-yun'yi, one of the Five Lower Towns, in the present Marion County, Tenn. Destroyed by Ore's men, 1794.

running the gauntlet, ayet'li; abbreviation of ayet-li un-tsi-gaya', "Between the lines of men."

scales, fish, awa-tsu'ska

sacred, holy, eti-kai-ere'

sad, unhappy, na-le-hay' le-gu-nu'

salt, a'ma, first syllable prolonged to distinguish from a-mo', water.

salt lick, gada'uni-ğis-ti-yi', they lick the ground there.

same, a-yun'sti

sand, na-yu'

Saluda, Tsalu-di-yi, Corn Place; the extreme eastern town of the Cherokees on Saluda River, S. C. Glen's treaty, 1755, was held there.

sassafras, ganu-sta'ği

Savannah, Shawa'noe, or Shawnee. Sewanne, same.

scalp, uska-ni-gili, the hair of his head; scalping, uska-ni-giga'luda', taking his head blood.

scent, galu'nusti'; small, same.

scissors, talita-ya-sti', two sharps.

Scolacuta, Skwala-gu'ta; Hanging Maw, Principal Chief, 1782-1794, the name means *fat,* or *hanging stomach.*

scraper, gatsu-wa-sta-di'

scratch, kanu'ka; scratcher, kanu-ka-ski', scratcher of rattlesnake teeth with which ballplayers were scratched before game to lend strength to muscles.

see, he-go-wa'ta; abbreviation of hegowa-akta, what the eyes do.

Seneca, Ani-Sen'iku; an important town on Keowee River at the mouth of Conneross Creek, Oconee County, S. C. The Cherokees were of Iroquoian descent, and this town was probably the original seat of those of the Seneca branch.

Sequatchie, sikwa'utset'tsi, "o'possum, he grins," or grinning o'possum.

Sequoyah, Tsis-kwa'ya, the Sparrow, or Principal Bird. The inventor of the Cherokee alphabet.

sewing, ye-wi'ya; I am sewing, tsi-wi'ya

sharp, as a weapon, ga-sta'yi

sharp words, u-tlun'ta

sheep, awi'unade'na, wooly deer.

shelf, or flat place, daya-tana-lun'ti

shell, u-ya'ska; mussel shell, dagu'na

shoals, usta-lana'li, hence Oostanaula.

shoot, na-da'a-sti-ya-li'; shot, ada-sti-ya-li', "shooting arrow."

shooting with the bow, daga-lo' sta-na-hah'

shooting at a mark, agwa-naha'

short, uska'li; abbreviation of tsus-kwa'li

shout, ta-hi-yu; I shout, ga-ta-hiyu

sinew, used for thread, uwa-du-na'

sinker for fish net, ali-tsi'

sitting, wa-la-tla'; to sit, a-gwa-la-sti'; sit down, tsa-la-di'

skinny, kalu-hu, all bones.

skunk, di-la'; not to be confused with beads, a-day'la

sky, galun-la'ti; clear sky, galun-lati-yi-ga'

skin, ga-nĕ'ga; skinning, da-gane-ga lato-di'

slanting or leaning, gul-galu'

slave, or captive, ahu'tsi

Slave Catcher, Ahu'tsi-di-ski', one who has taken a captive. War title.

sleep, hilu'nu; I am asleep, tsi-li-hu'; go to sleep, ega-si-nu'; gone to sleep, ahu'la

small, us-di'; plural, tsuns-di'

small pox, unu-da-kwa'la, holes in face.

smile, u-tse'tsi

snake button root, unaste'tsisti-yu', Aristolochia serpentaria, remedy for snake bite.

smilax, dunu'ski

smoke, tsus-du'; smoky, du-tsus-du'; rising smoke, tsuna-lu-gi'

smoker, ga-ski'; I am smoking, ga-gis-ku'

smooth, tawi'ska, flint.

snake, i-na'du; the snake family, ani-ada'wehi, supernatural people.

snipe, or killdeer, dasku-dalena-he-da'

snow, un-tsi'; it is snowing, gun-tsi-ha'

snow bird, tu-ti'

son, atsu-sti uwa'gi

soon, natla'gu-kwo'; soon after, ani-kwo'

song, daga-no'ge-da'; to sing, dagano'giski'; he is singing, dagano'ge-ah'

sore, uya'sti, it hurts

sorrel or sour grass, suna-tsa-ya-sti', sharp tasting.

sorrow, abe'le

soul, or spirit, adan'ta

sour, uga'sita

South, uga-la-ya-i', warm there

sparrow, tsis-kwa-ya, principal bird, because so numerous.

spear, dada-sto-di'; or da-tli-de-gwa', big arrow.

speech, wani-hu'; I am speaking, tsi-wa-ni-hu'

spider, kana-nĕ'ski, weaver

split, unest'li

spoil, asti-hu'; spoiler, aya-sti'; I spoil, or make bad, tsi-astihu'

Spring, season, ga-gă-i'

spring, of water, amo-gwa'

spruce tree, nu'na

squash, wa-tsi-gu'

stand, to-ga'; standing, ga-to-ga'

squirrel, gray, sala'li; ground squirrel, ki-u'ga; flying, te-wa'

star, nakwi'si, hence Nequassee

stem, as of pipe, gu-ha-la'hi

stick, da-ga-lo'sti

stickers, cockle burs, etc., uni-sta-lun'sti, sharp people.

sting, dasun-tali'

stomach, u-skwa'li

stone, nun-yu'

storm, unu'la

store house, adana-nu-hi'

straight, gatsi-no-sta'

stream, ste-wa'ya; up stream, ge-i'; down stream, tsa-gi'

Stecoyee, Sticoy; U-tsu'ti-gwa'yi, big fish place, or good fishing place. The name of several towns in the Cherokee country; on Tuckasegee River near Whittier, Swain County, N. C.; near Clayton, Rabun County, Ga.; on Stekoa Creek, Graham County, N. C., and at Lookout Mountain Town, near Trenton, Dade County, Ga. Same as Citico or Settaco.

strike, ka-ya-ne-ga'

strayed, ula-yu-tsi'

straw berries, a-nuh'

strong, uhu'sti

stump, tsun-alu'ga

succotash, salu-tuya-na-dela-nuhi', corn, beans, and pumpkin.

sugar, gulse'tsi

Sugar Town, Gulse-tsi-yi, a town on Keowee River, Fannin County, S. C., also at the present Cullasaja, near Franklin, N. C.

sumac, galo'kwa

Sun or Moon, nun'da; distinguished as nunda-egi-hi', day dweller; and nunda'sunna'yehi', night dweller.

sunrise, de-galun'yi, he comes up there.

sunset, udi-galun'yi, he goes down there.

sunny, uda-ha-lee'

sunny side, udahalee-yi

Summer, Tsa-gu'tsi

swallow, in eating, u-tsis'ka

swallow, bird, tso-dekwa-tlo'tsi, wings crossed.

swamp, ega'tega'wi, thicket place.

sweat, ali'alu'; sweat bath, ali-alu uta-wa'sti

sweet, aga-na'sti

sweet gum, tsi-lalu'

swim, yu-ni'

Swimmer, A-yu-ni'ni, a prominent chief of the Eastern band who assisted James Mooney in compiling his Cherokee data.

sycamore, tsu-wa'tsune'ga, white bark

Sycamore Shoals, Watauga, from the Creek we-to'ga, broken waters.

tabu, a prohibition, gatun'ta; I am observing a tabu, tsi-ga-tigu'

Tahlonteeskie, Ata-lun-ti'ski, "He throws him down;" a chief who emigrated to the West about 1808 and became Principal Chief of the Western band. Brother of John Jolly, brother-in-law to Doublehead.

tail, u-ta-na'

Talking Rock, (echo) Nunyu-guwani'ski, a town near the present town of that name on Talking Rock Creek, North Georgia.

tall, uni-gati'ya-wi', tall person.

Taliwa, Creek, Tali-we-wuh', Watertown; site of battle between Creeks and Cherokees in 1755; on Long Swamp Creek near the present Canton, Ga.

Tallulah, an ancient settlement on Tallulah River, Rabun County, Ga. The name probably means "Frog Place" from the cry of the frog, tu-lu-lu-yi, meaning, "The frogs cry there."

tame, uluni'ta

Tamassee, Creek, Tamaha-si, Little Town; a town on Tomassee Creek, Oconee County, S. C.; and on Little Tennessee River near the mouth of Burningtown Creek, Macon County, N. C.

Tamotley, or Timotley; from the Creek Tamaha-tala, "Hewed Timber Town," i.e. of log houses; a settlement near the present Tamotla, above Murphy, N. C.; and on Little Tennessee River in the present Monroe County, Tenn.

tassel, corn, utsi-tsa'lu

Tassel, Old, Kai-ya-tsa-tahee'; succeeded Attakullakulla as Peace Chief, 1777; killed under flag of truce, 1788. Uncle of Watts.

taste, ana-tlu-di-i'

tanning, utsa-da'wi

Tellico, Tla-le-kwa, peace. An important town on Tellico River at the present Tellico Plains, Tenn., Monroe County. The name indicates that it was originally a town of refuge, or peace town.

Tennessee, from the Creek Talua, town, and ahassee, old; Old Town. The term was frequently applied to any old, well beloved settlement; and was used, too, to indicate a place once settled and later abandoned. Same as Tallissee, Tallassee, Tallahassee, Talisi, etc.

terrapin, tuck-si'

thank you, wa-dan'

that, na-ski'

there, locative, indicated by suffix yi

they, tsu-nu'; they say, tsunu-di-ska'

thirsty, da-sti-hay'

thief, kuna-ska'si

thong, gano'tsi halu-sa-du'dee

thorn, ata-di-u'sti; thorny, da-sti-yu'sti

thread, a'sti

throwing, agwa-digu'

throwing the tomahawk, udagu' galoya-sti'

thunder, una-la'ski; abbreviation of ani-hyun-tikwa-li-ski-hu', "People who make a rolling sound."

tired, gia'wuga; I am tired, da-gia-wuga'

time, ale-ye-su'

titmouse, tufted, utsu'tsi; from utsa'hi, topknot.

toadstool, duwa-lu'

tobacco, tsa-lu'

Toccoa, Ta-gwa'hi, Catawba Place, a town on Toccoa Creek, near Clarksville, Habersham County, Ga.

Tomassee, see Tamassee.

tomorrow, suna-lay'i

tongue, ganu-ga'; forked tongue, ganuga tsulo-tso-tsi'

topknot, u-tsa'hi

Toquo, Dakwa, mythical great fish. A town on Little Tennessee River, Monroe County, Tenn.

torture, ada-gilu'di

tough, astu-hi'

town, gatu'gi

town house, gatu'yi; see council house.

Toxaway, Tuksi-wa'yi, Big Terrapin Place; a town on the headwaters of Keowee River, in South Carolina.

tracks, uta-sinun'yi

Track Rock Gap, Datsu'na-las-yun'yi, where there are tracks; Track Rock Gap, near Blairsville, Ga.

trail, or road, nuna'hi

trailing, gala-nu'ni

Trail of Tears, nuna-da-ut-sun'yi, Trail where they cried.

trade, dana-li'ska

trader, dana-ti'ski

transparent, ulun-tsu'ti

trash, guna-sa'ta, applied to trash floating in water.

treasurer, a-day'la-gaya'; keeper of the beads, or money.

tree, tsali-gu'; forest, tsalu'yi

trout, tsuna'ga

true, truth, to-e-u'; lie, untruth, atsi-ska-lay'

Tsul-kalu', Slanting Eyes, a mythical giant.

tuber place, ulun'yi, see potatoes.

Tuckasegee, Tuck-si'yi, Terrapin Place; a town near the forks of Tuckasegee River, above Webster, N. C.

# CHEROKEE VOCABULARY 547

Tuskega, or Tuskegee; from the Creek, meaning Warrior Place. The name occurs twice in the Cherokee country; on Little Tennessee at Fort Loudoun; and on Williams Island, below Chattanooga, Tenn.

Tuckalegee, Di-gwa-li'tsi-yi', "They have much green there," a town at the location of the present Bryson City, N. C.

turkey, kana' or kala'; gobbler, kala-gi'na; hen, kala-gi'sa

Turkey Town, Kana-gatu'gi, a settlement on Coosa River opposite Center, Ala., Cherokee County. Birthplace of John Ross.

turnip, duksu'ni

Turnip Town, Ulun'yi, tuber place; a town on Turniptown Creek above Ellijay, Ga. Home of Chiefs Whitepath and Little Turkey.

Tugaloo, Amo-tu-gwa-lun'yi, "Water rolling over rocks there," a town at junction of Tugaloo and Toccoa Rivers, Habersham County, Ga.

turtle, land terrapin, tuck'si; water, saligu'tsi; soft shell, uli-nawa'

turtle dove, gule-diska-nahi', "They cry for acorns," so called because their cry resembled the word for acorn, gu-le'

twilight, usun-hi-yi'

twist, ukun-tsu'sti

Uchees, Ani-utsi', a tribe occupying certain villages on Tennessee River in the present Rhea County, Tenn. Driven southward by Cherokees, and absorbed by the Creeks.

ugly, mean, a-sga'si-ti. The Cherokee language contained no profanity. The word a-sga'siti, ugly, was their worst term of abuse. Synonymous with dreadful, awful, etc.

uncle, adu'tsi, an abbreviation meaning "mother's brother."

unlucky, u-kwa-legu'

valley, uwa'tla-uh'

vegetables, awi-sa'ni

venison, deer's meat, awi-hawi'ya

vine, u-talun-la'ti, it climbs high.

violet, dinda-skwa-tsu'ski; they pull each other's heads off. From a child's game played with violets.

vomiter, dalik'sta, the Spreading Adder.

wahoo tree, tsuwa-donah'

walnut, tsa-de'; walnut oil, tsade-ka'i; walnut hominy, kanŭ'tsi

walk, ada'sti; walking stick, uda'la-nu-sti'

war, danawa'

warrior, aya-sti-gi', fighting man.

war chief, nu-gu-we-u-suh'

war club, ata'si

war ford, danawa-stun'yi

war hatchet, danawa'ahee-galu'sti

war path, danawa'nunnehi'

war pole, ata-de-dawa-sto'di

war stick, chief's banner, ada-skwa'lune-sto'di

war whoop, u-wa-hoop-p!

warm, de-la-ka'; hot, delaka'yu

was, past tense, gese-i'

Watts, John, Kunnessee-i', green corn top, or Young Tassel. A seceding chief, 1777; war chief of the Chickamaugas, 1792-1794, died about 1808 at Willstown.

wash, ada'wa-sti'; to baptize, ada'wa-hi'

Washington, Wasi-tŭ'ni, son of Charlie, who was spared when his father and brothers were killed for murder of soldiers during removal.

watch, watching, aka-lu'ga, "I am doing it with my eyes."

watching place, ak-ta-diyi'

water, a-mo'

water beetle, dayu'nisi', beaver's grandmother.

water cress, gur-ahi', hence Currahee Mountain.

water dog, mud puppy, tsu-wa'

water fall, or falling water, amo-aska'gahi'

water jar, diwa'li or unti'ya; western dialect, atle'sti

water lily, amo-ye-du-hi'

water rolling over rocks, amo-tu-gwa-lun'yi

water spirits, amo-yine'hi, water dwellers.

Watauga, from the Creek Weto'ga, broken waters. A town on Watauga Creek a few miles below Franklin, N. C.; also Watauga Old Fields near Elizabethton, Carter County, Tenn.

Wauhatchie, Waya-tsi', mighty or terrible wolf. A chief of the Lower Towns at the time of the French and Indian War, 1756.

weaver, tsu-o'la; also spider, kaně'ski

we, indicated by prefix di

weep, de-tlo-ya'sti

West, Usun-hi-yi', twilight land; or udi-li-gun'yi, it goes down there.

wet, amo', same as water

wheel, di-kwali-hu'

wheel and stick game, see chunky

Where they Cried, day-u-tsun'yi, where the captives cried for mercy; see Mooney, 336. It is probable that this myth refers to the defeat of Montgomery's force by the Cherokees in 1760.

whippoorwill, wagu-li', from its cry.

whiskey, amo-atsi'la, fire water.

White Man Killer, Unega-dihi', usually written Unacata. A frequent male name; a brother of John Watts was so called; as was a chief killed at Buchanan's Station, 1792. A chief named Unacata ambushed and captured the Scott boats at Muscle Shoals in 1794, taking about twenty captives.

wife, ada-lee'i

wild, gaya-dahi'

wild cat, or bob cat, guhe'ya

wilderness, ena-gaya'hi

willow, dele-gali'ski

will o' the wisp, atsil-diye'hi, fire carrier.

Willenawah, Awali-na-wa', Big Eagle, a chief active during the siege of Fort Loudoun, 1760, and afterwards.

wind, unu-lay'; the Four Winds, nungi-tsunulay'

winter, kaw-la'

wise, aga-tana'i

witch, tsi-ki-li, screech owl.

wolf, wa-ya'

woman, a-gi'ya, my beloved; man, asga'ya

wood, a-ta'

woodpecker, ku-gu-tsa'; downy, or flicker, tsu-kwa-na'tsi, scalped.

wool, uwanu'tala'la; wooly, unu-duna'

worm, gaska-ya'

worn out, old, uwa'ta

wound, injury, asa-nuda'i; wounded, asa-nunu'

year, uda-ti-yahu'

yellow, dalaw'nega

yellow hammer, uni-gada', ground person.

yellow jacket, d-ska'i

yellow money, gold, aday'la dalaw'nega

yell, gay-luhu'ska

yes, affirmative, um-ska-ga'; or ase-hi'

yes, sir! strong affirmative, ha-yu! "It is true!"

yesterday, u-sha-hi'

yi, locative, it happened there.

Yona-gun'ski, Drowning Bear; a chief of the Eastern Cherokees during
and after the removal. He died in 1839, age 80.

you, ne-hi'; me, aya'

young, ni'ta; abbreviation of awa-ni'ta

# APPENDIX B

## LAND CESSIONS OF THE CHEROKEES

### AFTER ROYCE, FIFTH ANNUAL REPORT,
### BUREAU OF AMERICAN ETHNOLOGY. (*See* MAP)

### COLONIAL PERIOD

| Number  Date | With Whom | Description of Cession |
|---|---|---|
| 1. 1721 | Gov. Nicholson of S. C. | Tract in S. C. between Santee, Saluda, and Edisto Rivers. |
| 2. Nov. 24, 1755 | Gov. Glen of S. C. | Tract in S. C. between Wateree and Santee Rivers. |
| 3. Oct. 14, 1768, | John Stuart, British Indian Superintendent, | Tract in S. W. Virginia. |
| 4. Oct. 18, 1770, | John Stuart, at Lochaber, S. C. | Tract in Virginia, West Virginia, Tenn. and Ky. |
| 5. 1772. | Governor of Virginia | Tract in Va., W. Va., and Eastern Ky. |
| 6. June 1, 1773 | John Stuart | Tract in Georgia, North of Broad River. |
| 7. Mar. 17, 1775 | Richard Henderson et al, | Kentucky, Virginia, and Tennessee. |
| 8. May 20, 1777 | S. Carolina and Georgia, | N. W. South Carolina. |
| 9. July 20, 1777, | Virginia and N. C., | Western N. C. and N. E. Tennessee. |
| 10. May 31, 1788, | Georgia | Tract in Georgia between Oconee and Tugaloo Rivers. |

### FEDERAL PERIOD

| | | |
|---|---|---|
| 10-A. Nov. 28, 1785 | United States | Tract in Western N. C. |
| 10-B. Nov. 28, 1785 | United States, (Treaty of Hopewell) | Tract South of Cumberland River in Ky. and Tennessee. |
| 11. July 2, 1791 | United States | East Tennessee and Western North Carolina. |
| 12. Oct. 2, 1798 | United States | East Tenn., between Hawkin's Line, Tenn. River, and Chilhowie Mountain. |
| 13. Oct. 2, 1798 | United States | N. C. between Picken's and Meigs' Line. |
| 14. Oct. 2, 1798 | United States | Tennessee, between Clinch River and Cumberland Mtn. |
| 15. Oct. 24, 1804 | United States | A small tract in Georgia known as Wafford settlement. |
| 16. Oct. 25, 1805 | United States | Kentucky, and Middle Tennessee North of Tennessee River. |
| 17. Oct. 27, 1805 | United States | Southwest Point, in Tennessee. |

| Number Date | With Whom | Description of Cession |
|---|---|---|
| 18. Oct. 27, 1805 | United States | First Island in Tennessee River above the Mouth of Clinch. |
| 19. Jan. 7, 1806 | United States | Tract in Tennessee, between Tennessee and Duck Rivers. |
| 20. Jan. 7, 1806 | United States | Long Island of Holston River. (The Beloved Treaty Ground.) |
| 21. Mar. 22, 1816 | United States | Extreme N. W. corner of S. Carolina. |
| 22. Sept. 14, 1816 | United States | Tract in Alabama and small portion of Mississippi. |
| 23. July 8, 1817 | United States | Tract in Georgia East of Chattahoochie River. |
| 24. July 8, 1817. | United States | Tennessee, along Sequatchie River North of Little Sequatchie. |
| 25. July 8, 1817 | United States | Small tract in Alabama, North of Tenn. River, bet. Cypress and Elk Rivs. |
| 26. July 8, 1817 | United States | Small tract in Alabama, on Tenn. River above Mouth of Spring Creek. |
| 27. Feb. 27, 1819 | United States | Tract in Tenn. and Alabama, South of Little Sequatchie to Guntersville on Tennessee River. |
| 28. Feb. 27, 1819 | United States | All North of Tennessee River from Hiwassee to Sequatchie Rivers. |
| 29. Feb. 27, 1819 | United States | Two tracts; in Tennessee between Hiwassee and Little Tennessee; and in North Carolina and Georgia. |
| 30. Feb. 27, 1819 | United States | Jolly's Island in Tennessee River. |
| 31. Feb. 27, 1819 | United States | Small tract at Mouth of Clinch River. |
| 32. Feb. 27, 1819 | United States | 12 sq. miles on Tenn. River in Ala. |
| 33. Feb. 27, 1819 | United States | Talotiskee's tract, 1 sq. mi., Tenn. |
| 34. Feb. 27, 1819 | United States | Talotiskee's tract, 1 sq. mi., Tenn. |
| 35. Feb. 27, 1819 | United States | 3 sq. mi. opposite Mouth of Hiwassee. |
| 36. Dec. 29, 1835. | United States | Final Cession in Ala., Ga., and Tenn. All lands East of Mississippi River. |

For details of cessions, see Royce, *Cherokee Nation of Indians, Fifth Report, Bureau of American Ethnology.*

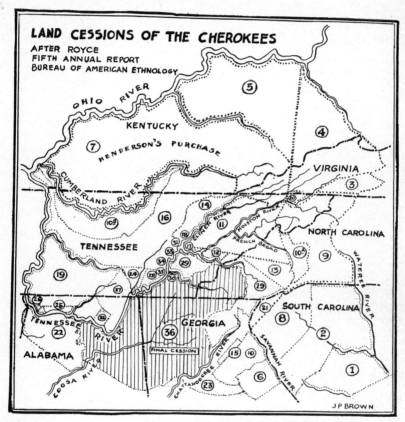

Approximate Scale, one inch equals 150 miles.

# APPENDIX C

## TREATY OF SYCAMORE SHOALS, MAR. 17, 1775.[1]

### THE CHIEFS OF THE CHEROKEES TO RICH[d] HENDERSON AND CO.

This Indenture, made this——day of————of the year of our Lord one thousand Seven Hundred and Seventy-five, between Oconistoto, Chief Warrior and first representative of the Cherokee Nation or tribe of Indians & Attacullacullah & Savanooka, otherwise Coronoh, Chiefs appointed by the Warriors and other head men to convey for the whole Nation, Beying the Aborigines and sole owners by occupancy from the Beginning of time of the lands on the waters of the Ohio River from the mouth of the Tennessee River up the said Ohio to the mouth or emptying of the Great Canaway or New River, and so across by a Southward line to the Virginia line by an intersection that shall strike or hit Holston River six English miles above or Eastward of the Long Island therein and other land or territorys thereunto adjoining, of the one part; and Richard Henderson, Thomas Hart, Nathaniel Hart, John Williams, John Luttrell, William Johnston, James Hogg, David Hart, and Leonard Hendley Bulloch, of the Province of North Carolina, of the other part;

WITNESSETH, that the said Oconistoto for himself and the rest of the said Nation of Indians, for and in consideration of Ten Thousand Pounds Lawfull money of Great Britain, to them in hand paid by the said Rich[d] Henderson, Thomas Hart, Nathaniel Hart, John Williams, John Luttrell, William Johnston, James Hogg, David Hart, and Leonard Hendley Bulloch, the Receipt Whereoff the said Oconistoto and his whole Nation do and for themselves and their whole people hereby acknowledge, have granted, bargained, sold, aliened, enfeoffed, Released & Confirmed & by these presents do Grant, bargain & sell, alien, enfeoff, Release & Confirm unto the said Rich[d] Henderson, Thomas Hart, Nathaniel Hart, John Williams, John Luttrell, William Johnston, James Hogg, David Hart, and Leonard Hendley Bulloch, their heirs and assigns forever, all that Tract, Territory, or Parcel of Land.

*Beginning on the Holston River where the course of Powel's Mountain strikes the same, hence up the said River as it meanders to where the Vir-*

---

[1] This copy of the Treaty of Sycamore Shoals is evidently that given by Richard Henderson to Parker & Carter for Carter's Valley, to compensate them for the loss of goods stolen from them by the Cherokees. It is a duplicate of the grant deed for the entire tract bought by Henderson, but defines specifically the bounds of the present Carter's Valley where the city of Rogersville, Tenn., is located. The deed was filed for recording at Rogersville, Hawkins County, Tennessee, on Nov. 1, 1794. It was transferred from the original book to the present Book E-127, where it may be consulted.

*ginia line crosses the same, thence along the line run by Donelson & Co. to
a point Six English Miles Eastward of the Long Island in the said Holston
River, thence a direct course towards the Mouth of the Great Canaway until
it reaches the top ridge of Powel's Mountain, thence Westward along the
said ridge to the Beginning.*[2]

and also the Reversion and the Reversions, Remainder and Remainders,
Rents and Services thereoff and all the Estate Rights, Title, Interest, Claim,
and Demand whatever of them, the said Oconistoto and the aforesaid whole
band or Tribe of People of, in, and to the said premises, and of, in, and to
Every Part and Parcel through, To Have and to Hold the said Messuage
& Territory and all and singular the Premises above mentioned with the
appurtenances above mentioned,[3] unto the said Rich^d Henderson, Thomas
Hart, Nathaniel Hart, John Williams, John Luttrell, William Johnston,
James Hogg, David Hart, and Leonard Hendley Bulloch, their heirs and
assigns in Severalty & Tenants in Common and not as Joint Tenants, that
is to say:

One eighth part to Rich^d Henderson, his heirs and assigns forever;
One eighth part to Thomas Hart, his heirs and assigns forever;
One eighth part to Nathaniel Hart, his heirs and assigns forever;
One eighth part to John Williams, his heirs and assigns forever;
One eighth part to John Luttrell, his heirs and assigns forever;
One eighth part to William Johnston, his heirs and assigns forever;
One eighth part to James Hogg, his heirs and assigns forever;
One sixteenth part to David Hart, his heirs and assigns forever;
One sixteenth part to Leonard Hendley Bulloch, his heirs and assigns
    forever;

To the only proper use and behoof of them, the said Rich^d Henderson,
Thomas Hart, Nathaniel Hart, John Williams, John Luttrell, William
Johnston, James Hogg, David Hart, and Leonard Hendley Bulloch, their
heirs and assigns forever, under the yearly rent of four pence or to be
holder of or the Chief Lord or Lords of the fees of the Premises by the
Rents and Services thereoff due and of right accustomed; and the said
Oconistoto and the said Nation of themselves do covenant and grant to the
said Rich^d Henderson, Thomas Hart, Nathaniel Hart, John Williams, John
Luttrell, William Johnston, James Hogg, David Hart, and Leonard Hendley
Bulloch, their heirs and assigns, that they, the said Oconistoto and the Rest
of the said Nation or People now are lawfully and rightly seized in their
own right of a good Fee Simple of and in all and singular of the said
Messuage and premises above mentioned and of all and every part and
parcel thereoff with the appurtenances without any manner of conditions,
mortgages, limitation of use or uses, or other matter, cause or thing to
alter, change, charge or determine the same, and also the said Oconistoto and

---

[2] The Virginia-North Carolina line had not been surveyed in 1775, but
was supposed to lie some miles southward of the present Kingsport (Long
Island). The present Powell's Mountain does not strike the Holston, but
its eastern spur, Clinch Mountain, does, at a point a few miles south of
Rogersville, where the above described line would begin.

[3] *Messuage* was a term used in old deeds to indicate good title, or
ownership.

the aforesaid Nation now have good right, full power, and lawful authority in their own right to Grant, Bargain, and Sell and Convey the said Messuage and Premises above mentioned with the appurtenances, unto the said Rich<sup>d</sup> Henderson, Thomas Hart, Nathaniel Hart, John Williams, John Luttrell, William Johnston, James Hogg, David Hart, and Leonard Hendley Bulloch, their heirs and assigns; and they shall and may from time to time hereafter peaceably and quietly have, hold, occupy, possess, and enjoy, all and singular the said premises above mentioned to be hereby granted with the appurtenances, without the lett, trouble, interference & molestation in occupation and denial of their right thereto, by the said Oconistoto & the rest or any part of the said Nation, their heirs and assigns and of all and every other person whatsoever, claiming or to claim, by, from, or under them, or any of them; and further, that the said Oconistoto, Attacullacullah, Savanooka, otherwise Coronoh, for themselves and in behalf of their whole Nation and their heirs and all & every other person or persons and his and their heirs, anything having or claiming in the said Messuage, Territory, or any part thereoff, by, from, or under them, Shall and will at all times hereafter at the Request and Cost of the said Rich<sup>d</sup> Henderson, Thomas Hart, Nathaniel Hart, John Williams, John Luttrell, William Johnston, James Hogg, David Hart, and Leonard Hendley Bulloch, their heirs and assigns forever, make, do, and execute, or cause or procure to be made, done, or executed, all and every further and other lawfull and reasonable Grants, Acts, and Assurances in the Law whatsoever for the further better and more perfect granting, conveying, and assuring of the said premises hereby granted with the appurtenances unto the said Rich<sup>d</sup> Henderson, Thomas Hart, Nathaniel Hart, John Williams, John Luttrell, William Johnston, James Hogg, David Hart, and Leonard Hendley Bulloch, their heirs and assigns forever according to the true intent and meaning of these presents, and to and for none other use, interest, or purpose whatsoever;

And lastly, the said Oconistoto, Attacullacullah, Savanooka, otherwise Coronoh, for themselves and the whole Nation aforesaid, have made, ordained, constituted, and appointed, and by these presents do make, ordain, constitute and appoint Joseph Martin and John Sevier their true and lawfull Attorneys, jointly and in either of them severally, for them and in their names unto the said Messuage, Territory, and Premises and Appurtenances hereby granted, conveyed, or mentioned, or to be granted or conveyed, or unto some part thereof in the name of the whole, to enter in full and peaceable possession and Seizen thereoff, for them and in their names to take and to have such possession and seizure to thereafter seize and hold the lawfull and peaceable possession and Seizure thereoff, or of some part thereoff in the name of the whole, unto the said Rich<sup>d</sup> Henderson, Thomas Hart, Nathaniel Hart, John Williams, John Luttrell, William Johnston, James Hogg, David Hart, and Leonard Hendley Bulloch, or their certain attorney or attorneys in their behalf, to Give and Deliver to hold to them, the said Rich<sup>d</sup> Henderson, Thomas Hart, Nathaniel Hart, John Williams, John Luttrell, William Johnston, James Hogg, David Hart, and Leonard Hendley Bulloch, their heirs and assigns forever according to the purpose, true intent, and meaning of these presents, Ratifying, confirming, and allowing all and whatsoever their attorneys or either of them shall do in the premises.

In Witness Whereof, the said Oconistoto, Attacullacullah, Savanooka otherwise Coronoh, the three chiefs appointed by the warriors & other head men to sign for and in behalf of the whole Nation, hath hereunto Set their Hands and Affixed their Seals, the day and the year above written.[4]

OCONISTOTO (His Mark)
ATTACULLACULLAH (His Mark)
SAVANOOKA
(Otherwise CORONOH) (His Mark)

Signed, Sealed, and Delivered, in the presence of

| | | |
|---|---|---|
| WM. BAILEY SMITH | LITTLETON BROOKS | VALENTINE SEVIER |
| GEORGE LUMPKIN | JOHN BACON | THOMAS PRICE |
| THO. HOUGHTON | TILMAN DIXON | |

---

[4] There is little likelihood that the Indians could understand the "purpose, true intent, or meaning of these presents," or that any interpreter could make them plain. Oconostota and other chiefs later claimed that Henderson had deceived them, and that they had sold him a much smaller tract than he claimed. They, however, signed the treaty, and accepted Henderson's goods, thereby binding the Cherokees.

# BIBLIOGRAPHY

BOOKS AND AUTHORITIES CONSULTED IN COMPILING
"OLD FRONTIERS"

ADAIR, JAMES, *History of American Indians,* Reprint S. C. Williams, Watauga Press, 1930.

*American State Papers, Indian Affairs,* Vol. 1, Government Printing Office, Washington, 1816.

ARMSTRONG, ZELLA, *History of Hamilton County, Tennessee,* Lookout Publishing Co., 1931.

———, *Notable Southern Families,* Vol. 4, Sevier, Lookout Publishing Co., 1926.

BANCROFT, GEORGE, *History of United States,* Little-Brown & Co., Boston, 1868.

BATTEY, GEORGE M., JR., *History of Rome and Floyd County, Ga.*

BARTRAM, WILLIAM, *Travels,* Reprint, Macy-Masius, 1928.

*British Colonial Documents,* Typed Calendar of, covering period of John Stuart's Agency, Lawson McGhee Library, Knoxville.

BRUNSON, REV. ALFRED, *A Western Pioneer,* New York, Carlton & Lanahan, 1872.

*Bureau of American Ethnology,* Various Reports and Bulletins.

*Calendar of Virginia State Papers,* Publication of Virginia Historical Society, Richmond.

CATLIN, GEORGE, *North American Indians,* London, by Author, 1841.

COLLINS, LEWIS, *Historical Sketches of Kentucky,* J. A. and U. P. James, Cincinnati, 1850.

CURTIN, J. and J. N. B. HEWETT, *Seneca Legends and Myths,* 32nd Report, Bureau of American Ethnology.

DE SOTO, *CONQUEST OF FLORIDA,* Gentleman of Elvas, Biedma, Ranjel, Garcillasso; Translations of E. G. Bourne and Theodore Irving.

DINWIDDIE, ROBERT, *Correspondence,* Publication of Virginia Historical Society, Richmond.

DRAKE, BENJAMIN, *Life of Tecumseh,* Cincinnati, 1850.

DRAKE, SAMUEL G., *Indians of North America,* Hurst & Co., New York, 1882.

*Draper Manuscripts,* Wisconsin Historical Society, Madison; Tennessee Documents, Lawson McGhee Library, Knoxville.

FOREMAN, GRANT, *Indians and Pioneers,* Yale University Press, 1930.

——, *Indian Removal,* University of Oklahoma Press, 1932.

——, *Advancing the Frontier,* University of Oklahoma Press, 1933.

GARRETT & GOODPASTURE, *History of Tennessee,* Brandon, Nashville, 1900.

GILMORE, JAMES R., (Edmund Kirke) *Rear Guard of the Revolution, John Sevier, Commonwealth Builder,* D. Appleton & Co., New York, 1887.

GOODPASTURE, ALBERT V., *Indian Wars and Warriors in Old Southwest,* Tennessee Historical Magazine, Vol. 4, Nashville, 1915.

GRINNELL, GEORGE BIRD, *Story of the Indian,* Appleton, New York, 1900.

HAMER, P. M., *British and Southern Indians,* East Tennessee Historical Society Publications, 1930.

——, *Fort Loudoun on the Little Tennessee,* Reprint, N. C. Historical Review, Raleigh, October, 1925.

HECKEWELDER, JOHN, *Narrative,* Edited by William Elsey Connelley, Burrows Bros. Co., Cleveland, 1907.

HEISKELL, S. G., *Andrew Jackson and Early Tennessee History,* Ambrose Printing Co., Nashville, 1918.

HENDERSON, ARCHIBALD, *Conquest of the Old Southwest,* Century Company, New York, 1920.

——, *Richard Henderson, Author of Cumberland Compact,* Tennessee Historical Magazine, Vol. 2, Nashville, 1913.

HAYWOOD, JOHN, *Civil and Political History of Tennessee,* Nashville, 1823; Reprint Methodist Publishing House, Nashville, 1891.

HEWETT, ALEXANDER, *Development of Carolina and Georgia,* London, 1789.

HAMILTON, P. J., *Colonial Mobile,* Houghton-Mifflin, Boston, 1910.

HODGE, F. W., *Handbook of American Indians,* Bulletin 30, Bureau of American Ethnology.

HOWE, HENRY, *The Great West,* Greeneville, Tenn., 1855.

HORRY & WEEMS, *Life of General Francis Marion,* Belford Clarke & Co., New York, undated.

HULBERT, A. B., *Boone's Wilderness Road,* A. H. Clarke & Co., Cleveland, 1903.

HUGHES, RUPERT, *Life of Washington,* W. Morrow & Co., New York, 1926.

JONES, C. C., *Antiquities of Southern Indians,* Appleton, 1873.

JAMES, MARQUIS, *The Raven, Story of Sam Houston,* Bobbs-Merrill, 1929.

——, *Andrew Jackson, Border Captain,* Bobbs-Merrill, 1933.

LEWIS, T. H., *Spanish Explorations in Southern U. S.,* Scribner's, 1927.

LOUGHRIDGE, R. M. and D. M. HODGE, *English-Muscogee Dictionary,* Westminster Press, Philadelphia, 1914.

MANSFIELD, R. E., *Life of Gen. Winfield Scott,* A. S. Barnes & Co., New York, 1846.

MOONEY, JAMES, *Myths of the Cherokees,* 19th Report, Bureau of American Ethnology.

——, *Sacred Formulas of the Cherokees,* 7th Report, Bureau of American Ethnology.

——, *The Ghost Dance Religion,* 14th Report, Bureau of American Ethnology.

MOORE, CLARENCE B., *Aboriginal Sites on Tennessee River,* Philadelphia Academy of Science, 1914.

MOORE, JOHN TROTWOOD and A. P. FOSTER, *Tennessee the Volunteer State,* S. J. Clarke Press, Nashville, 1923.

MOOREHEAD, WARREN K., *Exploration of the Etowah Site,* Yale Press, 1933.

MYER, WILLIAM E., *Indian Trails in Southeast,* 42nd Report, Bureau of American Ethnology.

*North Carolina Colonial and State Records.*

PILLING, C. C., *Bibliography of Iroquoian Tribes,* Government Printing Office, Washington, 1888.

PRESTON, JOHN HYDE, *Mad Anthony Wayne,* Garden City Publishing Co., New York, 1930.

PUTNAM, A. W., *History of Middle Tennessee, Life of Robertson,* Southern Methodist Publishing House, Nashville, 1859.

RAMSEY, J. G. M., *Annals of Tennessee,* Charleston, 1853, Reprint 1926, for Judge David Campbell Chapter, D.A.R., Kingsport Press.

RANCK, GEORGE W., *Boonesborough,* Publication of Filson Club, Louisville.

ROOSEVELT, THEODORE, *Winning of the West,* G. P. Putnam's Sons, New York, 1889.

ROTHROCK, MARY U., *Early English Traders among Cherokees,* East Tennessee Historical Society Publication, 1934.

ROYCE, C. C., *The Cherokee Nation of Indians,* 5th Report, Bureau of American Ethnology.

SMITH, JAMES F., *The Cherokee Land Lottery,* Harper & Brothers, New York, 1838.

SMITH, REV. SIBBALD, *Thomas Enrollment of Cherokee Indians,* Manuscript. Prepared for Confederate Government by Major W. H. Thomas, 1863.

SMITH, REV. W. R. L., *Story of the Cherokees,* Church of God Publishing House, 1928.

*South Carolina Colonial and State Records,* Typed Manuscripts relating to Indian Affairs, Lawson McGhee Library, Knoxville.

*Southwestern Monthly,* Published at Nashville by Wales and Roberts, 1852.

STARR, EMMETT, *History of the Cherokee Indians,* Warden Company, Oklahoma City, 1921.

SPARKS, JARED, *Writings of Washington,* Harper & Brothers, New York, 1847.

SWANTON, JOHN R., *Early History of Creek Indians,* Bulletin 73, Bureau of American Ethnology.

——, *Creek Social Organizations and Usages,* 42nd Report, Bureau of American Ethnology.

TAYLOR, OLIVER, *Historic Sullivan,* King Printing Co., Bristol, 1909.

THATCHER, B. B., *Indian Biography,* J. & J. Harper, New York, 1832.

THRUSTON, GATES P., *Antiquities of Tennessee,* R. Clarke & Co., Cincinnati, 1897.

TIMBERLAKE, HENRY, *Memoirs,* London, 1765, Reprint S. C. Williams, Watauga Press, 1927.

TURNER, FRANCIS, *Life of John Sevier,* Neale Publishing Co., Washington, 1910.

VAN DYKE, PAUL, *Washington, Son of his Country,* Scribner's, 1921.

WALKER, ROBERT SPARKS, *Torchlights to the Cherokees,* Macmillan & Co., New York, 1931.

WEBB, WILLIAM F., *Sequoyah,* Excerpt from John Howard Payne Mss., Newberry Library, Chicago.

WEEKS, STEPHEN B., *Gen. Joseph Martin and the Revolution in the West,* American Historical Association, Annual Report 1895, 401-477.

WHITAKER, A. P., *Spanish-American Frontier,* Houghton-Mifflin, 1927.

WILLIAMS, JUDGE SAMUEL C.,

——, *Early Travels in the Tennessee Country,* Watauga Press, 1928.

——, *Adair's History of American Indians,* Watauga Press, 1930.

——, *Memoirs of Henry Timberlake,* Watauga Press, 1927.

——, *Lost State of Franklin,* Watauga Press, 1924.

——, *William Tatham,* Wataugan, Vol. 2, Tennessee Historical Magazine.

——, *Gist the Father of Sequoyah,* Address, Chattanooga Times, Nov. 15, 1931.

Other Publications and Documents as Noted.

# INDEX